All
Made
of
Tunes

Yale
University
Press
New Haven
&
London

J. Peter Burkholder

Charles Ives
and the
Uses of Musical
Borrowing

All
Made
of
Tunes

Published with assistance from the National Endowment for the
Humanities, an independent federal agency, and the H. Earle Johnson
Fund of the Sonneck Society for American Music.

Set in Minion type by The Clarinda Company, Clarinda, Iowa. Printed in the
United States of America by Vail-Ballou Press, Binghamton, New York.

Library of Congress Cataloging-in-Publication Data
Burkholder, J. Peter (James Peter)
  All made of tunes : Charles Ives and the uses of musical borrowing
/ J. Peter Burkholder.
      p.   cm.
  Includes bibliographical references and indexes.
  ISBN 0-300-05642-7 (hc)
  1. Ives, Charles, 1874–1954 — Criticism and interpretation.
2. Ives, Charles, 1874–1954 — Sources.   I. Title.
ML410.I94B87   1995
780'.92 — dc20   95-13537
                                                                  CIP
                                                                   MN

A catalogue record for this book is available from the British Library.

The paper in this book meets the guidelines for permanence and durability
of the Committee on Production Guidelines for Book Longevity of the
Council on Library Resources.

10   9   8   7   6   5   4   3   2   1

To the memory of

JOHN KIRKPATRICK, 1905–1991

and

HOWARD MAYER BROWN, 1930–1993

I think there must be a place in the soul

all made of tunes,

of tunes of long ago . . .

CHARLES IVES

The Things Our Fathers Loved

Contents

Acknowledgments

Any book is a collaborative effort, and I am indebted to many people for helping me to write this one. All work on musical borrowing in Ives ultimately depends on the groundbreaking work of John Kirkpatrick in cataloguing Ives's music manuscripts and identifying hundreds of tunes and pieces that Ives used in his music. My own interest in musical borrowing as a subject began in a seminar with Howard Mayer Brown on the use of borrowed material in Renaissance masses, and the approaches I learned there provided new tools for examining Ives's uses of existing music. These two men were among my most important teachers, and I felt privileged to count them as friends. Both died while I was working on this book, which I would never have undertaken without their example and help. It is dedicated to their memory.

The community of Ives scholars continues to thrive, and many have offered help. Clayton Henderson's dissertation first led me to question received opinion about Ives's musical borrowings. He graciously provided me with a draft of his *Charles Ives Tunebook* before publication, which speeded my own work greatly. Geoffrey Block enthusiastically read the first draft, offered a detailed critique, and suggested many improvements. Jonathan Elkus and Larry Starr did the same for a later draft. Thomas M. Brodhead read and commented on drafts, offered numerous tips, and shared his work on the Fourth Symphony, *The Celestial Railroad,* and the *Four Transcriptions from Emerson* prior to publication. James B. Sinclair reviewed the manuscript, provided copies of new editions of Ives's music prior to publication, and answered many small questions. H. Wiley Hitchcock read the manuscript, shared it with his students, passed on their reactions, and offered constant encouragement. James Hepokoski shared his work on teleological genesis in Sibelius and Ives prior to publication and engaged me in several stimulating and useful exchanges on cumulative form and its significance. Kendall Crilly and others at the Yale Music Library were always cheerful and helpful. Most important of all, my students in classes on Ives and on musical borrowing provided fresh perspectives and helped me time and again to reexamine my views on Ives and his uses of existing music.

Gayle Sherwood generously provided estimated dates for the music paper and handwriting of each manuscript for the works considered here, a mammoth task. She also let me read portions of her dissertation-in-progress. David Birchler and Andreas Giger helped to locate sources on borrowing in the music of other composers and eras. Daria Depa, Carol Crowley, and Luiz Fernando Lopes assisted with bibliographic matters, and Kurt Messick and Thomas J. Mathiesen helped me find and learn the right computer equipment and programs. Lee Heritage beautifully prepared the musical examples.

My editors at Yale University Press deserve much of the credit for seeing this book into print, from the gentle prodding of Edward Tripp and Harry Haskell to the helpful editing of David Schulenberg. Thanks also to Indiana University for a sabbatical leave, during which I was able to finish the book, and for helping to pay for the musical examples. Subventions from the National Endowment for the Humanities and the H. Earle Johnson Fund of the Sonneck Society for American Music helped to support publication. Last but not least, my deepest thanks to my husband Doug McKinney and the rest of my family for their unending patience and support.

The following copyright holders have generously given permission to reprint musical examples of copyrighted works by Charles Ives. Acknowledgments for some additional works appear under several of the musical examples.

String Quartet No. 1. © Copyright 1961 and 1963 by Peer International Corporation. International Copyright Secured. All Rights Reserved. Used by Permission.

Evening. Copyright © 1970 by Associated Music Publishers, Inc. (BMI). International Copyright Secured. All Rights Reserved. Reprinted by Permission.

Symphony No. 1. © Copyright 1971 by Peer International Corporation. International Copyright Secured. All Rights Reserved. Used by Permission.

Symphony No. 2. © Copyright 1951 by Southern Publishing Co., Inc. Copyright Renewed by Peer International Corporation. International Copyright Secured. All Rights Reserved. Used by Permission.

Third Symphony. Copyright © 1947 (Renewed) by Associated Music Publishers, Inc. (BMI). International Copyright Secured. All Rights Reserved. Reprinted by Permission.

The Camp-Meeting. © Copyright 1958 by Peer International Corporation. International Copyright Secured. All Rights Reserved. Used by Permission.

Sonata No. 1 for violin and piano. © Copyright 1953 by Peer International Corporation. Copyright Renewed. International Copyright Secured. All Rights Reserved. Used by Permission.

Second Violin Sonata. Copyright © 1951 (Renewed) by Associated Music Publishers, Inc. (BMI). International Copyright Secured. All Rights Reserved. Reprinted by Permission.

Editor's Note

Standard abbreviations for instruments are used in the musical examples and in Tables 10.1 and 10.2: Vn. for violin, Vla. for viola, Vc. for violoncello, Db. for double bass, Picc. for piccolo, Fl. for flute, Ob. for oboe, Eng. Hn. for English horn, Cl. for clarinet, Bsn. for bassoon, CBsn. for contrabassoon, Sax. for saxophone, Hn. for horn, Tpt. for trumpet, Trb. for trombone.

If a melodic figure or phrase includes a pickup, the measure range given here begins with the measure in which the pickup occurs, except that the first measure of a work is assumed to include its pickup. Thus, in the hymn tune *Beulah Land,* the verse, which begins with a pickup to m. 1, is designated as mm. 1–8; the refrain, which begins with a pickup to m. 9, is designated as mm. 8–20.

CHAPTER 1

Ives's Uses of Existing Music

Musical quotation is one of the most characteristic facets of Charles Ives's music. There are almost two hundred pieces or movements that incorporate music by other composers, spanning his entire career and representing more than a third of his output. Some borrow from a single source, others from more than twenty. The music Ives uses includes hymn tunes, patriotic songs, marches, bugle calls, drum patterns, popular songs, fiddle tunes, college songs and cheers, and classical pieces by composers from Bach to Debussy. The borrowings vary in extent and recognizability, from the hint of *Erie* ("What a friend we have in Jesus") in the song *Afterglow* to the appearance in *Decoration Day* of the entire trio from David Wallis Reeves's *Second Regiment Connecticut National Guard March*.

The great number of his pieces that use existing music and the amount of borrowed material in such well-known works as *Three Places in New England* have seemed to set Ives far apart from other composers. Listeners accustomed to European art music from Corelli to Webern may experience Ives's borrowings as a kind of aesthetic dissonance, violating the expectation that compositions should be original, self-contained, and based on newly invented ideas. Some borrowings are readily understood; when the song *Down East* recalls the sound of an "old melodeon" playing "Nearer, my God, to Thee," we hear the tune with pleasure along with the words. But other borrowings may make little sense if we cannot perceive their purpose or relation to the surrounding music. If the borrowings have no clear function, we may like the music or not, but it will remain for us a jumble of apparently arbitrary gestures. And as the quotations stick out inexplicably from the musical texture, Ives's music in turn will seem to stand apart from the European tradition as an unintegrated mixture of heterogeneous elements.[1]

Ives's borrowings have inspired a great deal of comment, perhaps more than any other aspect of his music. This is in part a response to the aesthetic dissonance just described, as we seek to resolve in our minds a tension that seems to remain unresolved in the music between the quotation and the piece, or between the acts of quotation and composition. The essential groundwork for the study of Ives's borrowings has been laid by John Kirkpatrick and Clayton Henderson, who have catalogued the known appearances of borrowed material in Ives's music. Kirkpatrick's 1960 catalogue of Ives's music manuscripts includes a list of borrowings for each piece, and he continued to discover others throughout his life.[2] Henderson's *Charles Ives Tunebook* has made the tunes Ives used available in a single volume and provides quotation hunters with a helpful though not infallible field guide.[3] Although Kirkpatrick and Henderson have made clear the extent of borrowing in Ives's music, the reasons for it have been widely debated. Some studies stress the musical relationships of the borrowed material to its surroundings, showing how motives from the quoted tunes pervade the piece or link several borrowed tunes through common motives.[4] Others emphasize the psychological or extramusical significance of quoting tunes with texts or strong emotional associations.[5] A third group argues that both musical relationships and extramusical meanings play vital roles.[6]

Yet the entire discussion of this topic has been skewed by a misdefinition of the problem. All of Ives's uses of existing music have typically been regarded as examples of a single technique, for which various names have been used. But not all of them are "quotations," although he does at times quote familiar music in passing, as one might quote Shakespeare in a speech. Nor can Ives's practice be consistently described as "parody," in analogy to the Renaissance parody mass, as one writer suggests.[7] Not even the term "bor-

IVES'S USES OF EXISTING MUSIC

sonata-style development. This became the predominant procedure for Ives's concert music, particularly in the Third Symphony, the violin sonatas, and the First Piano Sonata.

Several works from 1899 on feature brief programmatic quotations, and some are humorous quodlibets. In techniques developed after 1902 and practiced increasingly in his mature music, Ives combined medley with paraphrase to produce patchworks from fragments of many tunes, as in *The Last Reader* and *The Things Our Fathers Loved,* and blended the ideas of quodlibet and programmatic quotation with modeling, paraphrase, and cumulative setting to produce the giant collages of *The Fourth of July* and the Fourth Symphony. Finally, a few pieces from 1908 on, such as *The Housatonic at Stockbridge,* are extended paraphrases of a single tune.

These later pieces, particularly those that use many tunes, seem to us most typical of Ives. But to hear his earlier music with expectations formed by his later music is to mishear and misunderstand it. We hear each work best when we hear it in context, against the backdrop of the music that Ives had composed to that point and of the music he knew and used as models. As we sort Ives's uses of existing music into categories and trace his path from those techniques that he learned first to his later, more complex approaches, we not only see the logical development of progressively more elaborate methods of reworking his sources, but also come to appreciate each procedure and each piece in its own terms.

The Plan of the Book

The purpose of this book is to make sense of Ives's uses of existing music, on three levels: first, by explaining the role of the musical borrowings in individual works; second, by showing the roots for each procedure in the musical traditions Ives knew; and third, by tracing the development of the later, more unusual procedures from the earlier, commonplace ones. The ultimate aim is to help us hear the music better. When we know the function of each allusion in a work and its relation to the whole, when we understand each work in the context of Ives's career, and when we understand Ives's music and his uses of existing music in the context of the traditions he inherited, we will be many steps closer to hearing the music as he meant it to be heard, sharing the experience he sought to share with us.

The discussion will proceed by category, treating works of each type together. The greatest concentration is on the categories that are the most unusual in respect to tradition (cumulative setting, patchwork, and collage) or least understood (modeling, paraphrase, stylistic allusion, and programmatic quotation). All of these are also highly characteristic of Ives. The other traditional types — variations, settings, cantus firmus, medley, quodlibet, and transcriptions — are both more familiar from the music of other composers and less common in Ives's music, and are treated chiefly as they relate to the other categories.

The major categories are arranged in a continuum from uses of existing music that are primarily structural, through those that are both thematic and characteristic, to the purely programmatic, ending with collage, a blend of all these types. Ives's use of models to learn a style or genre is treated in chapter 2, followed in the next two chapters by the development of paraphrase in Ives's early variations and settings and its application in the paraphrased themes of his first major works. Cumulative setting is described as a thematic form in chapter 5, while chapter 6 traces the origins of this procedure and shows that most cumulative settings are character pieces, not programmatic works. Chapter 7 treats Ives's uses of modeling and stylistic allusion for commentary or expression. Works based on patchwork and extended paraphrase, which are also more character pieces than program music, are discussed in chapter 8. Quotation for the sake of a program or text is taken up next, followed in chapter 10 by collage, in which programmatic quotation, quodlibet, and other procedures such as modeling, paraphrase, and cumulative setting converge. This ordering is also roughly chronological, with chapters 2–4 focusing on Ives's early works, chapters 5–6 on the form most characteristic of his mature music, and chapters 7–10 on other procedures used in his mature and late works. The final chapter reviews Ives's path and considers the significance of borrowing in his music.

Within each category, some pieces are treated in detail as examples, and others are discussed more briefly. As Ives's practice often varies from piece to piece, an accurate account of his methods requires some attention to every work. Unfinished works are included when sufficiently complete to be sure of his intentions.[11] All sketches and versions for all compositions with borrowed material have been studied, and findings that clarify Ives's compositional process or choice of tune are reported in the text or notes. Previous studies that offer fuller analyses of particular works or suggest different borrowings are cited in the notes.

Every major work based on existing music is discussed in some detail. When all movements of a work use similar procedures, as in the First, Second, and Fourth Symphonies, the two string quartets, and the *Concord Sonata,* they are discussed together; when movements fall into different categories or subgroups, as in the Third Symphony, *Three Places in New England,* the Second Orchestral Set, the four violin sonatas, the Trio, and the First Piano Sonata, they are treated separately. Thus, the book can be used both as a history of Ives's borrowing procedures and as a reference book. Readers interested in a particular work are directed to the index of Ives's compositions, where major analyses are indicated in boldface. Readers interested primarily in an overview of Ives's practices are invited to skim or skip later examples in each category. Readers interested in particular types of borrowing may wish to read the relevant chapters first.

Proceeding by category not only facilitates discussion of each piece and highlights commonalities among similar works, but also acknowledges the uncertain chronology of Ives's music. A number of early works are lost, making it impossible to identify Ives's first uses of several techniques. Most of his surviving music lay unperformed and unpublished for years or even decades after it was written, leaving no outside witnesses to when it was composed. During most of his career, Ives was not a professional composer working toward a deadline, but an evenings-and-weekends composer writing mostly for himself. In the case of some of his works, he had the idea for the piece at one point, finished a draft years later, and polished it and had a professional copy made years after that. This makes it difficult to put pieces in order of composition, since most were worked on over many years, and the first notations toward many works are apparently lost and cannot be reliably dated. Style is not a dependable criterion for dating the music of a composer who was capable of writing in the same year such different pieces as the tonal song *The One Way*, the atonal-impressionistic song *Yellow Leaves*, and the experimental *Three Quarter-tone Pieces* for two pianos (all securely dated ca. 1923).

The widely accepted dates that John Kirkpatrick supplied in his catalogue of Ives's manuscripts and refined in the work-list appended to his article on Ives in *The New Grove Dictionary* rely on the sometimes contradictory dates that Ives offered and on annotations on the manuscripts, including addresses of his residences and business offices. These are supplemented by evidence from letters, diaries, music paper, the order in which pieces were entered on a page, a comparison of Ives's handwriting to that in manuscripts whose dates can be established by other means, and other sources.[12] Kirkpatrick's dates generally estimate the year of the first draft for each work, not of later revisions or of earlier works that used some of the same material when either of these is part of the piece's history. But now Kirkpatrick's dates are in question. The dates Ives gave and the addresses he recorded on manuscripts have been challenged by Maynard Solomon, who argues that Ives dated many pieces too early and concealed significant later revisions in order to claim priority as an innovator over European composers who used similar techniques.[13] Even if Ives did not intend to deceive, most of the dates and addresses on his manuscripts were entered long after the music and must be treated with caution. Studies of Ives's sketches, analysis of his handwriting, and other approaches are now being undertaken to resolve these questions.[14]

The most reliable dates currently available are those offered by Gayle Sherwood, who has carefully dated when the types of music paper Ives used were available, establishing in many instances a firm date before which a manuscript cannot have been written. Using this new information, she has refined the estimated dates of the various forms of Ives's handwriting developed by Kirkpatrick and Carol K. Baron, and by combining paper type and handwriting she can date most manuscripts to within a brief span of years.[15] These methods often confirm, support, or refine Ives's dates, but in other cases they show that most or all of the extant sketches and copies of a piece were written five or even ten years after the date Ives supplied. It is not yet possible to determine in each instance whether Ives's date is erroneous or refers to the year in which he first conceived the piece and started to work on it, perhaps developing his ideas at the keyboard without writing them down or in sketches since discarded. Even when there is good reason to believe that earlier versions existed, however, it cannot be assumed that they used existing music in the same way as in the surviving manuscripts, since extant sketches for many works show that Ives added or changed musical borrowings as he revised. In order to relate a credible history of Ives's practices, a study like the present one must rely on the best date available for each surviving manuscript. Thus, the dates given here for most works are estimated dates for the surviving sources — often a range of dates, reflecting the combined research of Kirkpatrick and Sherwood, including preliminary estimates Sherwood generously provided for this study. It must be stressed that these dates remain open to refinement and revision. Lost works and works for which no manuscript exists could not be independently dated, and dates for these works follow Ives's own.

Given these difficulties, this book can offer only a preliminary history of Ives's uses of existing music, not a definitive one. Yet even Sherwood's redatings do not substantially change the order in which the major works that use existing music were composed: the *Variations on "America,"* marches, and other early works that use common-practice techniques such as modeling, variation, and setting; the First String Quartet and the First and Second Symphonies, based on paraphrased themes; the cumulative settings, including movements of the Third Symphony and the violin sonatas; and the later works such as the *Holidays Symphony, Three Places in New England,* the *Concord Sonata,* the late songs, and the Fourth Symphony, which use a variety of procedures contemporaneously, including programmatic quotation, patchwork, and collage. An unimpeachable chronology would make Ives's path clearer. But it would likely confirm the trends in his development suggested here: from common-practice techniques to increasingly individual ones; from primarily structural and thematic functions to increasingly extramusical ones; and from modeling and variation through paraphrase to cumulative setting, patchwork, and collage.

Musical borrowing is a central aspect of Ives's music, and the borrowed material is usually central to any work that uses it. Ives occasionally added tunes near the end of his process of composition, particularly when revising works that were already rich in borrowing, such as the Second and Fourth Symphonies. But this is rare. In most instances, Ives's original musical ideas and the forms that his music takes grow organically out of the way in which he uses his sources. Thus, the relationship between the "quotation" and the context is usually exactly backwards from what seems at first to be the case: it is the quotation, in the sense that it represents the existing music that Ives used as a starting point, that has priority over the surrounding musical material. Moreover, musical borrowing is frequent in Ives's mature songs and choral works and pervasive in his instrumental compositions from 1896; apart from pieces such as *The Cage, The Unanswered Question, Tone Roads,* and others whose experimental conception in working out a single concept or technique provides an alternative starting point to that provided by existing music, only the Largo for violin and piano (or violin, clarinet, and piano) and the first movement of the Trio for violin, cello, and piano among the completed, surviving instrumental works written after the First Symphony do not exhibit significant use of existing music. Ives depends on his sources not only for motives and tunes but in many cases for the very structure of his works or of his themes, as well as for their overall character or style. Thus, his use of existing music is the most important factor to consider in tracing the compositional process or in analyzing the form and meaning of any work based on another. Taken together, these factors demonstrate that Ives's reworking of existing music is central to his process of creation.

One of the goals of this study is to discover why and how this reworking became so important, such a fruitful path for Ives to pursue. But our first task is to see how he actually used existing music. The journey begins with the imitation of models in his early works, and to that we turn first.

CHAPTER 2

Emulating Models and Learning Musical Styles

For centuries, Western composers have used existing music as models for new works. Renaissance composers based chansons, masses, magnificats, and motets on existing chansons or motets, borrowing one or more voices and reworking them in ways that range from simple embellishment to realigning the parts in new contrapuntal relationships. Baroque and Classical composers drew on models in many ways, from imitating a general style to reworking a complete composition. Johann Sebastian Bach adapted for the keyboard instrumental concertos by Vivaldi and Telemann, and the young Mozart arranged sonatas by Johann Christian Bach into keyboard concertos. Handel often borrowed music by other composers, sometimes with little change, sometimes greatly transforming his sources. François Couperin wrote tributes to Corelli and Lully, imitating their styles, and Mozart wrote a prelude and fugue and keyboard suite after discovering the style of J. S. Bach. Haydn drew on Handel, Mozart, and other models in his oratorios, which served in turn as models for Beethoven and later composers. In the nineteenth century, despite growing demands for originality in musical material, Beethoven, Schubert, Mendelssohn, Brahms, Mahler, Debussy and many other composers modeled works on compositions they admired. For example, the finale of Brahms's Fourth Symphony draws on works by Bach, Beethoven, Buxtehude, and Couperin, and Debussy's opera *Pelléas et Mélisande* is modeled on Wagner's *Tristan und Isolde*. The imitation of past music is a recurring feature in the music of our own century, from the bow to Haydn in Prokofiev's *Classical Symphony* to the hidden emulation of Schubert's String Quartet in A Minor in Schoenberg's Third String Quartet.[1]

There are at least two aspects to this practice in Western music and in Ives's career. First, young artists learn through imitation, and Ives was no exception. During his youth and apprenticeship, Ives learned many genres, styles, and techniques in both classical and vernacular traditions, from march and parlor song through art song and symphony, by imitating the best examples he knew of each type. Second, for a mature composer, emulating and reworking existing music is a way to say something about music within music itself, as in Couperin's tributes to Corelli and Lully or Stravinsky's half-affectionate, half-critical recasting of Tchaikovsky in *The Fairy's Kiss*.[2] Having assimilated many styles and genres as a young man, Ives later wrote dozens of pieces that are *about* music in various styles, particularly about the experience of hearing music and responding to it emotionally. In these works he often relied on models of the musical types he sought to evoke.

In many and perhaps most cases of modeling, Ives's dependence on one or more existing compositions is revealed only in general terms — in style, gesture, figuration, or procedure. In some instances, however, when using a specific work as a model for another, Ives borrows characteristic details of melody, rhythm, harmony, or form. When this happens, a recognizable allusion to the source may result at any level from surface quotation to inner structure. It was in cases such as this that the earliest "quotations" appeared in Ives's work, and it was in extending the idea of alluding to a model that Ives was to develop the highly individual forms of borrowing typical of his later music. Thus, modeling had a double influence in Ives's music: as a stimulus for "quotations" and other explicit references to existing pieces, and as a technique first for learning and imitating traditional styles and genres and later for evoking them, whether in a nostalgic, celebratory, or satirical mood.

This chapter considers how Ives used models during his youth and apprenticeship, as he sought to master the many types of music he encountered. Chapter 7 will treat modeling after 1902, showing how it made possible the allusions to styles and to individual pieces that are so much a part of Ives's mature musical rhetoric and exploring the meanings those allusions have in his music.

Early Examples of Modeling with "Quotation"

From his earliest compositions, Ives wrote in standard genres and prevailing styles. By his fourteenth birthday in late 1888 or shortly thereafter, he had written a march called *Holiday Quickstep* for theatre orchestra or band, a Polonaise for two treble instruments and piano, a *Fantasia on "Jerusalem the Golden,"* a Minuet and a *New Year's Dance* for piano, two simple hymns, two songs, and several works now lost, including two marches and two organ voluntaries.[3] Each of the nine works that survive from this period shows a determined effort to meet the standards of a given style and genre. Each conforms closely to its type, and there is not a radical experiment among them. Despite revealing the awkwardness of a beginning composer, these works already show traces of the acute sensitivity to musical style and type that is evident in Ives's mature music, as he imitates band music in the march, Italian opera in the Polonaise, fiddle-tune style in the *New Year's Dance*, hymns in the hymns, and parlor songs in the songs. Of these nine early pieces, four are clearly modeled on specific works, at least in part: *Holiday Quickstep*, the Polonaise, one of the hymns, and the song *Slow March*.

Ives wrote *Holiday Quickstep* in late 1887, when he was thirteen.[4] The last strain is modeled on the trio of David W. Reeves's *Second Regiment Connecticut National Guard March* (H84), itself a quickstep.[5] (Throughout this study, when a source work is first mentioned, its number in Henderson's *Charles Ives Tunebook*, in this case H84, will be indicated to facilitate comparison with the original.) The two passages are compared in Example 2.1. (In this and the following examples, where passages from Ives are compared with their sources, Ives's versions are marked with an open bracket at the beginning of each system.) The phrase structure of each passage is the same, the distinctive rising arpeggiations in the cornet melodies are virtually the same, and Reeves's grace notes, missing from Ives's cornet tune, appear instead in the accompanying piccolo and violin parts. Despite these strong similarities, the second half of each four-measure phrase and the closing phrase of the sixteen-measure strain are quite different in the two passages. A listener familiar with both melodies would identify them as similar, but Ives's tune is not a "quotation" of Reeves's. Yet the passage is clearly based on Reeves's trio, whether the young Ives intended such a modeling or not. That the modeling

Ives

Reeves

Holiday Quickstep. © 1975 by Merion Music, Inc. Used by Permission.

EXAMPLE 2.1: *Holiday Quickstep,* final strain, and Reeves's trio, third strain

was intentional is suggested by another allusion to the Reeves. As shown in Example 2.2, Ives's brief introduction resembles both phrases of Reeves's closing tag (aligned vertically in the example), beginning with the same fanfare figure and continuing in similar rhythm. Perhaps Ives intended this as a deliberate echo to signal his use of Reeves as a model.

Ives knew the Reeves march well and loved it all his life. It appears to have been both his and his father's favorite march. He used it again in three later works, *Yale-Princeton Football Game* (ca. 1899, rev. ca. 1914–19), the Trio for violin, cello, and piano (ca. 1911–14), and *Decoration Day* (ca. 1913–19). He mentions it in his most important writings, *Essays Before a Sonata* (1919) and *Memos* (1931–34), and Charlotte Ruggles recalled Ives and her husband Carl marching around the table shouting Reeves's tune during a visit around 1950, when both composers were in their seventies.[6] It was Reeves's most famous

Holiday Quickstep. © 1975 by Merion Music, Inc. Used by Permission.

EXAMPLE 2.2: *Holiday Quickstep,* introduction, and Reeves's trio, closing tag

march, envied and emulated by no less a composer than John Philip Sousa.[7] Its melodic similarities to Ives's march, together with its popularity and life-long importance for Ives, make virtually certain that the Reeves was Ives's model.

A similar though more primitive case is the brief work that Ives called "First Hymn, Op. 2, No. 1," modeled on the *Crusaders' Hymn* ("Fairest Lord Jesus").[8] Ives's untexted hymn quotes the first phrase exactly, modifies the second, and then heads in new directions. This may be Ives's earliest piece to quote its model; he dated it July 1887, when he was twelve, and its infelicities of voice-leading, including parallel fifths and octaves, an occasional fifth voice, and cadences on inverted forms of the tonic, suggest that it was among his first attempts at composition.[9]

Slow March (1887 or 1888) features a different kind of modeling, more of mood than of tune or structure.[10] Ives's song is a memorial march for the family pet, yet there is nothing march-like or funereal about his melody, which could serve as well (or, as Ives might have said, as badly) for a love song or hymn. Ives uses the theme of the "Dead March" from Handel's *Saul* (H182) as prelude and postlude, lending the seriousness of a funeral march to the otherwise commonplace tune.[11] As Laurence Wallach comments in his study of Ives's early music, "The intent is not to underline the banality of the subject [a eulogy for a dead dog] with the pomposity of the music, but just the opposite: to enlarge the meaning of the seemingly ordinary event by 'pro-claiming' it gravely and seriously."[12] The Handel was no less a model for Ives of how a funeral march should behave than the Reeves was a model of a quickstep. In both cases, Ives places his piece within the relevant genre by incorporating a passage from his model, but the Handel reference remains a quotation, less well absorbed into the fabric of Ives's own music. David Gooding has suggested that parts of the vocal melody are borrowed from the spiritual "Were You There (When They Laid Him in the Grave)" (at the

EMULATING MODELS

words "we laid him in the grave," mm. 10–12) and Arthur Sullivan's "The Last Chord" (mm. 17–21).[13] These may be coincidental parallels or further examples of borrowing from appropriate models.

The most interesting instance of modeling in Ives's early music is the Polonaise in C (ca. 1887 to 1889) for two solo instruments (probably cornets or violins) and piano.[14] Only one page of an ink copy in George Ives's hand survives, containing an eighteen-measure double period and a cadenza with two endings, one leading to a da capo and the second changing key and implying a different continuation, now apparently lost. The main section is modeled on the sextet from Donizetti's *Lucia di Lammermoor*, particularly its first eighteen measures, a duet for Edgardo and Enrico; the openings of the Ives work and of its model appear in Examples 2.3 and 2.4 respectively. Ives

EXAMPLE 2.3: Polonaise, mm. 1–7

EMULATING MODELS

EXAMPLE 2.4: Donizetti, sextet from Act II of *Lucia di Lammermoor*, mm. 1–6

may have known the sextet or its opening duet in an instrumental arrangement like the ones given for other excerpts from *Lucia* in Stephen Foster's *The Social Orchestra* (1854), but no such transcription has been found.[15]

The only material quoted exactly is the opening accompanimental figure, marked "staccato" and "pizz[icato]" to simulate Donizetti's pizzicato strings; perhaps Ives planned an orchestral arrangment. Yet Ives's melodies evoke Donizetti's at several points.[16] As shown in Example 2.5, the initial motive is similar both rhythmically and melodically to Edgardo's. The two are aligned vertically in the example to highlight the parallel melodic contour, and Edgardo's rhythm is written under Ives's opening motive to show the rhythmic similarity. The continuations are different, but the second segment of the Ives melody parallels a later moment in Edgardo's line (mm. 16–17); the resemblance is even closer in the flute and clarinet line, which ends with a descend-

EMULATING MODELS

ing fifth, as does the Ives. Ives takes the long note on the first beat of Donizetti's m. 16 down an octave and uses as an upbeat the dotted figure from the opening motive, sung by Enrico at this point. The result is a very neat variation on Ives's initial motive. As shown in Example 2.6, mm. 15–16 of the Ives copy from the Donizetti sextet a descending scale in parallel thirds but substitute for its final flourish a dotted figure with a double chromatic appoggiatura to the tonic triad, borrowed from another spot in the sextet (mm. 7–8) and used once before in the Ives (mm. 8–10). The continuations of the two passages (mm. 12–13 of the Donizetti and 16–17 of the Ives) are also similar.

Polonaise. © Copyright 1977 by Peer International Corporation. International Copyright Secured. All Rights Reserved. Used by Permission.

EXAMPLE 2.5: Opening phrase of the Polonaise compared with the sextet from *Lucia*

Polonaise. © Copyright 1977 by Peer International Corporation. International Copyright Secured. All Rights Reserved. Used by Permission

EXAMPLE 2.6: Later passages from the Polonaise compared with the sextet from *Lucia*

EMULATING MODELS

19

In addition to these specific correspondences, both works feature frequent motion in parallel thirds (or sixths, in the Donizetti) and a pervasive dotted figure that appears most often on the third or first beats of the measure and at the beginning or end of melodic units. There is a wealth of similarities, from exact quotation and close allusion to these general features. But the mix of elements in the Polonaise is different, and Ives introduces some new ideas, notably the imitative texture in his opening phrase. It is as if Ives had challenged himself to create a new work that simultaneously resembled its model as closely as possible and yet was as distinct from it as it could be. The exact quotation and strong allusions challenge us to recognize the model and compare it with the Polonaise, yet the differences call attention to Ives's growing skill as a composer. Such reshaping of given material is an ancient and effective method for learning composition through imitation. Perhaps the idea of imitating the Donizetti sextet while transforming it came from Ives's father, who was training the young Ives in theory and composition.

The close relation between composition and model in these four cases suggests that Ives used a single main source as he composed each piece. Other works from this early period may also have been based on one principal model, but no other direct borrowings have been identified.

A slightly later work shows both melodic and structural borrowings from its model. Ives's setting of *Rock of Ages* (ca. 1891 or 1892) for solo voice and organ bases its middle section on *Rathbun*, a hymn tune by Ithamar Conkey that appears with several texts in the hymnal used at the Methodist Church in Danbury, which Ives attended and where he occasionally performed until 1889.[17] The first and third phrases of Ives's middle section (mm. 31–34 and 39–42) follow almost exactly the third phrase of *Rathbun*. There is a formal resemblance as well; the hymn tune is in four phrases in a pattern of ABA'B', and the first four of Ives's six phrases follow a similar ABAB pattern.

Along with Ives's two variation sets and several marches that include popular tunes, the five works examined above are the earliest of Ives's surviving works known to incorporate existing music.[18] It is significant that the "quotations" in all five derive from Ives's use of particular pieces as models for his own. Such dependence on models also lies behind several quotations in his later music, and the practice of using models underlies many of Ives's later techniques of reworking existing music.

Modeling Without Quotation

Not every case of modeling involves quotation. Ives soon learned to veil his reliance on models, and from about 1890 through the next decade direct

EMULATING MODELS

quotation from models is rare.[19] Indeed, most of Ives's pieces based on models do not quote them directly, emulating instead their style, form, or procedures, and in some cases following a similar melodic contour or rhythmic pattern.

There seem to be two main factors behind this change. First, as Ives learned each genre by familiarizing himself with a wide range of examples, often by performing them or studying them in his lessons, he came to depend less on single models than on the conventions of each style and type. By using several models, he limited the resemblance to any one. Second, about 1889 Ives apparently began deliberately to avoid quoting his models, seeking greater independence in respect to melody, the most prominent element of music. This meets the common expectation in the nineteenth century that new music should be based on original material.[20] Ives was no less dependent on models than he had been in his earliest works, but he became increasingly able to grasp musical ideas in an abstract sense, imitating and transforming models in gesture, procedure, form, or style rather than surface melody.

When no quotation appears, a new work's resemblance to its model or models may vary from obvious to obscure. Sometimes the strongest relationship between work and model is a negative one, as when Ives avoids copying a salient characteristic or takes a different approach to the same text or musical procedure used in the model. Models for some pieces may be suggested by external evidence. Where none exists, identifying models and proving their relationship to the new work is difficult, making it unlikely that the extent of Ives's reliance on models will ever be fully known.

Variations on "America"

The *Variations on "America"* for organ (ca. 1891–92), the earliest of Ives's works to become well known and widely played, draws on a number and variety of models far beyond his works of three to four years earlier.[21] Laurence Wallach has inferred Ives's models for this piece from the organ variation sets he had performed in concert, studied in lessons, or acquired for his collection of scores. These include variation sets by Dudley Buck, John Knowles Paine, and Johann Christian Heinrich Rinck, particularly Rinck's variations on *God Save the King*, the same tune as *America*.[22] Wallach notes several parallels between the Ives work and its models:[23]

1   the fragmentation of the theme in Ives's introduction may have been inspired by a similar procedure in an interlude before the finale of Rinck's variations, "in which the opening of the theme, harmonized in various tentative ways, seems to seek an adequate continuation";

2 the running sixteenth notes in Ives's first variation echo similar effects in Rinck's sixth variation and in the second variation in Paine's *Concert Variations on the Austrian Hymn*;

3 the second half of Ives's first variation accelerates to chromatic runs in thirty-second notes, recalling the third of Buck's *Variations on a Scotch Air* and the string obbligato in the Pilgrims' Chorus from Wagner's *Tannhäuser*, which Ives had performed;[24]

4 Ives's second variation harmonizes the tune with chromatic lines and chords, like the first and several subsequent variations in Rinck's set;

5 Ives's third variation sounds more like a circus calliope than like any of his distinguished models of variation sets;

6 the fourth variation is a minor-key polonaise, combining the mood, key, and style of the second variation in Ives's earlier variations on *Jerusalem the Golden* (1888 or 1889) with an accompanimental figure like the one that Ives's Polonaise borrowed from Donizetti; and

7 The running pedal line in Ives's fifth variation recalls the pedal variations of the sets by Paine and Buck.

Even the bitonal interludes after the second and fourth variations, apparently added about 1902, have models in Ives's polytonal experiments, particularly his canons in two or more keys.[25]

These links between the Ives work and its models are all matters of style or procedure, never of melodic resemblance or unequivocal allusion. The third and fourth variations may be heard as comments about musical style, witty nods to styles that seem out of place in a serious work. But the other variations show Ives's determination to master the variation genre and the prevailing styles and procedures of organ composition, using the best models he knew.

Works Modeled on Previous Settings of the Same Text

For most of Ives's pieces from the 1890s, individual models have not been found. Yet in broad outline his models are clear: Reeves, Sousa, and other march composers for his marches; the music he played and heard in church for his choral and organ works; Bach for his canons and fugues; and nineteenth-century European composers for his art songs and symphonic works. As Ives grew more skilled in imitation, distinctions of style and genre became more sharply focused, and he developed more than one native tongue as a composer. During his late teens and college years, Ives was equally at home writing pieces in several traditions, from marches and fraternity shows to organ sonatas and symphonies, choosing in each case the appropriate models to follow.

EMULATING MODELS

For one class of compositions from this period, a possible model can usually be identified. Ives frequently set to music a text already well known in another setting, often so familiar that the words alone could summon up the music in a listener's mind. The challenge was to compose a new work that would allow listeners to forget for the moment the other music they associated with the text. Although the earlier work may serve to some extent as a model, Ives usually shows its influence in a negative way, trying to create a setting quite unlike that of his predecessor while remaining true to the text and to the conventions of the appropriate style. By avoiding direct references to the earlier work, Ives highlights the new musical setting and the fresh insight it may bring to the familiar text.

During his teen and early college years, most resettings were pieces based on hymn texts and intended for performance in church.[26] These involve a change of genre, from a hymn sung by the congregation to a work for soloist or choir. Even when there are similarities in form, suggesting that the hymn tune served as a model, Ives pointedly rearranges the elements. For example, in Ives's setting of Henry F. Lyte's hymn text "Abide with me" (ca. 1890–92), there are no melodic traces of William H. Monk's *Eventide* (H19), the tune traditionally sung with this text.[27] Although *Eventide* could hardly be more hymnlike, moving diatonically within the range of a sixth, Ives's melody has the shape of a vocal solo, with twice as wide a range, expressive dynamics, some chromaticism, and a leap of a seventh up to the high point, just before the close. The only resemblance between the two settings, apart from their common meter and phrase structure, is a formal detail. *Eventide* features a sort of musical rhyme, as the first, third, and fourth phrases each end with a stepwise descent through a fourth, a step lower each time; the second phrase closes with a stepwise ascent of a fourth. Ives echoes the idea of a musical rhyme, ending all but the third phrase with the same turning motive. Whether or not Monk's rhyme suggested Ives's, parallels between the two settings are few and faint. In this as in many other cases of reusing a familiar text, Ives avoided obvious allusion, seeking instead to demonstrate originality through a different approach to the same words.

When there is a melodic echo of the model in these hymn resettings, it is quite subtle. *Turn Ye, Turn Ye*, probably composed early in Ives's Yale years, is an anthem for choir and organ on stanzas of a hymn by Josiah Hopkins.[28] John Kirkpatrick has suggested that the soprano line in mm. 2–3 "was intended as a recognizable variation" of the first phrase of Hopkins's tune for this hymn, *Expostulation* (H21).[29] Example 2.7a shows the similarity in contour, with parallel notes marked by crosses, although Kirkpatrick exaggerates its recognizability in light of the differences in rhythm. A closer but still minor parallel occurs in the soprano at m. 9, shown in Example 2.7b. These

a.

b.

EXAMPLE 2.7: *Turn Ye, Turn Ye* and Josiah Hopkins, *Expostulation*

passing resemblances could be dismissed as coincidental or insignificant if another feature did not confirm that Ives modeled his setting on Hopkins's tune. Most hymn tunes for stanzas of four lines, if they repeat musical phrases, fall into patterns of AABA, AA'BA', or ABAC, so that the two middle phrases are always different. But *Expostulation* repeats its middle phrase, yielding the apparently unique pattern of ABBA'.[30] Moreover, the tune follows this pattern despite the contrary rhyme scheme of matched couplets (aabb). The musical form of Hopkins's tune is reflected in Ives's setting. The middle two lines of both stanzas are sung to the same musical phrase, with only slight alterations. Although the first and fourth lines receive individual treatment in each verse, a variant of the opening phrase appears as a refrain at the ends of both verses to produce an overall form of ABBCA' DBBEA', with an organ interlude between the verses. This form closely follows that of the hymn tune. Together with the hints of borrowed melody, this formal correspondence shows that Ives used Hopkins's tune as a model, more for structure than for melody.

During his college years and his first years in New York, Ives wrote over two dozen songs to lyrics set previously by Schubert, Mendelssohn, Schumann, Franz, Cornelius, Brahms, Dvořák's, Massenet, Grieg, and about ten other European composers.[31] As in the other examples of modeling we have

EMULATING MODELS

seen, Ives was seeking to learn both a style and a genre — here, the Romantic lyric style and the art song genre, encompassing both German *Lied* and French *mélodie* — and turned for guidance to the works of recognized masters. Comparing Ives's songs with theirs shows both how assiduously he sought to absorb the language of the Romantic art song and how shrewdly he distinguished each song from its immediate model.

His setting of Peter Cornelius's poem *Ein Ton* (ca. 1898) provides an excellent example.[32] The poet hears a tone in his heart, asks rhetorically if it is the sound of his dead beloved's last breath or the funeral bell that rang for her, and swears it sounds as full and clear as if her spirit came down and sang to quiet his grief. In his own setting from 1854 (Op. 3, No. 3), shown in Example 2.8, Cornelius restricts the voice to recitation on a single pitch, literally "ein Ton," giving the melody to the piano. This clever text-painting poses a special problem for the student seeking to emulate Cornelius's setting and to reflect the text, yet wishing to avoid mere imitation. Such a one-note melody cannot be imitated without being duplicated, yet the references in the text virtually

EXAMPLE 2.8: Peter Cornelius, *Ein Ton*, mm. 1–8

EXAMPLE 2.9: Ives, *Ein Ton*, mm. 1–6

require that the music reiterate a single tone. Ives's solution, shown in Example 2.9, is to reverse the roles of piano and voice and to limit repetition to three successive measures at the most, thereby conveying a sense of reiteration without copying Cornelius's approach in either part or even hinting at such recitation in the voice. Melodic interest, given to the piano in the Cornelius setting, is restricted to the voice in Ives's, where the piano echoes in its syncopated right-hand chords, tolling bass notes, and recurrent rolling figures the dulling repetition of Cornelius's vocal line. Ives simultaneously emulates the central conception of his model and avoids alluding to it overtly, a neat trick.

Beyond the idea of reiteration in one part against melody in the other, Ives also borrows from his model the opening rhythmic figure in the voice (three short notes and a long one, as suggested by the text); the contour of the opening phrase, with a 3–2–1 descent followed by a rise to an appoggiatura at the peak; perpetual motion in the piano, broken only at the most important

EMULATING MODELS

points of articulation; and the tendency for phrases to move from minor to relative major (Ives's song closes in the relative major, Cornelius's returns to tonic minor). The songs differ in form; the Ives is a modified strophic form with a two-measure introduction before each strophe, and the Cornelius is set in couplets separated by two-measure interludes and closed by a postlude that echoes the main theme — a modified ABA pattern. Yet both composers set off the final couplet by a soft dynamic preceded by the dynamic and melodic high point of the song. In sum, Ives's song is clearly modeled on the Cornelius in conception and certain details, but shows its distinctiveness by reversing the roles of voice and piano and adopting a different melody and form. The result is a work that is simultaneously like and unlike its model, without the least hint of "quotation."

Ives seems to have begun resetting German texts in his studies with Horatio Parker at Yale. Parker presented the music of the European masters as models for form, style, phrasing, harmony, counterpoint, and instrumentation. Students were expected to imitate and absorb these models while writing music that was original within the given style. The resetting of texts from well-known European art songs seems to have been a favorite assignment of Parker's and a favorite exercise for Ives, for all of Ives's songs of this type were apparently written during his last year or two of college and his first four years in New York.

Ich grolle nicht and Feldeinsamkeit

What Parker and Ives were after is suggested by an anecdote from Ives's last semester, in spring 1898. The eminent American composer George Whitefield Chadwick, Parker's former teacher, visited Parker's composition class one afternoon, when Parker was commenting on two of Ives's songs on German models: Ich grolle nicht (ca. 1898), after Schumann's setting in Dichterliebe (Op. 48); and Feldeinsamkeit (ca. 1898), which Ives called by its English title In Summerfields, after Brahms (Op. 86, No. 2).[33] As Ives noted the story on a copy of Ich grolle nicht,

> When Chadwick came in, Parker [was] objecting to the too many keys in the middle [of Summerfields] — Geo. W. C. grinned at it and [at] H. W. P. Of this song, Prof. Horat[io] P[arker] said it [was] nearer to the G[rolle] of Schumann than the Summerfields was near to Brahms.
>
> But Chadwick said the Summerfields was the best. C. said "The melodic line has a natural continuity — it flows — and stops when [rounded out] — as only good songs do. And [it's] different from Brahms, as in the piano part and the harmony it takes a more difficult and almost opposite [approach] to Brahms, for the active tranquillity of the outdoor beauty of

nature is harder to express than just quietude. In its way [it's] almost as good as Brahms." He winked at H. W. P. and said "That's as good a song as you could write."[34]

These remarks, together with a look at the music itself, show what Parker and Chadwick thought Ives was doing. Their comments concern not only the quality of the music and its aptness for the text, but also the relationship of Ives's songs to their models. To be like their models is good, as Parker affirms, for it shows Ives's ability to reproduce the style of European art song. But to be different, even to take an opposite approach, is also good, as Chadwick argues. Mastering the genre required not only studying and imitating the art songs of leading composers, but also finding new, individual solutions to the same problems of text declamation and characterization. Both songs illustrate Ives's attempts to balance these concerns.

Schumann's setting of *Ich grolle nicht,* shown in Example 2.10, is moderately fast and loud, with a piano part consisting entirely of pounding octaves in the bass under pulsating eighth-note chords. Ives's version, shown in Example 2.11, is altogether different in character: much more lyrical, slower, and softer, with more varied figuration in the piano.[35] One of the most striking differences is the treatment of the opening line, "Ich grolle nicht, und wenn das Herz auch bricht" (I bear no grudge, although my heart may break): defiant and ultimately hollow in the Schumann, as if the speaker were trying to conceal his breaking heart and wounded pride behind a laugh of triumph; soft, almost tender, and full of an opposite but equally poignant irony in the Ives.

Yet there are striking similarities between the two settings. Schumann radically alters the structure of Heinrich Heine's poem, repeating each half of the second line, grouping the opening words of the second quatrain ("Das weiss ich längst") with the first stanza of the song, repeating the first line of the poem as a refrain at the beginning of the second half, and closing with two statements of the poem's opening phrase, already heard several times. Ives deploys the text in almost exactly the same way, with some additional repetition to close the first half. He even follows Schumann in a small detail, changing "Traum" and "Raum" in the second stanza to "Traume" and "Raume." Clearly Ives did not work directly from Heine's poem; either he had Schumann's song in front of him, or Parker supplied him the text as Schumann actually set it.

These strong textual parallels are joined by musical ones, showing beyond any doubt that Ives used Schumann's setting as a direct model. There are similar rhythms and melodic contours at many spots in the text. The opening phrases are full of examples: the same interval contour at the first "grolle nicht"; a retrograde-inverted contour at "und wenn das Herz auch bricht"; similar contour in the repeated "ewig verlor'nes Lieb"; and similar rhythm in

EXAMPLE 2.10: Schumann, *Ich grolle nicht*, mm. 1–12

all three spots. These are not "quotations" but correspondences prompted in part by the rhythms and accents of the text. Other parallels include the frequent use of repeated pitches in the melody and repeated chords in the accompaniment; a shift to minor at the second line; a change in character for the third and fourth lines, with a rising sequence, a higher dynamic level, and

EXAMPLE 2.11: Ives, *Ich grolle nicht*, mm. 1–15

EMULATING MODELS

virtually the same rhythm in both songs; a varied reprise of the first eight measures of the first stanza at the beginning of the second; and a crescendo in the second stanza beginning at the words "Ich sah dich ja im Traume" (I saw you in a dream), although the Ives setting reaches its climax sooner and makes a diminuendo to a quiet close.

Despite the great differences in character and sound, the two songs are quite similar in structure and in their reading of the poem. This must have been part of the assignment from Parker: to write a song that closely follows the structure of Schumann's setting and is true to the text, yet achieves individuality in both musical material and expression. Ives's success in this is no doubt what earned Parker's approval.

The two versions of *Feldeinsamkeit* are also different on the surface, yet have a number of parallels.[36] Brahms's setting, shown in Example 2.12, is slow and chordal, with a dotted pulsation in the bass and a gently moving inner line in eighths. As usual, Ives chose quite a different tempo and figuration for his set-

EXAMPLE 2.12: Brahms, *Feldeinsamkeit*, mm. 1–8

Feldeinsamkeit. © 1935 by Merion Music, Inc. Used by Permission.

EXAMPLE 2.13: Ives, *Feldeinsamkeit*, mm. 6–13

ting, shown in Example 2.13: allegretto with running sixteenth-note arpeggiation reminiscent of the C-major prelude in the first book of Bach's *Well-Tempered Clavier*.[37] Here is one aspect of the "active tranquillity" Chadwick admired. Although Brahms changes figuration, Ives deviates only briefly from the initial pattern, creating a rhythmic consistency more typical of Schumann than of Brahms. Ives did the reverse in *Ich grolle nicht*, whose accompaniment is much more varied than that of its model, and this suggests that in both cases Ives intentionally took a contrary approach, imitating Brahms's rhythmic variety in resetting a Schumann text and Schumann's regularity in treating one from Brahms.[38] The two songs differ also in form and harmonic plan; the second strophe of the Brahms varies the first, whereas Ives introduces new music and an extensive modulation (prompting Parker's complaint about "too many keys") and closes with a reprise of the opening text and music.[39]

Yet there are many similarities. Both songs feature soft dynamics and generally slow harmonic rhythm. Both repeat segments of text, with Ives following all the repetitions in his model and adding new ones, as he did in *Ich grolle nicht*. Among several parallels in declamation, perhaps the clearest are the rhythm and contour at "nach oben, nach oben" and a rising seventh-chord arpeggiation at "schöne stille Träume" (m. 22 in the Brahms, m. 28 in the Ives); among the less obvious are the sly reversals in the first vocal phrase, where Ives follows Brahms in alternating even and dotted rhythms, but reverses their placement, and echoes the triadic sound of his model's melody, while adopting a very different contour. In the harmony, both songs shift to a minor chord at "Unterlass" (tonic minor in m. 11 of the Brahms, a more surprising minor lowered seventh in m. 16 of the Ives) and move into the flat region at "schöne stille Träume" (notated enharmonically in the Ives). Finally, both songs include passages that pass through a string of chromatically altered chords on the way from the tonic through the subdominant to the dominant (mm. 21–25 of the Brahms, mm. 14–18 of the Ives); the bass in the Brahms moves up by half step, that in the Ives mostly down by whole step in what is, characteristically, a less predictable progression.[40] Although the dissimilarities are striking and the parallels more subtle, the two songs have enough in common to prove that Brahms's setting served Ives as a model even as he sought to distinguish his own song from it.

When Ives published ten of his French and German songs in *114 Songs*, he acknowledged their nature as stylistic studies in a somewhat defensive footnote to *Ich grolle nicht*:

> The writer has been severely criticized for attempting to put music to texts of songs, which are masterpieces of great composers. The song above and some of the others, were written primarily as studies. It should be unnecessary to say that they were not composed in the spirit of competition; neither Schumann, Brahms or Franz will be the one to suffer by a comparison, — another unnecessary statement. Moreover, they would probably be the last to claim a monopoly of anything — especially the right of man to the pleasure of trying to express in music whatever he wants to. These songs are inserted not so much in spite of this criticism as because of it.[41]

Despite Ives's protestations, competition was the point of the exercise. His songs are so different from the original settings that they suggest a deliberate attempt not to repeat the same ideas and indeed to take a contrary path, seeking opposite solutions to the problems posed by the text. At the same time, he frequently incorporates elements from the model and makes them function in a new way. Ives clearly aimed to write a song that was at once like his model and as distinctive as possible. In doing this, he was not simply using a text he liked, as his next-to-last sentence implies. Rather, he was publicly inviting comparison with the earlier setting, as a test of his ability to create a convincing yet individual setting of a well-known text and as a demonstration of his growing capabilities as a composer.

Ives here is like the young Mozart, who once wrote to his father that he had set to music an aria text already "beautifully composed" by Johann Christian Bach: "Just because I know Bach's setting so well and like it so much, and because it is always ringing in my ears, I wished to try and see whether in spite of all this I could not write an aria totally unlike his" — and, by implication, equally good or better.[42] What this involves is not imitation but emulation, the attempt to equal or surpass the achievements of another. Ives's modest statement that "neither Schumann, Brahms or Franz will be the one to suffer by a comparison" belies his hope that the quality of his art would be proven by meeting the great German Lieder composers on their own ground. Chadwick's comments that Ives's song was "almost as good as Brahms" and "as good a song as [Parker] could write" must have been music to his ears.

That these songs were more than classroom exercises for Ives is clear both from his later inclusion of them in *114 Songs* and in his continuing even after graduation to write songs to texts drawn from European art songs. Although the relationship to the previous setting of the same text varies, it appears that most and probably all of Ives's songs of this type use the existing setting as a model, at least in part. Ives's purpose in each case must have been essentially the same: to demonstrate his skill as a composer of art songs by inviting comparison with some of the masters and masterpieces of the genre.

The Celestial Country

When Ives tackled the late-Victorian choral cantata soon after graduation, he again turned to the most appropriate model, this time in his teacher's own work. *The Celestial Country* (ca. 1898–1902) is modeled on Parker's masterpiece, the oratorio *Hora novissima* (1893).[43] Victor Fell Yellin has noted similarities in scope, musical language, performing forces, formal procedures, and even text, for Ives thought that his text, a processional hymn by Henry

EMULATING MODELS

Alford, was based on the Latin poem by Bernard de Morlaix that Parker had used.[44] Both works include antiphonal and a cappella movements, fugato sections that state the theme in unison toward the end (No. 11 in the Parker, No. 3 in the Ives), choral movements to open and close the work, and separate movements for solo singers, solo quartet, and soloists with the choir. The mix is different in each work, but the ingredients are substantially the same.

In addition, some movements in the Ives appear to be modeled on specific movements in the Parker. Ives's fifth movement, for double quartet a cappella, resembles Parker's eighth movement for double chorus and orchestra in both its choral antiphony and its triple meter and characteristic rhythms. Ives's opening soprano melody echoes the rising and falling arch and the alternately even and dotted siciliano rhythms of the first main idea in the Parker (at m. 5, varied in the soprano at m. 19). A later theme in the Ives (mm. 47ff.) begins with a strong hemiola like that in the opening measures and first choral entrance of the Parker.[45]

The most conspicuous instance of modeling is Ives's third movement, for accompanied solo quartet, which draws on Parker's third movement "Spe modo vivitur," an aria for bass and orchestra. Both are moderatos in D minor and begin in $\frac{3}{4}$ time, and in each the middle section in the relative major features a striking pattern of alternating $\frac{4}{4}$ and $\frac{3}{4}$ measures, continuing with occasional interruptions for nineteen measures in the Parker and about twice as long in the Ives.[46] The melodies are similar in pitch and rhythm, featuring arpeggiation, half notes, and dotted figures, and both are accompanied by syncopated quarter-note figures and a counterpointing line (a real obbligato in the Parker, merely accompanimental in the Ives). Even without direct quotation, it is clear the Ives is using his teacher's work as a model. Significantly, the movement from Parker's oratorio upon which Ives draws most heavily is the one he almost certainly heard in performance; "Spe modo vivitur" was performed at a concert of Parker's New Haven Symphony Orchestra on 4 March 1897, the year before Ives began his cantata.[47]

Here again, Ives follows a model both to assimilate a new genre and to compete with a master composer on his own ground. Parker, though still young (only eleven years older than Ives), was one of America's best known composers, and *Hora novissima* was his most famous work. The emulation in this case was apparently not only musical, but also professional. Yellin has suggested that through the 1902 premiere of his cantata Ives sought recognition as a composer in the Parker mold, identifying himself to the newspapers and music journals as a recent Yale graduate and Parker student, and that the work's failure to obtain better than pleasant reviews or to prompt offers of publication or a teaching position may have led to Ives's decision to leave the profession of music and make his living elsewhere.[48] I have argued that in the four years after college Ives tried to establish a musical career, one that necessarily would include performing as an organist and teaching, since no American composer outside popular music could make a living strictly through composition.[49] Parker had such a career, working simultaneously as professor of music at Yale (since 1894) and as organist and choirmaster at the prestigious Trinity Church in Boston (since 1893). The success of *Hora novissima* since its 1893 premiere had helped him secure those positions and win a national reputation. In 1902, Ives was organist at Central Presbyterian Church in New York and was just two years younger than Parker had been when his oratorio was premiered. The close resemblance of Ives's cantata to Parker's oratorio and the parallels in their careers to that point strongly suggest that Ives strove to match Parker's attainments, both compositionally and professionally, and that he hoped to increase his reputation by emulating Parker's masterpiece. His sudden resignation from his position as organist, barely a week after the cantata's premiere, suggests that he saw in the mild reviews or recognized in the lesser quality of his own work a failure to achieve those aspirations.[50]

This marked a turning point for Ives, the end of his apprenticeship. After 1902, when Ives imitated models, it was no longer to assimilate a new style or genre. The modern composers he encountered after 1902 — Debussy, and perhaps also Mahler and Stravinsky — seem to have provoked not emulation but a mixture of admiration and repulsion, as he absorbed some ideas and strongly rejected others.[51] Such a reaction might be expected from a composer already thoroughly trained in the late-nineteenth-century German mainstream who is seeking his own expressive path.

Yet Ives did not stop using models or alluding to specific models; only the purpose changed. When Ives alludes to a certain piece or broad musical style after 1902, he does so most often as a comment on that piece or style, in music whose subject is music and the ways in which we perceive it and experience it emotionally and socially. The sense of competition and of proving his mettle as a composer disappears and is replaced by a celebration of the music that he evokes. The prominence of classical and European models gives way to an evocation within classical genres of American music in all its diversity, energy, and spirit. Instead of marches modeled on marches and art songs on art songs, there is a sometimes dramatic difference in genre between the new work and its models, a difference that is often fundamental to the meaning of the new work. These aspects of modeling are explored in chapter 7. But before taking up these later developments, let us return to his early years as a composer to pick up another thread in the tapestry: the art of melodic paraphrase.

CHAPTER 3

The Art of Paraphrase

In *Holiday Quickstep* and the Polonaise, Ives was both learning a style and genre through imitation of an existing piece and using that same piece as a source for melodic ideas to rework. In some respects, this represented a conflation of categories. Using another work as a model was common for all types of music in the nineteenth century. This might involve some melodic resemblance, but the similarities between a new piece and its models tended to lie more in procedure, form, or gesture than in outright quotation. The art of reworking existing material was primarily the province of variations, resettings, and transcriptions, from variations on popular tunes to Liszt's paraphrases for piano of operas by composers from Mozart to Wagner.

So it is striking that around the time Ives began to avoid direct borrowing from his models in the late 1880s or early 1890s, he wrote two sets of variations and a series of marches that include new settings of popular tunes. These are, of course, standard procedures in both European and American traditions, from Mozart's *Variations on "Ah, vous dirai-je, Maman"* to Dudley Buck's *Variations on "Old Folks at Home"* and from Beethoven's settings of Irish, Welsh, and Scottish folk songs to settings for band of popular tunes such as "Yankee Doodle" and "Listen to the Mockingbird." A comparison of Ives's variations and settings with his works from the early 1890s that are based on models, such as *Abide with Me*, shows that he had begun to observe the traditional dichotomy between using an existing work as a model and using it as a source of melodic material.

Thus Ives's interest in reworking borrowed melodies did not disappear when he stopped citing models overtly. It continued especially in his variation sets, which served as laboratories for exploring techniques of melodic transformation. Over the next decade, his interest in reworking existing melodies led to thematic paraphrase, the most important stage after modeling in the development of his borrowing procedures. This chapter will follow Ives's path from his first variation set through the use of paraphrased themes in the First String Quartet and will conclude with a look at the ambiguities inherent in Ives's frequent use of paraphrase.

Variation, Transcription, and Paraphrase

As Laurence Wallach points out in his study of Ives's musical education, Ives probably first encountered variation form in his organ lessons.[1] He began to study organ at about age eleven; by August 1888, he was playing church services, and in February 1889, at fourteen, he became the regular organist at Danbury's Second Congregational Church.[2] Wallach notes that variation sets, though rarely played in services, were "a mainstay of organ pedagogy," and lists those Ives played in lessons and recitals in 1890–91.[3] As we have seen, these served as models for *Variations on "America"* (1891–92). But Ives's first variation set, from 1888 or 1889, shows little if any influence from them.

Fantasia on "Jerusalem the Golden"

Ives never mentioned a variation set for organ on *Jerusalem the Golden* (H20, also called *Ewing* after its composer Alexander Ewing). But he twice referred to a piece for band on the same hymn, which he called "Fantasia (or Paraphrase) on *Jerusalem the Golden*."[4] There is only one surviving Ives work that uses this tune, consisting of the hymn and three variations, and only one extant source, an ink fair copy in George Ives's hand written on two and sometimes three staves.[5] This is listed among Ives's organ works in Kirk-patrick's *Catalogue* as *Variations on "Jerusalem the Golden,"* but it probably represents a short score of the piece for band. Although it can be played on the organ, several unidiomatic passages suggest a conception for instrumental ensemble. In particular, the second variation has such an active accompaniment that it could be played on the organ only with an assistant or by shortening the bass notes and played the uppermost melody on the pedals, which Wallach observes "would involve sophisticated couplings."[6]

In truth, the title "Fantasia (or Paraphrase)" better describes this piece than does "Variations," for the first and third variations seem too little varied to qualify for the term, and the second is so greatly altered that it might better be called a paraphrase. The work opens with the hymn, taken almost straight from the hymnal. A four-measure codetta features cascading eighth-note triads, an effect better suited to an ensemble than to the organ; one can imagine choirs of instruments trading arpeggiations and cadential gestures like echoes. The first variation avoids the virtuosic figuration typical of the organ variations that Ives studied and of his later *Variations on "America"* and instead presents the tune unadorned, with a few harmonic changes and a longer codetta. Rising triads appear over the final chord of each phrase, again suggesting the entrance of a new instrumental choir.[7] The third variation is even more austere than the first, simply a harmonization of the hymn, usually in five parts, with a running bass line in the last phrase and a closing amen.

The avoidance of real variation in the other sections sets off the elaborate second variation as a point of real contrast, as do the change of mode from F major to F minor and the change of texture from a hymn to something like an aria. This variation appears on three staves, with a lyrical melody alone in the top staff (shared elsewhere by two or more voices), bass notes and pulsating chords in the middle, and an arpeggiating figure in the bottom staff, like an instrumental obbligato. The top melody paraphrases Ewing's tune.

As shown in Example 3.1, Ives's melody follows its source closely at times but freely omits notes, interpolates new material, changes keys in midstream, and reorders the phrases. (In this and other examples, where the ends of phrases in the source tune do not occur at barlines, they are indicated with vertical strokes to aid comparison.) Ives's third phrase is virtually identical to Ewing's second phrase in A♭ major. The last phrase begins with a clear reference in A♭, adds embellishment, displaces the tune an octave through a rising scale, changes key to C major, and ornaments the cadence. The key change is smoothed over by elision, with the cadence in A♭ left incomplete and the same cadential figure in C embedded within it. The variation's first two phrases are more distant but still derive much of their shape from the hymn tune. As the example shows, Ives's first phrase is closest to Ewing's third but

EXAMPLE 3.1: *Fantasia on "Jerusalem the Golden,"* second variation, with Ewing's hymn tune

THE ART OF PARAPHRASE

shares enough with the hymn tune's first phrase in F, the key of the other variations, to link this variation to the rest of the set. Although both the variation and its source are in four-measure phrases, Ives does not preserve a measure-by-measure correspondence, as in a typical variation; for instance, his second phrase, based on the first phrase of the hymn, abbreviates the opening figure, then expands later in the phrase. (To facilitate comparison, notes that parallel more than one point in another melody are repeated here and in later examples, enclosed in vertical brackets.)

Ives's term "paraphrase" fits this melody perfectly, and "fantasia" suits the overall form, with exact statements of the hymn framing an elaborate paraphrase. Melodic paraphrase of this sort soon came to play an important role in Ives's music, and from this point on, Ives seldom borrowed tunes exactly but either varied or paraphrased them. Although both techniques involve melodic transformation, paraphrase differs from variation in that the melody is not merely ornamented, refigured, or accompanied by new material, but may be radically recast: events may be reordered, repetitions eliminated, portions omitted, new material inserted or appended, the length changed, and the whole made so distant from its source that it may not be recognized as related. The tension between the new and the old, the changed and the familiar, that lies at the heart of variation form is heightened in such a paraphrase. When the new melody appears side by side with its source, as it does here, the relationship of the two melodies is sure to be felt, even if the depth of similarity is not immediately grasped. We will see that in Ives's later uses of paraphrase, outside variation form, he provides enough clues that we can still detect the source in the paraphrase and retrace the path of transformation.

March No. 1 in F and B♭

A yet more distant paraphrase occurs in Ives's *March No. 1 in F and B♭*, with "The Year of Jubilee" (ca. 1890–92). This survives only in a version for piano, but it may also have been scored for band or theater orchestra.[8] This work is significant for several reasons. It is the first of his marches to incorporate a popular tune, a common procedure in nineteenth-century America; these marches will be discussed with Ives's early settings in chapter 6. Unlike his other marches of this type, *March No. 1* includes not one but two songs, and so represents Ives's only surviving medley.[9] The second tune, a variant of "That Old Cabin Home Upon the Hill" (H141), is set in long notes against a more quickly moving original theme.[10] This is Ives's first use of cantus firmus style, used again in a later march and in all four symphonies. Most important for our present purposes, the first popular song in the march, "The Year of Jubilee," is drastically reworked.

Example 3.2 compares Ives's paraphrase with the song's verse, which is all he uses. Ives preserves the general outline of the melody, including the opening and closing contours and the peak on the sixth scale degree, while doubling its length to sixteen measures. He also changes it radically in style. The rapid repeated notes of the original are typical of minstrel patter songs but out of place in a march tune. Ives replaces the repeated notes at some spots with sustained tones and at others with a chromatic neighbor-tone figure,

EXAMPLE 3.2: "The Year of Jubilee" as paraphrased in *March No. 1*

THE ART OF PARAPHRASE

repeats or interpolates other figures, and so creates a melody with the spaciousness and shapeliness one expects from a march theme. This demonstrates Ives's concern, as a composer fluent in many idioms, that a tune borrowed from one genre to be used in another be recast to suit its new context, while keeping its overall shape and something of its distinctive character.

So distant is this melody from its source that, had he not labeled it "Air (The Year of Jubilee) etc." in the manuscript, it would be difficult to believe that he conceived it as a paraphrase of that tune. This shows how far Ives was willing to take the art of paraphrase, even at an early stage.

Variations on "America"

Variations on "America" offers another example of recasting a tune to suit a new function. For all its high spirits, this is a more typical variation set than *Fantasia on "Jerusalem the Golden,"* with an introduction, theme (*America*, H69), five variations, and coda (plus two bitonal interludes added ca. 1902). Each variation has a new accompaniment, while the tune itself is little changed beyond tempo, meter, key, and mode. But the introduction presents a complete paraphrase of the tune, as shown in Example 3.3. The role of the introduction is to prepare us for the theme without being a variation. Ives's paraphrase reflects this function, for it follows the theme's contour and quotes some motives without stating a single phrase complete and unchanged. It shares the overall shape and character of *America* but cannot be heard as a variation. This is a neat trick, accomplished in several ways.

First, Ives repeats, alters, reorders, and develops parts of the theme. Its opening motive appears twice, at mm. 1 and 9; in mm. 2 and 10, rising steps change to skips; and in m. 5, a figure from m. 13 of the theme appears early and is treated in sequence. Ives also omits notes and adds new material.

Second, Ives develops a rhythmic pattern characteristic of the theme. The dotted figure from mm. 2, 4, 8, 10, and 12 of *America* appears literally in mm. 18 and 20 of the paraphrase, in diminution in mm. 2, 4, 10, 12, 14, and 22, and displaced to the second beat in mm. 1, 3, and 9. By transforming the pattern and using it to vary the original rhythm, Ives creates a new and distinctive rhythmic profile that still is clearly derived from the rhythm of the theme.

Third, Ives changes keys in midcourse, as in the second variation of *Fantasia on "Jerusalem the Golden."* The introduction begins in F major, then veers off to the relative minor and its parallel major. In Example 3.3, Ives's paraphrase is in the middle, aligned with *America* in F major above it and in D major below, with accidentals beneath the staff where Ives uses D minor instead. Once again, notes between brackets are repeated; notes in parentheses are not used in the paraphrase. For several measures around the key

EXAMPLE 3.3: *Variations on "America,"* introduction, compared to *America*

change in m. 12, one can trace through the paraphrased melody the contour of *America* in either key, like a common-tone modulation. Measures 9–13 follow the tune in F, dropping into the lower octave at m. 12; meanwhile, hints in mm. 5–9 of the hymn in D minor are confirmed in mm. 11–16, as the tune appears at first paraphrased, then exactly in D major.[11] Measures 17–24 follow the second half of *America* in D, yet Ives alters the melody, particularly in

THE ART OF PARAPHRASE

Variations on "America," for Organ. © 1973 by Mercury Music Corporation. Used by Permission.

EXAMPLE 3.3, continued

mm. 19–23, to resemble the hymn's last phrase in F. Measures 25–32 (not shown) repeat mm. 1–8, restoring F major and leading directly to the theme.

Finally, the introduction varies greatly from measure to measure in the extent to which it resembles the source tune. It begins with a clear reference, but mm. 3–4 already are more obviously related to the previous motive than to the parallel spot in *America*, and mm. 5–8 develop a relatively insignificant motive from later in the tune into something that sounds entirely new. Near the midpoint, Ives's melody swings back to follow the hymn exactly, then again wanders away, only to return at the cadence.

THE ART OF PARAPHRASE

All these procedures are typical of Ives's paraphrases. He freely repeats, omits, reorders, develops, transposes, and elides material from the source, often adding new material as well. Many of his paraphrases change keys in midcourse, using the sort of "common-tone modulation" we see here. Finally, the fluctuation in levels of resemblance to the source, from direct borrowing to subtle transformation, characterizes almost all his paraphrases.

As in the *Fantasia*, the paraphrase is juxtaposed with its source. Here the paraphrase appears first, tantalizing us with fragments and distortions of the familiar tune, so that when the hymn enters at last it sounds satisfyingly fresh, straightforward, and complete. The introduction also prepares us for the variations, presenting a range of sounds and styles from diatonic to chromatic, loud to soft, and bombastic to playful that embraces many of the contrasts to come. To begin with the theme itself would not have been as strong.

Ives ends with the paraphrase as well. In the coda, the tune appears almost complete but gets stuck, repeating and varying the portion just before the end as if unable to find the final cadence. This leads to an abbreviated and elaborated reprise of the introduction that serves as the culmination of the entire piece. The first eight-measure unit is varied, the second omitted, and the third transposed to F major over a pedal part in running sixteenths. The two segments used here provide an almost complete paraphrase of the tune, and the last two measures supply the cadence missing from the tune twenty measures earlier.

In both variation sets, the teenaged Ives shows a sophisticated understanding of how much change variation technique will allow, as he includes variants of the theme at several levels of recognizability from the obvious to the obscure. Later this becomes a trademark of Ives's paraphrases. A listener may hear the second variation of the *Fantasia* or the introduction to *Variations on "America"* as snatches of quotation mixed with new ideas. Yet the source tune is present throughout, even when transformed beyond immediate recognition. The interplay between varying degrees of recognizability is a fundamental issue in Ives's music, and such shifting back and forth between literal borrowing and radical reconstruction becomes characteristic of his later uses of existing melodies.

Transcribing a Beethoven Sonata Movement

The sensitivity to style and function that Ives shows in reworking a minstrel song as a march theme and a hymn tune as an introduction is also typical of his transcriptions. About 1898, he transcribed a piano work by Beethoven for string quartet and piano works by Schubert and Schumann for orchestra, probably as part of his studies with Parker.[12] The arrangement of the Adagio from Beethoven's Piano Sonata in F Minor, Op. 2, No. 1 was apparently Ives's first work involving string quartet, perhaps an exercise to explore the medium.[13] What is interesting is what Ives changes. There are, of course, many minor alterations of the idiomatic keyboard music to suit a quartet: changes of articulation and dynamics, dropped octave doublings, parts moved up or down an octave to fit instrumental ranges, and the addition, omission, and redistribution of notes, especially in the inner parts. But at two points the changes go beyond adaptation to a new medium.

Both passages involve the opening section's second period. At its varied reprise (mm. 39–43), Ives inverts the texture, placing the melody in the cello, two octaves down, and raising the arpeggiated accompaniment into the octave above it. Perhaps this was suggested by Beethoven's own quartets, where the cello often echoes ideas first played by the first violin, as in the slow movements of Op. 18, No. 1 and Op. 59, No. 1. At the first appearance of this phrase (mm. 9–12), there is a more drastic change, as Ives alters the accompanimental figure from arpeggiation to a mostly stepwise line tinged with chromaticism, as shown in Example 3.4. Both figures have the same function: to maintain a sixteenth-note pulse in an inner part while the melody moves more slowly. Yet Beethoven's simple arpeggiation was old-fashioned by 1890, and so Ives replaces the late-eighteenth-century cliché with a late-nineteenth-century equivalent. The result is stylistically coherent, for the new figuration recalls the chromatic touches in the first period of Beethoven's melody, and a direct transcription would have been pedestrian.

Ives seems concerned to preserve the original effect. Paradoxically, this leads him to change some details to fit not only a new medium but a new age. In making these alterations, the young composer shows a growing sensitivity to what is appropriate or desirable in a given style and to the potential interchangeability of differing materials that perform the same function. Although this is a transcription, not a melodic paraphrase, it reveals ways of thinking that also underlie Ives's uses of paraphrase in the next several years.

Transcription of the music of other composers did not become an important category in Ives's music. Perhaps the most significant result of his early transcriptions was his willingness to recast his own music in a new medium. Other than his early marches, several of which were cast in more than one guise, the first fully realized piece of his own that he transcribed was apparently the Postlude in F for organ, orchestrated about 1898, at about the same time as the Beethoven transcription.[14] Such arrangements and even more extensive reworkings of his own earlier works became frequent in his music: almost a third of the songs in *114 Songs* are arrangements of earlier works in other media; most of the orchestral works and piano sonata movements are reworkings of earlier material; and some pieces went through several differ-

EXAMPLE 3.4: Beethoven, Piano Sonata in F Minor, Op. 2, No. 1, second movement, mm. 8–13, and Ives's transcription

ent guises, such as the organ postlude that was adapted as the Third Symphony finale and then reworked as the song *The Camp-Meeting*, or the Emerson music, which began as an overture or concerto, was reworked into the first movement of the *Concord Sonata*, reappeared in the *Four Transcriptions from Emerson*, and continued to be revisited in Ives's improvisations at the piano for the rest of his life. This reworking recalls Bach's frequent reuse of his past music.[15]

Thematic Paraphrase in the First String Quartet

In *Variations on "America,"* Ives uses paraphrase to convert a hymn tune into an energetic prelude and a climactic coda, retaining the melody's general shape and character while changing its function and style. The First String Quartet (ca. 1898-1902) represents a fuller application of the same idea, for here the main themes are all paraphrased from hymn tunes.[16]

Adapting a vernacular song as a theme for a classical work was not new. One could find examples as far back as Haydn's use of folk melodies in his last two symphonies and the Russian themes in Beethoven's Razumovsky Quartets, and more recently in Tchaikovsky's First (1866–74) and Second Symphonies (1872–80), Smetana's *Tábor* (1878) and *Blaník* (1879) from *Má vlast*, Brahms's *Academic Festival Overture* (1880), Dvořák's *Hussite Overture* (1884), D'Indy's *Symphony on a French Mountain Air* (1886), and the funeral march of Mahler's First Symphony (1888). Ives's purpose, like theirs, was twofold: to introduce the character of vernacular melody into a classical form with a tune that might have special meaning for some listeners, yet to create a melody that had the structure of a classical theme and could be developed like other themes, resulting in a movement that is motivically coherent whether or not one recognizes the borrowed tune.

According to Ives, some of these movements were first played in church, where the listeners would have known the hymns used. Ives later removed the first movement, retitled the quartet "A Revival Service," and called the remaining three movements "Prelude, Offertory, and Postlude."[17] In this incarnation also, the nature of the themes as adapted hymns was an important part of the piece's meaning. The problem for Ives lay in the second concern just named: recasting a hymn tune as a classical theme.

Ives understood that hymn tunes do not make good themes. The short phrases, plain rhythm, simple harmony, frequent cadences, and melodic and rhythmic repetition that make a hymn tune emotionally powerful and easy to sing make it a poor way to start a piece in a classical form and a poor stimulus for further development. That Ives was already aware of this is evident in his choice to begin *Variations on "America"* with a paraphrased introduction rather than with the hymn tune itself. Indeed, of the about one hundred movements in which Ives uses hymns, only *Fantasia on "Jerusalem the Golden"* begins with the tune complete and unaltered.

Third Movement, First Theme

The third movement theme illustrates Ives's solution to this problem. It is based on *Nettleton* (H42, "Come, thou Fount of every blessing," attributed to Asahel Nettleton or John Wyeth), as shown in Example 3.5. Several things make this tune unsuitable as a string quartet theme. There is a strong cadence after each phrase, stopping the music dead in its tracks just as it should be building momentum. Each phrase begins and ends on the tonic, killing the tonic through overemphasis. Without motion to the dominant (or anywhere) and back, there is little feeling of a sustained melodic arch and no preparation for later modulation. Finally, the tune is full of repetition: the first phrase has the same rhythm in each measure, the end of the phrase recalls the opening motive, the second and fourth phrases are identical to the first, and even the contrasting third phrase has internal repetition. The motives, however interesting in themselves, are used up before the piece gets underway. For all these reasons, a movement in sonata or ternary form that begins with such a theme is in danger of collapsing in exhaustion, unable to proceed and without any sense of where to go.

In reshaping the melody, Ives eliminates most of the repetition, cutting the length virtually in half. The rhythm becomes quite varied, with no two measures the same, and the motives that are most characteristic of the hymn and most contrasting from one another are emphasized by stripping away repetitions and inessentials. Ives evades harmonic closure in m. 4, substituting a half cadence, and delays the return of the opening motive until the end of the theme. As if to compensate for the material he has cut, Ives stretches the theme in the middle (mm. 5–8) and echoes the opening motive in the lower parts (mm. 1–2 and 11–12).[18] He injects a mild chromaticism into the lower parts (mm. 3–4), lets the harmony wander to a repeated C♯-major triad (mm. 6–7), and then returns to the tonic through smooth yet unexpected chromatic shifts. These harmonic and melodic changes help sustain the melodic arch over the entire eleven-measure theme, avoiding the collapse of forward motion after each phrase of the hymn.

The result is an elegantly tailored theme that closely resembles its source yet has the interest and expansiveness of a classical theme. Redundancy and predictability are eliminated to produce the sort of "musical prose," marked by asymmetrical phrasing and lack of repetition, that Schoenberg praised in

EXAMPLE 3.5: First String Quartet, third movement theme, compared to *Nettleton*

Brahms and that Ives must have learned from Brahms as well.[19] Avoiding repetition leaves enough unsaid to allow the music to develop. Yet all the motives from *Nettleton* that appear during the movement are present in the theme, so the movement is motivically coherent even to a listener unfamiliar with the hymn and unaware of Ives's borrowings. This is typical of Ives's works on paraphrased themes. Similarly, making the theme more varied har-

THE ART OF PARAPHRASE

monically allows a wealth of harmonic development to ensue. Indeed, Ives evades the tonic at the end of the theme through a deceptive cadence and quickly modulates into new regions, so that after m. 1 another tonic chord in root position does not appear until m. 73, shortly before the reprise. Nothing could be further from the source tune's inability to escape the tonic.

In short, Ives's melody is as perfectly suited in style and structure to be a theme in a late-Romantic quartet as is *Nettleton* for singing in church, and as inappropriate at a revival as is *Nettleton* as a classical theme. Despite radical reworking, Ives's theme preserves the hymnlike character and highlights the main motives of its source. Ives once wrote of *Nettleton*, "I used it, or partly suggested it, in a string quartet,"[20] his wording hinting that it involved neither literal borrowing nor vague allusion but something in between.

Having stated his theme, Ives goes on to develop it throughout the first section of this movement in modified ternary form. Later appearances of motives from *Nettleton* are references back to the theme, such as would occur in any thematic form.

Second Movement, First Theme

The second and fourth movements use similar paraphrase procedures. Both are in ternary form, share the same middle-section theme, repeat their first sections almost complete, and have extensive codas.

The main theme of the second movement is based on John R. Sweney's gospel song *Beulah Land* (H8). This has a longer arch and more varied melody than *Nettleton*, including chromatic touches and strong motion to the dominant, but it is even more monotonous in rhythm, with the same bouncy figure in every measure. Ives's paraphrase completely recasts it, drawing primarily on its verse (mm. 1–8) for the opening period, shown in Example 3.6, and on its chorus (mm. 8–20) for the continuation, shown in Example 3.7.

The opening period begins and ends as does the hymn verse (mm. 1 and 7–8), framing the theme with direct references to the source. Between these, the derivation is less obvious, due in part to the change from triple meter in the hymn to common time in the quartet. Ives varies Sweney's characteristic dotted figure by making the pickup into two eighth notes, then shifts the pattern one beat later in mm. 2–4 (marked by horizontal brackets in Example 3.6), echoing the rhythmic repetition of the original without its complete monotony. The meter change and displacement of the dotted figure make these measures resemble George A. Minor's *Bringing in the Sheaves* (H10), as the example shows; however, the resemblance may be unintended, since there is no unambiguous reference to this tune in the quartet.[21] The first phrase of the Ives (mm. 1–4) follows the melodic curve of the first six measures of *Beulah Land*,

EXAMPLE 3.6: First String Quartet, second movement, opening period, compared with the verse of *Beulah Land* and other possible sources

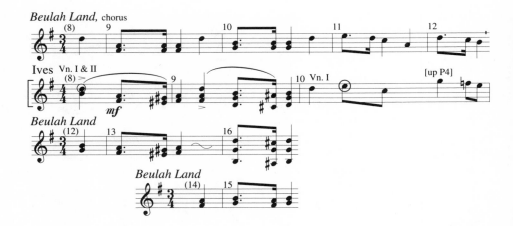

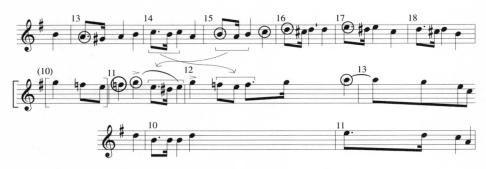

EXAMPLE 3.7: First String Quartet, second movement, continuation of theme, compared with the chorus of *Beulah Land*

springing up three times from low D and culminating on high D over tonic harmony. The B–C–B–A–G motion in the theme's first measure is both a variant of mm. 1–2 of the hymn tune and a distillation of the contour of both first and second phrases of the hymn tune (the notes circled in Example 3.6). There may be another source as well; as the example shows, Ives's opening resembles that of the Beethoven Adagio he had transcribed for string quartet some time before. The second half of Ives's theme (mm. 4–8) completes the verse of the source, but takes advantage of a musical rhyme in the hymn to borrow as well from the closing phrase of its chorus (mm. 16–20).

Despite these similarities, Ives's theme is far from being a "quotation." Everything from the change of meter to the omission and addition of material gives Ives's paraphrase the sense of a new melody. Even listeners who know *Beulah Land* are less likely to recognize the opening period as being derived from the hymn than they are to hear it as vaguely familiar.[22] Once again, Ives reshapes a melody to fit a new function and in the process changes

THE ART OF PARAPHRASE

its style as well, from a gospel song to a neatly constructed string quartet theme with an American character.

In the continuation, references to *Beulah Land* become more obvious, confirming its role as a source for the opening period. As shown in Example 3.7, the motive in mm. 8–9 of the Ives derives its overall shape from the beginning of the chorus (mm. 8–10) and its chromatic neighbor-note motion from a later phrase (mm. 12–16; inner voices shown where relevant). Since the hymn tune is in triple time, Ives uses these more direct references to disrupt the metric flow and establish long-range metric displacement.[23] After m. 10, Ives continues to follow the chorus, but shifts the pitch level up a fourth (and briefly up a sixth), exchanges the order of two measures of the source, and condenses the climb to a peak on high A. (As the example shows, this contour may owe something to mm. 9–11 of the source as well.) This stepwise rise of a fifth in mm. 8–12 of the Ives follows the similar rise in the hymn chorus, as shown by circled pitches in the example. The paraphrase breaks off as the music moves in new directions, including development of material already introduced. It is only in the coda that Ives presents the complete chorus, rhythmically altered and split into two segments (violin I, mm. 165–76 and 181–85, counting the last measure as 186).

Finale, First Theme

The main theme of the finale draws on three hymn tunes, as shown in Example 3.8. Most prominent are two segments from *Webb* (H62) by George J. Webb, best known to the text "Stand up, stand up for Jesus." Its opening motive appears twice in sequence in mm. 2–5 (in C major and E minor), and a motive from mm. 10–12 of the hymn tune pervades the latter part of the theme, with two complete statements (the second in B♭ major, the first modally altered) and several overlapping fragments (marked with horizontal solid and dashed brackets). The opening motive of *Webb* returns several times in the first section (cello, mm. 16–18; violin I, mm. 17–19, 23–25, and 28–29) and again in the middle section as a secondary idea (violin I, mm. 82–85 and 94–97). The two parts of the hymn tune that Ives selects are simultaneously the most recognizable segments and the most distinct from each other, the first being martial in character, the second more lyrical. In choosing these two segments and stating each twice in the theme, Ives emphasizes the melodic contrast inherent in his source while eliminating the less interesting cadential formulas and repetitions of the original. His procedure here is similar to that in the principal themes of the two previous movements, where the most salient and individual features of the source tune are stressed while redundant and unremarkable parts are trimmed.

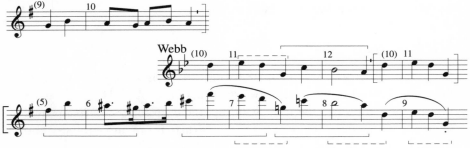

EXAMPLE 3.8: First String Quartet, fourth movement, first theme and its sources.

As shown in Example 3.8, the first two measures of this theme are based not on *Webb* but on a part of Oliver Holden's *Coronation* (H13, "All hail the power of Jesus' name!") that is also used in the quartet's first movement: the beginning of the last phrase, to the words "Bring forth the royal diadem." Ives later uses this motive with the opening of *Webb* (mm. 24–25 and 28–29, violins) and in canon with itself in inversion (mm. 100–104). The opening measures are also similar in contour to the cadence of *Shining Shore* (H54) by George F. Root, shown in Example 3.8 on the staff below Ives's theme.[24] The overall shape of the first half of the theme seems to draw on another part of *Shining Shore*, shown in the bottom staff of the example, whose main pitches link the two statements of the motive from *Webb*.

The coda of the movement presents a complete statement of *Webb* in the cello, in counterpoint with the theme of the middle section of both second and fourth movements (altered to fit with *Webb*) in the first violin and with motives from *Shining Shore* interspersed with free material in the inner parts. The cello and second violin are in $\frac{4}{4}$, the first violin and viola in $\frac{3}{4}$ (with quarter-note constant) — the earliest instance of polymeter in Ives's works.[25]

The coda serves two important functions. First, the four-square periodicity of the hymn tune resolves the metric tension of the first section, whose theme and continuation are both extremely irregular in phrasing. Asymmetrical phrasing is common in Ives's music from this time on, but this is the only movement of this quartet whose principal theme elides its articulations so completely that the structure of antecedent and consequent phrases is obscured. Second, the complete statement of *Webb* satisfies the implications raised by its fragmentary appearances throughout the movement, and its combination with the main theme of the middle section creates a climax of thematic intensity that leads to a satisfying close. In presenting a complete statement of *Webb* in counterpoint with another important theme, this coda looks forward to the form of cumulative setting discussed below in chapters 5 and 6.

The Middle-Section Theme of the Second and Fourth Movements

The principal theme of the finale is clearly based on *Coronation* and *Webb*. The connections to *Shining Shore* are less obvious. Yet there are other indications that this tune is an important source of melodic material for this movement and for the quartet as a whole. Its opening motive appears several times in the coda, as noted above, and the entire opening phrase, somewhat paraphrased, appears in the second violin as the coda begins, as shown in Example 3.9. Fragments of this tune also show up rather unexpectedly amidst other material in the second and third movements.

EXAMPLE 3.9: First String Quartet, fourth movement, coda, violin II, and *Shining Shore*

In the second movement, clear references to *Shining Shore* appear in the first violin at several points of articulation: at the mid-point of the first section (mm. 12–14 and, on its reprise, mm. 143–45);[26] twice in the central section, introduced by a motive from *Beulah Land* in the viola and cello and framing the repetition of the section's main theme (mm. 59–62, both first and second endings); and in the coda, where the latter combination reappears just before the complete rendition of the chorus of *Beulah Land* (m. 164). The first two of these are shown in Example 3.10, with the most direct references indicated by horizontal brackets above the staff.[27] Both of these segments peak on the sixth degree of the local tonic (the high A in mm. 12–13, B in mm. 60–61), a gesture that seems to derive from a figure near the opening of the hymn tune's chorus, marked with a bracket below the bottom staff of the example.

Each of these references to *Shining Shore* is unmistakable and marks a significant point in the form. When Ives so consistently and obviously pre-

EXAMPLE 3.10: First String Quartet, second movement, passages derived from *Shining Shore*

THE ART OF PARAPHRASE

sents fragments from a tune, he draws attention to that tune as an idea and makes us expect to hear more of it. In almost every instance where this happens in his music, the tune has a greater importance for the work than we may realize at first. The explicit references to *Shining Shore* throughout the second movement and in the coda of the finale suggest this tune as a possible source for the theme that is shared by the middle sections of both movements.[28]

The analysis in Example 3.11 bears out this suspicion, although the changes that Ives makes in his paraphrase make it difficult to recognize his theme as a variant of *Shining Shore*. The example presents the theme as it first appears in the quartet (second movement, mm. 32–45). The theme is in two seven-measure periods (shown in the third and fourth staves respectively), the second a variant of the first an octave lower. These follow the two eight-measure periods of the hymn tune (shown in the second and fifth staves, omitting mm. 1–2). The form of the source tune is AA'BA', and the Ives follows a somewhat similar pattern of ABA'B; in both cases, only the second and fourth phrases are exactly the same. Ives omits the opening motive of the tune, easily the most recognizable portion, and substitutes an opening gesture that owes its shape to the third measure of the tune, transposed up a perfect fourth (shown on the top staff of the example). The repeated D–E–F♯ motion in mm. 5–6 and 13–14 of the hymn tune is trimmed to a single statement each time, and the closing gesture of each period is modified to create a sequence on a figure from m. 4 of the hymn

EXAMPLE 3.11: First String Quartet, second movement, theme of middle section, compared with *Shining Shore*

tune, marked with horizontal brackets in the example. The similar figure in mm. 8–9 and 10–11 of the tune (marked with horizontal braces) is omitted, perhaps because its resemblance to Ives's m. 36 makes it redundant. Throughout, the rhythm is greatly changed and metric accents are displaced. All these changes make Ives's theme sound quite different from *Shining Shore*, yet the many similarities strongly suggest that it is a paraphrase of the hymn tune. What we have seen of Ives's ability to transform *Jerusalem the Golden* and "The Year of Jubilee" into scarcely recognizable paraphrases makes such an assertion far from implausible.

This thematic paraphrase is unique among those so far discussed in that the most characteristic and recognizable element of the tune, the opening motive, is not emphasized but rather suppressed. However, Ives stresses this motive elsewhere, at structural articulations in the second movement and in combination with this paraphrased theme and *Webb* in the coda of the finale, as shown above. Clearly, the motive is missing from the theme because it is being saved for another purpose. We will see in later examples as well that Ives occasionally eliminates the head-motive in paraphrasing a tune, saving the most recognizable element of the tune for later.

The Middle-Section Theme of the Third Movement

Shining Shore also plays a role in the third movement. This movement is in modified ternary form, with the return of the first section limited to the opening period and a brief coda that alludes to the middle section. In the middle section, after its theme is presented and repeated (mm. 33–57), the opening motive of that theme is developed in tandem with a motive derived from the opening of *Shining Shore*, shown in Example 3.12.[29] The latter's appearance at this point, like the overt references to *Shining Shore* in the second and fourth movements, is a clue that the middle section theme itself is based in part on this hymn tune.

EXAMPLE 3.12: First String Quartet, third movement, motive related to *Shining Shore*

THE ART OF PARAPHRASE

Clayton Henderson and Laurence Wallach have noted that this theme is rhythmically and melodically related to *Nettleton*, the source for the movement's first theme.[30] Yet the middle section theme is more closely patterned on the rhythm and contour of *Shining Shore*. The two hymns share a characteristic rhythm of two eighth and two quarter notes in triple meter, but in *Shining Shore* this begins on the downbeat, as in the theme. Example 3.13 compares the opening of Ives's theme with both hymn tunes. Although there are similarities to *Nettleton*, notably in m. 36, the relationship to *Shining Shore* is closer; Ives's tune is a modified inversion of Root's. The confusion here is no accident, for Ives chose these particular tunes as sources for his themes in part because of their melodic similarities. The paraphrased theme is a meeting ground for the various source tunes, where Ives explores the possibility of transforming one into another.[31]

After the opening measures, the theme continues as a rough paraphrase of *Shining Shore*, with contributions from *Beulah Land* and *Nettleton*, as shown in Example 3.14.[32] In this example, the similar pitch contour in the first two measures is stressed at the expense of the rhythmic and inversional similarities shown in the previous example. Drawing a parallel between the falling fifth in the first measure of Ives's theme and the rising fourth that opens the hymn tune is not unreasonable, for Ives similarly converts the rising fourth in the second measure of his theme to a falling fifth (by taking the first note up an octave) when he repeats the idea in mm. 58–59 and 64–65.[33] At m. 39, *Beulah Land* supersedes *Shining Shore* as the principal source for the pitch contour, though not for the rhythm, and at m. 42 it is superseded in turn by *Nettleton*, whose opening motive pervades mm. 44–49 (as indicated with horizontal brackets in Example 3.14). Once they are introduced as sources, all three tunes continue to influence the course of Ives's melody, and all three contribute to the theme's close in mm. 47–48.

EXAMPLE 3.13: First String Quartet, third movement, opening motive of middle section theme, compared with *Nettleton* and *Shining Shore*

THE ART OF PARAPHRASE

61

EXAMPLE 3.14: First String Quartet, third movement, middle-section theme and its sources

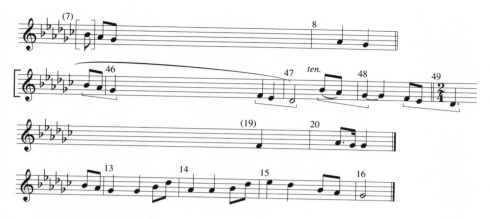

EXAMPLE 3.14, continued

What the Sketches Reveal

Much of this analysis can be verified by comparing the final version of this theme to Ives's earlier attempts. Sketches for the quartet are not complete, and those that survive for the other themes are so like the final versions that they apparently cannot help to confirm or to contest the analyses offered here. But several early sketches survive for this theme, and they illuminate Ives's thinking: they confirm that he was thinking of these three hymns as sources; they indicate that he intended *Shining Shore* as the main source for the first part of the theme; they show that he removed the most obvious reference to *Shining Shore* from the theme itself and relocated it to a later developmental passage; and they reveal a process of revision in which the latter portion of the theme was gradually saturated with the opening motive of *Nettleton*.

The early drafts of this theme are preserved on two pages of sketches, both arranged for the most part in systems of two staves.[34] At the top of the first page, transcribed in Example 3.15, there appear fragments of *Nettleton* (mm. 9–10) on the left and *Beulah Land* (mm. 1–2, without the pickup) on the right, as if Ives were announcing his intention to use those tunes.[35] Next, in the third and fourth staves, is a tentative try at a melody based on the opening motive of *Nettleton*. The rest of the page contains a first draft of almost the entire middle section, transcribed in Example 3.16. Where this corresponds to the final version, measure numbers of the latter are supplied in brackets to facilitate comparison. Ives made few changes to the developmental section that comprises the second half of this sketch (mm. 53–72), but it took several drafts to settle on the theme itself (mm. 35–52).

The theme begins as in the final version (mm. 35–36), complete with accompaniment. But it continues with the first two measures of *Shining*

EXAMPLE 3.15: First String Quartet, third movement, middle section, transcription of initial sketch, staves 1–4

Shore (shown in brackets above the sketch for comparison) and a rising sequence based on the second measure, shifted relative to the barline to produce the rhythm of *Nettleton*. It is apparent from this sketch that Ives intended to use *Shining Shore* as the basis of his theme, and it seems likely from the metric shift and the previous notations on the page that his choice of this tune was prompted, at least in part, by its rhythmic resemblance to *Nettleton*.

In the middle of staves 9–10 (mm. [53]ff.), the theme's opening motive returns and is developed. It is here, in sketching the development, that Ives finds the second segment of his theme. When the theme reappears after the repeat (mm. [58]–[62]), its first two measures are the same as before, but the reference to *Shining Shore* is less obvious, its opening motive simplified to a rising figure with a similar contour: G–C–E–D rather than G–C–C–D–E–C–D. This imitates a figure in the bass one measure earlier; erasures on the sketch suggest that both theme and bass line were altered to create this brief point of imitation. At the next appearance of the theme (mm. [64]–[67]), the combination of theme and lower line is modified to produce what will become the opening four measures of the final version of the theme; compare the upper voice in mm. [64]–[65] and the lower voice in m. [66] and the downbeat of m. [67] in Example 3.16 to mm. 35–38 in Example 3.14. All subsequent drafts of the middle section accept these four measures as the first phrase of the theme. Thus, Ives recasts the theme as he sketches its development, and as he revises he removes the most obvious reference to *Shining Shore* in favor of the subtler similarities of rhythm and contour charted in Example 3.14.

THE ART OF PARAPHRASE

Stricken from the theme, the opening motive of *Shining Shore* finds a home in the development. Between this sketch and the final version, Ives revises the figure treated in imitation in mm. 59ff. to make its derivation from the hymn's opening gesture more obvious; compare the first draft of mm. [59]–[61] in Example 3.16 with the figure in Example 3.12. The figure introduced in m. [68] and subsequently developed may also derive from *Shining Shore*. As in the middle section of the second movement, Ives withholds the most recognizable element of his source tune to the development that follows the theme, so that we may hear this theme as familiar but may not think specifically of *Shining Shore* until the latter is quoted more directly.

EXAMPLE 3.16: First String Quartet, third movement, middle section, first draft

EXAMPLE 3.16, continued

Finally, the sketches show a process of gradually saturating the end of the theme with the opening motive of *Nettleton*. It is clear from the first draft that Ives intended to recall this tune, the source of the movement's first theme, at the end of the middle section theme, for the reference to *Nettleton* in the lower parts in mm. 53–54 is already present (see Example 3.16).[36] But the references to *Nettleton* that pervade mm. 44–49 of the final version are absent from the first draft. There is a gap after the material from *Shining Shore*, as if Ives did not know how to proceed. The next segment of music, on the remainder of staves 7–8 and the beginning of staves 9–11, is a contrasting passage that does not seem to be based on borrowed material. Its middle segment becomes the duple-time Allegretto section of the final version (mm. 49–52), changing little in subsequent drafts, although the rest is discarded.[37]

The second page of sketches is concerned with finding the right link from the opening of the theme to this passage in mm. 49–52, and it is here that *Nettleton* comes into play. Example 3.17 transcribes Ives's five attempts, with corresponding measures aligned vertically for comparison; the music in each later version was meant to substitute for the music that lies above it in the example.[38] The example includes the measure numbers that Ives added to the sketch to show the course of the final version through the many alternatives he had considered (nos. 1–18 correspond to the theme itself, nos. 35–52 to the final version of the whole movement). The first draft on this page, shown as version A, presents the first eight measures almost exactly as they appear in the final version and joins the two ends of the theme with a one-measure transition.[39] This is amended in version B to add chromatic chordal motion in m. 44 and a new link to mm. 5off. This is amended again in versions C, D, and E, as Ives gradually works out mm. 45–49, with their many references to the opening motive of *Nettleton*, marked with horizontal brackets in the example. It appears that the reference in mm. 44–45 occurred in version B by an accident of voice leading, and then Ives seized on it as the solution to the problem of linking the front end of the theme to its conclusion, which had vexed him from the first sketch. In the process of solving this compositional problem, he solves another: how to relate this theme to the first theme, based on *Nettleton*, and thereby to draw the whole movement into tighter motivic unity.

The resulting theme sounds like none of its three source melodies, yet it reminds one of all of them. This is an excellent illustration of the suppleness of Ives's sense of melodic transformation. It is a question not only of motivic development but of reconstructing a melody by rearranging its most basic elements. When we have sketches, we can watch this process of reworking as the theme takes shape, but in other cases we can only see the end result. What is most surprising about these melodic paraphrases is how well disguised

EXAMPLE 3.17: First String Quartet, third movement, middle-section theme, comparison of sketch versions

THE ART OF PARAPHRASE

many of them are, how fundamentally they differ at times from the shape or rhythm of their sources. Both motivic development and this subtle sense of melodic reshaping remain very important for Ives throughout his career.

Cyclic Form

There is an extraordinary motivic unity among these three movements, due to innate similarities among the source tunes — similarities Ives carefully exploits — and to the appearance in each movement of material that appears in the others. In both respects, *Shining Shore* is the most important factor, present in all three movements and linked through melodic transformation or resemblance to the four other source tunes. In each movement, it is the main source for the middle–section theme, and its opening motive appears explicitly at some other point. Whenever two or more tunes are mixed, it is present: joined with *Beulah Land* and *Nettleton* in the middle section of the third movement, blended with *Coronation* and *Webb* in the principal theme of the finale, and combined contrapuntally with *Webb* in the coda.

The return in later movements of material from earlier ones is the basis of cyclic form, a device Ives learned from late-nineteenth-century composers such as Dvořák and Tchaikovsky, as we shall see in the next chapter. The strong influence of this procedure on Ives is apparent not only in his obvious concern to unify this quartet through such means, but also in the many works written over the next two decades that use cyclic unification, including the first three symphonies, the two piano sonatas, and the Third Violin Sonata.

The First Movement

The first movement of the quartet stands apart from the others in several respects, including the way in which the source tunes are used. It was written about 1897 or 1898 as a fugue for a class with Parker, and the other movements were composed about 1902, perhaps based on music played in church as early as 1896.[40] Ives later removed the first movement and scored it as the third movement of his Fourth Symphony. The key scheme of the four-movement quartet, C–G–D–G, is less traditional than that of the three-movement version, G–D–G; although unusual key schemes appear in some slightly later works, such as the Second Symphony, the key scheme of the First Symphony is the very normal d–F–d–D. These considerations suggest that the last three movements were conceived as a group, that the first movement was joined to them and remained somewhat extraneous, and that its later removal lent the work greater unity. Yet the first movement is linked to the finale through cyclic repetition. The same phrase of *Coronation* used in the opening theme of the finale appears in the first movement as a fugal countersubject (mm. 25–29, viola) and provides part of an episodic motive (mm. 17 and 19–20). A later episode on this motive (mm. 69–72) recurs transposed in a developmental passage just before the reprise in the finale (mm. 103–106).[41]

The first movement is interesting as an example of fugal paraphrase. Laurence Wallach has suggested that Ives's studies with Parker, particularly the study of fugue, prompted Ives to adopt "a thoroughly motivic approach to composition," relying on the manipulation and transformation of borrowed tunes to create motivically unified structures.[42] This connection between fugue and paraphrase is explicit in Ives's two fugues on borrowed tunes. The *Fugue in Four Keys on "The Shining Shore"* (ca. 1902) is a cumulative setting with aspects of paraphrase, discussed below and in chapter 5. The first movement of the First String Quartet presents a complete paraphrase in fugal style of Lowell Mason's *Missionary Hymn* (H38, "From Greenland's Icy Mountains"), with episodes and a countersubject derived from *Coronation*.[43] Example 3.18 shows the Mason tune and the paraphrased segments as they appear in the movement, together with the countersubject from *Coronation*.

The first phrase of *Missionary Hymn* forms the fugue subject, its cadence altered to fit smoothly with the answer in the dominant. The hymn's second phrase begins like the first but has a different second half. This phrase never appears complete in Ives's fugue but is represented by repetitions of the fugue subject (which drops some of its final notes, making its identification with the first phrase of the hymn less exact) and by the development in the first episode of a motive related to its second half, introduced by the second violin (see Example 3.18, mm. 21–25) and imitated by the first violin and cello. Reinbert de Leeuw has shown that this episode in three-part counterpoint is directly borrowed from an episode in J. S. Bach's "Dorian" Toccata and Fugue in D minor BWV 538, a work Ives had performed in Danbury.[44] The third phrase of Mason's tune arrives in the first violin at the climactic pedal point in the cello (mm. 81–89), its first half explicitly stated and the rest paraphrased.[45] After this climax, the opening motive of the fugue subject returns in combination with its own inversion (mm. 92–96), leading to a closing chorale-like statement of the hymn's final phrase (mm. 101–9), which begins like the first and second phrases but has a new second half, cadencing on the tonic.

Thus, over the course of the movement, all four phrases of the hymn tune appear in order. Indeed, this is much more a paraphrase in fugal style than it is a genuine fugue, shaped more directly by its source tune than by the usual fugal expositions and episodes. Significantly, what we hear when the tonic

EXAMPLE 3.18: First String Quartet, first movement, fugal motives and their sources

returns at the climax (m. 82) is not the fugue subject, as we might expect, but the one phrase of the hymn that does not resemble the subject. And the counterpoint is too free for a fugue, with extra voices entering and disappearing at will, parts reinforcing a single line in octaves or unison or moving for several measures in parallel thirds or sixths, and lower parts functioning often as harmonic support for the main melody rather than as independent lines.[46] Clearly, the presentation of the hymn tune is the focus of the movement. In this sense, it is like the chorale preludes and chorale fantasias of J. S. Bach, and indeed Ives called it "a kind of Chorale-Prelude," showing his awareness of Bach's procedures.[47]

THE ART OF PARAPHRASE

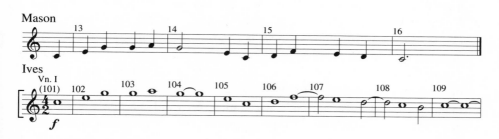

EXAMPLE 3.18, continued

The Significance of the Paraphrased Themes in the First Quartet

It is hard to find a common theme among the texts of these hymns that could account for their being brought together in this quartet, or an interpretation that could amount to a program for it. Yet there is a logic to their arrangement. The hymns used in the middle movements speak of redemption (*Beulah Land* and *Nettleton*), death (*Shining Shore*), and the afterlife (*Beulah Land* and *Shining Shore*) — all concerns of the individual — and all three use the image of at last coming safely to an eternal home. The outer movements, by contrast, use hymns that call the community to action in the world, spreading the gospel (*Missionary Hymn*), glorifying Jesus (*Coronation* and *Webb*), and soldiering for Christ (*Webb*). These hymns are filled with images of crowds and words of exhortation, whereas *Beulah Land* and *Nettleton* speak almost exclusively of "I" and Jesus, and *Shining Shore*, true to its

THE ART OF PARAPHRASE

role as a unifying force and its presence in both middle and final movements, alternates between first person singular and plural, between solitude and crowds.[48] Ives said he played the last two movements or their prototypes as prelude and postlude to a revival service, and he later titled the last three movements "Prelude, Offertory, and Postlude."[49] It is appropriate that a prelude to worship should center the worshiper's attention on personal salvation and that a postlude should exhort the congregation as they return to the world to take up the banner of the Lord. Gathered into a quartet, particularly in the three-movement format, these movements have something of the shape of the inner drama of a Protestant service.

This analysis of the texts may explain in part why Ives chose these hymns rather than others to use in his quartet, but it cannot explain why he uses the tunes as he does. Many of the links between these hymns are musical rather than textual, such as the ability of a phrase of *Coronation* to combine in counterpoint with the opening of *Missionary Hymn* or the rhythmic resemblance between *Nettleton* and *Shining Shore*. Most importantly, Ives treats the tunes, not as textual or programmatic elements, but as basic melodic material from which motives, themes, and entire movements can be developed. The drastic pruning of *Nettleton* in the third movement theme, the transformation of *Beulah Land* at the opening of the second movement, and the distant paraphrase of *Shining Shore* in the middle themes of both movements make it impossible to concentrate on the texts of these hymns while hearing the themes, even if the fragments that Ives makes immediately recognizable evoke a few key words or a general subject or spirit. Attention is focused instead on the tunes of these hymns and on their musical potential.

Here Ives goes beyond Bach's organ chorales, and beyond most previous uses of hymn melodies, in placing musical values above textual ones. Most of Bach's pieces based on chorales were intended for church, where the music is subordinate to the words; even in the instrumental preludes, however complex, the tune is never completely obscured and the words and their significance are never far from the listener's mind. But when a tune appears only in a fragment, or is stripped of internal repetitions, interwoven with another tune, or changed into a new shape, how can one still hear the text?

It is typical of Ives's uses of borrowed tunes from this point on that, although the overall character of the tune is important and the subject or spirit of the text may be as well, the specific words tend not to be. Perhaps this, like much of paraphrase technique itself, comes from his experience with variation form. In variations, the tune is treated solely as a musical entity. Although the words may be known, they do not determine what will happen to the melody as it is varied. If they play any role in the listener's apprehension, it is to lend

THE ART OF PARAPHRASE

the tune a certain character and thus, for example, provide a mild shock when one hears *America* rendered in circus calliope style.

The First String Quartet is an extraordinary achievement, a unified and coherent multi-movement work whose themes are all paraphrased from hymn tunes and developed in classical forms through traditional procedures. Among the many nineteenth-century classical works based on hymn, folk, or popular tunes, it is unusual in using so many; more unusual still in being a multi-movement cyclic work whose every theme draws on such sources; perhaps unparalleled in the degree to which its sources are transformed. And yet the techniques of paraphrase it uses are logical extensions of both the tradition of paraphrased themes, represented by works such as Brahms's *Academic Festival Overture* and Dvořák's *Hussite Overture*, and the methods of melodic restructuring that Ives had developed in his variation sets, *March No. 1*, and other early compositions.

In applying paraphrase to the creation of themes, Ives was setting out on a path that would eventually lead to a renovation not only of individual tunes but of traditional forms as well. Ives understood that the core of Western art music lay not in its themes but in their variation and elaboration, skills he learned in his variations and fugues and applied to the hymn tunes he adapted as themes. Like Beethoven in the *Diabelli Variations*, Ives demonstrates his great originality in the First Quartet not in his starting material but in what he does with it. Ives also came to understand that the compositional tradition that he sought to enter was itself one of variation and elaboration, within which each generation and each significant composer extended inherited conventions and enhanced them with new ideas. Perhaps paradoxically, one of Ives's most original ideas lay in his discovery of the potential of variation outside variation form. He borrowed and paraphrased, not because he was too poor a melodist to think up his own themes, but because reworking existing melodies allowed him to reach his audiences through music that was familiar, perhaps to evoke particular feelings or associations, and to engage his listeners in the process of thematic transformation in a way virtually impossible to do with newly invented material. In exploring the possibilities of this approach through paraphrase and later, more novel techniques of adaptation, Ives was weaving new variations on variation, one of the oldest strands of the web of tradition.

We will take the story of paraphrase further in the next chapter. But first it will be helpful to consider two issues raised by the First Quartet: the linear combination of tunes through melodic resemblance, and the problem of how to determine whether a tune is actually present, perhaps in a distorted version, or a resemblance to it is only coincidental. Both issues turn on the question of ambiguity.

Melodic Resemblance and Linear Combinations of Tunes

Many of the tunes that Ives uses feature similar or identical motives or rhythms, and he often exploits these relationships in his music. In some pieces, he transforms one tune into another or overlaps parts of two tunes in a single melodic line, using elements which they share to "modulate" from one tune to the other. This process is similar to that of paraphrasing individual tunes as new themes, and the two devices appear at about the same time in Ives's music.

One of Ives's earliest pieces to juxtapose two similar tunes, and apparently the first whose point depends on the transformation of one recognizable melody into another, was a novelty number for clarinet and piano played in a Yale fraternity show in 1896, later arranged as a song and published in *114 Songs* as *The Side Show*.[50] The piece turns on the resemblance between the chorus of Pat Rooney's immensely popular comic song "Is That You, Mr. Riley?" (or "Are You the O'Reilly," H97, 1883) and the quintuple-time waltz theme from the second movement of Tchaikovsky's *Pathétique* Symphony (H187). The symphony was current and probably familiar to least some Yale students, for it had just been composed in 1893, published the next year, and played in New York and Boston several times between 1894 and 1896.[51] Ives may have been struck at first hearing or seeing the second movement both by its unusual $\frac{5}{4}$ meter and by the similarity of its theme to Rooney's tune, so well known at the time.

As shown in Example 3.19, the first two phrases of Ives's song render the first half of Rooney's chorus but turn every second measure into a $\frac{2}{4}$ bar, giving the waltz a decided limp. This is itself a joke that would have been appreciated by the collegiate audience. The latter part of Ives's song paraphrases the second half of Rooney's chorus, reversing the order of the two phrases, as the example shows. When this lame "Riley" turns into the Tchaikovsky theme, anticipated by other fragments of the movement, the joke is made even richer, as Ives points out Tchaikovsky's inadvertent evocation of a bad performance of a humorous and trivial popular song. The transformation is subtle, as the *Pathétique* theme gradually becomes more apparent. At mm. 16–18, the last few notes of "Riley" move into the accompaniment (the circled notes) while the voice presents a melodically similar fragment from the Tchaikovsky, followed by a quite recognizable allusion at the words "Russian dance." Then in mm. 19–21 the voice returns to "Riley," ornamented by the neighbor-note figure that Ives introduced at the start of his song, which makes the resemblance to Tchaikovsky quite pointed. Meanwhile, the piano brings together two strands of the Tchaikovsky melody (cellos, mm. 1–2 and 3–4), originally related to each other as a melodic sequence but now forming parallel thirds, and a later accompanying figure

THE ART OF PARAPHRASE

EXAMPLE 3.19: *The Side Show* and its sources

EXAMPLE 3.19, continued

THE ART OF PARAPHRASE

Ri - ley,   they   speak   of   so   high - ly,

high - ly,   as   they   do   of   Ri - ley!

EXAMPLE 3.19, continued

(strings, mm. 11–12, introduced as a counterpoint to m. 3 of the theme in the winds) to create unmistakable multiple references to the *Pathétique*.

If we view the references to "Riley" and to the *Pathétique* as "quotations" and explain them as illustrations of the text,[52] we will miss the point of this very clever song, for the text merely comments on the transformation taking place in the music. What the song is about is the resemblance between the popular song and the symphonic theme, and the metrical change that transforms one into the other. Having established this relationship, Ives can achieve another level of comment in his text, pointing out slyly that "some think of [Tchaikovsky] so highly as they do of Riley" — punning on Rooney's original words to make a comparison between the relative values of popular song and European art music. Whatever Ives's view of these individual works, his comments elsewhere about Tchaikovsky suggest he might have thought more highly of "Riley," particularly for its economy and lack of pretension.[53]

The association of two or more tunes because of their melodic similarity became a frequent feature of Ives's music. The presence of common rhythmic patterns or interval contours helps to explain the choice of multiple source tunes for the First String Quartet, discussed above, and for the Second Symphony, treated in the next chapter. Similar opening gestures account for references to the hymn tune *Azmon* (H5, "O for a thousand tongues," arranged by Lowell Mason from Carl Gotthelf Gläser) in works based on *Shining Shore*—the *Fugue in Four Keys on "The Shining Shore*," the central section of *Thanksgiving*, and the song *Religion* — as well as the occasional confusion between the two among taxonomers of Ives's borrowings. Motivic similarity also helps explain the conjunction of the hymn tunes *Federal Street* (H22) and *Duke Street* (H16) in the outer sections of *Thanksgiving*; the allusions to *Where is My Wandering Boy?* (H64) in the first movement of the First Piano Sonata, based on *Lebanon* (H33); the linking of *Happy Day* (H27), *Bringing in the Sheaves* (H10), and *Welcome Voice* (H63) in the second and fourth movements of that sonata and the other pieces derived from the *Ragtime Dances*; the wedding of *Jesus Loves Me* (H30), "Old Black Joe" (H128), and "Massa's in de Cold Ground" (H121) in the first movement of the Second Orchestral Set, and the similar mixing of the latter two with "Marching Through Georgia" (H79) in *The "St.-Gaudens" in Boston Common*; the interweaving of the motto from Beethoven's Fifth Symphony (H173) with elements of *Missionary Chant* (H37) and *Martyn* (H35) in the *Concord Sonata*, and the linking of the last two with *Dorrnance* (H15) in the Fourth Symphony finale; the blending of parts of "Oh, My Darling Clementine" (H126), the college song "Few Days" (H150), and "Marching Through Georgia" (H79) in *The Gong on the Hook and Ladder*; and the combination of *Bethany* (H7) and *Westminster Chimes* (H170) in the finales of the Second String Quartet and Fourth Symphony. These will be discussed in later chapters.

One special case of transforming one tune into another is what Clayton Henderson has called "fusion," in which elements from one or more tunes are fused into a single melodic line.[54] The *Fugue in Four Keys on "The Shining Shore"* offers a good example. Near the end, the flute renders *Azmon* complete, while the cornet or trumpet begins to play *Shining Shore*, swerves off to *Azmon*, and returns to complete the second phrase of *Shining Shore*, as shown in Example 3.20. This is one of the earliest pieces to exhibit such fusion, overlapping different tunes through common intervals.[55]

Questionable Quotations and Phantom Allusions

This kind of paraphrase, which transforms one tune into another or overlaps segments of two tunes, depends on ambiguity, the ability of a melodic fragment or rhythmic pattern to sound like two or more different tunes. This same ambiguity, along with Ives's tendency to paraphrase or vary his bor-

Fugue in Four Keys on "The Shining Shore." © 1975 by Merion Music, Inc. Used by Permission.

EXAMPLE 3.20: *Fugue in Four Keys on "The Shining Shore,"* Shining Shore elided with *Azmon*

rowed tunes rather than state them exactly, allows a listener to hear what may be called questionable quotations and phantom allusions — tunes that may not have been in the mind of the composer but are suggested to the listener. Consideration of four works and their relationship to Lowell Mason's *Bethany* (H7, "Nearer, my God, to Thee") will illustrate this problem.

Down East, discussed in chapter 8, is an extended paraphrase of *Bethany* and at one point quotes its first phrase exactly, both music and text. There can be no mistake about the source for this song, which alludes to this and to no other tune.

The vocal line of *Religion* (adapted between 1910 and 1920 from a lost version of about 1902) is based primarily on *Shining Shore*, as Ives indicates in a footnote in the published score.[56] But as shown in Example 3.21, the song closes with a reference to *Azmon* in voice and piano, and the piano postlude seems to transform the second measure of the latter tune into the first mea-

EXAMPLE 3.21: *Religion* and its sources

THE ART OF PARAPHRASE

EXAMPLE 3.21, continued

sure of *Bethany*.[57] The reference to *Bethany* is vague and rhythmically distended, but the harmonic motion in m. 12 of the Ives song to the local subdominant, as in the second measure of *Bethany*, strengthens the allusion; it is
highly probable that a recognizable citation of this tune was intended.
Whether or not this is the case, once the resemblance is pointed out it is
almost impossible not to hear the final notes as the first six notes of *Bethany*.
One begins to wonder whether the opening phrase is also derived from this
tune, overlapping with *Shining Shore* (as shown in Example 3.21, first system).
Or are the first six notes of Ives's song an inversion of the opening of *Shining
Shore*? *Bethany* owes its presence in this song, if it is indeed present, to its
melodic similarities to the other two tunes, just as *Azmon* appears due to its
similarity to *Shining Shore*, yet it makes its presence felt in a very subtle way.

In the song *Evening* (1921), the allusion is even briefer and more subtle.
Henderson notes that the last four notes in the vocal line correspond to the
opening of *Bethany*, yet includes this allusion in a list of possible quotations
where "the very brevity, nebulous quality, and lack of distinctiveness" of the
similarity between the Ives work and its putative source suggests that what is
involved is not quotation but a coincidental resemblance of "standard
melodic patterns."[58] The case for *Bethany* can be made stronger than Henderson states. The opening gesture in the voice (m. 3) corresponds in rhythm
and contour to the opening of *Bethany* (in its alternate metric form, $\frac{4}{4}$ instead
of $\frac{6}{4}$), as shown in Example 3.22, and variants of this rhythmic pattern occur

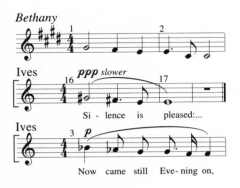

EXAMPLE 3.22: *Bethany* as a source for *Evening*

at several points during the song. The second section begins with two descending whole steps in the voice (m. 7), echoing the first three notes of *Bethany*, and that figure returns in the bass at the next section (mm. 11–13) and at the end (mm. 16–17). Once one hears these connections to *Bethany*, the figures of a descending whole or half step that pervade the song may come to sound like references as well. Moreover, Ives's song has the same reverent, simple, slow, stately, and quiet character as the hymn, and the evening imagery of the text, from Milton's *Paradise Lost* (book 4, lines 598–604), has parallels in the second verse of "Nearer, my God, to thee," which mentions sunset, darkness, and rest. The more links one finds, the more likely it seems that *Bethany* was a source for this song. Yet none of the references is obvious, and all of them could be nothing more than "standard melodic patterns," as Henderson observes. Without surviving sketches it may be impossible to prove a relationship with complete certainty.[59] If *Bethany* was a source for this song, it is clearly not essential to recognize the source in order for the song to be coherent and meaningful. Equally, if no allusion was intended, it does no harm for a listener to hear in Ives's song reminiscences of the hymn tune.

Finally, in the first movement of the Second String Quartet (ca. 1911–13), allusions heard by one analyst may be illusory.[60] *Bethany* plays a major role in the work's finale, as a principal theme and as a source for accompanimental figures. Its importance for the finale has led Wolfgang Rathert to identify numerous melodic gestures in the first movement that somewhat resemble the opening of *Bethany*, which he calls "the secret theme of the movement."[61] Some simply outline a descending major scale from the third to the fifth degree, like the mostly scalar descent that opens the hymn tune (mm. 7-9, cello, and 9–10, violin I); others extend or ornament this scalar motion (mm. 43–45 and 102-4, violin I); others he cites are nothing more than stepwise fig-

THE ART OF PARAPHRASE

ures, some not even descending or diatonic, that seem to have little relation to *Bethany*. None shows any clear rhythmic similarity to the tune. There is no doubt that the scalar figures are significant, for the contrast between diatonicism and chromaticism, in both melody and harmony, is an essential expressive and form-building element in this movement. But are they allusions to *Bethany*? They could equally well refer to other tunes, or to none at all. When Ives borrows all or part of a tune as a main theme, he is never this vague. Nor does this movement feature a theme or leading motive that might be derived from the hymn tune through paraphrase, in the manner of the themes of the First String Quartet. Although Rathert's suggestions cannot be completely disproven, there is simply too little evidence to establish even the likelihood that Ives intended to refer to *Bethany* in this movement. That does not mean that a listener will not hear it, particularly one who is primed by Ives's usual practices to listen intently for references to other music.

It is precisely because of the blurred boundaries between what is borrowed, what is paraphrased, and what is merely common musical property, illustrated in these pieces, that Ives can achieve the transformation of one familiar tune into another or the overlapping of two similar tunes as described in the previous section. The ambiguity is the key. Just as tonal modulation would not work without a pivot chord of dual or ambiguous function, so Ives's interweavings of various sources would not work if individual melodic fragments could not seem to be related to two or more source tunes at once. In the examples cited above from the *Fugue in Four Keys* and *Religion*, Ives uses shared elements to "modulate" from one tune to another, in the same way in which earlier composers used shared harmonies to move from one key to another. Ives invites us to draw relationships between tunes, to anticipate potential "modulations," by initiating the process, but he does not and cannot end it. Once he has made us hear the similarity between *Azmon* and *Shining Shore*, it becomes difficult to hear one without thinking of the other. And this is only one of several such melodic relationships Ives plays upon in his music. Indeed, it is typical of Ives to paraphrase or alter his borrowed tunes, rather than to state them exactly, and to use melodically related tunes and highlight their similarities. Both practices introduce an element of melodic ambiguity, which is as much a part of Ives's music as is ambiguity of harmony or rhythm.

This ambiguity of allusion opens up Ives's music to the possibility of being heard as making references to other tunes where none were intended. In part, this is because the process of ambiguous reference, once begun, has no clear ending point. If a musical fragment was not intended to evoke a certain tune and yet is heard that way by a listener, the latter is simply continuing in his or her own mind the process of allusion and transformation that Ives began, taking a direction in which Ives's music might have moved but does not. In the earlier works based on one or two sources, which are formally as closed as a Bach chorale prelude or Mozart variation set, we may safely ignore as coincidental what fleeting phantom allusions might occur; the same is true of later works that are saturated with references to one or two tunes, making their sources obvious. But in many of Ives's other mature works, the open-ended and ambiguous nature of allusion is part of the point. The vast swirl of quoted tunes being transformed into one another and overlaid on each other in a work such as the Fourth Symphony naturally points the listener's ear toward tunes that are not overtly stated but may be suggested by some fragment of melody that rises out of the crowd. So it is far from surprising that listeners — including those who catalogue and study Ives's borrowings — may hear "quotations" that Ives probably did not intend. Although idiosyncratic and beyond the composer's control, these hearings cannot be called wrong, for they are within the range of responses that the work allows and stimulates, part of each person's unique experience of the work. Indeed, the creativity that a listener employs in hearing relationships that are not "there" in the music is precisely the creativity that Ives requires of a listener in order to hear the motivic relationships that he reveals between tunes. Ives was clearly such a listener himself, hearing unintended similarities between tunes, and among the things his music does is to teach us to hear in the same way.

This does not mean that we cannot know what is borrowed and what is not borrowed in any piece by Ives, but it does suggest that the answers are far from straightforward. First and foremost, it should remind us that a study of musical borrowings must include both what the composer intends and what listeners perceive. These are different, particularly when a composer transforms his borrowed material as radically as does Ives; some of Ives's reworkings are unlikely ever to be recognized by ear, and individual listeners may hear in his music evocations of tunes he did not even know. The degree of ambiguity that Ives cultivated should make us suspicious of any claim that a certain work "quotes" a certain tune without a demonstration of how the tune is used and how much is actually present, for a listener's detection of a resemblance is not necessarily proof of Ives's intent. And it should convince us that in Ives's music it is not "quotation" that should receive so much attention but rather his remarkable gift for melodic transformation, whether used to turn a borrowed tune into a well-rounded theme, to disguise a familiar tune through elision and omission, or to link several tunes by exploiting their innate similarities. It is this technique of melodic transformation that is fundamental to Ives's later music, in his cumulative settings, patchworks, and collages.

In light of this discussion, let us return to the First String Quartet and consider an issue that was not explicitly addressed earlier in this chapter. Did Ives consciously plan to paraphrase all the themes of this work as suggested

THE ART OF PARAPHRASE

in Examples 3.5–18, and did he intend that his paraphrases be recognized? When there are references to his sources as clear as those for the opening themes of each movement, there can be little doubt on either score that he did. For the theme of the middle section of the third movement, the sketches reveal his intention to use all three source tunes and show his thinking as it develops, and the prominence of *Beulah Land* in the preceding movement, *Nettleton* in the first theme of this movement, and *Shining Shore* all around make it difficult not to hear them in this section as well.

Perhaps the weakest case is that for the derivation from *Shining Shore* of the middle-section theme of the second and fourth movements. It could be argued that the note-by-note comparison offered in Example 3.11 is speculative, that one might as well derive Ives's melody from any other largely pentatonic hymn tune or indeed from none at all, or that the suggested relationships between these two tunes may have been unintended. These objections would carry more weight if Ives had not been so consistent in paraphrasing themes throughout the quartet and so careful to leave us clues to his sources. If the opening motive of *Shining Shore* were not so prominent in both movements, one would be less inclined to hear that tune as a source for this theme, which appears at first to be very different in character and shape. It may be that Ives had no awareness of the similarity of his theme to *Shining Shore*, although this is difficult to believe in light of his subtle allusions and radical transformations elsewhere in this and in several earlier works. Even if he intended no allusion to *Shining Shore* in this theme, he cannot have been unaware, at least intuitively, of the close motivic relationship of this theme to the tune he was quoting overtly in such close proximity to it.

There are individual cases where it is far from clear what Ives may have intended to do and what he meant us to hear. But it seems certain, for the First String Quartet and for many later works, that Ives did indeed seek to create themes, motives, and other segments of melody from familiar tunes in very subtle ways, that he left enough clues in the music to allow us eventually to recognize his allusions, after many hearings if not at first, and that the kind of close analysis and sketch study attempted here is the key to understanding what his sources were and how he used them. This quartet and most of Ives's other works based on existing material make perfect musical sense even for a listener who does not recognize a single tune, because Ives develops his borrowed and paraphrased themes as he would a completely original idea. Yet for a listener, gradually discerning Ives's sources through their transformations is part of what gives this music its lasting appeal and joyful play, rewarding us for our concentration and our willingness to struggle with it, pulling us through its challenge and the pleasure of discovery deeper and deeper into Ives's musical world.

CHAPTER 4

Modeling and Paraphrase in the First and Second Symphonies

The *First String Quartet* was an extraordinary work with far-reaching implications for the use of vernacular tunes within classical genres. Meanwhile, in his studies with Parker and during his first years in New York, Ives sought to ground himself in the tradition of art music. As we have seen for his art songs, this meant imitating models of excellence and publicly inviting comparison with the European masters while asserting his individuality by offering a new twist on each borrowed idea.

This same stance toward the European Romantic tradition can be seen in Ives's First Symphony, and it assumes a more defiant, nationalistic, and self-confident form in his Second Symphony. Both draw heavily on European symphonic models, and both include paraphrased themes. The main difference between them is that the First Symphony borrows almost exclusively from other symphonies, and the Second uses a wide range of vernacular music from minstrel songs to bugle calls as well as classical sources. If the First String Quartet shows the potential of thematic paraphrase for infusing a classical genre with vernacular tunes and the First Symphony demonstrates Ives's command of the symphonic tradition, the Second Symphony does both. It represents the high-water mark of Ives's willingness to bend American vernacular material to fit the requirements of European classical forms. After this work, it was the form that was reshaped to fit the material.

Sources for the First Symphony

The critic Thomas Willis has commented that in writing the First Symphony "Ives was doing his homework."[1] This is literally true; he began it in 1897 or 1898 during his studies with Parker, although he apparently continued to work on it after leaving Yale and finished it by 1902.[2] But it is also figuratively true, in that Ives was studying the great nineteenth-century symphonies, drawing ideas from them, and learning his craft through emulation. Willis says of this symphony, "in its four movements can be found echo after echo of the European symphonists, transferred to paper by an incredible and eclectic ear and a pen which, disinterested or not, was nonetheless accurate."

Some of these echoes are specific, some general, some hazy. Seldom does a passage truly *sound* like another composer. More often, an effect may sound familiar but prove difficult to trace with certainty, or one may be reminded of another piece yet find on comparison that Ives has worked out a parallel idea in a rather different way. Sometimes a wealth of similarities may make a strong case for a certain symphony or movement as a model. In those rare cases in which the resemblance to another piece is unmistakable, the reference seems to have been deliberate, part of the intended effect.

The "New World" Symphony

There is a close relationship between Ives's First Symphony and Dvořák's Symphony in E Minor, "From the New World." That Ives knew the Dvořák is certain; he owned a keyboard arrangement and entered performance marks in the second movement, the famous Largo, suggesting that he played it.[3] It is hardly surprising that an American attempting his first symphony would choose the "New World" Symphony as his primary model. Dvořák had just returned to Europe in 1895 after three years as director of the National Conservatory in New York. The importance of the post and his prestige as a European composer had made him for a time the most prominent classical musician in the United States. Parker had taught at the conservatory the first year Dvořák was there. The "New World" Symphony premiered in New York in December 1893 and was an immediate success with both critics and public, quickly becoming one of the most popular symphonies ever composed. As the newest European symphony Ives knew, as the most significant symphony composed in and identified with the United States, and as an enormously popular work, it was an obvious model for emulation.

The clearest similarities between the two symphonies lie in their second movements. Both are slow, mostly soft, in ABA' form, and in a major key, with the middle section in a closely related minor key (parallel minor in the Dvořák, relative minor in the Ives). The A section in each features a largely pentatonic melody in the English horn over sustained chords in the strings, played near the beginning and again near the end of the opening section after interjections by strings and winds. In the final section, the English horn plays only one segment of its original melody (at the beginning of the section in the Dvořák, at its end in the Ives), and the rest of its music is reassigned to other instruments. In both movements, the return of the English horn immediately follows the dynamic and dramatic climax. Ives's use of the English horn, from the manner of its first appearance through the preparation for its final return, is directly and entirely modeled on Dvořák's.

Moreover, Ives's English horn melody paraphrases Dvořák's.[4] Example 4.1 shows that the first five measures of Ives's melody almost exactly follow the pitch contour of Dvořák's closing phrase (mm. 15–18), beginning with the last two notes of the preceding phrase. Since the final phrase of the Dvořák theme is a variant of the first phrase (mm. 7–10) with the cadence transposed up an octave, Ives's opening measures paraphrase both the first and final phrases of the Dvořák. The shape, internal stresses, articulation, and dynamics of the Ives are very like those of the final phrase of the Dvořák.

EXAMPLE 4.1: First Symphony, second movement, opening of English horn theme, compared with theme of Dvořák's "New World" Symphony, second movement

MODELING AND PARAPHRASE

Yet Ives carefully differentiates his melody from its source. He avoids the dotted rhythm that pervades the Dvořák while creating a new motive in m. 2 and repeating it in inversion in m. 4.[5] This motive propels the melody through the low and high points of the line, where Dvořák allows a break between melodic units. These elisions in the Ives contrast with the measure-to-measure segmentation of the Dvořák and make the two melodies sound less similar than they otherwise might. Ives also deemphasizes the articulation between mm. 2 and 3, although there is still a sense of a breath just before the upward arpeggiation of mm. 3–4. By avoiding the dotted rhythms, four-square phrasing, and short melodic units of the Dvořák, Ives makes his melody more supple and less folklike while keeping its charm and simplicity.

The pitch material that Ives omits (from Dvořák's mm. 15, 16, and 18) is both highly recognizable as part of Dvořák's melody and melodically somewhat repetitive, stressing the same pitches as the surrounding music. Leaving out these elements tightens the melody and makes it more Ives's own. As if to compensate for these omissions, Ives uses in his opening gesture the same pentatonic set (a perfect fourth enclosing a major second and minor third) that pervades all three segments of his source that he omits or abridges.

The rest of Ives's theme is derived from mm. 14–15 of the Dvořák, as shown in Example 4.2. Here Ives repeats more than he omits, reiterating in m. 7 the descent in mm. 5–6. After avoiding in the first half of his melody the dotted rhythm characteristic of Dvořák's, Ives finally states it once in m. 6. However, the second note repeats the first and the next note drops a third, yielding a contour different from that of any of the dotted figures in his source.[6] When the pitch contour is like the source, as in mm. 3–4 of Ives's theme, the rhythm is changed; when the rhythm is at last the same, as here, the shape is different. In the first four notes of m. 7, both rhythm and pitch are simultaneously like and unlike those of the source: the rhythm is retained, but in diminution; pitches

EXAMPLE 4.2: First Symphony, second movement, continuation of English horn theme, compared with portion of Dvořák theme

MODELING AND PARAPHRASE

are paired as in the source, but their order is reversed. Throughout, Ives preserves much of his source while making his melody distinctive.

Taken as a whole, Ives's theme is an elegant condensation of Dvořák's, which is three times as long. Dvořák's melody is a tiny ternary form (ABA′), with repetitions in each phrase; in the Ives, nothing essential is missing, but most repetitions within and between phrases are trimmed. We have seen that the first half of the Ives paraphrases both the first and final phrases of the Dvořák. Since the latter's middle phrase (mm. 11–14), shown in the top line of Example 4.3, presents the same pitch sequence in each measure, and the last of these is paraphrased near the end of Ives's melody, every measure of the Dvořák is represented in the Ives, and the omissions simply avoid redundancy. The order of events in Ives's theme is somewhat different from that of its source; the peak, which Dvořák places in the last two measures, arrives in the second two measures of the Ives, followed by material from the middle of the Dvořák. Despite the reshuffling, the overall shape is similar in an important respect. The Dvořák melody is exclusively pentatonic in its outer phrases but in its middle phrase repeatedly touches the leading tone. The Ives follows the same shape in abbreviated form: its first six measures are pentatonic; it touches the leading tone just once (m. 7), corresponding to the middle of Dvořák's melody; and it closes with a descending pentatonic scale. Finally, while the Ives condenses and reorders the Dvořák, it adds nothing to it, for there is not a note of the Ives that does not derive from the Dvořák.

The English horn tune forms the first and last of four eight-measure units in Ives's first section. The second section is a lovely contrasting melody in the violins. The third unit is divided between winds and strings, and its first half (mm. 17–20), shown in Example 4.3, presents a longer paraphrase of the mid-

EXAMPLE 4.3: First Symphony, second movement, third period of opening section, compared with portion of Dvořák theme

MODELING AND PARAPHRASE

dle of Dvořák's theme (mm. 11–14), which was severely abridged in Ives's English horn tune. This passage in the Ives, like its source, features winds over sustained chords, although Ives substitutes flute and oboes over low winds for English horn and clarinets over strings; as in its source, the parts move in parallel intervals, although Ives uses sixths and Dvořák tenths; and, as in its source, the intervals in the melody appear in exact inversion in the lower line about two beats later (marked with brackets in Example 4.3). This last similarity is telling, for Ives borrows directly what is least likely to be heard — an arcane motivic relationship in a middle phrase — while altering the main part of his source in often radical ways to create a distinctive theme.

Comparing Ives's theme with Dvořák's shows both how similar and how different they are. This movement represents an act of homage to one of the great modern symphonies, but it is also a challenge, declaring that Ives is not afraid to compete with Dvořák on his own turf. Recognizing that Dvořák's theme is an elegant and famous tune, Ives cites it and tries to improve on it. As in his condensation of *Nettleton* in the First String Quartet, Ives recasts a very repetitive melody in the musical equivalent of prose. This constitutes an implicit critique of Dvořák's theme as redundant and rhythmically uninteresting and an implicit assertion of Ives's superiority as a composer. No doubt this was sincerely felt, for outside of his early marches Ives never wrote a melody, original or paraphrased, that is as repetitive in rhythm and pitch or as predictable in phrasing as this Dvořák theme, and his later writings stress the wealth of ideas and minimal repetition in his music and complain of repetitiveness and dearth of ideas in music by others.[7]

As in the theme, so in the movement and the symphony as a whole, Ives takes ideas from the "New World" Symphony and extends them. In both slow movements the climax juxtaposes themes in a similar way. In Dvořák's Largo, the peak comes at the end of the middle section (mm. 96–100), just before the English horn returns with its theme (rehearsal no. 5). Here themes from the first and second movements come together: the first measure of the English horn melody appears in the trumpets in parallel thirds; this is joined in counterpoint with the opening phrase of the first movement's closing theme (from reh. 5, mm. 149–52), begun by horns and violins and completed by the winds; and this complex alternates with the opening motive of the first movement's main theme in the trombones. The climax of the Ives movement occurs in the reprise of the A section (reh. 8, m. 81) rather than just before it, but follows similar procedures. The first period of the reprise, the English horn theme, appears in horns and trombones in parallel thirds, combined with the middle-section theme of this movement in the upper strings. The second unit of the A section follows in the upper strings (reh. 9, m. 89), combined with itself in the winds in double diminution and with the opening period of the first movement's main theme in the horns. Both composers notate the first-movement material in diminution, so that it sounds at about the right speed in the slower tempo. The procedures Ives uses here are all borrowed from Dvořák; even the idea of counterpointing a motive with itself in diminution, not used in Dvořák's Largo, appears in his first movement (at reh. 7) and finale (just before reh. 8). But Ives takes each device to greater lengths, as if to prove his command of the technique. The young composer has not yet learned restraint, and the starkness of the Dvořák, in which themes are recalled only by their opening motives and all the motives are rhythmically similar, is arguably more effective. Yet the impulse to elaborate on his model and show off his skill in contrapuntal combination is obvious.

Several uncommon procedures in Ives's first movement have parallels in Dvořák's. In the Ives, part of the second theme (rehearsal letter I, flutes, the second idea of the group that begins at reh. H) is anticipated in the preceding transition (mm. 83–87, five bars before reh. F, and 98ff., four before reh. G, violins alternating with flutes and oboes). This is an extremely rare procedure. Yet the same process occurs in Dvořák's first movement, where the opening motive of the second theme (reh. 3, m. 91, flute and oboe) is heard twice in the transition before it (mm. 74 and 76, three measures before reh. 2, strings).[8] As might be expected, in the Ives the motive is longer and treated more extensively, even being combined in counterpoint with the first theme. In both works, in the recapitulation the transition is cut, removing all references to the second theme. Ives's exposition closes with a brief fugato on another element from the second theme (*Più moto*, mm. 201ff., eight measures before reh. M; cf. m. 131, four after reh. I), perhaps suggested by the much briefer canon on the closing theme that ends Dvořák's exposition (mm. 171–76). Both development sections begin with a diminuendo to very soft and with harmonic ambiguity based on symmetrical partitioning of the octave; as usual, Dvořák's approach is simple (an augmented triad sustained for twelve measures) and Ives's more interesting and unusual (a series of minor triads whose roots descend through a complete whole-tone scale while the notes themselves are rising, so that each successive triad is in a different inversion). Both include passages at the end of the development and at the beginning of the coda (in the Dvořák, mm. 257–72, sixteen measures after reh. 8, and mm. 396–403, at reh. 13; in the Ives, mm. 303–23, at reh. R, and mm. 432–46, eight before reh. Z) in which material from the first theme is combined contrapuntally with material, sometimes in diminution, from the second theme (Ives) or closing theme (Dvořák). Once again, the Ives is more elaborate; one passage in the coda (reh. Z, mm. 440–45) combines three strands, one in diminution. The large number of similarities shows that Ives drew on Dvořák's first movement for many technical details, always seeking to outdo his model.

Ives's third movement scherzo owes less to the "New World" Symphony than to the scherzo of Beethoven's Ninth Symphony, arguably also the model for Dvořák's scherzo. But the opening of Ives's trio hints at the violin melody from m. 9 of his second movement, and Dvořák's scherzo also has a theme (at the *Poco sostenuto*) that echoes his second movement theme, although neither similarity is strong enough to be sure that a reference was intended.

In the finale, Ives brings back the violin melody from mm. 9–16 of the second movement near the end of the exposition (mm. 102ff., four bars before reh. G, violins, and 110ff., winds) and at the parallel spot in the recapitulation (mm. 267ff., four before reh. S), in counterpoint with parts of the finale's second theme. In the recapitulation, the main theme of the first movement is tucked into the transition to the second theme (mm. 219ff., two before reh. O, horns and violins) and reappears in the coda (mm. 295ff., eight after reh. T, winds). Thus, Ives's symphony refers to the opening theme of the first movement in both the second and fourth movements and uses part of the theme of the second movement in the finale as well. As a cyclic symphony, it is in the late-nineteenth-century mainstream. But its pattern of thematic repetition seems closest to that of the "New World" Symphony, which introduces themes from the first movement in the second (and, unlike the Ives, in the third movement as well, in the bridge to the trio and in the coda) and recalls the opening ideas of movements 1, 2, and 3 in the development and coda of the finale, in counterpoint with motives from the latter. Finally, the closing measures of the two symphonies are much alike, sharing a rising 1–3–5–6 bass figure in quarter notes moving through two octaves (on the tonic, rising and falling, in the Dvořák; on the subdominant, rising only, in the Ives) and an almost identical rhythm of closing tonic chords (Ives adds two chords five measures from the end).

Through it all, Ives is trying to match or exceed Dvořák's achievement. The English horn theme in Ives's second movement signals his intention to challenge and if possible to best Dvořák at his own game, but there are signs of this competition elsewhere as well. Particularly important are the devices that Ives borrows. Cyclic form, diminution or augmentation of themes, and contrapuntal combination of themes from one or several movements or of a theme with itself in diminution are all procedures in Dvořák's symphony that Ives uses prominently in his own, sometimes at much greater length. Some of these later became trademarks of Ives's music.

Other Models

Other symphonies also served as models for Ives. A prominent model for the finale is the third movement of Tchaikovsky's *Pathétique* Symphony (1893), another recent and successful European symphony. The two movements share very similar tempos (Allegro molto and Allegro molto vivace, respectively) and characters. Part of Ives's coda (reh. X, mm. 330–39) directly echoes a passage in the Tchaikovsky (reh. X, mm. 221–32), with sweeping scales in octaves alternating between strings and winds, followed by a march-like tune over a descending bass.[9] Example 4.4 shows the opening of both passages. As shown

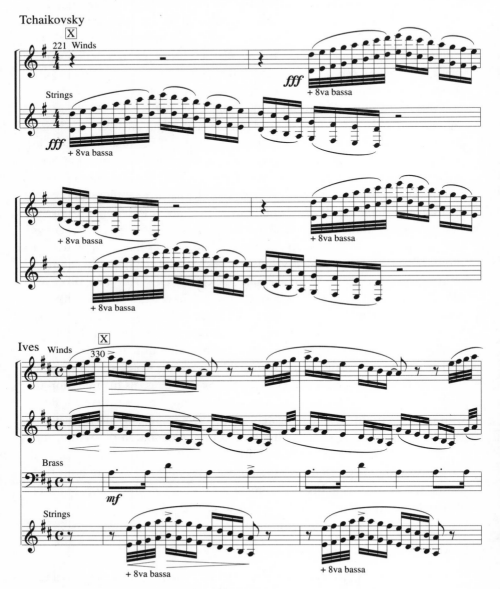

EXAMPLE 4.4: First Symphony, finale, mm. 330–31, compared with Tchaikovsky, *Pathétique* Symphony, third movement, mm. 221–24

MODELING AND PARAPHRASE

EXAMPLE 4.5: First Symphony, finale, segment of principal theme, compared with theme from Tchaikovsky's *Pathétique* Symphony, third movement

in Example 4.5, part of Ives's first theme paraphrases the opening of Tchaikovsky's main theme; while not close enough to constitute a "quotation," the resemblance helps make Ives's theme sound "Tchaikovskian." There are many other Tchaikovskian touches throughout Ives's symphony, including sudden exclamations in the brass, passages that pass quickly through series of unexpected and colorful chords, and sequences in which a motive is repeatedly transposed up by minor thirds (as in the Ives finale, mm. 51–54, horns and strings), perhaps inspired by the trip up the full circle of minor thirds in the first theme of the first movement of the *Pathétique* (at reh. A, m. 31).

Ives's third movement is a scherzo in D minor that starts with canonic entries and ends with a stretto, like the scherzo of Beethoven's Ninth Symphony in the same key, and its principal subject parallels that of its model, as shown in Example 4.6.[10] Both themes open with descending octaves, and the

EXAMPLE 4.6: First Symphony, third movement theme, with scherzo theme from Beethoven's Ninth Symphony

MODELING AND PARAPHRASE

pitch contour of the first three measures of Ives's subject follows that of the second through fourth measures of the Beethoven. The backbone of Beethoven's tune, pointed out by single notes in the oboe, falls a fifth and then rises by step through a third; similarly, Ives's tune outlines a stepwise ascent, continuing all the way up to the fifth. One parallel is rather subtle. The fourth measure of the Beethoven is a retrograde of the second measure, framing the rising gesture between them. Ives imitates this interesting detail in his first and third measures and makes the retrograde more striking because of the octave leap.

The first movement of Schubert's "Unfinished" Symphony may have been a model for Ives's first movement, for the two share several features: both are minor-mode, triple-time first movements in similar tempos (Allegro moderato and Allegro, respectively); in each, a vamp in the strings introduces and accompanies the first theme in the clarinet (in the Schubert, the clarinet is in unison with the oboe); in the exposition of each, both first and second themes are repeated immediately after their first presentation and in the same key, although the Ives themes are longer and more complex. There may also be a motivic link, for a figure from the end of Ives's second theme group resembles motives in the Schubert. The top three staves in Example 4.7 show the similar pitch contour of the Ives motive, the opening notes of the Schubert, and the second four-measure phrase from Schubert's first theme. The bottom four staves show the rhythmic resemblance of the Ives motive (in the bottom staff) to the rhythm in Schubert's mm. 18–19 and its later echoes in the transition and second theme; the shared rhythmic pattern is marked with a horizontal bracket. These passages are all similar in character, articulation, and dynamic level, making the family resemblance even stronger. There is also a possible parallel between the opening phrases of Schubert's second theme and Ives's first theme, compared in Example 4.8. Both begin with a leap of a fourth and back, feature dotted rhythm on the first beat of the second and a later measure, have two stepwise rising gestures in the third measure, and end with a descending fourth. Moreover, they are presented in similar ways by similar instrumental forces: the Schubert theme, played by the cellos, is introduced and accompanied by pulsating violas and clarinets over pizzicato downbeats in the basses, while the Ives, played by the clarinet, is introduced and accompanied by a pulsating figure in the violas over pizzicato downbeats in the cellos. None of these parallels is strong enough alone to confirm that Schubert's "Unfinished" served Ives as a model, yet all these similarities taken together suggest that it did. Moreover, Ives had the opportunity to hear the Schubert in May 1895 and April 1896 at concerts of the New Haven Symphony Orchestra under Parker, so he is virtually certain to have known the work and likely to have had it in his ears while working on the First Symphony.[11]

MODELING AND PARAPHRASE

EXAMPLE 4.7: First Symphony, first movement motive, compared with motives from Schubert's "Unfinished" Symphony, first movement

Amid all the allusions to European symphonies, at least one theme shows an American ancestry, using material from two hymn tunes. The opening melody of the first movement is in three eight-measure units, played by clarinet, second violin, and winds in turn. The middle segment (mm. 10–17) features two statements, in A and C, of a four-measure phrase derived from *Shining Shore*, as shown in Example 4.9.[12] This is accompanied

EXAMPLE 4.8: First Symphony, first movement, opening phrase, compared with Schubert's "Unfinished" Symphony, opening phrase of second theme

EXAMPLE 4.9: First Symphony, first movement, middle segment of first theme, with *Shining Shore* and *Beulah Land*

by a neighbor-note figure in the flute, adapted from the fourth phrase of *Beulah Land*; the segments that are borrowed, from the soprano, alto, and tenor of the hymn setting, are marked with horizontal brackets in the example. This same neighbor-note figure, developed in sequence, provides the material for the final eight-measure segment of Ives's theme, as shown in Example 4.10.[13]

EXAMPLE 4.10: First Symphony, first movement, final segment of first theme, with motive from *Beulah Land*

MODELING AND PARAPHRASE

The reasons Ives cites these tunes are not clear. There are textual links between them, and especially between the passages Ives uses here. Both hymn texts are about the afterlife, and both describe it as an eternal home: "our home, / Forever, O for ever" in the fourth stanza of *Shining Shore*, and "My heav'n, my home forever more" in the refrain of *Beulah Land*. Moreover, the words of the *Beulah Land* passage from which Ives borrows the neighbor-note figure develop the same image as the refrain of *Shining Shore*:

> I look away across the sea,
> Where mansions are prepared for me,
> And view the shining glory shore,
> My heav'n, my home forevermore. [*Beulah Land*, refrain]

> For, O we stand on Jordan's strand;
>   Our friends are passing over;
> And, just before, the shining shore
>   We may almost discover. [*Shining Shore*, refrain]

These similarities of word and image may explain the conjunction of the two hymns, but the reason for their appearance in the symphony is still obscure. There are no other apparent allusions in the symphony to music associated with words.[14] Ives used the first sixteen measures of this theme, including the *Shining Shore* motive but not the material from *Beulah Land*, in the song *On Judges' Walk* (ca. 1902), later retexted as *Rough Wind*. It is unclear whether the earlier song was adapted from the symphonic theme or the reverse, and neither song text provides any clues that might explain the presence of *Shining Shore*.[15] Ives may have included these hymns in the symphony because of motivic links to the surrounding material: the characteristic rhythm of *Beulah Land*, with a dotted figure on the downbeat, pervades the entire first theme (see Examples 4.8–10), and the opening gesture of *Shining Shore* is the inversion of a motive used three times in the first segment of the theme (mm. 3, 5, and 7; see Example 4.8).

Whatever the presence of these hymns may signify, the allusions throughout the symphony to some of the most popular symphonies of the nineteenth century reveal a composer who is far from shy about his purpose. The relationship of Ives's First Symphony to its models is that of a new symphonic composer elbowing his way into the crowded concert repertoire, seeking to match the achievement of the masters of the genre and contribute something fresh. The echoes in this symphony of its European forebears are deliberate allusions, not the result of inexperience. Ives is doing more than his "homework"; he is both demonstrating and announcing his command of the European symphonic tradition, his strong affiliation with composers like Dvořák and Tchaikovsky, and his ability to say something new and individual.

Ives may also have been following his teacher's lead. Parker was an eclectic composer, particularly in the 1890s. His biographer William K. Kearns has suggested that among composers of his time, Parker "seems to have been the most susceptible to other composers' mannerisms."[16] Critics of the day noted the influence on *Hora novissima* (1893) of composers from Josquin, Palestrina, Bach, and Handel to Mendelssohn, Gounod, and Dvořák, and Kearns has found borrowings from Wagner, Mendelssohn, and Franck in *Hora novissima* and *A Wanderer's Psalm* (1899–1900), works that chronologically frame Ives's studies with Parker.[17] While the critics disagreed on whether this showed a praiseworthy emulation of the masters or a lack of individuality, Kearns argues that it represents an aesthetic stance in which the ability to integrate ideas from diverse sources and eras into a distinctive, unified work was highly valued, as it was in the art and architecture of the time.[18] In this spirit, Ives's symphony can be seen as a summation of the nineteenth-century symphony, from Beethoven's Ninth and Schubert's "Unfinished" through the great symphonies of the 1890s, the "New World" and *Pathétique*. Indeed, Ives's allusions seem more successful than Parker's, which, according to Kearns, occur for no apparent musical or textual reason. By contrast, Ives's borrowings from other symphonies are never mere surface phenomena or stylistic mannerisms; an explicit allusion to another work always indicates deeper similarities of form or procedure. Even Ives's melodic allusions often reflect reworkings that, like those in his English horn theme adapted from Dvořák, constitute a critique of his model. Perhaps Ives's more deliberate, rigorous, and thoroughgoing approach to using borrowed material, if it indeed owes something to Parker, may serve as a critique of his teacher and model.

The First Symphony has been too often ignored or briefly dismissed in discussions of Ives's music, and it is played too seldom. It is an important late Romantic symphony, a compelling and endlessly interesting work that stands up well to a comparison with the symphonies of his principal models, Dvořák and Tchaikovsky. Like the tonal music of Schoenberg, Ives's exact contemporary, it proves his ability to work within the forms and procedures of his forebears, and it provides a backdrop against which his later music can be heard as an extraordinary, individual development that is nonetheless deeply rooted in the nineteenth-century European tradition.

"Quotation" and Paraphrase in the Second Symphony

Having claimed a place in the symphonic tradition in his First Symphony, Ives now tried to establish an individual identity as a composer. In the Second Symphony, he achieved a distinctive voice in two ways: by using American material, and by emphasizing allusion and quotation, taking what had been a common feature of the tradition and intensifying it.

Indeed, the Second Symphony is crowded with "quotations." Borrowed material appears on almost every page, some immediately recognizable, some disguised, some taken from American hymns, fiddle tunes, and popular songs, some from European art music. The extent, variety, and differing shades of recognizability of these borrowings reveal Ives's purpose: to create a symphony in the European Romantic tradition that is suffused with the character of American melody, wedding the two traditions in a single work.

According to Ives, the symphony was written and scored in 1900–1902, based in part on overtures and organ works written earlier, and was revised and professionally copied in 1909.[19] Gayle Sherwood has dated the work a bit later by music paper and handwriting, placing the earliest extant sketches for the first and third movements between 1902 and 1907 and the rest of the work about 1907.[20] The symphony has five movements, of which the first and fourth serve as slow introductions to the second and fifth.[21] The key scheme is unusual. In the middle is a slow ternary movement in F major. The finale is a modified sonata without development in F, with a second theme in A♭, recapitulated in the tonic. The second movement is in sonata form, with a first theme in A♭, a second theme (m. 72) in F, and a transitional theme that mediates between the two keys, appearing first in A♭ minor/major and immediately repeating in F minor/major. In the recapitulation, both main themes are in F, and the transitional theme is at the same level as before. The tonic is restored only in the coda, with the appearance in A♭ of the second theme and then of both main themes in counterpoint. The tonal polarity in both the second and fifth movements is thus between F and A♭ rather than between tonic and dominant.

Thematic links between the movements create a tight cyclic form. Both main themes of the second movement return in the finale. Moreover, the fourth movement is a shortened reprise of the first, sharing the same themes and several identical passages; the first movement is a slow sonata form with the order of themes reversed in the recapitulation, and its first theme and recapitulation return in the fourth movement to create a modified ternary form with a new coda. Both of these introductory movements begin in B minor — an unorthodox key in relation to the keys of the following movements — and move to D major; the first movement closes in D, while the fourth movement ends on the dominant of F. The four principal keys of the symphony — B minor, D major, A♭, and F — are all related by minor thirds, and F major ultimately prevails. On one manuscript, Ives noted this intricate key structure in a prospective title: "Sym #2 / in F Maj — A flat Maj / also in D B min."[22]

The borrowings in this symphony have attracted attention since its 1951 premiere. By now, most of the borrowed material has been identified, and several interpretations of the significance of the "quotations" have been offered.[23] Yet our view of the work and our understanding of its meaning are still incomplete, for three essential points have been missed.

First, what is involved here is not quotation but paraphrase, in which a borrowed melody or passage is reshaped to create a new one. If little is changed, the result may strike someone who knows the source as a direct "quotation," yet if the transformation is more complete, the new tune or passage may sound only vaguely familiar. This means both that more is borrowed than is obvious at first hearing, and that it may be hard to determine whether a passage is paraphrased from another piece or only coincidentally resembles it.

Second, the borrowed material is not inserted into an existing framework but forms the very basis of the music. Virtually every idea, theme, or transition in the piece is paraphrased from other music or is conceived as a counterpoint to or extension of such a paraphrase.

Third, Ives uses his sources in a thoroughly systematic way. Every one of his themes paraphrases an American vernacular tune. These are developed in turn, providing material for transitions and development sections. At the same time, many transitional sections, including at least one in each movement, paraphrase transitions or episodes in the music of Bach, Brahms, or Wagner. The American sources, then, are identified with the thematic material, the European sources with episodes and transitions.

Unaltered, the American tunes that Ives uses as sources would not serve well as symphonic themes, for the same reasons that a literal statement of *Nettleton* would not have been a satisfactory theme for his First Quartet: their four-square periodicity and strong tonic cadences brake forward momentum, their frequent repetitions of rhythmic patterns and even whole phrases exhaust material before it can be developed, and they resist extension because they are complete in themselves. Here as in the quartet, Ives reshapes his raw material into themes of an almost Brahmsian character, with phrasing that is more often irregular than periodic. Through paraphrase, Ives (1) eliminates plainness and redundancy while (2) preserving the rhythmic spark and American sound of each source tune, (3) isolates motives for development, (4) emphasizes common melodic and rhythmic patterns that link his themes, and (5) creates themes and countermelodies that work well in counterpoint, allowing him to suffuse the music with borrowed material and to achieve climaxes in which themes first presented separately are played simultaneously.

Themes Paraphrased from American Tunes

First- and Fourth-Movement Themes

Example 4.11 shows the first movement's first theme (mm. 1–7). At its repetition in m. 7, the theme is joined in counterpoint by part of the chorus of

EXAMPLE 4.11: Second Symphony, first movement, first theme, compared with part of Stephen Foster's "Massa's in de Cold Ground"

Stephen Foster's "Massa's in de Cold Ground" (H121). Colin Sterne has shown that Ives's theme is derived from this phrase of Foster's song, and Sydney Robinson Charles has suggested the same for the motive that initiates the following transition (shown here as it appears in mm. 13–14). Thus the entire opening passage is permeated with this Foster phrase.[24]

In the earliest surviving sketch of this movement, transcribed in Example 4.12, the first theme is based not on the Foster tune but on *Nettleton*.[25] The opening presents an abridged paraphrase of the hymn tune, with two embellished statements of the initial motive, each echoed in another voice (marked with brackets in Example 4.12), which stand for the first two phrases; the contrasting third phrase, with some rhythmic alterations and its second half transposed up a third and extended in sequence; and a return to the opening motive, representing the fourth phrase. The first three measures of this draft were later replaced by mm. 1–9 of the published version, but the rest of the passage, slightly reworked, was kept as part of the transition to the second theme. In the final version, without an overt reference to *Nettleton* in the preceding material, the hymn tune motives in mm. 4–13 of this sketch (mm. 10–19 of the published score) are likely to go unheard.

Besides bringing to light a borrowing that might have gone unobserved, this sketch raises questions about the relation of "Massa's in de Cold

MODELING AND PARAPHRASE

Nettleton

f0353

[corrected to A♮]

EXAMPLE 4.12: Second Symphony, first draft of first movement, opening, compared with *Nettleton*

MODELING AND PARAPHRASE

Ground" to the transition. The sixteenth-note figure that pervades the transition (mm. 13–14 of Example 4.11) is already present in this initial sketch, showing that it was first created, not as a paraphrase of the Foster, but as a counterpoint to and perhaps as a variant of the third phrase of *Nettleton*. The resemblance of this motive to the "Down in de cornfield" phrase of the Foster may have suggested using the latter as a source for the first theme, rather than the reverse, as might be assumed from their order in the final version.[26]

What is most telling about this substitution of the Foster melody for *Nettleton* as the source of the first theme is how little else is different: both tunes are paraphrased, not merely quoted; both are linked motivically to the following transition; and both are American tunes, reshaped to fit a pseudo-Baroque contrapuntal texture. These similarities show that Ives did not change *how* he planned to use the borrowed melody, even when the source itself changed. This is strong evidence that Ives intended from the start to write a movement in the European tradition on themes paraphrased from American tunes.

The second theme of this movement paraphrases the fiddle tune "Pig Town Fling" or "Warm Stuff" (H167). As shown in Example 4.13, the first violins have most of mm. 1–3 of the source, the violas supply missing notes, and the neighbor-note motive from mm. 2–3 (C♯-B-C♯-A) is developed in the continuation. The sources for the first and second themes share a similar intervallic contour, as the example shows.[27] In addition, the second theme shares with the preceding transitional motive a rhythm of an eighth and two sixteenths, marked in Examples 4.11 and 4.13 by horizontal brackets. These

EXAMPLE 4.13: Second Symphony, first movement, second theme, with "Pig Town Fling" and "Massa's in de Cold Ground"

MODELING AND PARAPHRASE

links of contour and rhythm illustrate Ives's preference for themes that are melodically related and suggest his ability to turn one idea into another through progressive variation. Both are typical features of nineteenth-century music in the tradition of Beethoven, Liszt, Wagner, and Brahms.

Both tunes return in later movements, "Massa's in de Cold Ground" in movements 3 and 5, "Pig Town Fling" in movements 4 and 5, and the first theme, based on the Foster, in movement 4. Two other passages in the first movement also forecast later events. In mm. 33–36, low strings and bassoons anticipate the finale's second theme (horn, m. 58 of the finale), changed from common to triple time.[28] And in mm. 66–68, the horns present the opening of "The Red, White, and Blue," better known as "Columbia, the Gem of the Ocean" (H75, attributed to both David T. Shaw and Thomas à Beckett). This tune appears complete in the coda of the finale, after being hinted at throughout that movement and heralded in the fourth movement by a reprise (m. 16) of the first-movement passage where it is first heard.

Both of these forecasts in the first movement of material from the finale appear in counterpoint with motives from "Pig Town Fling." This also anticipates the finale, for there a countermelody based in part on "Pig Town Fling" accompanies both the horn theme and the patriotic tune. Besides contributing to the symphony's cyclic network, the references to these tunes in the first movement alert us to the dual role of "Pig Town Fling," as the source for a theme in that movement and for a countersubject in the finale, and to the multiple roles of the first movement itself, which is at once a slow sonata form, complete in its own right; an introduction to the second movement; a longer variant of the fourth movement (which leads into the finale); and thus an introduction to the entire symphony.

Second-Movement Themes

The first theme of the second movement paraphrases the verse of Henry Clay Work's Civil War song "Wake Nicodemus" (H144). Example 4.14 compares the song's first phrase with the first period of Ives's theme. By repeating the opening gesture and treating the cadential motive in sequence (marked by horizontal brackets), Ives achieves several goals at once: he emphasizes the opening and closing motives of his source, marking them as material for development and revealing their relationship by inversion; he relieves the unrelenting rhythm of the original while preserving and even highlighting its characteristic pattern of dotted eighth and sixteenth leading to a quarter note; he maintains the pentatonicism and jaunty American character of his source; and he avoids the tonic cadence and introduces a colorful harmonic excursion that extends the phrase to double its original length. On repeating the phrase, Ives varies it to include the low C and rising arpeggiation in mm.

MODELING AND PARAPHRASE

EXAMPLE 4.14: Second Symphony, second movement, first theme, with "Wake Nicodemus"

1–2 of his source, which he previously omitted, and spins out the end of the phrase in a new extension based on the opening motive. In immediately developing material he has just introduced, Ives follows the example of Beethoven and Brahms. At the same time, he lays out his first theme area (mm. 1–41) in an AA'BA' format, corresponding to the AABA structure of the verse of Work's song. Here Ives integrates into the classical European framework not only the melodic shape but also the form of an American vernacular tune.

The transitional theme at m. 42 paraphrases George A. Minor's *Bringing in the Sheaves* (H10), as shown in Example 4.15. As is usually the case with Ives, the paraphrase continues beyond the point where the derivation is obvious. Like the second theme of the first movement, this theme is motivically anticipated; as Example 4.14 shows, *Bringing in the Sheaves* shares several motives

EXAMPLE 4.15: Second Symphony, second movement, transitional theme, with *Bringing in the Sheaves*

with the first theme.[29] Similarly, the latter part of this transitional theme refers back to "Wake Nicodemus" by adopting its unrelenting dotted rhythm, a sameness that Ives avoids in his first theme but deems appropriate in a transition.

As Example 4.16 shows, the second theme presents the college song "Where, O Where Are the Verdant Freshmen?" (H157, adapted from David Walker's hymn tune *The Hebrew Children*), slightly altered for smoothness and elegance.[30] The theme's middle section (mm. 80–89) is based on the same tune, with the second half transposed down a fourth to prepare the half cadence, after which the first section repeats. Just by changing the repeated notes and skips of his source into stepwise motion, Ives changes the whole character of the melody, making it hard to recognize the middle section as a variant of its source despite the many common tones (marked by crosses in the example). The theme is anticipated in mm. 59–69 by the viola obbligato that accompanies it, in counterpoint with motives from the first theme. In addition, the pickup added to the second theme echoes that of the first. The significance of these links between themes is made clear by later events.

In the development at mm. 137–66, under a rhythmically augmented statement of the first theme, the trombones play a cantus firmus comprised of alternating phrases from two hymn tunes: the first and third phrases of *Hamburg* (H26, at mm. 137 and 153) and the second and fourth phrases of *Naomi* (H40, at mm. 146 and 161). The two hymn tunes are similar in structure and character, sharing a basic long-short-short rhythm, and both were arranged by Lowell Mason from existing tunes.[31] At m. 166, the violins repeat the first phrase of this cantus firmus three times, answered each time by the final phrase in the horns. In the coda, the first cantus firmus phrase returns at m. 329, now in counterpoint with the second theme.[32] This leads to the climactic

MODELING AND PARAPHRASE

EXAMPLE 4.16: Second Symphony, second movement, second theme, with "Where, O Where Are the Verdant Freshmen?"

simultaneous presentation of both themes (mm. 342–46, anticipated at mm. 340–41) over a variant of the cantus firmus's first phrase.

The first theme was thus designed as a counterpoint to the second theme and to the first phrase of *Hamburg*. Ives bends his source tunes through paraphrase so that they will combine well and adds the pickup to the second theme as a foretaste of the contrapuntal climax to come. The rich web of linear and contrapuntal relations recalls procedures that Ives used in the First Symphony and again shows his allegiance to the late Romantic tradition.

Third-Movement Themes

The main theme of the third movement is shown in Example 4.17. It is based primarily on *Beulah Land*, whose distinctive rhythm, a dotted figure on the downbeat, is present from the start. Measures 13–14 of the hymn appear at mm. 11–12 of the Ives, initiating a paraphrase of the last eight measures of the hymn's refrain. At the cadence, the flute briefly joins the paraphrase, as shown by dotted lines in the example. The resemblance to *Beulah Land* is

EXAMPLE 4.17: Second Symphony, third movement, opening theme and its sources

MODELING AND PARAPHRASE

closer in the sketches, particularly the early ones, than in the final version, suggesting that as the piece took shape Ives sought to make the evocation more subtle. The middle staff of Example 4.18 (marked "First version") shows mm. 11–18 as they appear in one early sketch, possibly the first.[33] Here the contour follows *Beulah Land* closely, varying the third and fourth measures and changing the next two to adopt the figuration of mm. 11–12 of the hymn, which is not included elsewhere in the theme.

EXAMPLE 4.18: Second Symphony, portion of early sketch for third movement, opening theme, and its sources

The paraphrase of the hymn's refrain in mm. 11–18 interlocks with a paraphrase of the second half of its verse. The entire theme (mm. 7–18) is framed by mm. 5–8 of the hymn. As shown in Example 4.17, mm. 7–9 of the Ives movement follow the rising contour of mm. 4–6 of the hymn, adding new notes around the borrowed tones. Because the hymn's verse and refrain end alike, the cadence of Ives's theme completes both this paraphrase of the verse and the refrain-paraphrase embedded within it. The final reprise of this theme is followed by a coda (mm. 119–30) that presents the complete refrain, the beginning of which is shown in Example 4.17; here, mm. 5–20 of *Beulah Land* are heard in order, while the middle of Ives's theme is heard as an interpolation, a bit of the refrain tucked inside the verse.[34]

Embedded in this interpolation is another. In both theme and coda, mm. 17–18 of *Beulah Land* are replaced by a variant of mm. 13–14 of *Materna* (H36) by Samuel A. Ward, followed by a hint of *Materna*'s cadence in the flute. This tune was usually sung in Ives's day to the words "O Mother dear, Jerusalem," but has since become identified with "America the Beautiful," whose popularity makes this brief reference leap out of context to startle modern listeners with what may sound like a sudden, unmotivated quotation. Yet the substitution serves two important musical purposes: it provides a more satisfying climax by touching the upper octave, and it avoids the neighbor-note figure that pervades mm. 13–18 of *Beulah Land*, which appears earlier in the theme and would be anticlimactic to repeat at the peak of the phrase. That Ives sought to avoid this repetition is clear from the early sketch in Example 4.18, in which mm. 17–18 of *Beulah Land* are replaced by a descending motive from mm. 11–12 of the hymn. Just above this in the sketch, on staves previously left blank, is a later alternative (marked "Revised version" in the example) with the fragment of *Materna*, as in the final version. These two measures of *Materna* are similar in rhythm, implied harmony, and decorated 6–5 melodic motion to mm. 17–18 of *Beulah Land*, and they also resemble mm. 9–10 of *Beulah Land*, transposed and reordered, as Example 4.17 shows.[35] Thus the *Materna* excerpt is completely absorbed into the paraphrase of *Beulah Land*, as Ives exploits their melodic similarities to move from one to the other and back.

Others have found in this theme part of the Valhalla motive from Wagner's *Die Walküre* (mm. 9–10) and a cadential figure from the second movement of Brahms's First Symphony (H175, shared between flute and first violin at mm. 16–17 of the Ives), and part of the hymn *There is a Happy Land* (H57, arranged by Lowell Mason) in the accompaniment to it (violin II, mm. 15–17).[36] Each of these alleged references is quite brief and very different in rhythm or harmonic context from its putative source, and nothing in the sketches suggests that any resemblance was intended. These may be arcane

MODELING AND PARAPHRASE

allusions or private jokes, yet it seems more likely that they are not "quotations" at all, only musical commonplaces that remind some listeners of other music. The rich web of allusion in the Second Symphony almost inevitably leads us to hear in it things that Ives did not intend, as noted in the discussion of "questionable quotations" in the previous chapter. More likely, though still uncertain, is a possible reference to the refrain of *Cleansing Stream* by Mrs. Joseph F. Knapp at mm. 38–40, replacing the final cadence in the solo cello's partial restatement of the theme.[37]

The middle section of the third movement uses three tunes, each first quoted in part and then paraphrased. Clayton Henderson has shown that Charles Zeuner's *Missionary Chant* (H37, "Ye Christian heralds"), partly stated in the horns (mm. 45–46) and the strings (mm. 47–48), is later partly paraphrased in the strings (mm. 59–67). A phrase from the same hymn returns in the horn at the close of the movement, counterpointing the *Materna* fragment in the flute.[38] The first two measures of *Nettleton* appear in the horn in mm. 49–51 while the winds embellish it with neighbor and passing tones (as in the sketch of the first movement shown in Example 4.12). Measures 46–51 are repeated, followed by an abridged paraphrase of the second half of *Nettleton* in the first violins, echoed in canon by the violas (mm. 51b–56); since the hymn is in AABA form, this completes a condensed paraphrase of the source tune. At m. 59, over the *Missionary Chant* paraphrase in the strings, horns and winds play the phrase from "Massa's in de Cold Ground" that appeared in the first movement, followed by a new tune paraphrased from the Foster melody (mm. 65–67, flute). The pattern is like that in the second movement, where each of the three themes begins with a direct reference to its source and moves toward less explicit paraphrase, but the process here is concentrated into a much shorter timespan.

Fifth-Movement Themes

The finale features a still more intricate web of themes. As in the first two movements, each new theme is anticipated by previous material. Instead of one chain of ideas, however, there are three.

1. The first theme area is based on Foster's "De Camptown Races" (H100). The first half of the chorus ("Gwine to run all night") appears in the horns in the tonic in mm. 14–15; recurs in the dominant in low strings in m. 31, answered by a paraphrase of the remainder of the chorus in the flute at m. 33; and repeats several times in the tonic in low strings and bassoons starting at m. 35, while the first trombone states the whole chorus, somewhat altered. The statement in the trombone is a late addition, appearing first in the 1951 score and parts; perhaps Ives felt a need to make the allusion more explicit.

EXAMPLE 4.19: Second Symphony, finale, direct references to the chorus of "De Camptown Races"

Example 4.19 compares both complete renditions of the chorus with the chorus as it appeared in Foster's original 1850 print.[39]

These overt statements of the chorus follow a disguised but complete paraphrase of Foster's verse in the opening theme (mm. 1–14), moving from tonic to dominant and back, as shown in Example 4.20. As is typical of Ives's paraphrases, there are elisions, overlaps, insertions, and omissions: the opening C is lacking (made unnecessary, perhaps, by the prominent C at the close of the previous movement), and the paraphrase is less recognizable because several of its first few notes are missing or displaced; the middle segment in C major overlaps the first segment in F (mm. 3–6 of the Ives); and mm. 5, 9, and 10 of Foster's tune are elided to avoid redundancy (mm. 6–9 of the Ives). In the recapitulation, mm. 6–7 of the theme are dropped, reducing the overlap while further condensing the paraphrase.

The shape of the theme is determined in part by its ultimate use as a countermelody to "Columbia, the Gem of the Ocean" in the coda. Like the first theme of the second movement, this theme serves as both main theme and countersubject, and the parallel is made explicit when the second-movement theme briefly joins the fray as the coda begins (m. 253, trumpets). A bit of "Columbia, the Gem of the Ocean" in the cellos and basses at mm. 11–12 provides a hint of the first theme's final destiny during its initial presentation. Given the twin restraints of counterpointing one borrowed melody while paraphrasing another, it is remarkable that Ives's theme is so appealing and shapely in its own right.

MODELING AND PARAPHRASE

EXAMPLE 4.20: Second Symphony, finale, opening theme, compared with "De Camptown Races"

EXAMPLE 4.20, continued

In fact, it took Ives several tries to find a suitable theme, and paraphrasing "De Camptown Races" was not part of his original conception. The early sketches for the theme all show it in counterpoint with "Columbia," making clear that finding a good countermelody for the latter was Ives's first concern. What appears to be the earliest surviving sketch, partly transcribed in Example 4.21, shows that his first attempt had little or nothing to do with "De

MODELING AND PARAPHRASE

EXAMPLE 4.21: Second Symphony, finale, preliminary sketch toward opening theme, showing it as a countermelody to "Columbia, the Gem of the Ocean"

Camptown Races."[40] Only mm. 3–4 and 11–12 match the final version, and these are the segments of the theme that least relate to the Foster tune.[41] At the bottom of the same page, after several intervening attempts, mm. 1–2 of the final version appear over the first two measures of "Columbia." It was apparently at this point, after mm. 1–4 and 11–12 were decided on, that Ives discovered he could paraphrase "De Camptown Races" in his theme, for the segments most obviously based on the Foster tune — the whole-tone oscillations in mm. 6–9, 10, and 13 — were added last.[42] Perhaps this in turn suggested following his theme with a paraphrase of Foster's chorus. Both the necessity to fit well in counterpoint with "Columbia" and the gradual cobbling together of his theme from fragments help to explain why Ives's theme sounds so distant from the Foster, its principal source.

There are traces of the chorus as well as of the verse in this theme, as Example 4.20 shows. The link between the openings of Ives's theme and of Foster's chorus is made explicit when they appear together in m. 43. Similarly, mm. 11–12 of the main theme counterpoint the paraphrased chorus in mm. 33–34. Like the first movement theme derived from "Massa's in de Cold Ground," these elements of the theme not only paraphrase the Foster but serve as counterpoints to it.

The verse's cadence in m. 14 elides with the opening motive of the chorus in the horns. The first four measures of the theme return at m. 20, leading to an episode and the two full statements of the chorus at mm. 31 and 35, and then Ives modulates suddenly, marking the transition to the second theme.

Thus, the entire first theme area is an extended paraphrase of both verse and chorus of "De Camptown Races," each beginning in the tonic, moving to the dominant, and returning to the tonic. What appear to be fragmentary quotations of the chorus are only the most conspicuous moments in this process, clues to the more subtle transformations around them. This complete rendition of the song's verse and chorus again parallels the second movement, where the AABA structure of "Wake Nicodemus" is likewise reflected in the layout of the first theme area. In both cases, Ives integrates into his classical symphonic structure not only the melodic motives but the very form of his vernacular American source.

2. In addition to the paraphrase of "De Camptown Races," the opening theme initiates a second motivic chain. Measure 1 recalls a rhythmic cell of one eighth and two sixteenths that played a prominent role in the first movement (see Examples 4.11, 4.13, and 4.20). This cell recurs throughout the theme and soon develops into a fife tune for flutes and piccolo (mm. 27–29) over the traditional marching band "street beat" or "street cadence" in the drums. The fife tune sounds like a quotation but is apparently only a variant of mm. 3–4 of the theme; however, the street beat is a quotation, one Ives uses frequently.[43] The rhythmic cell recurs in the countermelodies that accompany the chorus of "De Camptown Races" in mm. 31–42, first in a fragment of the first theme (violins, m. 33) and later in the passage shown in Example 4.22, in which the violins present the verse of the fiddle tune "Turkey in the Straw" (H169), off the beat in mm. 37–40 and then, in part, in its normal metric placement in mm. 41–42.[44] The motive returns in the transition to the second theme (mm. 43–57) and leads to a melody based on "Pig Town Fling" (at m. 52), which uses the same rhythmic cell. At the second theme (m. 58), the principal countermelody in the first violins consists of elements from "Pig Town Fling" and both verse and chorus of "Turkey in the Straw," so that the rhythmic cell and its retrograde continue to be prominent. Another melody based on the same rhythmic cell, Thomas Haynes Bayly's popular song "Long, Long Ago" (H119), appears in flute and oboe in mm. 70–71, punctuating the end of the theme's middle phrase.

Except for the opening theme, the melodies linked by this rhythmic cell are all secondary ideas, counterpointing the main themes. Since the first theme ultimately serves as a countermelody to "Columbia, the Gem of the Ocean," this motive can be said to link all the important countermelodies of the movement. Both main themes and countersubjects are paraphrased, not quoted verbatim, but reshaped to fit contrapuntally and motivically into the context of the symphony while retaining their individual characters.

Several countermelodies did not coalesce into allusions to existing tunes until later stages of composition. In many cases, Ives first sketched a suitable

EXAMPLE 4.22: Second Symphony, finale, first theme group, countermelody, compared to "Turkey in the Straw" and to an earlier sketch

countermelody using a variant of the common rhythmic cell and only later found a tune that he could adapt for the purpose while simultaneously deepening the motivic links between countermelodies. We have seen this already for the first theme, in which the rhythmic cell was present from the first sketch but became more prominent as Ives revised the theme into a paraphrase of "De Camptown Races." The first sketch of the countermelody in mm. 37–42, shown on the bottom staff of Example 4.22, is less clearly related to "Turkey in the Straw" than is the final version but shares with it the same rhythm of two sixteenths and an eighth, the retrograde of the rhythmic cell common to all the countermelodies.[45] The first version may have resembled the fiddle tune only coincidentally; the revised version is both more clearly a borrowing and more closely tied to other themes through its greater use of the rhythmic cell. A parallel and even more drastic revision can be seen in the countermelody to the middle period of the second theme. Example 4.23 compares the beginning of this phrase in the final version, which follows the contour and rhythm of an off-beat rendition of "Turkey in the Straw," with the parallel passage in the earliest surviving sketch, in F major.[46] The main melody (in the middle of the texture) and the harmony are identical, but the countermelody in the sketch is based on a repeated ornamental figure rather than on any existing tune. The bridge after the middle period underwent similar changes; Example 4.24 compares the final version (flute, m. 70), which quotes "Long, Long Ago," with the corresponding line in the same earlier sketch, based on a variant of the ornamental figure used before. In both cases, Ives replaced the ornamental figure, only vaguely related to the other motives in the movement, with the rhythmic cell common to the other countermelodies. Because of these and similar revisions, the final version of the movement is both more unified motivically and more filled with allusions to existing tunes.

3. A third chain of linked motives begins with the second theme, a stately, mostly pentatonic horn melody in ABA form. The A phrase resembles but

EXAMPLE 4.23: Second Symphony, finale, second theme, opening of countermelody to its middle period, with "Turkey in the Straw" and an earlier sketch

EXAMPLE 4.24: Second Symphony, finale, second theme, bridge before reprise of first period, compared to "Long, Long Ago" and to an earlier sketch

does not quote the opening of Foster's "Old Black Joe" (H128).[47] The B phrase paraphrases the same segment of "Massa's in de Cold Ground" used in the first and third movements. The last four notes of this phrase (mm. 69–70) are developed after m. 78, transformed into motives that suggest "Joy to the World" (Antioch, H3, adapted from Handel by Lowell Mason) as well as "Massa's in de Cold Ground." The B phrase and part of its later development are shown in Example 4.25 together with these two source tunes.

In the recapitulation, the horn theme initiates a series of references to earlier movements. The first and second themes of the second movement appear briefly in mm. 181–82, just before the reprise of the horn theme. The reprise of the extension that follows the horn theme leads to a passage from the third movement (mm. 228–33 recast mm. 59–67 of the third movement), including a prominent statement of this same phrase from "Massa's in de Cold Ground," part of Missionary Chant, and the theme based on the Foster tune that first appeared in mm. 65–67 of the third movement.[48] This leads in turn to a fuller reference to the opening theme of the second movement (at m. 235), in counterpoint first with itself and later with the countermelody based on "Turkey in the Straw." Fragments of "Columbia, the Gem of the Ocean" mix with elements from the first theme of the finale amid a general crescendo, leading to the climax at m. 253. Here all of "Columbia" appears in counterpoint with the first theme of the finale and the countermelody to its second theme, with the opening bars of the first theme of the second movement thrown in for good measure.

"Thrown in" is literally true, for the sketches show Ives adding material to this climax as he revised: the earliest sketch shows "Columbia" and the movement's first theme, accompanied only by the bass line and horn chords; in the next version, Ives adds the second theme's countermelody (based on "Pig

EXAMPLE 4.25: Second Symphony, finale, second theme, middle period, and a later variant, with "Massa's in de Cold Ground" and "Joy to the World"

Town Fling" and "Turkey in the Straw"), altered to fit the new harmonic context; finally, he adds the first two measures of the first theme of the second movement (based on "Wake Nicodemus") in the trumpet, omitting the rest of that theme because it does not fit the harmony.[49] Another addition at this late stage is the bugle call "Reveille" (H83), which appears in the trumpet in mm. 251–52, just before the triumphant entrance of "Columbia" and its entourage. In these closing minutes, beginning at m. 228 with the passage from the third movement, which itself quotes a theme from the first movement, the entire symphony is summed up.

Synthesizing American and European Musical Traditions

We have seen that all the themes and principal countermelodies of this symphony are paraphrased from American tunes. But these tunes are recast to eliminate repetition, to isolate motives for development, to highlight common motives that link themes together, and to create melodies that work well in counterpoint. Through paraphrase, these American tunes are reworked to fit the forms and textures of European art music, from the Bach-like

MODELING AND PARAPHRASE

polyphony of the first movement to the Dvořák-like second theme of the finale, while maintaining their American character. Once presented, the themes are developed and combined using procedures common to Ives's First Symphony and the European works he took as models, woven into a thematic tapestry that is coherent and compelling even if none of the source tunes is recognized.

Yet we do recognize these tunes, at least in part. The character of each type of tune is preserved in Ives's paraphrases; no matter how drastic the changes, the themes based on hymns sound like hymns, the Foster paraphrases like Foster, and the melodies taken from fiddle tunes like fiddle tunes. Clearly, it was Ives's intention to evoke the styles and feelings associated with these different kinds of music, whether or not the specific tunes are identified. Furthermore, though they vary in the degree to which they resemble their sources, it is striking that each paraphrased theme or countermelody includes at least one overt quotation from its source. Most veer between levels of allusion from the obvious to the obscure. This variability pulls us into the music, catching our attention with fleeting gestures we can identify and inviting us to delve deeper. That the level of recognizability was a major concern is clear from Ives's sketches, which show that he changed several passages to make their resemblance to their sources either more or less obvious, apparently seeking the proper balance. Although the thematic substance of this symphony would surely sound cohesive even to a listener who recognizes not a single borrowed tune, the process of gradually recognizing Ives's source tunes through their transformations is part of this music's appeal.

Why did Ives base the themes of this symphony on American vernacular tunes? One clue lies in the work's adaptation from music he had composed between 1896 and 1898, while he was at Yale. None of the earlier works survives. According to Ives's annotations, the first movement is adapted in part from an organ sonata, the third movement from an organ prelude, and apparently all movements but the third from a pair of overtures titled "Down East Overture" and "Town, Gown and State," grouped under the collective title "In These United States."[50] According to Ives, the finale's second theme is older still, having been performed in 1889 as a short piece, now lost, called *The American Woods*.[51] The origin of the third movement in a piece for church explains the presence of several hymns (though not the allusion to Foster), and the descriptive titles of the overtures suggest both why Ives based his themes on vernacular tunes and why he chose the popular, college, and patriotic songs he did. Perhaps he conceived these overtures as an American reply to Brahms's *Academic Festival Overture* (1881), a comparable treatment of familiar tunes with specific extramusical associations in a classical format.

Whereas Ives's other early orchestral music — the Postlude in F, the unfinished Overture in G (both ca. 1898),[52] and the First Symphony — had shown no nationalist traits, the titles of these overtures and of *The American Woods* show that in these works Ives was trying to write music that sounded American and reflected American life. He logically turned to the types of melody that he knew his listeners would recognize as distinctly American and would associate with particular aspects of American life: the songs of Stephen Foster, patriotic songs, traditional fiddle tunes, and gospel hymns. These are, of course, the types of American melody that return again and again in his later music.

But the Second Symphony is not exclusively American in origin. Although its themes are adapted from vernacular tunes, transitional sections in every movement borrow from similar passages in European classical masterpieces. By this means, Ives emphasizes at once what the two traditions have in common and what is most distinct about them. Whereas vernacular music is full of potential themes, it offers few models for transitions, because its forms seldom require them. Yet vernacular tunes contain motives that are just as susceptible to extension and development as are those of art music, and in his transitions, as if to prove the point, Ives changes part of a fiddle tune into a passage from Brahms and an episode from a Bach fugue into a Foster song.

The second theme of the first movement, derived from "Pig Town Fling," includes a lower-neighbor-note figure that resembles a motive from the main theme of Brahms's First Symphony finale, particularly as that motive appears in diminution and sequence at mm. 94–96. At the return of Ives's second theme, the similarity is made explicit, as the fiddle-tune figure is developed (mm. 76–78) in a transition that paraphrases a passage in the Brahms (mm. 273–78), transposed down a semitone. Both source and paraphrase play the same role, appearing in transitions that lead to a thematic return. Ives's transition develops so naturally out of his theme that the allusion to Brahms is not at all obvious. Indeed, Ives's first draft has at this point a simple rising sequence on the fiddle-tune figure; this is crossed out and replaced by the Brahms, a substitution clearly prompted by its resemblance to Ives's first thought.[53] This same passage reappears in the fourth movement (mm. 26–28) in virtually the same context.

Near the end of the first movement, Ives borrows an episode from Bach's Sinfonia or Three-Part Invention in F Minor BWV 795 (m. 93 to the downbeat of m. 94 quotes from mm. 28–29 of the Bach, transposed up a whole step). Ives immediately repeats it a minor third higher to create a rising sequence that leads to the climactic statement of a figure derived from the movement's opening theme; this parallels the shape and function of the borrowed Bach episode, a rising sequence that leads to a restatement of the

MODELING AND PARAPHRASE

opening material in the tonic. The passage reappears in the fourth movement (mm. 34–36) and, transposed and somewhat altered, in the middle of the first theme area of the fifth (mm. 25–27 and 127–29), as part of an excursion that effects the modulation from tonic to dominant. Like the earlier allusion to Brahms's First Symphony, these borrowings from Bach were afterthoughts, apparently suggested by their similarity to ideas Ives had already sketched.[54]

Measures 126–39 of the second movement present and develop a figure from another Brahms symphony, the Third (first movement, mm. 47–48), transposed, transformed, and metrically recast.[55] This motive leads from second-theme to first-theme material in both movements. In the Brahms, it appears in the exposition and the recapitulation between the second theme, of which it is a transformed inversion, and the closing material, which is based on arpeggiating figures from the first theme; in the Ives, it leads from the closing material, based on second-theme motives, into a reprise of the first theme. Ives uses it as the closing tag of the exposition and the recapitulation and develops it at the start of the development, just as Brahms treats the exposition's closing tag in his first movement.[56] These structural similarities show that Ives is using the Brahms not only as a melodic source, but also as a formal model. Sydney Robinson Charles has noted a resemblance between the opening figures of the two movements, which may partly explain the allusion.[57]

There is yet another allusion to Brahms in this movement. At m. 186, shortly before the recapitulation, Ives paraphrases and extends a passage from the end of the exposition of Brahms's First Symphony, first movement (mm. 181–88, developing a figure introduced in m. 161).[58] Once again, source and paraphrase have the same function: here, leading back to the first theme. A similar passage in diminution appears near the end of the coda (mm. 355–66).

Two passages in Ives's third movement use motives from the prelude to *Tristan und Isolde*, notably the descending figure first heard in Wagner's mm. 20–22 and the quickly rising scale that answers it on its reappearance at mm. 62–63 (H191). The latter leads directly to the return of the opening chord and motive at the original pitch in m. 66 of the Wagner. Both Ives passages that are based on this material likewise lead to restatements of opening material in the tonic: the first (mm. 23–32) follows the main theme and leads to a partial reprise of that theme, and the second (mm. 93–106) leads from the middle section to the return of the main theme. Wagner's descending figure shares the falling contour of the "Massa's in de Cold Ground" theme used in the middle of the movement, a resemblance that may have suggested the borrowings. At mm. 44–45, just before the middle section, another brief reference to the *Tristan* prelude (H190, from mm. 39–40, oboe I and clarinet I) marks the cadence.

A climbing figure of rising fourths and falling thirds from Brahms's First Symphony finale (mm. 385–88) appears in mm. 246–47 of Ives's finale, transposed down a fifth. In both cases, the figure lies over a dominant pedal and leads into a triumphal conclusion; in the Ives, it introduces "Columbia, the Gem of the Ocean" and returns at its cadence (mm. 267–68). The same figure appears in more complete form at the close of the fourth movement (mm. 37–40), where it is preceded in mm. 36–37 by another Brahms allusion: a dramatic cadence from the third of the *Vier ernste Gesänge* (mm. 29–30), marked by interlocked descending augmented triads in the melody. The harmony is similar to that in Brahms's song — A minor and E minor triads leading to a half-cadence (on a B major triad in the Brahms, a C dominant seventh in the Ives) — but Ives transposes the melody down a major third, producing the same augmented triads in a slightly more pungent harmonic context. This in turn is preceded by the sequence adapted from Bach's F Minor Sinfonia. Thus, in the last eight measures of the fourth movement, Ives presents three short allusions to European composers back to back.

Finally, in the reprise of the finale, the transition from the first theme to the second is greatly expanded, serving as a replacement for the development. It includes two passages (mm. 147–57 and 168–76) that cite episodes from the middle of Bach's E-minor fugue from book 1 of *The Well-Tempered Clavier* (mm. 13–14, 15–17, and 22), interspersed with Bachian figuration that may or may not be borrowed. Example 4.26 shows the two direct citations in the first of these passages. Ives carefully underlines the similarities between Bach's figuration and that in his own themes. The first passage directly follows a statement of the movement's opening motive, the second follows references to "Pig Town Fling," and in both cases the sixteenth-note motion of the Bach seems to grow naturally out of the preceding material. Even more striking is the transformation in mm. 154–55 of Bach's arpeggiated figure into a reference to the chorus of "De Camptown Races." In Example 4.26, Bach and Stephen Foster — the two kinds of "great music" that George Ives taught his son from an early age — meet on equal terms.[59]

Each classical allusion is woven into the texture through its resemblance to other material in the movement, making its presence far from obvious even for those familiar with Ives's models. As is true for the paraphrased themes, the degree to which the source can be recognized varies considerably. From the sketches, it is clear that many of the allusions to European music were afterthoughts, prompted by their resemblances to passages that Ives had already roughed out. This is true also of many of Ives's allusions to American music, particularly in his countermelodies; he clearly added references to both types of music as he revised, until the symphony was saturated with borrowed material. Finally, every paraphrase of classical material functions in

EXAMPLE 4.26: Second Symphony, finale, episode based on Bach's E-minor fugue
from *The Well-Tempered Clavier*, Book I

a way similar to its source, as an episode between thematic statements, and
often the parallel of function is quite close.

These allusions are clearly neither accidental nor incidental but a vital part
of Ives's purpose: the integration of American melody with European form.
Borrowing transition sections from well-known European works and weaving them through paraphrase into the fabric of his music allows him to
emphasize what is lacking in American vernacular music: symphonic devel-

MODELING AND PARAPHRASE

129

opment and elaborate formal schemes that require transitions and episodes between thematic statements. By citing transitional material from classical masterworks in his transitions and episodes, Ives acknowledges these non-thematic sections as the most distinctively European formal elements in the symphony, underlines his allegiance to European models of symphonic form, and provides an audible sign of a deeper aesthetic and structural kinship between his symphony and its European models.

The unmistakable classical borrowings are confined to these transitions. But every movement includes one or more apparent passing allusions to classical music within the themes themselves. Two of these have been mentioned: the presence in the second theme of the first and fourth movements of a neighbor-note figure akin to one in the finale of Brahms's First Symphony, and the motive shared by the first theme of the second movement and the opening of Brahms's Third Symphony. If these are not phantom allusions, they may be intended to prepare the listener for more explicit borrowings from the same sources later on — and perhaps even to demonstrate parallels between vernacular American and classical European tunes. Some analysts find hints of Wagner's *Die Walküre* and Brahms's First Symphony in the main theme of the third movement and of Beethoven's Fifth Symphony in its coda;[60] these seem too brief and vague to be clear citations. The allusion to one of Brahms's *Vier ernste Gesänge* near the end of the fourth movement suggests that the similar figure introduced in m. 3 as a counterpoint to the first theme (anticipated at m. 79 of the first movement) may also derive from that source.

In the finale, two ideas may refer to both vernacular and classical sources. The opening figure, part of a theme paraphrased from "De Camptown Races," is also related to the pizzicato theme of the scherzo of Tchaikovsky's Fourth Symphony, also in F major, as shown in Example 4.27. Similarly, the figure in the first violin at m. 60 (part of the countermelody to the second theme), taken from the chorus of "Turkey in the Straw," resembles a motive in the first movement of Dvořák's "New World" Symphony, as shown in Example 4.28. Given

EXAMPLE 4.27: Second Symphony, finale, opening motive, compared to Tchaikovsky's Fourth Symphony, third movement, opening theme

MODELING AND PARAPHRASE

EXAMPLE 4.28: Second Symphony, finale, part of countermelody to second theme, with motives from the "New World" Symphony and "Turkey in the Straw"

the many references to "Turkey in the Straw" in the surrounding measures, this motive must belong to that tune. But Ives may have intended it to sound like Dvořák as well.[61]

These may be phantom quotations, similarities that we may hear but that have no significance, like the appearance of the opening idea of Mozart's *Bastien und Bastienne* in the first theme of Beethoven's *Eroica Symphony*.[62] But other parallels between Ives's symphony and these by Dvořák and Tchaikovsky suggest that these apparent melodic allusions may have been intentional. Both Tchaikovsky's Fourth Symphony and the "New World" Symphony are cyclic works, models for the kind of piece Ives was attempting. The linear and contrapuntal combination of themes from previous movements in the "New World" finale is similar to that in the Ives, and Ives's presentation of themes in diminution and augmentation echoes procedures in his First Symphony that were directly modeled on the Dvořák. The principal motive of the "New World" is a rising arpeggiated triad not unlike Ives's "Camptown Races" figure, and the closing passages of the Dvořák and Ives symphonies are very much alike.[63] Ives's key scheme, based on the keys of F major, A♭ major, B minor, and D major, may have been inspired by that of the first movement of Tchaikovsky's Fourth Symphony, in which themes presented in F minor, A♭ minor, and B major are recapitulated in D minor and F major, completing the circle of minor thirds.[64] These parallels suggest that the hints of Dvořák and Tchaikovsky in the finale's themes may be double entendres designed both to point to broader relationships between Ives's symphony and theirs, and also to show once again — as with Ives's transformations of Bach into Foster and "Pig Town Fling" into Brahms — that the European and American traditions, however different, are closely akin.

Finally, there is a close formal resemblance between Ives's last two movements and the finale of Brahms's First Symphony, which may be signaled by another pun. Ives first conceived of the fourth and fifth movements as a single movement with a slow introduction,[65] and in that format they closely parallel the Brahms finale. Both slow introductions start in a minor key (C minor in the Brahms, B minor in the Ives) with a majestic idea in octaves, in the horn and violins in the Brahms and in the horns in the Ives. As Example 4.29 shows, Ives's motive resembles Brahms's, particularly at the latter's repetition in mm. 12–14.[66] In both slow introductions, the opening idea is repeated prior to a transition leading to a second idea, marked *Più andante*, in a closely related major key (parallel in the Brahms, relative in the Ives). The following Allegro is a modified sonata form without development in both works, with numerous parallels between them: the second idea from the introduction returns just before the second theme; an extension following the second theme leads to a reprise of the first theme in the tonic; there follows a greatly expanded transition that includes new material and takes the place of a development section; the second theme returns in the tonic, again preceded by the second idea from the slow introduction; and a long coda brings the movement to a fortissimo close. In the coda, Ives even borrows the climbing figure mentioned above (mm. 385–88 of the Brahms, in mm. 246–47 of the Ives) and ends in a similar manner, with descending octaves syncopated across the barline, a rising subdominant arpeggio, and dry tutti chords (mm. 431–57 of the Brahms and 269–77 of the Ives). Movements 4 and 5 are as closely modeled on the Brahms finale as is the second movement of Ives's

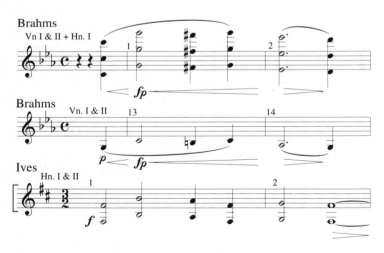

EXAMPLE 4.29: Second Symphony, fourth movement, opening motive, with opening motive of Brahms's First Symphony finale

MODELING AND PARAPHRASE

First Symphony on the slow movement of Dvořák's "New World," and the number of references in these and other movements to Brahms's First Symphony makes clear that the latter was the principal model for Ives's Second, as the "New World" was for his First. Here as in the First Symphony, an explicit allusion to another work in the same genre indicates deeper similarities of form or procedure.[67]

The Significance of the Borrowed Material in the Second Symphony

What Ives is doing in this symphony is using models: Brahms for thematic design, Bach and Dvořák for counterpoint, Brahms, Dvořák, and Tchaikovsky for form, and all four, plus Wagner, for texture, rhetoric, and motivic development.[68] His themes are paraphrased (not quoted) from American tunes. In using models and alluding to their music directly and indirectly, Ives was following a strong tradition in nineteenth-century European art music. His methods and ideals are European. The form of the work, though novel in several respects, is still entirely determined by traditional notions of symphonic form. Despite the diverse origins of his borrowed material, the symphony exhibits the thematic unity characteristic of contemporary European art music. Even paraphrase technique itself, as we have seen, grew out of Ives's earlier work with melodic transformation in variation sets and fugues, both European forms. And the purpose of his music is European too; this is nationalist music, asserting the value of the music of his homeland, but it is nationalist music in an international style, like that of Dvořák, Tchaikovsky, and Brahms.

Is there an extramusical explanation for Ives's use of so much borrowed material in this symphony? In a fascinating stream of metaphor, Colin Sterne has suggested that the Second Symphony reveals Ives's "shrewd appraisal of his position as a composer": "He accepts the fact that he is a 'cornfield' composer in a 'cornfield' country — one without its own musical tradition, but one that, for that very reason, offers him a unique challenge. He is then, as he himself tells us in his music, a verdant freshman, bringing in the sheaves from an American cornfield, betting his money on the bobtail nag while somebody else bet on the bay."[69] The vernacular tunes, Sterne believes, are used to evoke their texts, from the "Down in de cornfield" segment from "Massa's in de Cold Ground" to the chorus from "De Camptown Races," and the classical references are present because Ives is proclaiming the death of the European tradition, particularly the actual death in 1897 (the year Ives dated his first work on the symphony in a note in the published score) of Johannes Brahms, the classical "Massa" whom Ives quotes most thoroughly and most often.[70]

It is a wonderful theory, impossible to disprove and equally impossible to credit. Perhaps we could extend the notion to include borrowings that Sterne does not explain, imagining that Ives considered himself "hot stuff" endowed with "missionary" fervor to proclaim "the great Jubilee" ("Wake Nicodemus") in the "New World," "the land of corn and wine" (*Beulah Land*) and "fount of every blessing." Maybe *Hamburg* is a sly reference to Brahms's birthplace. But one could assemble such a program for almost any random collection of texts and titles. If, in the early 1900s, Ives truly believed that the European tradition was dead, when all around him composers were busily continuing that tradition, as was he in his own works, he was ahead of even the most progressive European composers. More importantly, a psycho-programmatic interpretation such as this directs our attention away from the music itself, lending credence to the regrettable view that Ives's music lacks purely musical logic and coherence. Finally, if Ives is so eager to have us recognize his allusions, why is he so coy about making the references explicit? If Sterne were correct, surely bald quotation would have served Ives's purpose better than such subtle paraphrase.

The Second Symphony is not a program symphony but a character piece. When it is so difficult to recognize the source tunes, and when they are so transformed that in most cases only brief fragments appear in their original forms, it is clear that the intended meaning is carried by the melodies themselves, not by their associated texts. It is their character as hymns, fiddle tunes, popular songs, and other representative American types that is most important in Ives's themes, just as it is the European character of the material borrowed from Bach, Brahms, and Wagner that makes the juxtaposition of the European with the American material so witty and poignant. By interweaving American and European sources in the ways he does, Ives proclaims the unity of his musical experience as an American exposed to both traditions.

The growing importance of "quotation" in Ives's music from this point on probably stemmed from his experience with paraphrase technique in the First Quartet and Second Symphony. At the time they were begun, paraphrase was still a relatively uncommon procedure for Ives; most of the other music he was working on, including the Postlude in F, the unfinished Overture in G, the Largo for violin, clarinet, and piano, *The Celestial Country*, about ten other choral works, and about forty songs, had nothing to do with paraphrase or with any other overt references to existing melodies. In attempting to incorporate American tunes into European genres, Ives apparently discovered that he enjoyed reworking familiar tunes, and he certainly demonstrated that he was good at it, possessing a sense of melodic reinvention of rare subtlety. As he explored the ramifications of transforming one

MODELING AND PARAPHRASE

melody into another through fragmentation and reconstruction, he developed methods of motivic development that allowed him to manipulate the level of recognizability of a source tune or to draw several tunes together by exploiting their innate melodic similarities. The resulting music inevitably had extramusical connotations because of the associations carried by the tunes, but its logic depended solely on the musical relationships Ives was learning to establish. In other words, almost by accident, Ives discovered new procedures for organizing musical form based on familiar melodies. In his later music, he found the extramusical connotations of his borrowed tunes more and more useful, yet he continued in most cases to organize his music in purely musical terms.

The Second Symphony is thus both a pinnacle and a turning point, Ives's most successful attempt to integrate American melody into European forms and a springboard for developments still to come. If it had been performed when finished and received well, its success might have prompted Ives to write more in the same vein. As it was, the symphony lay unperformed for almost half a century, and Ives went no further down that path.

After completing the Second Symphony, Ives abandoned both the received forms of European art music and the simple nationalism of Dvořák and Tchaikovsky. Instead of placing national melody in an international frame, as in this work, Ives moved toward a celebration of American individuality, first of particular tunes, later of specific people, places, and events: the idealism of *Emerson* or of *Lincoln, the Great Commoner*; the stories of *Putnam's Camp, Redding, Connecticut* or *The "St.-Gaudens" in Boston Common*; the sound and spirit of *Decoration Day* in a small town or of a hymn rising *From Hanover Square North* over the noise of New York's rush hour.

These pieces use new approaches to form to match their new subject matter. In the extended ruminations on individual hymn tunes in most movements of his Third Symphony, violin sonatas, and First Piano Sonata, Ives used a kind of cumulative form, discussed in the next chapter, in which his theme, a borrowed or paraphrased tune with one or more countersubjects, appears complete only at the end of a movement, preceded by fragments and paraphrases of it. In this new form, the ability to fragment, disguise, and slowly reveal a source tune, evident in every movement of the Second Symphony, was of fundamental importance. In his immense but tightly integrated collages such as *Washington's Birthday* and *The Fourth of July* (discussed in chapter 10), the structure depends upon motivic and contrapuntal links between the many tunes Ives borrows, as in the Second Symphony, and the meaning of these works, much more specifically programmatic than the symphony, relies on the extramusical connotations of the tunes.[71] These pieces are often unique in form, yet they too follow a few simple formal ideas — variation, verse-refrain,

ABA, arch, climax-release, rondo — whose roots lie deep in the European tradition. As received forms are replaced by novel and synthetic forms, the self-conscious nationalism of the Second Symphony fades as well, replaced by music that seeks to capture the individual musical experience — all of it — of one man from Connecticut and is therefore both international and American in its essence. Its sense of place is no longer forced but quietly understood, and its New England regionalism is offered as "a local color that will do all the world good," "a true pigment of the universal color."[72]

In this reconception of both musical form and extramusical content, paraphrase technique was fundamental. In the Second Symphony, as we have seen, paraphrase allowed Ives to achieve several apparently contradictory objectives at once: to pay homage to the European tradition of art music at the same time that he saluted the American vernacular tradition; to integrate the two while emphasizing what is most distinctive about each; to write unmistakably nationalist music within an international idiom; and to create an extraordinarily original symphony based on borrowed tunes. But the same skill in reworking existing material that permitted him to remake "Wake Nicodemus" into a theme of Brahmsian shape and potential also made it possible in his later music to create pieces with strong extramusical associations whose structures, like that of the Second Symphony, nonetheless depend squarely upon musical relationships. These mature works are still Romantic in ethos; Ives was still committed to the formal and expressive aesthetic of art music he had learned from Parker. Yet they move beyond Ives's nineteenth-century models as decisively as do contemporary works by Debussy, Schoenberg, and Stravinsky. In these later compositions, the tension between European and American traditions that is so palpable in the Second Symphony is no longer felt. Ives has absorbed all his influences and has found his true subject: the idealism that he attributed to Emerson and Beethoven, Lincoln and gospel singers, Bach and Stephen Foster alike.

CHAPTER 5

Cumulative Settings

The ternary and sonata forms that Ives used in his First String Quartet and first two symphonies depended upon the presentation, development, and reprise of themes. But from about 1902, he turned increasingly to forms that did not use large-scale repetition and did not present their themes at the outset. The most significant of these new forms is *cumulative setting*. This is a variety of *cumulative form*, a thematic, non-repetitive form in which the principal theme is presented, not at the beginning as in traditional forms, but near the end, and is preceded, not followed, by its development. In cumulative form, there is no repetition of long segments of music, as there is in ternary, sonata, rondo, and many other forms, but rather a continual development that leads up to the definitive statement of the theme. Since Ives invariably uses as a theme an existing tune, sometimes slightly varied, or a melody paraphrased from two or more tunes, we may best describe his particular procedure as a *setting* of this tune in cumulative form, or a *cumulative setting*.[1] In a cumulative setting, the borrowed or paraphrased theme is first heard in fragments, often varied; is gradually assembled and clarified; and appears in full for the first time near the end of the movement. In most instances, the full statement of the theme is accompanied by a countermelody that is developed in a similar manner and usually appears complete before the theme itself. In a cumulative setting, Ives uses paraphrase not only to create themes and countermelodies, but as part of a process of discovery, as the theme slowly emerges from the fragments and variants that precede its culminating appearance. The elements of the theme, its countermelody, and their accompaniment gradually accumulate until the borrowed tune and its setting appear together in their entirety — hence the name "cumulative setting."

In their pioneering book on Ives, Henry and Sidney Cowell noted his tendency to save the first complete statement of a tune or idea for the end of a movement and offered a philosophical explanation: "He feels that music, like other truths, should never be immediately understood; there must always remain some further element yet to be disclosed. A complete musical statement, in all its clarity and simplicity, like any absolute truth, is an ultimate, not a beginning. Ives reserves it, therefore, for the culmination of a work."[2] Many studies have noted this as a tendency in Ives's music, but none has defined his typical pattern as a distinct form.[3] Lacking a formal paradigm for these movements, analysts have tried to press them onto the procrustean bed of ternary or sonata form, have treated each as a unique form, or have failed to differentiate cumulative settings from works in other forms that happen to end with a complete statement of a borrowed tune, such as the finales of the First Quartet and the Second Symphony. Once cumulative setting is recognized as a form, many difficulties in analyzing, understanding, and performing these works disappear, and both the overall design and the individual features of each movement come into sharper focus.

Cumulative setting is by far the most common form in Ives's concert music between about 1907 and 1920, including the Third Symphony, the four violin sonatas, and the First Piano Sonata. More than two dozen instrumental movements and songs use this form, about a sixth of Ives's completed movements that incorporate existing music and about one-eighth of his finished works after 1902 (other than arrangements). Although the procedures that underlie Ives's cumulative settings can be found in music by earlier composers and are anticipated in his own, there appear to be no previous works that follow his typical pattern in every respect. Ives may have invented the form, and his frequent use of it defined cumulative setting as a new and distinctive type.

Cumulative setting for Ives, like ritornello form for Vivaldi or sonata form for Beethoven, is not a rigid mold but a flexible set of devices used in various ways to create movements that differ from one another yet share a common form. Each of Ives's settings in cumulative form has unique features, but all follow similar procedures. A close look at three examples, followed by a survey of the other works in this form, will reveal both the elements they share and the variety of shapes they assume, including five distinct subtypes. The evolution of cumulative form in Ives's music and the models he may have drawn upon for his procedures are discussed in chapter 6, which also explores the relationship of cumulative setting to program music, including two cumulative settings inspired by a text (*General William Booth*) and a program (*From Hanover Square North*). Two movements that combine cumulative setting with collage (*The Fourth of July* and the Fourth Symphony finale) are treated in chapter 10.

What is most important in understanding a movement in any thematic form is to identify the themes and discern how they are deployed and transformed. The descriptions here focus on these concerns. Given the number of works to cover and the growing complexity of Ives's harmony and rhythm, there is not space for fully rounded analyses.[4]

Three Cumulative Settings with Paraphrased Countermelodies

In the most common type of cumulative setting, Ives takes as a theme an existing tune or a theme paraphrased from one or more tunes, adds a figured accompaniment and a countermelody paraphrased from the same or another tune, and places this complex near the end. This is preceded by fragments and variants of both theme and countermelody, often including a full statement of the countermelody and accompaniment without the theme. The key is often vague or unstable until the theme appears near the end in the tonic. Thus instead of stating a theme and then developing or varying it, as in traditional forms, Ives begins with fragments and paraphrases and gradually assembles the theme and its accompaniment before our ears.

Three movements will illustrate Ives's procedures. All three are based on lost organ works from 1901, which may or may not have been in cumulative form. Of the extant works in this form, the outer movements of the Third Symphony appear to be among the earliest, and the Third Violin Sonata finale is the first whose form Ives appears to have described in writing. The plan of each movement is outlined in Table 5.1.

TABLE 5.1: Three Cumulative Settings

T indicates Theme
CM indicates Countermelody
>: indicates final statement of T with CM
> indicates significant statement of T (partial or paraphrased)
: indicates complete statement of CM

Third Symphony, third movement (ca. 1908–11, based on lost organ communion piece from 1901)
T: *Woodworth* (H67)
CM 1: Main countermelody, paraphrased from *Azmon* (H5)
CM 2: Subsidiary countermelody, original

Section		Measure		
1		1	Fragments of T and CM 1	B♭, many passing modulations
		12	First half of CM 1 and 2	F, modulating to B♭
2	:	20	CM 1 and 2 complete, with accompaniment as at m. 49	E♭
		25	T fragments	modulatory
3	>	29	Paraphrase of T	modulatory
		37	Fragments of T and CM 1, with varied reprise of opening at mm. 39–41	modulatory, closing on V of B♭
4	>:	49	T complete, with CM 1 and 2 and accompaniment	B♭
		57	Extension of T and final cadence	

Table 5.1, continued:

Third Symphony, first movement (ca. 1908–11, based on lost organ prelude from 1901)

T: *Azmon* (H5)

CM: Paraphrased from *Erie* (H17)

CS a (Countersubject a): Derived in part from a segment of *Erie*

CS b (Countersubject b): Derived from a segment of *Erie*

Secondary idea: *Woodworth* (H67), first phrase

Section		Measure			
1		1	Mixture of CM, T	$\frac{3}{2}$ Andante maestoso	Bb, many passing modulations
	>	8	Fragments of T with CS a and b		
		22	T mm. 1–6, fugato with CS a	con moto	Eb, Bb, modulatory
		38	CS b enters, fugato continues		final statement on Bb
2		54	*Woodworth*, first phrase, with CS b		D Mixolydian
		60	Further development of fragments of T, CS a and b		modulatory, closing in D Dorian
3	:	75	CM complete, with a few T fragments	$\frac{4}{2}$ Adagio cantabile	modulatory, ending in Bb
		88	Development of fragments of CM, CS b, T, and CS	più mosso	Bb, with passing modulations
		101	Development continues	$\frac{3}{2}$	Bb, modulating to F
4	>:	117	T complete, with CM	largamente, Adagio cantabile	F

Table 5.1, continued:

Third Violin Sonata, third movement (ca. 1914, based on lost organ prelude from 1901)

T: *Need* (H41), refrain (mm. 8–16)

CM: Paraphrased from *Need*, beginning of verse´ (mm. 1–4) and end of refrain (mm. 14–16)

Section	Measure		
1	1	Piano introduction on fragments of T, CM, verse of *Need*	modulatory
	13	Violin enters, development continues	
>	68	Paraphrase of T in piano, twice (**pp**, then **mf**), with fragments of CM (violin, then piano alone)	D♭
2	85	Piano interlude on fragments of T, CM, verse of *Need*	modulatory
:	103	CM complete in violin, accompaniment in piano	A♭
	110	Development of CM	modulatory
	145	Piano postlude on fragments of T and CM (varied reprise of mm. 40–46)	
3	154	Piano interlude (small ABA´) on T fragments, including paraphrase of T (166–74)	modulatory
>	180	T fragments, later CM fragments as well	modulatory over F pedal point
>:	208	T complete in violin I, twice (**ff**, then **pp**), with CM and accompaniment in piano	B♭
	222	Codetta on T, m. 1, in piano	

Third Symphony, third movement ("Communion"), and The Camp-Meeting

The Largo finale of the three-movement Third Symphony (ca. 1908–11, adapted from a lost organ communion piece of 1901) is based on William Bradbury's hymn tune *Woodworth* (H67, "Just as I am") and is in four sections defined by the thematic and harmonic process.[5] Although the chord-to-chord motion is rapid, with much chromatic voice-leading, the harmony is largely triadic and functional, and the borrowed tunes often help to clarify the local key. The first and final sections center on the tonic, B♭ major; the second is in subdominant regions, moving from E♭ to C major, the dominant of the dominant; and the third is modulatory, beginning on an implied F-minor triad and ending on a strong half-cadence in the tonic, yielding an overall tonal scheme based on a greatly elaborated I–IV–V–I progression. Since the theme appears complete only at the end, after earlier sections refer to and develop it, let us take up these sections in reverse order.

Example 5.1 shows the opening of the final section (mm. 49–62), where the hymn tune theme appears at last, complete and in the tonic, played by the cellos with a solo cello and flute doubling an octave higher (not shown). The first violins simultaneously present the main countermelody, paraphrased from the hymn tune *Azmon* (H5, "O for a thousand tongues"). The only segment of *Azmon* that is immediately recognizable in Ives's reworking is mm. 5–6 of the hymn, which are presented exactly. The rest is subtly altered, following the course of the tune as if transposed up a major second for the first segment of the hymn and then by a perfect fourth. In mm. 50–52, the bassoon plays a subsidiary countermelody, not based on an existing tune. Missing from the example are the bass and inner parts, which provide the accompaniment and fill out the harmony. *Woodworth* is stated complete, but its cadence is delayed: the cellos and flute break off (m. 57) just before the last three notes of the hymn; the violins repeat the hymn's third phrase a step higher, then return to the fourth phrase in the tonic; and the solo cello presents the concluding two-note motive over a dominant-tonic cadence. This is played twice and echoed a tritone away by soft orchestral bells in parallel minor triads, imitating the characteristic harmonics of church bells.[6]

At the beginning of the third section (m. 29), about halfway through the piece, we hear an almost full but very distorted paraphrase of *Woodworth*, shown in Example 5.2. The paraphrase modulates upwards as it goes, from A♭ through B, F, B♭, and E, reflecting the quickly-moving harmony. A stringendo on the main countermelody leads to a *forte* reprise of the opening bars of the movement (m. 39) and a climax based on fragments of both theme and countermelody (mm. 42–45). This relaxes into a repeated ii[7]–V (or ii[9]–V) half-cadence in the tonic B♭, preparing the appearance of the complete theme in the following section.[7]

EXAMPLE 5.1: Third Symphony, finale, principal themes in counterpoint

EXAMPLE 5.2: *Woodworth*, with paraphrase from Third Symphony, finale, third section

The second section (m. 20) presents the two countermelodies and accompaniment as they appear in the final section, but without the theme and transposed down a fifth or up a fourth into the subdominant E♭. Every element of the final setting is present here but the theme itself. After the main countermelody is stated, fragments of the theme provide a transition to the next section.

At the very beginning of the movement, fragments of *Woodworth* and its countermelodies are tossed around like scraps of themes in the development of a Beethoven symphony, as the harmony alternates swiftly between the tonic and other keys. Several instruments play the hymn's opening three-note motive in imitation. The cellos, which will present the entire theme at the end, play its first phrase, in the tonic but distended, as shown in Example 5.3. Other fragments appear, notably the peak of the hymn tune from its third phrase (violins, mm. 4–5). Then part of the main countermelody appears in the woodwinds (mm. 6–7), we cycle back to the opening idea (m. 8), and these fragments develop until the first parts of both countermelodies are pre-

EXAMPLE 5.3: Third Symphony, finale, opening phrase in the cellos

sented in combination, slightly varied, beginning in the dominant and moving to the tonic (mm. 11–16). A brief transition then leads to the second section.

This movement is typical of Ives's later music in its gradual motion from complexity to clarification, as fragments and paraphrases of the theme and countermelodies are assembled into complete statements and as the most important secondary idea, presented independently at first, is ultimately revealed to be a countermelody to the main theme. This process depends upon paraphrase technique, particularly on the different levels of recognizability Ives had explored in previous compositions. Here he uses paraphrase not only to create themes, deriving the main countermelody from *Azmon*, but also to allude to the principal theme and countermelodies in ways that gradually become more complete and recognizable: in the first section, fragments of the main thematic ideas, sometimes unchanged and sometimes greatly reworked; in the second section, presentation of the theme's accompaniment and countermelodies, without the theme itself and in a different key; in the third section, further development, including an almost complete but greatly distorted paraphrase of the main theme; and finally the theme complete and in the tonic, fully clad in its countermelodies and accompaniment, providing a satisfying point of arrival for both thematic and harmonic progressions.

The form here is of particular interest. It is something like the development and recapitulation of a sonata form without the exposition. The two forms share the presence of two themes of contrasting characters; the process of developing these themes through fragmentation, variation, transposition, and recombination; the sense of arrival at a subsequent statement of the principal theme; and the harmonic closure created by presenting the secondary theme at the end in the tonic, after first presenting it in another key. Yet Ives avoids both the clear exposition of themes at the outset and the exact thematic repetition of traditional sonata form.

CUMULATIVE SETTINGS

The avoidance of large-scale repetition is what most differentiates this movement from what appear to be its immediate antecedents, the finales of the First String Quartet and Second Symphony. In those works, the concluding presentations of *Webb* and of "Columbia, the Gem of the Ocean" occur in codas appended to traditional ternary or sonata forms based on the presentation, development, and reprise of themes; the main theme appears at the outset, and the major signal of impending formal closure, the reprise of the first section, has already been heard before the coda begins. In the Third Symphony finale, there is no important thematic return before the final statement of the complete source tune and its countermelodies. Although there is a recollection of the movement's opening phrase in the third section, this is not a point of arrival, of sectional division, or of "recapitulation"; it occurs as a new propulsive element in the middle of a rise in tension, dynamic level, register, and tempo that leads to the climax of the movement in m. 45. In the absence of any previous thematic return of any significance, the closing presentation of *Woodworth* with its countermelodies becomes the formal goal of the whole movement. It combines the long-awaited appearance of the principal theme, foreshadowed by fragments and variants, with the reprise of a secondary theme presented earlier and the return to the tonic to fulfill all our expectations at once and achieve a very strong sense of closure. It is striking that this presentation of the theme and countersubject together occurs at a soft dynamic level, far from the bustle and noise of the codas to the First Quartet and Second Symphony finales.

Saving the full presentation of the theme for the end of the movement reverses the sequence of other thematic forms, such as sonata or variation form. However, as one might expect, the surviving sketches show that Ives first worked out a countermelody and harmonization for the theme and then drafted the earlier sections in which those ideas were developed.[8] Sketches for a number of other cumulative settings show a similar process, suggesting that it became Ives's typical practice to draft the theme, countermelody, and accompaniment in combination before sketching the earlier sections of the movement.[9] The compositional process is not unlike that of other composers or of Ives's own earlier music, as it relies on common procedures of elaboration and development. What has changed is the order of events within the piece; we do not hear the parts in the order in which they were conceived, but rather begin with the peak of fragmentation and variation and work toward the relative clarity and directness of the theme itself.

This idea of leading up to the theme instead of presenting it at the outset had precedents in both European and American music, explored in chapter 6. Perhaps closest to home, for a form that developed in movements adapted from organ works Ives had played in church, are two improvised genres used in religious services and revivals that have a shape similar to cumulative setting. It is a practice of long standing for church organists to improvise a fantasy on motives drawn from a hymn tune that concludes with a full statement of the melody, as a prelude to worship or to singing the hymn. Since Ives was a church organist for thirteen years, this may have been one of the most important inspirations for his use of the form. There is also a parallel between his practice in music and the improvised sermons of American folk preachers, particularly in the Appalachian and African-American traditions. The closing statement of the hymn tune as the culmination of all that has gone before is reminiscent of the way folk preachers frequently end improvised sermons by quoting the words of a hymn or gospel song that distills the essence of what they have said. A famous example is the last speech of Martin Luther King, Jr., in which he reviewed the history of the civil rights movement, vowed that "we as a people will get to the Promised Land," and concluded by trumpeting, "Mine eyes have seen the glory of the coming of the Lord!," the opening line of "The Battle Hymn of the Republic."[10] If the preachers Ives heard at the revivals and camp meetings he attended as a youth followed a similar strategy in their improvised sermons, he might have based the structure of his cumulative settings in part on their model. Although the form of Ives's Third Symphony finale is too complex to have been improvised, the sense of groping gradually towards clarity and completeness gives it an improvisatory cast, and the work may have roots in Ives's improvisations at the organ.

This progression from complexity to clarity and from fragments to wholeness relates directly to the meaning of this movement. The Third Symphony is not explicitly programmatic. Ives gave descriptive titles to the symphony ("The Camp Meeting") and to each movement ("Old Folks Gatherin'," "Children's Day," and "Communion") that reveal the general mood or character he sought to capture, but he did not seek to describe a scene or depict a sequence of events.[11] This music is no less concerned with purely musical matters than are the First String Quartet or the Second Symphony. What this movement is about is the hymn tune itself.

A cumulative setting like this may be compared to an extended gloss on a text, a ruminative, interpretive sermon on a verse of scripture that is stated in full only at the end. Such a setting explores and gradually clarifies the implications of the tune taken as its subject, as a sermon might explore the ramifications and clarify the ultimate meaning of a text. Part of the purpose of such scriptural exegesis in a gloss or sermon is to encourage a similar struggle with the meaning of the text on the part of the reader or listener, inviting a continuation of the process that the interpreter only begins. For a listener who knows the text of the hymn that Ives uses for his theme or who recalls the feelings associated with singing or hearing the tune, the way is open for associating verbal and emotional meanings with the music.[12] For a listener who does not know the text and has no particular memory of the hymn, the work can still be both comprehensible, since the processes involved are entirely musical and non-programmatic, and emotionally affecting, since the rumination on a tune that this movement embodies resembles the effort of trying to grasp an idea that seems at first too hard to express and only gradually assumes a coherent form.

No matter how we may have experienced the hymn tune before, the Third Symphony finale changes the way we perceive and understand *Woodworth*. Just as we read a passage from scripture differently once we have heard it interpreted in a sermon, so the process of fragmenting, paraphrasing, and reconstructing *Woodworth* in cumulative form focuses our attention on aspects of the melody we might otherwise have ignored and makes connections we might otherwise have missed. Ives does not present the hymn first, which would allow us to respond to it directly and form our own opinions of it; he gives it to us in parts and paraphrases, offering his interpretation first, so that when it appears whole at last we recognize in it the elements he has so carefully shown us, as if we were hearing it through his ears.

The change in the way we hear and understand *Woodworth* that results from the preceding development is highlighted in the music and text of *The Camp-Meeting* (1912), Ives's recasting of this movement as a song. Although the music is abbreviated and reordered, the essential parts of the cumulative setting are all present.[13] The piano introduction is based on the first section of the symphony finale, presenting first the countermelody (from mm. 12–16 of the finale) and then the original opening measures, with their many references to the theme. The finale's second section is omitted, and the voice enters in m. 10 with the paraphrase of *Woodworth* from the third section of the symphonic movement. From here to the end, the song is very close to its source, omitting only eight measures from the third section and a few inner voices, among them the second countermelody at the final statement of the theme.

The original first verse of the hymn text, by Charlotte Elliott, is sung when the hymn tune finally appears. It is preceded by Ives's own text, which sets the scene and suggests how to hear the hymn, text and tune:

Across the summer meadows fair,
there comes a song of fervent prayer,
It rises radiantly o'er the world,
Exulting, exulting, in the power of God!
Exalting Faith in life above
but humbly, yielding, yielding, yielding to His love.

Just as I am without one plea,
But that Thy blood was shed for me,
and that Thou bidd'st me come to Thee,
O Lamb of God, I come! I come!

The narrator is not singing the hymn but hearing it and naming the feelings it embodies. When at the end he quotes it (or, as it were, stops speaking so we can listen to it ourselves from "across the summer meadows"), he invites us to hear that same exultant yet humble spirit behind the words. The long extension before the hymn's closing notes now becomes an interlude in the piano, so that when the final words "I come! I come!" appear at last, they suggest that the narrator himself has been swept up in the spirit of the hymn.

Just as Ives's musical exegesis points to aspects of the tune that we might have missed, his added text focuses our attention on the spirit behind the words and the singing. Both music and text create a drama whose denouement is the hymn itself. This makes it impossible to dismiss either the tune or the words of the hymn as banal and beneath notice, as sophisticated listeners might do if we heard it without such preparation. We listen to the hymn differently in the context that Ives gives it: with greater concentration, awareness, and empathy. We do not hear the hymn alone and respond to it directly; we hear it in the context of an art song, clothed in an artful accompaniment and in counterpoint with the melody we heard at the outset, which may represent the narrator, the scene he describes, or our own sense of separateness as we hear a hymn being sung by others. The song is wholly within the tradition of the nineteenth-century art song, which always represents an individual point of view, and outside the traditional role of the hymn as the collective expression of a group. What we experience through the song, then, is not the hymn itself but the narrator's experience of hearing the hymn, recognizing it as the embodiment of deep feelings, and being moved.

The meaning of the Third Symphony finale is less specific, as it lacks a text or explicit program. But if the song is about the experience of hearing the hymn sung from a distance, this movement is also about the experience of hearing the hymn. The process of development gives the tune associations that are psychologically similar to those it might acquire for a person who sings or hears it on many occasions, noticing now one aspect, now another. It has at its final appearance a richness and depth gained through our experience of its many earlier manifestations, combined with a sense of rightness as it achieves its ultimate form.

This is an entirely musical process with clear spiritual parallels, like the progression from minor-mode turbulance to major-mode triumph in Beethoven's Fifth and Ninth Symphonies. The process would carry a similar

CUMULATIVE SETTINGS

meaning whether the theme were original or borrowed, and if borrowed whether it were recognized or went unnoticed. Of course, there are added levels of meaning for one who knows the tune and its text, just as a listener who knows of Beethoven's struggle with deafness or of Schiller's original intention to write an ode to freedom (*Freiheit*) rather than joy (*Freude*) may hear additional meanings in the Fifth and Ninth Symphonies.

The point deserves emphasis. Ives's hymn-settings in cumulative form rely purely on musical procedures for their structure. Yet the process they embody, of gathering the themes from fragments and variants until their definitive appearance at the end, and the material they use, hymns with particular texts and liturgical uses, inevitably have extramusical associations. This combination of clear musical structure and open-ended extramusical meaning is part of the richness of cumulative setting as a form and no doubt a prime reason Ives used it so often, more than any other form in his major works after the Second Symphony. The extramusical associations of this and the other cumulative settings are considered more fully in chapter 6.

Third Symphony, first movement ("Old Folks Gatherin'")

The first movement of the Third Symphony (ca. 1908–11, based on a lost organ prelude of 1901) resembles the finale in using a hymn tune as its main theme, paraphrasing another hymn tune for its countermelody, presenting the latter in a middle section, combining it at the end with the first complete statement of the theme, and anticipating both melodies with fragments and variants. Here *Azmon* is the theme, appearing at the end in F major in the first violins (mm. 117–25, with an echo of its last phrase in mm. 126–28). Above it in the flute, assisted briefly by the oboe, is a countermelody based on Charles Converse's *Erie* (H17, most often sung to the hymn "What a friend we have in Jesus," although Ives once linked it to "There's a wideness in God's mercy").[14] This is presented in quadruple meter over the triple-meter *Azmon*, as shown in Example 5.4. Most of *Erie* appears in either flute or oboe, but rhythmic changes, the omission of repetitions of the opening motive (in mm. 5–6 and 13–14 of the tune), and some added notes give Ives's melody a distinctive shape. The countermelody appears in a $\frac{4}{2}$ Adagio cantabile section about midway through the movement, first in a distorted fragment in the oboe (mm. 75–77), then complete in the flute (mm. 78–85), where it differs in some details from its final form and modulates from A♭ to B♭ major. The accompaniment includes brief references to *Azmon*: the closing phrase of the countermelody is counterpointed by the closing phrase of *Azmon* in violin I (mm. 83–84, echoed in the viola and horn in mm. 86–87), and the first segment of *Erie* (mm. 75–76 and 78–79) by a figure in violin I that resembles the opening of the main countermelody from the symphony's finale, which is based on *Azmon*.

EXAMPLE 5.4: Third Symphony, first movement, concluding passage with *Azmon* and countermelody based on *Erie*

CUMULATIVE SETTINGS

In other respects, this movement's form differs from that of the finale. The key scheme centers on B♭ major, with excursions to E♭, D, and A♭, and ends in F. The beginning of the movement foreshadows the episode in which the countermelody appears complete (mm. 1–5 parallel mm. 78–81 transposed down a fourth), but the first measure of *Erie* is missing, making its counterpoint, the opening of the finale's *Azmon* paraphrase, the first motive of the leading melody.[15] This upper line continues with part of the countermelody on *Erie* and the descending thirds from *Azmon*'s third phrase (mm. 5–6), for a composite opening melody that hints at both source tunes without directly stating their distinctive initial motives. There follows a passage based on fragments of *Azmon* and of two important countersubjects, a and b, that are partly derived from *Erie*, as shown in Example 5.5. Next is a fugato on the first six bars of *Azmon*, joined first by countersubject a (mm. 22ff.) and later by countersubject b (mm. 38ff.). An episode that combines the latter with the first phrase of *Woodworth*, theme of the finale (mm. 54–59, played twice), leads to further development of the opening figure of *Azmon* with fragments of both countersubjects. After a grand pause, the main countermelody is introduced in a new meter and tempo, and subsequent development combines elements of *Erie*, *Azmon*, and both countersubjects before reaching the culminating statement of the theme and its countermelody.

EXAMPLE 5.5: Third Symphony, first movement, countersubjects derived in part from *Erie*

The similarities and differences between this movement and the finale illustrate both the common features of cumulative settings and the individual traits that make each one distinctive. Previous analyses have described these movements as different in form, the first in modified ternary or sonata form, the last through-composed.[16] But both are in cumulative form, with a hymn tune as a principal theme; a countermelody paraphrased from another hymn tune; complete presentation of the two together at the end and of the countermelody alone near the middle of the movement; and development of both themes prior to their presentation, using techniques common to development sections of traditional symphonies, including fragmentation, variation, transposition, recombination, and fugato. Once the paradigm of cumulative setting is recognized as the formal principle behind both movements, they can be seen to have as much in common as any two sonata-form movements of Beethoven's middle period. The differences between them make them as interesting in their varying realizations of a single form as are the first movements of Beethoven's "Waldstein" and *Appassionata* sonatas.

Third Violin Sonata, third movement

The finale of the Third Violin Sonata (ca. 1914, based on a lost organ prelude of 1901) is also a cumulative setting but takes yet another distinctive shape.[17] It is in three large sections. Each begins with the piano alone before the violin enters, and the first two close with a brief piano postlude. The theme is the refrain of Robert Lowry's hymn tune *Need* (H41, "I need Thee ev'ry hour"), presented twice at the end in the violin in B♭ major, first *fortissimo* and then *pianissimo*, with a countermelody and arpeggiated accompaniment in the piano. The final statement appears in Example 5.6. The countermelody is derived from the beginning of the verse and the end of the refrain of *Need*, as shown in Example 5.7. The movement closes with a brief piano codetta that echoes the first measure of the theme as the violin sustains its final note.

At the beginning of the movement, the piano introduces in quick succession the motives that will play the most significant roles: the initial motive of the hymn verse; the opening of the countermelody, based on that motive; the figure from mm. 12–13 of the hymn's refrain (or mm. 2–3 of its verse); the part of the countermelody paraphrased from the next portion of the refrain, mm. 14–15; and the opening of the refrain. All appear in the topmost melody, shown in Example 5.8, and most are echoed in the lower parts. The alternation of motives from the hymn tune with segments of the countermelody makes the derivation of the latter from the former audible from the start.[18] After the violin enters, motives from the theme (the hymn's refrain) and countermelody are developed, with occasional appearances of ideas from the

Sonata No. 3 for Violin and Piano. © 1951 by Merion Music, Inc. Used by Permission.

EXAMPLE 5.6: Third Violin Sonata, third movement, final statement of theme with countermelody and accompaniment

hymn's verse (notably variants of mm. 3–5 and 7–8 at mm. 55–62 in the violin). The harmony throughout this opening section is chromatic, with rapid changes of implied key. At the end of the first section, a complete though disguised paraphrase of the theme appears twice in the piano in D♭, accompanied by fragments of the countermelody (first in the violin, then in the piano's bass line). Example 5.9 shows the piano and violin melodies in the

Sonata No. 3 for Violin and Piano. © 1951 by Merion Music, Inc. Used by Permission.

EXAMPLE 5.7: Third Violin Sonata, third movement, countermelody compared with *Need*

first of these passages, with the violin's final notes providing a more overt statement of the hymn's closing cadence.

The second section begins at m. 85 with a piano interlude on motives from the theme, countermelody, and opening of the hymn verse. The violin enters with the complete countermelody in A♭, over the same figuration in the piano as at the final statement of the theme. An added line in the piano, derived from the countermelody, enriches the texture. The rest of the section is based primarily on motives from the countermelody until the piano postlude that closes the section, a varied reprise of mm. 40–46. In this section, as in the first, the harmony is chromatic and suggests frequent changes of key; only the appearances of the movement's main ideas, the theme and the countermelody, are in stable keys. Thus, in this movement Ives maintains the traditional association of thematic statements with tonal stability and of motivic development with modulation, typical of thematic forms since the eighteenth-century ritornello and sonata forms.

CUMULATIVE SETTINGS

Sonata No. 3 for Violin and Piano. © 1951 by Merion Music, Inc. Used by Permission.

EXAMPLE 5.8: Third Violin Sonata, opening of third movement, topmost melody, with *Need* and countermelody

After the focus on the countermelody in the second section, the last section emphasizes the theme. The piano interlude (m. 154) is a small ABA′ form that includes another paraphrase of the theme, given in Example 5.10. This paraphrase is modulatory, moving from E♭ through D♭ to close on G major. The bass line settles onto an alternating figure with a repeated F as a pedal point, and the violin and upper parts in the piano develop fragments of the theme and then of the countermelody, building to the presentation of the complete theme in B♭ with countermelody and accompaniment.

Here is another cumulative setting, sharing the traits common to the outer movements of the Third Symphony (save that the countermelody is based on

Sonata No. 3 for Violin and Piano. © 1951 by Merion Music, Inc. Used by Permission.

EXAMPLE 5.9: Third Violin Sonata, third movement, paraphrase of theme with fragments of the countermelody

Need

Ives Piano 166

Sonata No. 3 for Violin and Piano. © 1951 by Merion Music, Inc. Used by Permission.

EXAMPLE 5.10: Third Violin Sonata, third movement, paraphrase of theme

the same tune as the theme) while again taking an individual shape. Although this and similar movements may give some listeners the impression of a jumble of random quotations, Ives has created a very simple structure: three sections — each an extended statement in violin and piano framed by piano solos — which present and develop in turn (1) the motives from which the two main themes are built, (2) the countermelody, and (3) the theme itself.

This movement is a perfect example of two characteristics that are typical of Ives's mature music. First, the surface complexity is almost invariably based on a simple underlying formal plan.[19] All the details fit, and the work is perfectly coherent, but one must understand the plan, whether intuitively or through analysis. This is made more difficult because Ives's forms are unusual, often (as in this case) of his own invention, although simple once one grasps them. The difficulty for most of us lies in the second characteristic this movement exemplifies, noted by the Cowells in the passage quoted at the beginning of this chapter: for Ives, simplicity is a place one gets to, not where one starts.

In his program note for the sonata's 1917 premiere, Ives described this movement in these terms: "The last movement is an experiment: The free fantasia is first. The working-out develops into the themes, rather than from them. The coda consists of the themes for the first time in their entirety and in conjunction."[20] Ives's reference to this as "an experiment" should not be taken literally. In 1917, this approach was not experimental but was the most common formal procedure for his instrumental works of the previous decade. Ives sometimes used the word defensively, as a way to deflect potential criticism; he once described his most central work, the *Concord Sonata*, as "but an experiment" in a letter responding to criticism of it from Elizabeth Sprague Coolidge.[21] Since the Third Violin Sonata was among the first of his mature pieces to be performed, Ives no doubt used the word here to alert his audience to the unorthodox form of the movement.

His description makes clear that the presentation of the themes is not an appendage to the form, as the term "coda" normally implies, but the culmination of the thematic process, with all the weight of both exposition and reprise in more familiar forms. The movement does not follow the shape of an oration in which the point is made at the start and subsequently developed, as do most eighteenth-century forms, but models the inner thoughts of one who is trying to distill his experience into speech and finally arrives at an aphorism, deeply felt because it is weighted with all the thought and struggle that went into its formulation. Just as the theme becomes clear only over the course of the movement, so too the form and the role of each part becomes clear only over the course of repeated hearings or study of the score, as we learn to recognize the themes and the motives and variants that derive from them. Our very process of coming to understand this music is modeled for us in the movement itself.

Ives's description of the form shows that he considered it a *thematic* form in which the themes appear at the end. The terms he uses invoke a comparison with sonata form, in which the themes are presented first and are developed in the "working-out" or "free fantasia" that follows. Sonata-form movements by Beethoven, Brahms, and others must have been his primary models for thematic development even as he reordered the sequence of events. Most significant is that Ives did not consider this a *motive*-based movement that happened to culminate in a complete statement of the tune from which some of the motives were derived, but saw it as a *theme*-based movement in which most or all of the important motives were derived from the theme.[22] The model is sonata form, not such works as the prelude to *Tristan und Isolde*, which creates a quasi-ternary form from the interplay of several short motives but never arrives at a theme. Ives's reference to "themes" in the plural and to their presentation in conjunction at the end shows that he thought of both *Need* and its countermelody as themes. This movement is also reminiscent of sonata form in featuring two themes of contrasting contour, character, and key that are ultimately reconciled.

Once the structure of the Third Violin Sonata finale is understood, its formal coherence becomes clear, for virtually everything in the work relates to the themes. This would be true whether or not the theme and countermelody were based on existing tunes. In addition, it shows both Ives's strong adherence to the compositional tradition of Beethoven and Brahms and the significant departure he represents: they are renowned for creating large-scale structures in which the most significant material is presented at the outset and later events unfold through developing variation, and Ives does the same in reverse, as it were, elaborating the events of the movement from material presented in its "original" form only at the end.[23]

In reversing the order of events, Ives achieves a new solution to the problem of working with hymns and other popular tunes. We have seen that in his First String Quartet and Second Symphony, Ives reworked his source tunes into themes better suited for subsequent development: less foursquare, predictable, repetitive, and harmonically restricted. But the very traits that make such a tune a poor beginning for a movement in a developmental form make it an excellent ending, providing stability and clarity after a long, uncertain, and sometimes difficult journey. So, rather than alter the tune to fit the form, Ives alters the shape of the piece to capitalize on the strengths of the tune. In the process, the tune gains a new stature, as the logical result of the gradually unfolding developments that lead up to it. What some might disdain as a trivial or uninteresting melody is presented at the end as the goal of all our aspirations.[24]

In his program note, Ives characterizes the entire sonata as "an attempt to express the feeling and fervor — a fervor that was often more vociferous than religious — with which the hymns and revival tunes were sung at the Camp Meetings held extensively in New England in the [18]70's and 80's."[25] Like the descriptive titles of the Third Symphony, this indicates that Ives sought to capture a particular feeling but was not writing music to a program. The same is true of most of his cumulative settings. With the exception of the explicitly programmatic works described in chapters 6 and 10, Ives's cumulative settings are extended meditations on the tunes themselves. Through the process of development and gradual accumulation, they raise the hymn tunes that he uses to the level of art music, allowing us to hear in them something of the spirit Ives felt when he heard them sung.

Varieties of Cumulative Setting

The preceding examples have illustrated the outlines of cumulative form and the flexible way in which Ives applied it to produce a variety of shapes. The largest group of cumulative settings follows the same pattern as the three movements discussed so far: (1) the principal theme is a borrowed tune or a melody paraphrased from borrowed material; (2) it appears complete for the first time in the final section; (3) it is joined there by a countermelody paraphrased from the same or another tune; and (4) this is preceded by sections that develop fragments from both theme and countermelody, that paraphrase or partially present the theme, and that present the complete countermelody without the theme. There is a good deal of variation of this basic structure, and each movement assumes an individual shape.

There are also several smaller groups of movements that deviate from this description in some significant respect, constituting different subtypes: movements in which the countersubject is partial or rudimentary and is not paraphrased from an existing tune; movements that lack a countermelody; one instance of a double cumulative form; and works that combine cumulative setting with verse-refrain form. We will take up each type in turn, roughly in order of increasing distance from the most common pattern. Each movement in cumulative form is described here, at least briefly, because each is unique in some way and thus deserves attention both in itself and as an illustration of how flexible Ives's paradigm was for him. We will find it convenient for now to group movements by category; in chapter 6, we will consider the multi-movement cycles as whole entities.

Because of the large number of works, the complex harmonies and harmonic structure that many of them exhibit can only be hinted at here. Although all preserve the association we have seen so far of fuller thematic statements with more stable key areas, in several cases naming the diatonic keys in which the themes appear cannot adequately describe the harmonic framework in which they are placed. Many of these works exemplify Ives's interest in combining tonal and posttonal procedures side by side, an aspect of his music that deserves more extensive discussion than is possible here.

Other Cumulative Settings with Paraphrased Countermelodies

The other instrumental movements with paraphrased countermelodies are as varied in shape as the three considered so far, although they follow the same general plan. Their forms are synopsized in Table 5.2, which is arranged in rough chronological order according to the approximate date of the earliest existing draft of each movement. Some of these, like the three movements above, were said by Ives to have been adapted from previous works that have been lost, but it is not known whether these were in cumulative form. Ives dated several of these movements earlier than the dates given here; if there were earlier sketches, they have not survived.

Fugue in Four Keys on "The Shining Shore"
The *Fugue in Four Keys on "The Shining Shore"* (ca. 1902) is one of several experiments in writing a polytonal canon or fugue.[26] It uses only the verse of

Shining Shore (mm. 1–8), with *Azmon* as a countermelody. It begins as a fugal paraphrase, like the first movement of the First String Quartet. Each of the four voices enters with *Shining Shore*, in the keys of C, G, D, and A major, respectively, and continues through the fifth, sixth, or seventh measure of the tune before developing into free material. After some motivic development, the top line presents an abbreviated paraphrase of *Azmon* in A major (mm. 36–44, eliding parts of mm. 1–2 of the hymn and omitting the last phrase). The two hymn tunes share the same rhythmic pattern and several melodic features, which no doubt suggested the combination, but here the most distinctive parts of *Azmon* are emphasized. After a climax that presents the middle of *Azmon* directly (mm. 2–6 appear in mm. 52–55 of the Ives in B major over a C pedal), a cadence is reached, and the two source tunes appear simultaneously over a C/G double pedal (m. 59), with a portion of *Azmon* spliced into the A-major statement of *Shining Shore* in the trumpet (as discussed in chapter 3 and shown in Example 3.20) and with *Azmon* as a countermelody in G major in the flute.[27] This differs from the movements discussed so far in its fugal opening and polytonal harmony, but it is clearly based on the same formal idea.

First Violin Sonata, first movement

The first movement of the First Violin Sonata was composed between about 1907 and about 1914.[28] It is based mainly on *Shining Shore*, a hymn in AA'BA' form, the second half of which is a refrain. The main theme is the A or A' phrase; it occurs in both forms, which differ only in their penultimate note. The last statement of the theme (mm. 126–30), shown in Example 5.11, includes both endings over an accompaniment permeated by the closing motive of the A' phrase, marked with a horizontal bracket in the example. The contrasting B phrase of the hymn is paraphrased in the countermelody, shown in Example 5.12 both as it appears with the theme in mm. 101–6 and in its somewhat fuller form when stated alone in mm. 62–69.[29] The movement begins with a long slow introduction based on three main ideas, shown in Example 5.13: the opening figure, motive W (almost identical to and probably derived from the opening figure of the countermelody in the first movement of the Second Violin Sonata, discussed below); a pentatonic motive from mm. 11–12 of *Shining Shore*; and fragments of the countermelody, which appear in context to derive from the other two motives.[30] A faster section at m. 34 develops these ideas further, culminating in the full statement of the countermelody at m. 62. Variants of the theme and the return of motive W herald the complete statement of theme and countermelody at m. 101. After this climax, the music quiets down as fragments and variants of the theme, countermelody, and motive W provide a transition to the final statement of

TABLE 5.2: Other Instrumental Cumulative Settings with Full Countermelodies Based on Borrowed Material

Fugue in Four Keys on "The Shining Shore" (ca. 1902)

T: *Shining Shore* (H54), verse (mm. 1–8)

CM: *Azmon*

Section	Measure		
1 >	1	Fugal exposition on mm. 1–6 of T	C, G, D, A
2	26	Development/episode	A
:	36	CM, abbreviated and paraphrased	
	44	Further development of CM	
3 >:	59	T (in A, with part of *Azmon* interpolated) with CM (in G)	A/G over C pedal

First Violin Sonata, first movement (between ca. 1907 and ca. 1914)

T: *Shining Shore* (H54), principal phrase (mm. 1–4 or 5–8)

CM: Paraphrased from *Shining Shore*, first phrase of refrain (mm. 8–12)

Secondary material: T variant, Motive W

Section	Measure			
1	1	Slow introduction: Motive W, variants of *Shining Shore* mm. 11–12, CM fragments	$\frac{6}{4}$, Andante	modulatory
2	34	Varied fragments of W, *Shining Shore* mm. 11–12, CM	C, Allegro vivace	modulatory
:	62	CM complete, repeated, developed	$\frac{6}{4}$, Con Moto	G, C
	81	Hints of T in violin	$\frac{4}{4}$	E pedal
>	83	T paraphrased in piano, then violin with W in piano		c♯, C

Section	Measure		Description	Tempo	Key
	91		T variant in violin, then in piano with W in violin		modulatory
	101	>:	T complete in piano, CM in violin		G
	108		T variant in piano, joined at m. 112 by CM variant in violin		modulatory
	116		T opening contour in violin, W in piano		C
	126	>	T in violin, with mm. 7–8 of T in piano		D
	134		Varied reprise of slow introduction		modulates to e
3	146		W ostinato in piano, violin anticipates next movement theme ("The Old Oaken Bucket," H96)	$\frac{6}{4}$, Andante	

Second Violin Sonata, first movement ("Autumn") (between ca. 1907 and ca. 1914, rev. ca. 1919)

T: *Autumn* (H4), slightly paraphrased and missing mm. 9–10

CM: Paraphrased from *Autumn*, mm. 6–11

Section	Measure		Description	Tempo	Key
1	1		Slow introduction: Parts of CM and T in piano, opening of CM in violin	Adagio maestoso	F♯, A♭
2	10	:	Fragments of T, CM	Allegro moderato	modulatory
3	33		CM in violin (first half only, somewhat different from final version), part of T in piano	largo	A♭
4	43		Small ABA developing T and CM	Allegro risoluto con brio	modulatory
5	67		Further development, primarily of CM, closes with part of T	Meno allegro con moto	modulatory
6	95	>:	T complete in violin, CM in piano	maestoso	A

Table 5.2, continued:

Third Violin Sonata, second movement (ca. 1914, based on lost organ toccata from 1901 and/or lost ragtime piece from 1902–3)

T: Paraphrased from *There'll Be No Dark Valley* (H58), mm. 1–3 and 9–12, and *The Beautiful River* (H6), mm. 3–4
CM: Mostly original, but begins like T and like CM from third movement
Secondary ideas: Harmonization of T+CM, Motive X, Motive Y

Section	Measure		
1	1	Piano introduction: melodic variations of Harmonization, with opening motives of T (m. 4), CM (m. 8)	F
	15	Violin enters with fragments of T, motives X (m. 17) and Y (m. 20); piano continues to develop Harmonization and CM	F, modulatory
2 :	22	Piano interlude: fantasia on CM, comprising an expanded statement with interpolations and portions of Harmonization	F, modulatory
	41	Violin enters with varied end of T as piano completes CM	modulates to F
>:	47	T complete in violin, with CM and Harmonization in piano	F
3	54	Repetition of first two measures of T, CM, and Harmonization leads to further development of T, CM, and motives X and Y	E, modulatory
>:	78	T complete in violin, with CM and Harmonization in piano	E♭
	86	Bridge	modulatory
>:	89	T complete in violin, with Harmonization and most of CM in piano	D
	95	Codetta: opening of T in violin, CM in piano (mm. 98–99)	D

Table 5.2, continued:

Fourth Violin Sonata, first movement (ca. 1914, based on lost sonata for trumpet and organ from 1900 or 1901)

T1: *Old, Old Story* (H45), refrain (mm. 17-24)

T2: Paraphrased from *Old, Old Story*, second (or fourth) phrase of verse (mm. 5-8)

CM1: Exposition of *Fourth Fugue in B flat* by George E. Ives (H184)

CM2: Original

Secondary material: Material from hymn verse and fugue omitted from themes

Section		Measure		
1	:	1	CM2 complete in piano, most of T2 in violin	B♭
		8	Opening motives of T1, T2	B
2		16	Opening motive of CM1 in piano, part of T2 in violin	B
		21	Episode, including fragments of T2 and hymn verse (mm. 24–25 in piano and 36–38 in violin present mm. 11 and 9 of hymn) and motives from the fugue	C
3	>	44	Opening motives of CM1, CM2, first half of T1	B♭
	:	47	CM1 complete (second fugal voice in violin) with accompaniment (from CM2)	B♭
		52	Fugue continues in piano (mm. 47–56a derived from mm. 1–19 of George Ives's fugue), hymn verse fragments in violin (mm. 52–55 present mm. 9–10 and 2–4 of hymn)	modulates to F
		56	Episode on motive from fugue, mm. 20–21, piano and violin	C
		59	Fugue continues in piano (mm. 59b–69 derived from mm. 22–42 of fugue), violin develops first half of T1, end of hymn verse (mm. 68–69 present mm. 15–16 of hymn)	F, modulates to B♭
4	>:	70	T1 in violin, CM1 in piano with accompaniment (from CM2) and fugal episode (mm. 76–77 derived from mm. 44–47 of fugue)	B♭
	>:	78	T2 in violin, CM2 in piano	B♭

Table 5.2, continued:

Fourth Violin Sonata, second movement (ca. 1914)

T: *Jesus Loves Me* (H30), refrain only (mm. 9–16)

CM: Paraphrased from *Jesus Loves Me*, refrain

Secondary idea: Middle-section theme (MT), related to *Jesus Loves Me*, mm. 9–10

Section	Measure			
1	1	Piano introduction: opening ideas of T, CM, MT	Largo	vague
	2	Violin enters; opening ideas of T, MT CM somewhat abbreviated, violin		vague, countermelody in E
	>	Paraphrase of T, violin	a tempo	theme in D, undercut by harmony
		Development of ideas from T, CM		
	: 5	CM (violin) and Accompaniment (piano)	cantabile	E
2	9	Piano alone: contrasting middle section on MT	Allegro (conslugarocko)	chromatic, C prominent in bass
3	> 30	T in piano, part of CM in violin (both varied)	Andante con spirito	D (over G major ostinato)
	>: 34	T in piano, CM in violin, with varied Accompaniment	Adagio cantabile	A
	>: 38	T in violin, CM and Accompaniment in piano	Largo cantabile	E

Thanksgiving and Forefathers' Day (1910s, rev. 1932–33)

T: *Duke Street* (H16), somewhat varied

CM: *Federal Street* (H22), with mm. 9–12 replaced by mm. 9–12 of *Duke Street*

Table 5.2, continued:

Secondary ideas

MT1: Middle section, main theme; *Shining Shore* (H59), slightly varied

MT2: Middle section, secondary theme; paraphrase of *Shining Shore*

HWT: "Harvest Work Theme"

Section	Measure			
1	1	Opening ideas of CM, MT1, HWT	Adagio maestoso	modulatory
	25	CM mm. 1–4, in imitation; shadow lines with other hymns	Poco Adagio	
	51	T fragments (mm. 1–4, 9–12), with CM mm. 1–4	Poco con spirito	mostly E♭
:	69	CM, distorted paraphrase	A little faster	chromatic, A pedal point
	88	HWT	Andante maestoso	
	98	*Duke Street* mm. 9–12 (part of T and CM) paraphrase	Slow Down	polytonal
	106	transition		
	118	transition continues with MT1 mm. 1–8	Meno mosso	A♭
2a	129	MT1	Adagio cantabile	G
b	154	MT2	Più moto	
	165	MT2 repeats; shadow lines with other hymns	Allegro con moto	
	180	transition	Adagio con moto	
a'	186	MT1, fragmented between strings and winds	Slightly faster	
	210	transition, with HWT, CM mm. 1–4	animando poco a poco	
3	222	*Duke Street* mm. 9–12, HWT	Andante con moto (at 219)	E♭, B♭, modulatory
	230	*Duke Street* mm. 9–10, HWT, CM mm. 1–4 paraphrase (horns)		
>:	244	T complete, CM	Maestoso	A
	259	extension on last phrase of CM		

EXAMPLE 5.11: First Violin Sonata, first movement, final statement of theme, compared with verse of *Shining Shore*

the theme at m. 126. A varied reprise of the slow introduction rounds out the movement, which ends with an ostinato on motive W in the piano beneath an anticipation in the violin of the theme of the following movement ("The Old Oaken Bucket," H96, by George Kiallmark).

This movement is unique among cumulative setings in several respects. The reprise of the slow introduction at the end frames the cumulative form itself. The theme is quite brief in comparison to the movement and is dwarfed by its countermelody, which is stated and varied in a long passage in the center of the movement (mm. 62–79). The double appearance of the theme at the end (mm. 101 and 126), the second time without the counter-melody, is also rare, and may have been calculated to redress the imbalance created by the prominence of the countermelody. However, the last statement is typical of the violin sonatas in giving the theme for the first time to the violin, which previously played only the countermelody. Ingenious ears may even find a hint of the countermelody in the accompaniment to this final statement, hidden in the upper line of the piano.

Second Violin Sonata, first movement ("Autumn"), and His Exaltation

The first movement of the Second Violin Sonata was written between about 1907 and about 1914 as the finale of Ives's first attempt at a violin sonata, known as the "Pre-First" Violin Sonata, and was revised about 1919.[31] As usual, the theme appears at the end in the violin; it is based on *Autumn* (H4, variously attributed), which gives the movement its title. As shown in Example 5.14, the theme is somewhat varied: mm. 13–14 of the hymn elide with mm. 11–12, and mm. 9–10 are missing. The omission is significant, for, as

EXAMPLE 5.12: First Violin Sonata, first movement, theme and countermelody in combination, with earlier statement of countermelody and refrain of *Shining Shore*

EXAMPLE 5.13: First Violin Sonata, first movement, motives in the slow introduction

the example shows, the countermelody is paraphrased from mm. 6–11 of the hymn and uses the figure from mm. 9–10 prominently and repeatedly, even at the point where it is missing from the theme. References to this motive should be understood as fragments of the countermelody rather than of the theme.[32] The movement begins with a slow introduction that states the most important motives: in the piano, the headmotives of the countermelody (mm. 1–2) and theme (mm. 3–6) and mm. 9–10 of the hymn (mm. 6–8); in the violin, the opening of the countermelody, somewhat varied (mm. 5–7).[33] A fast section then develops fragments of both theme and countermelody.[34] A slow interlude in mm. 33–42 presents the first half of the countermelody, somewhat altered, in the violin, with the opening of the theme in the piano (mm. 33–35) hinting at its ultimate destiny; the first half of this interlude harks back to mm. 5–8 of the introduction. Then a fast section paraphrases

EXAMPLE 5.14: Second Violin Sonata, first movement, final statement of theme and countermelody

CUMULATIVE SETTINGS

173

and develops the headmotives of both theme and countermelody in a small ABA form. Further development based mostly on the countermelody (mm. 67ff.) leads to the climactic final statement of theme and countermelody at m. 95, anticipated in mm. 90–94 by the opening idea of the theme.

In 1913, Ives arranged the last quarter of this movement as the song *His Exaltation*.[35] The song's second half (mm. 12–26) is adapted from the final section of the sonata movement (mm. 95–109), with the theme in the voice. The text, "For the grandeur of Thy nature," is the second verse of a hymn by Robert Robinson ("Mighty God! while angels bless Thee") sung to *Autumn*. The fifth and seventh lines are omitted, corresponding to the elision in the sonata theme of mm. 9–10 and 13–14 of the hymn. The first half of the song is a piano introduction that begins with two newly composed measures, loosely based on the opening motives of the theme and countermelody, and continues with mm. 86–94 of the sonata movement, which include motives from the countermelody and the opening segment of the theme. Although both theme and countermelody are anticipated in the piano introduction, the song lacks the other hallmarks of cumulative setting, such as presentation of the whole countermelody, the theme in paraphrased form, or extensive development of motives from the theme before the culminating statement. This song might better be considered an adaptation of the latter part of a cumulative setting than a cumulative setting in its own right.

Third Violin Sonata, second movement

The second movement of the Third Violin Sonata (ca. 1914, based on a lost organ toccata of 1901 and/or a lost ragtime piece of 1902–3) has something of a ragtime feeling, with off-beats and shifting emphases over a regular beat in the bass. This helps create the character Ives intended for this movement, which he said in his program note "may represent a meeting where the feet and body, as well as the voice, add to the excitement."[36]

The form is unusual in that there are three statements of the theme with its countermelody and harmonization, not just one. The first statement is in F major and arrives about half-way through the movement, in the passage shown in Example 5.15. The theme is paraphrased from parts of the verse and refrain of Ira D. Sankey's *There'll Be No Dark Valley* (H58) and ends with a phrase of *The Beautiful River* by Robert Lowry (H6, "Shall we gather at the river").[37] This borrowing from another hymn may have been motivated by musical factors, as it provides a kind of half-cadence before the first part of the theme repeats. But it also creates an interesting sequence of texts (ignoring repetitions): "There'll be no more sorrow when Jesus comes / To gather his loved ones home, / Where bright angel feet have trod."[38] The countermelody appears to be mostly original, although portions derive from Ives melodies that are themselves paraphrased: its first five notes imitate the opening of the theme; its first eight notes are identical to part of the countermelody in this sonata's finale, which was paraphrased from *Need* (cf. Example 5.7); and similar rising motives recur later in the countermelody (mm. 48, 50–51, 52, and 53). The countermelody may also derive in part directly from *There'll Be No Dark Valley*, for it consists mainly of two kinds of figuration from the hymn's verse: rising scale figures of three or more notes (mm. 47–48 and 51–53), most often in whole tones, like those that begin each segment of the verse; and descending scale figures (in mm. 48–50), again most often in whole tones, like the figures that end each four-bar phrase of the verse (m. 4 and mm. 7–8) and are omitted from the theme itself. The left-hand harmonization in mm. 47–49 plays an important and at times independent role in the movement. In the opening measures, it appears in a melodic form, as shown in Example 5.15.

The movement opens with a piano solo that introduces and develops the melodic form of the harmonization, the opening motive of the theme, and the first dozen notes of the countermelody, all in F major over a repeated F pedal tone. The violin enters in m. 15 with fragments of the theme as the piano further develops the harmonization and countermelody. Soon the violin introduces two motives, labeled X and Y in Example 5.16, that seem, from contour and context, to be based on part of the hymn refrain, including a segment (mm. 12–14) not used in the theme. There follows an extensive piano interlude (mm. 22–41), a fantasia on the countermelody that introduces and develops its various segments in turn. This replaces the complete statement of the countermelody that is usually part of Ives's cumulative form. At m. 41 the violin reenters, playing ideas from the end of the theme as the piano completes its development of the countermelody. A bridge leads to the climactic statement at m. 47 of the complete theme in the violin in F, over the countermelody and harmonization in the piano.

So far, the movement has followed the typical pattern for cumulative settings, in most respects. But now it pursues a unique path, repeating the theme twice more as it moves into new keys. The beginning of a restatement in m. 54 swerves off instead to further development of motives from the theme and countermelody and motives X and Y, modulating through several keys. The theme, countermelody, and harmonization reappear at m. 78 in E♭ and, after a brief bridge, at m. 89 in D; at this final statement, part of the countermelody is omitted in order to allow the harmonization to appear in large, resonant block chords. A brief codetta touches on the opening gestures of theme and countermelody and closes in D major. When one is familiar with the typical structure of cumulative form and knows what to expect, the restatements of the theme and its countersubjects are surprising yet satisfy-

Hymn verse

Hymn refrain

The Beautiful River

*Repeat if "ragged."

EXAMPLE 5.15: Third Violin Sonata, second movement, first statement of complete theme with countermelody and accompaniment

ing, like the "second recapitulations" in the first movement codas of Beethoven's Third and Fifth Symphonies. The unique shape of this movement shows again the flexibility of cumulative setting as a form, a flexibility that springs from the simplicity of its basic ingredients and procedures.

Fourth Violin Sonata, first movement

The first movement of the Fourth Violin Sonata (*"Children's Day at the Camp Meeting"*) was revised about 1914. According to Ives's note on one copy,

There'll Be No Dark Valley

Sonata No. 3 for Violin and Piano. © 1951 by Merion Music, Inc. Used by Permission.

EXAMPLE 5.16: Third Violin Sonata, second movement, motives X and Y

it was based on a lost sonata for trumpet and organ from late 1900 or early 1901.[39] As usual, the theme appears complete and with its countersubjects only at the end of the movement, shown in Example 5.17. The theme is in two parts, designated as T1 and T2 in Example 5.17 and in Table 5.2. The first half (mm. 70–77) is the refrain of William H. Doane's *Old, Old Story* (H45, "Tell me the old, old story"), little changed but for a repetition at the cadence. Its countersubject (CM1) is the exposition of a fugue in B♭ by Ives's father, the fourth of seven fugues that George Ives wrote while studying music as a young man and the only one to survive in an ink copy.[40] The second half of the theme (mm. 78–84) is paraphrased from part of the same hymn's verse (the second or fourth phrase, the two being identical) and closes with a brief reference to the fugue subject. The countersubject to this part of the theme (CM2) is a simple chordal pattern, a variant of which also accompanies the beginning of the first half of the theme and its countermelody.

Although only parts of the hymn verse and fugue appear in the themes, the missing elements of the hymn and virtually all of the fugue are included in the preceding development, as shown in Table 5.2. The first section of the movement introduces in turn CM2 complete, most of T2, and the opening motive shared by the hymn's verse and refrain. The fugue subject enters at m. 16, joined by part of T2, and the second section continues with an episode that includes fragments of the hymn's third phrase, which is missing from the theme. The third section includes almost all of the fugue but its closing phrase. This section begins at m. 44 with the opening motives of the theme and countermelodies and proceeds at m. 47 to present the first counter-melody, the exposition of the fugue, with the violin taking the first answer. This leads to a long episode in which the piano part is taken almost entirely and literally from the fugue, while the violin line is based on motives from the third and first phrases of the hymn verse, the opening phrase of the refrain, and the closing notes of the verse (which are inexactly paraphrased in the theme by the first five notes of the fugue subject). Since the hymn's verse starts with the same motive as the refrain, all parts of the verse have been

CUMULATIVE SETTINGS

EXAMPLE 5.17: Fourth Violin Sonata, first movement, final statement of theme with countermelodies

EXAMPLE 5.17, continued

heard at least once before the entrance of the complete refrain in the final
section. The refrain's closing cadence is accompanied in the piano by the
closing measures of the fugue, so that all but two of the fugue's forty-eight
measures are included in the sonata movement. This wholesale borrowing is
rare for Ives, matched only by the inclusion in *Decoration Day* (1912) of the
entire trio from David Wallis Reeves's *Second Regiment Connecticut National
Guard March*.

Ives seems to have begun work on this movement with the discovery in
about 1892 that the first five bars of the hymn refrain fit in perfect counterpoint with the first ten bars of the fugue. A pencil sketch of this combination
appears on the ink copy of his father's fugue, along with other notations
toward the sonata movement.[41] The program that Ives offers for this movement in the published score tells of an incident at a camp meeting in which a
boy's organ practice (presumably Ives's) and the children's hymn-singing "got
to going together, even joining in each other's sounds."[42] Ives played for camp
meetings in about 1890–93. It is hard to credit the idea that the fugue and
hymn combined accidentally in the way that Ives describes, but it is certainly
possible that he noticed how they fit together as he was trying things out at
the organ, sometime in his teens. Whether this incident was real or imagined,
it reflects the work's origin in the fortuitous contrapuntal fit of two existing

CUMULATIVE SETTINGS

pieces. If Ives did make this sketch in the early 1890s, it was his earliest quodlibet. We will address quodlibet in chapter 10.

In an illuminating analysis of this movement's motivic structure, Lora Gingerich points out the close resemblance between the fugal answer and the figure from mm. 5–6 of the hymn verse, both of which first appear in the violin in the same key and register (mm. 48–49 and 4–5, respectively).[43] This resemblance probably prompted Ives to highlight this figure from the verse in his opening theme (T2) and to combine it in counterpoint with the opening of the refrain (T1, mm. 8–9) and with the fugue theme (mm. 18–19).[44] Ives seems to have designed this movement to exploit to the fullest the contrapuntal and melodic links between his sources, revealing them gradually over the course of his cumulative form. This parallels the process of relating and combining two similar source tunes in the *Fugue in Four Keys on "The Shining Shore,"* but in a more complex way.

Fourth Violin Sonata, second movement

The second movement of the Fourth Violin Sonata (ca. 1914) uses as its theme the refrain (mm. 9–16) of William Bradbury's *Jesus Loves Me* (H30), slightly altered in rhythm.[45] Example 5.18 shows the final statement of the theme, in E major in the violin over the countermelody and arpeggiated accompaniment in the piano. The countermelody is based on the same hymn, as Example 5.19 shows. The relationship is complex, involving three transpositions of the hymn. The most direct reference is in notes 5–8 of the countermelody, which match notes 2–5 of the hymn refrain in B major. This similarity is made explicit at the outset of the movement, where the opening notes of the hymn are inserted into this segment of the countermelody. Meanwhile, the first nine notes of the countermelody follow the contour of mm. 9–10 of the hymn in A, with embellishing tones. The falling lines in mm. 38–40 resemble the pentatonic descending figures in mm. 11–12 and 14–16 of the hymn in either key. Near the end of the countermelody is a figure drawn from mm. 13–15 of the hymn in E, and the first part of the hymn refrain in that key is outlined in the upper register in the previous measures. *Jesus Loves Me* is wholly pentatonic, yet the combination of references to it in B, A, and E yields all seven notes of the E major scale and creates a supple diatonic melody (with a passing reference to the E Phrygian scale near the end). Indeed, the pentatonic material of *Jesus Loves Me* is so elemental that some of the similarities between the countermelody and the hymn tune suggested in Example 5.19 may be the coincidental result of writing a melody in E major that begins and ends with clear references to the hymn and includes falling figures like those in mm. 14–16 of the hymn. This melody is among Ives's most beautiful, combining simplicity with

CUMULATIVE SETTINGS

EXAMPLE 5.18: Fourth Violin Sonata, second movement, final statement of theme with countermelody and accompaniment

EXAMPLE 5.19: Fourth Violin Sonata, second movement, countermelody with refrain of *Jesus Loves Me*

unpredictability. Any closer resemblance to its source might have disrupted the balance.

Cumulative form is blended with ternary and variation forms in this movement, which features a contrasting middle section in a faster tempo and several varied statements of the main theme. The first section, marked *Largo*, is mostly unbarred. The initial motives of the countermelody, theme, and middle-section theme appear in the piano and then in the violin, which plays a truncated version of the countermelody in the tonic E major, though the piano obscures the key. The violin then presents a complete paraphrase of the theme in D, made difficult to recognize by octave displacement and ambiguous harmony.[46] After further development of theme and counter-melody in the violin, the first section ends with a full statement of the coun-termelody in E in the violin over the arpeggiated accompaniment in the piano. The contrasting middle section for piano solo, marked "Allegro (con-slugarocko)," presents and develops a theme that is motivically related to mm. 9–10 of *Jesus Loves Me*, as shown in Example 5.20.[47] According to Ives's pro-gram note, this section evokes the point in the Children's Day services when the boys would "run out and throw stones down on the rocks in the brook" before being gathered again into the hymn singing.[48] In the third section, the principal theme is heard three times, each time slower, softer, and in a key a fourth lower, until the tempo returns to the original Largo and the key returns to E for the final statement. The first time, the tune is in D, somewhat varied, in chords high in the piano over an ostinato, with a distant variant of the countermelody in the violin. The second time, the tune is again in the piano, little varied, in A, with the countermelody beneath it in the violin. In the final statement, the theme is at last in the violin, with the countermelody above it for the first time as a descant, and the final note of the counter-melody resolves at the end in a soft plagal Amen. The three statements of the theme at the end, each clearer than the last, combine with the paraphrase of the first section to create what Eugene Gratovich has called "a reverse varia-tion form."[49] Yet the movement is not merely in variation form, nor in ternary form. It has all the classic features of cumulative setting, including a complete statement of the countermelody and accompaniment without the theme and an opening section that develops fragments of the themes. Thus it is truly a synthesis of all three forms.

EXAMPLE 5.20: Fourth Violin Sonata, second movement, middle-section theme with refrain of *Jesus Loves Me*

CUMULATIVE SETTINGS

Thanksgiving and Forefathers' Day

Thanksgiving and Forefathers' Day (1910s, rev. 1932–33) also blends cumulative and ternary forms. The middle section is adapted from an organ Prelude Ives played at an 1897 Thanksgiving Day service at Center Church in New Haven, where he was organist, and the outer sections derive from a Postlude for the same service. Of the two organ works, only the first page of the Postlude survives, making it impossible to determine their shapes or to ascertain how much Ives altered their forms as he reworked them.[50]

The middle section is a small ternary form on *Shining Shore*, with a cantabile statement of the hymn, slightly varied (reh. K, mm. 129–53); a more active theme paraphrased from the hymn (reh. L, mm. 154–79); a brief transition (reh. N, mm. 180–85); and a return to the cantabile hymn, now more fragmented (mm. 186–209). Like the movement itself, this middle section achieved its ternary form through insertion; the central episode was added after the ink score-sketch was complete.[51] At the climax of this section (reh. M, m. 165), as the paraphrased theme repeats, the oboes softly play variants of two hymn tunes, *Azmon* and *In the Sweet Bye and Bye* (H29, by James P. Webster), which are melodically related to the theme and to *Shining Shore*. These "shadow lines" may have been added as late as Ives's 1932–33 full score, for no earlier full sketch of this passage survives.

The outer sections, taken together, have the shape of a cumulative setting. At the climax (mm. 244ff), John Hatton's hymn tune *Duke Street* (H16), slightly altered, is sung by unison chorus and reinforced by trumpets and bassoons. The text is adapted from Leonard Bacon's hymn "O God, beneath Thy guiding hand," with which this tune appears in the hymnal Ives used at Yale.[52] The main countermelody, in horns and trombones, is the rhythmically and melodically similar hymn tune *Federal Street* (H22) by Henry K. Oliver, with its third phrase replaced by that of *Duke Street*; since this phrase in the theme is shifted forward by a measure, the result is a brief canon between theme and countermelody. Two other ideas appear here as well: a descant in violins and upper winds, and a sweeping motive in the clarinet, like the swinging of a scythe, that Ives identified on the first page of the Postlude as the "Harvest Work Theme."[53]

The first section introduces and develops motives from the themes. The Adagio maestoso opening highlights the Harvest Work Theme and the initial motives of *Federal Street* and *Shining Shore*. In the next passage (reh. A, mm. 25–50), the first phrase of *Federal Street* is developed in imitation, while several other melodies paraphrased from hymns appear as "shadow lines" that Ives directs should be played "Faintly — as choirs (practising before church) in the distance."[54] These include *Laban* by Lowell Mason (H31, muted violins, mm. 29–35 and perhaps through m. 60), *Nettleton* (flute, mm. 34–37), *Valen-*

tia, arranged by George Kingsley (oboe, mm. 42–44), *Arlington* by Thomas Arne (solo violas, mm. 50–52), and perhaps others not yet identified (e.g., flutes, mm. 38–41 and 48–60, oboe, 45–47, and solo violas, 44–50). The presence of all these added tunes gives this passage something of the quality of a collage, except that they are all shadow parts, much softer than the other lines, and only dimly heard.

Elements of *Duke Street* are introduced and developed in the next subsection (reh. C, mm. 51–87), which culminates in a paraphrase of the countermelody in horns and trumpets (mm. 69–87). Then the Harvest Work Theme returns (reh. G, mm. 88–105), followed by a transition to the middle section, including an anticipation of its theme, *Shining Shore*, in oboe and flute (mm. 118–28). After the middle section, the tempo and dynamic level gradually increase, and further development of the Harvest Work Theme, the first phrase of *Federal Street*, and the third phrase of *Duke Street* leads to the climactic appearance of the theme with its countermelodies.[55]

Ives changed his mind about what the theme and countermelody would be and which was which. The earliest extant draft of the end of the work shows *Federal Street* as the theme, combined with a countermelody paraphrased from *Shining Shore* and a descant like that in the final version (mm. 244ff.). After this was written out, the third phrase of *Federal Street* was cancelled and replaced by the third phrase of *Duke Street*, creating what would become the countermelody of *Thanksgiving*.[56] In the score-sketch for the corresponding place in *Thanksgiving*, this composite melody is treated as the theme, with the descant still above, but *Shining Shore* is missing. Ives then added in pencil *Duke Street* as a countermelody, rhythmically adjusted as in the final version.[57] Only in the full score did he make *Duke Street* the most prominent line at this point by adding the unison chorus, making it by implication the theme and changing the composite former theme into the countermelody. This history helps to explain the prominence of *Federal Street* and *Shining Shore* in the first section of the movement and the lack of an earlier paraphrase of the theme as in other cumulative settings.

Thanksgiving is not programmatic, as are the other three movements of the *Holidays Symphony*, but it evokes its two holidays with some extramusical symbolism: Thanksgiving, which celebrates the colonists' first harvest, with the Harvest Work Theme, and Forefathers' Day, which commemorates the Pilgrims' landing in 1620 and is observed in New England on December 21 or 22, with the text sung to *Duke Street* ("God! Beneath thy guiding hand / Our exiled fathers crossed the sea") and perhaps some of the words to *Shining Shore* ("a pilgrim stranger" and "the shining shore / We may almost discover").[58]

Cumulative Settings with Original Countermelodies

The movements examined so far are all individuals, as different from one another as are middle- and late-period sonata-form movements of Beethoven. Yet each follows the same basic plan, ending with a borrowed or paraphrased theme and its paraphrased countermelody and preceding this with sections that present the theme in part or in paraphrase, state the countermelody, and develop fragments of both. These movements gain their individuality in harmonic structure, in the order of events prior to the final statement of the theme, and in modifications to the basic plan. These modifications include paraphrasing or developing the countermelody instead of presenting it in full, as in the *Fugue in Four Keys* and the middle movement of the Third Violin Sonata; following the first full statement of theme and countermelody with further development and restatement in new keys, as in that movement and in the first movement of the First Violin Sonata; framing the cumulative setting with a slow introduction that is recalled in a slow coda, as in the latter movement; or blending cumulative setting with ternary or variation forms, as in *Thanksgiving* and in the second movement of the Fourth Violin Sonata.

The three movements to which we turn now differ more significantly from the typical pattern of cumulative setting, yet still conform to it in most respects, suggesting that they represent a distinctive subtype. The main difference in these movements is that their countermelodies are apparently not based on existing tunes. Interestingly, this seems to be linked with another trait, for these same movements are also those in which the countermelody is only partial, accompanying the initial phrase rather than the entire theme (First Piano Sonata, first and third movements), or is rudimentary, less a melody of its own than simply part of the accompaniment to the theme (Fourth Violin Sonata, finale). The forms of these movements are synopsized in Table 5.3.

First Piano Sonata, first movement

The first movement of the First Piano Sonata, composed between about 1909 and about 1914, is grouped into five main sections by changes of tempo, character, and musical material.[59] The main development in the cumulative form takes place in the first, third, and final sections, with the others serving as contrasting episodes based in part on the secondary thematic material.

Example 5.21 shows the melody of the final section (mm. 98–103). It ends with a statement in B major of *Lebanon* (H33, "I was a wand'ring sheep") by John Zundel. The third phrase is altered to resemble the opening of Robert Lowry's *Where Is My Wandering Boy?* (H64), punning on both the musical

TABLE 5.3: Instrumental Cumulative Settings with Partial or Rudimentary Countermelodies Not Based on Borrowed Material

First Piano Sonata, first movement (between ca. 1909 and ca. 1914)

T: *Lebanon* (H33), with a reference to *Where Is My Wandering Boy?* (H64)

Secondary theme: Original (comprising M, M+N, then CM complete)

CM: Original; only as long as one phrase of T

Secondary ideas: Motive M, Motive N (M+N is a countermelody in the third movement of this sonata)

Section	Measure		
1	1	Fragments of CM, M, T, N	Adagio con moto
2 :	21	Episode on M, T variant	slower and freely (largo)
3 :	28	Secondary theme: M, M+N, then CM complete	Andante con moto
	35	Development of these plus fragments of T	
4	72	Episode on motive derived from CM (including N), M	Allegro risoluto
5 :	98	Secondary theme: M, M+N, then CM complete	With a certain kind of poise . . .
>:	100	T with CM, echoes of M	

First Piano Sonata, third movement (ca. 1914)

T: *Erie* (H17)

CM: Original (combines motives M and N from first movement of this sonata); only as long as one phrase of T

Secondary ideas: Countermelody from first movement appears in fragments

Section	Measure			
1 :	1	CM, part of T (mm. 1–4)	Largo	unstable; hints of E
	2	Fragments of first-movement CM, parts of T (mm. 1–2 and 9–12)		
2	3	Development of T fragments (mm. 1–2, 9, and 11) and CM	Allegro	

Table 5.3, continued:

	Measure			
>	27	T complete, somewhat paraphrased, with varied CM		A
	42	Evaded cadence, extension		
	49	Further development of CM, T, first-movement CM		
3 >:	62	T complete, somewhat paraphrased, with CM	Largo	E, with passing modulations
	71	Final cadence, with part of first-movement CM		

[The first two "measures" are an unbarred rhapsody, lasting almost as long as the final section. The middle section is about half again as long as each of the outer sections in playing time.]

Fourth Violin Sonata, third movement (ca. 1914, based on 1905 sketch of piece for cornet and strings)
T: *The Beautiful River* (H6)
CM: Original (rudimentary)

Section	Measure		
1 >	1	Fragments of T (piano, then violin), constituting partial paraphrase	E♭
	14	Extension	
2 :	19	CM in violin, with Accompaniment in piano	E♭
	27	End of T in violin; CM and Accompaniment continue in piano	
	33	Extension (equals mm. 14–18)	
3 >:	37	T complete in violin, CM and Accompaniment in piano (expanded to fit theme)	E♭
	56	Closing tag (first measure of T+CM)	

CUMULATIVE SETTINGS

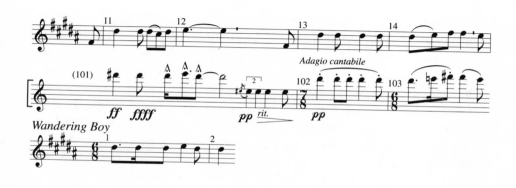

EXAMPLE 5.21: First Piano Sonata, first movement, melody of final section and its sources

parallel between the two tunes, whose first measures are related by inversion, and the links between their texts, particularly at this point; in the first verse of "I was a wand'ring sheep," the third line reads "I was a wayward child, I did not love my home."[60] This is a rare instance among Ives's cumulative settings in which textual similarities prompted the choice of source tunes.

The countermelody (marked CM in Example 5.21) is apparently not based on an existing tune and accompanies only the first phrase of the hymn. The countermelody suggests the key of A rather than B major. This is typical of the movement, whose advanced harmony often has a polytonal sound, making the key structure difficult to describe. Before the theme, Ives presents a composite melody (mm. 98–99) based on two motives that play a significant role in the movement, here labeled M and N, and then the countermelody alone, transposed up a semitone. Motive M may be related to two brief motives in *Lebanon* (as shown in Example 5.21), and it shares the dotted rhythm of *Where Is My Wandering Boy?*. Motive N is also present in the countermelody, and the combination of motives M and N in a single phrase appears as a countermelody in this sonata's third movement.

This same composite melody from mm. 98–99 begins the third section of the movement at m. 28, transposed a third lower. The full statement of this melody near the middle of the movement is akin to the presentation of the countermelody in most of the works we have examined, establishing it as the main secondary theme of the work. The third section proceeds to develop these motives plus fragments of the theme, in particular the opening motives of the two source tunes. The first section introduces fragments of the countermelody, motive M, the theme, and motive N and develops them in a free fantasia. The second section (mm. 21–27) is a slow episode on motive M and a new tune, perhaps a variant of the theme. The fourth section (mm. 72–97) is a fast episode mostly based on a motive woven from part of the countermelody (compare the top line of mm. 72–73 to notes 5–12 of the countermelody, transposed down a whole step) and the rising fifths of motive M; this thematic idea is anticipated at mm. 50–53, where its rhythmic character is different.[61] This movement is more episodic than the finale of the Third Symphony, but it still has the effect of gradual clarification that is characteristic of cumulative settings, and the final section provides all the thematic material for the rest of the movement, both borrowed and original.

First Piano Sonata, third movement

Like the first movement, the sonata's third movement (ca. 1914) has only a partial countermelody, but it takes quite a different shape.[62] The theme is the hymn tune *Erie*, also used in the countermelody of the first movement of the Third Symphony (see Example 5.4). This tune is composed of two-bar units in the pattern ABAB′CDAB′. In the present movement, Ives consistently modifies motive A so that the last note in the first measure is the second scale degree rather than the tonic, smoothing out the descent to become more pentatonic and less triadic. He does the same at several spots in the first movement of the Third Symphony.[63] This may reflect a local performance variant, or may be influenced by the opening of Foster's "Massa's in de Cold Ground," which has a similar rhythm and pitch contour (though a different alignment between rhythm and pitch) and includes the second degree. In the sonata movement, some statements of this motive follow the Foster in rhythm as well as pitch, suggesting that Ives intended a sort of musical pun.[64]

In the slow, soft final section (mm. 62–71), *Erie* appears in E major, complete and recognizable despite some altered intervals, brief changes of key, omissions, and interpolations. Its first phrase is accompanied by a short countermelody combining motives M and N from the first movement (see Example 5.21), and parts of this idea also accompany the hymn's second and fourth phrases, which are variants of the first. The closing plagal cadence is embellished with the first few notes of the first-movement countermelody. The movement's first section is also slow and quiet, an unmeasured rhapsody in two subsections marked off by a barline. The first subsection presents in turn the countermelody, a distorted version of the hymn's first phrase, and a variation of the countermelody, and the second develops parts of the first-movement countermelody and the most distinctive portions of *Erie*: its opening motive (mm. 1–2) and the two halves of the contrasting third phrase (mm. 9–10 and 11–12). Between these slow, pensive outer sections, the middle section is fast, active, and loud. It begins with a development of these same motives from the theme intermixed with ideas from the countermelody. This leads at the center of the movement to a complete, somewhat varied statement of *Erie* in A over an accompaniment based on ideas from the countermelody. After an evaded cadence, more development follows, including part of the first-movement countermelody alongside elements of the theme and countermelody. With its clear sectional contrasts and three statements of the theme (including the partial one in the first section), this movement exhibits aspects of variation as well as cumulative form, though not to the same degree as the middle movement of the Fourth Violin Sonata.

Fourth Violin Sonata, third movement, and At the River

The Fourth Violin Sonata finale (ca. 1914, based on a 1905 sketch of a piece for cornet and strings) uses as a theme Robert Lowry's *The Beautiful River* ("Shall we gather at the river?"), slightly altered.[65] As usual, the theme first appears complete in the final section, presented by the violin in E♭ major over the countermelody and accompaniment in the piano (m. 37). The hymn's verse and refrain both end with the same two-bar motive (mm. 7–8 and 15–16 of the hymn); at the corresponding spots in Ives's theme (mm. 43–45 and 52–55), the penultimate measure is changed intervallically and then, after the cadence, repeated in original form without the cadential measure. This indefinite ending heightens the sense of questioning in the text of the verse and undermines the affirmation expressed in the refrain ("Yes, we'll gather at the river"). The countermelody here is rudimentary, consisting of the top line of the chord progression in the piano.[66] The opening section presents motives from the theme over repeated figures in the accompaniment.[67] The chords are chromatic, but the key is clearly E♭, with the bass line centered on B♭. The middle section (m. 19) presents the countermelody in the violin and the accompaniment in the piano, both somewhat truncated. At m. 27, the violin plays the end of the theme as the piano completes the countermelody. Both second and final sections are solidly in the tonic E♭, despite many chromatic chords, and both first and second sections end with the same extension that serves as dominant preparation for the following section.

As he had done with the first movement of the Second Violin Sonata, Ives arranged the latter part of this movement as a song, *At the River* (1916).[68] The song corresponds exactly to mm. 33–57 of the sonata movement, with a four-bar piano introduction and the hymn tune in the voice. The text is that of the hymn, with part or all of the opening line ("Shall we gather at the river?") repeated at the end of both verse and refrain with the melodic figure from the penultimate measure. The text repetition reinforces the sense of questioning present in the music, and this gives an interesting new slant on the text; as Kevin O. Kelly comments, "What happens beyond death remains an unanswered question, despite the religious faith in an afterlife put forth in the preceding verse."[69] The song is just a setting and reworking of the hymn tune, not a cumulative setting, for only the brief introduction precedes the tune itself.

Cumulative Settings Without Countermelodies

The presence of a countermelody, developed and presented independently before appearing in counterpoint with the principal theme, is usually one of the hallmarks of Ives's cumulative settings. Yet three settings in cumulative form have no obbligato countermelody at all, and they constitute another distinctive subtype. Their forms are summarized in Table 5.4.

In the most common type of cumulative setting, the countermelody serves not only as a counterpoint to the principal theme but also as the main secondary theme. In the movements just examined, the countermelody is not substantial enough to serve in this role, and in the next group, there is no countermelody to use. In the first movement of the First Piano Sonata, as we have seen, Ives includes the countermelody in a longer secondary theme that anchors the middle section and returns in the final section, just before the main theme. In contrast, the third movements of the First Piano Sonata and Fourth Violin Sonata are so dominated by material from their principal themes that they seem monothematic, relieved only by brief episodes when the theme is absent; here the countermelody is more a contrasting motive than a true second theme. Of the three works in the next group, the first is brief and essentially monothematic, and the other two alternate between contrasting segments of their principal themes. "The Alcotts" also introduces a middle section on new themes and in a new key to create a kind of ternary form. Among these six movements, the first movement of the First Piano Sonata is alone in continuing the nineteenth-century sonata principle of two contrasting themes of almost equal weight, as do the cumulative settings of the most common type.

Adagio cantabile (The Innate)

Adagio cantabile was written about 1908 for string quartet, piano, and optional string bass and revised in 1916 as the song *The Innate*.[70] It is a short cumulative setting of the first phrase of *Nettleton*, heard at the end in the upper strings in G major (mm. 21–24) over a repeated chord with a chromatic neighbor-tone figure in the bass line. The accompaniment is not, strictly speaking, a countermelody, but it is used in a similar way, appearing transposed in the opening measures (mm. 1–7) and echoed after the final statement of the theme (mm. 24–26). At the beginning and end of the work, it accompanies a motive apparently taken from mm. 1–2 of *The Beautiful River*, used as a framing device. Fragments of the theme's first half, both literal and paraphrased, appear within the accompaniment in mm. 2–7. There follows a passage in mm. 8–11 that seems to be based on the third phrase of *Nettleton* (mm. 8–12) — the one contrasting phrase of the hymn, which is in AABA form. Fragments of the theme return in m. 12, and the music builds to a climax on the neighbor-tone figure from mm. 2–3 of the hymn (mm. 19–20), preparing the culminating appearance of the theme and accompaniment.

Second Piano Sonata (Concord Sonata), *third movement ("The Alcotts")*

"The Alcotts," the third movement of the *Concord Sonata*, was adapted around 1914–19 from a lost, unfinished *Orchard House Overture* (1904?).[71] The sonata is famous, among other reasons, for using the first four notes of Beethoven's Fifth Symphony (H173) in a prominent way in all four movements. What is seldom noted is that the Beethoven motive is part of a longer theme, the main theme of "The Alcotts" and the unifying theme of the whole sonata, and usually appears in conjunction with other elements of this theme. Since this theme is new and is not an existing or paraphrased tune, despite its incorporation of borrowed material, this is the one Ives work that might more justifiably be called a cumulative form than a cumulative setting.

Example 5.22 shows the theme in its first complete appearance in the sonata, at the end of the first section of "The Alcotts." The first half of the theme is apparently not based on borrowed material, but the second half is adapted from no fewer than four sources: two famous Beethoven tunes, the opening motives of the Fifth Symphony (transposed) and "Hammerklavier" Sonata, Op. 106 (at pitch), and two hymns that are motivically related to the Fifth Symphony motto, Charles Zeuner's *Missionary Chant* (H37, "Ye Christian heralds") and Simeon B. Marsh's *Martyn* (H35, "Jesus, lover of my soul").[72] Here and in several other places in this and other movements, the melody is soft and lyrical, quite the opposite of the two Beethoven motives. The resemblance to the "Hammerklavier" Sonata is even stronger at the theme's restatement at the end of the movement, where huge hammered triads in both hands echo the texture of the Beethoven. The entire theme is permeated by the rhythm of the Fifth Symphony motto, and intervallic similarities between segments also give the theme a unified cast.

TABLE 5.4: Instrumental Cumulative Settings Without Countermelodies

Adagio cantabile (The Innate) (ca. 1907–8)

T: *Nettleton* (H42), first phrase only (mm. 1–4; equals second and fourth phrases)

CM: none

Secondary idea: Adapted from mm. 1–2 of *The Beautiful River* (H6)

	Measure		Key of tune
	1	Prelude: Accompaniment with mm. 1–2 of *The Beautiful River*	Db
	2	Fragments and paraphrases of T, mm. 1–2, with Accompaniment	modulatory
	8	Hints of *Nettleton*, third phrase (mm. 8–12)	
	12	Fragments and paraphrases of T, mm. 1–2 (piano)	G, D
	17	Bridge based on T, mm. 2–3	modulates to G
>	21	T complete, with Accompaniment	G
	24	Postlude: Accompaniment with mm. 1–2 of *The Beautiful River*	B

Second Piano Sonata ("Concord, Mass., 1840–1860"), third movement ("The Alcotts") (ca. 1914–19, based on lost *Orchard House Overture* of 1904)

T: Partly original, partly derived from the opening motives of Beethoven's Fifth Symphony and "Hammerklavier" Sonata and from the hymn tunes *Missionary Chant* (H37) and *Martyn* (H35)

CM: none

Secondary ideas: Themes of contrasting middle section (possibly based on existing tunes)

Section	Page/System		
1	53/1	Opening motives of Fifth Symphony, *Missionary Chant*	Bb
	53/2	T, first part incomplete, second part almost complete	Bb over Ab triad
>	53/4	T, missing final segment	Bb
	54/1	Development of Fifth Symphony motive, leading to a climax on mm. 5–7 of *Missionary Chant* (55/1)	modulatory

Table 5.4, continued:

Section	Measure	Description	Key
>	55/1	T complete (*mf* and *p*)	B♭
2	55/3	Contrasting middle section; new themes	E♭
	56/5	Transition to reprise	
	57/1	Opening motive of T developed	
3 >	57/4	T complete (*ff* and diminuendo), chordal accompaniment	C
	57/4	Codetta on opening of T	

Second Violin Sonata, third movement ("The Revival"; ca. 1914–19)

T: *Nettleton* (H42)

CM: none

Section	Measure	Description	Tempo	Key
1	1	Fragments of T, mm. 1–2 (piano and violin)	Largo	unstable key
2	15	T, mm. 1–4, in canon (piano)	very slowly	E major and B♭ major
	17	T, mm. 8–10, varied, repeated (piano)		G Dorian/Mixolydian
	19	T, mm. 1–4, in canon (piano and violin)		E major and B♭ major
	21	T, mm. 8–10, varied, repeated (violin)		G Dorian/Mixolydian
3	25	T, mm. 1–2, varied, repeated (piano)	Allegretto	A major
	27	T, mm. 2–4, varied, repeated (violin)		C major
	33	T, mm. 8–10, varied, repeated (violin)		G Dorian/Mixolydian
	36	T, mm. 1–3, developed (canon in violin and piano)	allegro assai	F major
	38	Extension (violin)		G major
4 >	41	T complete, last phrase incomplete, repeated with diminuendo (violin)		G major
	50	Codetta; T, mm. 1–2 (violin)		F major (ends on V)

*B♭ (or transposed equivalent) in all other statements of theme

EXAMPLE 5.22: Second Piano Sonata *(Concord Sonata),* third movement ("The Alcotts"), theme and its sources

Given the prominence of the Fifth Symphony motive in both theme and sonata, it is striking that two sketches show the theme without this motive but otherwise virtually complete.[73] Perhaps Ives only inserted the Beethoven idea after noticing its motivic resemblance to the rest of his theme.

Like the slow movement of the Fourth Violin Sonata and *Thanksgiving,* "The Alcotts" blends cumulative with ternary form. The opening and closing sections, based on the principal theme, are mostly unbarred; thus, locations will be indicated by page and system numbers in the 1947 second edition, rather than by measure numbers.[74] The movement opens with a reference to the Fifth Symphony, reharmonized to resemble a hymn. On its repetition,

CUMULATIVE SETTINGS

one note is changed, and it becomes *Missionary Chant* in B♭ major. There follows a statement of the theme in B♭ over a repeated A♭ major triad, the first half of the theme lacking its final notes, the second complete but for its last note (p. 53/systems 2–3).[75] A second statement in B♭ follows over a descending bass line (pp. 53/4–54/1). Here the theme is almost complete, but it breaks off to develop the motives derived from the Fifth Symphony and *Missionary Chant*. This leads to a climactic statement (at p. 55/1) in E♭ of the third phrase of the hymn (mm. 5–7), which begins with the Beethoven motive. The first complete statement of the theme, again in B♭, concludes the opening section.

The middle section is in E♭ and presents two new ideas that may be based in part on borrowed material. The cadence of the first of these (p. 55, last measure) sounds like the opening of the Wedding March from Wagner's *Lohengrin*, but the echo is too brief for certainty.[76] H. Wiley Hitchcock points out that the beginning of the second idea (p. 56, m. 1) resembles the opening of Anthony F. Winnemore's 1843 minstrel song *Stop That Knocking at My Door* (H136).[77] After these ideas are played twice, a rhapsodic transition leads to the final section, with a development of the principal theme's opening motive (p. 57/1–3) and the reprise of the complete theme, now in C major and in large block chords, slower and louder than before. There is a brief codetta based on the opening motive of the theme, presented in C major over a repeated B♭-major triad. The latter harks back to the key in which the theme appeared in the first section of the movement and to the polytonal sound of its first partial appearance in B♭ over a repeated A♭ major triad, and the closing C-major chord resolves the remaining harmonic tension.

Like Ives's other movements in cumulative form, "The Alcotts" is thematically coherent, and would be so if none of the borrowings were recognized. The outer sections are derived from the theme, which is presented in whole or large part four times, enough to establish it as a unit. Only the familiarity of the Fifth Symphony motto has led us to hear it as a thing apart when it first appears, rather than as the very center of Ives's theme. Several studies have identified the first half of the theme, the part that is not borrowed, as the "human-faith-melody" that Ives mentions in his essay on this movement.[78] But if this is the melody to which Ives refers, surely the Beethoven motives are part of it, both because the theme is treated as a unit throughout the movement and the sonata, and because Ives mentions Beethoven later in the same sentence, describing the human-faith-melody as "a tune the Concord bards are ever playing while they pound away at the immensities with a Beethoven-like sublimity."[79] "Pounding away" aptly describes the opening of the "Hammerklavier" Sonata as well as the Fifth Symphony, even if Ives's presentations of the theme vary from the large block chords at the end of "The Alcotts" to the soft, dreamy statement colored by a whole-tone ostinato that closes the movement's first section. What is crucial is the incorporation of Beethoven's motives into Ives's theme, so that by the end of the sonata we hear them not as borrowings but as the core of the unifying theme of the *Concord Sonata* itself, not as Beethoven but as Ives.[80]

Second Violin Sonata, third movement ("The Revival")

The finale of the Second Violin Sonata (ca. 1914–19) is a cumulative setting of *Nettleton*.[81] There is no countermelody, and almost all the significant motivic material is drawn from the theme.[82] The theme appears at the end in G major, complete except for its closing phrase. The first section develops motives from the theme's opening bars, in various keys and in both instruments. In the second section, the final tone center of G is forecast by unorthodox means: the piano states the hymn's first phrase in canon at the tritone in two keys equidistant from G—E and B♭ major—while the violin plucks open G and D strings. The piano then presents a variant of the hymn's third phrase in G with a flatted leading tone, over a spare accompaniment in the violin and the piano left hand that mixes B♭ and B to produce a G Dorian/Mixolydian sound. This section repeats, with the violin taking one voice of the canon and playing the third-phrase variant that follows.[83] The third section is faster and changes key frequently, developing fragments of the tune in an almost complete paraphrase: mm. 1–2 in A in the piano, the remainder of the first two phrases in C in the violin, the third phrase in G Dorian/Mixolydian in the violin, and the last phrase in F in canon between the instruments. After a brief extension, the final section presents the theme in G in the violin over a pounding chordal ostinato in the piano. The last phrase is left incomplete, perhaps because it would merely have repeated the first two phrases, and is converted into a repeated figure that slows and quiets. A brief codetta shifts the key down to F and ends on a C-major triad in one of Ives's frequent off-key endings. The graduated increase in tempo and dynamic level over the course of the movement and the shift in melodic focus from piano to violin reinforce the thematic process to create a terrific momentum forward to the climactic statement of the theme.

Double Cumulative Setting

Although the previous two subtypes usually lack a strong secondary theme, the next two subtypes retain the idea of two contrasting themes that underlies both the nineteenth-century concept of sonata form and the most common type of cumulative setting. However, instead of a principal theme and a subordinate countermelody, here there are two independent themes with different functions. The first example to be considered is unique among

CUMULATIVE SETTINGS

Ives's works in being a double cumulative setting, one inside the other, in a structure akin to ternary form. The final subtype combines cumulative setting with verse-refrain form, using one theme for the verses and another for the refrains.

First Violin Sonata, third movement

The First Violin Sonata finale (ca. 1914) combines the idea of a middle section in cumulative form, used in the first movement of the same sonata, with that of outer sections comprising a single, interrupted cumulative setting, used in the middle movement of the Fourth Violin Sonata, which was composed about the same time.[84] The result is the only double cumulative setting in Ives's output, whose form is outlined in Table 5.5.

The middle section (mm. 41–111) is a cumulative setting of a theme paraphrased from Lowell Mason's *Watchman* (H61, "Watchman, tell us of the night"). The theme appears complete in the violin in mm. 91–109, in $\frac{6}{8}$ and D major over an accompaniment in $\frac{3}{4}$ that emphasizes a B-minor triad. As shown in Example 5.23, the first ten bars of the theme are changed in small ways, and the second half is more distant from the source: m. 11 of the hymn tune elides with m. 10; m. 12 is altered and repeated to create a caesura; the similarity of mm. 13–14 of the hymn to its opening motive is exploited to introduce a repetition of the first phrase; a striking new motive, labeled Z (mm. 107–8), is based on mm. 13–16, most closely resembling the retrograde of mm. 15–16; and a closing tag reorders the descent to the cadence to suggest the opening motive again and leave the music a bit up in the air. These changes make the theme more diverse in rhythm, less four-square, less lilting, and thus more contemplative. Although there is no independent countermelody, the accompaniment to the theme is permeated by a stepwise descending figure that may derive from the cadential gesture of *Watchman* (compare mm. 91ff. in the piano with mm. 8 and 16 of the hymn). This figure may be considered the countersubject, for it receives substantial development prior to its appearance with the theme, as is typical of Ives's countermelodies.

The complete *Watchman* theme is preceded by a long development. Here the most prominent motives are two elements of the theme, mm. 1–2 of *Watchman* and motive Z, and the countersubject. The development is in a rough ternary form, delineated by the reprise of mm. 41ff. at m. 75. The middle part, mm. 56–74, includes varied statements of the first and third phrases of *Watchman* in the violin (at mm. 57 and 66) over variants of the countersubject, both times leading to further development. This passage takes the place of the theme paraphrase or statement of the countermelody that is typical of cumulative settings.

TABLE 5.5: Double Cumulative Setting

First Violin Sonata, third movement (ca. 1914)

T1: Paraphrased from *Watchman* (H61)

T2: *Work Song* (H68), mm. 1–8

CS1: 3–2–1 figure perhaps drawn from *Watchman*, m. 8 and 16

CS2: Ostinato based on figure taken from the countermelody from the Second Violin Sonata, first movement, ultimately derived from *Autumn* (H4); the first movement of the First Violin Sonata uses a variant of this motive

Section	Measure			
1	1	Piano introduction based on T2 mm. 1-2 (with mm. 3–4 at mm. 21ff. and mm. 9–10 of *Work Song* at mm. 10ff.)	$\frac{4}{4}$, Allegro	F, modulatory
	26	Violin develops T2 mm. 1–2; piano has other material, then varied reprise of opening of movement		modulates to F
2a	41	Fragments of T1 (mm. 1–2, Motive Z) in violin, CS1 in piano	Più Allegretto	B, modulatory
	47	First phrase of T1 (mm. 1–4) in piano, in parallel triads (mm. 47–49), distorted intervals (mm. 51–55)		
b >	56	First phrase of T1 in violin, CS1 variant in piano	$\frac{6}{8}$, Con Moto	G, modulatory
>	66	Third phrase of T1 (mm. 9–12) in violin, CS1 and variant of T1 mm. 1–2 in piano, developed	$\frac{4}{4}$	C, modulatory
a´	75	Varied reprise of mm. 41–46	meno mosso	D, modulatory
	81	Fragments of T1 (mm. 1–2, Motive Z) in violin, first phrase of T1 in piano, further development	meno mosso	
:	87	CS1 in piano, then violin (meter change at m. 90)		
c >:	91	T1 in violin, CS1 in piano (tempo: Andante cantabile)	$\frac{6}{8}$ over $\frac{3}{4}$	D

EXAMPLE 5.23: First Violin Sonata, third movement, theme based on *Watchman*

This theme paraphrased from *Watchman* had an interesting career. Ives wrote that it was taken from a 1901 song for soprano and organ, now lost.[85] Soon after writing the sonata movement, he transcribed mm. 86–111 almost without change as the song *Watchman*, and later he reworked mm. 89–111 as the second half of the Fourth Symphony first movement.[86] Like *At the River* and *His Exaltation*, both arrangements are settings of the paraphrased melody rather than cumulative settings. All the surviving works on this melody use the same text, adapted from the first verse of the hymn.[87]

The outer sections of the movement comprise a cumulative setting of the first half of Mason's *Work Song* (H68, "Work, for the night is coming"). The theme, mm. 1–8 of the hymn tune, appears in full for the first time near the end, at mm. 189–98 in the violin in F major. It is accompanied by a four-bar ostinato in the piano that twice states a figure identical to the opening two measures of the countermelody from the first movement of the Second Violin Sonata (see Example 5.14). A variant of this appears prominently in the first movement of the First Sonata (motive W in Example 5.13), so that it functions here as a reminiscence of material from an earlier movement; it plays almost no prior role in the finale. After the theme has been stated, while the violin repeats variants of the theme's opening motive, the piano ostinato gradually changes into a variant of mm. 6–8 of *Autumn* (mm. 208–9). This is the segment from which the ostinato figure is paraphrased (see Example 5.14), and its presence here suggests that this movement was once intended as the finale of the Second Violin Sonata, whose first movement is based on *Autumn*, rather than of the First. Indeed, in *114 Songs*, the song *Watchman* is identified as adapted from the Second Violin Sonata, not the First.[88]

The first section of the movement, centered loosely on the tonic F major, begins with a long piano solo based primarily on mm. 1–2 of *Work Song*. Two other parts of the hymn tune are cited briefly, mm. 9–10 and 3–4 (at mm. 10 and 21, respectively); the first of these is not part of the theme but does return later in the movement. The violin enters at m. 26 with more development of the theme's first motive, while the piano has other material and then reprises the opening of the movement. There are fleeting suggestions of the middle section to come: part of motive Z in mm. 21–22 and hints of motive Z and the countersubject in mm. 36–40, at the end of the first section. After the middle section, a bridge (m. 112) links mm. 3–4 of *Watchman* with mm. 1–2 of *Work Song* by punning on their common motivic elements (5–3 and 5–6–5 in major), and a chromatic transition accelerates and crescendos to the opening Allegro tempo and *forte* dynamic. There follows a varied reprise of most of the first section of the movement, culminating in the first complete statement of the first phrase of *Work Song* at m. 153. Hints of the middle-section theme then lead to an extended paraphrase of that theme in the violin at m. 164 over the opening motive of *Work Song* in augmentation. The return of mm. 9–10 of *Work Song* at m. 176 and a C pedal point a few bars later prepare the climactic presentation of the *Work Song* theme in F major.

In this movement, both the middle section individually and the outer two sections taken together function as cumulative settings of their respective themes. In some respects, this is like the Third Symphony finale, which presents each theme in fragments and variants before it appears in full. But in that work the first of the themes to be stated fully is ultimately revealed to be a countermelody to the other, the principal theme. In the First Violin Sonata finale, each theme retains its independence as the theme of a separate section. At the same time, the anticipation of motives from the middle section in the first, the linking of motives from both themes in the bridge to the third section, and the extensive paraphrase of the middle-section theme in the third section in counterpoint with a motive from the other theme weave the two cumulative settings together into a unified movement.

Combinations of Verse-Refrain Form with Cumulative Setting

The First Violin Sonata finale combines cumulative setting with ternary form, as do the middle movement of the Fourth Sonata, *Thanksgiving*, and "The Alcotts," each in a unique way. This composite form may constitute another distinctive subtype of cumulative setting, overlapping the others.

Another composite form that Ives used combines cumulative setting with verse-refrain form. This presents a series of "verses" based on a hymn tune theme, with the last verse stating the theme in its most complete and recognizable form, as in a cumulative setting. Each verse is followed by a much briefer "refrain" based on a different hymn. The refrain theme is stated relatively complete each time and undergoes little development, as befits a refrain. For these pieces, Ives used hymns that were themselves in verse-refrain form, which no doubt suggested the procedure.[89] There are only two such works: the first movement of the Third Violin Sonata, with four verses, and the *Ragtime Dances* in its two forms as an independent work and as the two scherzo movements of the First Piano Sonata.

Third Violin Sonata, first movement

The first movement of the Third Violin Sonata dates from the same time as the other two movements (ca. 1914) and like them was based on an earlier work, a lost set of organ preludes from 1901.[90] It is laid out in four verses, each followed by a brief refrain. Its thematic structure, outlined in Table 5.6, is among the most intricate of Ives's cumulative settings.

The theme of the verses (T) is stated most directly at the end of the final verse, shown in Example 5.24, where it appears in F major. It is paraphrased from the refrain of *Need*, the hymn also used in the sonata's finale. The meter and rhythm of T are changed from the hymn, and two motives are added: the dotted figure from m. 15 of the hymn (motive t3) is inserted in the second and fourth bars of the theme, and a variant of the hymn's cadential motive (t2) is embedded in the double stops in the sixth and seventh bars of the theme. These motives appear frequently in the preceding development, along with the opening motive of the theme (t1). Motive t3 is part of both other motives and is also developed independently.

The theme of the refrain (R) is partly paraphrased from the refrain of *Beulah Land*. Example 5.25 shows its final statement. Although T is constantly varied before its final complete appearance, R is the same each time, changing only in instrumentation and accompaniment: the first refrain is for piano

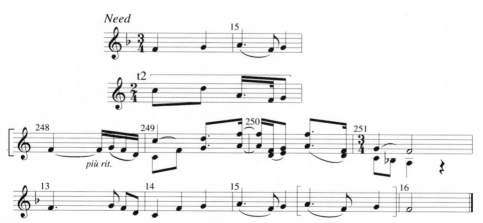

EXAMPLE 5.24: Third Violin Sonata, first movement, verse theme with refrain of *Need*

TABLE 5.6: Combination of *Verse–Refrain* Form with
Cumulative Setting in a Single Movement

Third *Violin Sonata*, first movement (ca. 1914, based on lost organ prelude from 1901)

Themes:

T, main theme of verses: Paraphrased from refrain of *Need* (H41), mm. 8–16
  Motives derived from T: t1, t2, t3
R, theme of refrains: Partly paraphrased from refrain of *Beulah Land* (H8), mm. 8–20

Countermelodies:

T′: Variant of T, used as countermelody to first half of refrain at its final appearance
T′′: Variant of T′ (and thus of T), used as countermelody to first half of refrain at its third appearance
CM, countermelody to second half of refrain at its final appearance: Perhaps related to *Beulah Land*, mm. 13–16
Secondary ideas: A (arpeggiated chord), B (meandering motive), C (lyrical tune based on t2), D (accompaniment to T)

		Measure				
Verse I	>	0	T′ in violin, A in piano	$\frac{2}{4}$	Adagio	E (chord implies c♯/d♭)
		11	B in piano, t1 developed in violin			modulatory
		26	C in violin			G
		29	Development of C/t2 in violin, t1 and B in piano			modulatory
	:	44	CM in violin, D in piano, then developed			B♭, modulatory
		54	C in violin			A, modulatory
	>	64	T′/T paraphrase in violin, A and B mixed in piano			F
Refrain	R	77	R, piano alone			B♭, closes on V of A
Verse II		88	Piano alone: T incomplete paraphrase, A	$\frac{3}{4}$	Andante	D♭ (chord implies b♭)
		95	Development of *Need*, m. 13, other T fragments	$\frac{5}{4}$		modulatory

Table 5-5, continued:

Refrain	R	111	Episode on fragments of R, *Beulah Land*	$\frac{4}{4}$	Con moto	closes in B♭
Verse III		149	R, alternating between violin and piano	$\frac{2}{4}$	Adagio	E♭, closes on V of D
		160	t1 in violin, A in piano	$\frac{6}{8}$	Allegretto	D♭ (chord implies b♭)
	>	166	T′′ in canon			F
		175	Varied reprise of Verse I, mm. 44–56, including T′′, C			modulatory
		191	Develop T′′, fragments of T			closes in F
Refrain	R>	231	R in violin, T′′ in piano (abbreviated)	$\frac{4}{8}$	Adagio	B♭, closes on V of A
Verse IV		242	Piano alone: New T′/T paraphrase, A	unbarred	Adagio	D♭/b♭, modulatory
		243	Varied reprise of Verse II, mm. 95–98	unbarred	Poco rubato	
	>	244	T in violin, D in piano	$\frac{2}{4}$ $\left(\frac{4}{8}\right)$	Adagio	F
Refrain	R>:	252	R in violin, T′ and CM in piano	$\frac{2}{4}$		B♭
		262	Codetta	$\frac{5}{8}$	Largo	closes on A

Sonata No. 3 for Violin and Piano. © 1951 by Merion Music, Inc. Used by Permission.

EXAMPLE 5.25: Third Violin Sonata, first movement, refrain theme with countermelodies and sources

CUMULATIVE SETTINGS

alone, the second passes R back and forth between the instruments, and the last two statements give the melody to the violin and new accompanimental figuration to the piano. All but the second refrain are in Bb major, ending on the dominant of A; the second is a fourth higher. The last refrain adds the note and chord of resolution and a short codetta.

The verse theme does not have a countermelody, but R is joined by countermelodies at its last two appearances. At its final statement (Example 5.25), the first half of R (mm. 252–57) is accompanied by a variant of the verse theme (T′) that is built up from varied statements of t1 and t2. This variant is first heard at the beginning of the movement (mm. 3–10, violin), and at the end of the first verse it is expanded into a full paraphrase of the verse theme (mm. 64–76, violin). Near the outset of the third verse, T′ is transformed into a new melody (T″), shown in Example 5.26, that is treated in canon (mm. 166ff.), developed later in the verse, and presented in slightly abbreviated form as a countermelody to the first half of the following refrain (mm. 231–35). The contrapuntal combination of the refrain theme with two different variants of the verse (T″ and T′) thematically unifies the verse and refrain sections of the movement. The second part of R at its final statement is accompanied by a countermelody (CM) that may be related to the middle phrase of the refrain of *Beulah Land*, as Example 5.25 suggests. It has been heard twice before, in the middle of the first verse and again in the third (mm. 44 and 175, violin). Both earlier statements are in rather different rhythm, and both lead through extension and development to the figure from mm. 11–12 of *Beulah Land* that is used in R itself (at mm. 53 and 185–86, respectively), making the derivation of CM from that hymn somewhat more likely. Interestingly, the first statement of CM is accompanied by the same figuration used for the final statement of T (motive D), a small detail that further binds verse and refrain together.

The verses are alike in certain respects: each begins with a variant of T, preceded and accompanied by an arpeggiated chord (motive A) that gives a minor-mode cast to the melody; and each ends with a cadence on the domi-

Sonata No. 3 for Violin and Piano. © 1951 by Merion Music, Inc. Used by Permission.

EXAMPLE 5.26: Third Violin Sonata, first movement, T′ and T″

CUMULATIVE SETTINGS

nant of the following refrain, using t2 as a cadential figure. But each verse is also distinctive in meter, tempo, and melodic material, and alternate verses are paired by common melodic elements. The first verse, Adagio ($\frac{2}{4}$), is characterized by two ideas besides T′ and CM: a chromatic wandering motive in octaves in the piano (B) introduced in mm. 11–12, and a lyrical tune based on t2 in the violin (C), introduced and developed at m. 26 and repeated at m. 54. The second verse, Andante ($\frac{3}{4}$), begins with a paraphrase of T, repeats and develops the motive in its fifth bar (m. 13 of *Need*, developed in mm. 95ff.), and proceeds to a long episode (Con moto, $\frac{4}{4}$) on motives from *Beulah Land*, particularly those included in R. The third verse, Allegretto ($\frac{6}{8}$), introduces and develops T″ but also presents a varied reprise of part of the first verse (mm. 175–90 adapt mm. 44–56, transposed by a tritone), including CM and C. The fourth verse, Adagio, is at first unbarred, presenting another paraphrase of T and a varied reprise of part of the second verse (m. 243 adapts mm. 95–98) before stating the full theme at m. 244. Although each verse is individual, the third verse recalls the first and the fourth recalls the second, and all begin and end in similar ways.

The verse-refrain structure makes this movement quite different in shape from other cumulative settings yet like them in several important respects. The verse theme, paraphrased from a hymn tune, is presented in fragments and variants before finally appearing in a form most like its source; this exactly parallels the process of gradual clarification in the other movements. Although there is no countermelody per se for the verse theme, the refrain theme serves an analogous function; like the countermelody in a typical cumulative setting, the refrain theme is a secondary theme that appears in complete form relatively early in the work and is ultimately combined with a form of the main theme (here, T″ and T′, both derived from the verse theme). In short, this movement is different from the others we have studied in its combination of verse-refrain and cumulative forms, yet it shares a similar process of development and thus may be considered to represent another subtype of cumulative setting.

Ragtime Dances *and First Piano Sonata, second and fourth movements*

Ives wrote a number of pieces based on ragtime rhythms, including a four-movement set that exists in two forms, as a *Set of Four Ragtime Dances* for theater orchestra (ca. 1907 or 1911?) and as the scherzo movements IIa–IIb and IVa–IVb of the First Piano Sonata (ca. 1914–23). The score of the *Ragtime Dances* is mostly lost, but James Sinclair has reconstructed the orchestration from indications on the sketches.[91] As a set, they resemble the first movement of the Third Violin Sonata in combining four pairs of verse and refrain with cumulative setting.

Each movement features themes paraphrased from the hymn tunes *Bringing in the Sheaves* and *Happy Day* (H27, "O happy day," anonymous) and closes with a brief "Chorus" based on the refrain of Lewis Hartsough's *Welcome Voice* (H63, "I hear Thy welcome voice").[92] As Dennis Marshall has shown, these three tunes are melodically related, sharing a 2–1–3–2–1 cadential figure.[93] The first two also share another motive, the rising 5–1–2–3 figure that opens *Happy Day* and appears three times in *Bringing in the Sheaves* (mm. 7, 11, and 15) at the words "We shall come rejoicing." These common elements make it difficult to ascertain which of these two tunes is being used at several points, and Ives was clearly interested in exploring the ambiguity between them. Yet *Happy Day* never appears complete or in unambiguous paraphrase, whereas *Bringing in the Sheaves* is paraphrased extensively in every movement, making it the principal theme of the verses.

Of the paraphrased themes in the verses, the opening theme of the first movement (mm. 1–14) recurs in all four movements in various guises, and another first-movement idea (mm. 64–66) reappears in the finale (mm. 46–49). Both themes seem to derive from a motive in *Happy Day* that is not shared by the other two hymns, the 3–4–3–2 figure from its second phrase (mm. 2–3), spun out into much longer melodies. The other themes are unique to each movement. Most important, all four movements include one or more lengthy passages that paraphrase *Bringing in the Sheaves*, giving it a different rhythm and character in each movement, as in a set of variations. The most complete and recognizable statement of the hymn is at the end of the verse section of the fourth movement (m. 63); here the hymn's verse is repeated before its refrain is stated, and the repetition is accompanied by the refrain of *Welcome Voice* in the piccolo, stated as an ostinato in altered rhythmic diminution, probably moving too quickly to recognize. The following chorus includes a paraphrase of *Bringing in the Sheaves* as a countermelody to the *Welcome Voice* refrain, uniting in counterpoint the two main themes of the set.

Many factors join the *Ragtime Dances* into a unified work, including the verse-chorus structure of each movement, thematic links, similar choruses, and the omission from all but the last chorus of the final note and chord of *Welcome Voice*, so that the first three movements end on the local dominant and sound incomplete. Taken as a whole, these four movements comprise a single form combining verse-refrain structure with cumulative setting, culminating in the most conclusive statement of the principal theme of the verses and in the contrapuntal combination of the verse and chorus themes.

Like Brahms and Mahler, Ives frequently reworked his own pieces into new forms. The *Ragtime Dances* and related works have one of the most complex histories of this sort.[94] Ives dated his first work on the set at 1902, and sketches toward two related works, *Drum Corps or Scuffle* and *Skit for Danbury Fair*, survive from about that time. Only one page of a full score survives for the *Ragtime Dances* (ca. 1907 or 1911?). About 1914, Ives revised them as the second and fourth movements of his First Piano Sonata. Together, these comprise a single scherzo that combines verse-refrain and cumulative form, with four verses (marked IIa, IIb, IVa, and IVb) divided in the middle by the slow third movement.[95] Around this time, he replaced the third of the four original dances with "a study in 'Rag' for 5s 3s & 2s together," a much more abstract composition linked to the other verses by a reference to the *Welcome Voice* refrain in its closing measures (mm. 48–51).[96] An ink and pencil manuscript of about 1919 restored the original third verse and switched the order of the first two; this was the basis for Sinclair's reconstruction of the *Ragtime Dances*. Meanwhile, Ives revised and orchestrated two of the dances for other works: movement IIb of the sonata, titled "In the Inn," as the middle movement of the *Set for Theater or Chamber Orchestra* (ca. 1914, rev. ca. 1923), and the third of the original dances, omitted from the sonata, as *The Rockstrewn Hills Join in the People's Outdoor Meeting*, the middle movement of the *Second Orchestral Set* (between ca. 1914 and 1929). The first of these adds a number of borrowed tunes and will be treated with collage in chapter 10, but the second merits consideration here.

The title of this movement suggests that Ives sought to reflect the spirit of outdoor revivals, though there is no specific program. The movement differs substantially from the earlier version, omitting some portions and adding several new sections. One significant change is that the opening motive of the refrain (the chorus of *Welcome Voice*, with an added neighbor-note figure) is hinted at and developed from the start (e.g., mm. 4–5, 9, 18, and 23–25 in the winds and mm. 25–27 in violin II) and appears as a prominent line at m. 127, long before the "Chorus" itself begins at m. 172. Thus, the refrain theme is treated in cumulative fashion, which does not occur in the *Ragtime Dances*. There are also some brief references to other tunes: a variant of *Welcome Voice* in the trumpet (mm. 77–82) seems to hint at "The Girl I Left Behind Me"; "Rock-a-bye Baby" (H132, by Effie I. Crockett) appears in the flute, clarinets, and piano over *Welcome Voice* in violin I (mm. 127–31); and a few notes of "Massa's in de Cold Ground" are hidden in trumpet I near the end (mm. 153–54).[97] Only the second of these is at all prominent, and the others may be unintended.

Cumulative Setting as a Thematic Form

The cumulative settings described above are a remarkable series of movements, all composed within a period of about twenty years. Each is unique in some respects, yet all follow similar procedures. Together they establish cumulative setting as a distinctive form with several subtypes.

Cumulative setting is a thematic form with a distinctive and predictable shape, like sonata, ternary, rondo, or variation form. Like these other forms, it is both sufficiently individual and sufficiently flexible to retain its identity while assuming many different shapes, including combinations with other forms such as ternary, variation, or verse-refrain form. The thematic development in Ives's cumulative settings differs little from nineteenth-century practice, involving fragmentation, variation, transposition, recombination, and other means of transformation. What is different is the order of events: the themes are presented at or near the end, preceded by their development. In general, the themes are borrowed or paraphrased from existing tunes, but it is the *themes* that are developed in the course of the work, not the borrowed tunes themselves (although some movements include fragments of the latter that do not appear in the themes). In this respect, Ives's cumulative settings are like his earlier movements based on paraphrased themes, in which it was also true that the themes, not the source tunes themselves, provided the material for subsequent development. Like the First String Quartet and the Second Symphony, Ives's cumulative settings are thematically and motivically coherent in themselves, without reference to the sources of the themes. All that has changed is the form.

CHAPTER 6

The Development
and Significance of
Cumulative Settings

The previous chapter established the formal paradigm for cumulative setting and delineated the various subtypes. Yet the definition of the
form is only half the story. Several important issues remain: Where did the
idea for cumulative setting originate? How did the form develop in Ives's
music? Did he invent it? What role do these movements play in the multi-
movement works of which they are a part? How does cumulative setting
relate to program music? With a sense of cumulative setting as a form, we are
now prepared to treat its sources and evolution, its role in Ives's music, and
its extramusical significance.

Just as in a cumulative setting the various constituents of the culminating
thematic complex are introduced one by one and gradually combined, so we
can trace through Ives's career the gradual confluence of the ideas upon

which his cumulative form is based, all of which have ample precedent in the music of earlier composers:

the very idea of setting a tune in new surroundings;

procedures of variation, paraphrase, and thematic transformation;

adding a countermelody to an existing tune;

presenting the countermelody before the tune itself;

combining in counterpoint in the coda of a movement in sonata or ternary form two main ideas that were originally presented separately, as a way of shifting the formal weight of the movement to the end;

eliminating the standard reprise, so that the final presentation of the two themes in counterpoint also serves as their restatement; and

foreshadowing the first appearance of an important theme with a variant, fragment, or gradual accumulation of the theme from its elements.

By combining these ideas in cumulative setting, Ives solved several problems at once. Cumulative form provided a new way to create an end-weighted movement in the sonata tradition. It avoided the large-scale repetition that weakened some movements of Ives's first two symphonies while preserving the tradition of developing variation and thematic transformation that he had inherited from nineteenth-century composers. As was mentioned in chapter 5, it solved the problem of working with vernacular tunes by using the very qualities that made them unsuitable as themes in sonata or ternary form, such as their regular periodicity, tonal simplicity, and repetitiveness, to provide stability and clarity at the end of a movement. By including his source tunes whole and preceding them with an elaborate development, Ives found a new significance for American hymn tunes within European art music. For those who knew the hymns, their texts and religious associations gave extramusical resonance to the music, while the musical structure remained independent of any program. Finally, in some works in this form, Ives found the progression from fragments to wholeness and from complexity to clarity that is typical of cumulative setting to be a perfect musical analogue for the sequence of events in a text or program.

Sources for Cumulative Setting

Perhaps the most basic source for cumulative setting was Ives's experience with more straightforward ways of setting a tune to a new accompaniment. Much of the music that he heard and played in his youth involved settings of tunes, from hymn harmonizations in church to transcriptions of popular airs for band or theater orchestra. If he made any such arrangements in his teens, they do not survive, although several variations in each of the two variation sets are little more than settings of the tune against a new accompaniment. What do survive are his marches and early experimental works, which include a number of settings of familiar tunes.

The experimental settings need only be briefly mentioned, for their use of borrowed material is quite simple: the tunes are presented without alteration, and only the accompaniment is changed. In these pieces, Ives used the simple format of placing a familiar tune in new surroundings to prove that the traditional rules of harmony and counterpoint are not the only ones that can establish a pitch center and convey tonal progress and resolution within a logical system.[1] One group explores polytonality through settings of "London Bridge" (H118) over chordal accompaniments in keys a half or whole step away from the key of the tune.[2] In another group, four brief interludes on *Nettleton, Bethany,* an unidentified tune, and *Woodworth,* one phrase of the hymn is played *mezzoforte* or *forte* in the pedals (coupled to the great) in the octave below middle C, accompanied in the treble by a stream of parallel chords of stacked major and minor thirds (e.g., D–F♯–A–C–E♭–G–B♭–D♭ over a D in the pedal), played very softly in the swell. These chords are so soft and lightly registered that they tend to sound like overtones, altering the perceived timbre of the fundamental pitch, rather than standing out as parallel dissonant chords.[3] Although these pieces hold great interest for later developments in Ives's harmonic procedures, what is most important about them in terms of his uses of existing music is that they foreshadow his later tendency to set off his tunes from their accompaniment more drastically than is typical in more traditional settings, such as a new harmonization of a hymn. Here, the accompaniments to "London Bridge" are set off by being placed in a different key and, in some cases, by rhythmic displacement as well. Similarly, the chords in the hymn interludes are at a distant dynamic level and suggest quite a different harmonic practice from the traditional tonality implied by the hymn tunes themselves. Several cumulative settings use similar effects, including the polytonal sections of the *Fugue in Four Keys on "The Shining Shore,"* the finale of the Second Violin Sonata, and "The Alcotts," and the combination of tonal tunes with largely atonal accompaniments in the first movement of the First Piano Sonata and *Adagio cantabile (The Innate).*

Marches with Borrowed Tunes

The most prevalent use of borrowed melodies in Ives's early music is in his marches. Ives no doubt became interested in writing marches through his father George, who had led a regimental band during the Civil War and later led a band in Danbury.[4] However, most of Ives's marches survive in versions not for band but for theater orchestra or simply for piano.

Sixteen marches survive in whole or large part from his years in Danbury and New Haven, including five that are reworkings of his own previous marches. Most follow the standard march form for the time, with a short introduction, first and second strains, and trio in a closely related key. There are a few variants: *Holiday Quickstep* has three strains, all in the same key; some marches have a "break" strain or interlude before or in the middle of the trio; and the *March "Intercollegiate"* repeats the first part of the march after the trio.

Of these sixteen marches, nine incorporate a popular tune as a principal melody, most often in the second strain. The tunes were familiar to Ives's audiences, as was the device of including a popular song in a newly composed march. Two other marches use parts of familiar tunes in their introductions, and five do not use popular tunes. The marches are listed by type in Table 6.1, with the tunes they borrow. Since some marches share similar titles and others exist in two or three quite different versions, each march is identified by its number in Kirkpatrick's *Catalogue*.[5]

The practice of incorporating a popular song as one of the strains in a march dates back at least to the mid-nineteenth century. Amateur brass bands sprang up throughout the United States soon after the development of valved brass instruments early in the century, and they often played pieces based on popular songs. Some were simple arrangements, like those of "The Star-Spangled Banner" and "Auld Lang Syne" in Allen T. Dodworth's *Brass Band School* (1853), one of the earliest and most influential of the manuals and collections published for the growing amateur market. Others were medley marches, with a different tune in each strain; Ives's one medley march, *March No. 1*, is of this type. But many marches included original material in addition to the popular song, which appeared verbatim or slightly embellished in one section, most often the trio. Examples appear in G. W. F. Friederich's *Brass Band Journal* (1853–55), including marches with Stephen Foster's "Ellen Bayne" and "Farewell, My Lilly Dear."[6] This was one of the most popular types of march from mid-century through the Civil War. Although marches based solely on original themes became increasingly common thereafter, marches incorporating popular tunes continued to be written and played into the early twentieth century. Even John Philip Sousa, better known for marches on original themes, continued the practice, beginning with his first march, *The Great Revival March and Salvation Army Rally* (1876), which uses in its trio the gospel hymn *In the Sweet Bye and Bye*. Of Sousa's one hundred thirty-six marches, twenty-four use existing tunes, not including those Sousa arranged from his own songs and operettas.[7] Thus,

TABLE 6.1: Ives's Marches and the Popular Tunes They Use

* countermelody introduced before tune

Tune in First or Second Strain, Presented Whole or Slightly Abbreviated

March No. 1 in F and B♭ for piano, 3B4 (ca. 1890–92)
>First strain: "The Year of Jubilee" (H145), verse, very freely paraphrased and with interpolations
>>in bass line
>>no countermelody
>
>Second strain: "That Old Cabin Home Upon the Hill" (H141), verse (without repeat) and chorus
>>in topmost melody, in long notes
* >>with countermelody in middle voice, introduced before tune

March No. 2 in C and F for piano (source fragmentary), 3B5 (ca. 1892–98)
>Second strain: "The Son of a Gambolier" (H135), probably complete
>>in bass line
>>with countermelody in upper voice

March No. 2 in F and B♭ for theater orchestra, 1C4 [revision of 3B5] (ca. 1892–98)
>Second strain: "The Son of a Gambolier" (H135), complete
>>in middle of texture (cornet and trombone)
>>with countermelody in upper voice (first violin, flute, and clarinet)

March No. 3 in F and C for theater orchestra, 1C6 (ca. 1892–98)
>Second strain: "My Old Kentucky Home" (H123) verse (without repeat) and chorus
>>in middle of texture (cornet and trombone)
* >>with countermelody in upper voice (first violin, flute, and clarinet), introduced before tune

March No. 5 or *March "Intercollegiate" in C and A♭* for band, 1D5 (ca. 1892, published 1896)
>Second strain: "Annie Lisle" (H95), verse (without repeat) and chorus
>>in middle of texture (trombones and baritone horn)
>>with countermelody in upper voice (cornets, clarinets, and piccolo)

March No. 5 in D and B♭ for piano, 3B10 [alternate version of 1D5] (ca. 1892–98)
>Second strain: "Annie Lisle" (H95), verse (with repeat)
>>in bass line
>>with countermelody in upper voice

Table 6.1, continued:

March in G and C for piano (incomplete; missing introduction and first strain), first (?) version of 3B13 (ca. 1892–98, closer to 1898)
Second strain: "Here's to Good Old Yale" ("Bingo," H148), first eight bars (A section)
   in topmost melody, in long notes
*   with countermelody in middle voice, introduced before tune

March No. 6 in G and D for piano, second (?) version of 3B13, with new second strain and trio (ca. 1892–98, closer to 1898)
First strain: "Here's to Good Old Yale" ("Bingo," H148), first eight bars (A section)
   in topmost melody, in long notes
   with countermelody in middle voice

March in F and C for band, 1D6 [revision of 3B6] (ca. 1892–98, closer to 1898)
Intro: "Omega Lambda Chi" (H156), first phrase, unison
First strain: "Omega Lambda Chi," twice through
   in bass line
   with one countermelody first time, two second time, in upper parts

Tune in Introduction, Partial or in Fragments

March in F and C for piano, 3B6 (ca. 1892)
Introduction: "Omega Lambda Chi" (H156), fragments with interpolations
   in bass line
   no countermelody

March in G and C for piano, 3B11 (ca. 1892–98, closer to 1898)
Introduction: "See the Conquering Hero," from Handel's *Judas Maccabaeus* (H181), opening eight-measure period, with interpolation (form: first phrase of Handel, new answer, first phrase repeats, new answer in treble in counterpoint with second phrase of Handel in bass — or A B A B+C)
   first phrase in melody, second phrase in bass line
   with walking bass under first phrase, counterpoint to second phrase in treble, introduced before tune's second phrase

No Borrowed Tune

Holiday Quickstep for theatre orchestra, 1C1 [third strain modeled on Reeves, *Second Regiment Connecticut National Guard March*] (1887)

March in F and C for theater orchestra (incomplete; missing introduction
and trio), 1C5 (ca. 1892–98)

March in G and D for piano, third version of 3B13 [revision of second (?)
version, with new first strain replacing "Here's to Good Old Yale"] (ca.
1892–98, closer to 1898)

March in F and C for theater orchestra (incomplete; missing latter part of
second strain and trio), 1C7 (ca. 1898)

March: "The Circus Band" for piano, 3B12 (ca. 1899)

Ives's use of popular tunes is far from unusual, although the preponderance
of such marches in his output is perhaps a bit old-fashioned.

Ives's usual procedure is to present the borrowed tune whole, sometimes
omitting internal repetitions. The tune is often slightly altered and in two
cases ("My Old Kentucky Home" and "Annie Lisle") is changed from duple
meter to $\frac{6}{8}$, but remains easily recognizable. The distant paraphrase of "The
Year of Jubilee" in *March No. 1,* discussed in chapter 3, is exceptional. In the
marches for piano, the tune appears either in the bass or in the topmost
melody, guaranteeing its prominence. When it is on top, as in the march
strains based on "That Old Cabin Home Upon the Hill" and "Here's to Good
Old Yale" ("Bingo"), the tune is in long notes, in the style of a cantus firmus,
with each measure of the march corresponding to one beat in the tune's original meter. In the versions for orchestra or band, the tune is usually stated in
octaves in the middle of the texture by prominent instruments such as trombone and cornet; in the band march with "Omega Lambda Chi," the tune is
in octaves in the bass line. Wherever the borrowed tune is, it does not perme-
ate the texture; the other parts do not imitate or develop motives from the
tune, which stands out as a foreign element against its accompaniment.

In most instances, the borrowed tune appears with a countermelody.
When the tune is in the top voice, the countermelody is in the middle of the
texture; otherwise, it is on top, acting as a descant. The countermelody usually moves more quickly than the tune itself. In featuring prominent countermelodies, Ives shows the influence of David Wallis Reeves (1838–1900), who
added countermelodies to the simple texture of melody and accompaniment
used in earlier marches and who has been called "the creator and first great
master of the modern, contrapuntal military march."[8] As we saw in chapter 2,
Reeves was one of Ives's favorite march composers and provided the model
for *Holiday Quickstep.*

Anticipating the Borrowed Tune with Its Countermelody

In three marches, marked by asterisks in Table 6.1, Ives introduces the "countermelody" *before* the tune it accompanies. In effect, the borrowed tune appears as a countermelody to Ives's original theme, although Ives's theme was conceived as a counterpoint to the given melody. In these marches, the borrowed tune appears in the second strain, which is not repeated (departing from the usual practice) and is three or four times as long as the usual sixteen measures. The second strain of each march is outlined in Table 6.2. In the march with "Here's to Good Old Yale," the same countermelody fits both halves of the tune's first period, creating a form of AA′A″ for the strain. But

TABLE 6.2: Marches in Which the Countermelody is Presented First

March No. 1 in F and B♭ for piano, 3B4
Tune used: "That Old Cabin Home Upon the Hill," verse (AA) and chorus (BA)
Form of second strain: 64 measures, AA′BA′
- A: countermelody a
- A′: verse (without repeat) + countermelody a
- B: 1st phrase of chorus + countermelody b
- A′: 2nd phrase of chorus + countermelody a

March No. 3 in F and C for theater orchestra, 1C6
Tune used: "My Old Kentucky Home," verse (A1 A2 A1 A3) and chorus (B A3)
Form of second strain: 48 measures, A1 A2 A1′ A2′ B A2′
- A1: countermelody a1
- A2: countermelody a2
- A1′: 3rd phrase of verse + countermelody a1
- A2′: 4th phrase of verse + countermelody a2
- B: 1st phrase of chorus + countermelody b
- A2′: 2nd phrase of chorus (equals 4th phrase of verse) + countermelody a2

March in G and C for piano, first (?) version of 3B13
Tune used: "Here's to Good Old Yale" ("Bingo") melody in ABA form (uses A section only)
Form of second strain: 48 measures, AA′A″
- A: countermelody a
- A′: 1st half of tune's A section + countermelody a
- A″: 2nd half of tune's A section + countermelody a

in the marches with "That Old Cabin Home Upon the Hill" and "My Old Kentucky Home," a new countermelody is used for the contrasting element of the tune.[9] Here Ives omits the tune's first phrase or period and instead introduces the main countermelody alone. As a result, the strain follows a form similar to that of the tune itself.

In at least one instance, the sketches show that stating the countermelody before the tune was an afterthought. The first sketch of the march with "My Old Kentucky Home" includes the borrowed tune in the bass clef with the countermelody in the treble, with chords indicated by Roman numerals between the staves. The sketch is in C major but is otherwise close to the final version, except that it lacks the initial statement of the countermelody alone. This proves what could be presumed from the music itself: that Ives's theme was conceived from the start as a countermelody to the existing tune and only later was given an independent presentation.[10]

Ives's song *A Son of a Gambolier*, adapted about 1920 from the first (piano) version of the march on this tune, uses a procedure similar to that of these three marches.[11] The borrowed tune first appears in the second strain, with a countermelody. The unusually long and complex trio begins with a thirty-two-measure first strain. A twenty-four-measure break strain leads to the repetition of the trio's first strain, now joined in counterpoint by two statements of "A Son of a Gambolier" in an instrumental line marked "Kazoo Chorus: Flutes, fiddles and flageolets" and, at the second statement, "add piccolos, ocarinas and fifes." The first statement of the tune is altered to end inconclusively, preparing the repetition, and both statements are somewhat varied. Then the break and final strains are repeated. This song is particularly interesting because it first introduces the borrowed tune in the second strain with a countermelody, then presents a new countermelody in the first strain of the trio, and ultimately combines the tune and new countermelody in the final strain.

One march features a related procedure on a smaller scale. The march with "See the Conquering Hero" from Handel's *Judas Maccabaeus* uses only the most recognizable element of the tune, its opening eight-measure period.[12] Both halves of the sixteen-measure introduction begin with the first phrase of the tune in the treble over a walking bass. The first time, Ives supplies a new answer; the second time, Handel's original second phrase appears in the bass, with Ives's answer as a countersubject in the treble.

This procedure of presenting a tune's countermelody before the tune itself is not original with Ives, but it appears to have no precedent in the march repertoire. Ives may have been inspired by examples in classical music, such as Bach's organ chorale on "Wachet auf, ruft uns die Stimme" BWV 645 (arranged from Cantata 140, fourth movement) and his setting of "Jesu, Joy of Man's Desiring" (from Cantata 147, part 1, closing movement). Examples of a similar procedure used for original themes include the finale of Beethoven's *Eroica* Symphony and his "Eroica" Variations for piano, Op. 35, both of which introduce and vary the bass line before presenting the theme it accompanies, and the slow movement of Beethoven's Seventh Symphony, in which the bass line and a countermelody are heard before the lyrical main theme is superimposed upon them.

Related Procedures in Later Works

Whatever its origins, the anticipation of the borrowed tune by its counter-melody became typical of Ives's later settings. It is a key part of cumulative settings with countermelodies, where the countermelody always appears before the theme itself. There are also several other works, not cumulative settings, in which a borrowed tune is stated for the first time near the end, preceded by its countermelody.

Two of these are quite simple in form, presenting the countermelody, then combining it with the tune, and ending with a short coda. The song *The Collection* (1920), based on George Kingsley's hymn tune *Tappan* (H56), may be adapted from an earlier work for church. In *Adeste Fideles in an Organ Prelude* (ca. 1897–99), the countermelody is an exact inversion of the hymn itself (H1).[13]

Two other works join this treatment of borrowed tune and countermelody with other formal procedures. *In the Night* (ca. 1914), the finale of the *Set for Theater Orchestra*, begins with a paraphrase of the chorus of Thomas P. Westendorf's "De Little Cabins All Am Empty Now" (H117) in the horn and concludes (at m. 11, reh. C) with the first six measures of William H. Monk's *Eventide* ("Abide with me") in the solo cello. The latter appears in counterpoint with the "Down in de cornfield" phrase from Foster's "Massa's in de Cold Ground" in the bells over ostinatos that sound throughout the piece.[14] The final section is a reworking of an earlier setting of *Eventide* over the same bass ostinato but without the other borrowed tunes. In its first form, as a Prelude for trombone, two violins, and organ (ca. 1899), *Eventide* is preceded by two measures of the ostinato as a vamp. A revision of this as a *Hymn-Anthem* for male chorus is lost.[15]

The finale of the Trio for violin, cello, and piano (ca. 1911) is a much longer movement in ternary form with coda. It is a reworking of Ives's song *The All-Enduring* (ca. 1896–1900) with new material interpolated.[16] In addition to a new introduction (mm. 1–12) and two short bridges based on it (mm. 41–45 and 126–29), this new material centers on two themes, called here for convenience X (mm. 46–57, in canon) and Y (mm. 68–76). These are presented, combined in paraphrased versions (mm. 83–90), and repeated as part of a *dal segno* reprise of mm. 6–76. In the coda that follows this reprise, theme Y reappears, slightly varied, in combination with Thomas Hastings's hymn tune *Toplady* (H60, "Rock of Ages"). Thus theme Y is revealed as a counter-melody for both *Toplady* and theme X.[17]

In these works, combining a borrowed tune with a theme that was heard before and is now being repeated helps to weave the tune more fully into the texture of the piece, making it sound less foreign and more like the logical result of what has preceded it. When the first statement of the tune coincides with the restatement of the countermelody, the tune's appearance becomes a strong point of arrival, a formal and contrapuntal climax. Ives's preference for preceding the full statement of the tune by its own development or by part of its accompaniment is evident in the small number of settings from after 1902 that do not use this idea: three songs adapted from cumulative settings, *His Exaltation*, *Watchman*, and *At the River*, and two simple song harmonizations, *Christmas Carol* by his daughter Edith (1925) and an anonymous black spiritual, *In the Mornin'* or *Give Me Jesus* (1929).[18]

Contrapuntal Combination in End-Weighted Movements

Ives was clearly interested in achieving strong endings through final sections that reach a peak of rhythmic density and contrapuntal complexity. Several movements introduce two or more themes in separate sections and combine them in counterpoint near the end, often in the coda. This procedure has long precedent, from the finales of Mozart's "Jupiter" Symphony, Beethoven's Ninth Symphony, and Berlioz's *Symphonie fantastique* through the symphonic works of Ives's teacher Horatio Parker.[19] Ives used this idea in the first movement of his First Symphony and the second movement of his Second, which are both in sonata form and combine in the coda elements of the first and second theme groups in counterpoint.

The first movement of Ives's "Pre-First" Violin Sonata (ca. 1907), perhaps his first work for the medium, extends this idea by hinting at a contrapuntal combination of the two main themes during the reprise of the first and then stating both together in the coda.[20] This is a fast ternary movement on paraphrased themes, with a brief piano introduction and longer coda. The first section theme (m. 12, violin) begins with the first two measures of the chorus to William G. Tomer's hymn tune *God Be with You* (H24) and continues with new material. The second section begins at m. 51 with a syncopated figure that seems to derive from the last phrase of "Tenting on the Old Camp Ground" by Walter Kittredge (H88, mm. 17–18), but its main material is from another Civil War song, George F. Root's "The Battle Cry of Freedom" (H71).

DEVELOPMENT AND SIGNIFICANCE

This song is in two-measure units in the form ABAB′CC′AB′, and the A and B′ motives are used here, introduced respectively by the violin at mm. 58–62 and by the piano in mm. 69–71. A bridge that mixes elements from both sections (m. 91) prepares the varied reprise of the first section at m. 99, where the theme is now accompanied by a figure adapted from the opening of "The Battle Cry of Freedom." The themes of the first and middle sections are linked even more closely in the coda. This begins with the first section theme shared by piano and violin (mm. 126–31), counterpointed by the "Tenting Tonight" figure and the opening segment of "The Battle Cry of Freedom." After further developing both motives from the latter song, the coda closes with a final reminder of the first section theme.

Here, as in his symphonies, it is clear how much Ives was heir to the Beethoven tradition of extended codas that shift the weight to the end of a movement and create a sense of forward motion and accomplishment rather than mere formal closure. The combination of the two main themes, together with an increase in activity and dynamic level, provides a strong climax in the coda. This is akin to the arrival of the theme and its countermelody in a cumulative setting, but it differs in one crucial aspect: one or both themes have already been recapitulated, so that the first return does not coincide with the combination of the two themes in counterpoint.

Although these movements in sonata and ternary forms rely on loud and busy codas to create an end-weighted quality, Ives also tried out forms that do so naturally by making the combination of themes simultaneous with their first reprise. The simple form of *The Collection* and *Adeste Fideles in an Organ Prelude*, which stated a melody and then united it in counterpoint with a familiar tune, was one such procedure. Another was the second strain and trio of *A Son of a Gambolier*, which presented the borrowed tune, then the countermelody, then both together. This form had precedents in popular music Ives might have known, such as the scene from *The Pirates of Penzance* (1879) in which the police prepare to attack the pirates: the Sergeant and his men admit their fears ("When the foeman bares his steel"); Mabel and the women urge them off to a glorious death ("Go, ye heroes!"); each strain repeats, varied and transposed; and finally the two melodies join in counterpoint, complete and in their original key. Similar numbers can be found in other Gilbert and Sullivan operettas and in those of John Philip Sousa, such as the choruses "Onward, patriotic son" in *El Capitan* (Boston, 1896) and "We cannot see the reason why" in *The Bride Elect* (New Haven, 1897), showing its currency in 1890s America.[21] Ives's most ambitious early work to combine two themes contrapuntally at their reprise is the First Symphony, in which the middle-section theme of the second movement accompanies the return of the first section, acting as a countermelody to the opening theme. This moment may have been modeled in part on a passage in the slow movement of Dvořák's "New World" Symphony, in which the reprise of the principal theme is anticipated by combining its opening motive with ideas from the first movement (see chapter 4). But Ives may also have been following the lead of pieces that more closely parallel his procedure, such as the Prelude to Wagner's *Tristan und Isolde*, in which the reprise of the opening material is accompanied by a motive from the second main idea, interjected between the phrases. Finally, two works that do not use borrowed themes are entirely based on this idea of contrapuntal accumulation. The first movement of the Trio for violin, cello, and piano (ca. 1914) presents a passage for cello and piano right hand, then a passage for violin and piano left hand, and then combines them, for a form that might be diagrammed A B A+B.[22] *Halloween* (ca. 1911), for string quartet and piano, is played several times, louder and faster each time: the first time, only second violin and cello play their parts; the second time, first violin and viola only; the third time, all strings with only the outer notes of the piano chords; the fourth time, all strings, full piano, and optional drum, ending with a coda.[23]

All of these are rudimentary cumulative forms, in which the definitive statement of the entire contrapuntal complex appears only at the end, after a gradual accumulation of elements. This is a fundamental idea behind Ives's cumulative settings, an idea he first explored in his marches and later tried out in other formats. But Ives was apparently unsatisfied with contrapuntal combination alone as a device for achieving forward motion to a point of arrival near the end of a movement. If all the elements have been heard before, as in the first movement of the Trio, the ending can feel static and reiterative instead of climactic. Yet if they have *not* all been heard, or at least hinted at, it is impossible to anticipate the climax or to know what to expect, making the progress of the piece seem arbitrary. The climax of *Halloween* is satisfying, but other climaxes would be equally satisfying, and there is nothing to prevent yet another repetition, still faster and louder, with trumpets and firecrackers added. Whatever his reasons, Ives did not use this simple additive format very often and abandoned it after *Halloween*. In his full-fledged cumulative settings, he combines this procedure of contrapuntal combination with techniques of development derived from European music that lend an even greater sense of forward momentum and ultimate arrival at a long-awaited goal.

European Precedents for Cumulative Form

The most crucial procedure in a cumulative setting is the presentation of fragments or paraphrases of the main theme before the theme itself. This idea is foreign to most eighteenth-century forms but has a significant place in the chorale settings of Bach and in the nineteenth-century tradition leading from Beethoven. Three particular procedures that contribute to cumulative setting are the paraphrase or variation of a melody before it is stated in its original form; the anticipation of a melody in fragments before it is stated in full; and the gradual accumulation of a theme or motive from its elements.

In *Variations on "America,"* Ives prefaces the theme with an introduction that paraphrases the theme. An early parallel may be found in the Bach chorale settings that anticipate each phrase of the chorale with a point of imitation based on that phrase in diminution, such as the chorale prelude *Vor deinen Tron tret' ich hiermit (Wenn wir in höchsten Nöten sein)* BWV 668. Two organ chorales, *Wer nur den lieben Gott lässt walten* BWV 690 and *Fantasia super Christ lag in Todesbanden* BWV 695, follow a setting of the chorale tune in paraphrase against a contrapuntal background with a simple statement over basso continuo, perhaps reflecting the practice of playing an elaborate prelude before the congregation sings the chorale. This type of structure, whether written out or resulting from performing tradition, may have suggested Ives's typical procedure of ending with a full, relatively simple statement of the hymn. Similarly, the progression in Bach's Cantata 4 (*Christ lag in Todesbanden*) from chorale paraphrases in the early movements to a simple harmonization of the chorale at the end resembles in some ways the gradual emergence of *Need* in the Third Violin Sonata finale, although Bach's series of variations differs in form and approach from the thematic development within a single movement typical of Ives's cumulative settings.

We have already seen that another element of cumulative setting, the presentation of a countermelody alone before the borrowed tune appears with it, also has a precedent in Bach's chorale settings. Since almost all of Ives's cumulative settings are based on hymns and in many cases are adapted from organ works he played in church, these parallels with Bach may be more than coincidental. Perhaps the Bach chorale settings suggested some of Ives's procedures. Chorale or hymn settings by nineteenth-century composers may also have served Ives as models. One that he played, the first movement of Mendelssohn's Organ Sonata No. 1 in F Minor, Op. 65, No. 1, introduces the chorale only after a long opening section, and it becomes the most prominent melody only in the last third of the movement.[24] This is like Ives's typical pattern in some ways, although it differs in presenting the chorale before varying it. As mentioned in chapter 5, Ives may also have been influenced by the tradition among church organists of ending an improvised prelude on motives drawn from a hymn tune with a complete statement of the tune. However, this practice cannot be the only source for Ives's cumulative settings. His procedure of presenting a countermelody whole earlier in the prelude and then joining it with the hymn at the end is hard to improvise and is not part of the improvisatory tradition. The great length of Ives's cumulative settings, in comparison to the usual hymn prelude, and his practice of using the form as the basis of movements in sonatas and symphonies, outside of church, also suggest that Ives had other influences besides improvised preludes.[25]

Later parallels to Ives's procedures can be found in two French symphonic works of the late nineteenth century. Like the *Variations on "America,"* Franck's *Variations symphoniques* (1885) begins with an introduction that paraphrases its main themes. The gradual process of clarification typical of Ives's cumulative settings, and especially of the "reverse variation form" in the second movement of the Fourth Violin Sonata, is anticipated in d'Indy's tone poem *Istar* (1896). This is a set of variations on a theme that does not appear in its simplest, unison form until the end of the work, and each successive variation hints more strongly of the theme to come. Ives admired both Franck and d'Indy, and by the time he began to compose cumulative settings in the early 1900s he may have been aware of these relatively recent works, which were first performed in the United States in 1898.[26]

A number of nineteenth-century works foreshadow a theme or present it in part before stating it whole. The finales of Beethoven's Ninth Symphony and Berlioz's *Symphonie fantastique* quote the opening of the main theme before it appears in full. Chopin's Third Impromptu, Op. 51, and *Polonaise-Fantasie*, Op. 61, both arrive at their first real theme after preliminary development of some of its motives.[27] Many slow introductions, such as those to Schumann's Fourth Symphony and Tchaikovsky's *Pathétique* Symphony, allude to the initial motive of the following theme. In works that use thematic transformation, from Liszt tone poems to Wagner's *Ring*, it is not uncommon for fragments of a theme to anticipate the theme itself. For instance, the Transfiguration theme in Richard Strauss's *Death and Transfiguration* (1888–89) is anticipated several times before its definitive appearance near the end. In the first movement expositions of both Dvořák's "New World" Symphony and Ives's First Symphony part of the second theme appears in the transition that precedes it (see chapter 4). Dvořák's *Husitská (Hussite Overture)*, Op. 67 (1883), presents and develops fragments of two Czech hymn tunes in its slow introduction and states the hymns more fully (though not complete) as subsidiary themes in the following exposition. Franck's *Prélude, choral et fugue* for piano (1884) combines the foreshadowing of a theme with the presentation of its countermelody before the theme itself; the fugue subject is hinted at in the two previous sections, and the chorale theme from the middle section returns at the end of the fugue in counterpoint with the fugue subject.

DEVELOPMENT AND SIGNIFICANCE

In each of these cases, the melody that is anticipated is subsequently repeated and developed as a theme. Closer to Ives's typical practice of fore-shadowing a borrowed tune that is stated only once are two works of Schumann. A quotation from Beethoven's song cycle *An die ferne Geliebte* near the end of the first movement of Schumann's Piano Fantasy in C Major, Op. 17, is prepared by numerous gestures that have a similar shape.[28] In *Die beiden Grenadiere*, Op. 49, No. 1, the vocal melody repeatedly hints at the opening notes of "La Marseillaise" and then uses its first few phrases, somewhat reworked, in the climactic final section.

There are several symphonic works in which a theme gradually accumulates from its elements. This is closer to Ives's cumulative settings than is the simple foreshadowing of a theme. An early and simple example is the opening of the finale of Beethoven's First Symphony, in which the rising scale that begins the theme is introduced note by note—the first three notes; after a pause, the first four; then five, six, and seven notes, each time slightly faster—until the full octave scale launches the theme. Far more complex is the Ninth Symphony, in which, as Maynard Solomon has shown, the "Ode to Joy" theme is prefigured by melodic ideas of similar shape in all movements and thus functions as "the culmination of a series of melodies aspiring to achieve an ultimate, lapidary form."[29] In the third movement of Tchaikovsky's *Pathé-tique* Symphony, the main theme appears complete at m. 71 (reh. H), only after its principal elements have been presented and developed, its opening melodic and rhythmic motive at mm. 9–10 and the descending scale (mm. 77–78) at m. 45 (two after reh. E). In Mahler's First Symphony, the first movement development begins with a passage in which a new theme in the cellos slowly grows from fragments (just after reh. 12) through incomplete variants to its complete form some fifty measures later (four before reh. 16). This resembles some of Ives's procedures, and Ives may have known the work after its American premiere in 1909 under Mahler himself.

In all these cases, once the themes are introduced they are treated as normal themes in forms based on thematic repetition. Ives's cumulative form differs from these in its non-repetitive structure: once the theme appears complete, in most cases, the movement is over. More like Ives's procedure is the first movement of Sibelius's Second Symphony (1901–2), in which thematic fragments introduced in the exposition coalesce into a broad melody in the development; this is not repeated, although there is an abbreviated recapitulation. One work that avoids large-scale repetition, though probably too late to have served Ives as a model, is the third movement of Sibelius's Fourth Symphony (1911). This is a full-fledged cumulative form whose main theme emerges more clearly, completely, and emphatically with each statement until its final climactic appearance.[30]

Perhaps the work that is most similar to Ives's approach is Smetana's *Tábor* (1878), the fifth movement of *Má vlast*, which is based on a Hussite chorale, *Ktož jsú boži bojowníci* ("Ye who are God's warriors").[31] In the Lento introduction, the chorale is introduced and developed by segments (mm. 3, 25, 59–61, and 63–66 introduce all but the last phrase, and other passages develop what has preceded them) until the entire chorale appears, slightly altered, at the end of the slow section (mm. 87–103). The ensuing Molto vivace uses themes based on motives adapted from the chorale (such as the figures in mm. 108–9, 128–29, 134–36, 184, and 234–35), and at the climax the chorale is stated with maximum force in its pure form (mm. 332–45). In effect, both the slow introduction and the fast main body of the movement are cumulative in form. Despite its strong similarities to Ives's cumulative settings, there is no indication that Ives knew this work; he never mentioned Smetana or showed familiarity with his music.

Many other compositions might also be cited here. Whether or not any of these served Ives as models, it is clear that the idea was very much in the air of a movement or passage in which "the working-out develops into the themes, rather than from them."[32] This idea, in Ives's music as in that of his European counterparts, drew on the general interest in the nineteenth century in thematic transformation and in shifting weight toward the end of a work.

Yet Ives's cumulative settings still seem to be unique. Of the works listed here in which a theme is anticipated by fragments or variants, in none is the complete appearance of that theme accompanied with a countermelody, as is Ives's usual practice, and only Franck's *Prélude, choral et fugue* uses a countermelody at all. Nor do the works cited earlier in which a theme is preceded by its countermelody, such as Bach's organ chorale on *Wachet auf* (BWV 645) and the slow movement of Beethoven's Seventh Symphony, anticipate the theme motivically. Ives seems alone in combining the two ideas.

Moreover, Ives is by far the most consistent composer to use these procedures in his or any preceding generation. Although the works cited above are exceptional within the outputs of their respective composers, settings in cumulative form make up the largest group of Ives's compositions in the traditional genres of sonata and symphony in the period 1907–19, and more than two dozen of his surviving works use this form. It is no exaggeration to say that cumulative setting replaced sonata and ternary forms as the principal formal paradigm for Ives's instrumental music after the Second Symphony.

The many precedents in Ives's music, from his marches to the finales of the First String Quartet and Second Symphony, show that cumulative setting was the solution to a problem with which Ives had struggled for years: how to write a movement based on borrowed material with the developmental intensity of sonata form, but with the formal weight shifted to the end and without lengthy repetition that could weaken the second half of the movement. The many solutions that he attempted and the wide variety of sources on which he may have drawn suggest that there was no single model for Ives's form. Rather, he seems to have woven together several threads from the tradition into a new, naturally end-weighted form that goes beyond any of his models.

The Development and Role of Cumulative Setting

If Ives invented cumulative setting as a distinctive form, drawing on precedents in chorale settings, the symphonic tradition, and his own earlier works, it should be possible to trace the development of the form in his music. Unfortunately, the chronology of Ives's works is uncertain, and many are missing. Many of his cumulative settings were worked on over several years, and the dates Ives gave to them often predate the extant sketches, suggesting that there may have been earlier versions that were worked out by memory at the keyboard or were lost or discarded once replaced by later drafts. He often based new works on pieces composed years earlier, many of which do not survive; in such cases, it is impossible to tell which aspects of the later piece are shared with the earlier one and which are new. This includes the fundamental issue of whether the earlier composition was in cumulative form or was simply a source of themes and ideas for the later work. With all these difficulties, a detailed and dependable chronology is impossible. Yet the broad outlines of an orderly development can be discerned. There are two aspects to consider: the individual movements that use this form, and the multi-movement cycles of which they are a part.

The Development of Cumulative Settings

According to Ives, a number of his cumulative settings were adapted from works composed and performed in 1897 or 1901: the organ *Prelude* and *Postlude for a Thanksgiving Service* (November 1897), combined and reworked in *Thanksgiving*; a sonata for trumpet and organ (January 1901), used in the first movement of the Fourth Violin Sonata; an organ toccata (May 1901), the prototype of the middle movement of the Third Violin Sonata; two organ preludes (November 1901), early versions of the other two movements of that sonata; and a prelude and a piece for a communion service (June and December 1901), revised as the first and final movements of the Third Symphony.[33] None of these works survive. We know of their existence only through Ives's comments on the works that he later adapted from them and one page of a copy from around 1899 of the Thanksgiving *Postlude*. Yet there is reason to believe that the others existed as well. All these movements of the Third Symphony and Third and Fourth Violin Sonatas are tonal and relatively consonant, despite innovations in harmony, and this, together with their relative simplicity and clarity, distinguishes them stylistically from the other cumulative settings and from other works composed after the Second Symphony; this may suggest an origin in earlier music. Their use of hymn tunes links them to church services, as does their form to the tradition of improvised preluding before a hymn. Indeed, transcribed for organ, these movements would be marvelously suited for church performance.

However, without copies of the earlier works, it cannot be assumed that they were in the form of fully developed cumulative settings. Indeed, for at least two of them, there is manuscript evidence that the countermelody, a crucial part of the form, was not devised until much later. A draft for the end of *Thanksgiving*, written between about 1907 and about 1914, shows *Federal Street* as the main tune, with a countermelody paraphrased from *Shining Shore*; the third phrase of *Federal Street* was then replaced by the third phrase of *Duke Street* to create a new theme. In later drafts, this theme became the countermelody, *Duke Street* became the theme, and the melody based on *Shining Shore* was dropped.[34] The earliest sketch toward the Third Symphony finale, on paper not available before 1907 and in a hand of around 1908–9, shows two settings of *Woodworth* in the same key and register as it appears at the end of the movement; the first setting features a free descant, replaced in the second by the countermelody based on *Azmon* in a form close to the final version.[35] Since the countermelodies were created only after about 1907, the thematic content of the organ works on which these movements were based must have been different, and it is reasonable to assume that the form may have been different as well.

Ives hinted that at least some of the earlier works were only settings of the borrowed hymn tunes, not cumulative settings. This seems to have been true of the song *Watchman* (1901), later reworked as the theme of the middle section of the First Violin Sonata finale. The clearest suggestion that this might also have been true of one of the organ works is a memo on the ink manuscript of the Third Violin Sonata finale, where Ives wrote that the movement was "finished as is 1914, last 2 pages from about [m. 180] from an organ piece & played in C. P. Ch. [Central Presbyterian Church] NY 1902."[36] It may be that the organ piece comprised only this final segment, and the earlier sections were added later; a similar process of expansion forward can be seen in *In the Night* (discussed above), where Ives added a new first section to a Prelude for trombone, two violins, and organ from about 1899. The portion of

DEVELOPMENT AND SIGNIFICANCE

the Third Violin Sonata finale that Ives identifies as coming from the organ piece—the last fifth of the movement—moves from stating fragments of the theme and later the countermelody to a complete presentation of the two together. If this is all that was in the organ prelude, it had much of the shape of a cumulative setting but was not fully developed. Perhaps some of these organ works had a rudimentary cumulative form, as does the one surviving prelude from this period, on *Adeste fideles* (ca. 1897–99). But there is no evidence, nor any strong indication, that these works of 1901 and earlier were full-fledged cumulative settings.

Without these earlier works, and without earlier drafts of the surviving works, the first stages of Ives's development of the form cannot be known. But if the surviving manuscripts include the first complete, written drafts of each work, a logical chronology can be traced. The first extant cumulative setting is the *Fugue in Four Keys on "The Shining Shore"* from about 1902, an experiment in form as well as in polytonal counterpoint and the melodic blending of related tunes. It may have remained a unique experiment until about 1907 or 1908, when Ives wrote *Adagio cantabile (The Innate)* and the orchestral version of the *Ragtime Dances* and began work on the outer movements of the Third Symphony, which were probably finished by 1909 and copied by 1911. Around the same time, he began the first movements of the First and Second Violin Sonatas and the First Piano Sonata, which were finished by about 1914. This first group includes five cumulative settings of the most common type, with countermelody, and one each of the types with a partial countermelody (First Piano Sonata, first movement), without countermelody (*Adagio cantabile*), and with a blend of cumulative setting and verse-refrain form (*Ragtime Dances*). The years around 1914 produced many cumulative settings of all five types, including all movements of the Third and Fourth Violin Sonatas, the First Violin Sonata finale, the revision of the *Ragtime Dances* as the second and fourth movements of the First Piano Sonata, the third movement of that sonata, the song *General William Booth Enters into Heaven* (discussed below), "The Alcotts," and the first versions of the Second Violin Sonata finale, *Thanksgiving*, and *The Fourth of July* (discussed in chapter 10). Two works round out the roster of Ives's cumulative settings: *From Hanover Square North* (ca. 1915–19, rev. ca. 1929, discussed below) and the Fourth Symphony finale (ca. 1919–23 with later revisions, discussed in chapter 10).

Cumulative Settings in the Context of Multi-Movement Cycles

There were three main stages in the evolution of the cumulative setting: initial exploration in individual movements; finding a place for the form in the multi-movement works Ives wrote after the Second Symphony; and the emergence of cumulative setting as the standard form for his concert works of the 1910s. Perhaps the crucial step was Ives's use of cumulative settings to replace his earlier practice for weighty movements in multi-movement genres: a ternary or sonata form on paraphrased themes with a climax in the coda, often created by combining the two main themes in counterpoint. In Ives's "Pre-First" Violin Sonata and Third Symphony, we can trace the process of change from one paradigm to the next.

"Pre-First" Violin Sonata (ca. 1906–10)

Ives's first attempt at a violin sonata is notable, not because it was a success, but because of the way it was a failure. Ives was never able to put it into satisfactory form, and he eventually abandoned it, moving most of the movements once planned for it into other works. The main issue seems to have been the sonata's coherence as a multi-movement cycle, for two of the five movements originally written for it were replaced or rejected, and as a group these five movements represent a jumble of different forms, keys, sources for themes, and approaches to musical borrowing.

The first movement (ca. 1907), in C major, was described above as a fast ternary movement on paraphrased themes that ends with a climactic coda in which the two main themes are combined in counterpoint. The first-section theme uses part of the hymn *God Be with You*, and the middle section draws on portions of two Civil War songs, "Tenting Tonight" and "The Battle Cry of Freedom." The original second movement (ca. 1906–7), a slow ternary form in G with a faster middle section, is not based on paraphrased themes; since all the other movements composed for this sonata use themes drawn from vernacular music, perhaps Ives removed this movement because it seemed too unlike the others to work with them in a multi-movement cycle, despite similarities of style.[37] The new second movement, composed ca. 1908–9 and later used as the middle movement of the First Violin Sonata, has a similar shape but uses themes based on vernacular songs: in the outer sections, George Kiallmark's 1822 popular song "The Old Oaken Bucket" (also known as "Araby's Daughter," H96) in D, and in the middle section, George F. Root's Civil War song "Tramp, Tramp, Tramp" (H89) in F.[38] Ives began a scherzo movement for this sonata about 1907, using a theme in the style of fiddle tunes and directly borrowing parts of three traditional dance tunes, "Sailor's Hornpipe" (or "College Hornpipe," H161), "Money Musk" (H166), and "The White Cockade" (H171). Whether Ives intended this as the final movement or the third of four is not clear, but the key of the opening section is again C major. He seems not to have finished the movement before deciding not to include it in this sonata; he

DEVELOPMENT AND SIGNIFICANCE

reworked it sometime between 1914 and 1919 as the second movement of the Second Violin Sonata, incorporating passages from the *Ragtime Dances* and the first movement of the "Pre-First" Sonata as well. The last movement of the "Pre-First" Sonata to be begun was the finale. This is a cumulative setting of *Autumn* in A major, perhaps begun about 1910, that was later revised as the first movement of the Second Violin Sonata.[39]

Ives was clearly concerned with the coherence of the "Pre-First" Sonata, but he seems never to have solved the problem to his satisfaction. The original three movements (counting the rejected scherzo as the third) had a logical key scheme of C–G–C, but the new second and final movements, in D and A, do not fit any scheme.[40] The original second movement, which did not use borrowed material, seems to have been too different from the others. Its replacement relates more directly to the first movement, as both include a theme based on a Civil War tune, and the tunes are melodically related. The combination of a hymn with Civil War songs in the first movement—which seems an odd mixture of musical types—may be explained motivically, for they share a similar rising arpeggiation. But the hymn tune in the finale is related more distantly, if at all, and the fiddle tunes in the scherzo are more distant still. Neither the type of music used nor the motivic relationships between these specific tunes gives coherence to the work as a whole, which ends up sounding like a suite with movements of quite disparate character.

Beyond the keys and the character of the themes, Ives also may have been dissatisfied with the balance between the movements in the way they use their material. Because the first movement's opening theme uses only two measures of the hymn tune before continuing with original material, there are long stretches of the first and third sections in which no borrowed material appears. By contrast, both the new second and the third movements are saturated with borrowed material. In retrospect, the gulf between the two approaches may have seemed too large.

Finally, the forms of the opening allegro and the finale are dissimilar, making this work unlike Ives's previous multi-movement cycles. The first movement is one of several in which two contrasting themes are introduced separately and ultimately combined in counterpoint. The other opening allegro movements in which Ives had used this idea—the first movement of the First Symphony and the second movement (the first allegro) of the Second Symphony—were in sonata form and were balanced at the end by sonata-form finales that found other ways to create climactic codas. In the First String Quartet, the second movement (again, the first allegro, after the opening fugue) is in ternary form, with an extensive coda that includes a complete paraphrase of the chorus of *Beulah Land*, the source for the principal theme. This is balanced by a ternary-form finale whose coda presents a complete statement of *Webb*, a source for the first theme, in counterpoint with the middle-section theme. In all three works, the slow middle movements, like both middle movements composed for the "Pre-First" Sonata, are in ternary form without large codas, and the outer fast movements are consistently parallel in form. Given this pattern, one would expect the "Pre-First" Sonata to conclude with a ternary-form movement with varied reprise and a long coda, like the first movement. Instead, the finale is in cumulative form.

Ives's choice of this form for his finale and the parallels in structure between this sonata and his earlier multi-movement cycles confirm that cumulative setting was essentially a replacement for his earlier custom of writing movements in ternary or sonata form with extensive paraphrase or contrapuntal combination of themes in their codas. In particular, it was the next logical step after the finales of the First String Quartet and the Second Symphony, in which the coda includes a complete statement of a borrowed tune that has been foreshadowed in the previous music, in counterpoint with a major theme now revealed as its countermelody. These movements differ from cumulative form primarily in preserving a complete reprise of the first section or exposition before the full borrowed tune is heard in the coda. Moving from this type of form to cumulative setting solved the problem Ives had been wrestling with for years: how to create an end-weighted movement with sonata-style development and without excessive repetition. However, in the "Pre-First" Violin Sonata, it created a new problem on the level of the three-movement work, for it left the first movement more closely matched in form to the second, which was also in ternary form, than to the finale, as had been Ives's consistent practice. This appears to have been the difficulty that led Ives to disassemble the sonata after its completion and to incorporate individual movements into other works.

Third Symphony ("The Camp Meeting," *ca. 1907–11*)

The solution to the problem posed above is simple: use cumulative setting in the first and last movements and include a middle movement in ternary form. Indeed, this is the shape of the Third Symphony, begun during work on the "Pre-First" Violin Sonata and completed and scored by about 1911.

The outer movements are described in chapter 5. The middle movement, "Children's Day," is a fast ternary form on paraphrased themes. This is the standard pattern in Ives's earlier instrumental music based on hymns, and in fact this movement was begun about 1907, before the outer movements.[41] The first section is in E♭ major and combines the hymn tune *Naomi*, stated in augmentation as a cantus firmus, with a theme based on a continuous spinning out of motives from *Fountain* (H23, "There is a fountain filled with blood"), using mm. 1–4 with *Naomi* and mm. 6–8 thereafter (at mm.

DEVELOPMENT AND SIGNIFICANCE

32–49). The faster middle section opens with a theme paraphrased from *There Is a Happy Land* (H57).[42] The second half of the hymn (mm. 9–16) appears first, in B♭ (flute alternating with violin I, mm. 50–53); the flute in m. 52 alters mm. 13–14 of the hymn to resemble a figure found in m. 3 of *Fountain* and m. 1 of *Erie*, yielding a passing reminiscence of the first section of the movement and the first movement of the symphony (whose countermelody is based on *Erie*). After an extension, the first half of *There Is a Happy Land* appears paraphrased (mm. 59-62), alternating between lower strings in D major and upper strings in F. An echo of the hymn's last phrase in the horn (mm. 64–66) is accompanied in the winds by a segment of George F. Root's popular song "There's Music in the Air" (H142, mm. 13–14), part of a theme begun in the first violin in m. 62. A fugato and a marchlike figure lead to a repetition and then further development of the middle-section themes.[43]

The reprise of the first section (m. 120) begins in A major, a tritone from the original key, but moves back to E♭ for the second half of *Naomi* and the accompanying part of the theme based on *Fountain*. The last part of the first section, based on mm. 6–8 of *Fountain*, is replaced at m. 150 by a coda in which all of *Fountain* appears in paraphrase, overlapping itself and with many repetitions and reorderings (mm. 1–4 of *Fountain* appear in strings and brass in mm. 150–53; mm. 5–16 in violin I in mm. 150–68). Mixed into the coda are fragments of the middle-section theme based on *There Is a Happy Land* (mm. 161–65 and 169–76, upper winds and strings), recalling the combination of themes from the first and middle sections in the first movement coda of the "Pre-First" Violin Sonata. As in the second movement of the First String Quartet, the complete paraphrase of the source tune in the coda does not make this a cumulative setting but rather rounds out a movement in a clear ternary form.

The Third Symphony is satisfactory in all the ways that the "Pre-First" Sonata was not. The key structure is logical: the first movement centers on B♭ with an episode in E♭ and closes in F; the second movement is in E♭, with a central section beginning in B♭; and the finale is in B♭, passing through E♭ and F. The level of musical borrowing is consistent, with all three movements infused with borrowed material in almost every measure. The forms of the first and final movements are parallel. The unusual tempo sequence, with two slow movements framing a fast middle movement, may have resulted in part from this concern for balance, for it seems to have been primarily in slow hymn settings, such as the *Fugue in Four Keys*, *Adagio cantabile*, and the outer movements of this symphony, that cumulative form was worked out.

Most importantly, this symphony shows Ives's continued interest in the cyclic unification of multi-movement works, already evident in his First String Quartet and first two symphonies. The motivic links between *Erie*,

Fountain, and *There Is a Happy Land* have already been noted, but there are even stronger ties between the outer movements. *Woodworth,* the main theme of the finale, appears in part in the first movement, while *Azmon,* the first movement's main theme, is the source of the finale's countermelody, whose opening motive is present from the beginning of the first movement. In addition, *Naomi,* used as a cantus firmus in the middle movement, is melodically very similar to the opening phrase of *Woodworth.* When *Woodworth* appears complete at the end of the finale, it harks back to its incomplete appearance in the first movement and to the related tune *Naomi* in the second; in this sense, there is a kind of cumulative setting operating over the whole three-movement work, drawing it into a tighter unity.[44]

Alternative Paths Not Taken: The Trio and the Three-Page Sonata

Around the same time as the Third Symphony, Ives tried other approaches to form in the Trio for violin, cello, and piano (ca. 1911–14) and the *Three-Page Sonata* for piano (between 1907 and 1914).[45] As noted above, the first movement of the Trio is an additive form (A B A+B), without apparent borrowings, and the finale is a long ternary form on original themes, with a coda in which a theme heard earlier is combined with *Toplady* ("Rock of Ages"). The middle movement, Ives's most extensive quodlibet, is discussed in chapter 10. All three movements are highly developed examples of forms that Ives rarely or never used again. *The Three-Page Sonata,* in three connected movements, is equally anomalous. It has been described by H. Wiley Hitchcock as an "anti-sonata."[46] Its first movement resembles a sonata exposition (repeated) and development without recapitulation. The thematic material is based largely on the BACH motive (B♭–A–C–B), which also plays a role in the later movements.[47] The slow second movement is in two sections, Andante and Adagio, over gradually descending arpeggiated triads in the bass; the Adagio repeats and varies two motives from *Westminster Chimes,* and the Andante may draw on this or other tunes.[48] The finale mixes march, waltz, and ragtime figures, none apparently based on existing melodies, in a modified ternary form in which part of the middle section replaces part of the reprise. This can be summarized as below.[49]

A1 A2 A3 A4 A5   B1 B2   A1′ A2 A3 B2 A5   Codetta

This form joins the first and second sections together in a blended reprise, as does the first movement of the Trio, but it does so by interpolating part of the second section into the first rather than by playing both at once. This is a less revolutionary idea, going back at least to Beethoven's string quartets.

Both the Trio and the *Three-Page Sonata* are clearly attempts to find new solutions to the problem of musical form in extended works. But both explore paths that Ives was not to pursue further. It was the Third Symphony that provided the pattern for future multi-movement works.

The Violin Sonatas

Having solved the formal problem of using cumulative settings in multi-movement works in the Third Symphony, Ives returned to the violin sonata around 1914. At about that time, he revised two earlier movements, one in cumulative form; wrote eight new cumulative settings for the medium, some based on earlier works in other media; and assembled the First, Third, and Fourth Violin Sonatas. Over the next five years, he revised one of the new cumulative settings and two movements from the "Pre-First" Sonata to create the Second Violin Sonata. These four sonatas form a consistent group, yet each is individual in character.[50] All are in three movements, adopting either the traditional fast-slow-fast pattern (in the First and Fourth Sonatas) or the slow-fast-slow pattern Ives had tried out in the Third Symphony and would use again in most of his later three-movement sets (including the Second and Third Violin Sonatas). The first two sonatas follow the pattern of the Third Symphony in placing two cumulative settings around a middle movement in another form, and the Third and Fourth consist entirely of cumulative settings of various types.

Among the cumulative settings, the first and last movements of the First Sonata are each unique in significant ways (as discussed in chapter 5), the first for its reprise of the slow introduction at the end, the finale for its double cumulative form. The slow middle movement, written as the second try at a second movement for the "Pre-First" Sonata (described briefly above), is a fantasia in ternary form on two borrowed tunes. The first section theme (mm. 1–9) is paraphrased from "The Old Oaken Bucket," specifically from the four-measure phrase used as the chorus and as the first, second, and fourth phrases of the verse. The whole phrase is paraphrased in D major at the outset (the first half in the violin, mm. 1–2, the remainder in the piano, mm. 2–3) and is subsequently varied and developed, passing through several keys. The faster middle section (mm. 30–68) presents portions of the Civil War song "Tramp, Tramp, Tramp," first introduced in the piano in m. 30 as the violin concludes a variant of the first section theme, then taken up by the violin in F at m. 40. The section closes as the violin spins out these ideas while the piano turns back to motives from the first section (mm. 58ff.). A return to the opening tempo, meter, and key in m. 69 marks a varied reprise of the movement's opening theme. Another repetition of the phrase from "The Old Oaken Bucket" in D at m. 76 in a very soft dynamic is interrupted by a sudden loud statement in the violin of the opening theme and key of the next movement, *Work Song* in F. This fades, and a calm D major is restored with the end of the phrase from "The Old Oaken Bucket," missing only its final note.[51]

The First Violin Sonata is very carefully unified. Both outer movements blend cumulative and ternary form in unique ways. The opening motives of the second and third movements are anticipated in the appropriate key at the end of the preceding movements, and the opening idea of the first movement is recalled at the end of the finale. There are melodic links between the source tunes as well; for instance, the opening of the refrain of *Shining Shore* resembles mm. 3–4 of *Watchman* and, more distantly, the opening of *Work Song*. Important keys for the sonata are D major, the key of the final statement of *Shining Shore* in the first movement, the outer sections of the second movement (on "The Old Oaken Bucket"), and the middle section of the third movement (on *Watchman*); and F major, the key of the middle section of the second movement (on "Tramp, Tramp, Tramp") and the outer sections of the finale (on *Work Song*). The first sketch of the first movement began in E minor, the key in which the movement closes, but when the cycle was assembled the opening was transposed up into F minor to fit the key scheme of the whole work.[52]

Neither the Second nor the Fourth Violin Sonata is unified by motive or key scheme in this way. The Second Sonata draws on three movements from the "Pre-First" Sonata, reworking the finale as its first movement and combining the rejected scherzo with the first movement coda in its second movement, resulting in a patchwork discussed in chapter 8. The close relationship of this sonata to the "Pre-First" shows that it is essentially a revision of the earlier work, whose main structural problems Ives solves by recasting the former finale as the first movement and pairing it with a new finale that is also a cumulative setting on a mostly pentatonic hymn tune in triple time. The two hymns, *Autumn* and *Nettleton*, have a few similar motives, but none of the movements cites material from the others. The key scheme is not a strong unifying force; although the first and final movements both begin by suggesting F# major, the most prominent keys in each movement are A, C, and G major respectively. The coherence of this work derives mainly from the balance of characters among its three movements, with two serious cumulative settings on hymn tunes framing a scherzo on an original theme in fiddle-tune style that also includes dance tunes, ragtime, and "The Battle Cry of Freedom." The Fourth Violin Sonata is similar: there is no unifying key scheme (the keys are B♭, E, and E♭ respectively), there are no allusions in one movement to themes from the others, and the sense of a whole proceeds mainly from the similar march-like character of the outer movements around the more contemplative middle movement.

Like the First Violin Sonata, the Third has strong cyclic features. Its first and final movements are both based on *Need*, and secondary ideas from the first two movements recur in the finale: from the first movement, motive B (mm. 11ff., piano), found in mm. 9–10 and 35–36 of the finale; and from the second movement, the opening notes of the countermelody, identical to a segment of the finale's countermelody. There are also key relationships that unify the work, as both outer movements center most prominently on B♭ and include important passages in D♭, and the middle movement is primarily in F (dominant of B♭) and closes in D major to outline a similar minor-third relationship.

Ives called the Third Violin Sonata "a weak sister," considering it "a slump back" after harmonically more adventuresome works.[53] Nothing could be more wrong. The Third may be the best of the sonatas, with wonderful themes and clear forms that convey deeply felt emotions. Its simpler harmonic language is not surprising, given its origin in organ pieces from 1901, but the relative harmonic simplicity also makes the melodic development more easily understood and contributes to the clarity of the whole. Ives must have recognized the strengths of this work, for it was the first of his mature compositions that he arranged to have performed, in a private concert at Carnegie Chamber Music Hall in 1917.[54]

First Piano Sonata

Ives worked on the First Piano Sonata between about 1909 and about 1919, contemporaneously with the violin sonatas. In contrast to the three-movement structure of those sonatas, this work has five movements, in a sort of arch. Like the Third Symphony and the First and Third Violin Sonatas, it is unified by cyclic return of melodic material. The slow third movement on *Erie* is at the center, linked to the first movement in two ways: its own countermelody is based on motives from the first movement (M+N in Table 5.3), and portions of the first-movement countermelody also appear. The second and fourth movements together comprise a scherzo in four verses based on *Happy Day*, *Bringing in the Sheaves*, and *Welcome Voice*. The first and fifth movements are both serious in mood, with a long central development and many episodes of changing character, and there is a melodic link as well. The finale, written about 1919, is the only movement not in cumulative form and not based primarily on a borrowed theme, and its presence makes this sonata the only multi-movement cycle in which cumulative settings predominate that does not both begin and end with a movement in that form. The main part of the finale is a series of episodes, most of them atonal and based on a recurring motive of a falling half step, minor third, and half step, often lacking the fourth note.[55] Framing these episodes are the opening theme (mm.

1–14) and its varied reprise (mm. 208ff.). The beginning and end of this theme are composed of repeated statements of the principal motive, but the middle phrase (mm. 5–9) is an atonal harmonization of a melody paraphrased from mm. 14–15 of *Lebanon*, the main theme of the first movement. Since this phrase apparently plays no part in the succeeding episodes, its role seems to be to recall the first movement, rounding out the piece with a hint of cyclic return. In addition, the main motive of the finale is related to motives in earlier movements.[56]

The Musical Functions of Cumulative Settings

From this survey of the predecessors to and the development of cumulative setting in Ives's music, the musical functions of this form are clear. In giving shape to a movement, this form combined four principles, all inherited from the European Romantic tradition, that were of utmost significance for Ives in his concert music: that music is best which is *thematic, developmental, goal-oriented*, and *minimally repetitive*.

First, all of Ives's instrumental music in European genres conforms to the nineteenth-century conception of musical form as fundamentally thematic rather than harmonic or merely motivic, so that each movement is based on one or more melodic themes that are memorable, recognizable, and distinctive in both shape and feeling.

A second principle required these themes to undergo development through fragmentation, variation, transposition, recombination, and other methods that allow a melodic idea to be transformed without completely losing its identity. The development of themes with strong affective characters provided a way to achieve emotional expressivity without a program or text. Here the music of Beethoven was the principal model, joined by the later Romantics. Like the principle of thematicism, this is characteristic of all of Ives's instrumental music in European forms.

The third principle held that a movement should not simply achieve formal balance and closure, in the manner of a Haydn minuet, but should move forward to a point of culmination, as if envisioning and achieving a goal. Here again the model is Beethoven, joined by the many later composers who amplified this idea. This principle appears as early as the *Variations on "America,"* with its gradual increase in activity culminating in a long, climactic finale, and becomes more characteristic of Ives's music over time.

The final principle was the avoidance of exact repetition, as exemplified in the formal elisions in some of Beethoven's later sonata movements, the Liszt tradition of constant transformation, and the terse musical prose of

DEVELOPMENT AND SIGNIFICANCE

Brahms.[57] Ives had earlier revealed his interest in this idea when he reworked very repetitive sources into themes with minimal repetition, as in the opening themes of the third movement of the First String Quartet and the second movements of his first two symphonies. As was suggested in chapter 5, placing the theme at the end made the repetitiveness of Ives's source tunes a virtue rather than a defect, providing stability and simplicity at the end of a movement. At the same time, reserving the complete theme for a single appearance at the end avoided the repetition inherent in ternary and sonata forms, which tended to weaken the sense of approaching climax near the end of a movement.

Cumulative setting provided a unique application of all four of these formal principles without sacrificing any of them for the sake of the others. This was a balance of virtues that none of the forms Ives had previously used was able to achieve.

Once Ives had settled on cumulative setting as a form for individual movements, he adopted it in his multi-movement cycles as a replacement for the weightiest forms he had previously composed, the sonata forms of his first two symphonies and the fast ternary forms with large codas of his chamber music. The new form accommodated his interests in cyclic unification and in achieving congruence of form between first and final movements. Finally, all the multi-movement works in which cumulative settings occur feature movements of strongly contrasting character. In this sense too, they continue the European tradition of the symphony and sonata cycle. Cumulative setting could replace sonata and ternary forms in Ives's music, not only because it relied on the same compositional principles, but also because it served the same functions in his multi-movement works.

The Extramusical Significance of Cumulative Setting

Cumulative setting served more than purely musical functions for Ives. Because the themes were drawn from American hymn tunes, they carried extramusical associations, from the specific words and images of the hymn texts to the feelings evoked by hymn singing or the flavor of American song. Together with the form itself, which embodies a progression from fragments to wholeness and from vagueness to clarity, these associations give Ives's cumulative settings three kinds of extramusical significance: a celebration of American melodies; a sense of the spirit in which these hymns were sung and the feelings they inspired; and, in two works, a perfect musical parallel to the experience described in the text or program.

Cumulative Settings and Americanism

The use of cumulative settings of hymns in Ives's secular instrumental works marks a significant change in his approach to working with American tunes in the genres of European art music. He had already asserted the value of American hymnody in adapting hymn tunes as themes in his First String Quartet and first two symphonies, but here he goes much further. In a work like the finale of the Third Symphony, the American tune on which it is based is not reworked into a theme suitable for a sonata form, as in the Second Symphony, nor is it the subject of variations, as in *Variations on "America."* Rather, it becomes the goal of symphonic development. When we hear the theme at last, we hear in it the ideas that have been so thoroughly developed in the preceding music, and it strikes us as something achieved only after intense struggle. Through this process, similar to the questing that leads at last to the "Ode to Joy" theme in Beethoven's Ninth Symphony, the simple American tune is raised to a level of seriousness we associate with art music.

This reflects changes in Ives's understanding of the music of his native land. In his teens, he participated in it gladly, if naively, writing marches and playing hymns in church; in his twenties, he gained a command of European art music; and then he returned to the music he had known as a youth and found in it riches he had scarcely suspected were there, riches he found because of what he had learned of art music. If the First String Quartet and Second Symphony show Ives introducing the character of American melody into European form, the cumulative settings of the Third Symphony, violin sonatas, and First Piano Sonata show him investing American hymn tunes with all the seriousness and profundity of the greatest art music. He has taken a decisive step away from European models, not only by abandoning sonata and other received forms, but by placing American tunes at the center of his music. Rather than pay homage to Europe, as in his First and Second Symphonies, he uses the techniques and ethos of European art music to pay homage to the music of America.

Such a work has a strong nationalist character and, like much nationalist music of the late nineteenth and early twentieth centuries, has social and political overtones as well. For the hymn tunes Ives used in his cumulative settings were not a type of folk music, which had established itself as a frequent and generally accepted source for art music, but rather a kind of popular music, music that was created and sold as a commodity, from hymnals and sheet music to band concerts and player piano rolls. This was the music most familiar to the urban and small-town population of America, the music Ives had grown up with, but it was little valued by the social and educational elites who controlled art music in America. By placing a hymn or other popular tune in a work of art music, he was endorsing it as music worthy of attention, much as European composers had done for the ethnic music of Spain, Bohemia, and Russia. By making a popular tune the thematic goal of the entire movement, he was doing something still more radical: inverting the presumed social hierarchy in which art music had the highest status and popular music the lowest. A concert audience that might have rejected *Woodworth* as banal and beneath contempt, had Ives quoted it directly at the outset, is compelled to hear in it at its final appearance in the Third Symphony finale the feelings and meanings Ives has invested in it through development over the course of the movement. Here, Ives does more than claim an identity as an American within the European tradition. He asserts the value of the American vernacular tradition in its own right, and he uses the methods of European art music to do that.

Cumulative Settings as Character Pieces

At the same time that the structure of these movements proclaims the value of American popular music as a whole, the specific choice of hymn tunes as themes introduces a religious element into the normally secular genres of the symphony and sonata. Sensing that an audience accustomed to works in traditional forms with newly composed themes might not know how to react to a piece of art music based on hymns, Ives provided guidance through programs, texts, or evocative titles for all of the cumulative settings save the first, the experimental *Fugue in Four Keys on "The Shining Shore."*

In the development of cumulative setting as a form, programmaticism seems to have played no part. The cumulative settings that were conceived from the start with a text or program in mind—*General William Booth Enters into Heaven, The Fourth of July,* and *From Hanover Square North*—were written in 1914 or later, after the form was already well established. Many cumulative settings were derived from works intended for performance in church, where musical elaborations of liturgical melodies have a long tradition but instrumental program music has no traditional role. When Ives reworked these pieces as secular concert music, he created movements that can best be understood as character pieces, in which the particular tune being used and the way it was treated lent the music a certain mood. Although meant to evoke a certain feeling, they were not written to a program or to a text. These movements are no more programmatic than are the First String Quartet and the Second Symphony. The programs Ives later offered for several of them were created after the music, and the same is true of the texts for those songs which did not simply adopt the text of the hymn being set.

Thus, attempts to interpret these pieces in programmatic terms get it exactly backwards. The programs or texts did not inspire the music, suggest the use of particular tunes, or determine the sequence of musical events, as is true of Ives's explicitly programmatic works such as *Decoration Day*. Rather, they comment on or interpret music that was already extant, indicating the general character of the music or the feeling Ives wished to capture.

Such programs have roots deep in the Romantic tradition, in the picturesque imagery that E. T. A. Hoffmann, Schumann, and Berlioz used to describe music they heard, in Wagner's interpretations of the inner meaning of Beethoven's music, and in other evocative descriptions of the spiritual and emotional content of music. Ives's programs share with these an emphasis on the listener's emotional response and a reliance on images to suggest the feelings the music evokes. In short, the retrospective "programs" that Ives provided for several of his cumulative settings resemble the programmatic interpretations that nineteenth-century musicians and concertgoers offered for their experiences of absolute music. They have little or nothing in common with the explicit programs of such composers as Richard Strauss, or indeed with the explanations Ives supplied for his own programmatic pieces.

The First Piano Sonata provides a good illustration of the nature and function of Ives's retrospective programs. He offered at least two different interpretations of the work. John Kirkpatrick recalled that Ives once described to him "one possible aspect of the scenario: the family together in the first and last movements, the boy away sowing his oats in the ragtimes, and the parental anxiety in the middle movement."[58] Ives made this comment long after writing the music, since Kirkpatrick first wrote Ives in 1927 and had no close contact with him until the mid-1930s. The other interpretation also postdates the music, as it appears in a memo made on an ink copy of the sonata after that page had been photocopied in the late 1920s or later.

> What is it all about?—Dan S. asks. Mostly about the outdoor life in Conn. villages in the '80s & '90s—impressions, remembrances, & reflections of country farmers in Conn. farmland.
>
> On page 14 back, Fred's Daddy got so excited that he shouted when Fred hit a home run & the school won the baseball game. But Aunt Sarah was always humming *Where Is My Wandering Boy*, after Fred an' John left for a job in Bridgeport. There was usually a sadness—but not at the Barn Dance, with their jigs, foot jumping, & reels, mostly on winter nights.

DEVELOPMENT AND SIGNIFICANCE

In the summer times, the hymns were sung outdoors. Folks sang (as *Old Black Joe*)—& the Bethel Band (quickstep street marches)—& the people like[d to say] things as they wanted to say, and to do things as they wanted to, in their own way—and many old times . . . there were feelings, and of spiritual fervency![59]

This program sounds quite specific, but even if it matched the music it would not go beyond the evocation of certain states of feeling connected with Ives's memories of his Connecticut youth. In fact, there is no barn dance in the First Piano Sonata, nor anything that sounds like one, nor any fiddle tunes; there is no allusion to "Old Black Joe"; there is no hint of a band playing a march or anything else; and the incident "on page 14 back" apparently refers to a rejected sketch, not included in the final version, that has an entirely different character from the calm and flowing moment it might have replaced.[60] There are hymn tunes in the sonata, including the opening measure of *Where Is My Wandering Boy?*, introduced into the first movement theme because of its melodic and textual relationship with the theme's main source, *Lebanon* ("I was a wand'ring sheep"). But there is no attempt to evoke either the sound of outdoor singing or the wistfulness of a mother missing her children. Indeed, Ives's use of *Where Is My Wandering Boy?* could not be less appropriate to a picture of "Aunt Sarah's humming": it appears at the loudest moment in the entire movement, marked "in a kind of furious way" and *con furore*.[61] In short, Ives's "program" does not fit the music that it purports to interpret in any of its details. The interpretation that Ives offered Kirkpatrick fits no better: there is no "parental anxiety" in the middle movement, only the setting of a hymn, and playing the movement in an "anxious" manner would destroy its calm assurance; moreover, if the family is together in the first movement, why should the source tunes refer to "wandering"?

The only relation between either of these "programs" and the piece itself is one of overall mood or character, the evocation of certain kinds of music and certain states of feeling. That evocation, and only that, is the extent of Ives's extramusical concerns in his violin sonatas and Third Symphony as well. The titles of movements in the symphony and Second Violin Sonata suggest a character, a setting, or a mood, and do not imply a program; they recall the titles of character pieces by the early Romantic composers or the French clavecinists. Ives's "programs" for the First, Third, and Fourth Violin Sonatas, and even for the "Alcotts" movement of the *Concord Sonata*, were all composed after the music, sometimes long after, and should be understood as explaining only the character of the music, not its structure, form, or meaning.[62] What happens in these pieces is based on musical rather than programmatic ideas, and primarily on the formal plan of cumulative setting.

Ives's titles and programmatic interpretations nonetheless have an important purpose. We saw in *The Camp-Meeting* that the text of that song aided us in hearing *Woodworth* and *its* text, "Just as I am," in the way Ives intended. By describing a place, a situation, a way of hearing the tune (from a distance, across the fields), and the feelings the tune inspires, Ives prepared us to hear in the tune what he wished us to hear and what he experienced in it. The programs and titles that Ives offered for these movements have much the same function; he provided them because he wanted the borrowed tunes to be heard in the right spirit. We are not to imagine that we are hearing in the music a literal translation of events, even when the program lists specific occurrences, as for the First Piano Sonata and the Fourth Violin Sonata. Rather, the purpose of Ives's titles and descriptions is to suggest the emotional resonance which the music that he used had for him, to put us in a particular frame of mind or to set the stage, as does the text for *The Camp-Meeting*.

The mood described in these programs is often concrete, but the events are vague, and words like "impression," "reflection," "remembrance," "express," and "suggest" are common. That of the First Violin Sonata is typical:

This Sonata is in part a general impression, a kind of reflection and remembrance, of the peoples' outdoor gatherings in which men got up and said what they thought, regardless of consequences—of holiday celebrations and camp meetings in the '80s and '90s—suggesting some of the songs, tunes and hymns, together with some of the sounds of nature joining in from the mountains in some of the old Connecticut farm towns.

The first movement may, in a way, suggest something that nature and human nature would sing out to each other—sometimes. The second movement, a mood when *The Old Oaken Bucket* and *Tramp, Tramp, Tramp, the Boys are Marching* would come over the hills, trying to relive the sadness of the old Civil War days. And the third movement, the hymns and actions at the farmers' camp meeting, inciting them to "work for the night is coming."[63]

Such a program does not explain what happens in the music, though it cites some of the songs that are used. What it does is suggest the feelings Ives wants to convey and the spirit in which he asks us to listen. As stated above, the musical form raises the borrowed tunes to the level of art music by making them the goal of the thematic development. A program like this prepares an audience for this process. In both program and music, Ives tells us that there is something of great value in these songs of the common people, if we will only listen for it in the right way.

DEVELOPMENT AND SIGNIFICANCE

The words to these hymns and songs, when we know them, are not unimportant. Mark Harvey has shown that the hymns Ives used, with few exceptions, were among the most widely known in nineteenth-century American Protestantism, dating back to before Ives was born and often generations earlier. Most were used both in regular church services and in the camp meetings Ives attended in his youth; very few were identified with the more modern evangelical revivalism begun by Dwight Moody and Ira D. Sankey in the last quarter of the century.[64] Thus Ives must have expected many in his audience to know these hymns and their texts.

But the texts are never the central focus; that is on the tune itself and its emotional associations, including its melodic character and the feelings of those who sing and hear it. In his programs and in comments on the hymns that he uses, Ives consistently emphasizes the feelings carried by the music, not the words or images of the texts. Knowing the words and the occasions, times of year, or types of service or revival in which a hymn was sung is helpful because it gives a deeper appreciation of what those feelings might be. Yet it is not necessary to know the texts or uses of these hymns in order to understand the music and the feelings Ives sought to convey.[65] Although knowing a hymn's text or context might make the meaning of a movement in which it is used more concrete, the melodic and rhythmic character of the tune and the way Ives treats it are enough to give the music a general emotive flavor that any listener can recognize. Most significant of all for Ives was the spirit in which these hymns were sung: "It was the *way* this music was sung that made them big or little—and I had the chance of hearing them big. . . . it all came from something felt, way down and way up."[66]

Among the feelings Ives wished to evoke in his music were those he felt in the camp meetings of his youth, when, as he recalled it, "great waves of sound used to come through the trees—when things like *Beulah Land, Woodworth, Nearer My God to Thee, The Shining Shore, Nettleton, In the Sweet Bye and Bye* and the like were sung by thousands of 'let out' souls. . . . There was power and exaltation in these great conclaves of sound from humanity."[67] Mark Harvey suggests that the way in which these hymns were sung at camp meetings embodied for Ives the strength and vitality of the common people who had built the nation, and individual variations between singers within the mass of sound represented for him the free expression of each person within a group united by a common fervor. For those who had shared this experience of vigor and unity, the hymns could evoke that same spirit, even when sung alone or in a small group or merely remembered.[68] When Ives used these hymns in his music, they carried these associations of strength and of a group feeling in which the individual is merged but not erased.

In these pieces, Ives does not represent the singing itself. Unlike *Decoration Day, The Housatonic at Stockbridge*, and other works that recreate the sound of group music-making and the order in which musical events occur, the Third Symphony, violin sonatas, and First Piano Sonata are not sound-pictures, and the sequence of events in a cumulative setting has nothing to do with the way hymns were sung at camp meetings.

What these works evoke is not the sound of singing hymns but the feelings of strength and unity associated with singing them. These are feelings that could not be conveyed without using the tunes themselves, any more than the feelings of dynamism and triumph signified in eighteenth- and nine-teenth-century music by fanfare figures could have been depicted in any other way. Thus, criticisms of Ives for borrowing hymn tunes as themes miss the point; no other kind of theme could serve, not even a new melody in the style of hymns, for such a tune would too closely resemble the hymn-like themes of nineteenth-century art music, which carry very different meanings.[69] But it is equally true that those feelings could not be conveyed by the hymn tunes alone. It is the way in which the tunes are treated in the music that recreates the spirit Ives wished to capture. The vigor of hymn singing is represented in these works by subjecting the hymn tunes to extensive motivic development, a symbol of vitality in European art music on many levels: as a source of energy and forward momentum; as an evocation of a struggle or quest; as testimony to the strength of the thematic material, which can undergo such transformation without losing its identity; and as the procedure most characteristic of Bach, Beethoven, and Brahms, Ives's principal models and the composers he considered the strongest. The coming together of individuals in a shared group feeling is symbolized by the gradual coming together of the theme, in which all of the fragments and variants heard over the course of the movement are still present, their individuality intact, but are merged in a common expression of feeling. In short, cumulative form itself is what conveys the spirit of strength and unity Ives associated with the hymn singing at camp meetings.[70]

Thus, the most important experience these works have to offer is not in the programs, nor in the words of the hymns, nor even in the associations carried by the tunes, but in the music itself, particularly in its form: the process of gradual revelation, discovering and mulling over fragments of a theme and its accompaniment until they come together in a moment of great clarity. The sense of strength and unity that this conveys can be felt by a listener who has no background in Protestant religion and no experience of hymn singing at camp meetings, simply because the musical process embodies it so clearly. Indeed, many of the tunes Ives used have now fallen out of common parlance, and many listeners in younger generations or from non-Protestant backgrounds have learned them from Ives's works themselves. We may know intellectually the importance they had for Ives and for the people of his place and time, and his programs may help us in this, but we cannot know it emotionally. Fortunately, the emotion is in these pieces, both in the form they follow and in the particular way in which Ives develops each tune, reflecting its individual rhythmic and melodic characteristics and textual associations. Ives has interpreted the tunes he uses by reworking them in these cumulative settings, and after a few hearings we know them inside and out through his eyes and ears and hands. His exegesis has found treasures in utterances now forgotten or disdained as trivial or parochial. It is the treasures he found in these tunes that we hear in his music, far more than the tunes themselves.

Cumulative Settings Based on a Text or Program

Although most cumulative settings are character pieces rather than program music, two were originally inspired by a text or a program: *General William Booth Enters into Heaven* and *From Hanover Square North*. No doubt Ives chose this form for these pieces, not only because it was the one he used most often, but also because it was uniquely suited to the text or program, matching the sequence of events in the story he sought to tell. In these works, it was the program or text that determined the use of particular hymns as themes and the choice of countermelodies.

General William Booth Enters into Heaven (1914)

There was probably no living poet better suited for Ives's musical idiom in his fortieth year than Vachel Lindsay (1879–1931), nor any composer better prepared to capture the spirit of Lindsay's poetry than Ives. As Ives brought the sounds and styles of American hymns, ragtime, and popular songs into his music, Lindsay infused his poetry with the rhythms and performing styles of hymns, ragtime, vaudeville, and jazz. "General William Booth Enters into Heaven," the poem that made Lindsay's reputation, imagines the triumphant march into Heaven of the English revivalist William Booth, at the head of the Salvation Army he had founded and the souls he had saved. The poem demands a dramatic performance akin to a staged production number, for Lindsay directed that it is "to be sung to the tune of 'The Blood of the Lamb' with indicated instrument," from bass drum to banjos to sweet flutes.

The hymn Lindsay mentions ("Are You Washed in the Blood?" by Elisha A. Hoffman) has a verse-chorus structure, with the second line of the verse repeated as a refrain:

Have you been to Jesus for the cleansing pow'r?
Are you washed in the blood of the Lamb?
Are you fully trusting in His grace this hour?
Are you washed in the blood of the Lamb?

Chorus:
Are you washed in the blood,
In the soul-cleansing blood of the Lamb?
Are your garments spotless, are they white as snow?
Are you washed in the blood of the Lamb?

The first four lines of Lindsay's poem follow the pattern of the hymn's verse:

Booth led boldly with his big bass drum—
(Are you washed in the blood of the Lamb?)
The Saints smiled gravely and they said: "He's come."
(Are you washed in the blood of the Lamb?)[71]

The poem continues in the rhythm of the first and third lines (three long stressed beats, three short weak beats, and three strong beats again), with the parenthetical question returning as an occasional refrain. The rhythm has all the choppy energy of a gospel tune, and even though the entire poem cannot literally be sung to the hymn tune without adding the refrain after each line, Lindsay begins his recording of the poem by singing the opening lines to this tune and chants much of the rest in the same rhythm.[72]

Ives did not hear Lindsay read it. He read excerpts (the first, second, and fourth stanzas) in a review of Lindsay's first book of poems that appeared in *The Independent* for 12 January 1914.[73] Though the stage directions were lacking, the rhythm and spirit were unmistakable, and Ives took over much of the dramatic quality of the performance.

He did not use the indicated hymn, however, but adapted another one in the same style and on the same subject: the hymn tune *Fountain*, adapted from an early American melody by Lowell Mason.[74] This too is in verse-refrain form, and like Lindsay, Ives uses only the verse:

There is a fountain filled with blood,
Drawn from Immanuel's veins,
And sinners plunged beneath that flood
Lose all their guilty stains.

Both texts link baptism with the washing away of sins by the sacrifice of Jesus in a graphic set of images. There is also a melodic similarity, for both tunes arpeggiate the tonic chord at the beginning and throughout. Thus, Ives's sub-

DEVELOPMENT AND SIGNIFICANCE

stitution of one hymn for the other is natural, enriching the associative content by mixing the text of one hymn with the tune of a closely related one, while avoiding a mere transcription of the recitational scheme indicated by the poet.

As shown in Example 6.1, the song begins by imitating Booth's bass drum in the piano, using the dissonant chords with bass afterbeat that Ives had devised for playing drum parts on the piano and quoting the "street beat" or "street cadence" rhythm that drummers use to coordinate marching troops.[75] This figure becomes the countermelody to *Fountain* at the end of the song. Above this, the voice borrows the rhythm of "Are You Washed in the Blood?" and paraphrases the melody of *Fountain*. The parade-like character of the music exactly matches the poetry and further extends the unity of sound and sense that Lindsay achieves through his choice of words and rhythms, exemplified in the phrase "big bass drum," which sounds like its subject.

In setting the first two lines, Ives makes explicit a tension that will develop later in the poem between the spectacle that Booth creates and the inner faith that prompts his actions. The first line, representing outward action, is *forte* and marcato, but the parenthetical question of faith in the second line is suddenly *piano* and legato, the "softening" effect reinforced with a harmonic shift from D to C major. The music gradually returns to the character of the parade and arrives at the half-cadence *forte* and marcato once more, making clear the function of faith as the basis for Booth's militance.

The poem proceeds by a series of images, and Ives sets off each new scene or group with a new musical idea. When these are not drawn from the opening drumbeat and paraphrased hymn, they tend to be dissonant ostinatos and meandering scalar motions, sufficiently abstract and similar in character that we see the people whom Booth is leading and the heavenly citizens who welcome them, not as individuals, but as masses of bodies that function as outward manifestations of Booth's own personality and experience. The refrain "Are you washed in the blood of the Lamb?" returns periodically, each time with a new variant of the melody paraphrased from *Fountain* in the voice and a new figuration in the piano.[76] After its first return (in C♯ minor) in mm. 34–38, the drumbeats fade, and the first of the three main sections of the song draws to a close.

The middle section, setting the poem's second stanza, begins with piano ostinatos and rising and falling whole-tone scale segments in the voice. These convey a sense of undirected but constant motion, suggesting that the parade has arrived at the central square of Heaven and the participants are milling about. Several programmatic quotations illustrate the scenes that follow. At the line "Big-voiced lassies made their banjos bang" (mm. 52–55),[77] the piano paraphrases the minstrel tune "Oh, Dem Golden Slippers" by James A. Bland

General William Booth Enters into Heaven. © 1935 by Merion Music, Inc. Used by Permission.

EXAMPLE 6.1: Opening of *General William Booth Enters into Heaven*, with its sources

DEVELOPMENT AND SIGNIFICANCE

(H125). This type of music captures perfectly the change from a parade to something like a revival, and the choice of this tune is explained in part by its text; the song speaks of preparing to go to heaven, and the second verse begins "Oh my ole banjo." The banjo players reach a fever pitch as they sing, "Are you washed in the blood of the Lamb? Hallelujah!" (mm. 58–65) with a new variant of the refrain tune in G major.[78] "Loons with trumpets blowed a blare" is depicted by a paraphrase of "Reveille" in the voice with another trumpet call in the piano (mm. 70–73), and the next few notes in the voice, to the words "On, on, upward" (mm. 73–74), resemble the opening notes of Ira D. Sankey's gospel song *Onward, Upward* (H47) to an almost identical text.[79] The middle section closes in E♭ major with the refrain text again sung to a new variant of the melody paraphrased from *Fountain*, as the accompanying ostinato slows and softens.

Although Lindsay's poem has five more stanzas, *The Independent* printed only one more, the fourth. But this is the center of the poem, describing the change that makes the sinners spotless and the wounded whole:

> Jesus came from the court-house door,
> Stretched his hands above the passing poor.
> Booth saw not, but led his queer ones there
> Round and round the mighty court-house square.
> Yet in an instant all that blear review
> Marched on spotless, clad in raiment new.
> The lame were straightened, withered limbs uncurled
> And blind eyes opened on a new, sweet world.[80]

As the stanza begins, the preceding E♭ sonority moves as a dominant to A♭ major. The verse of *Fountain* appears mid-range in the piano in A♭, slightly altered in rhythm, while the voice repeats a descending C–B♭–A♭ figure twice for each line of text. This is the first almost wholly diatonic passage in the song, and its simple tonal harmony, soft dynamic level, much slower tempo, and smooth melodic lines convey the serenity of Jesus at the center of the dynamic action of Booth and his followers. The voice sticks on the words "round and round" (the rest of that line of text appears in an *ossia* passage, not usually sung), and the fourth line of *Fountain* is rhythmically adjusted to create an endless series of syncopated quarter notes circling around the same three notes as the voice but ascending instead of descending. Thus both voice and piano go round and round, illustrating the image in the text and creating a hypnotic effect that evokes Booth's trance-like faith.

The instant transformation of Booth's legions into citizens of the holy city is perfectly shown by a sudden change back to the march, at a dramatic soft dynamic, on the word "yet." A gradual crescendo and accelerando leads to bugle calls in the voice (repeating the words "marched on") over drumbeats in the piano, and finally the culmination of Booth's work is reached, as each soul is saved and every body healed, including his own "blind eyes."[81] Example 6.2 shows this moment, the song's climax. The triumphant tune for these triumphant words is of course the verse of *Fountain*, now back in C major as it was near the beginning of the song, with a hint of the refrain on the last word, "world." This is the culmination of the cumulative form, with the drum pattern serving as countermelody and harmonization. The double appearance of the hymn tune in the third section, first in the piano and then in the voice, recalls the first movement of the First Violin Sonata and the middle movement of the Fourth Violin Sonata, in which the theme appears more than once in the final section but is played by the soloist only at its last appearance.

What is interesting about the use of this tune for these words is that they do not go well together at all. There are three lines of text, nine, ten, and ten syllables long, following the pattern of three stressed, three unstressed, and three stressed syllables that Lindsay took from "Are You Washed in the Blood?" These three lines are perched precariously on the four lines of *Fountain*, with eight, six, eight, and six syllables respectively in even iambs. These are irreconcilable in accent and scansion despite an almost equal number of syllables, and the result is a kind of dissonance between melody and text which might appear comic or simply incompetent.

Yet this dissonance is not a defect and is almost certainly deliberate. Ives presents two events, both appropriate to the moment—the tune as the culmination of everything that has come before in the music, and the words as the culmination of the action described in the text—that do not fit together at the most basic level. In Ives's mature work, such a deliberate breaking of rules is almost invariably a call for interpretation.[82] Here, through the conflict in scansion, a single melodic line is broken up into two separate layers, two simultaneous yet independent events, that illustrate the contradictions Booth has had to overcome.

The poem's words express the miracle of transfiguration, when by the grace of God even the least mortal is made whole both in spirit and, as a sign of God's power, in body. In essence, the poem is the promise. The hymn tune recalls two things: its original words, and the spirit that moves the singing of the hymn. The words of the hymn (printed above) refer to the miracle taking place in Lindsay's poem but go beyond the promise to detail the method: salvation (the washing away of "guilty stains") is gained by the sacrifice of Jesus on the cross (the "fountain filled with blood, / Drawn from Immanuel's veins") and by the sinner's acceptance of Christ as redeemer. The spirit behind the singing is that of a firm commitment to the will of God, a belief in the promise and a willingness to pay the price of total faith.

These are three different things: the promise, the method, and the fervor. Because poem and music do not fit together nicely, we sense the force of will that Booth must exert to unite them, to motivate himself and his followers to accept the sacrifice, make the commitment, and thus achieve salvation. The potential contradictions between inner faith and outer practice disappear through Booth's decision to accept God's plan for mankind and act on his faith. These are contradictions familiar to many believers, to Lindsay, and to Ives, and they lie at the very center of the poem's meaning. The dissonance between text and music at this point gives Booth's achievement its power and significance; were the tensions he faces not dramatized in the musical setting, the song's triumph would be hollow, too easy a resolution to take seriously.

Although Ives did not have the complete poem, he shows how deeply he understands it by repeating the refrain at the end. In the last line of the poem, Lindsay takes the question "Are you washed in the blood of the Lamb?" out of the parentheses that have contained it from the start, indicating its place in the background as part of the underlying tune, and addresses it directly to the reader: Are you washed in the blood of the Lamb? Are we, indeed? Could we do what Booth did? Are our actions determined by our perception of the will of God? The question is a bit shocking, catching us off-guard, as after several minutes of being observers we are suddenly called to choose sides. Instead of focusing on Booth, the poem suddenly focuses on us, and that is Lindsay's purpose. We are forced to assimilate the entire experience we have been only watching, with its conflicts fully developed, and relate it to our own lives.

Ives also turns to question us directly. As seen in Example 6.2, he sets off the question by a rest, a change of key, and a slower tempo that recalls the Adagio at the appearance of Jesus. But the most important change is in the dynamic level; as the voice sinks to *pianissimo* in this, the softest moment of the song, we must listen more closely, and we sense that the poet is speaking to each of us alone. The repetition of the question, using m. 3 of *Fountain* in the piano, is harmonized as a hymn in four parts, the only time such harmony occurs in the song. The change from the drumbeat of a parade to the organ of a church (for that is the association we have with such harmony) drives home the change in tone in the poetry, and we are called to respond. The return of the drumbeat in the closing measures, soft and fading away, now seems slightly ironic, as if it had been calling us into the parade, demanding a response, all along.

General William Booth Enters into Heaven. © 1935 by Merion Music, Inc. Used by Permission.

EXAMPLE 6.2: Closing passage of *General William Booth*

DEVELOPMENT AND SIGNIFICANCE

EXAMPLE 6.2, continued

Cumulative setting is the ideal form for this text because the gradual progress toward a full statement of the theme after fragments and paraphrases parallels the spiritual progress in the poem from brokenness to wholeness, from a vision of salvation to its achievement. At the same time, the clear structure of the form keeps the music somewhat independent of the text, and the tension created when both music and text reach their culmination simultaneously and yet do not fit together comfortably adds layers of meaning beyond simple programmatic parallels. Cumulative form was useful to Ives in setting this poem, not only because of its shape or its familiarity, as his most common procedure for working with a hymn-tune theme, but because of two traits we saw repeatedly in our survey of his instrumental works in this form. On the one hand, the simple, wholly musical process of development that leads to the theme provides a frame that is strong enough to contain the programmatic imagery of the text and its musical representations. But combined with this strong structure is a great flexibility that allows it to adapt to the shape of the poem, following the divisions between stanzas and the succession of images in a series of episodes interspersed with textual and musical refrains, without losing its own fundamental shape. The result is one of Ives's greatest works and indeed one of the masterpieces of song, combining his most innovative and individual musical form with his characteristically sensitive interpretation of a text.

From Hanover Square North (ca. 1915–19, rev. ca. 1929)

The finale of the *Second Orchestral Set* was composed between about 1915 and 1919 and fully scored in the late 1920s.[83] Its full title is *From Hanover Square North, at the End of a Tragic Day, the Voice of the People Again Arose.* This ungainly title, together with the bland title of the *Second Orchestral Set* itself, has no doubt contributed to this movement's being relatively unfamiliar and seldom heard in comparison to works like *Three Places in New England*. Ives himself called it "one of the best [movements] that I've done."[84]

The work is a cumulative setting with introduction and coda. According to Ives, it depicts an experience he had on an elevated train platform in New York. As Ives tells the story, this incident is the urban equivalent of the camp meetings of his youth, as people from many backgrounds came together to express a shared emotion through the singing of a hymn. It was May 7, 1915, the day the *Lusitania* was sunk off the coast of Ireland by a German submarine with a loss of over a thousand lives, including 128 Americans.

Everybody who came into the office, whether they spoke about the disaster or not, showed a realization of seriously experiencing something. (That it meant war is what the faces said, if the tongues didn't.) Leaving the office and going uptown about six o'clock, I took the Third Avenue "L" at Hanover

DEVELOPMENT AND SIGNIFICANCE

Square Station. As I came on the platform, there was quite a crowd waiting for the trains, which had been blocked lower down, and while waiting there, a hand-organ or hurdy-gurdy was playing in the street below. Some workmen sitting on the side of the tracks began to whistle the tune, and others began to sing or hum the refrain. A workman with a shovel over his shoulder came on the platform and joined in the chorus, and the next man, a Wall Street banker with white spats and a cane, joined in it, and finally it seemed to me that everybody was singing this tune, and they didn't seem to be singing in fun, but as a natural outlet for what their feelings had been going through all day long. There was a feeling of dignity all through this. The hand-organ man seemed to sense this and wheeled the organ nearer the platform and kept it up fortissimo (and the chorus sounded out as though every man in New York must be joining in it). Then the first train came in and everybody crowded in, and the song gradually died out, but the effect on the crowd still showed. Almost nobody talked—the people acted as though they might be coming out of a church service. In going uptown, occasionally little groups would start singing or humming the tune.

Now what was the tune? It wasn't a Broadway hit, it wasn't a musical comedy air, it wasn't a waltz tune or a dance tune or an opera tune or a classical tune, or a tune that all of them probably knew. It was (only) the refrain of an old Gospel Hymn that had stirred many people of past generations. It was nothing but—*In the Sweet Bye and Bye.* It wasn't a tune written to be sold, or written by a professor of music—but by a man who was but giving out an experience.

This third movement is based on this, fundamentally, and comes from that "L" station. It has its secondary themes [and] rhythms, but widely related, and its general make-up would reflect the sense of many people living, working, and occasionally going through the same deep experience, together. It would give the ever changing multitudinous feeling of life that one senses in the city.[85]

In the Sweet Bye and Bye is a gospel funeral hymn, made doubly appropriate to the tragedy by the central image of its text:

There's a land that is fairer than day,
    And by faith we can see it afar;
For the Father waits over the way,
    To prepare us a dwelling place there.

Refrain:
In the sweet bye and bye,
    We shall meet on that beautiful shore. *(sung twice)*

The image of a beautiful shore that one can see but not yet reach must have been particularly heart-rending for a crowd singing a funeral hymn for people who had perished at sea, torpedoed only a few miles offshore.

The work begins with an invocation by a distant unison chorus, using a variant of the second Gregorian psalm tone to intone the opening words of the Te Deum in English: "We praise Thee O God; We acknowledge Thee to be the Lord. All the Earth doth worship Thee." Surrounding this D Dorian chant are chromatic ostinatos in and around D major and minor, played in various rhythms by a distant choir of two violins, viola, piano, harp, chimes, and string basses. These ostinatos continue with little change throughout the piece, evoking through free dissonance and rhythmic complexity the background noises of rush hour in New York. A horn, also part of the distant choir, joins in as the chorus begins its second phrase and continues after they are silent, playing a mournful tune in D major spiced with a raised second degree that suggests an alternation of D major with D minor. This tune may be distantly related to *In the Sweet Bye and Bye*, having a similar form (AABB, compared to AA′BB′) and a similar stepwise rise from the third to the fifth degree at the start of the B phrases. This first section, played entirely by the distant choir, serves as an introduction, representing the sounds of the city and the mood of the day.

As the distant horn cadences (reh. 2), the main orchestra enters, beginning a section based on the verse of *In the Sweet Bye and Bye*. Over a sustained D in the basses, the cellos, soon joined by clarinet, vary the opening of the hymn's verse in the key of B♭. A brief interlude follows (reh. 3), as a horn in the main orchestra plays a contrasting melody in B♭ that sounds like a distant paraphrase of the hymn. Variants of the hymn verse return in clarinet, violas, and cello in B♭, while the solo piano works with the same ideas in A♭ (reh. 4). The violins join (reh. 5) with bits of the verse in D, adding a new timbre and key while the others continue. The pedal point in the basses sinks to C, then to B♭, and finally to A (reh. 6), where the hymn drops out and the contrasting horn idea returns in another brief interlude. Fragments and variants of the hymn verse return in four contrasting timbres and keys (reh. 7, cello in B♭, piano in A♭ and D, violins in D, and horns in F) to bring this section to a close.

The rest of the movement is based on the hymn's refrain. At the Più moto (reh. 8), the pedal point falls to low D, an octave below its first pitch. Above this, the violins play all but the last few notes of the refrain in D, and the trumpets play the same in F. Both are augmented and somewhat distorted in rhythm, and the trumpets are slightly behind the violins; as one might expect in a widely dispersed crowd of singers, there is more than one key and sense of the rhythm. Other instruments accompany with ostinatos or hints of the hymn. Next, the pedal point shifts to F and the violins play the complete refrain, again in D and in augmentation, but now less altered in rhythm (reh. 9); flutes and clarinets follow in canon a measure later, in F. Beneath this, soft and almost unheard in violas and cellos, is a distorted variant of the "Down in de cornfield" phrase from "Massa's in de Cold Ground," which Ives had used in the Second Symphony, *In the Night*, and perhaps a dozen other pieces.[86] This tune is so common in Ives's music that its appearance here may be interpreted programmatically as a musical symbol for his presence among the crowd.[87]

A bridge based on repeated ostinatos and a crescendo over a pedal C leads to the climactic statement of the hymn's refrain in F (reh. 11), fully harmonized and with embellishments. Besides a pedal F and the background ostinatos, this is accompanied by two other versions of the refrain: a faster, metrically displaced statement in F in an accordian or soprano concertino, and a triple-time variant in B major in the flutes and clarinets. This is a gloriously noisy moment in which everyone is doing something slightly different, as in the miscoordinations and improvised descants and harmonies of group singing, yet the hymn tune comes through loud and clear. There is no countermelody, no doubt because none would be appropriate to the program; in its place, the background ostinatos of the distant instruments continue, all but drowned out by the hymn. Virtually inaudible in the texture, like the private thoughts of people in the crowd, are two other tunes: a distorted paraphrase of most of *Ewing* ("Jerusalem, the golden") in the organ (reh. 11–12) and a phrase from "My Old Kentucky Home" in cello II (beginning two measures before reh. 12). When the refrain is completed (reh. 12), the music slows and fades. Bits of the hymn are softly hummed by several instruments in various keys until it disappears. All that remains is a sustained F-major triad and the repeated figures of the distant choir that evoke the sound of traffic, and these gradually quiet as well.

Ives's music captures the feelings described in his program note and follows the same sequence of events. The introduction sets the scene, depicting background noises and thoughts. The following sections suggest the way in which a tune, starting in one part of a crowd, is picked up by others, using polytonality and metrical displacement to evoke the effect of many voices singing from many directions, joining first in the verse and then in the refrain. The climax is a wonderful orchestral equivalent of the impromptu performance Ives describes, "as though every man in New York must be joining in it," and the quiet coda evokes the continuing effect on the crowd as they sing or hum snatches of the tune or stay reverently quiet. Thus, unlike the cumulative settings in his sonatas or Third Symphony, this movement directly represents a series of events and evokes in both sound and structure the way in which the hymn was actually performed.

Yet the shape of the movement is determined by musical factors. Although cumulative setting is the perfect formal analogue to the events Ives describes, the piece is not a literal rendition of the sounds he heard. The fragmentation, paraphrase, and spinning out that is typical of his cumulative settings occurs here as well, driving the music forward through the traditional devices of symphonic development. The pedal points provide a tonal underpinning that helps delineate the form, as does the gradual progress from D through B♭ and mixtures of B♭, A♭, D, and F to the final goal of F major. As is true of most excellent program music, both the form and the mood are sufficiently strong and clear to be grasped without reference to the program.

General William Booth and *From Hanover Square North* take the overall progression of cumulative settings, from fragments to wholeness and from vague intimations to direct statements, and adapt it to a specific sequence of events. Among the other cumulative settings, only *The Camp-Meeting* and *The Innate* have texts, and only *The Fourth of July* and the Fourth Symphony finale (discussed in chapter 10) are programmatic. The others (discussed in chapter 5) are essentially about the tunes they adopt as their themes, and the emotional resonance that these hymn tunes had for Ives is conveyed principally by the musical form. Although open to extramusical interpretation, this approach continues the primacy of musical over extramusical concerns seen in the other borrowing procedures discussed so far: using an existing work as a model for a piece in the same genre and style; writing variations on a given tune; setting a tune to a new accompaniment or using it as a cantus firmus; transcribing a piece for another medium; or reshaping a tune into a theme for a work in traditional form. But in a number of smaller pieces, Ives by the early 1900s was already trying out ways of using borrowed music in which extramusical concerns were as strong as musical ones. In some works, treated in the next chapter, he used allusions to specific pieces or to general musical types as a kind of rhetorical effect, sometimes for text-painting, sometimes to make a comment about musical style or about how people experience and respond to music. Other works, discussed in chapter 9, use quotation as a programmatic device, telling a story through borrowed tunes and the associations they evoke. These literary ideas of rhetoric, commentary, and storytelling converge in Ives's later music with the ideas of musical transformation through modeling, paraphrase, and cumulative setting to create a diverse body of works marked by structural integrity, depth of meaning, and extraordinary individuality.

CHAPTER 7

Modeling and Stylistic Allusion to Evoke a Style or Genre

Ives used models throughout his career, but his purposes broadened and changed. In his early works, he assimilated a wide range of musical styles and types through imitation. In the works of his apprenticeship, he added an element of competition, as he invited comparison with the masters of European art music and sought to prove himself their equal on their own ground. Yet after the premiere of *The Celestial Country* in 1902 failed to win him recognition as a composer and Ives abandoned his hopes for a career in music, he began to move away from established styles and genres, inventing new forms and synthesizing a varied, flexible, and very personal idiom from the many styles he had assimilated.[1]

Within this new idiom, Ives continued to use models. But instead of imitating models to produce new works of the same kind, Ives in his mature

267

music is interested in evoking a familiar musical type within a piece in a different genre and style, such as an art song that suggests hymn style or an orchestral piece that recreates the sound of band music. Several works from the 1890s through the mid-1920s are *about* music in various styles, and thus take other music as their subject matter rather than simply as models for composition. Others use the associations that listeners have with a certain type of music to create an image or lend a particular mood or character to a passage. This chapter will explore these new uses for modeling as a way, not to learn traditional styles and genres, but to evoke them.

Ives's later pieces based on models divide into three general categories according to the nature and specificity of the allusions:

1 using one or more specific pieces as models and quoting them;
2 using one or more specific pieces as models without quoting them; and
3 alluding to a certain style or musical type without unmistakably alluding to any particular piece (although it is often hard to establish that Ives did not have a particular, still unidentified model in mind).

However, these differences in procedure, or in the degree to which the new piece incorporates ideas and material from a specific model, should not obscure the similarity of purpose and effect. In all these cases, Ives uses the familiar style as a rhetorical device, knowing that the style will bring with it a wealth of emotional associations and remembered experiences.

Music About Music

Several works use these associations to comment on music itself. Some of these pieces critique certain styles and genres; others are about the experience of hearing music and responding to it emotionally; still others demonstrate the characteristics of a new procedure, such as polytonality or quarter tones, by juxtaposing it with familiar musical styles and types.

Modeling as Commentary to ca. 1907

Commentary about music within music appears as early as Ives's *Waltz* (ca. 1895, rev. 1921).[2] It emulates the very popular waltz song "Little Annie Rooney" by Michael Nolan (H115) and quotes snatches of both tune and text, including the title character's name. The opening of Nolan's chorus is quoted in Ives's piano introduction (mm. 1–6); in mm. 25–28 of the Ives song the words "Little Annie Rooney" are set to a phrase that recalls the setting of the same words in Nolan's chorus; the final phrase of the Nolan song (mm. 25–32) appears slightly altered in the piano at the end of both verses of the Ives (mm. 39–45, both endings); and the voice joins in at the end of the second verse with the last four notes of Nolan's chorus to the words "An old sweetheart," a take-off of Nolan's words "is my sweetheart." Ives also borrows in the closing phrases the short-long rhythmic pattern (quarter note, half note in triple meter, the short note on the downbeat) that pervades Nolan's song.

The spirit of Ives's song can be sensed by comparing the two texts. Nolan's is breezy but sentimental:

> A winning way, a pleasant smile,
> Dress'd so neat but quite in style,
> Merry chaff your time to wile,
> Has little Annie Rooney.
> Ev'ry ev'ning, rain or shine,
> I make a call twixt eight and nine,
> On her who shortly will be mine,
> Little Annie Rooney.
>
> *Chorus:*
> She's my sweetheart, I'm her beau;
> She's my Annie, I'm her Joe,
> Soon we'll marry, never to part,
> Little Annie Rooney is my sweetheart![3]

Ives's text is mildly satirical, imagining a later stage of the same relationship in the first hours after the marriage itself:

> Round and round the old dance ground,
> Went the whirling throng, moved with wine and song;
> Little Annie Rooney, (now Mrs. Mooney,)
> Was as gay as birds in May, s'her Wedding Day.
>
> Far and wide's the fame of the bride,
> Also of her beau, everyone knows it's "Joe";
> Little Annie Rooney, (Mrs. J. P. Mooney,)
> All that day, held full sway o'er Av'nue A!
> "An old sweetheart."

Although Nolan's song is about Annie from the point of view of "her Joe," Ives's narrator is completely detached. The first character introduced is not Annie but "the whirling throng," and we see Annie through them and as one of them, "moved with wine and song" rather than by deeper feelings. We are allowed none of the sentiment that suffuses Nolan's song, and we see none of the virtues enumerated by Annie's lover; we see the scene from a distance, knowing only her public actions and not her private thoughts. The musical borrowings reinforce this detachment. Ives could assume his listeners would know Nolan's song, and enough of the model appears to show that we are dealing with the Annie Rooney we know. But much is changed. Like most waltz songs, Nolan's is infectious and catches us up in its spirit. Ives's is just as frothy, but by quoting another waltz song and showing its characters in a new light, it reveals the power of popular forms like the waltz to delude us with sentiment and intoxicate us with artificial high spirits. Nolan's narrator is a starry-eyed lover, but Ives's is a realist. By commenting on a sentimental song, *Waltz* becomes the opposite of sentimental: it makes us think.

An Invention or Allegretto in D for piano (ca. 1898) may also comment on its genre, or it may be another example of Ives's learning through imitation.[4] The piece shows the influence of Bach's keyboard music, and it refers briefly to Bach's Sinfonia (Three-Part Invention) in A Minor BWV 799 (H172) and extends the borrowed material sequentially: mm. 49–50 of the Bach appear, slightly altered, as mm. 20–21 of the Ives, repeated and varied in mm. 24–25. This may be a student piece, an assignment to write an invention in the style of Bach.[5] Yet the lapses in counterpoint, the frequent appearance of a fourth voice, touches of barbershop chromaticism, and cadences more classic than Baroque show that Ives is not following Bach's style closely. Rather than trying to imitate Bach, Ives may have sought to evoke Bach's style in a piece that mixed Baroque counterpoint with salon music, perhaps as a commentary on one or both of the styles he was borrowing. If so, this piece would deflate the prestige of Bachian counterpoint by mixing it with a more trivial, popular style, as the roughly contemporary song *The Side Show* does to Tchaikovsky by revealing his symphonic theme as a limping "Is That You, Mr. Riley?"

Stylistic Allusion as Commentary

In his other music before 1908 that comments on musical style, Ives tends to refer not to a single model but to a general style. Allusion to a style in order to invoke a type of music and the people or activities associated with it is, of course, common in operas and program music; examples include the evocations of shepherds' dances and hunting calls in Vivaldi's *Four Seasons*, Berlioz's depiction of a ball through a waltz in the *Symphonie fantastique*, and numerous operatic scenes that portray musical performances, from the wedding songs and dances in Monteverdi's *Orfeo* to the tavern piano in Berg's

Wozzeck. Ives uses stylistic allusion both to evoke the sound and spirit of music-making and to comment on musical styles.

The two songs paired as *Memories, A, Very Pleasant, B, Rather Sad* (1897) both relate an experience of hearing music and responding to it emotionally, and each imitates the kind of music the narrator is hearing.[6] In the first, children in a theater waiting excitedly for a show whistle, hum, and beat time with the pre-curtain music, and Ives writes a presto in $\frac{6}{8}$ in a jaunty operetta style. In the second, the narrator overhears "the tune my Uncle hummed" and recalls the way the sweet but sad little tune "seemed to slow up both his feet," while the music imitates the style of sentimental parlor songs. In a similar vein, *The Circus Band* (music by 1902, words by 1921) sets words to Ives's *March: "The Circus Band"* (ca. 1899), turning a march into an art song in march style about watching a circus parade.[7] For the song, Ives added four bars of dissonant chords hammered on the piano in imitation of the sound and rhythm of a drum corps beginning a parade, quoting the same "street beat" figure he used in *General William Booth Enters into Heaven.*[8]

Memories and *The Circus Band* are sincere celebrations of styles with which Ives sympathized. In contrast, *Romanzo di Central Park* (ca. 1900 or 1907) turns a spoof of bad poetry into a satire on bad songs.[9] At the top of the score, Ives quotes Leigh Hunt: "how many 'poems' are there . . . of which we require no more than the rhymes, to be acquainted with the whole of them? You know what the rogues have done by the ends they come to."[10] Hunt offers the following example, which Ives adapts for the text of his song: "Grove, Night, Rove, Delight, Heart, Prove, Impart, Love, Kiss, Blest, Bliss, Rest."[11] In setting this "poem," Ives borrows the clichés of late-nineteenth-century salon style, all earnest yearning and sentiment, with modified strophic form, standard piano figuration, a treble melody in counterpoint with the vocal line, and the mild dissonance and chromaticism typical of the style. The first half of the song is shown in Example 7.1.

The satire is evident particularly in the way conventional elements are distorted. Perhaps because each word is to be heard as the end of a line whose other words are missing, most words enter just after the downbeat rather than on it or on an upbeat, lending a panting quality to the vocal melody. The effect is heightened by the piano melody, which begins with an anacrusis and thus seems to end its gesture just as the voice enters. This gives a sense that the two are never exactly together, and when the voice rushes to catch up at the cadence in mm. 3–4, the piano blithely begins the next phrase before the voice has finished ornamenting its cadence. The song begins with a four-measure phrase that oscillates between tonic and dominant harmonies embroidered with appoggiaturas and chromatic tones; Ives goes a bit over-

EXAMPLE 7.1: *Romanzo di Central Park,* first half

MODELING AND STYLISTIC ALLUSION

board in m. 3, offering us the raised, natural, and lowered sixth degree (D♯, D♮, and D♭) in quick succession. The second phrase collapses into a long downward chromatic slide through a series of seventh-chords (mm. 5–12), an overblown Chopinesque ooze that drains the music of momentum and exceeds boundaries of taste even salon composers would have observed. The second half is a varied reprise of the first, with a different second phrase (which threatens to get stuck in mindless repetition and is deftly rescued by the cadence) and a coda recalling the chromatic ooze.

Ives observes in a postscript:

> Some twenty years ago [i.e., ca. 1900], an eminent and sure-minded critic of music in New York told a young man that _____ was one of our great composers; what he meant by "our" is not recorded, nor is it remembered that this profound statement was qualified by the word "living"—probably not, as this arbiter of tears and emotions is quite enthusiastic over his enthusiasms. The above collection of notes and heartbeats would show, but does so very inadequately, the influence, on the youthful mind, of the master in question.[12]

Ives later identified the composer as "Victor Herbert!!—lily-white hands and diamonds!"[13] Ives's exaggeration here of Herbert's style is in some ways like the intensification in his First Symphony of Dvořák's symphonic techniques, not least in the competition of a young man with an established composer. But Ives's intentions are as opposite in the two works as satire is from homage.

Two works from between 1902 and 1907 are about hearing music out-of-doors. This is a theme to which Ives returns frequently in his later music: in *The Camp-Meeting* (discussed in chapter 5); in *From Hanover Square North* (discussed in chapter 6); and in several works that use programmatic quotation or collage (discussed in chapters 9 and 10). But in the present two pieces, Ives creates the effect of hearing music outdoors without borrowing any given tune.

In the song *Walking* (ca. 1902–7), Ives describes a brisk walk on "a big October morning" and marks changes of scene with changes of music.[14] At the indication "up the valley,—a road-house, a dance going on," an episode in the piano imitates first the gestures and syncopations of ragtime (mm. 51–56), depicting the roadhouse through the music one might hear there, and then the lilt of a fiddle tune (mm. 56–58), suggesting a dance.

Another piece that uses stylized references to distinctive types of music is *From the Steeples and the Mountains* (ca. 1902–7) for trumpet, trombone, and four sets of church bells or chimes.[15] A note at the end of the score reads: "From the Steeples—the Bells!—then the Rocks on the Mountains begin to shout!" The chimes evoke the pealing of church bells by loosely imitating change ringing, an English (and now American) art in which bells are rung in constantly changing patterns.[16] In the first half of the piece, each set of bells, starting at a different time and in strict canon with the others, runs down a major scale repeatedly, faster and louder with each reiteration.[17] At the peak of activity the pattern changes to chains of falling thirds (scale degrees 8–6–4–2 and 7–5–3–1 within one octave), and the pace gradually slows. Each set of bells is in a different key or register from the others (including high bells in C and B and low bells in D♭ and C), suggesting the ringing of bells from four different steeples. Ives's imitation is not as complex as the real thing, as he simply repeats two of the thousands of patterns possible with eight bells, but the written-out accelerando and the canon between the four sets of bells creates a great rhythmic complexity at the climax. Meanwhile, the trumpet and trombone lines include, among other music, many statements of a fanfare figure resembling the first three notes of "Taps" (H87), at constantly changing pitch levels. While the bells imitate change ringing, evoking the steeples of a town, the brass suggest bugle calls answering each other from a distance, evoking the open country nearby and perhaps "the Rocks on the Mountains" from which the human sounds echo. There are similar allusions to bells and bugle calls in many of Ives's pieces, sometimes using a specific tune, such as *Westminster Chimes* in the Second String Quartet finale or "Taps" in *Decoration Day*, and sometimes with no clear reference to any tune.

The pieces discussed so far comment on music by critiquing a certain style, as in *Waltz* or *Romanzo di Central Park*, or by recreating the experience of hearing music, as in *Memories* or *Walking*. Ives also wrote dozens of small experimental works that comment on technical aspects of music, critiquing traditional procedures by trying out new ones.[18] Early examples, discussed in chapter 6, are the polytonal settings of "London Bridge" and the hymn interludes that use parallel streams of eight-note chords.

Between about 1898 and about 1902, Ives wrote about a dozen experimental sacred works for chorus, most of which echo traditional choral styles.[19] Several include sections that imitate the style of Anglican chants, formulas used in Anglican, Episcopal, and some other Protestant churches for reciting psalms and canticles on slowly changing chords under a simple melody. Example 7.2 shows such a passage, the closing bars of *Psalm 67* (ca. 1898, revised by ca. 1902), which differs from Anglican chant only in substituting bitonal chords for the usual tonal ones. Not surprisingly, this style appears most often in Ives's settings of psalms; further examples can be found at mm. 59–62 of *Psalm 14* (ca. 1902, revised ca. 1914), mm. 23–27 of the first of *Three Harvest Home Chorales* (begun ca. 1902, finished or reconstructed between ca.

1914 and ca. 1919), and at mm. 16–20 and 66–67 of *Psalm 90* (earlier version lost, reconstructed ca. 1923). The opening of *Psalm 67* also imitates Anglican chant, but here the rhythms are written out.[20] By evoking Anglican chant style, these passages create a churchly atmosphere and link these works, whose other music is often very complex and dissonant, with a past tradition of liturgical music. At the same time, by using a different system of harmony, they highlight the new techniques that Ives is trying out in these works. In a similar way, passages in unison chant (as in *Psalm 90*, mm. 6–12, 26–34, and 93–98) or in imitative counterpoint (as in the middle sections of *Psalm 67* and *Psalm 150*, both ca. 1898, revised by ca. 1902) evoke liturgical music of previous centuries. The styles that are alluded to help to highlight the words, as in *Psalm 67*, in which the passages in Anglican chant style address God or describe God's blessings in a serious liturgical tone, and the middle section, to the words "O let the nations be glad and sing for joy," represents the many nations in its imitative texture and expresses joy in its jaunty rhythms and rising arpeggiations. Simultaneously, this evocation of traditional styles and procedures provides a foil for Ives's innovations, using the familiar to emphasize what is distinctive in the new. In this sense, these experimental works are also about music, reflecting more on musical procedures than on the experience of hearing music and responding to it.

Modeling as Commentary after 1907

After 1907, Ives continued to use models to comment on musical style and to showcase new techniques. For his pieces about the experience of hearing music and responding to it emotionally, he turned increasingly to procedures that employ more explicit borrowing, from cumulative setting to programmatic quotation and collage. Stylistic allusion, formerly used for this purpose, is used in his later music primarily for expressive ends, to lend a passage a certain mood or character associated with the style being evoked; this is discussed in the final section of this chapter.

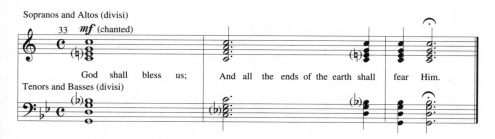

EXAMPLE 7.2: *Psalm 67*, mm. 33–35

After resigning from his last position as a church organist in 1902, Ives changed the focus of his experimentation with new procedures from choral music to works for small ensemble or for piano. Among the latter, there are some that use borrowed material in traditional styles to highlight the special qualities of the techniques being explored.

Study No. 21: Some South-Paw Pitching! (ca. 1914), a study for rapid left-hand passagework, draws most of its melodic material from the third and fifth movements of Ives's Second Symphony, including themes based on "Down in de cornfield" from "Massa's in de Cold Ground" and on *Antioch* ("Joy to the World") and a transition based on part of Bach's Three-Part Sinfonia in F Minor.[21] The simple tonal material of the themes is set against rapid chromatic lines and chords that tend to obscure any sense of key, thus emphasizing the stylistic gulf between this work and the Second Symphony of a few years earlier.

The second and third of the *Three Quarter-tone Pieces* for two pianos (1923–24) rework parts of several existing pieces, mostly Ives's own, to show how they might sound if diatonic or chromatic music were enriched with quarter tones.[22] The second movement, Allegro, borrows and varies the opening two bars of Ives's *The New River*, the first half of his song *The Indians*, the opening of the chorus of "The Battle Cry of Freedom," and, in an extended ragtime episode covering the second half of the movement, ragtime figures from three of Ives's works, the song *The Seer* and movements IIb and IVb of the First Piano Sonata.[23] More than half the movement is borrowed, all but one brief passage from Ives himself. The finale reworks the opening of *America* in various quarter-tone contexts and cites the phrase "Aux armes, citoyens" from "La Marseillaise" (H80) near the end in counterpoint with *America* (mm. 56–57), recalling the combination of these two songs in Ives's *In Flanders Fields*. Jeffrey Gibbens has suggested that Ives quoted "La Marseillaise" as a tribute to the Franco-American Music Society, sponsors of the concert in which the *Three-Quarter-tone Pieces* were premiered.[24] But the other borrowings have no apparent extramusical significance; they simply represent a variety of traditional styles. According to Ives, the quarter-tone pieces "were not presented as definitely completed works of art (or attempts at works of art)," but "were simply studies within the limited means we had with which to study quarter tones."[25] Adapting a wide range of musical types, from a hymn and a patriotic song to ragtime figuration and Ives's own innovative idiom, was a perfect way to explore what quarter-tone music can do and how it differs from diatonic or chromatic music.

What is most interesting in these three pieces is not the manipulation of the borrowed material, which is usually what is of interest when Ives borrows, but the way in which it interacts with its context to throw into relief the most distinctive features of the new procedures. Thus, these pieces also use models to comment on music, here specifically on its basic materials and procedures.

Two other studies for piano seem to comment more directly on musical style through the use of models. The trio (middle section) of Ives's *Study No. 20* (ca. 1908–14) includes a ragtime song in four phrases, played twice. This is modeled on the chorus to Harry Von Tilzer's popular ragtime song "Alexander" (H94, from 1904), identifiable from the drawling figure on "[Alex]ander" at the end of its first two phrases. Although Ives copies this figure almost exactly, the rest of his song is not a direct quotation or even a variant of Von Tilzer's chorus.[26] The piece seems to be about musical genres and styles, juxtaposing march and ragtime sections with a quodlibet (discussed in chapter 10) of fragments of popular songs from earlier generations. *Study No. 23* (ca. 1914 or later) also includes ragtime sections, partly new, partly paraphrasing the chorus of Joseph E. Howard's ragtime song "Hello! Ma Baby" (H107, from 1899), and partly based on a ragtime-derived ostinato figure Ives had earlier used in *Take-Off No. 3 ("Rube trying to walk 2 to 3!!")* (ca. 1906–7), *Scherzo: Over the Pavements* (ca. 1906–13), and movement IVa of the First Piano Sonata (ca. 1914).[27] Later, the same piece uses a ragtime-style melody that also appears in the second movement of the Fourth Symphony, which John Kirkpatrick identifies as a blend of Edward S. Ufford's hymn *Throw Out the Life-Line* (H59) with "Hello! Ma Baby."[28] In this study, Ives seems interested primarily in creating the effect of ragtime and uses a famous ragtime song as a model.

One of Ives's most interesting commentaries on musical style is the song *Grantchester* (1920), to a text excerpted from Rupert Brooke's poem "The Old Vicarage, Grantchester." Ives carefully indicates in the score that the song quotes Debussy's *Prélude à "L'après-midi d'un faune"* (H178), even printing a note that he has obtained permission to use the work from Debussy's publisher.[29] The quotation in the piano is inexact but extensive, including all of mm. 1–5 of the Debussy (omitting the repetition of m. 1 in m. 2). At first it appears that this is an instance of text-painting, illustrating the words at this point:

And clever modern men have seen
A Faun a-peeping through the green,
And felt the Classics were not dead,
To glimpse a Naiad's reedy head . . .

The overt quotation in the piano begins at the word "Faun," linking that word with the most famous musical depiction of a faun, and the voice at "clever modern men" echoes the opening figure of the Debussy as if to suggest that the French composer was just such a man. The borrowings fit the text, certainly, but the text also comments on the music. Indeed, Jeffrey Gibbens has shown that the entire song is suffused with allusions to Debussy. These include direct references to the *Prélude*, from the rough inversions of its opening motive in the first two vocal phrases to the echo in Ives's closing ostinato of the whole-tone oscillation in the horn near the start of the Debussy. There are also more general allusions to Debussy's style, including whole-tone chords, modal scales, and recitation on repeated pitches. Gibbens's analysis suggests that the work is a comment on Debussy's music. Far from using musical quotations to depict Rupert Brooke's text, Ives seems to have used the poem as a vehicle for a musical critique.[30] Ives's stance toward Debussy in this song seems ambivalent, absorbing much of his language and aesthetics while rejecting his polish, characteristic detachment, and choice of subject-matter in this work, which in the decade after Nijinsky's scandalous 1912 choreography was inevitably associated with decadence. Here as in the *Essays Before a Sonata* written a year earlier, Ives uses Debussy as a foil, defining himself in part through a critique of the composer Gibbens has called "the last contemporary musician to be of major impact on Ives."[31] Gibbens's thesis suggests that Ives knew Debussy's music better than has been supposed and took Debussy seriously, rejecting parts of his aesthetic, adopting some ideas and procedures, and finding in others confirmation for his own views.

Ives is less ambivalent in his wholehearted rejection of other styles of composition, as shown in two late songs about songs. Both of these refer directly to individual models without quoting them.

On the Counter (1920), written as Ives was assembling his book of *114 Songs* (printed 1922), satirizes parlor songs of the 1890s—"Tunes we heard in 'ninety two,' soft and sweet" (the text is Ives's own)—and chides 1920s songwriters for failing to move beyond "the same old chords, the same old time, the same old sentimental sound." In a self-deprecating manner, Ives targets his own *A Song—for Anything*, which he included in *114 Songs* and dated 1892, the only song in the collection dated that year. The earlier song's title is a tribute to its adaptability: the music was first composed about 1888 to a religious text (the words printed last in *114 Songs*); the second text, a love song (printed first), dates from about 1892; about 1898, a third text (printed second), a farewell to Yale, was set to the same tune.[32] This song shares with the later one a similar vocabulary of chords and harmonic patterns, the same meter and phrase structure, virtually identical melodic rhythm, and several details of melodic contour. Example 7.3 compares the two vocal lines, showing the close rhythmic modeling, and marks with horizontal brackets the melodic gestures in the later song that are most overtly borrowed. *On the Counter* even has a plagal final cadence, evoking the "Amen" that, Ives tells us in a footnote, was "tacked on" to the church performance of the earliest version of the model.[33] That the later song is modeled on the earlier, and thus intended to satirize it, is clear from the many similarities, but it does not "quote" the earlier song. It does, however, quote two other pieces. The last line of the text opines that "Shades of Nevin, Smith & Hawley in new songs abound," referring to three salon composers of a prior generation: Ethelbert Nevin (1862–1901), Charles Beach Hawley (1858–1915), and possibly Wilson George Smith (1855–1929), all best known for sentimental songs and short piano pieces. Their names are clear in Ives's manuscript but are coyly replaced by blanks in *114 Songs*, perhaps to avoid insult or libel.[34] But there is a clue for the informed and alert listener, for the music at this point makes a sly reference to both melody and harmony of a brief passage from *Narcissus* (H185, 1891), a best-selling piano piece by Nevin, whose lyrical, sweetly chromatic style made him one of the most popular American composers of the late nineteenth century and a prime target for Ives's satire. The short piano postlude quotes "Auld Lang Syne" (H98), adapted to the triple meter and prevailing rhythms of the rest of the song, over the final Amen. This is a transparently programmatic gesture, a wicked hint that at least in some cases "old acquaintance" should have been forgotten long ago.

The One Way (1923) is another satirical song about song-writing.[35] Here, the relationship to the model involves resemblances not of melody, but of rhythm, style, and mood. John Kirkpatrick has noted that the chorus "starts suspiciously like the middle of the chorus of *On the Road to Mandalay* (1907) by Oley Speaks."[36] A memo Ives added to the manuscript long after the song was composed seems to confirm the connection, for he mentions as apparent inspiration a "concert in Aeolian Hall some 20 years or so ago—one afternoon a young man with a dumb look sang some songs by Frank LaForge and Oley Speaks."[37] The two songs share a pompous, expansive character, frequent drum-like triplet figures on the second and fourth beats, and thick chords tinged with chromaticism, but no obvious melodic similarities. Ives's chorus includes a brief modulation marked by a change in figuration and a reduction in dynamic level, followed by a powerful crescendo and a return to the triplet figure as the home key is regained and the main tune of the chorus returns. This sequence of events is almost exactly the same as that at the end of Speaks's verse, leading up to the chorus. Ives's text reads: "Now a softer cadence, / Now we change the key, / Just to stage a come-back / To the main strain of our glee." The harmonic "come-back" to which Ives refers is literal in both songs, but he may also be punning on Kipling's words at this point in the Speaks: "Come you back, you British soldier; come you back to Mandalay!"

EXAMPLE 7.3: The vocal lines of *On the Counter* and *A Song—for Anything*

On the Counter and *The One Way* allude not only to particular songs but
to the style and genre they represent, and thus comment on that type of song
as a whole. The close relationship in these two songs between a new work
and a single model that is not directly quoted is rare in Ives's mature music.
However, the broader idea of evoking familiar styles or types and their conventional gestures is a basic element of his approach.

Modeling and Genre: The Example of *Serenity*

In Ives's early music, a work and its model were usually of the same genre,
as he learned how to compose by imitating examples. Later works show a

more sophisticated stance, from the parody of *Waltz* to the allusion in *Study No. 20* and *Study No. 23* to popular styles in the context of a genre associated with art music, evoking the characteristics of one genre while writing a piece in another. This evolution is typical of Ives's compositions in general, for his early efforts, diverse as they are, follow fairly closely the parameters of a given genre and style, whereas his mature works in the genres of European art music incorporate a vast range of styles and allude to many genres and types.

The importance of genre in creating meaning is illustrated by *A Song—for Anything*, mentioned above as the model for *On the Counter*. Its three texts were originally set to the tune in apparent sincerity, and each text belonged to a different popular genre: church solo, love song, or college song. Ives's decision to print the song with all three texts in *114 Songs* resulted in a new, composite work that fit none of these genres and was instead an art song *about* different types of popular song. As Joseph W. Reed has observed, in this form it is a "disquisition on genre," one that demonstrates that the music can manipulate the listener in exactly the same way no matter whether God, a beloved, or Yale is the object of the singer's devotion.[38] With each new text, the song changes genre. With all three, it changes function, from a sentimental song in one or another traditional genre to an ironic commentary that exposes the power of sentimental music to influence our feelings.

The tension between the genre of a work and the genre of its model is central to the meaning of Ives's *Serenity* (1919), a "unison chant" or solo song arranged from a lost version with orchestra (ca. 1909).[39] This song, whose opening is shown in Example 7.4, is based on a hymn text and on hymn tunes and has something of the character of a hymn, both in its style and in its use of unison voices. But it is not a hymn and is not intended to be sung by a

EXAMPLE 7.4: *Serenity*, mm. 1–6

MODELING AND STYLISTIC ALLUSION

congregation. This is not even church music, to be sung by a choir or soloist in a service, though it is sometimes sung in church today. It is conceived as concert music, as is clear from its original scoring with orchestra. It is close to the hymn tradition yet separate from it. This is art music *about* hymns, and that makes it particularly interesting.

The piece is a setting of two stanzas from John Greenleaf Whittier's hymn "Dear Lord and Father of Mankind," traditionally sung to the tune known as *Whittier*, by Frederick C. Maker, shown in Example 7.5. Ives's tune is like Maker's in several ways: both are slow, simple, and mostly stepwise, moving within a range of an octave or less, with one sudden peak a phrase or two before the close. If anything, Ives exaggerates these traits, as his vocal line is very slow and simple and exclusively stepwise except for the skips that set off the high point of the line at the word "ordered" (mm. 20–21). Other than these general similarities and a shared phrase structure that follows the shape of the poem, melodic resemblance between Ives's tune and this model is slight.

The Ives song is more directly related to another hymn tune that shares with *Whittier* and with Ives's song the general characteristics listed above. This is *Serenity* (H53), from which Ives's song clearly derives its name. The music is adapted from a melody by William V. Wallace and exists in two metric variants: one in $\frac{3}{4}$, which is more widely known, and one in $\frac{6}{8}$, shown in Example 7.6, which Ives uses here and in *The Rainbow*, discussed below. The tune appears with many hymn texts but is perhaps best known as the setting

EXAMPLE 7.5: *Whittier*, by Frederick C. Maker

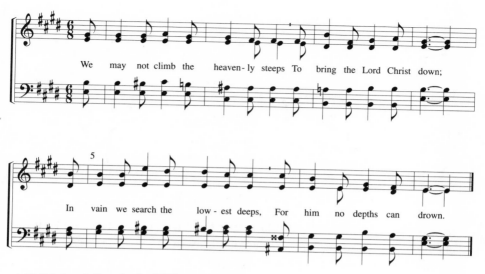

EXAMPLE 7.6: *Serenity*, by William V. Wallace

for stanzas from Whittier's "Our Master," beginning with the words "Immortal Love, forever full" or with the next stanza (shown in Example 7.6).[40] The two hymns are very similar in both text and music. The texts, both by Whittier, use similar images of eternity, love, Galilee, and living according to the example of Jesus. The music of the two hymns has several points of resemblance: the opening melodic motion from the repeated third degree to a note that is removed by a semitone (down in the Maker, up in the Wallace) and back; a similar use of secondary dominants with chromatic motion in the tune or in the tenor; parallel climaxes in the third phrase, in which the tune leaps from the fifth degree up to the octave and descends stepwise to the sixth degree, harmonized by a I^6–V^7/vi–IV progression with an appoggiatura on the downbeat; and a fall from the fifth to the tonic near the beginning of the final phrase of both tunes. By joining the words of one hymn to music taken from another, Ives hints at these relationships between the two hymns.[41]

At the opening of both stanzas in the Ives, the vocal line paraphrases the first two bars of Wallace's hymn over an ostinato in the piano. The hymn's opening bars then appear intact in the last measure before the cadence in each verse, the voice quoting the melody and the piano the accompanying chromatic harmony.[42] The borrowing is more extensive in the piano than in the voice, spilling over into the ostinato chords before and after the explicit quotation. As shown in Example 7.7, where notes derived from one of the four voices of the original hymn are large while other notes are small, every one of the pitches in the two-chord ostinato serves as part of the quotation

EXAMPLE 7.7: Quotations of Wallace's hymn in Ives's *Serenity*

from Wallace's hymn at the end of one or the other verse, sometimes with a change of octave (indicated by arrows on the example).[43]

Thus, every element in the work ultimately derives from the models. The overt quotations from Wallace's hymn are not afterthoughts nor something extraneous to the piece; rather, they represent the very source of the music. In the piece, the direct quotation comes at the end of the verse, so we only gradually become aware of the relationship of Ives's song to its model; from a compositional standpoint, the direct quotation must have been one of Ives's first decisions, part of the original idea for the piece and a source for the notes in his ostinato. In both these respects, this work recalls Ives's cumulative settings, though on a much smaller scale.

All these similarities make Ives's song hymn-like, but it remains a piece of concert music. Classical concert music functions as art for its own sake, whereas hymns are purely utilitarian. We are trained to listen to art music with concentration, but we may consider hymns to be simple and uninteresting in their texts, tunes, and harmonies—appropriate for use in church but not deserving of our rapt attention *as music*. By making an art song out of material drawn from hymns, Ives subverts these distinctions. We hear the hymn tradition in its text, its melody, and its chords, and our sense of that tradition is—must be—transformed.

To evoke the emotional overtones of singing hymns together, without sounding trite, Ives makes the familiar sound unfamiliar. Most obviously, he sets old words to a new melody and strange harmonies. But even the familiar music of Wallace's hymn, when it appears near the end of each stanza, surprises us: we do not expect to hear hymns in the concert hall; nor are we led to expect a hymn by the opening of the song, which is in a very different style; finally, the hymn tune is not even the right one for the text. The song is new and original, as art music is supposed to be, while conveying the musical and emotional character of an old and familiar type of music.

MODELING AND STYLISTIC ALLUSION

The borrowings from the hymns help to illustrate the text, but the text also implies something about the hymns. Whittier's poem offers a lesson about keeping the Sabbath, imitating Jesus in his silent prayer, experiencing divine love, ceasing to strive and strain, coming into order and peace. The calm vocal line, soft dynamics, and gently rocking ostinato echo the images of calm and eternity, and the hymn references, by invoking singing in church, suggest the ideas of the Sabbath, ceasing our worldly busy-ness, and coming together as a group to experience peace from a common divine source. The music of the song models that serenity. Yet that music is entirely based on hymns, from the stepwise undulations of the vocal line to the structure of the accompanying chords. This suggests that a path to communion with God, a way to touch the silence of eternity, to rest from the stress of life and achieve peace, may lie in the simple act of singing hymns.

This is an art song that treats hymns in an unfamiliar way. The rich set of interrelationships here, involving text, music, and genre, may change the way we hear these two hymns and perhaps all hymns. From this song, we may return to hymns with fresh eyes and ears, paying attention to them as we would to art songs, aware of the power of their texts and the serene simplicity of their tunes. The idea of this song, then, is not only to convey the text, nor simply to create a piece based on material from the hymn tune *Serenity*, but to argue for the power of the simple hymn as a form of religious experience and to refresh our jaded ears so that we may be open to that experience.

In this work, Ives shows how far he has come. The technique of modeling is little changed from his student works, but his stance toward the model and hence the meaning of its relation to the new work is quite different. His early pieces represent attempts to master the genres he encountered, from marches to art songs, and he adopts the assumptions and limitations of those genres without question. For the most part, the relation of the new work to its model is primarily of historical interest; there is no hidden meaning in Ives's dependence on a Donizetti duet for his Polonaise or a Parker oratorio for *The Celestial Country*. But *Serenity*, far from adopting the assumptions of a given genre, offers a commentary *about* genre, specifically about the different ways we approach and experience hymns and art songs. Moreover, *Serenity* uses the conflicting conventions of the art song and the hymn to convey emotions—those Ives experienced in singing hymns or hearing them sung— that could not be conveyed in any other way. To present the hymn without comment would not convey these emotions, since the listener could not be expected to share the same sense of its emotive power. Yet to try to depict those emotions in entirely new music without referring to the music that evoked them would be to lose the special character of the experience of responding to music, which is part of the experience Ives is seeking to capture. So Ives deploys his references to the hymn tradition within the foreign genre of the art song to convey the inner meaning these hymns had for him. Here, the tension between the content and the frame, between the model and the work drawn from it, is intrinsic to the song's meaning.

This relation of piece to model is typical of Ives's later works, many of which comment in some way on music and the act of hearing it, whether they are based on single models or on broader stylistic types. In his mature pieces, Ives sought to convey the emotional side of his own experiences with all kinds of music. He found in modeling and in other borrowing techniques the tools he needed to recreate, within music itself, the inner experience of hearing music.

Modeling and Stylistic Allusion for Expressive Ends

The pieces described so far are all about music in some way, whether they comment on musical style and genre, demonstrate what an innovative technique can do with familiar musical procedures or materials, or depict the experience of hearing music. But several of them also suggest an image, mood, or character through the associations connected with the types of music they use as models, from the frothy *Waltz* to the meditative *Serenity*.

Many of Ives's other works allude to individual models or to familiar styles for just such expressive ends, without engaging in direct commentary on music. These pieces are not primarily about music, but they use musical references as signs for emotions, situations, or types of people. This use of modeling and stylistic allusion for purely expressive purposes seems to have developed late in Ives's career, for almost all the works that use this approach date from after 1910, and most were composed in the 1920s.

Modeling with Quotation

In two late songs, Ives seeks to capture the spirit of the folk or popular style most closely associated with his narrator, and he cites examples of the genre in passing. As Anne Timoney Collins's poem "The Greatest Man" echoes the language of common folk, so Ives's song to her words (1921) evokes the vernacular of American folk music. Two folk-like songs are alluded to directly, though briefly: the opening of "I've Been Working on the Railroad" (H109) in mm. 16–17, and the first phrase of the chorus to Paul Dresser's "On the Banks of the Wabash" (H130), expanded in mm. 9–13. Both models share with other folk and folk-like songs a characteristic dotted rhythm, which becomes pervasive in Ives's song; in context, the musical allusions are hardly noticeable.[44] *Charlie Rutlage* (1920 or 1921) uses a text from a collection of cowboy songs and mimics both the kind of declamation common to these songs (limited range, recitation on a single pitch, and simple diatonic or pentatonic figures) and the pluck and strum of a cowboy's guitar, imitated by alternating bass notes and treble chords. At one point (mm. 24–29), Ives places in the piano a rhythmically tranformed version of "Git Along Little Dogies" (H103), one of the best-known cowboy songs. He alerts the performers to its presence by including the opening words of the chorus in the score above the piano part, though these words are not meant to be performed.[45]

In trying to capture the flavor of a whole type of song, these songs have something in common with certain examples of collage (discussed in chapter 10), such as the Barn Dance in *Washington's Birthday*, in which a cluster of borrowed tunes makes explicit the general models for a section's main theme. It is the character of the music that is most important, and the specific model used is often less significant than the general type it represents. This can be seen by comparing several songs that feature hymnlike melodies, whether directly borrowed or more ambiguously related to a possible model.

The Rainbow (So may it be!) sets a short poem by Wordsworth, using a change to hymn style to delineate its form and meaning. The text and vocal line appear in Example 7.8. Like many Ives songs, it exists in two versions, an earlier one for instrumental ensemble, in this case chamber orchestra (sketched in 1914), and a later arrangement for voice and piano (1921) made for *114 Songs*.[46] When the instrumental version of a song was written first and the words are by Ives himself, as is true of *The Innate* (discussed in chapter 5), the text may have been added after the music was composed. But when the words are taken from existing poetry or prose, as in *The Rainbow*, there are seldom any significant changes in the music to accommodate the text, suggesting that Ives had the words in mind as he wrote the instrumental work. Indeed, in the published score of *The Rainbow*, the vocal melody of the song is given verbatim to the basset horn or English horn, and the text is provided underneath. Ives recalled in his *Memos* a concert his father gave of songs by Schubert and Franz performed on the basset horn or trombone, with the words printed on a sheet for the audience to follow along, and wrote that "hearing him play these songs got me, to a certain extent, writing songs for the horn or some instrument, with the words underneath, which should be sung. Some of the songs in the book of *114 Songs* were first written in this way, partly because singers of the time made such a fuss about the unfamiliar 'awkward intervals' they called them."[47] *The Rainbow* is clearly such a song, and its musical content reflects the text. The first six lines of the poem are dynamic, calling forth an arching vocal melody accompanied by thick, impressionistic chords. The last three lines of Wordsworth's poem then change character:

> The Child is father of the Man;
> And I could wish my days to be
> Bound each to each by natural piety.

Ives matches the more contemplative tone of these lines with a change to a more reserved style. Perhaps prompted by the reference to "natural piety," he bases the melody here on the hymn tune *Serenity*, the same tune used in his song *Serenity*. As Example 7.8 shows, the first half of the tune is paraphrased twice, in mm. 13–14 and 15–16 of the Ives, changing keys at each phrase to pass through A, E, E♭, and D major. The frequent changes of key and the slight rhythmic alterations make the tune less recognizable, so that the melody is heard less as a quotation of a particular tune than as an evocation of hymn tune style that creates the appropriate mood of reverence and humility.

Luck and Work (ca. 1920), shown in Example 7.9, also changes styles to match a shift of tone in the text.[48] The first half, marked *forte* and "Fast and hard," depicts the undisciplined activity of the adventurer through an angular, chromatic melody and a meandering chromatic figure, nine sixteenth notes long, in two-part counterpoint in the accompaniment (marked by braces in the example). Each time the figure repeats, it shifts rhythmically against the beat and expands outward in register, its upper line transposed up a tritone and its lower line down a tritone, as Ives creates sophisticated musical symbols for aimless wandering. By contrast, the second half, marked *piano* and "slower and easily," illustrates the simple, grounded, and disciplined life of the farmer with a hymnlike, mostly diatonic melody accompanied by unmoving, diatonic ostinatos in D major and then by mildly chromatic chords that lead to a tonal cadence on B major. Both melody and accompaniment seem to borrow the opening motive of *Nettleton*, whose occurrences are bracketed on the example. This motive is so brief and so commonplace that an allusion to this hymn may not be intended.[49] What is most significant is the change to a hymnlike style, for which *Nettleton* and other hymn tunes served as models. The sketch for this song is revealing; the first phrase of the song's second half was originally set in an atonal, chromatic style, which did not offer sufficient contrast with the preceding music; this is canceled and replaced with the final version, which does.[50]

In several late songs that apparently use hymn tunes as models, Ives seems deliberately to limit the recognizability of the source in order to evoke the broader style of hymns, suppressing the specific model in favor of the general

EXAMPLE 7.8: Vocal melody of *So may it be!* (version of *The Rainbow* for voice and piano), compared to William V. Wallace's hymn tune *Serenity*

type and resulting in allusions too subtle and fleeting to be certain that they are intended. The possible use of *Bethany* as a model for *Evening* (1921), discussed in chapter 3, is an example of such an allusion. Other instances include possible references to *Erie* in *Afterglow* (1919), shown in Example 7.10, to the last phrase of Lowell Mason's *Olivet* (H46, "My faith looks up to Thee") in *Disclosure* (1921), and to Alexander R. Reinagle's *St. Peter* (H52) in *Immortality* (1921) and *Two Little Flowers* (1921).[51] In each case, the opening and closing vocal phrases seem to follow the opening melodic contour of the putative model, with one reference an exact though brief quotation of four to eight notes and the other a less direct paraphrase (in *Disclosure,* both are

Luck and Work.© 1933 by Merion Music, Inc. Used by Permission.

EXAMPLE 7.9: *Luck and Work*

MODELING AND STYLISTIC ALLUSION

paraphrased). In every instance, except for *Two Little Flowers,* the more exact reference comes at the end. But even when Ives's melody matches the hymn exactly, the identity is so brief and the melodic line so commonplace that one cannot be sure whether the resemblance is deliberate or coincidental. Perhaps these somewhat ambiguous allusions reflect a conscious attempt around this time to convey the general mood of a hymn tune or to suggest a hymnlike character while avoiding a reference so blatant that recognizing the quotation would distract the listener from the song at hand. What seems to matter in these songs is that a phrase *sound like* a hymn, whether or not it reminds us of a particular tune or text.[52] In deemphasizing the individual tune used as a model, Ives focuses our attention on the overall hymnlike quality of the passage.

The same is true in *The White Gulls* (1921), where a change of musical style from impressionistic to hymnlike in both sections of the song helps to convey the text. In the second half, shown in Example 7.11, the chromaticism and constant harmonic motion of mm. 17–22—musical images for the aimless, unceasing movement described in the text—give way in the closing section to harmonic stasis and a hymnlike, diatonic melody, which represent the steady, comforting, "all-receiving breast" of God. This change of style resembles those in *The Rainbow* and *Luck and Work,* suggesting that Ives is after a similar effect. Example 7.12 compares this hymnlike melody to excerpts from several hymn tunes that share a similar contour and that Ives used in other works. This final phrase of *The White Gulls* most resembles *Shining Shore:* both two-measure segments follow mm. 9–10 of that hymn with minor changes, and the whole phrase parallels mm. 8–12 of the hymn. But the

Afterglow. © 1933 by Merion Music, Inc. Used by Permission.

EXAMPLE 7.10: *Afterglow,* opening and closing vocal phrases, compared with *Erie*

The White Gulls. © 1933 by Merion Music, Inc. Used by Permission.

EXAMPLE 7.11: *The White Gulls,* second section

　　　MODELING AND STYLISTIC ALLUSION

The White Gulls. © 1933 by Merion Music, Inc. Used by Permission.

EXAMPLE 7.12: *The White Gulls*, final phrase, compared with similar passages from several hymns

phrase also shares elements with *Bethany, Nettleton, Dorrnance, Expostulation*, and *Watchman*, without matching any tune exactly. The A in m. 24 lends a particularly haunting quality, deviating from all possible hymn models and contradicting the implied local key of E♭ major. If *Shining Shore* was the main model, the omission of the 3–5–3 melodic skips at the beginning of each unit renders it far less recognizable.

Ives modeled this phrase of *The White Gulls* on familiar hymn tunes in order to obtain the appropriate rhetorical effect, but he seems to have made the reference deliberately ambiguous. Yet this only heightens the effect. Ives apparently wanted to avoid the specific programmatic or motivic associations that might be stimulated by an unambiguous reference to a single hymn tune, and to focus our attention instead on the associations aroused by the general style of hymn tunes. The texts of these hymns are not irrelevant, but any particular text would be too precise. For instance, a direct reference to *Shining Shore* would invoke its text about the afterlife and its associations with funerals and death, which in turn would suggest that the image in the poem of sinking to rest on the breast of God could only occur at death; this unnecessarily narrows the meaning of these words, which otherwise could apply as well to seeking solace during life. Instead of this specific set of associations, Ives was after a general mood of comfort, of humble bending to the will of God, and of trust in God's mercy conveyed by this whole cluster of hymns and by slow hymns in general.

Stylistic Allusion

The difficulty in determining whether *The White Gulls* is an instance of modeling with quotation or of stylistic allusion demonstrates that Ives often used these techniques for similar expressive purposes. The effect may be the same whether a single model can be identified or not, for what is usually most important is the meaning created by evoking a style or type associated with a certain group of people, type of event, or mood; we will associate *Charlie Rutlage* with cowboys, *Waltz* with dancing, and the latter part of *The Rainbow* with reverent contemplation because we recognize the styles evoked, no matter whether we recognize the individual models or not. In a number of works, Ives conjures up the associations carried by a particular musical style by alluding to it within a piece in another style. What Ives borrows in these instances is not the individual tune or the unique structure of a single source but the most characteristic elements of an entire type.

In some pieces, allusion to a certain style fulfills a program or illustrates a text. For example, in the middle of the second movement ("Arguments") of the Second String Quartet (ca. 1911–13), a highly dissonant, polymetric ruckus is interrupted when the second violinist, who represents conservativism in Ives's scenario, plays a solo cadenza in high Romantic style marked *Alla Rubato Elman* and *Andante emasculata* in Ives's manuscript. This is shouted down by violent, insistent chords in the other instruments (marked "Cut it out! Rollo!"), as they continue the argument.[53] The vocal line of the song *The New River* (between 1913 and 1921) imitates the lilting dotted rhythms of Tin Pan Alley at the words "only the sounds of man, phonographs and gasoline, dancing halls and tambourines" and a horn call at "the blare of the hunting horn."[54] *The Indians* (orchestral version ca. 1912–14, song version 1921) evokes the songs of American Indians in its diatonic, chant-like melody, centered around a note in the middle of its small range and composed of figures that repeat with slight variation. *Majority* (written for unison voices and orchestra ca. 1915, arranged as a song in 1921) echoes the sing-song of children to illustrate the words "The Masses are singing."[55] The song *Paracelsus* (1921) meditates on power and its relation to love. At the words "I learned my own deep error," the music changes from dense dissonance to the tonal, chordal style of hymns, evoking all that that style carries with it, from simplicity and clarity to prayer and humble submission. And in *On the Antipodes* (ca. 1915–23), the contrast of the commonplace with the extraordinary reaches an extreme. Ives's words reflect on nature, and the music is largely an essay in variation based on a cycle of dissonant chords, each a stack of similar intervals. Tonal music appears only once, at the words "Sometimes Nature's nice and sweet, as a little pansy" (mm. 14–17), where we hear the "nice and sweet," gently chromatic lyricism of late-nineteenth-century parlor songs. This is interrupted just as suddenly by a return to the full-force dissonance of the song's opening bars and a wild, angular melody as the poet observes, "And sometimes 'it ain't.'"[56] To this list might be added several works in which bare major triads suddenly appear in an otherwise post-tonal context, whether with serious intent, as at the end of the songs *Majority* and *Duty* (arranged 1921 from a choral version from the 1910s), where a tonal cadence symbolizes rightness and certainty, or as a joke, as at the end of *Halloween* and before the last variation of *Varied Air and Variations* for piano (ca. 1914–23).[57]

Ives's stylistic allusions can be quite subtle. *Resolution* (1921), shown in Example 7.13, features a series of changes of figuration coordinated with images in the text. No part is *in* a conventional style, but each segment *refers to* elements of a familiar style. In the first two bars, the melody's folklike opening gesture, dotted rhythms, and pentatonic sound suggest the style of folk songs, whose associations with rugged strength and the outdoors reinforce the text. The melody in m. 2 becomes too angular to be truly folklike, but this only reinforces the sense of rough-hewn strength, while the large intervals reflect the sense of space described in the poem. The piano also conveys spaciousness through factors not associated with folk music: the wide outer interval of a major seventh and the wide spacing between the hands, emphasized by the close thirds within each hand. The voice is in the middle of this texture, like a lone person under a vast sky. The reference to faith in the second line of the poem is matched with a sudden change to hymn-like harmonies in the piano: closely spaced, functionally tonal, and with the chromatic touch of secondary dominant chords, in contrast to the widely spaced, static, wholly diatonic chords of the previous phrase. The words "needs to mark the sentimental places" prompt an undulating vocal line in dotted rhythm using only steps and skips, a melodic style Ives associated with sentimental parlor songs in both their shopworn style and their expressions of true feeling; compare his setting of the words "the same old sentimental sound" in *On the Counter* (shown in Example 7.3), and the similar style throughout much of *The Greatest Man*. Accompanying this phrase in the voice, the piano chords alternate B♭ and B♮ paired with E♮ and E♭, suggesting the chromaticism of the parlor song style without directly imitating it. Up to this point, each phrase has used a different collection of six or eight notes, demarking each image in the text with a change of harmony. The next phrase returns to the same collection of notes found in the opening bars (later adding B and F♯), but the harmony is different—a minor seventh-chord on D instead of a major seventh-chord on F—and the melody here is diatonic rather than pentatonic, evoking the soaring intensity of Romantic song through an upward leap and diatonic descent. The last two measures return to the opening music and the opening image ("journey" harks back to "walking").

These shifts of figuration serve a rhetorical purpose, using stylizations of familiar musical types in order to highlight each image of the poem. But they also serve a formal purpose, dividing the song into segments marked off by changes of figuration and arranged in a kind of stylistic arch. The song moves from quasi-pentatonic through diatonic to somewhat chromatic and back, hinting at the styles of folk song, hymn, sentimental parlor song, Romantic air, and folk song again. The pitch content and harmony are coordinated with this arch, balancing a move to the flat side in m. 3 with one to the sharp side in m. 6. The music is perfectly suited to the changing images of the text but is coherent in itself. This is typical of Ives. As Larry Starr has shown, changing style from section to section is a basic element of Ives's method in many mature works, where it plays both a rhetorical and a formal role.[58]

Ives's allusions to familiar styles, the division of his music into segments marked off by changes of style, the coordination of pitch content and harmony with these changes, and the congruence of musical rhetoric and structure all have precedents in the core of the European classical repertoire, from Haydn and Mozart through Mahler and Debussy. Although the music of Haydn and Mozart may sound stylistically consistent to modern ears, that is only because we are no longer familiar with the great variety of musical styles current in their day, each of which carried its own associations. Much as the styles of waltzes, hymns, church bells, cowboy songs, Anglican chants, parlor songs, piano rags, and marches each evoked for Ives and his contemporaries a particular group of people in particular circumstances engaged in a particular activity, so too did various types of music for people in the eighteenth century: dance styles were associated with certain social classes and moods (the minuet and sarabande with courtly formality and elegance, contradanses and Ländler with boisterous rural folk); various march styles with ballrooms,

EXAMPLE 7.13: *Resolution*

parade grounds, or funerals; fanfares with the military; horn calls with the hunt and therefore with the upper classes and with nature; bagpipe music with shepherds and pastoral scenes; and so on.[59] Composers evoked various types to set a mood, illustrate a text, or delineate a character in an opera. In the later eighteenth century it became common to shift from style to style, marking off the rapid changes of mood and situation in a vocal work or the sections of an instrumental work. The opening scene of Mozart's *Don Giovanni* shifts between comedy and tragedy and between low- and high-born characters, and the music reflects each character and twist of the plot. In Mozart's Piano Sonata in F Major K. 332, the changes of style have a more purely formal role, marking off each part of the exposition with a unique figuration and style: legato yet angular, as in an aria, for the opening idea; like a horn call for the following period; minor-mode and dramatic, almost stormy, for the transition; songlike for the second theme; and so forth, with a new musical character every few measures. In works like these, the contrast of style and type is part of the musical rhetoric, leading the listener through a series of moods that unfolds like a drama, and also of the musical structure, demarcating sections, phrases, and major harmonic goals. Beethoven, Wagner, Mahler, Debussy, Strauss, and younger composers such as Berg and Bartók all show this same use of diverse styles to evoke particular associations while delineating the musical structure. In every case, as with Ives, continuities of motive, pitch content, and harmony help counterbalance these changes of figuration and type, but the very strength of the contrasts helps to make the form clear. Ives's music is very much part of this tradition.

Stylistic Allusion and Explicit Borrowing as Ends of a Continuum

Ives's ability to evoke the character of an entire genre or type in a few notes or chords depended upon his command of a great variety of musical styles, styles that he assimilated during his youth and apprenticeship by imitating models. What unites Ives's early dependence on models with his mature practice of alluding to existing music is his focus on imitating recognizable elements of a style or type; what changes over time, besides his level of familiarity with various musical types and his skill in manipulating and combining elements of the styles he knew, is his awareness of the associations carried by each stylistic convention and his sophistication in juxtaposing them to create multiple levels of meaning.

At all stages of Ives's career, there is a continuum between his citations of particular pieces and his evocations of broad conventions. The quotation of a familiar tune, the use of a familiar turn of melody, the appearance of a familiar sound or rhythmic pattern, all play similar roles: in his early works, as part of his attempt to write successful music in many genres by imitating pieces of each type; in his mature works, as techniques used to recreate the experience of hearing music, to comment on musical style, to convey a feeling, or to lend a certain character to the music. An identifiable tune may carry additional meanings because of its unique text or associations, but the primary meanings carried by most allusions to existing music derive from the associations listeners have with the type of music alluded to, rather than with the particular piece.

It is in the context of this approach, in which modeling and stylistic allusion create meaning through the associations listeners have with various types and styles of music, that the more overt borrowings of Ives's later music can be understood. Patchwork and extended paraphrase, treated in the next chapter, also derive their meaning primarily from the types of music evoked but create most or all of the melodic substance of a work through paraphrase, either from many tunes (in patchwork) or from a single one (in extended paraphrase). Programmatic quotation, examined in chapter 9, also depends on our knowledge of general musical types to evoke a feeling or depict an event, but it carries even more specific meanings for those who know and recognize the music that is quoted. Collage, discussed in chapter 10, relies on the same approach as the works considered in this chapter, but uses many more existing tunes, as if to multiply the effect. These procedures gave Ives a number of options, allowing him to tailor his methods to the requirements of each piece. Yet in most pieces and for most listeners, the exact tune used, the number of tunes used, the amount of borrowed material, and the extent to which this material is reworked through paraphrase all matter less than the feelings, people, places, situations, or events we associate with the types of music these borrowed tunes represent. As different as these procedures are from each other, Ives turns them all to similar ends and particularly to the two purposes served by modeling and stylistic allusion in the works considered in this chapter: to comment on music, especially by recreating the experience of hearing it and responding to it emotionally; and to evoke a certain feeling, mood, or character.

CHAPTER 8

Patchwork and
Extended Paraphrase

Among the new procedures that Ives began to use after 1902 are two extensions of paraphrase technique that create an extended melody by reworking one or several borrowed tunes. In *patchwork*, a melody is stitched together from fragments paraphrased from many tunes.[1] In *extended paraphrase*, the main melody of an entire work is paraphrased from an existing tune. The latter has roots as far back as the introduction to the *Variations on "America"* (1891–92), and the former builds on the idea of joining related tunes into a composite melody, such as the blend of *Shining Shore* with *Azmon* in the *Fugue in Four Keys on "The Shining Shore"* (ca. 1902) But patchwork has another source as well, in the American popular music of Tin Pan Alley.

Patchwork

In a patchwork, fragments of several tunes are joined into a single melody, sometimes elided through paraphrase and sometimes interspersed with new music. The sources for any one piece are usually drawn from a single genre, making this in many respects an extension of modeling, perhaps influenced by medley or quodlibet. The effect is like that of stylistic allusion, but with direct borrowing. This connection is especially clear in works, such as *Old Home Day*, that intermix references to general types and to particular tunes.

Patchworks Based on Hymn Melodies

A good example of patchwork is *The Last Reader*, a song without words for theater orchestra from the early 1910s, recast for voice and piano in 1921.[2] The words are serious and hymnlike, and the music draws on several hymn tunes. The opening bars of *Cherith* (H11), arranged from Ludwig Spohr, and *Manoah* (H34), adapted from Haydn by Henry W. Greatorex, are quoted directly, as Ives indicates on the score. Example 8.1 shows that a complete paraphrase of *Cherith* appears in mm. 1–8, with two motives, marked by a horizontal brace and bracket, transferred to the piano. This tune's movement from the tonic F major to the dominant C major and back recalls the similar effect in the Second Symphony finale theme paraphrased from "De Camptown Races." Into this paraphrase are woven bits of melody that suggest other tunes: fragments of *St. Peter* in various keys, missing only mm. 3–4 of the hymn; motives from *Bethany*; and perhaps part of the sentimental song "The Old Oaken Bucket." At m. 8, *Manoah* appears, at first in the voice and then in the piano, repeating fragments from mm. 4–6 and 10–11 of the hymn. This is succeeded by a close paraphrase of the third phrase of *Bethany* in mm. 14–17. *Manoah* returns in mm. 17–19, sounding in context somewhat like *St. Peter* in a different key. The cadence is based on both *Manoah* and *Cherith*, possibly influenced by *Watchman* or other hymns with similar cadences. Measures 8–22 include an almost complete, modulating paraphrase of *Manoah*, with interpolations. This list of borrowings runs the gamut from the explicit and acknowledged citations of the two main sources through the clear but unacknowledged reference to *Bethany* to possibly coincidental similarities; there may be others, or some of these may be illusory.[3]

The borrowed tunes do not illustrate the text. *Cherith, Manoah,* and *St. Peter* are each sung to several hymn texts, none of which is clearly linked to the words of this song. Rather, the hymn tunes lend a particular mood, dignified, reverent, and a bit nostalgic. The piece may be heard as a hymnlike song

EXAMPLE 8.1: *The Last Reader* and its sources

PATCHWORK AND EXTENDED PARAPHRASE

EXAMPLE 8.1, continued

EXAMPLE 8.1, continued

modeled on hymns or as a quodlibet based on existing tunes.[4] In fact, it is both; it is a patchwork, a cento—"a composition formed by joining scraps from other authors," in Samuel Johnson's definition of the latter term— which succeeds on its own, without requiring that the scraps be recognized, because the sources all share a similar character.

Ives wrote several other patchworks, most associated with a text. Some are based on tunes of a single type, either hymns or patriotic and military music;

Manoah in D

Cherith in D

Watchman in D

steal - ing half its snows a - way.

l.h. r.h.

r.h.

pp   morendo   ppp

EXAMPLE 8.1, continued

these pieces typically use the associations that type of music carries to create a certain mood, as does *The Last Reader*. Other works mix tunes of various types, and these are about the music they describe.

The patchworks based on hymns are similar to the works described in chapter 7 that allude to hymn style or to a particular hymn in order to set a reverent mood but differ from the latter in the number of hymns used. For instance, *Religion* (discussed in chapter 3) blends *Azmon, Shining Shore*, and *Bethany*, rather than relying on only one source. Unlike *The Last Reader*, whose melody is almost wholly derived from hymn tunes, the other patchworks based on hymns interpolate much free material between borrowed or paraphrased passages.

Largo cantabile (Hymn) for string quintet or string orchestra (between ca. 1904 and ca. 1914, recast in 1921 as *Hymn* for voice and piano) uses the initial motives from three hymn tunes.[5] The most important is the opening of W. H. Doane's *More Love to Thee* (H39), which pervades the introduction (mm. 1–13, or mm. 1–7 of the song), begins the main melody (mm. 14–15, cello, or 8–9, voice), returns twice to accompany the other two hymn fragments, and is paraphrased in the eighth-note figure that lends a whole-tone cast to the accompaniment. After beginning with this hymn, the principal melody continues freely through the first half of the song. The second half begins with the second hymn tune (mm. 21–23/15–17), which may be *David*, adapted from Handel, or *Hexham*, from Mendelssohn's Song Without Words, Op. 30, No. 3 ("Consolation").[6] The song concludes with the opening of *Olivet* ("My faith looks up to Thee," in mm. 27–29/21–23).

In *Adagio sostenuto* for chamber ensemble (ca. 1919, arranged 1921 as the song *At Sea*), the main melody includes several segments that recall hymn tunes, including *Azmon* at mm. 6–8, the third phrase of *Missionary Chant* at mm. 8–10, and *Bethany* or perhaps Samuel Webbe's *Come, Ye Disconsolate* in the opening motive and its later variants (mm. 2–3, 5–6, and 11–12). The resemblance to *Bethany* is made stronger by the song's form, which is like that of the hymn: four phrases, all but the third beginning with a similar figure.[7]

In none of these patchworks based on hymns is there any apparent intent to illustrate the text, nor is there a significant correspondence between the song's words and any text associated with the hymns used. Their function seems simply to lend the music the character and dignity of hymns.

Songs About Popular Music

Two songs about popular music use patchwork. *The Things Our Fathers Loved* (ca. 1917, from a lost orchestral work of ca. 1914), shown in Example 8.2, is a virtual catalogue of the types of popular song Ives used in his music.[8] The opening melody has been identified as Dan Emmett's "Dixie" (H76), but when Ives uses this tune in other works he retains its rapid tempo and, in most cases, its initial downward arpeggiation. Here the slow tempo and initial stepwise descent, imitated in the piano, suggest instead a phrase from Stephen Foster's "My Old Kentucky Home," its first four notes inverted to recall *Nettleton*. Indeed, the early sketches show several versions of a melody that resembles the Foster tune and is recast by stages into the opening as it stands in the song.[9] After the Foster phrase repeats in another key, again slightly altered, we hear in succession fragments of Paul Dresser's "On the Banks of the Wabash, Far Away"; *Nettleton;* George F. Root's "The Battle Cry of Freedom," its verse paraphrased and then quoted in the voice and accompanied by its chorus in the piano; *In the Sweet Bye and Bye,* with a figure from "The Battle Cry of Freedom" continuing in the accompaniment; and a return to the opening idea. Each of these fragments represents a specific type of tune: popular songs from the mid-nineteenth century (the Foster, from 1853) and the turn of the century (the Dresser, from 1897), hymn tunes from

EXAMPLE 8.2: *The Things Our Fathers Loved* and its sources

Sa - rah hum- ming Gos - pels; Sum - mer eve - nings, The

"The Battle Cry of Freedom"
(chorus)

"The Battle Cry of Freedom"

faster and with more emphasis   *in a gradually excited way*

vil- lage cor- net band, play - ing in the square. The town's Red, White and Blue,

EXAMPLE 8.2, continued

In the Sweet Bye and Bye

all Red, White and Blue _____ Now! Hear the

più accel.

l.h.

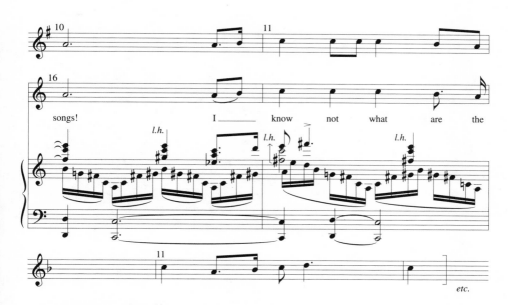

songs! I _____ know not what are the

l.h.   l.h.   l.h.

etc.

EXAMPLE 8.2, continued

EXAMPLE 8.2, continued

the early and later nineteenth century (*Nettleton* from ca. 1812 and *In the Sweet Bye and Bye* from 1868), and patriotic songs from the Civil War era. The text of Ives's song is about these different kinds of music and the values they represent, from religion to patriotism. It is not crucial to the song's meaning that a listener identify the borrowed songs or think of their words; what is most important is the character of the songs, each of which represents a type of song that played a distinctive role in American society in Ives's day and is endowed with a particular emotional resonance.

What Ives's song is about, ultimately, is the power of tunes, even without a text, to embody and remind us of what we value. As Ives says in his poem,

Now! Hear the songs! I know not what are the words
But they sing in my soul of the things our Fathers loved.

The next to last line makes clear that it is not the words but the tunes themselves that carry the meaning Ives celebrates in his song. The song's subtitle, "and the greatest of these was Liberty," makes clear that "the things our Fathers loved" Ives has in mind are not merely the tunes themselves, but the values they represent. Here is where knowing the texts for the songs Ives borrows adds meaning, for they name these values: home; the natural beauty of one's homeland; religious faith; patriotism and group feeling; and hope for a future reunion with those we love, in Heaven if not on earth. These are the things our fathers loved, the fruits of liberty. This is not an exercise in nostalgia for the songs and scenes of the past; rather, Ives regards the songs he uses as reminders of the virtues that we inherit from the past and still need in the present.[10]

Another song about popular music, *Old Home Day* (ca. 1913–14, rev. 1920), also with a text by Ives, mixes patchwork with stylistic allusion.[11] It begins with an impressionistic setting of a line from Virgil, "Go my songs! Draw Daphnis from the city," like an operatic prologue played before the curtain. When the curtain opens, we hear "A minor tune from Todd's opera house": not a borrowing, but a melody that suggests an operetta or music hall song in a syncopated turn-of-the-century style. At the words "We boys used to shout the songs that rouse the hearts of the brave and fair," Ives turns to a paraphrase, then direct quotation of part of "The Battle Hymn of the Republic."[12] An imitation of drums playing the "street beat" introduces the chorus: "As we march along down Main street, behind the village band," set to an apparently original tune in march style.[13] For a phrase that mentions "an Irish song," Ives's melody turns to the triplet lilt of Irish dance tunes, again without borrowing any particular song. The chorus ends wistfully: "underneath's a note of sadness, 'Old home town' farewell," set to H. S. Thompson's song "Annie Lisle" (H95), the tune for the "Alma Mater" of many colleges. The vocal line is based more on stylistic allusion than on actual borrowing. But after the second verse, the chorus is accompanied by an optional obbligato for fife, violin, or flute composed entirely of fragments borrowed or paraphrased from folk or traditional tunes: the fiddle tune "Arkansas Traveler" (H158, in m. 21) and the army song "The Girl I Left Behind Me" (H102, in mm. 22–28) accompanying the march; the Irish dance tunes "Garryowen" (H163, in mm. 28–30) and "Saint Patrick's Day" (H168, in mm. 31–32) at the mention of "an old breakdown" playing an "Irish song"; "Auld Lang Syne" (in mm. 33–36c) at the closing nostalgic phrase; and, in a brief coda, the bugle call "Assembly" (H70) and a recollection of the opening motive of Ives's chorus tune.[14] This song is about the place of music in a small town and the memories it may evoke, and the elevated tone of the opening music and the respectful references that follow lend a dignity to small-town life, music, and memories. This is reinforced by the invocation from Virgil, with its classical atmosphere (the original Latin is printed in the score, like an epigraph) and its tribute to the power of songs to draw us out of the city and, by implication, back to our small-town roots.[15]

Songs and Choral Works on Patriotic Subjects

The remaining songs and choral works that use patchwork are on patriotic subjects and draw almost exclusively on patriotic tunes. *Lincoln, the Great Commoner* for voice and piano or for unison chorus and orchestra (ca. 1921) sets lines from Edwin Markham's poem that tell of Lincoln's idealism, the saving of the Union, and the nobility of his death.[16] The vocal melody is mostly original, but in three passages it borrows or paraphrases fragments of several patriotic tunes: "Hail! Columbia" (H77, adapted from "The President's March" by Philip Phile) in mm. 12–13 and 28; "The Star-Spangled Banner" (H86, adapted from a song by John Stafford Smith), present but hard to recognize in mm. 15–16 and 44–45; the middle phrase of *America* at mm. 16–18 and 32–34; and brief snatches of the opening of "Columbia, the Gem of the Ocean" and the cadence of "The Battle Hymn of the Republic" at mm. 28–31.[17] In addition, motives from "The Battle Hymn" play a significant role in the accompaniment near the beginning and end (mm. 4–13 and 35–44 in various instruments), and most of the other tunes used in the voice also appear briefly in the accompaniment.[18] None of these fragments seems intended to make a listener think of the text of the borrowed song, and indeed several are hard to recognize, as the borrowed segment is either distorted or taken from a less memorable part of the tune. Rather, the reminiscences of these tunes lend a patriotic atmosphere to the piece, whether they are consciously identified or heard as familiar-sounding snatches in the style of patriotic song.

The First World War inspired the other three songs or choral works that use patchwork. The first was *Sneak Thief*, sketched ca. 1914 in protest against Germany's invasion of Belgium and apparently left unfinished.[19] It is mostly atonal, angular, and dissonant, capturing Ives's outrage. But near the end is a patchwork of patriotic and military tunes, starting in the accompaniment with a blend of "Reveille" (under the words "get up") and the opening figures of Henry Clay Work's "Marching Through Georgia" (H79) and *America*. In the chorus, as the words express hope for creating a "People's World Union," the voice borrows the first phrase of "The Star-Spangled Banner" while a trumpet obbligato melds motives from "Columbia, the Gem of the Ocean," "Marching Through Georgia," "Assembly," and "Reveille."[20]

In 1917, Ives's business partner Julian Myrick suggested that Ives set to music John McCrae's war poem "In Flanders Fields," and in April 1917, just as the United States was entering the war, Ives's song was performed at a luncheon for managers associated with the insurance company Ives and Myrick represented.[21] Both voice and piano alternate borrowed and original material. At the climactic words "Take up our quarrel with the foe!" (mm. 29–33), the "Aux armes, citoyens" phrase of "La Marseillaise" in the voice is joined by *America* in the piano, symbolizing the passing of the torch from the dead French soldiers to the Americans. Other borrowings are less directly related to the text, with "Columbia, the Gem of the Ocean" prominent at beginning and end (mm. 2–4, 8–10, 34–35, and 37–39) and *America* (mm. 14–17 and 34–37), "The Battle Cry of Freedom" (mm. 6 and 18–19), and bugle calls ("Reveille" in mm. 20–21 and what may be "Taps" in m. 14) all playing a role. The beginning, climax, and end are all signalled by an imitation of the "street beat" pattern of drums (mm. 7–8, 28–29, and 40–42).[22] The only non-military source is a hymn whose text is replete with martial imagery, *All Saints New* (H2, "The Son of God goes forth to war," tune by Henry S. Cutler). Its third phrase seems to be quoted at "Short days ago we lived, felt dawn" (mm. 22–24); perhaps the sentiment of these words required a hymnlike rather than patriotic setting.

He Is There! was written later that spring and arranged both as a song and as a work for unison chorus and instruments. In 1942, Ives revised the song, wrote new words, and retitled it *They Are There!* to fit the new World War, and this version was later arranged for chorus and orchestra by Lou Harrison.[23] Like *Old Home Day*, this song combines original and borrowed material in the vocal melody and adds to the song's chorus an obbligato for violin, flute, or fife that is almost entirely paraphrased from existing tunes. Most tune fragments cited in the voice and piano are linked with appropriate words in the first verse and chorus of Ives's poem: parts of Ives's *Country Band March* appear in the piano introduction (mm. 1–2) and at the words "Marched beside his granddaddy" (mm. 8–9); a phrase from "Marching Through Georgia," a Civil War song, sets the words "The village band would play those old war tunes, and the G. A. R. [Grand Army of the Republic] would shout" (mm. 12–14); "Tenting on the Old Camp Ground" is paraphrased twice, at "sounded on the old camp ground" (mm. 18–19) and "Tenting on a new camp ground" (mm. 34–38 and 40–44, numbering the second ending as m. 40); three excerpts from "Columbia, the Gem of the Ocean" appear (mm. 19–21, 27–30, and 32–33), the first to the words "That boy has sailed o'er the ocean"; and both text and music of "The Battle Cry of Freedom" are quoted at the end of the song (mm. 44–48, hinted at in mm. 38–39 at the end of the first chorus and anticipated by the words "shout the Battle cry of Freedom" in mm. 32-33, set to part of "Columbia"). Only one tune, "Tramp, Tramp, Tramp," appears with words unrelated to its original text (mm. 23–25). In addition, two phrases repeat the title words "He is there" three times in a rhythm that recalls George M. Cohan's "Over There" (H82), although the melody is different (mm. 21–23 and 25–27). Since Ives wrote the text, the many correspondences between music and words suggest that Ives set out to create a patchwork of allusions, both textual and musical. That Ives conceived of these as something other than direct quotations is indicated by his footnote to this song in 114 Songs, which refers to the tunes "suggested" in the music.[24] The obbligato is almost entirely based on borrowed tunes: "Dixie" (mm. 21–23), "Marching Through Georgia" (mm. 23 and 25–26), "Yankee Doodle" (m. 24), fanfare motives (mm. 28–29), "Maryland, My Maryland" (H81, to the traditional German tune "O Tannenbaum," mm. 29–30), "La Marseillaise" (mm. 31–35), "The Battle Cry of Freedom" (mm. 43–47), and "The Star Spangled Banner" (mm. 48–49).[25] In the choral version, the trombone adds the opening of "The Battle Hymn of the Republic" (mm. 20–23) at the beginning of the chorus, and in They Are There! the coda includes more extensive quotations of "The Star-Spangled Banner" (mm. 48–51) and "Reveille" (mm. 51–53).[26]

The appearance of Civil War songs in two songs about World War I may seem odd from a distance of three generations. But in 1917 the Civil War was the last great war the United States had experienced, and many of its veterans were still alive. Ives makes the connection explicit, recalling in his text to He Is There! how "a little Yankee with a German name" marched with his grandfather in the Decoration Day parade commemorating the Civil War dead, heard his grandfather tell of leaving Germany after the failed 1848 revolutions, and now as an adult is going back to "finish up that aged job." In the first draft of the second stanza, Ives reinforced this connection by referring to Carl Schurz, who was involved in the 1848–49 German revolution, fled to the United States, worked against slavery and for Negro rights, and was a Union general in the Civil War.[27] In a typewritten note, Ives writes,

> The second verse was inserted in the realization of the added strain that American soldiers of German descent are under.
> The forbears of many of them were exiled from Germany after the revolution of 1848, and came to the United States as a country where their

ideals could be realized. Carl Schurz was an example of this kind of patriot; like him, many of them fought under the Stars and Stripes against slavery in this country. The hope of a "free Germany" was always with them, and now their boys are fighting for the fulfillment of that hope.[28]

Thus Ives placed this song firmly in the context of the ideals that nurtured past struggles for justice and freedom, rather than of the anti-German sentiment then rife in the United States. The many allusions to Civil War songs deepen this sentiment, emphasizing idealism rather than jingoism.

Instrumental Patchworks

Most of Ives's patchworks are vocal works or instrumental versions of works with text, but three are solely instrumental. Here the relationship between patchwork and modeling is especially clear. There are no texts and no real programs, only attempts to capture a mood. To this end, Ives weaves together borrowed fragments with original material modeled on the same musical type, from fiddle tunes to Stephen Foster songs.[29]

The second movement of the Second Violin Sonata (ca. 1907–19), titled "In the Barn," combines a barn dance episode, adapted from the rejected scherzo of the "Pre-First" Violin Sonata, with a fantasia on a Civil War tune. After a brief introduction, the barn dance opens with an original Ives quadrille theme in the violin. Bits of two traditional fiddle tunes drop into the melody: "Sailor's Hornpipe" (mm. 15–16, 24–27, 30–31, and 40–43) and "Money Musk" (mm. 35–39). After a ragtime episode partly borrowed from *Ragtime Dance No. 1* (mm. 40 and 43–62), two more fiddle tunes appear: "The White Cockade" (mm. 64–68, piano, and 68–71, violin) and a modified "Turkey in the Straw" (mm. 70–71 and 73–83, violin, and 71–73, piano).[30] The fiddle tunes are all in duple meter, and each shares melodic ideas with one or more of the others. The violin continues with fragments of "Turkey in the Straw" and "Money Musk" mixed with original fiddle-tune figuration in a continuous stream of sixteenth notes. A change of meter, tempo, and mood marks a new section (mm. 108–74), based primarily on an extended paraphrase of "The Battle Cry of Freedom" in the violin (verse in mm. 108–20 and 140–57, chorus in mm. 125–37 and 158–62). The fiddle tunes return in fragments, mixed with phrases from the Civil War song, until "The White Cockade" appears in the violin over the verse of "The Battle Cry of Freedom" in the piano (mm. 194–98), the latter adapted from the first movement coda of the "Pre-First" Sonata. From here to the end, motives from "The Battle Cry of Freedom" are developed in both instruments, continuing to draw on the earlier sonata movement coda. Like the other violin sonata movements, this is a character piece, not a programmatic work. The first half wonderfully recreates the spirit of a barn dance, the presence of ragtime and a Civil War tune pays homage to other American musical traditions and the spirit they convey, and the intermingling of material at the end recalls the closing sections of cumulative settings and other movements in which the various themes come together. The particular mix of tunes may be explained by motivic interrelationships, including a resemblance between the openings of "The White Cockade" and "The Battle Cry of Freedom."

Another patchwork, in a much more solemn mood, is the first movement of the Second Orchestral Set (ca. 1914–15, revised in the 1920s), now entitled *An Elegy to Our Forefathers* but originally called *An Elegy for Stephen Foster*.[31] Here Ives reduces his source tunes to basic pentatonic gestures and recombines them in a haunting work that seems to evoke a procession of ancestors, slowly approaching, coming into focus, and retreating into the distance. Over a bed of ostinatos and mostly static harmony appear three main melodic strands: a leading melody in the trumpet and violins; a softer descant in the flute and violins; and a continuous melody in the zither, almost inaudible in the recordings. The piece opens very softly, as if just coming into earshot, and the zither enters with a partial paraphrase of the chorus of Foster's "Old Black Joe" (H128) at the words "I'm coming, I'm coming, for my head is bending low." At m. 13 (reh. A), the muted trumpet and violins begin a paraphrase of the chorus of William Bradbury's *Jesus Loves Me*, which closely resembles the Foster melody, while the zither continues its paraphrase of the latter, reworked to sound like part of the verse of Foster's "Massa's in de Cold Ground." All three source tunes are primarily pentatonic melodies that emphasize the third, fifth, sixth, and eighth scale degrees and sound a bit alike, and Ives capitalizes on this throughout to move seamlessly between tunes. A brief motive in the second trumpet and violins in m. 15 may be a reference to the spiritual "Oh, Nobody Knows de Trouble I've Seen" (H43). Fanfares based on "Assembly" or "Reveille" in the flutes and violins (reh. B, m. 20) signal the middle section, which grows in dynamic level and then recedes. Here the trumpet and first violins blend the last phrase of *Jesus Loves Me* (mm. 21–25 and 29–31) with part of the chorus of "Massa's in de Cold Ground" (reh. C, mm. 25–29, the dynamic high point of the movement); the flute and second violins present and extend the first half of the chorus of "Massa's in de Cold Ground" (mm. 24–27 and 30–35); and the zither presents the chorus complete (mm. 21–31).[32] As these ideas conclude and the music softens, the zither returns to the chorus of "Old Black Joe," at first indistinctly and then with a clear statement of its first half (reh. E, mm. 37–40), together with the first half of the chorus of "Massa" in the harp and bells. The work fades to a close, repeating two- and three-note figures from the source tunes.

This entire process unfolds over a bass ostinato of a falling and rising minor third, derived from the opening motive shared by the choruses of "Old Black Joe" and *Jesus Loves Me*.

The *"St.-Gaudens" in Boston Common (Col. Shaw and his Colored Regiment)* (composed between ca. 1915 and ca. 1923 and revised 1929), the first movement of *Three Places in New England*, is similar to *An Elegy* in sound, mood, and thematic sources.[33] It is a tribute to the Civil War monument by Augustus Saint-Gaudens at the northeast corner of Boston Common and to the people depicted there, the first regiment of black soldiers in the Union Army and their white commander, Col. Robert Gould Shaw. The Fifty-fourth Massachusetts Regiment was formed in late 1862, and in July 1863, in an assault on Fort Wagner in South Carolina, half the regiment was killed, including Shaw.[34] Ives's piece captures the slow pace of their march south to battle, yet is more descriptive than programmatic. Like *An Elegy to Our Forefathers*, it builds to a dynamic high point and then recedes, but there is a real climax here and a more sudden falling away, perhaps a hint of the regiment's fate.

Just as Saint-Gaudens presents the most distant figures in faint outline, nearer ones in relief, and the closest, including Shaw on horseback, in full sculpture, so Ives presents gestures and tunes in varying levels of audibility and recognizability, throwing some into relief and leaving others as wisps in the background. Throughout most of the piece, the main melody in the first violin is a patchwork of motives from Foster's plantation tunes "Old Black Joe" and "Massa's in de Cold Ground" and the Civil War song "Marching Through Georgia," and fragments of these tunes also appear from time to time in other instruments. Example 8.3 shows the opening melody as an amalgam of motives drawn from these tunes, sometimes overlapping.[35] Here the links between patchwork, paraphrase, and modeling are particularly clear, for although almost every note is borrowed, the individual motives are obscured and elided through paraphrase, so that one hears in this melody, not specific tunes, but the general style of lyrical pentatonic melodies, the archetypal American sound from which mid-nineteenth-century songwriters drew. We do not listen for borrowed tunes here, and we may not even notice them, but we can sense in this melody of pentatonic fragments over hazily chromatic harmony the tone of wistful remembrance of a Stephen Foster song.

The piece unfolds in a sort of lopsided arch.[36] The opening melody appears over a bass ostinato of a rising minor third in uneven rhythm. This both suggests the slow trudge of a regiment on the march and echoes the repeated figures that open the choruses of "Old Black Joe" and "Marching Through Georgia." Example 8.4 shows this ostinato and related motives in

"Massa's in de Cold Ground"

Hear dat mourn - ful sound;

"Old Black Joe" in C

I'm com - ing,   I'm com - ing,

Ives   Vn. I, upper line

"Old Black Joe" in G

I'm   com - ing,   I'm com - ing, for my head   is

cresc.

"Marching through Georgia"

Bring the good old   bu - gle, boys! We'll sing an - oth - er   song,

"Marching through Georgia" (chorus)

"Hur - rah! Hur - rah!   we   bring

"Old Black Joe" in C

I'm com - ing   I'm com - ing, for my head is bend - ing   low:

the Ju - bi - lee!"

From *Three Places in New England.* © 1935 and 1976 by Mercury Music Corporation. Used by Permission.

EXAMPLE 8.3: *The "St.-Gaudens" in Boston Common, opening melody, and its sources*

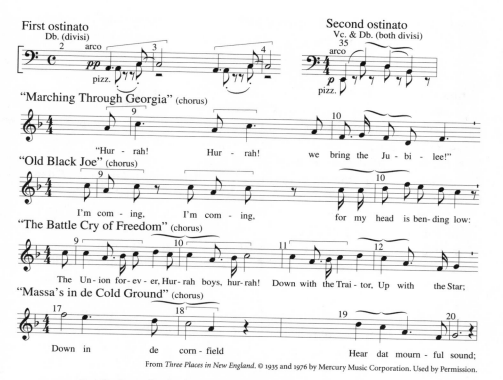

From *Three Places in New England*. © 1935 and 1976 by Mercury Music Corporation. Used by Permission.

EXAMPLE 8.4: Ostinato figures in *The "St.-Gaudens" in Boston Common* and similar motives in the four source tunes

the source tunes, marked with horizontal square brackets. At mm. 24–27 (reh. B), this ostinato ceases and the first violin melody coalesces into a complete paraphrase of the first half of the chorus of "Old Black Joe." Throughout the first section, other instruments occasionally echo the tunes in the main theme, and hints are heard of the chorus of "The Battle Cry of Freedom" (mm. 14 and 18–19, violin I, and 27–28, flute and oboe), which will play a significant role later on. This is another Civil War song, and it shares the motive of the falling and rising minor third (here decorated by a passing tone), as Example 8.4 shows.

A new section begins at m. 35 (reh. D) with a paraphrase of the first half of the chorus of "Marching Through Georgia" in the violins. Here the drums begin the "street beat" pattern, which continues to the end of the work; this conveys the sound and feeling of a slow but steady march, now less uneven and more determined. Here too begins a second bass ostinato whose motive of a falling major second and minor third echoes figures from all four source tunes (marked with horizontal braces in Example 8.4).[37] A brief ragtime episode at m. 42 (reh. E), apparently without borrowed material, may suggest the black soldiers, not through Foster's plantation songs, but through the syncopations of their own music. The next section develops motives from the verse of "Marching Through Georgia" (reh. F, mm. 48–65), building to a climax through ever more forceful repetition of a rising motive (m. 5 of the tune, at mm. 50, 53, 58, and 60). Other tunes appear briefly: in the horn, "Reveille" (m. 54) and what sounds like part of a spiritual, perhaps "Deep River" (H14, at mm. 56–57);[38] and at the peak, a trombone countermelody based on "The Battle Cry of Freedom" (mm. 58–62).

After the climax, the rest of the movement briefly recalls earlier material in reverse order. First is the partial paraphrase of the chorus of "Marching Through Georgia" (over the same ostinato as at reh. D), now with most of the chorus of "The Battle Cry of Freedom" in the flute as a countermelody (mm. 66–72). This passage is somewhat akin to the final thematic statement of a cumulative setting in texture, form, and feeling. The movement closes with reminiscences of the opening section and further variants of the three main sources for the opening melody, including the most direct allusions to the verse of "Marching Through Georgia" (mm. 71–72, clarinet and horn) and to "Massa's in de Cold Ground" (mm. 72–73, violin I).[39] If the opening of the movement invokes the general style of nineteenth-century American melody, the closing section sets specific tunes in greater relief than elsewhere in the movement, as if through the experience of the music and its evocation of the black regiment's march a memory had come into stronger focus.

Melodic Interrelationships, Thematic Unity, and Levels of Meaning

Like the other two instrumental patchworks, The "St.-Gaudens" in Boston Common depends on Ives's exploitation of resemblances between existing tunes to create a continuous melody from borrowed and original elements. The borrowed tunes are more often fragmented and altered than stated directly, and Ives uses the resulting ambiguity to join them together or gradually turn one into another. In this movement, the two ostinatos that Ives abstracts from his sources highlight the remarkable fact that all four tunes feature pitch motives based on a minor third and on a major second and minor third, and that these motives appear in the first half of the chorus of each tune in the same order that the ostinatos are introduced in the work itself. This striking yet subtle similarity shows that Ives was thinking in terms of pure interval motives shared by all four tunes and rendered in rhythmically simple form in the ostinatos. Each tune presents these pitch motives in a different rhythm and metrical position (and in one case in inversion) for a

PATCHWORK AND EXTENDED PARAPHRASE

unique contour and feel. The way Ives combines these songs in this work both highlights their commonalities, by blending them into a patchwork melody and deriving ostinatos from motives they share, and points to the uniqueness of each, as it emerges from the thematic tapestry as a temporarily prominent quotation.

Ives clearly chose these tunes, not only for their extramusical associations, but also for their melodic similarities. Indeed, Ives is almost always attuned to such motivic connections between his sources. We have already seen examples in the First String Quartet, Second Symphony, Third Violin Sonata, First Piano Sonata, and *Serenity*, to name only a few, and we will see more in the *Concord Sonata, The Fourth of July*, the Fourth Symphony, and other works discussed in the following chapters. There has not been space to demonstrate such motivic links for all the pieces considered here. Yet such links have been shown often enough, in a wide enough range of pieces, that it must be taken as characteristic of Ives that he motivically relates each fragment he borrows to other tunes and to the surrounding music.

The view is occasionally still heard that, as Kurt Stone wrote of the Fourth Symphony at the time of its premiere and first recording, the tunes Ives uses in a work "have no apparent musical relevance to the whole of the work, nor do they even have any musical interrelationships among themselves," so that "one cannot escape the suspicion that musically speaking any other tunes would have done just as well, a somewhat disturbing thought."[40] Such a view rarely if ever holds up to close examination of the music and was long ago refuted for the Fourth Symphony.[41] It is clearly untrue for The *"St.-Gaudens" in Boston Common*, for although Ives may have begun with the idea of combining tunes of the Union cause with tunes that symbolize the slaves on the plantation, the ones he chose show strong motivic links and give rise to an intricate, unified motivic structure that works in purely musical terms.

In typical fashion, Ives makes it possible to approach the music in many different ways. If we recognize the tunes, we may recall their words and relate them to the program of a black regiment marching south to save the Union and end slavery: "I'm coming, I'm coming" (from "Old Black Joe"); "Hurrah! Hurrah! we bring the Jubilee!" (from "Marching Through Georgia"); "The Union forever, Hurrah boys, hurrah!" (from "The Battle Cry of Freedom"). These words add a level of irony, contradicting the somber, almost mournful music that depicts the slow march south to great loss of life. If we do not recall the words, but recognize the tunes and know them as Civil War and plantation songs, we still catch their import and relevance to the program. If we do not know the tunes, but recognize their character as patriotic and sentimental songs, that helps us to catch the special mood of this work, a mixture of patriotic devotion and touching sadness that is unusual in music. And if we do not notice any of the references to existing music, every motive will still sound like part of the thematic complex, integrated into the whole.

This is why, to quote Kurt Stone again, "it makes really not the slightest difference for the understanding of the *music* whether there are twenty-five popular melodies in the Fourth Symphony or thirty-two . . . or which tunes they are."[42] If one is concerned only with the music, not its meaning, Ives's works based on borrowed tunes almost always make perfect musical sense without one's recognizing a single tune. (The humorous quodlibets considered in chapter 10 represent a possible exception.) But there are multiple levels of meaning in each piece, and as we work from the musical material through the character of each melodic fragment, its musical type, and the associations that type of music carries, to specific associations with a particular tune, including its text, we may gain deeper insights.[43] The foundation is always the existing music itself and how it is used, for until we understand the full range of ways in which Ives draws on his borrowed material, we may misinterpret the more overt citations as mere quotations.

Patchwork in Tin Pan Alley Songs

Ives did not invent patchwork, nor did he find it in nineteenth-century art songs or instrumental works. Rather, his model seems to have been in popular song, most immediately in the patriotic songs of George M. Cohan. "The Yankee Doodle Boy," from Cohan's 1904 musical show *Little Johnny Jones*, was a great hit, and it is a classic example of patchwork, interspersing recognizable quoted or paraphrased tunes with original material. In the verse, shown in Example 8.5, both text and music refer to "Yankee Doodle," "Dixie," "The Girl I Left Behind Me," and "The Star Spangled Banner," with original ragtime-influenced phrases in between.[44] The chorus, not shown, is mostly original, with a final borrowing from "Yankee Doodle." The success of this song may have encouraged Cohan to repeat the procedure, for he wrote several more songs of this type. "You're a Grand Old Flag" (1906) uses fragments of text and music from "Dixie," "The Battle Cry of Freedom," and "Auld Lang Syne," and borrows music from Cohan's "Yankee Doodle Boy." "Under Any Old Flag at All" (1907) quotes from "Marching Through Georgia," "Dixie," "Maryland, My Maryland," and "Yankee Doodle" in the accompaniment, between phrases. "Yankee Doodle's Come to Town" (1908) paraphrases "The Girl I Left Behind Me" in the piano introduction and text and melody from "Yankee Doodle," "There'll Be a Hot Time in the Old Town Tonight," "Tramp, Tramp, Tramp," "Dixie," Cohan's own "Give My Regards to Broadway," and *America*. "Any Place the Old Flag Flies" (1911) uses "The Girl I Left Behind

"Yankee Doodle"

Cohan

I'm the kid that's all the can-dy, I'm a Yan-kee Doo-dle Dan-dy, I'm glad I am,

"Yankee Doodle"

Cohan

(chorus) (So's Un-cle Sam.) I'm a real live Yan-kee Doo-dle, Made my name and fame and boo-dle,

"Dixie"

"The Girl I Left Behind Me"

Cohan

Just like Mis-ter Doo-dle did, by rid-ing on a po-ny. I love to lis-ten to the Dix-ey strain, "I

"The Girl I Left Behind Me"

"The Star-Spangled Banner"

Oh

Cohan

long to see the girl I left be-hind me;" And that ain't a josh, She's a Yan-kee, by gosh. (Oh,

EXAMPLE 8.5: The verse of "The Yankee Doodle Boy" by George M. Cohan, with its sources

PATCHWORK AND EXTENDED PARAPHRASE

323

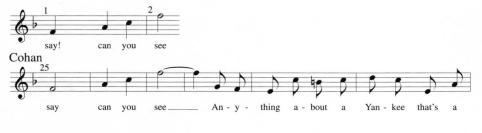

EXAMPLE 8.5, continued

Me" in the piano introduction and interlude, "Yankee Doodle" at the beginning of the verse, and "Dixie" near the end of the chorus.

Cohan was not the first or only songwriter to use this idea. Paul Dresser's "The Blue and the Gray" (1900), a tribute to a mother whose sons died in both Union and Confederate uniform, quotes "Yankee Doodle," the bugle call "Assembly," "Marching Through Georgia," and "Dixie" in the accompaniment to the chorus. A sequel on Irish soldiers in the Boer War, "The Green Above the Red" (1900), reworks Dresser's song of the Spanish-American War "We Are Coming, Cuba, Coming" (1898) and adds several Irish tunes to the accompaniment to the chorus. Harry Von Tilzer's "First Comes Your Duty to the Flag" (1901), a song about the Civil War, quotes "Dixie," "Marching Through Georgia," "Reveille," "The Star Spangled Banner," "Yankee Doodle," "Tramp, Tramp, Tramp," and "Hail! Columbia" in the piano. Later songwriters often quoted one or more tunes in their patriotic songs, though the extent of borrowing in Cohan's songs was rarely duplicated.

Among the many popular songs about music-making written in the era in which Ives was active as a composer, dozens quote a familiar tune, and a few use more than one. Charles K. Harris's "The Organ-Grinder's Serenade" (1897) quotes three of his own songs in the chorus: "After the Ball," "Creep, Baby, Creep," and "While the Dance Goes On." In the guise of celebrating "those dear sweet songs we used to play and sing" before ragtime and the tango took over popular music, Harris's "Songs of Yesterday" (1916) presents a virtual catalogue of his own works, stringing together excerpts from a dozen of his biggest hits from the previous quarter century. "Alexander's Ragtime Band" (1911) by Irving Berlin echoes a fanfare in the verse and Foster's "Old Folks at Home" in the chorus, and his sequel "Alexander's Bag-Pipe Band" (1912) quotes his own earlier song, "The Campbells Are Coming," "Auld Lang Syne," and "Old Folks at Home," the last a quotation of the quotation in the earlier song. These, like Cohan's patchworks, are extreme examples of Tin Pan Alley's fondness for quotation, especially in patriotic songs or songs about making music. This tradition will be discussed further in the next chapter.

Several conclusions can be drawn from this comparison of Ives with his contemporaries in Tin Pan Alley. First, the tunes used by Cohan, Dresser, and Von Tilzer include many of the same songs that Ives uses in his patriotic patchworks. The prominence of Civil War songs is especially notable. Second, Cohan, like Ives, often uses the same tunes repeatedly in different works. Third, Harris, Cohan, Dresser, and Berlin all borrow from themselves, as Ives does in using part of *Country Band March* in *He Is There!* Fourth, Ives appears to be exceptional in using hymn tunes, which are rarely used in the popular songs of his time.[45] But songs on patriotic subjects or about music are frequent in Tin Pan Alley, and these often feature one or more borrowed tunes; here Ives's patchworks find their closest parallel and most likely source. Fifth, although a complete survey of borrowing in American popular songs has yet to be undertaken, a preliminary survey of the works of several of the best known songwriters active between the 1840s and the 1920s shows a greatly increased use of quotation, including patchwork, from the turn of the century through World War I.[46] Ives follows a similar curve a few years later, suggesting that he was influenced by the trend in popular songs. He certainly knew the music of Harris, Dresser, Von Tilzer, and Cohan, for he quoted from all of them, and they were the leading figures of the first Tin Pan Alley generation.[47]

Finally, and most significant, Ives is writing art songs and instrumental art music, not popular songs. Of the Ives works surveyed here, only *He Is There!* is close in style to popular song. The others include sections of counterpoint, dissonance, impressionism, even atonality, all far from popular style. Even the tonal portions of *The Last Reader* and *The Things Our Fathers Loved* are allusive rather than fully tonal, as if tonality itself were a thing recalled from a distant time or place.[48] As in *Serenity* (discussed in chapter 7), this produces a feeling of remove. We are "in" one musical idiom, Ives's mature voice, talking about other idioms, those of hymns, popular music, or patriotic songs. By implication, the song speaks from one person's perspective about music that is part of a shared tradition, instantly recognizable by style if not by name.

The great stylistic gulf between the music that Ives borrows or paraphrases and the context that he creates around it emphasizes this sense of commentary. But there is a similar effect in Cohan's songs, although the difference in style is not so great. In "The Yankee Doodle Boy," between borrowings, Cohan sets the phrases "I'm glad I am, / So's Uncle Sam" and "that ain't no josh, / She's a Yankee, by gosh" in the ragtime-influenced idiom of the time. Because the Tin Pan Alley style of the early twentieth century is quite different from that of the eighteenth- or mid-nineteenth-century songs that Cohan borrows, we hear these phrases as if the singer is speaking in his own voice. The same effect is heard when Ives's *He Is There!* interleaves the current popular style with borrowed tunes from previous generations. The greater stylistic contrast in Ives's other works only heightens the effect of commenting in one's own voice on a type of music or on what that music represents.

This sense of speaking from one's own perspective, yet using music that is part of a common tradition to say what one means, seems central to much of Ives's late music, including his patchworks. According to John Kirkpatrick,

> Some instances [of musical quotation] are certainly for nostalgic evocation, . . . but most are probably due to a transcendentalist's faith in the validity of traditional or popular expressions to voice his own thoughts. In his setting of In Flanders Fields, for instance, he seems to be acting as a kind of musical scribe of the whole nation, being one with all those who had felt it deeply, and one with them in singing the old inspiring phrases. The result is anything but a pot-pourri.[49]

Ives does not presume to write from a universalist perspective; Kirkpatrick's view of his "acting as a kind of musical scribe of the whole nation" does not ring true. Rather, in these songs he seeks to capture a particular experience: reading one's own poems in *The Last Reader*; offering a private prayer in *Hymn*; recognizing the power of music to recall feelings, values, and memories in *The Things Our Fathers Loved* and *Old Home Day*. Even the national issues in *He Is There!* and *In Flanders Fields* are treated from an individual point of view. Only *Lincoln, the Great Commoner* adopts the voice of an omniscient narrator, and this of all these songs is the one in which the borrowings stand out least. But Ives clearly does "voice his own thoughts," as Kirkpatrick suggests, in part through the music that he shares with others who have similar backgrounds and experiences, music that he knows will speak to them at a level of feeling neither words nor his own original melodies could approach.

There is a great deal of variety in these works based on patchwork: in mood and character, in the stylistic range from popular song to radical modernism, in the number and types of songs used, in the proportion of borrowed to original material, and in the degree to which Ives's text draws on or relates to the texts of his sources, among other respects. And patchwork is only one of several borrowing procedures Ives was using in the years after

1902. The variety we see here reinforces one of the central points of this study: that there is not one procedure of quotation in Ives's music, but several procedures of using existing music, related by a common history yet different from one another in technique and intent. What we see in the development of Ives's procedures of borrowing is not a linear evolution but a branching, in which many different types become available, each suited for different purposes.

Extended Paraphrased Melodies in Ives's Mature Music

Paraphrase plays a role in many types of borrowing, from Ives's early variations to the recasting of tunes as themes in his First String Quartet and first two symphonies, from the gradual coming into recognizable form of a borrowed tune in his cumulative settings to the recombinations of familiar melodies in some of his patchworks. In a few mature works, Ives creates the leading melody through extended paraphrase of a single tune. Here the tune as a whole is used as a source; almost no elements are missing, although only the most direct references to the most characteristic parts of the source may be recognized; the entire substance of the principal melody is based on one or more statements of the source tune; and any introduction or postlude is partly derived from the source. This procedure differs in several respects from thematic paraphrase, in which a theme rather than the entire piece is based on a given tune, less salient parts of the source are often omitted, and both the theme and the movement as a whole may be structured differently from the source. Although there are only three works in this category, their importance and the distinctiveness of this procedure justify considering extended paraphrase as a separate type. Moreover, extended paraphrase plays a role in sections of some other works, such as the second movement of the Second Violin Sonata, whose middle section paraphrases two statements of "The Battle Cry of Freedom."

The Housatonic at Stockbridge for orchestra was begun in 1908, completed in the 1910s as the third movement of *Three Places in New England*, and arranged as a song in 1921 to lines excerpted from Robert Underwood Johnson's poem "To the Housatonic at Stockbridge."[50] The first sketch was inspired by a walk along the river that Charles and Harmony Ives shared in June 1908, soon after their marriage. Ives sought to capture the colors and motion of the mist, the waters, and the trees in dissonant, irregular ostinatos in the upper strings, and the sound of singing from a church across the river in the hymn-like melody in the horn, English horn, and violas, supported by the underlying harmony. This principal melody, shown in Example 8.6, is

EXAMPLE 8.6: The principal melody of *The Housatonic at Stockbridge*, analyzed as a four-verse paraphrase of *Dorrnance*

329

paraphrased from Isaac B. Woodbury's hymn tune *Dorrnance* (H15), also known as *Talmar* and *Chester*.[51] The example follows the vocal line of the song, rather than the orchestral version, because the principal melody in the latter passes between instruments during segments not directly paraphrased from the hymn and is occasionally slightly obscured. The two versions are otherwise quite similar, differing mainly in the length of some transitions inserted into the pauses in the principal melody.

A congregation normally sings several verses of a hymn after the organist plays the closing line as an introduction to set the pitch, and Ives's paraphrase follows a similar structure. The melody consists of four paraphrased verses of the hymn, with some added material, mostly scalar and chromatic, that forms a contrast to the pentatonic hymn tune. The verses are separated by rests and, in two cases, by changes of underlying key. An introduction paraphrases the second half of the hymn, and a two-measure postlude presents the opening motive, reharmonized as a kind of Amen. In Example 8.6, the two halves of the hymn are aligned vertically to show their similarity, and the four verses are numbered in the margin, with first and second phrases indicated by letters.

Ives's adaptation of *Dorrnance* adds a note at the beginning of the opening motive in most of its statements. This is primarily in response to the iambic scansion of the text. Ives clearly had the text in mind even while writing the orchestral version, for the principal melody is essentially the same in all surviving sketches and versions.[52] But the added note may also suggest the hymn tune *Missionary Chant*, which begins like *Dorrnance* but with the extra note.[53]

Ives's paraphrase works by rhythmic alteration, as in mm. 7–9 and 11–12; by omission, as in mm. 9–10 and 12–13; by repetition, as in mm. 17–19, where one unit of the source is repeated three times; by transposition, in the third and fourth verses; by elision, where a single note or pattern in Ives's melody takes the place of two notes or motives in the source, marked by brackets in Example 8.6; and by interpolation of new material, marked by parentheses. There is also a kind of developing variation, as segments paraphrased from the source are varied later in Ives's melody; for instance, the melodic idea in m. 23 reappears varied in mm. 35–36 and 37–38. The resulting melody is as extraordinary and beautiful as its model is plain. Through extended paraphrase, Ives preserves the character of the hymn tune, suiting the program of the piece, while transforming it utterly to fit the text.

The song *Down East* (1919) may seem at first to use quotation simply to illustrate its text.[54] The words, Ives's own, tell of the poet's home and mother and the tunes she played on the "old melodeon," including "Nearer, my God, to Thee" (*Bethany*), whose first line (both words and music) is quoted near

PATCHWORK AND EXTENDED PARAPHRASE

the end (mm. 35–38). This format resembles any number of Tin Pan Alley songs that mention a well-known piece and quote it near the end of the chorus, such as George M. Cohan's "The Story of the Wedding March" (1901, with Mendelssohn's wedding march) and "I've Never Been Over There" (1906, with *God Save the King*), or Irving Berlin's "Alexander's Ragtime Band" (1911, with "Old Folks at Home") and "I Love to Stay at Home" (1915, with "Silver Threads Among the Gold"). But Ives's use of the borrowed tune is more complex and pervasive. The song opens with an impressionistic, harmonically static invocation of songs of the past and the visions they evoke. This section begins and ends with chromatic variants of the opening of *Bethany* (mm. 1–2 and 7b). The mostly tonal main section then follows the melodic structure of the hymn.[55] The hymn has four phrases, in AA′BA′ form, and Ives's first verse (mm. 8–23) expands the first two phrases into a sixteen-measure period through paraphrase and interpolation. The varied repetition of this tune (mm. 27–42), shown in Example 8.7, is accompanied in the piano by the B phrase of the hymn, similarly expanded. Thus, in the course of the piece one complete paraphrase of *Bethany* is presented, shared between voice (A and A′ phrases) and piano (B phrase), and the explicit quotation at mm. 35–38 not only fits Ives's text but also marks the culmination of that paraphrase, through the appearance of the hymn's final phrase (complete with text, for in the original hymn the final phrase repeats the words of the first). The piano's closing bars hint at m. 9 of the tune, joining with the introduction to frame the paraphrase with fragmentary references. Ives also plays on the words of the hymn to suggest that memories of childhood may bring feelings of closeness to God. Addressing the "old, red farm house" of his childhood in the first stanza, the poet says "All that is best in me, lying deep in memory, draws my heart where I would be, nearer to thee." The echo of the hymn text in the last three words implies that thinking of his home and family brings him nearer to God, a point that is reinforced throughout the song as the poet's memories of home and family are set to a melody paraphrased from this famous hymn.

We have seen in other cases that a direct quotation may serve as a clue to a deeper connection between Ives's music and its source. Understanding this relationship can change our view of a piece in both musical and extramusical terms. Thus we must be cautious in ascribing extramusical significance to a quotation or allusion until we know exactly how the borrowed material is used in the piece. To view the direct quotation of *Bethany* in *Down East* as mere text-painting is to miss its presence throughout the song, representing the spirit of the poet's home and childhood through an evocation of the songs his mother played. Similarly, in *The Housatonic at Stockbridge*, the hymn sung in church is heard from across the river in snatches, sometimes

EXAMPLE 8.7: *Down East*, mm. 27–34, compared to *Bethany*

more and sometimes less distinct, but it is continuous. Ives's complete para-phrase, with an introduction, four verses, and closing Amen, is true to his program in a way that we miss if we hear this melody as a series of fragments from *Dorrnance* and *Missionary Chant* mixed with original material.[56] Here it is not the text of the hymn that is important to the program, for *Dorrnance* is sung with many texts, and the words Ives may have associated with it, if any, are unknown.[57] Rather, it is the form and melodic character of the hymn as preserved in the paraphrase that create the extramusical imagery Ives intended. Although the text of the hymn tune source is significant for the meaning of *Down East*, the lack of any particular text associated with *Dorrnance* makes the latter especially useful for a work about hearing hymn singing across a river, in which the sound and atmosphere are more impor-tant than any images a text might arouse.

Analysis and Interpretation: The Example of *West London*

The final example of extended paraphrase further demonstrates that an appropriate extramusical interpretation of a quotation requires a full under-standing of the way borrowed material is used throughout the work. In an essay on the meaning of Ives's uses of existing music, Christopher Ballantine analyzes the song *West London* (1921, adapted from a lost *Matthew Arnold Overture* for chorus and orchestra).[58] A piano postlude at the end of the song quotes the opening notes, fully harmonized, of the hymn tune *Fountain* ("There is a fountain filled with blood"), and Ballantine explains this as an instance of text association whose meaning derives from knowing the hymn text sung to this tune. The Matthew Arnold sonnet that Ives uses as a text tells of a London tramp who sends her daughter to beg from working men—members of her own social class—rather than from the rich. Arnold com-ments,

> Thought I: "Above her state this spirit towers;
> She will not ask of aliens, but of friends,
> Of sharers in a common human fate.
> She turns from the cold succor, which attends
> The unknown little from the unknowing great,
> And points us to a better time than ours."

Ballantine finds the "platitudinous optimism" of the closing line to be under-cut in Ives's song by the quoted hymn, whose text describes the fountain of Christ's blood which alone can wash a sinner pure. Presumably because of its implications of sacrifice and total religious commitment, Ballantine views the hymn as representing a more "difficult" path to a better world than that suggested by Arnold and comments that this "ironic reversal" is reinforced by the melodic similarity between Ives's setting of the climactic final line, stated three times fortissimo, and the quoted hymn tune, set off in a different key, pianissimo, in the piano postlude.[59]

Ballantine's interpretation depends on the assumption that the quotation from *Fountain* is extraneous and must be explained in terms of its text. In fact, almost the entire vocal melody of *West London* derives from *Fountain*, in the manner of an extended paraphrase. Examples 8.8 and 8.9 show the derivation of most of the vocal line from the two most striking elements of the hymn, the opening bars of the verse and the refrain. The music for the poem's last line is given at the top of Example 8.8, below the hymn's opening

West London. © 1933 by Merion Music, Inc. Used by Permission.

EXAMPLE 8.8: Parts of *West London* derived from the opening motive of the verse of *Fountain*

PATCHWORK AND EXTENDED PARAPHRASE

West London. © 1933 by Merion Music, Inc. Used by Permission.

EXAMPLE 8.9: Parts of *West London* derived from the first phrase
of the refrain of *Fountain*

phrase, to show the paraphrase in both rhythm and melody.[60] Several other
passages (including, as Ballantine notes, the song's opening phrase) are variants of this concluding melodic idea. Moreover, because of internal repetitions in the hymn tune, the entire vocal line of Ives's song can be analyzed as
a paraphrase of two complete repetitions of *Fountain*, where the first half,
setting the sonnet's octave (except for the eighth line, set to a repeated note
followed by a chromatic descent), is somewhat closer to the source than is the
second. Example 8.10 shows the first half of the song analyzed as a paraphrase
of the entire hymn tune.

The appearance of an exact quotation from *Fountain* at the end after a
number of paraphrases does not make this a cumulative setting. Like *Down
East* and *Serenity*, which also quote the main source in its most recognizable
form only near the end, *West London* lacks most features of a cumulative setting, for the final statement is only a fragment, is not used as a theme, and is
not developed before its final presentation. Rather, these songs relate to
cumulative form in a more general way. Having worked with the idea of
gradual clarification in his cumulative settings, Ives applied the same principle in these songs based on modeling or paraphrase. A number of pieces not

EXAMPLE 8.10: First half of *West London* as a paraphrase of *Fountain*

based on borrowed tunes, such as *Majority* and *Paracelsus*, use a similar idea, beginning at the height of complexity and ending with serene clarity. This tendency, often noted in Ives's music, seems to originate in his experience with cumulative settings, but it operates in many other works that relate to cumulative form only superficially or not at all.

If the hymn tune is the source for the song's entire melody, its partial appearance in the postlude can hardly be ironic in intent. It is there partly for musical reasons, because of its intimate relationship to the vocal line. For the analyst, at least, it functions as a clue to the character of the principal melody as a hymn paraphrase; without such a direct reference, the relationship of the song to its source might have gone unobserved. When he bases a work on an existing one, Ives seems always to provide such a clue. It is not chiefly the quotation that must be explained, then, but Ives's use of *Fountain* as the basis of his piece.

There are two related explanations, beyond the observation that reworking existing music is pervasive in Ives's music. He writes in the *Memos*, "I can find nothing left of the *Matthew Arnold Overture* but the first page—I have a hand-organ reflecting the London streets—a part of which is practically the same as the song, *West London*."[61] The hand-organ is reflected in the song both in the arpeggiating ostinato that opens the piano accompaniment and in the hymn tune, which Ives presumably imagined being played on the London streets.[62] In this respect, the tune helps evoke the scene much as the similar hymn paraphrase in *The Housatonic at Stockbridge* reflects the sound of hymn-singing across the water, and the piano postlude can be heard as a direct reference to the hand-organist.

Text association is also important, but apparently in a way exactly opposite to the "ironic reversal" seen here by Ballantine. Ives probably found the poem "West London" in a collection of Arnold's poetry given to his wife Harmony by her parents in 1898, ten years before their marriage.[63] The poem appears in collections of Arnold's works as one of a sequence of sonnets. The sequence emphasizes inner resources and the accomplishment of spiritual ends in this life rather than in the hereafter, including such statements as "The aids to noble life are all within" (from "Worldly Place"), and "Was Christ a man like us? *Ah! let us try / If we then, too, can be such men as he!*" (from "The Better Part," italics original). These are themes dear to Ives's heart, as is clear from reading his *Essays Before a Sonata* or his spiritual mentors: Emerson, Thoreau, the Reverend Joseph H. Twichell (his wife's father), and Horace Bushnell.[64] Had he considered Arnold's poem platitudinous, as Ballantine implies, it is unlikely he would have bothered to set it. There are no examples of his mocking a text in his musical settings except when the text is satirical, as in *Romanzo di Central Park* (see chapter 7). In footnotes in *114 Songs*, Ives does mock some of his early songs, music as well as text, but the original settings were sincere when they were made. This song seems perfectly sincere as well.[65]

It is less the exact words of the hymn "There is a fountain filled with blood" than their overall emphasis on salvation, Christ, and a personal relationship with God and with other humans that makes the tune *Fountain* appropriate to Arnold's point of view. Once we understand the context of the poem in both Arnold's and Ives's thinking and realize that *Fountain* is not a detached comment on the rest of the song but its source—the "fountain" from which all else springs—it becomes clear that Ives saw the connections between the poem and the tune as apt rather than ironic.

This discussion has assumed that Ives adapts *Fountain* for this song in part because of the meaning conveyed by its words and other associations. At the same time, it has shown that Ives's purpose is not simply programmatic but is structural as well. Thus, despite contradicting Ballantine's specific interpretation, it reinforces his larger point: that Ives's borrowings are best understood not solely on a musical level, as part of a piece's network of motives, nor on a purely programmatic level, but on a level that recognizes both the musical and the extramusical associations exploited or created by the composer.[66] Ballantine's sense of the interpretive problems that borrowing poses is both subtle and generally accurate. The flaw in his view of *West London* is more basic: one cannot interpret what one has not yet seen, and one cannot understand the significance of Ives's use of an existing piece of music until one understands how the borrowed material is actually used.

What we have seen so far of Ives's uses of existing music after 1902 attests to a great variety in both musical procedure and extramusical intent. In the pieces considered here and in previous chapters, the structural function of the existing work—as a model, a source for a paraphrased theme or melody, or a tune used in a variation set, new setting, or cumulative setting—equals or outweighs its extramusical functions. But this is not true for all Ives pieces. There are more than twenty works, discussed in the next chapter, in which Ives borrowed primarily to fulfill a program or illustrate a text. In most of these, both the musical borrowings and the programmatic interpretation are generally clear, involving little of the subtlety and interpretive difficulty we have seen in *West London*. In the collages discussed in chapter 10, neither programmatic nor musical analysis seems sufficient, as the multiplicity of quotations at varying levels of prominence and recognizability suggests a dream state or stream of consciousness. These pieces further exemplify the diversity of Ives's procedures and make clear that no single analytical approach can account for all cases.

What is ultimately most harmful to our understanding of Ives's uses of musical borrowing is to insist that what is true for one work is necessarily true for another. What is most helpful is to recognize the variety of techniques that Ives was using at the height of his career and to investigate first what actually happens in each piece, before settling on an interpretation.

CHAPTER 9

Programmatic Quotation

Much of Ives's later music is program music, and some of his borrowings are programmatic. Program music seeks to depict a scene, tell a story, or relate a series of events. Musical elements correspond to a specific happening, as in Beethoven's *Wellington's Victory*, or represent a person, object, or idea, as in some Strauss tone poems. Such representation may also occur in works with text, as in Schubert's song *Gretchen am Spinnrade*, in which a quickly moving figure in the piano represents the motion of the spinning wheel, at first rapid and constant, suddenly ceasing, then starting up again.

This direct relation between elements in the music and in the program distinguishes a programmatic work from a piece that merely evokes a mood or character.[1] We have seen, for instance, that despite its use of hymn tunes and descriptive titles, Ives's Third Symphony is not programmatic, because events in the music do not correspond to events in any program. Yet *From Hanover Square North* does follow a program, representing the spontaneous hymn-singing of commuters on a New York train platform as they gradually join in a shared expression of their feelings on a tragic day. Without the program, we would not know what the music is intended to represent; we could still hear it as a cumulative setting of *In the Sweet Bye and Bye*, but we would not hear the sounds of New York in the distant instruments, nor would we understand the significance of this particular hymn.

Programmatic quotation, whether in an instrumental or texted piece, is intended to represent an event, action, thing, or person mentioned in the text or in a given or implicit program.[2] In many of Ives's works, programmatic quotation represents a performance of the music being quoted, such as the hymn in *From Hanover Square North* or the drumbeats, minstrel tune, and fanfares in *General William Booth* (both discussed in chapter 6). In others, a tune may stand for a thing, person, or situation associated with it, as when "Massa's in de Cold Ground" symbolizes Ives's presence in *From Hanover Square North* or *On the Counter* alludes to Ethelbert Nevin by quoting his *Narcissus* (as described in chapter 7). In some pieces, a brief reference to a song is used to invoke its text, as in the appearance of "Auld Lang Syne" near the end of *On the Counter*. Sometimes this will work in reverse, and a work's text will suggest music associated with its words, as in the reference to the gospel song *Onward, Upward* at the words "On, on, upward" in *General William Booth*.

The great majority of Ives's borrowings do not fall into this category of quotations used to fulfill a program or text. As we have seen, he often uses other works as models or borrows or paraphrases existing tunes as themes, and this serves a primarily musical rather than extramusical role. In other cases, some of which were treated in chapter 7, a tune's type, mood, or character is more significant than specific programmatic connotations. In addition, some borrowings that have programmatic significance, such as the hymn in *From Hanover Square North*, also play a central role in the musical structure through techniques treated in other chapters. This chapter focuses on quotations that serve a clear extramusical purpose and are motivated primarily by programmaticism. Virtually all of them stand out from their context as obvious quotations, akin to quotations in literature.

Program Music

There was ample precedent for programmatic quotation, both to represent a musical performance and to symbolize people or ideas. Many operas feature scenes in which music is performed, and some use existing music, from the on-stage band in *Don Giovanni* that plays hits from three recent operas to the singing of *Ein' feste Burg* in *Les Huguenots*. Depictions of music-making exist also in program music, for instance, in battle-pieces, from *Wellington's Victory* to American piano works such as *The Battle of Trenton* by James Hewitt and *The Battle of Manassas* by Thomas Bethune (Blind Tom),[3] and in evocations of church music, such as the *Dies irae* in the *Symphonie fantastique*. But even here, the use of borrowed music verges on the symbolic, as the military songs represent the warring armies and the *Dies irae* the death of the protagonist. Other uses of quotation to symbolize people or ideas are frequent, including later uses of the *Dies irae* motive to evoke death in Liszt's *Totentanz*, Mussorgsky's *Songs and Dances of Death*, Saint-Saëns's *Danse macabre*, and many others; of national tunes to represent armies or national causes in Tchaikovsky's *1812 Overture* and Smetana's *Tábor*; and of self-quotation in *Ein Heldenleben* to represent Strauss himself.

What seems new with Ives is an attempt to capture the spirit of music-making in its own right. Most of his programmatic works that use quotation are about the act of making music, the way we hear music, or the role that music plays in our lives. But in a few major programmatic works, notably the Second String Quartet, the *Concord Sonata*, and *The Celestial Railroad*, and in the vast collages of the Fourth Symphony (treated in chapter 10), the musical borrowings have largely symbolic meanings and do not directly represent the act of making music.

Evocations of Music-Making

Ives's first work of program music appears to be *Yale-Princeton Football Game* for orchestra (ca. 1899, revised ca. 1914–19), a musical picture of the 1897 match between the two schools, with downs marked off by the referee's whistle (in the piccolo), the traditional flying wedge depicted by the musical equivalent of wedges (dissonant chords that contract in contrary motion to a single note or cluster), and the electrifying broken-field run for which this game became famous represented by zig-zagging scales in the trumpet.[4] The noise of the crowd is depicted by dissonant string ostinatos and by quotations of college cheers and songs. The cheers, such as "Bre-ke-co-ax, co-ax, co-ax" from *The Frogs* of Aristophanes, are rendered in clusters to suggest a chanting crowd. The songs pile in on top of one another in fragments: "Old Nassau" (H155, a Princeton song by Carl Langlotz), "Hy-Can Nuck A No" (H153), "Harvard Has Blue Stocking Girls" (H151), "Dear Old Yale" (H149, using the tune from Carl Wilhelm's "Die Wacht am Rhein"),[5] and "Hold the Fort, McClung is Coming" (H152, a football parody on Philip P. Bliss's hymn *Hold the Fort*), with the trio of Reeves's *Second Regiment Connecticut National Guard March* mixed in, no doubt to represent the college band. The effect is not a literal sound-image, but an evocation of the crowd through the songs they sing. The piece makes clear how important music is to the spirit of the event.

Another college piece is *Calcium Light Night* (late 1910s), evoking the Yale tradition in which members of the junior-class societies marched through campus with colored calcium lights before "tapping" sophomores chosen for membership in each society.[6] The piece depicts a parade, led by a band, that becomes louder as it approaches, passes, and moves into the distance until it fades from hearing. Over the "street beat" in drums and piano, fraternity songs join in one by one as the band approaches: "Few Days" (H150, a Psi Upsilon song by George Morris) in the trombone, the "Marching Song" of Ives's fraternity Delta Kappa Epsilon (H154, to the traditional tune "Jolly Dogs") in the piccolo, "A Band of Brothers in DKE" (H146, arranged by William G. Harris) in clarinet then trumpet, and "Tramp, Tramp, Tramp" in the clarinet, with part of "Marching Through Georgia" mixed in. These Civil War tunes may have served for college songs with new texts, as did many well-known tunes. As the band retreats, segments heard previously appear in reverse order, creating an elaborate arch form.[7] The effect is not a realistic one, but it captures the mood of the event by presenting the kinds of songs used and suggesting the raucous way in which they were performed, perhaps with various groups singing or playing different songs simultaneously, in different rhythms and keys.

The Gong on the Hook and Ladder or *Firemen's Parade on Main Street* for chamber orchestra (ca. 1914) also represents a march.[8] The main focus is on the rhythm, but altered fragments of three tunes are quoted, apparently to represent the band: "Oh, My Darling Clementine" (H126, mm. 13–15 and 32–34), the college song "Few Days" (mm. 20–27), and "Marching Through Georgia" (mm. 26–30). As usual, motivic similarities link the tunes with one another and with the surrounding music.[9]

The General Slocum (early 1910s) is more somber, depicting the explosion that destroyed the excursion boat *General Slocum* in June 1904.[10] The opening evokes the water, with gently rocking figures in the strings, and the pleasure-boat, imitating its horn and whistle with blasts in the low and high brass and its engine with machine-like ostinatos. Groups of instruments enter one by one, representing orchestras on different decks playing currently popular tunes in different keys and meters: Michael Nolan's "Little Annie Rooney" (1890), "The Sidewalks of New York" by James W. Blake and Charles B. Lawlor (H133, 1894), a variant of "Ma Blushin' Rosie" by John Stromberg (H120, 1900), and Ellen Wright's "Violets" (H143, 1900). The intensity builds until an alarm sounds and a rising roar recreates the malfunction and explosion of the engine. The noise suddenly ceases, and we hear again the quiet rocking of the waves. This is one of Ives's favorite effects in his program music, called "sonic exuviation" by Nicolas Slonimsky, in which a noisy climax suddenly cuts off to reveal another plane of sound, softer and more distant, representing something that has been going on all the time unheard.[11] The fate of the passengers and crew is signalled by two hymns: *Bethany* ("Nearer, my God, to Thee"), often sung at funerals, and *Throw Out the Life-Line*, whose normally metaphorical text may here be taken literally. In this work, the quotations of popular tunes represent actual performances, whereas the hymns are quoted to suggest their texts and to invoke the association of *Bethany* with death.

According to Ives's program note, *Central Park in the Dark* (ca. 1914) "purports to be a picture-in-sounds of the sounds of nature and of happenings that men would hear some thirty or so years ago (before the combustion engine and radio monopolized the earth and air) [i.e., ca. 1906, the date on the sketch], when sitting on a bench in Central Park on a hot summer night."[12] In fulfillment of this program, Ives superimposes several layers of music, each in an independent meter or rhythm, that represent various sounds coming from many directions. An impressionistic chordal ostinato in the strings represents "the night sounds and silent darkness." Over this we hear sounds of human society, represented by quoted or paraphrased popular tunes: a clarinet softly plays a waltz paraphrase of "Ben Bolt" by Nelson Kneass (H99, at mm. 12–17, 24–28, and 59–63), as if heard "from the Casino over the pond"; flute and oboe play an unidentified tune in canon and in different keys (mm. 28–34, 42–45, and 65–69), like "street singers coming up from [Columbus] Circle singing, in spots, the tunes of those days," the canon suggesting the echo of the song off the nearby buildings, following more quickly as the singers get closer; and a muted solo violin plays the opening phrases of "Violets" (mm. 44–47), representing "some 'night owls' from Healy's whistling the latest."[13] A piano enters with ragtime figures (mm. 47–51 and 60–62) and soon settles into a variant of the chorus of the ragtime song "Hello! Ma Baby" (m. 67), played four times, each time faster and louder. This begins the depiction of "pianolas [player pianos] having a ragtime war in the apartment house 'over the garden wall.'" A second piano answers with the "street beat" drum pattern (m. 91) and what sounds like a variant of "The Worms Crawl In" (m. 95), marked in the first sketch "another piano from another floor pushes Freshmen in Park" (perhaps a Yale song). As the "ragtime war" builds, other instruments take up these tunes; the flute plays fiddle-tune figuration based on the traditional tune "The Campbells are Coming" (H160, mm. 93–97); and piano II throws in a phrase from Sousa's *Washington Post March* (H90). The piling-up of ideas reaches a climax complete with a policeman's whistle in the flute and a fire engine siren in the trombone (mm. 114–18, as noted in the second sketch). Suddenly the noise stops; through sonic exuviation, "again the darkness is heard," as the string ostinato, which had continued throughout, again becomes audible; there comes "an echo over the pond" of the clarinet, flute, and violin tunes from the opening section; "and we walk home," as only the string ostinato remains and fades to a close. Here, each quotation, along with virtually every event in the music, is motivated by the program, and all of them represent actual sounds one might have heard while sitting in Central Park. As usual, it is not necessary for a listener to recognize each tune; what is most important is the general style and character of the tune quoted or paraphrased, with sentimental ballads in the opening and closing sections and the ragtime tune as the most prominent in the raucous middle section.

One of Ives's most powerful programmatic works is *Decoration Day* (ca. 1913–19), an orchestral sound-picture of a New England celebration of the forerunner to our present Memorial Day.[14] It follows the events of the day as described in Ives's program: gathering flowers for garlands, assembling on the village green for the parade, the slow march to the cemetary, a military salute and a hymn, a high-spirited march back to town, and a "shadow of the early morning flower-song" at sunset.[15] The flower-gathering is given its own brief motive (m. 5), apparently not borrowed.[16] Each of the other events is represented in part by music associated with it.

The mood of the gathering crowd is evoked by "Marching Through Georgia," a Union song about the decisive campaign of the Civil War, whose fallen were the heroes celebrated on Decoration Day. The opening of the chorus is heard softly in flute I and continued in bassoon I (mm. 37–39), answered by the opening of the verse in horn I, continued in flute and clarinet (mm. 39–42); each fragment is soft and in a different key, as if to suggest the private thoughts of many people.[17] As the march to the cemetary begins, "the roll of muffled drums and 'Adeste fideles' answer for the dirge." The latter tune, also known as *Portuguese Hymn*, was sung with many texts other than its familiar Christmas verses, including some appropriate to this occasion. The hymn is stated broadly in strings and horns, its intervals somewhat altered (mm. 54–61 and 69–74). The work's opening melody (mm. 1–4, violin I) is probably a paraphrase of this tune, foreshadowing its later appearance.[18] Inserted into the dirge are paraphrases of "Tenting on the Old Camp Ground" (mm. 61-64 and 68–69) and "The Battle Cry of Freedom" (mm. 65–68, violin I), well-known Union songs that evoke respectively the weariness felt near the war's end and the fervor felt near its beginning.[19]

At the cemetary, "after the last grave is decorated, 'Taps' sounds out through the pines and hickories, while a last hymn is sung"; an off-stage or muted trumpet plays "Taps" while soft tremolo strings play the first motive of *Bethany* three times. "Then the ranks are formed again, and we all march back to town to a Yankee stimulant": the entire trio of Reeves's "inspiring" *Second Regiment March* (in mm. 89–145), the longest and fullest direct quotation in all of Ives's music, enhanced with Ives's additions. However, according to the program, "to many a soldier the somber thoughts of the day underlie the tunes of the band"; this is suggested by reminiscences of "Taps" in solo viola and low bells and of *Bethany* mixed with "Taps" in two extra violins, playing almost unheard amid the strains of the march, and by the appearance late in the Reeves trio of "The Battle Hymn of the Republic" in oboes and clarinets (mm. 126–34), blending verse and chorus. When the march is over, a sonic exuviation reveals the flower-gathering tune once more, and the opening of "Taps" sounds quietly at the close; despite the euphoric march, the loved ones whose graves they have decorated are still in the minds of the townspeople. Almost every event in the music is accounted for in the program, including all the references to existing music, which either represent the actual music performed on that day or evoke the inner thoughts of the participants.

All the works discussed above seek to suggest the sounds and capture the spirit of an event in which music plays a central part. The role of music in our lives, the act of making music, and the way in which we hear music and respond emotionally to it are all part of the subject-matter of these pieces. Such program music is like a scene from a stage work in which music is used on two or three levels at once, as in the last act of Verdi's *Otello*: to represent actual music-making on stage; to convey the thoughts and feelings of the characters; and to frame the action or to suggest the reactions of the audience. Like musical theater, these works of program music have the quality of fiction, for they ask us as listeners to imagine ourselves in a particular setting, from a football game to a parade, hearing music and other sounds.[20] Our imagined position may be as part of the crowd, as in *Yale-Princeton Football Game* and *Decoration Day*, or at a distance, as in *The General Slocum* and *Central Park in the Dark*, but we are always observers, akin to an audience in the theater. Just as in operas, we recognize which music represents "real life" sounds, such as the popular songs in *The General Slocum*, and which is meant to set a mood or suggest our own reactions, as do the hymns at the end of that work. This distinction will become crucial when we consider Ives's collages in the next chapter.

Symbolic Use of Quotation

Although the works discussed so far and most of the collages treated in the next chapter are about making and hearing music, a few pieces use borrowed tunes to stand for a person, thing, idea, or event, rather than for the sound of music itself. The two hymns that close *The General Slocum* symbolize death and danger and the human responses of prayer ("Nearer, my God, to Thee") and seeking to help ("Throw out the Life-Line"). In *In the Night* (discussed in chapter 6), the closing citations of *Eventide* ("Abide with me") and "Massa's in de Cold Ground" likewise speak of loneliness, fear, death, and prayer at the end of a piece that paraphrases "De Little Cabins All Am Empty Now."[21] The faint rendition of "Taps" underneath the Reeves march in *Decoration Day* symbolizes "the somber thoughts of the day [that] underlie the tunes of the band." *Washington's Birthday*, discussed in chapter 10, uses hints of "Home! Sweet Home!" and "Old Folks at Home" to evoke the older generation sitting around the hearth while the young folks go to the barn dance, and quotes "Goodnight, Ladies" for the farewells at the end of the evening.

Ives's first piece to use borrowed tunes solely in a symbolic manner seems to be *Mike Donlin–Johnny Evers* for chamber orchestra (1907 or soon after), an unfinished "take-off" of a stirring moment in a baseball game between the Giants and the Cubs in the summer of 1907.[22] In the brief first section, Mike Donlin "jaunts out to C[enter] F[ield]," apparently signified by the first phrase of the verse of "Ta-ra-ra Boom-de-ay!" by Henry J. Sayers (H140), and Johnny Evers steps up to bat, symbolized by the opening of Patrick S. Gilmore's "When Johnny Comes Marching Home" (H91). After three balls and two strikes, each marked by the umpire's "slide down yell" in the trumpet, Johnny gets a hit, Mike goes "running in C[enter] F[ield] after [the] ball," indicated by running chromatic scales, and the first phrase of "When Johnny Comes Marching Home" appears in the cornet or trumpet to represent "Johnny running around Bases" and "Johnny making Home Run" over "great excitement" in the strings.[23]

Less clear in its meaning is the appearance of two hymns near the end of the *Robert Browning Overture* (ca. 1912–15): the opening notes of *Adeste fideles* (mm. 370–71, trumpets, imitated in the horns and in the bass instruments) and the first half of Handel's *Christmas* (H12), somewhat altered (mm. 371–76, trumpets, harmonized by horns 1 and 2, and imitated in the winds).[24] Perhaps this moment, which joins diatonic tunes with chromatic figuration in a rapid, loud, multi-layered march, represents the union of elements that were previously kept separate, as rapid, loud, multi-layered chromatic marches alternated with slower episodes that mixed diatonic and chromatic fragments. But Ives may also intend to link Browning to his countryman Handel, to one of the many texts sung to *Christmas*, or to the rousing spirit of the tune.

The most notable pieces to use programmatic borrowing in a symbolic way rather than to represent musical performances are the Second String

Quartet, the *Concord Sonata* and related works, and the Fourth Symphony (discussed in chapter 10). All are late works and are among Ives's best known compositions. They are programmatic, but less concrete than the pieces surveyed so far; not all of the borrowings have apparent musical or programmatic functions, and those that can be explained in terms of a program tend to allegory or philosophical abstraction rather than the direct representation of reality seen in the works discussed so far.

It is these late and famous pieces, together with the collages treated in the next chapter, that have formed public and critical views of Ives's borrowings. Given how different these are from most of Ives's other works, it is no wonder that most musicians, critics, and listeners misunderstand the purpose and meaning of the borrowings in his earlier music and in his other mature compositions. Recognizing that these pieces are exceptional helps us both to understand them and to fix their place in Ives's output as a whole.

Second String Quartet

The Second String Quartet (ca. 1911–14) is apparently the only one of Ives's mature finished multi-movement works to be conceived from the start as a whole, rather than being assembled from existing movements, as were the violin sonatas, *Concord Sonata*, orchestral sets, and last three symphonies.[25] Ives wrote that he began it after a Kneisel Quartet concert; feeling that string quartet music had become "weak, trite, and effeminate," he started writing the quartet "half mad, half in fun, and half to try out, practise, and have some fun with making those men fiddlers get up and do something like men."[26] On the sketch, Ives offered a brief program: "S.Q. [String Quartet] for 4 men— who converse, discuss, argue (in re 'Politick'), fight, shake hands, shut up— then walk up the mountain side to view the firmament!"[27] In line with this program, the three movements are titled "Discussions," "Arguments," and "'The Call of the Mountains.'"

Most of the work uses original material, largely atonal, with occasional triads, tonal progressions, and diatonic scale fragments. Some figures recall snatches of familiar melody but are too brief, vague, or commonplace to allow firm identification.[28] At one point in each of the first two movements, there is a quick jumble of fragments of familiar tunes that emerge one by one from the thick chromatic polyphony, as if to suggest a spirited conversation whose participants keep interrupting each other. In the first movement, the tunes used are patriotic songs: "Columbia, the Gem of the Ocean" (violin I, mm. 58–60), "Dixie" (viola, mm. 60–62), "Marching Through Georgia" (violin II, mm. 62–63, with a variant of "Turkey in the Straw" accompanying it in the viola), and "Hail! Columbia" (violin I and cello, mm. 64–66). This suggests a conversation about politics, with a statement of national pride

("Columbia, the Gem of the Ocean") provoking a response from a southerner ("Dixie"), who in turn is interrupted by a rather chauvinistic northerner ("Marching Through Georgia") before both are quieted by an appeal for unity in the name of the nation and in the spirit of its founders ("Hail! Columbia," whose tune was Washington's inaugural march and whose words, a salute to the unified purpose of the revolution, were written during the divisive years of John Adams's presidency).[29] In the next movement, an extensive four-part canon (mm. 42–65) includes a segment based on "Columbia, the Gem of the Ocean" (mm. 48–54). Near the end, classical fragments mix it up with the patriotic tunes, suggesting that part of the argument may be about relations with Europe, European versus American culture, or high versus low musical taste: "Hail! Columbia" (violin I, mm. 87–88) is followed by the march theme from the third movement of Tchaikovsky's Sixth Symphony (H188, cello, mm. 87–89, and violin I and II, mm. 89–91), the transitional theme from the first movement of Brahms's Second Symphony (H176, violin I, mm. 92–94), "Columbia, the Gem of the Ocean" (viola and cello, mm. 94–97), the chorale theme from the finale of Beethoven's Ninth Symphony (H174, violin II, mm. 96–97), "Marching Through Georgia" (violin I, mm. 97–100, mixing parts of verse and chorus), and the "Down in de cornfield" phrase from "Massa's in de Cold Ground" (violin I, mm. 101–4).[30] However one interprets these quotations, they are clearly not meant to represent the actual performance of pieces of music, as in the works treated previously in this chapter, but are intended to suggest the back-and-forth of a spirited conversation and to symbolize, through the contrasts between them, the disagreements among the participants.

The finale has a unique form. The first half uses mostly original material, almost all dissonant and atonal. There are brief hints of the opening motives of *Nettleton* (m. 9, in parallel major thirds in violin I and II) and *Bethany* ("Nearer, my God, to Thee," at mm. 35–36, violin I, in inverted canon with the cello), which are similar in pitch contour, and part of *Westminster Chimes* (m. 35, in violin II), which is melodically related to the first phrase of *Bethany*, especially to its second half (5–1–3–2).[31] Near the midpoint (mm. 56–79), over whole-tone scalar motion in the cello, most of *Bethany* appears in long notes in the viola, with segments of *Westminster Chimes* interpolated. Fragments and variants of both tunes appear intermittently in the ensuing passage. Near the end of the movement, the third phrase of *Bethany* followed by *Westminster Chimes* peals out high in the first violin over descending whole-tone scales on D in the cello and ostinatos in the other instruments (mm. 123–36); the viola ostinato and the whole-tone scales both derive from the descending whole steps that open *Bethany*. Here the music is suffused with the brilliant sound of a whole-tone-enriched but firm D major. A brief coda repeats the first and third phrases of *Bethany* in the inner instruments (mm. 136–43), the first in parallel major thirds, recalling the earlier, melodically similar figure from *Nettleton*. Like a cumulative setting, this movement arrives at a definite musical statement only near the end, but it has a different structure. At the end of the quartet, politics is forgotten in a shared moment of transcendence, as the resonance of D major, the suggestion of bells heard from across the landscape, and the sense of being "nearer, my God, to Thee" combine in a rich musical image of viewing the firmament from a mountaintop.[32]

Concord Sonata

The Second Piano Sonata (*Concord, Mass., 1840–1860*) (ca. 1914–1919, rev. 1940s) is a less obvious case. Ives described it and the *Essays Before a Sonata* written to accompany it as "an attempt to present (one person's) impression of the spirit of transcendentalism that is associated in the minds of many with Concord, Mass., of over a half century ago."[33] Each movement is a character study of a person or family important in the literary life of Concord in the two decades before the Civil War. Certain themes and motives are connected with these people, with events in their lives or writings, or with ideas. The result lies somewhere between a character piece and a programmatic work, neither as explicit in its sequence of events as the works examined in the first part of this chapter nor so far from program music as are Ives's Third Symphony, First Piano Sonata, and violin sonatas.

The unifying thread is the theme of "The Alcotts" (shown in Example 5.22). This seems to be the theme Ives refers to in his Essays as "that human-faith-melody—transcendent and sentimental enough for the enthusiast or the cynic, respectively—reflecting an innate hope, a common interest in common things and common men—a tune the Concord bards are ever playing while they pound away at the immensities with a Beethoven-like sublimity."[34] Each of the other movements has its own themes but also incorporates the "Alcotts" theme in a significant way. This is the only theme or motive that is used prominently in all four movements; thus, it carries the principal burden of unifying the disparate movements into a whole.[35] At each appearance (partial or complete), it serves on a musical level as a unifying theme and on a programmatic level as an emblem of human faith and of the "Concord bards" as a group.

The first movement, "Emerson," has no explicit program but offers what Ives calls an "impressionistic picture" of the writer.[36] It shares aspects of cumulative form in that every important theme appears in fragmentary or altered form before it is stated in full. The Emerson music originated between 1907 and 1914 as a concerto or overture for piano and orchestra, "opening with several cadenzas, and gradually becoming more and more unified," as Ives described it in his *Memos*.[37] The sonata movement likewise begins with a cadenza on the main themes. The significance of the motives interwoven there is likely to be understood only in retrospect, after one has heard or played the movement often enough to become familiar with the themes.

The "Alcotts" theme is present from the start and gradually comes into focus in the first section. Example 9.1 shows the opening of the movement. The initial motive of the "Alcotts" theme appears almost immediately (motive a, marked by a bracket). The opening motive from Beethoven's Fifth Symphony (motive b), which begins the second half of the "Alcotts" theme, soon appears (with a minor instead of a major third) and is repeated in the bass line in tandem with motive a. Shortly thereafter (mm. 5–6), the first two segments of the theme's second half appear in augmentation in A♭ major, in enharmonic spellings. The theme's opening motive appears several times in the upper voice, intermixed with other material (mm. 7–8 and 10, not shown in Example 9.1). Then both halves of the theme appear in counterpoint (m. 11), as shown in Example 9.2; the complete first half of the theme is paraphrased in C major over the first and final segments of the second half in the bass, again in augmentation and in A♭.

Once all parts of the "Alcotts" theme have been heard, albeit in fragments and rhythmically altered, the music turns to other themes. Yet motives a and b from the "Alcotts" theme return frequently, and the second half of the theme appears in altered form shortly before the movement's middle section (p. 6, systems 2–3).[38] In the closing section, the second half appears three times in its normal rhythm, in G major (p. 18, system 5), A (p. 19, systems 2–3), and E♭ (p. 19, system 4, anticipated by a partial statement in system 3). The first of these statements breaks off before the last three notes, and the others lack the final segment entirely. But it is this theme with which the movement ends, after each of the other themes has come to rest. There is something of the feel of a cumulative setting in this ending, with the direct statement of a theme that has been heard from the outset in fragmented or paraphrased form. However, the thematic plan of the movement is much more complex, combining elements of sonata and ternary forms with the ideas of continuous development and of incorporating several movements in one, in a manner reminiscent of Liszt's Sonata in B Minor.[39]

Other themes and motives that play a major role in "Emerson" are also introduced or foreshadowed in the opening cadenza, as shown in Example 9.1. Of these, three may be symbolic: the middle-section theme (m. 1, bass), which Ives wrote "may reflect some of Emerson's poetry rather than the prose"; the movement's principal motive (m. 2, top line), which may repre-

Middle–section theme (p.8)

"Emerson" motive

Fugue theme (p. 13)

Middle-section theme

"Emerson" motive

Second theme (p.5)

"Alcotts" theme, second half

EXAMPLE 9.1: *Concord Sonata*, parts of the "Alcotts" theme and other motives in the opening of "Emerson"

EXAMPLE 9.1, continued

sent Emerson himself; and the tune in clusters, whose opening few notes are shown in Example 9.3, which Ives told John Kirkpatrick "had something to do with the idea of tolerance," as suggested by its appearance in three keys simultaneously.[40] The tune may be paraphrased from *Crusader's Hymn* ("Fairest Lord Jesus"), which has a similar rhythmic and melodic contour, as Example 9.3 shows.[41]

Three of the most important motives in "Emerson" are melodically related to the "Alcotts" theme and may derive from it. The pitches of the "Emerson" motive (3-2-2-6-1 in major) can be seen as a reordering of the first four notes of the "Alcotts" theme (1-2-3-6). The first four notes of the second theme (1-3-3-2 in major) appear inverted in the "Alcotts" theme (3-1-1-2), marked with a horizontal brace in Example 9.1. The first five notes of the middle-section theme (6-5-4-2-1 in major) also appear inverted in the "Alcotts" theme (4-5-6-1-2), marked with a horizontal broken brace in Examples 9.1 and 9.2.[42] Both inversions involve not only exact intervallic inversion but the preservation of the same scale degrees in reference to the implied local key. This suggests that Ives heard the relationship and may have developed the "Emerson" themes from fragments of the "Alcotts" theme. Whether conscious or not, these subtle motivic interrelationships between his themes show Ives as continuing the Brahmsian tradition of developing variation, deriving themes from the main idea of the work.[43]

"Emerson" is loosely related to sonata form, but the second movement, "Hawthorne," is more episodic. John Kirkpatrick has suggested that it is a fantasy with "images following as if helter-skelter but actually in a symmetrical design: phantasmagoria–nocturne–ragtime–contrasts–ragtime–nocturne–phantasmagoria."[44] Once again, the "Alcotts" theme figures promi-

"Alcotts" theme, first half

"Alcotts" theme, second half

EXAMPLE 9.2: *Concord Sonata,* "Emerson," m. 11, with elements of the "Alcotts" theme

nently. Several appearances of motive a lead first to an incomplete paraphrase of the opening of the theme with the descending fifth inverted to an ascending fourth (p. 28, systems 2–3, varied at p. 29, systems 4–5) and then to an extensive paraphrase of the entire theme, with repetitions and interpolations, about a third of the way through the movement (p. 30, end of system 2, through p. 32, system 4). Further fragments occur throughout the subsequent episodes, with another, briefer paraphrase of most of the theme near the end (p. 49, system 4, through p. 50, system 3).[45]

PROGRAMMATIC QUOTATION

Crusader's Hymn

"Tolerance" theme (p.3)

EXAMPLE 9.3: *Concord Sonata*, "Emerson," the "Tolerance" theme and *Crusader's Hymn*

Ives gives only a sketch of a program, calling the movement "but an 'extended fragment' trying to suggest some of [Hawthorne's] wilder, fantastical adventures into the half-childlike, half-fairytale phantasmal realms" and naming several stories and incidents that may be reflected in the music.[46] One not attributed to any Hawthorne tale is "the old hymn-tune that haunts the church and sings only to those in the churchyard to protect them from secular noises, as when the circus parade comes down Main Street." This is depicted explicitly. Just after the first paraphrase of the whole "Alcotts" theme, a loud blur cuts off to reveal a soft hymn already sounding, suggesting through sonic exuviation that the hymn has been going on unheard and is audible now only because all other sounds have ceased. This occurs twice (pp. 33–34), and the effect is sufficiently eerie to suggest both the haunted church and the graveyard. The hymn begins like *Martyn* ("Jesus, lover of my soul"), but its continuation is only distantly related to that tune. *Martyn* is one of the sources of the "Alcotts" theme, and its text appropriately pleads for Jesus' protection. This episode is followed by "the circus parade" in the guise of passages from Ives's *Country Band March*, reworked and interspersed with new material (pp. 35–36) and closed by an imitation of the drum "street beat" (p. 36, bottom). *Martyn* returns twice (p. 42, systems 3–4, and p. 51, just before the end). After the first of these is a long episode on material from "Columbia, the Gem of the Ocean," first in distant paraphrase, then in recognizable fragments, but never coalescing into a complete statement (p. 43, system 3, through p. 46, system 4). This section ends with another self-borrowing, from the vocal line of *He Is There!* (1917), of a phrase that is itself based on part of "Columbia" (mm. 27–33 of the Ives song). This episode does not seem to correspond to any of the images in Ives's program. One other self-borrowing deserves mention; a passage just after the first incomplete paraphrase of the "Alcotts" theme (p. 28, end of system 3, through p. 29, first beat) reworks an idea from *Scherzo: Over the Pavements* (mm. 1–6 and 29–30).[47]

Ives wrote of the next movement,

we won't try to reconcile the music sketch of the Alcotts with much besides the memory of that home under the elms [Orchard House]—the Scotch songs and the family hymns that were sung at the end each day— though there may be an attempt to catch something of that common sentiment (which we have tried to suggest above)—a strength of hope that never gives way to despair—a conviction in the power of the common soul which, when all is said and done, may be as typical as any theme of Concord and its Transcendentalists.[48]

This "common sentiment" is represented musically by the "Alcotts" theme— or perhaps one should say that the latter becomes the "theme of Concord and its Transcendentalists" through its inclusion in all four movements of the sonata. The other elements Ives mentions suggest that he was trying to capture the sound and feel of family music-making as a way to evoke the house and its occupants. The music includes material from two hymns, *Missionary Chant* and *Martyn*, and several hymn-like passages. The middle section may stand for the "Scotch songs," for it adopts the style of popular music and includes a Scotch snap, although the tunes it appears to borrow, the Wedding March from Wagner's *Lohengrin* and the minstrel song "Stop That Knocking at My Door," are not Scottish.[49] In his essay on "The Alcotts," Ives also mentions "the little old spinet piano Sophia Thoreau gave to the Alcott children, on which Beth played the old Scotch airs, and played at the *Fifth Symphony*."[50] Beethoven's famous motive is much in evidence, as is the opening motive of the "Hammerklavier" Sonata, also a source for the main theme. Moreover, the style at the beginning of the first and middle sections is reminiscent of home piano playing of the pre-Civil War era, and the borrowings are historically appropriate, for the two hymns date from the 1830s and the apparent quotations in the middle section from the 1840s. Although the movement is closer to a character study than to representational works such as *The General Slocum* or *Central Park in the Dark*, it is like them in evoking the sounds and feelings of music-making in a particular place and time.

The last movement, "Thoreau," has the most explicit program, filled with images that are reflected in the music, from mist over Walden Pond to a train going by.[51] Near the end, "the poet's flute is heard out over the pond. . . . Is it a transcendental tune of Concord?" This is represented in the music by the entrance of a flute (an ossia for piano alone is provided) playing the "Alcotts" theme in its main key of B♭ major, first incomplete, then transposed and varied, and finally complete but for the last four notes (p. 67, top, to p. 68, system 1). The theme is not heard earlier in the movement; its musical function here is as a unifying element, and its programmatic role is to suggest the "common sentiment" shared by the Concord writers.

One other theme in "Thoreau" uses borrowed material. Partly para-phrased from the "Down in de cornfield" motive from "Massa's in de Cold Ground" and played over a slowly swaying ostinato (p. 62, recalled on p. 65, systems 3–4, and at the end), this theme seems to represent a passage that Ives paraphrased from Thoreau's *Walden* in this part of his program: "He grew in those seasons like corn in the night, and they were better than any works of the hands. They were not time subtracted from his life but so much over and above the usual allowance. He realized what the Orientals meant by contem-plation and the forsaking of works."[52] The slow, unchanging ostinato, the longest such passage in any of Ives's keyboard works, suggests precisely this mood of submissive meditation. The identification of this section with this part of the program is confirmed by the song *Thoreau* (1915), adapted from parts of this movement.[53] Its first line of text is "He grew in those seasons like corn in the night," set over an unrelated passage from the sonata (from p. 66, system 3) but followed by a transposed version of the final reprise of this theme paraphrased from "Down in de cornfield." Perhaps the reference to "corn" is the reason Ives used this tune as a source for this passage.

Some of the borrowings in the *Concord Sonata* evoke the experience of making or hearing music: the hymn and march in "Hawthorne," Beth Alcott playing the piano, Thoreau playing the flute. But other borrowed material is symbolic: the "Tolerance" theme in "Emerson," the episode on "Columbia, the Gem of the Ocean" in "Hawthorne," the "cornfield" theme in "Thoreau," and most important, the "Alcotts" theme throughout the sonata.

The symbolism of this sonata leaves its meaning open to interpretation, which Ives invites through his ruminations in *Essays Before a Sonata* on the nature and limits of program music and on his famous distinction between "substance" and "manner."[54] But this is not typical of Ives's program music, nor of his uses of existing music. The majority of Ives's programmatic works represent concrete things and happenings, not abstract ideas. Outside this sonata, only a few pieces operate on such a symbolic level, notably the Sec-ond String Quartet finale and the Fourth Symphony among works that use borrowed material, and *The Unanswered Question* and the unfinished *Uni-verse Symphony* among works that do not. These are among his most famous pieces, perhaps because audiences and critics find Ives's mystical side particu-larly appealing. But they should not lead us to misread mysticism into Ives's more down-to-earth musical pictures.

The Celestial Railroad

After the *Concord Sonata* was completed, its music continued to evolve. The first movement and the concerto on which it was based were reworked in the 1920s into *Four Transcriptions from Emerson* for piano, which incorporated material from both earlier versions and in turn contributed revisions to the 1947 second edition of the *Concord Sonata*.[55]

The "Hawthorne" movement has the most interesting history. According to the best account, by Thomas M. Brodhead, in the 1910s Ives began to sketch a piano concerto based on Hawthorne stories (now lost). Abandoning the concerto, he recast some of this material into the "Hawthorne" movement of the *Concord Sonata* and around the same time adopted or adapted the concerto draft as the second movement of the Fourth Symphony. After the sonata was engraved in 1920, he drew on the "Hawthorne" movement and on the original concerto to create a fantasy for solo piano now known as *The Celestial Railroad*, finished by 1923 and premiered in 1928 by Anton Rovinsky. This represented a substantial reworking of both earlier works. After Ives completed the fantasy, he orchestrated and slightly expanded it, adding other instrumental lines and perhaps incorporating ideas from the earlier concerto or symphony movement. This orchestrated version became the present second movement of the Fourth Symphony, premiered in 1927.[56]

Although *The Celestial Railroad* is based on "Hawthorne," it has a different shape, more borrowed music, and a more concrete program. It adapts the first half of "Hawthorne," presenting much of the same material in the same order, and inserts into this the episode on "Columbia, the Gem of the Ocean" from the second half. But it omits almost two-thirds of the sonata movement and interpolates new episodes, so that it is almost half newly composed.

As Brodhead points out, *The Celestial Railroad* and its orchestral adaptation closely follow the events of Hawthorne's satirical tale "The Celestial Rail-Road" from *Mosses from an Old Manse*, one of the stories that Ives mentions in his program for "Hawthorne" and part of the inspiration for that movement.[57] In the story, the narrator recounts a dream in which he is offered an easy way to Heaven, on a railroad, instead of the difficult journey pilgrims make on foot, an allusion to the allegory of John Bunyan's *Pilgrim's Progress*. Encouraged by his companion Mr. Smooth-it-away, he boards the train and it takes off. After passing by pilgrims and other sights, the train takes a rest stop at Vanity Fair. At last the train reaches Beulah Land, across the river from the Celestial City, as the foot-pilgrims arrive and are welcomed into the City. The sinful railroad passengers board a ferry to take them across the river, only to discover that they have been duped and are being ferried off to Hell. The narrator's desperate attempt to flee wakes him from his dream.[58]

The musical borrowings in the piano fantasy support the program, but in a way that is more allegorical than realistic. The hymn tune *Martyn* seems to signify the pilgrims who are traveling in the traditional way, or perhaps the heavenly goal itself. Its text is appropriate to the pilgrimage, asking "Jesus, lover of my soul, / Let me to Thy bosom fly; / . . . Safe into the haven

PROGRAMMATIC QUOTATION

guide; / O receive my soul at last." We hear hints of it near the beginning (mm. 15 and 17 of Brodhead's edition), just before the train starts up (at m. 20), interleaved with the benediction "God be with you till we meet again" (mm. 7–8 of *God Be With You*, in mm. 16–17 and 18–20). Toward the end, after a sonic exuviation, we hear a quiet fragment of *Martyn* (mm. 146–48), like a glimpse of the Celestial City from the railcar window. Soon afterward, the noise ceases again for a longer hymn-like section based on *Martyn* (mm. 157–66), representing, in Brodhead's interpretation, the arrival of the train at Beulah Land and the entrance of the foot-pilgrims into the Celestial City. A loud interruption signals the passengers' discovery that their shortcut to Heaven is leading them to damnation. The narrator wakes to reality, symbolized by a march (mm. 174 to the end) based on Ives's *Country Band March*, with a variant of the "street beat" imitating a drum corps (mm. 194–201) and a snippet of "Yankee Doodle" near the end (mm. 202–3). This entire passage, from the appearance of *Martyn* through the end of the piece, is based on the section of "Hawthorne" that includes the hymn and the march (pp. 33–36), though the apparent meaning of the events is different in the new context.

The relation of the other borrowings to Hawthorne's story is less clear. As the train starts moving quickly, we hear the opening of "Tramp! Tramp! Tramp!" ("In the prison cell I sit, / Thinking, Mother dear, of you," at mm. 36–38), joined with the beginning of the chorus of "Marching Through Georgia" ("Hurrah! Hurrah! we bring the Jubilee!," at mm. 38–40). Might this suggest liberation from sin, or hint that the Celestial Railroad is itself a prison because it offers false salvation? A lively episode paraphrases the chorus of "De Camptown Races" (mm. 48–67), perhaps to evoke its words ("Gwine to run all night! Gwine to run all day!") or its air of gambling and loose living. Later comes the chorus of "Old Black Joe" ("I'm coming, I'm coming, for my head is bending low," at mm. 65–73). The text of this song looks forward to "a better land," and perhaps this quotation is meant to suggest that idea. A substantial section (mm. 76–91, taken from "Hawthorne," p. 43, system 3, through p. 45, system 2) paraphrases "Columbia, the Gem of the Ocean," whose relevance is far from obvious. After a rest stop at Vanity Fair, the final leg of the rail journey is a fantasy based in large part on the "Alcotts" theme, its first portion varied in mm. 111–13 and 128–30 (after being anticipated in m. 3) and its second half, with the Beethoven Fifth Symphony motive, developed in mm. 136 and 138–43 (adapted from "Hawthorne," pp. 28–32). This, too, is hard to connect with Hawthorne's story. Between the two halves of the "Alcotts" theme is a tune (in mm. 131–37) that appears to paraphrase the chorus of *Throw Out the Life-Line*, perhaps symbolizing through its text ("Throw out the Life-Line! Someone is drifting away") the danger of damnation faced by the railroad passengers. Finally, a number of melodic fragments resemble hymns or other types of tunes and may be quoted or paraphrased.[59] Perhaps these borrowings help to suggest the diverse horrors that Hawthorne's protagonist sees through the windows of the train. Interestingly, Mr. Smooth-it-away (m. 94) and Vanity Fair (mm. 97–108) are depicted without borrowed material.[60]

The largely symbolic use of existing music in *The Celestial Railroad* suits its story, an allegory in which everything that seems real stands for a theological idea. Even episodes that were representational in "Hawthorne," such as the hymn and the march, here represent concepts or symbolic actions. The Fourth Symphony movement adds more layers and sections to this fabric, including several more borrowed tunes, creating a vast programmatic collage that will be discussed in chapter 10 with the rest of the symphony. As we shall see there, the entire symphony assumes the allegorical spirit of *The Celestial Railroad*, making it in many ways the most unusual of Ives's works.

The three pieces considered here all use quotation in a symbolic sense, but each does so in a different way. The Second String Quartet uses quick bursts of borrowed fragments to suggest rapid-fire conversation, and *Bethany* and *Westminster Chimes* to evoke the majesty and wonder of contemplating the heavens. The *Concord Sonata* uses various means to suggest incidents or concepts related to the literary figures it depicts, from representations of music-making to the symbolism of the "transcendental tune of Concord." *The Celestial Railroad* is allegorical, even when imitating the sounds of musical performance. Each is unique in what it tries to signify through quotation, and the kind of symbolism they use is one of the least common though most widely recognized forms of borrowing Ives practiced. The special nature of these pieces again reminds us of the diversity of Ives's procedures for reworking existing music and the danger of assuming that what is true for one work is necessarily true for another.

Works with Text

About fifty of Ives's songs and choral works use borrowed music. Of these, only about a dozen briefly quote familiar music to illustrate the text. The questions of representation and symbolism in these works with text are similar to those in the instrumental music, but the presence of words often makes it easier to understand what Ives intended to signify through the quotation of existing music.

The limits of programmatic quotation in Ives's songs may be illustrated by considering a problematic case. Ives wrote *The Pond* between 1906 and 1914 for voice, trumpet, or basset horn and small orchestra to his own brief text:

PROGRAMMATIC QUOTATION

A sound of a distant horn
O'er shadow'd lake is borne,
My father's song.

He later revised it as the song *Remembrance* (1921), removing the harp and string parts, which represent the gentle rippling of the pond's surface, and transferring the flute line to the piano. The flute echoes the voice at a distance of one measure later and an octave higher, "to suggest the echo over a pond," according to Ives's program note.[61] At the end, the first three notes of "Taps" sound high in the piccolo (or piano), soft and in a different key. This is clearly "my father's song," rendered not naturalistically by an offstage horn, but impressionistically, in a remote octave and key to suggest its distance.[62]

Stuart Feder has interpreted this piece as a memorial to Ives's father, identifying the principal melody as a variant of "Kathleen Mavourneen" by Frederick Crouch (H112), a popular song from about 1840 whose mention of "the horn of the hunter" and theme of parting Feder links to the text of *The Pond*.[63] Yet this identification is far from certain. Ives used the same melody in *Largo cantabile (Hymn)* from about the same time or slightly before (ca. 1904–14), later recast as the song *Hymn* (1921); as noted in chapter 8, the other melodic sources for this work are two hymns, *More Love to Thee* and *Olivet*. It is highly likely that this melody is also based on a hymn tune. Example 9.4 compares the principal melody of *The Pond* and the parallel passage in *Hymn* with "Kathleen Mavourneen" and two hymn tunes that may have served as the model. *David*, arranged from a tune by Handel, appears in a hymnal that Ives used at the Methodist Church in Danbury, where he attended and occasionally played organ until 1889.[64] A slightly different arrangement of the same Handel tune, called *Thacher* or *Thatcher*, appears in the hymnal used in the college chapel services that Ives attended during his years at Yale and in the one that Ives used in his last position as an organist at Central Presbyterian Church in New York.[65] Both adaptations share the parallel three-measure phrases of *The Pond*, although the hymn's second phrase is an inverted variant rather than a simple sequential repetition of the first phrase, as in *The Pond*. Perhaps the most likely candidate, as the only one of these possible source tunes to share the meter and rhythm used in *Hymn* and *The Pond*, is a hymn tune adapted from one of Mendelssohn's best-known Songs Without Words, No. 9 in E Major, Op. 30, No. 3, known popularly as "Consolation." There were several adaptations; the example shows *Hexham*, from the hymnal used in the Yale chapel.[66]

The difficulty in identifying the source of Ives's melody has a clear bearing on the programmatic interpretation of *The Pond*. None of these hymn tunes is linked with a text that is directly relevant to *The Pond*, and indeed, like many

"Kathleen Mavourneen"

The Pond

p

Hymn

pp

David

Hexham

EXAMPLE 9.4: Principal melody of *The Pond (Remembrance)* and its possible sources

hymn tunes, they are used with more than one text. The title of Mendelssohn's "Consolation" might be relevant, yet the resemblance has long gone unrecognized. No matter which of these tunes, if any, served Ives as a model, it seems clear that he was not concerned to make the reference recognizable. This makes it unlikely that we will ever find a programmatic explanation for his choice of some particular tune for the main melody of *The Pond*. Rather, Ives seems to have picked this tune because it combined well with itself in imitation, producing the desired echo effect. The meaning of the piece does not hinge on identifying the source of the principal melody but depends on the evocation of the scene through the arpeggiating figures in piano and strings, the open harmonies, the echo of the melody in the flute or upper octaves of the piano, and the almost ghostly reference to "Taps" at the end, carrying associations of evening, rest, and death. The main melody of *The Pond* is almost certainly not a programmatic quotation but another example of modeling, like those explored in chapter 7, in which Ives lends a quality of reverence or dignity to a passage by following the contour of a hymn.

As this example suggests, quotations whose main role is to illustrate a text tend to be as brief, direct, and recognizable as the words they reflect. The quoted material, through its particular words or associations, can carry a more specific meaning than can a reference to a general style or type.

Like several pieces discussed above and in chapter 8, *The Pond* is about hearing music and the emotions it brings; the song sets up the situation through its words and music, and we hear "Taps" over the pond at the end. Ives's first work to quote a tune referred to in its text is *The Bells of Yale* (ca. 1898) for male voices and accompaniment.[67] The poem, by another Yale student, Huntington Mason, salutes the Battell Chapel bells as a symbol of life at Yale, and Ives's setting quotes the tune of the Battell Chimes (H147) in the accompaniment to the chorus. In a satirical vein, *The New River* for chorus and chamber ensemble (ca. 1913–21, also for chamber orchestra as *The Ruined River*) briefly quotes the popular songs "Tammany" (H139, piccolo, mm. 7–8) and "Ta-ra-ra Boom-de-ay!" (words of chorus with music of verse, voices and trumpets, m. 13) to illustrate the "sounds of man, dancing halls and tambourine, phonographs and gasoline" mentioned in the text between the two quotations. The specificity of these quotations combines with stylistic allusions to popular song and horn calls (the latter illustrating the vanished "blare of the hunting horn"), discussed in chapter 7, to convey the images in the text. In the song *Requiem* (ca. 1911–14), Ives sets the familiar poem by Robert Louis Stevenson that ends

> This be the verse you grave for me,
> Here he lies where he longed to be;
> Home is the sailor, home from sea,
> And the hunter home from the hill.

To set the last line, Ives uses the opening motive of "Taps" repeatedly in the voice and accompanies it in the piano with soft echoes of the same motive in various keys. This not only reflects the closing image by evoking "the echoes of the hunting-horn in the hills," as he says in a note, but suggests evening, death, and interment through the associations we have with "Taps."[68] Indeed, in all four works under discussion, the quotation's intended meaning goes beyond the representation of musical performance to encompass ideas and feelings associated with the music performed.

In Ives's later works, quotations to illustrate the text often have only this symbolic purpose. In some cases, a quoted tune seems to have been suggested by a resemblance between its text and the words to Ives's song. We have seen examples of this in *General William Booth*, *Thoreau*, and *Grantchester*.

Ives's text for his World War I song *Tom Sails Away* (1917) begins with the words "Scenes from my childhood are with me" and ends with a similar phrase. Ives sets both to a melody based on "The Old Oaken Bucket," which begins "How dear to this heart are the scenes of my childhood."[69] He quotes the second half of this line of text but the music for its first half, thereby invoking the words he does not quote: "how dear to this heart." Through the familiar tune, its words, and the sentiment that both carry, Ives suggests what these childhood memories mean to his speaker, the older sibling of a man who has left today for the war.[70] This is more subtle, more powerful, and more true to life than it would be to name the speaker's feelings in the text, and it nicely captures the tradition, among families in New England and elsewhere, of leaving the most important feelings unspoken. The speaker's feelings about Tom's leaving are equally unspoken, hidden beneath the language of public patriotism. As she returns to the present and says, "But today! In freedom's cause Tom sailed away,"[71] the voice turns to the rising fourths of fanfares, beginning with a possible reference to "Taps," and the piano begins a fortissimo statement of "Columbia, the Gem of the Ocean." As she continues "for over there, over there, over there!," the music slows and softens; "Columbia" continues in the piano, then halts as if unsure; and the vocal line slowly quotes George M. Cohan's "Over There" from that same year of 1917. Nothing is said, but the changing dynamics and tempo hint first of pride, then of loss and grief, as Cohan's musical recruiting poster becomes, in this context, an emblem of separation; "over there" is a long way away, and Tom's return is uncertain. In this song, one of his most tender, Ives quotes both the music and the text of particular songs, using the emotions and other associations they carry to convey the feelings of his speaker with a precision that probably could not be achieved in any other way. The song can still be understood by a listener who does not know these songs; the dotted rhythm and lilting style of "The Old Oaken Bucket" can evoke sentimental songs and thus nostalgia, and "Columbia" and "Over There" are both based on fanfare-like figures that are widely recognizable as signs of patriotism and the military. But knowing the songs quoted and the words associated with them adds a deeper and more precise level of meaning.[72]

After the national elections in 1920, Ives vented his frustrations in a song, *Nov. 2, 1920* (1921, later arranged for male chorus and orchestra as *An Election*).[73] Here, all the quotations seem to be motivated by textual links: at the words, "over there [our men did not quit]," Ives again quotes "Over There"; at "'It's raining, [lets throw out the weather man']," he paraphrases the children's song "It's Raining, It's Pouring"; and at the end, he alludes to the lost spirit of Lincoln in two ways, through a verbal reference to Walt Whitman's poem "O Caption! My Captain!" and by incorporating the closing passage of his own setting of "Lincoln, the Great Commoner," including a paraphrase of the opening of "The Star Spangled Banner."[74]

Psalm 90 (1923–24, based on a lost earlier version) contains an interesting quotation, recently identified by H. Wiley Hitchcock, which is so brief and distinct from its surroundings that it must be meant to illustrate the text. Comparing men to grass, the psalm's sixth verse says, "In the morning it flourisheth and groweth up; in the evening it is cut down, and withereth." The second half of this verse is set to a melody derived from Louis Moreau Gottschalk's *The Last Hope* for piano (H180).[75] Hitchcock notes that this tune was arranged as a hymn by Edwin Pond Parker, and Robert Offergeld has traced the entertaining history of its arrangement as a hymn with various texts and has suggested how Ives's father might have come in contact with the Gottschalk work or with its first adaptation as a hymn tune, called *Gottschalk*, by Hubert Platt Main.[76] But Ives most likely encountered the tune in the later version by Parker, called *Mercy*, which appears in the hymnal Ives used at the Methodist Church in Danbury until 1889. Here it carries a text that begins "Softly now the light of day / Fades upon our sight away" and whose third and final stanza begins "Soon from us the light of day / Shall forever pass away."[77] These images of evening and death parallel those in the sixth verse of Psalm 90, which may explain Ives's intentions in quoting the tune.

One of Ives's last works uses part of a college song as a motive, a symbol, and a direct illustration of the text. *Johnny Poe* (ca. 1925–29) for male chorus and orchestra sets a poem published in fall 1925 in the *Yale Alumni Weekly*, a tribute by Yale graduate Benjamin Low to the heroism of Princeton's Johnny Poe on the football field and on the battlefields of Europe, where he was killed in action in 1915.[78] Where Low's poem mentions the Princeton song "Old Nassau," Ives quotes a phrase from it—significantly, a line from the chorus sung to the words "Her sons will give while they shall live" (mm. 12–14, quoted at mm. 43–46). This same phrase opens the work, is developed in the initial section (mm. 1–11), and returns at the end as the text speaks of Johnny Poe "calling numbers" in the afterlife (mm. 56–63). Thus the phrase illustrates Low's text, symbolizes Princeton's football hero, and serves as a unifying motive and formal marker. The only other reference to "Old Nassau" is the opening of its chorus (mm. 9–10, to the words "In praise of Old Nassau"), which appears at the end of the first section at the words "Back in the long ago" (mm. 10–11).[79]

Quotation in the Popular Song Tradition

Quotation to illustrate a text was quite rare in European art songs of the nineteenth and early twentieth centuries, and references tended to be symbolic, as in the appearances of "La Marseillaise" in Schumann's *Die beiden Grenadiere* and the *Dies irae* in Mussorgsky's *Songs and Dances of Death*. But it has strong precedents and parallels in American songs. Neely Bruce has noted that borrowing is common in nineteenth-century American music, citing as examples two mid-century songs: David Warden's setting of Longfellow's "The Village Blacksmith," in which a choir enters singing Handel's "Angels Ever Bright and Fair" to depict the village choir mentioned in the poem; and J. C. Baker's "My Trundle Bed," which quotes *Nettleton*.[80] The incidence of borrowing increases in the songs of Ives's own time.

Many American popular songs of the 1890s through 1920s are about singing, playing, hearing, or dancing to music, and some refer directly to well known tunes. For example, James Thornton's "Streets of Cairo" (1895) tells of a country maid who succumbs to the temptations of the city and is hired "To appear each night / In abbreviated clothes." The song's verse evokes erotic dancing by borrowing the tune, based on the old Algerian melody "Kradoutja," that accompanied the "hoochy-koochy" dance performed by "Little Egypt" at the 1893 World's Columbian Exposition in Chicago, and the chorus mentions the dance.[81] Irving Berlin's "In My Harem" (1913) used the same tune at the words "And the dance they do / Would make you wish that you [were in a Harem]." One of Berlin's first big hits was "That Mesmerizing Mendelssohn Tune" (1909), on the romantically intoxicating powers of Mendelssohn's "Spring Song" (Song Without Words No. 30, Op. 62, No. 6), whose opening figure is interleaved with new material in Berlin's chorus. Berlin used this tune again in "Stop, Stop, Stop" (1910) and "Tell Her in the Springtime" (1924) and wrote several more songs that represent a musical performance through quotation, from "Alexander's Ragtime Band" (1911) to "Oh! How I Hate to Get Up in the Morning" (1918), on a soldier's distaste for "Reveille."[82] Harry Von Tilzer uses a similar approach in a number of songs, such as "The Song That Stole My Heart Away" (1913, to lyrics by Andrew B. Sterling), which mentions and quotes the popular song "Ben Bolt."

Other songs quote music to symbolize something associated with it. Patriotic songs, from Walter Kittredge's "Tenting on the Old Camp Ground" (1864) to Berlin's "Goodbye France" (1918), use fanfares, bugle calls, or patriotic tunes to set the scene or stir patriotic feelings. Many songs use quotation to suggest a nation or region: for example, Charles K. Harris's "My Virginia" (1907), a love song to a southern sweetheart, begins with eight bars of "Dixie" in the piano; Berlin's "Alexander's Bag-Pipe Band" (1912) uses the Scottish song "The Campbells are Coming" to characterize a Scot; and "The Dixie Volunteers" (1917) by Edgar Leslie and Harry Ruby, on Southern soldiers in World War I, echoes the text and quotes the music of Stephen Foster at the words "They're coming! They're coming! From the land of Old Black Joe." This last also is an example of a quotation suggested by the words of the song (or of words suggested by an intended quotation), of which there were many; for instance, Sterling and Von

Tilzer's "When Kate and I Were Comin' Thro' the Rye" (1902) quotes the song mentioned in its title, and George M. Cohan's "Over There" (1917) begins by quoting music and text from an earlier song, "Johnny Get Your Gun."

As in the popular song tradition, many of Ives's vocal works about music and its emotional effects quote tunes directly, including the patchworks *The Things Our Fathers Loved* and *Old Home Day* and several works discussed here, *The Bells of Yale, The Pond, The New River*, and *Requiem*. Given the rarity of this type of borrowing in the art music that Ives knew, his models for this procedure probably lay in American popular song. Perhaps this habit of Tin Pan Alley also influenced his instrumental works about music-making, from *Yale-Princeton Football Game* to *Decoration Day*, for these show a concern for the sound and feel of music as it is experienced in daily life that is unusual in program music, yet is not so distant from the more sentimental approach to the same theme in popular songs of the time. In making an evocation of music and our experience of it the focus of so many works, Ives seems to assimilate into his art music not only the tunes but also part of the subject matter of American popular song.

What is perhaps most striking is how seldom Ives quotes a tune primarily because of a link between its text and his own. We have seen examples in *General William Booth, Thoreau, Tom Sails Away, On the Counter* (the reference to "Auld Lang Syne"), *Nov. 2, 1920, Psalm 90*, and *Johnny Poe*, a mere seven out of more than two hundred vocal works, all from late in his career (1914–29). This type of quotation seems to be no more common in Ives's songs and choral works than it is in the songs of Cohan or Von Tilzer, although all three composers appear to borrow more frequently than most songwriters of the time. Together with his focus in so many works on conveying the experience of music and his use of various types of music to suggest people, places, or ideas associated with them (as described in previous chapters), this shows that in most instances Ives was not primarily interested in making his listeners think of the texts of the tunes he borrowed, as has often been assumed. Rather, in the vast majority of works in which borrowed tunes were meant to carry extramusical meaning, it was the music, the situation it implied, and the emotions it evoked that were of greatest importance to Ives; the words, if any, were only part of that larger web of experience a listener might have with a tune.

Understanding this emphasis in Ives's use of quotations for fulfilling a program or illustrating a text will help clarify what he is after in his collages, treated in the next chapter. In these works, as many as thirty tunes may scurry across the musical landscape, in any form from complete to fragmentary, from directly borrowed to recast almost beyond recognition, and from prominent to all but unheard. Were we to try to hear each one and focus on its text, we would miss the experience Ives is trying to convey: a sense of the swirl of inner thoughts as we dream or remember. In these collages, Ives combines aspects of modeling, paraphrase, and programmatic quotation with quodlibet and medley, drawing on these traditional procedures and on his own long experience to create the most extraordinary and individual of all his methods of reworking borrowed material.

CHAPTER 10

Quodlibet and Collage

Perhaps the most extraordinary of Ives's works are his vast orchestral *collages*, such as *The Fourth of July, Putnam's Camp*, and the Fourth Symphony. In these and similar works, the uses of existing music that we have examined so far, including modeling, paraphrase, cumulative setting, and programmatic quotation, blend with procedures derived from quodlibet to create music based on many borrowed tunes, some more prominent than others, that resembles in another medium the stream-of-consciousness writing of James Joyce's *Ulysses* or *Finnegans Wake* or the interweaving of quotations and allusions in T. S. Eliot's *Waste Land* or Ezra Pound's *Cantos*.[1] The intended effect in most of Ives's collages is to convey the sense of an event, not as it actually might have happened, as in *Central Park in the Dark* or *Decoration Day*, but as it is remembered or envisioned, with the cloud of borrowed tunes representing memories or thoughts associated with the events being pictured.

What defines collage is not the number of tunes that are used. We have already encountered about twenty works that borrow from at least a handful of sources: most movements of the Second Symphony and the middle movement of the Third, which use paraphrased themes; half a dozen vocal works that join numerous fragments in patchwork (*The Last Reader; Lincoln, the Great Commoner; Old Home Day; In Flanders Fields; He Is There!* and *They Are There!*; and *The Things Our Fathers Loved*); and several works that use five or more tunes in the service of a program (*Yale-Princeton Football Game; The General Slocum; Central Park in the Dark; Decoration Day*; the first two movements of the Second String Quartet; and *The Celestial Railroad*).

What distinguishes Ives's collages from these is that tune fragments are overlaid atop a musical structure that is already coherent without them. Most borrowings in the Second and Third Symphonies are themes or significant countermelodies; the borrowed tunes in a patchwork are woven together to create the main melody or an important countermelody; and almost all the borrowings in the programmatic works described in chapter 9 are prominent tunes that relate directly to the program. In a collage, by contrast, only some of the borrowings are themes, leading melodies, or principal countermelodies, and the others add further layers to the music, thickening both the musical texture and the forest of borrowed material. The omission of these added tune fragments might simplify the texture and weaken the effect, but it would not harm the basic musical structure.

Collage is an apt term for this procedure because borrowed tunes are added to an underlying structure in the way assembled objects are fixed on a painted or prepared surface to create a visual collage. Yet the term may be misleading, in at least two respects. First, in a visual collage the added objects tend to be in the foreground, while in Ives's collages the swirl of added tunes typically is in the background or finds prominence at transitions, remaining subordinate to the principal theme or cumulative setting that occupies center stage. Second, materials in a visual collage tend to be disparate, their relation to each other imposed by the artist, as in the collages of Kurt Schwitters or the three-dimensional constructions of Joseph Cornell. By contrast, Ives's added tunes typically have some obvious link to the other material, through melodic resemblance, common genre, or shared association with the events being depicted in the piece.

These collages combine the principles explored already, from modeling and paraphrase to cumulative setting and program music, with procedures typical of quodlibet: the combination in a polyphonic context of a number of borrowed tunes, presented either simultaneously or in quick succession, as in the second movement of Heinrich Biber's *Battalia* or the last variation of Bach's Goldberg Variations. They differ from quodlibet in using one or more of the procedures discussed in previous chapters to create a musical structure based on existing music, to which further tunes are added. Before turning to collage, let us consider the small number of Ives's pieces that fit the traditional definition of quodlibet because of their apparently arbitrary, often humorous, combination of existing tunes. As we shall see, despite a superficial similarity, collages have an entirely different character.

Quodlibet

We have seen that most of Ives's works based on existing music use borrowed material within a formal and thematic structure that is coherent even if the listener does not recognize the borrowed tunes. Programmaticism plays a role in a relatively small number of works, and in only a few are the borrowings to be understood primarily as fulfilling a program or illustrating a text. Yet in addition to the works whose borrowings can be explained in terms of a musical procedure or extramusical program, there are several in which the process seems entirely arbitrary, like a joke or compositional tour de force. These are the works in the tradition of *quodlibet*, a small group in Ives's output but a significant influence on some of his greatest compositions.

There are two basic techniques of linking existing tunes in a quodlibet: contrapuntal combination, in which tunes are piled on top of one another, and successive combination, in which fragments of various tunes appear in quick succession, whether in the same or a different instrument.[2]

Contrapuntal Combination

The earliest instance of Ives's combining existing tunes in counterpoint appears to be a sketch from about 1892 that superimposes the chorus of W. H. Doane's *Old, Old Story* on George Ives's Fugue in B♭, a pairing that later formed the climax of the first movement of the Fourth Violin Sonata.[3] As this example shows, Ives found the idea useful in cumulative settings, most of which combine the main theme with a countermelody, often paraphrased from a different tune. But he also combined borrowed tunes contrapuntally in other works. In the opening fugue of the First String Quartet, the third phrase of *Coronation* appears as a countersubject to the fugal subject, taken from *Missionary Hymn*. The contrapuntal combinations of themes that close the First Quartet and the second and final movements of the Second Symphony also use this idea. The climax of *In Flanders Fields*, at the words "Take up our quarrel with the foe!," joins "La Marseillaise" with *America,* a combination that recurs near the end of the *Three Quarter-tone Pieces.* There are several more examples in the collages discussed below.

This kind of quodlibet apparently has a vernacular precedent. In the arrangement of *The Circus Band* for chorus and orchestra, made by George F. Roberts in the 1930s or 1940s under Ives's supervision, the final reprise of the closing strain incorporates as countermelodies parts of four songs: in the horn, "Marching Through Georgia" and the "Marching Song" of Ives's junior fraternity, Delta Kappa Epsilon (to the tune of "Jolly Dogs"), at mm. 81 and 89, respectively; and in the piccolo at the same point, a tune that may be a college song (to the words "Riding down from Bangor on the midnight train"), followed by a variant of "Reuben and Rachel" (H131, music by William Gooch) to a text ("I had a horse we'd called Napoleon, / All on account of his 'Bony parts'") that Ives writes in a footnote was "sung by Cully Kernochan in the 'Spot'—'Boule' 3:33 a.m. before our march to East Rock."[4] These songs follow, more or less, the harmony of the last sixteen-measure strain, but they do not fit together with Ives's own tune or with one another any better than other similar tunes might have done. Ives explains in a note: "In the cornet bands of the 70's, 80's, and 90's, (at least in Connecticut), these quicksteps, so-called, were usually played twice, and often during the last strain of the repeat a little extemporaneous fun would be allowed—partly to let the boys know that the parade was going to stop or, at least, that this quickstep was."[5] Whereas the combination of George Ives's fugue with *Old, Old Story* was not necessarily humorous, and could later be used in a movement that is full of good humor but not really comic, this sort of off-the-cuff counterpoint was certainly intended to show off wit and high spirits. A few passing bad moments in the vertical sonorities were permissible and expected; indeed, for some in the audience, the more incongruous the combinations the better. This kind of "extemporaneous fun" with multiple quotations in counterpoint eventually led to the true quodlibets or "jokes" considered next, which emerge in Ives's notated music only after 1907 but may have roots in improvisations from his youth and college years.

Multiple Quotation as a Joke

Good counterpoint, melodic similarity, or extramusical associations all give at least some justfication for combining tunes. In a handful of pieces, no such rationale is obvious. Presumably they are simply jokes—two are explicitly labelled as such—and thus they meet our expectations for quodlibets. Obvious quotation of a familiar tune in another context has long been heard as incongruous in Western music, and incongruity is a vital element in humor.

Ives may have experimented with this sort of humorous combination of tunes during his college years. He writes in *Memos* of composing pieces that were played by the Hyperion Theater Orchestra in New Haven: "Some had old tunes, college songs, hymns, etc.—sometimes putting these themes or songs together in two or three differently keyed counterpoints (not exactly planned so but just played so)—and sometimes two or three different kinds of time and key and off-tunes, played sometimes impromptu."[6] Ives mentions *Yale-Princeton Football Game* and *Calcium Light Night* as pieces that were later written out in the same spirit. These are like polytonal quodlibets in mixing several different tunes in various keys, both simultaneously and successively, but as pieces that try to represent specific events they also have a strong programmatic character.

Ives's longest and most impressive quodlibet is the second movement of the Trio for violin, cello, and piano (ca. 1914), titled "TSIAJ" (for "This Scherzo Is A Joke") or "Medley on the Campus Fence."[7] This consists mostly of a string of tunes, often in counterpoint, that would have been familiar to Ives's college friends. Although not programmatic, according to Ives it reflects "the games and antics by the Students on the Campus" through "some of the tunes and songs of those days."[8] It includes at least twenty-five tunes, of which six have not been identified; many and perhaps all the tunes were associated with campus life. As is usual with Ives, some tunes are quoted at length, others more briefly, some directly, others in altered form. They appear in various keys, sometimes changing keys as they proceed, sometimes in polytonal combinations. The borrowed tunes are almost always the most prominent lines, and the other parts harmonize with the melody or play accompanimental figures or ostinatos, often chromatic or dissonant but usually implying a tonal center.

The incongruities begin in the introduction as all three instruments scurry chromatically in and around G major and land hard on odd divisions of the beat. The quodlibet begins with all but the last phrase of "A Band of Brothers in DKE," a song of Ives's junior fraternity Delta Kappa Epsilon (violin, mm. 16–42). The pace quickens and the violin continues with parts of "Marching Through Georgia" (mm. 43–46), "Few Days," a Psi Upsilon song (mm. 47–64), and the variant of "The Worms Crawl In" that Ives later used in *Central Park in the Dark* and identified as "Freshmen in Park" (mm. 65–67).[9] The violin shifts to a chromatic ostinato while the other instruments play in counterpoint two old sentimental songs, the verse of "My Old Kentucky Home" in the piano and the verse and chorus of "That Old Cabin Home Upon the Hill" in the cello (mm. 68–83).[10] After a pause and a slow statement of the first phrase of *In the Sweet Bye and Bye* in parallel major thirds in the piano (mm. 84–86), the tempo picks up again and the violin plays part of

"Sailor's Hornpipe" (also known as "College Hornpipe") while the cello plays the opening of the trio of Reeves's *Second Regiment March*, which Ives noted was "always played by Brass Band at Games and reunions."[11] The following section uses three unidentified tunes (H214 in the violin, mm. 93–99, repeated an octave higher; another in the piano, mm. 93–99, repeated at mm. 100, at 107 in the violin, and at 114 in the piano; and the third in the cello, mm. 107–14), possibly fraternity songs, and ends with brief fragments of two dance tunes, "Pig Town Fling" (violin, mm. 118–19) and "The Campbells Are Coming" (cello, mm. 119–21).[12] A faster section brings "Long, Long Ago" in the violin (mm. 120–24c, counting as mm. 124a–124c the three measures omitted in the first edition and restored in the critical edition); *Happy Day* or "How Dry I Am" in canon in the strings (mm. 124c–29); a polytonal, modulating statement of "Ta-ra-ra Boom-de-ay!" in violin and cello (mm. 130–45); overlapping that tune's cadence, a distorted fragment of "Dixie" in the violin (mm. 145–47); another reference to "Pig Town Fling" in the violin (mm. 149–53); a chromatic passage not based on borrowed material; an unidentified tune in the piano (H215, about mm. 162–69); a vertical combination of fragments of three tunes, with "Hold the Fort, McClung is Coming" in the bass of the piano (mm. 169–74), an unidentified tune in the cello (mm. 169–72), and the fiddle tune "Saint Patrick's Day" in the violin (mm. 170–72); and, to close the section, a distorted version of "Reuben and Rachel" in the cello (mm. 173–77). The last major section presents what John Kirkpatrick suggests may be two songs of Wolf's Head, Ives's secret society for his senior year.[13] The first is an unidentified tune in the piano (H216, mm. 178–87); perhaps this is "The Gods of Egypt Bid us Hail!," a phrase noted on a sketch of this movement that fits the rhythm of this melody. The second tune is the hymn *Fountain*, presumably used with different words in the college song, presented almost complete as an off-key paraphrase in octaves in the piano (mm. 187-200). Its close dovetails with a reprise of the phrase from *In the Sweet Bye and Bye* (piano, mm. 200–2); perhaps, as Kirkpatrick hints, this is a sign of nostalgia for the old college years.[14] After a cadenza, the variant of "The Worms Crawl In" returns in parallel keys a semitone apart (mm. 212–15), and the movement closes with a tonal cadence.

This movement is unique in Ives's output. He did, however, write five other works that include much shorter passages with humorous quodlibets.

The Scherzo for string quartet (ca. 1907–14) uses as its trio an earlier musical joke entitled "Practice for String Q[uarte]t In Holding Your Own!," in which each player must hold to a different pulse and scale.[15] Although the trio section contains no borrowings, the main melody of the scherzo proper consists largely of a string of fragmentary quotations: in the cello, a paraphrased segment of *Bringing in the Sheaves* (mm. 2–4), the opening of the chorus from "Massa's in de Cold Ground" (mm. 5–10), and the beginning of "My Old Kentucky Home" (mm. 10–13, overlapping the previous tune); and in the violins and cello, the initial motive of "Sailor's Hornpipe" (mm. 14–15). The scherzo closes with a canon in all four instruments in four different keys (mm. 17–20) on the "hoochy-koochy" dance tune used in James Thornton's "Streets of Cairo" (H137).[16] In typical Ives fashion, this is melodically related to "My Old Kentucky Home," acting in context like the debauched city cousin of the Foster tune.[17] The other tunes that Ives borrows are not humorous but become so in context as they are played against syncopated chromatic ostinatos. The joke lies in juxtaposing brief quotations with impossible accompaniments, culminating in the raucous canon and a thick, dissonant final chord.

Study No. 20 for piano (ca. 1908–14?) is a march in arch form whose humorous central trio features a ragtime song modeled on Harry Von Tilzer's "Alexander" (discussed in chapter 7), introduced by a fleeting quodlibet of fragments of other tunes: the opening of the chorus to "The Battle Hymn of the Republic" (mm. 71–74), overlapping "I've Been Working on the Railroad" (mm. 72–77), which elides with "The Girl I Left Behind Me" (mm. 77–80), which in turn elides with "Turkey in the Straw," recast as an Irish jig tune in $\frac{6}{8}$ time (mm. 80–82). Beneath the first part of this composite melody is an unidentified tune in an inner voice (mm. 73–77).[18] The similar brief quodlibets in the first two movements of the Second String Quartet appear to have a programmatic motivation, as discussed in chapter 9.

The quodlibets in the *Waltz-Rondo* for piano (ca. 1911) are less obviously humorous than the other examples we have seen.[19] This is a rondo in waltz time, with a brief introduction, a main theme, six episodes alternating with exact repetitions of the theme, and a coda that presents what Ives calls a "Digest" or abridgement of the main theme and all the episodes.[20] The sixth episode (mm. 138–50) paraphrases part of Ives's signature tune "Columbia, the Gem of the Ocean" (mm. 1–5 and 9–15 of its verse) in the left hand, counterpointed by a medley of four fiddle tunes in the right: "Fisher's Hornpipe" (mm. 138–40), "Turkey in the Straw" (mm. 140–46), "Sailor's Hornpipe" (mm. 145–47), and "The White Cockade" (mm. 148–49). This material returns condensed near the end of the coda (mm. 193–98), heralded by a brief development of the opening of "Columbia" (mm. 188–91); here "The White Cockade" is omitted and the left-hand paraphrase of "Columbia" is infiltrated by m. 5 of "Marching Through Georgia" (mm. 196–97). In the context of Ives's music as a whole, his use of such material for an episode is less surprising than his writing a rondo in the first place. Whether his intent was humorous or not is uncertain, particularly since the fiddle tunes are distorted enough to be hard to recognize and the underlying paraphrase of "Columbia" gives these passages somewhat more coherence than the other works discussed in this section.

Collage in *The Fourth of July*

Quodlibets, whether intended as humor or as displays of compositional virtuosity, show Ives's occasional interest in quotation as an end in itself. But far more common in his music are pieces like those discussed in previous chapters, in which the borrowings form the basis of the musical structure, lend a particular character to a piece or section, or have a clear programmatic purpose. In his collages, most or all of these traits are combined. There are aspects of quodlibet in the presence of so many tunes, often presented simultaneously; most of the borrowings evoke a mood, establish a character, or correspond to events in a program; and the musical structure is based on existing music through modeling, paraphrase, cumulative setting, or in some other way. What distinguishes collage from quodlibet is the presence of this underlying structure derived from existing music through one of the procedures surveyed in the previous chapters. What distinguishes collage from these other ways of using existing music is the presence of anywhere from a handful to upwards of two dozen tune fragments added on top of the basic musical structure.

The Fourth of July

A typical collage is *The Fourth of July* (written ca. 1913–19 and scored and revised in the 1920s), the scherzo for the *Holidays Symphony*.[21] This is a tribute to the celebrations of Independence Day that Ives remembered from his youth, marked by parades, dancing, and fireworks. Over the course of the movement we hear patriotic songs and dance tunes and near the end the explosion of the fireworks. Ives called it "pure program music—it is also pure abstract music— 'You pays your money, and you takes your choice.' "[22] The program that he offers in a postface mentions a number of sounds, sights, and incidents of the day. But only a few of these correspond to events in the music, and the program does not account for the musical structure, the order of events, or the presence of most of the twenty or so borrowed tunes.

The piece is a cumulative setting of the verse of "Columbia, the Gem of the Ocean."[23] At the climax near the end (reh. S–X, mm. 99–114), the complete theme is stated in intricate heterophony by trumpets, trombones, and cellos. It is essentially in B♭ major and *fortissimo*, but the many "wrong" notes (marked at lower dynamic levels in the brass) and other variants between the instruments suggest the sound of a brass band in which not everyone plays all the notes and rhythms correctly and some members are prone to a little spontaneous improvisation. The main countermelody, also mostly in B♭, mixes elements from verse and chorus of "The Battle Hymn of the Republic" and interpolates part of the chorus of "Marching Through Georgia" (at mm. 108–11). The countermelody appears in flutes, oboes, clarinets, and cornet in counterpoint with the theme, again in a not-quite-unison ensemble that evokes the sound of amateur bands. These two main melodies are accompanied by a great mass of sound that includes supporting harmony in the bass instruments; waves of parallel diatonic clusters in A, B♭, and B major in the upper strings, like a wash of sound around the principal key of B♭; percussion; and several other tunes (discussed below). After a final triadic flourish that may invoke "The Star Spangled Banner" (mm. 114–15) and a brief pause, the work closes with a dissonant, noisy explosion in the entire orchestra, a sonic exuviation, and a soft, wispy descent in upper strings and flute, depicting the end of Ives's program: "and the day ends with the sky-rocket over the Church-steeple, just after the annual explosion sets the Town-Hall on fire."[24]

The earlier parts of the piece present and develop fragments of the main theme and countermelody, along with other material.[25] The first section (mm. 1–44) is concerned primarily with "Columbia." At the outset, the tune's opening segment appears softly and slowly in C♯ minor over a sustained F-major triad, with which it forms poignant dissonances (mm. 1–3). It then moves to the bass, first in B and then in C major. Here it is combined with a dissonant ostinato and quartal, quintal, and whole-tone chords, the latter perhaps derived from the perfect fourths and major seconds that comprise the first four intervals of "Columbia."[26] A cuckoo's call (m. 16) signals the shift of the tune to the upper winds and back to B major, and brief hints of the bugle call "Assembly" in the horn and "The Battle Cry of Freedom" in the cello (m. 27) mark the close of the first subsection. The next subsection (reh. E, m. 28), somewhat faster, presents a paraphrase of the first two segments of "Columbia," with much repetition, in flutes and piccolo in A minor and major (mm. 28–36), joined at the end by the opening of the chorus of "Marching Through Georgia" in the trumpet (mm. 34–36). After an extension, a second cuckoo call (m. 42) prepares the turn to new material in the middle section, in which "Columbia" appears only briefly.

The central third of the piece (reh. G–N, mm. 44–79) gradually increases in tempo. It uses a number of tunes, perhaps most importantly "The Battle Hymn of the Republic," the principal component of the countermelody.[27] The first subsection is based on the verse of Ives's song *Old Home Day*. Flute and clarinet play the original melody that opens the verse, to the words "A minor tune from Todd's opera house, comes to me as I cross the square" (mm. 9–13 of the song, at reh. G, mm. 44–48).[28] The borrowing continues as oboe, clarinet, and violins play the remainder of the verse, based on "The Battle Hymn of the Republic," with the piano accompaniment in the lower strings (mm. 14–18 of the song, at mm. 49–53). Added quietly in the background are two hornpipes, "Sailor's Hornpipe" (oboe, mm. 45–47) and "Fisher's Hornpipe" (flute and piccolo, mm. 49–51), and the "street beat" in the bass drum and timpani (mm. 49–53). The next subsection (mm. 53–63) centers on a series of single-interval chords generated by parallel chromatic and whole-tone scales. But it also includes altered fragments of a number of patriotic or military tunes: "The Battle Cry of Freedom" (horns and viola, mm. 53–55), "Reveille" (horns and trumpet, mm. 57–60), the first half of the chorus to "The Battle Hymn of the Republic" (winds, mm. 60–63), and "Columbia, the Gem of the Ocean" (trombones, mm. 62–63), whose combination here with "The Battle Hymn" presages the later pairing of the two tunes at the climax. The remainder of the middle section hints at a reprise of the first subsection, with several recollections of the verse of *Old Home Day* (violins, mm. 65–66, 69–70, 73–75, and 78–80, and horn, mm. 70–73). However, several tune fragments are more prominent: part of "Hail! Columbia" in clarinet and bassoons (mm. 64–66 and 73–74); the "street beat," both bass and snare drum patterns, in drums and piano (reh. L, mm. 66a-74); a fife tune in the piccolo, perhaps modeled on "The White Cockade" (mm. 66a–67a), elided with the chorus of "Tramp, Tramp, Tramp" (mm. 68a–70a) and "The Girl I Left Behind Me" (mm. 70a–72a); and "London Bridge," distributed pointillistically between piccolo, flute, oboe, and bassoon (reh. M, mm. 74–75).[29]

The third main section of the movement (from m. 80, one measure after reh. N) leads up to the climactic statement of the theme and its countermelodies. "Hail! Columbia" is heard again in horn and trumpet (mm. 80–81 and 83). Then the opening motive of "Columbia, the Gem of the Ocean" returns in various keys, both in the paraphrased form heard earlier at reh. E and in its original form, and is developed through canonic entrances and spinning-out (reh. O–S, mm. 86–98). The accompaniment recalls the earlier one at reh. E, including an ostinato that is here transformed into a variant of "Hail! Columbia" (cello I, viola, and clarinet, mm. 86–82). Meanwhile, the xylophone and piano introduce a pair of Irish dance tunes, "Garryowen" (mm. 82–83 and 86–88) and "Saint Patrick's Day" (mm. 88–90 and 93–94), the same Irish tunes used in *Old Home Day*;[30] the trumpet plays "Reveille" (mm. 91–92), joins "Saint Patrick's Day" (m. 94), and adds what may be "Irish

Washerwoman" (H164, mm. 95–96) and part of "Marching Through Georgia" (mm. 97–98); horn 4 contributes an unidentified tune (mm. 94–98); and the upper winds suggest two brief motives from "The Battle Hymn" (a three-note descending motive from m. 1 as part of the "Columbia" paraphrase in mm. 86–92 and the subsequent rising gesture from mm. 1–2 in mm. 96–97). Now, after developing and paraphrasing the theme and presenting the principal countermelody separately, Ives combines them in a complete statement, as described above. They are accompanied by several other tunes: "Yankee Doodle" in xylophone and piano, and later bassoon;[31] the sentimental song "Katy Darling" (H113, mm. 99–109), followed by a fusion of "Dixie" and Henry Clay Work's Civil War song "Kingdom Coming" (H114, mm. 109–14) in the piccolo; the "street beat" in the drums (timpani at m. 99, snare and bass drum from m. 101); and "Assembly," dropped in from time to time in various instruments (oboe, mm. 102 and 108–9; clarinet, mm. 102–3 and 104; and cello I, mm. 103 and 106). The final explosion has only one brief quotation, "Yankee Doodle" (cornet and trumpet III, m. 118), virtually inaudible in the melee.

The Function of Collage

The kind of texture described above has unfairly earned Ives a reputation as a composer who quoted indiscriminately and was not fully in control of his materials. But the underlying structure is very clear: a cumulative setting in three parts with coda, the first part developing the main theme, the second based on contrasting material that includes the principal countermelody, and the third returning to the theme and culminating in a complete statement of the theme and its countermelody. The main problem for listeners and analysts is the presence of so many tune fragments added to this relatively simple form.

The musical and extramusical function of these added tunes can best be understood by comparison with similar works that do not use collage. *From Hanover Square North* and *The Housatonic at Stockbridge*, like *The Fourth of July*, are programmatic works in which a main event, a cumulative setting or paraphrased melody, appears against a multi-layered background that can only be described as muddy. Ives defended Brahms from the charge of muddy orchestration by asserting that "the mud may be a form of sincerity which demands that the heart be translated rather than handed around through the pit. A clearer scoring might have lowered the thought."[32] Similarly, one can defend the necessity in many of Ives's own works of what may be called the "mud," the background figurations and transitional ideas that crowd his music but do not hold center stage. What is crucial is to understand what the "mud" is for and how it helps to communicate the experience Ives intends to convey.

For his pieces about life experiences, Ives had developed the convention of music sounding in at least two simultaneous layers. The foreground represents the events themselves, and the background, often in many layers of varying audibility, evokes the noises of the environment that one may notice or ignore but are nonetheless always there. Their presence in the music is an essential part of Ives's attempt to render the multi-layered feel of life.[33] But the nature of the background varies with each work. For pieces about recent experiences, the background noises are usually rendered as soft, dissonant ostinatos in complex rhythms, representing the sounds of the rustling leaves and swirling river in *The Housatonic at Stockbridge* or the hum of rush hour traffic and machinery in *From Hanover Square North*. In such works, the addition of a large number of tunes in the background would be distracting and untrue, for nothing like that happens in real life. In these works, Ives finds atonal and rhythmically suspended ostinatos to be the truest representation of his auditory and psychological experience.

But *The Fourth of July* captures a different kind of experience—not that of a boy participating in the Independence Day celebrations in his home town, but that of a man approaching middle age, remembering the Fourth of July celebrations of his boyhood and especially the role of music in the festivities. In a piece about remembered events, there is also a background hum, but it is not the hum of traffic or natural noises; it is the cloud of memory, as each remembered event, person, or thing recalls others aroused involuntarily by their association with or resemblance to the first. Ives signals this through quotation. When Ives is remembering, one tune will suggest another that resembles it in melody or rhythm, or with which it is associated by common genre or use in similar circumstances. The result is a collage of half-heard and half-remembered tunes that is a wonderfully true musical evocation of the way human memory works.[34]

Here the day's central events are represented by the cumulative setting of "Columbia, the Gem of the Ocean," which builds up to something resembling the sound of the town band marching down Main Street and playing at full force. The added tunes represent other memories recalled involuntarily or as part of the scene. Dissonant ostinatos alone would fail to capture the special quality of the experience of remembering; only the intrusion of events that have no parallel in an actual experience, like the combination of four loud tunes at the climax or the sudden appearance of hornpipes and Irish dance tunes in remote keys amid largely unrelated music, can suggest the leaps and fancies of memory. Ives can use music of various types to represent these memories, both because of the strong associations we carry with different types of music, from patriotic songs and bugle calls to Irish jigs, and because of the important role music plays in the public celebrations he seeks to depict in this work.

Characteristic of this and Ives's other collages is that they do not allow us to listen to the borrowed tunes naively. Instead of presenting them whole and unchanged, Ives alters them rhythmically and melodically, in varying degrees from slight variation to virtual unrecognizability. Moreover, with the exception of the main theme and countermelody, tunes combined vertically often make poor counterpoint. Ives wants them not to combine gracefully but to conflict with one another and retain their individuality, like simultaneous but not wholly related thoughts. So he lets them clash through casual dissonance, or places them in different keys, or displaces them metrically so that their accents fall on off-beats, and assigns each tune a different instrumental timbre, making each sound like an independent event. Without this distortion and conflict, we might enjoy hearing the familiar melodies, hum along with them, or admire Ives's clever combinations of tunes, as we do in listening to Peter Schickele's *Quodlibet for Small Orchestra* or *"Unbegun" Symphony*.[35] But the disruptions that Ives introduces force us instead to interpret his music, to seek to understand the purpose behind it.[36] Ultimately, Ives aims not to entertain us but to convey an inner experience through a musical metaphor, and the incongruous and unexpected elements of the music open us to an understanding of this experience.

These incongruous and unexpected elements also help to define the nature of that experience. For the altered tunes and the rough fit between them represent the way we remember pieces of music or past events. As we try to sing a melody or retell a story, we may recall and reproduce some of it accurately, but we may get other parts wrong, forget a detail, get lost, be unable to finish, or mix it up with another tune or tale. As we remember a day's events, some elements may be prominent, others blurry or in the background. Some memories may flit by half-unnoticed or distorted beyond recognition. All of this is modeled in Ives's collages, through the fragmentation and variation of his borrowed tunes and through the presence of simultaneous layers in different keys, timbres, and degrees of prominence.

The Process of Composition

As might be expected, the core musical structure of *The Fourth of July* was created first and most of the other borrowed tunes added later. The basic structure comprises the cumulative setting of "Columbia, the Gem of the

Ocean"; the principal countermelody adapted from "The Battle Hymn of the Republic" and part of "Marching Through Georgia"; a secondary countermelody, "Yankee Doodle"; and a middle section with parts of *Old Home Day*, "The Battle Cry of Freedom," and "Reveille," in addition to the main theme and countermelody. In his study of the first complete draft of the work, Wayne Shirley points out several additions to the earliest version through insertion or overlay, including the hornpipes at mm. 45–51, the composite piccolo tune in mm. 66–74, the Irish jigs in mm. 82–94, and the piccolo line at the climax with "Katy Darling," "Dixie," and "Kingdom Coming."[37] Other additions include the two cuckoo calls, the several references to "Assembly" and "Hail! Columbia," the first references to "The Battle Cry of Freedom" at m. 27 and "Marching Through Georgia" at mm. 34–36, and "London Bridge." Some of these were added to the ink score-sketch in pencil, and others may date from the 1920s or later.[38] The sketches thus reinforce the conclusion that the various borrowings have different functions, either as parts of the basic musical form or as added elements that evoke music, people, or happenings associated with the work's main event.

Why were these particular tunes chosen to add to the existing structure? First, there are motivic similarities between the main theme and some of the added tunes, including the cuckoo call, "Hail! Columbia," "Yankee Doodle," and "Katy Darling."[39] Several other tunes share melodic and rhythmic patterns, such as dotted rhythms, triadic motion, or descending scales. Second, many of the tunes are linked to the main material by genre and shared associations with the Fourth of July, including American patriotic songs, Civil War tunes, bugle calls, and tunes often played by fife and drum corps, such as "The Girl I Left Behind Me," "The White Cockade," and "London Bridge." Melodic resemblance and other types of association may also work in tandem; for instance, the neighbor-note motion in the verse of *Old Home Day* may have suggested the version of "Sailor's Hornpipe" that Ives uses, which begins with a similar neighbor-note figure, and this seems to suggest in turn the second hornpipe tune through its common genre and role. Finally, Shirley suggests that the Irish tunes, "Katy Darling" and the two jigs, may have been added as "Ives's homage to the Irish-American participation in a New England Fourth of July."[40] No one explanation accounts for every tune, but each is clearly connected to the main material through melodic similarity, common genre, or shared associations with the events or experiences the work is meant to convey, and often by more than one of these. The web of musical and extramusical associations created by the presence of all these tunes is what gives *The Fourth of July* its special character and allows it to represent the stream of thoughts one might have while remembering the Independence Day celebrations of one's youth.

Other Works That Use Collage

Nine other completed movements use collage, dating from ca. 1903 to the 1920s: *Washington's Birthday, In the Inn, Putnam's Camp* and its predecessors *Country Band March* and *Overture and March "1776,"* and the four movements of the Fourth Symphony.[41] Each is individual, as is typical of Ives's mature works, yet the collage procedure is similar in all of them. In each case, borrowed tunes are added over another musical process, such as modeling, paraphrase, cumulative setting, fugue, or a narrative program. All nine are scored for orchestra, for the differentiation between layers that is crucial for Ives's collages is best achieved in a medium with a large number of players, many diverse timbres, and a wide range of dynamic levels.

Washington's Birthday

Washington's Birthday (ca. 1913–19, scored and revised in the 1920s), the first movement of the *Holidays Symphony*, has three sections: a slow section representing the cold, bleak New England winter landscape and the "old folks" sitting at home by the hearth; an Allegro picturing "the barn dance at the Centre," where "the village band of fiddles, fife and horn keep up an unending 'break-down' medley, and the young folks 'salute their partners and balance corners' till midnight"; and a closing Andante, in which, "as the party breaks up, the sentimental songs of those days are sung half in fun, half seriously, and with the inevitable 'adieu to the ladies' the 'social' gives way to the grey bleakness of the February night."[42] All three sections use borrowed material, but only the middle section is a collage.

The first section fulfills its program with dissonant, mostly soft chords and wisps of melody that hint at times of two old songs of home: "Home! Sweet Home!" by Henry R. Bishop (H108, mm. 1–4, violin I) and Stephen Foster's "Old Folks at Home" (H129, mm. 5 and 7–8, horn, and m. 15, violin I). Late in the section (reh. J, m. 48), the music grows louder, parallel dissonant chords in the strings rise and fall to suggest hills and snowdrifts, and runs and glissandi evoke "the younger generation" as "over the hill road they go, afoot or in sleighs, through the drifting snow, to the barn dance." Snatches of dance tunes float by in the flute ("Turkey in the Straw" in mm. 50–51 and "Sailor's Hornpipe" in m. 52), as if heard from the barn as we approach, and the music slows and fades out.

In the final section, the first violins play a sentimental tune in G major (mm. 163–77).[43] This may be an old song, but given its length, which would be unusual in an Ives borrowing, and the fact that no one has recognized it since *Washington's Birthday* was first performed, recorded, and published in the 1930s, it is more likely an original tune in the style of "the sentimental songs of those days." It is packed with clichés, from the opening reminiscence of "Home! Sweet Home!" to the final climax, with lilting triplets, ornamental chromaticism, Scotch snaps, dramatic leaps, and other common figures along the way. Indeed, the diversity of figuration and relative lack of repetition set it apart from genuine popular songs and suggest that it is a gentle take-off on sentimental tunes, rendered "half in fun, half seriously." In the background, behind this melody, a single violin softly plays fiddle tunes, blending "Pig Town Fling" with "Turkey in the Straw" and wandering from key to key (mostly A♭ and B♭) before fading out. This may represent either sounds still coming from the barn dance or, more likely, memories of the dance just concluded. It also reinforces the programmatic nature of the final section by creating two simultaneous, mutually dissonant strands of music, making it impossible to listen to the violin melody as nothing more than a pretty tune and forcing us to interpret the music in terms of the program. At the end, we hear "Goodnight, Ladies" (H104, music by Edwin P. Christy, at mm. 178–81), Ives's "adieu to the ladies," and soft, dissonant music like that of the opening evokes "the grey bleakness of the February night."

The middle section recalls the barn dance in the second movement of the Second Violin Sonata but is set up as a collage in several instruments rather than a patchwork in two. A loud introduction in D major (mm. 56–59) signals the start of the dance. The main theme in the first half (m. 60) appears to be an original Ives melody in the character of a fiddle tune for a quadrille.[44] As the music develops, several other dance tunes infiltrate the texture, along with a few tunes of other types. As in several instances of modeling discussed in earlier chapters, Ives is referring to the models for his theme overtly; what is different here is that so many are cited. Above Ives's theme, fragments of what may be an unidentified tune appear in a shadow part a tritone away (mm. 65–72). After a brief rhythmic disruption, parts of "Sailor's Hornpipe" enter in violins and flute in various keys (mm. 80–84 and 89–91), joined by "De Camptown Races" in D in the horn, cellos, and later violin I (mm. 86–93), much as it appeared in Ives's Second Symphony finale (mm. 35–38, trombone). The flute adds "For He's a Jolly Good Fellow" in E♭ (H101, mm. 99–102), and soon the rhythm lurches to a stop. The second half of the barn dance uses the fiddle tune "The White Cockade" as the leading theme. This is first played complete in A♭ by violin I (reh. P, mm. 109–25), assisted by the Jew's harp, with bits of "Turkey in the Straw" and the chorus of "Massa's in de Cold Ground" in D in the flute. The chorus of "The White Cockade" repeats in D♭, somewhat altered (reh. Q, mm. 126–32), with the chorus of "Turkey in the Straw" in the same key in the flute and the opening of "Irish Washerwoman" in the horn in F♯ minor and E major. The complete

QUODLIBET AND COLLAGE

"White Cockade" returns in the violins two octaves higher than its first appearance (reh. R, mm. 133–48), joined by other tunes: in the flute and piccolo, "Turkey in the Straw," in and around A♭ (mm. 134–45), "Fisher's Hornpipe" in F (mm. 145–52, joined by the Jew's harp), and later an apparent variant of "Money Musk" (mm. 153–61); and, in the horn, a blend of "The Campbells Are Coming" (mm. 134–40, with the Jew's harp), "Garryowen" (mm. 141–45 and 149–50), and "Saint Patrick's Day" (mm. 145–49 and 150–52). Figures developed from these tunes spin out and repeat, and the texture thickens until the section ends in a loud dissonant chord, from which the final section emerges through sonic exuviation.

Ives recalled that dances would at times feature several bands, so that "in some parts of the hall a group would be dancing a polka, while in another a waltz, with perhaps a quadrille or lancers going on in the middle," and that "often the piccolo or cornet would throw in 'asides.' "[45] But he does not try to capture realistically this effect of several bands playing at once, as he did in *The General Slocum* or as Mozart did in the first act finale of *Don Giovanni*. Rather, the accumulation of tunes represents the telescoping of an entire evening's music or a lifetime's recollection into a three-minute swirl, as the event that takes center stage, whether Ives's original quadrille theme in the first half or "The White Cockade" in the second, is surrounded by tunes suggested through melodic resemblance, shared genre, or other associations.

In the Inn

Another collage that seeks to capture the feel of music-making is *In the Inn* (ca. 1914, revised ca. 1923), the second movement of the *Set for Theater Orchestra*. This is an orchestration of movement IIb ("In the Inn") from the First Piano Sonata. Virtually every note of the sonata movement is present, but other elements are added, including altered fragments of several tunes: "After the Ball" by Charles K. Harris (H93, mm. 29–34, violin), joined with "Reuben and Rachel" (mm. 34–40); the verse of "Ta-ra-ra Boom-de-ay!" (mm. 74–81, violin); the final phrase of Harry Von Tilzer's "With His Hands in His Pockets and His Pockets in His Pants" (mm. 91–94 and 117–19, violin); and three as yet unidentified tunes in popular style (mm. 57–61, clarinet and bassoon, and 101–4, clarinet; mm. 86–89, violin; and mm. 119–22, violin).[46] All or most of the added tunes are motivically related to the thematic material already present in the sonata movement.[47] All the identified borrowings are popular tunes, and the others are in a similar style, suggesting that Ives added them to evoke the atmosphere of a tavern through the music that might be heard there. The effect is much like the barn dance in *Washington's Birthday*, with the principal musical thread—here, the ragtime piano—colored by added tunes appropriate to the scene and mood.

As David Nicholls points out, a listener can approach this work in many ways, from hearing it as a succession of melodic fragments, to following the form created by statements of the main themes, to tracing a path marked out by changes of meter, texture, implied key, or other parameters, yet each of these different approaches conveys a sense of the whole.[48] This is typical of Ives's collages, and it perfectly captures the multifaceted nature of experience, especially as it is remembered.

Putnam's Camp and Its Sources

Besides *The Fourth of July*, two other compositions use collage to convey the sound and spirit of an outdoor band: *Country Band March* and a work later adapted from it, *Putnam's Camp, Redding, Connecticut*. The latter also incorporates part of *Overture and March "1776,"* a pastiche on patriotic tunes.

Country Band March for theater orchestra, composed between ca. 1905 and ca. 1914, is an affectionate picture of an amateur band playing with beats dropped or added, parts out of step, miscues, mistranspositions, spontaneous solos, and general high spirits. H. Wiley Hitchcock calls it "an American equivalent of Mozart's *Musical Joke*."[49] Its form is not that of a march, with several strains and a trio, but ABAB'A', in which B' is a transition to a modified reprise of A in a key a whole step lower, with two new countermelodies. But both the principal tune, first heard at mm. 8–17 and stated twice in each A section, and the more lyrical tune that begins the B section, first heard at mm. 64–68, are in the style of march themes and may have specific models.[50]

The borrowed tunes are laid on top of this form.[51] "London Bridge" appears most often, serving a role similar to that of the countermelody in a cumulative setting. It appears in fragments in the first section (mm. 24–26, flute and oboe, and perhaps mm. 28–30, violins); returns, is stated almost whole (its end altered), and is developed further in the B section (mm. 77–78, 87–93, 97–100, and 109–11 in violins and 94–96 in winds); and ultimately sounds in the piccolo at the climax, off the beat but almost complete, as a countermelody to the principal tune (mm. 131–40, recalled at mm. 181–83). The chorus of "Marching Through Georgia" appears twice in the violins, linked to other material through melodic similarity: just after the second statement of the principal tune (mm. 52–59), taking off of a similar rising minor third motive in that theme; and again in the B section (mm. 82ff.), where it leads to the melodically related "London Bridge" (mm. 87ff.). The Civil War tune's chorus, suggested by its motivic links to the main material, seems in turn to have prompted Ives to include the verse of the same tune, which appears in the flute at both spots

QUODLIBET AND COLLAGE

(mm. 50–51 and 82–85). A bit of "The Girl I Left Behind Me" (mm. 26–28, flute) follows the first appearance of "London Bridge," and a cluster of borrowings, mostly marches and patriotic tunes, surrounds the second statement of the principal tune: the fiddle tune "Arkansas Traveler" (mm. 44–46, cornet), both forms of the "street beat" in the drums (mm. 45–52), "Massa's in de Cold Ground" (mm. 44–50, flute; 51–52, cornet; and 62–63, violin I), Sousa's *Semper Fideles* march (H85, mm. 53–59, clarinet), "The Battle Cry of Freedom" (mm. 55–58, cornet and saxophone), and "Yankee Doodle" (mm. 59–61, cornet, piccolo, and violins). The dreamy B section includes at least two popular songs, "Violets" (cornet, mm. 76–79) and "My Old Kentucky Home" (mm. 105–8, flute and violin I), and ends with a snippet of "Yankee Doodle" (saxophone, mm. 111–12). A bit of "The British Grenadiers" (H73, mm. 160–62, violin I and clarinet) accompanies the final full statement of the main theme. In addition, there are ragtime figures in several places, including a possible allusion to Ives's *Ragtime Dances* (mm. 170–73).[52]

In this work, Ives is not trying to reproduce the way an amateur band actually sounds. But he is trying to capture the experience of listening to or remembering such a performance, on two different levels. Through the written-out "mistakes" and rough edges, he represents some of the traits of such bands through high spirited but affectionate caricature. And by adding a collage of tunes related to the main themes and to one another by melodic resemblance, genre, or extramusical association, he suggests the thoughts of the listener, who may be reminded of other tunes that sound similar, or of pieces the band has played before, or of other music he has recently heard, and may "hear" more or less extraneous music in his mind at different points, as his mind wanders and refocuses. The connections that Ives makes to other music are unique to him, but they are as logical as those another listener might make, and they neatly convey the experience of thinking while listening.

Overture and March "1776," (ca. 1903–8) was begun as an overture to a projected opera on a Revolutionary War theme, using a verse play by Ives's uncle Lyman Brewster as a libretto.[53] It is in a modified ternary form. The first section is principally based on melodic ideas paraphrased from the late-eighteenth-century patriotic tune "Hail! Columbia" (most prominently in mm. 5–6 and 8–10, oboe; mm. 28–31, violins, clarinet, and cornet I; and mm. 32–39, cornets). Oscillating melodies in other instruments may relate to the frequent back-and-forth stepwise motion in this tune. Added to this are "The British Grenadiers" in the flute (mm. 16–22) and bugle call figures in various instruments (mm. 23 and 34), creating a multilayered mixture of elements that derive from or are reminiscent of tunes of the Revolutionary War era. Ives knew "The British Grenadiers" as a tune used by both the British and the Americans, who gave it new words.[54] The second section, marked "Trio," pits

"Columbia, the Gem of the Ocean" in the cornets (mm. 42–57) against a somewhat distorted "Battle Hymn of the Republic" in the winds, in an early version of what would become the climax of *The Fourth of July*. Throughout this passage, one cornet plays in B♭ and the other in A, evoking amateur players whose "shanks get mixed up."[55] This unfolds over both forms of the "street beat" in the drums and a chromatic ostinato in the strings, and near the end the winds add "Tramp, Tramp, Tramp" (mm. 53–55). Here the elements are of nineteenth- rather than eighteenth-century origin, and the texture involves contrapuntal combination of a tune and countermelody rather than collage. The final section returns to material from the first section, including a theme paraphrased from "Hail! Columbia" (mm. 59–61, oboe, recapitulating mm. 8–10) and "The British Grenadiers" (mm. 63–66, clarinet, and 66–67, oboe and cornet). The flutes add the opening of "Hail! Columbia" in two parallel keys (mm. 61–67), elided with the end of "Columbia, the Gem of the Ocean" (mm. 67–72) through a common motive. Meanwhile, clarinet and oboe turn from "The British Grenadiers" to a disguised rendition of "Yankee Doodle" (mm. 67–69), again exploiting a melodic similarity. Near the end, cornets play triadic fanfares while the rest of the orchestra glides up and down in parallel triads, culminating in a polytonal statement of the opening of "The Star-Spangled Banner" just before the final dissonant chord. In this last section, patriotic and military tunes of different eras are woven together through melodic resemblance and counterpoint. This produces the dreamlike quality of a collage in the motivic and generic connections that it makes between tunes, but the setting and subject are not as well defined, nor the extramusical imagery as clear, as in the other collages we have seen.

Ives later combined parts of the previous two works in *Putnam's Camp, Redding, Connecticut* (composed between ca. 1914 and ca. 1923 and revised ca. 1929), the middle movement of *Three Places in New England*.[56] He cut out the center of *Country Band March*, from the middle of the B section to the transition before the varied reprise of the A section at the end; inserted most of the first section of *Overture and March "1776,"* as a replacement and wrote new transitions, creating a modified ternary form; and closed with references to both earlier works, including the raucous closing passage of the *Overture*.[57] The resulting composite features the same kind of collage as the two original movements, with a number of changes. The most important change is that Ives eliminates most references to "London Bridge" in the sections from *Country Band March*, substitutes "The British Grenadiers," and thus unifies the disparate sections through this common theme.[58] Indeed, the progress of this tune somewhat resembles that of the countermelody in a cumulative setting: from snippets (mm. 14–16, winds, and mm. 68–72, trumpet), to a fairly full statement (mm. 91–97, flute), to its appearance as a countermelody to the

QUODLIBET AND COLLAGE

main theme of *Country Band March* (mm. 126–30, winds) and subsequent restatements (mm. 133–37, trumpets, and mm. 144–45 and 148–55, violin I).

The extramusical imagery of *Putnam's Camp*, as outlined in Ives's program, is clearer than that of its prototypes. The piece is about the place near Redding, Connecticut, where General Israel Putnam's soldiers camped during the winter of 1778–79. Ives's program imagines a child attending a picnic at the small park that preserves the site, represented by the sounds of the band playing in the first section, and wandering away from the others as the band music fades. Here begins a kind of dream sequence, in the middle section: the child sees "the Goddess of Liberty" pleading with the soldiers not to abandon the Revolutionary cause, yet they march out of camp (to the drum's insistent "street cadence" and the trumpet's rendition of "The British Grenadiers" in mm. 68–72, part of a newly composed transition); the material from *Overture and March "1776,"* then represents General Putnam's return to the camp, as "the soldiers turn back and cheer." The child awakes from his reverie, hears the sounds of the picnic, and "runs down past the monument to 'listen to the band' and join in the games and dances," as the music suddenly returns to the *Country Band March* and builds to a noisy close.[59] Here Ives's use of collage helps convey the sense of viewing both real and imagined events through the eyes and ears of a participant.

The Fourth Symphony

The Fourth Symphony is Ives's most extraordinary work. Like the other collages, it conveys an inner experience rather than describing an outer one. The layering of events, from the most prominent lines in the foreground to various levels of background melodies, some unheard or unrecognized (at least consciously), evokes the multi-level nature of consciousness in an apt musical metaphor, and the often unpredictable sequence of events suggests a stream of consciousness like that in James Joyce's novels. But in this work, Ives uses collage to convey an impression, not of memory, but of mystical experience.[60]

Each movement was based on an earlier work by Ives: the first on the setting of *Watchman* in the finale of the First Violin Sonata and the song adapted from it; the second on *The Celestial Railroad*; the third on the fugal first movement of the First String Quartet; and the last on a lost memorial slow march and on the closing passage of the Second String Quartet.[61] Each of these was already based on borrowed tunes, primarily hymns. In reworking them for his symphony, Ives interpolated new music around and between existing passages, as was his frequent practice when revising. He also added new layers to the texture in each movement, including many more borrowed tunes, to create the multiple layers characteristic of his collages.

In a program note for the symphony's partial premiere in 1927, Henry Bellamann, who had become Ives's advocate and friend and was probably reporting Ives's own views, summarized the composer's "aesthetic program" for the work as "the searching questions of What? and Why? which the spirit of man asks of life. This is particularly the sense of the prelude. The three succeeding movements are the diverse answers in which existence replies."[62]

First Movement

The first movement, "Prelude," has three main sections, each serving to introduce the next, as the whole movement serves as prelude to the entire symphony.[63] Each successive section is about twice as long as the previous one. The first is a brief invocation, with two solemn motives proclaimed *fortissimo* in unison low strings and piano. Between them, a pause reveals a soft distant instrumental choir that hovers above most of the movement: a harp elaborating fragments of *Bethany* in two parallel keys and two muted violins with slow, elemental melodies that may derive from *Bethany* or *Nettleton*. In the second section (mm. 5–16), a solo cello plays the first phrase of *In the Sweet Bye and Bye* and then spins out another motive while other instruments accompany, the distant choir continues, and the celesta enters with another variant of *Bethany*. The main section (mm. 17–41) is an adaptation of Ives's song based on *Watchman*, with the vocal line sung by unison chorus, the accompaniment in the piano and strings, and a few modifications.

As in the song, and in accord with the program for this movement, the original hymn text is altered to end with a question and a call to see the distant star, creating an impression of a search still in progress, a promise made but not yet fulfilled, a goal in sight but not yet achieved:

Original (John Bowring):	*Ives's adaptation:*
Watchman, tell us of the night,	Watchman, tell us of the night,
What its signs of promise are.	What the signs of promise are:
Trav'ler, o'er yon mountain's height,	Traveller, o'er yon mountain's height,
See that glory-beaming star!	See that glory-beaming star!
Watchman, does its beauteous ray	Watchman, aught of joy or hope?
Aught of joy or hope foretell?	Traveller, yes, Traveller, yes!
Trav'ler, yes; it brings the day,	Traveller, yes; it brings the day,
Promised day of Israel.	Promised day of Israel.
	Dost thou see its beauteous ray?
	Traveller, see!

QUODLIBET AND COLLAGE

The musical setting has a similarly indefinite ending, deviating from the original tune at the sixth line of text, repeating the initial phrases, and closing on a repeated subdominant chord. To this are added the distant choir of harp and violins, now including an ostinato in solo viola; the "street beat" very softly in the timpani; and two other lines. The celesta links the third phrase of *Bethany* with *Westminster Chimes*, recalling the similar combination in the finale of the Second String Quartet and anticipating the same pairing in the symphony's finale. Meanwhile, the flute and first violin play a patchwork of motives from several hymns: the opening phrase of Theodore E. Perkins's *Something for Thee* (H55, in mm. 17–22 and 30–33), with the order of two notes reversed to create the first motive of *Proprior Deo*; a cadential motive shared by several hymns, including *Welcome Voice* (mm. 23–24); and a motive from *Crusader's Hymn*, mm. 9–10 (at mm. 25–26), identical but for its last note to part of *Bethany*. The earliest sketch of this passage shows *Something for Thee* as the descant here, converted by stages in subsequent sketches into the final composite.[64] At the close, the opening motive of *Bethany* appears for the first time in the main orchestra (mm. 38–39), and the distant choir is heard one last time.

Unlike the collages examined above, this movement does not try to reflect outward events, even as remembered. The distant choir does not create an impression of actual space, as does the distant choir in *From Hanover Square North*, because it does not evoke actual sounds. Rather, its soft dynamic, high tessitura, independent slow meter, and gentle timbres of harp and muted violins give a sense of both elevation and distance without implying location. This suggests an interior or imagined space, like a vision of luminous angels floating in the air or, as Kirkpatrick suggests, the "glory-beaming star" mentioned in the text of *Watchman*.[65] The allusion to *Bethany* strengthens this effect through association with its text, "Nearer, my God, to Thee," and its pentatonicism, a frequent musical image of purity, as in the nature themes of Wagner's *Ring* cycle. As the chorus sings *Watchman*, the presence of other lines in the flute and celesta expands the space in new directions.

Combined with this effect of an imagined, interior space rather than a real one is an effect of intuitive understanding, created through collage, rather than connections that can be articulated in words. The musical punning between *Something for Thee* and *Proprior Deo* (two notes' difference) and between *Bethany* and *Crusader's Hymn* (only one note) suggests that Ives is interested in ambiguity. Indeed, all the melodies and fragments that Ives borrows here are interrelated in a complex network of shared motives.[66] This helps to create the sense of a stream of thoughts, making quick, subtle, half-unnoticed links between ideas. One cannot describe exactly what transpires in this movement, but one is left with a definite impression of what it is about, involving reflection, searching, and notions of prayer ("Nearer, my God, to Thee"), eternity ("In the sweet bye and bye"), and salvation ("Traveler, yes; it brings the day, Promised day of Israel"). Through the illusion of visionary space, the fluidity of motion between thoughts, and these strong religious images, this movement recreates an inner, mystical, ultimately unnamable experience.

Second Movement

The impression of a stream of consciousness corresponding to an inner spiritual experience continues in the next movement. Bellamann calls this

a comedy in the sense that Hawthorne's Celestial Railroad is a comedy. Indeed this work of Hawthorne's may be considered as a sort of incidental program in which an exciting, easy, and worldly progress through life is contrasted with the trials of the Pilgrims in their journey through the swamp. The occasional slow episodes—Pilgrims' hymns—are constantly crowded out and overwhelmed by the former. The dream, or fantasy, ends with an interruption of reality—the Fourth of July in Concord—brass bands, drum corps, etc.

We have already seen the close relation of Ives's *Celestial Railroad* to the Hawthorne tale. This movement of the symphony is an orchestral expansion of the piano fantasy, with some new sections and many added layers.[67]

Table 10.1 outlines the movement in terms of its program and shows the borrowings that have been identified with reasonable certainty, with the instruments that perform them.[68] There are at least two dozen tunes by other composers (counting verse and chorus of a song as a single tune), plus two of Ives's own, the themes from "The Alcotts" and *Country Band March*. Most tunes are partial or fragmented, and most also are varied or paraphrased. Sometimes more than one variant of a tune appears at once; the later or less prominent variants are listed second (after the word "also"). Many borrowings are already present in the material derived from *The Celestial Railroad* (listed in the left-hand column of Table 10.1). These are almost always the most prominent line in the symphony, indicated in boldface in the table. But many more tunes are parts of interpolated episodes or added layers. A borrowed tune is the leading melody in most of the episodes, but few of the borrowings in the added layers assume the most prominent role. Most serve instead as part of a multi-layered background to the events taken from the piano fantasy. Some added tunes, particularly in the bells, appear in long notes, like a cantus firmus. Others are disguised by figuration or are represented by transpositions of an ostinato, as in the statement of *Nettleton* at

TABLE 10.1: Borrowed Tunes in Ives's Fourth Symphony, second movement

Borrowings extend approximately to next entry, unless otherwise noted
All instruments given; "also" indicates a different variant or paraphrase of the same tune
Boldface indicates most prominent line (which is not always borrowed material)
★ "Hidden" quotations, represented by transpositions of an ostinato or by prominent notes interspersed with an ostinato
' Borrowed tune that appears in autograph full score but not in previous versions or sketches
" Late addition, added after autograph full score was completed

Reh.	Measure	From *The Celestial Railroad*	Interpolated Episodes	Added Layers
Before the trip				
	1	[none]		
1	6	**Martyn**, Solo Piano		**Beulah Land**, Db.; 'God Be With You, Bsn.
2	7		**Martyn**, Vns.	
	9	**God Be With You**, Fl.		
	10		**Martyn**, Vns.	
	11		**Home! Sweet Home!**, Vns.	'Nettleton, Solo Piano & Vn.
	13	**Martyn**, solo pno		
3	14		**Martyn**, Vns.	'God Be With You (chorus), Vn. (m. 17)
	16	**God Be With You**, Fl.		
The trainride begins				
4	19	[none]		'God Be With You, Vn., continued (to m. 30)
	35	**Tramp! Tramp! Tramp!**, Trb.		Throw Out the Life-Line, Bsn. & low Strings; also Bells
	37	**Marching Through Georgia**, Trb.		

Table 10.1, continued:

Reh.	Measure	From *The Celestial Railroad*	Interpolated Episodes	Added Layers
		The pilgrims are seen out the window		
7	38		***In the Sweet Bye and Bye***, Vn. I (varied to m. 62); *Nettleton*, Solo Vns. (to m. 58)	
8	43		*★Beulah Land*, Fl. (to m. 51); also Trb., Bsn. (mm. 47–54); *'Throw Out the Life-Line*, Bells; *'The Beautiful River*, Solo Piano (mm. 48–50)	
		The train rumbles by		
10	55		*'Washington Post March*, Tuba (mm 56–59); *'Nettleton*, Bells (mm. 57–63); also Tpt. (mm. 60–62)	
		The train passes the pilgrims and continues		
12	62	[none]		*"Throw Out the Life-Line*, Sax.
	65	***Tramp! Tramp! Tramp!***, Trb.		*Throw Out the Life-Line*, Orchestra
	66	***Marching Through Georgia***, Trb. (to m. 69)		Piano II (mm. 68–71)

	m.		
	69	[none]	*In the Sweet Bye and Bye*, Trb. (to m. 74) *Turkey in the Straw*, Vns.
13	72		
14	75	***De Camptown Races***, Solo Piano & Cl. (to m. 80)	
	79	[none]	
15	81		'*Massa's in de Cold Ground*, Fl. (to m. 85) **Hail! Columbia**, Bsn. I & Tpt.; *Beulah Land, Db. I; Throw Out the Life-Line, Bells (mm. 84–85) '*Throw Out the Life-Line*, Bells; '*Nettleton*, Vn. I
16	86	*Old Black Joe*, Solo Piano (from m. 84)	

Another glimpse of the pilgrims

17	89		***In the Sweet Bye and Bye***, Vn. II, Cl., & Brass; '*Nettleton*, Vla., Vc., & Bsn.; also Bells in mm. 93–95; '*There Is a Happy Land*, Fl. (to m. 93); '*Westminster Chimes*, Celesta (90–93)

The trip continues

18	96	***Columbia, the Gem of the Ocean*** (variants), Brass	*Beulah Land*, Bells; *Yankee Doodle*, Picc.; "*Massa's in de Cold Ground*, Bsn. I & II;

Table 10.1, continued:

Reh.	Measure	From The Celestial Railroad	Interpolated Episodes	Added Layers
20	109	*Columbia*, (variants), continued, Tpts.		"street beat," Orchestra Piano I & Drums; *Throw Out the Life-Line*, Solo Piano (mm. 104–8); '*Reveille* (Tpt. III, mm. 105–6)
	112			*Beulah Land*, Solo Piano & Bells; *Nettleton*, Vns. (to m. 114)
21	114	*Columbia*, Trb. & Vc. (mm. 115–16)		*Columbia*, Picc. & Fl.; *The Beautiful River*, Solo Piano & Bells (to m. 115); *Throw Out the Life-Line*, *"Sax.; also Cl. in mm. 116–18)
Mr. Smooth-it-away				
22	119	[none]		
A rest stop at Vanity Fair				
23	122	[none]		'*In the Sweet Bye and Bye*, Extra Vla.
	134			*In the Sweet Bye and Bye*, Fls.
The train takes off again				
26	141	[none]		*In the Sweet Bye and Bye*, Brass (to m. 146)

	143	**"Alcotts" theme,** first half, Solo Piano, Orchestra Piano II, Vla., & Vcs.	
27	146	[none]	*Beulah Land* (rhythm only), Bells (to 149); "*Pig-Town Fling,* Bsn. (147–52); '*Westminster Chimes,* Bells (149–51); '*Long, Long Ago,* Cornet & "Orchestra Piano I (151–53)
28	154	[mm. 156–63 interpolated]	**Throw Out the Life-Line,** Vns.; also 'Bell I; '*Nettleton,* Bell II (to m.164); "*De Camptown Races,* Bsn. & Sax.
29	160	**Throw Out the Life-Line,** Tpts.; "*Pig Town Fling,* Bsn. & Sax.	
	164	**"Alcotts" theme,** first half, Solo Piano & Tpt. III	'*Massa's in de Cold Ground,* Fl.; '*Nettleton,* Bells (to m. 170)
30	167	**Throw Out the Life-Line,** Vns., Orchestra Piano I, & Fl. (to m. 170)	
	173	"Alcotts" theme, second half, Tpts. (to m. 178)	*Beulah Land,* Trb.; *Nettleton,* Vn. I, Orchestra Piano I, & *Cl.; also Bsn. & Bells; *In the Sweet Bye and Bye,* Picc.& Fl.; also Solo Piano; '*Massa's in de Cold Ground,* Cornet; *Throw Out the Life-Line,* Tpts. (178–80)

Table 10.1, continued:

Reh.	Measure	From *The Celestial Railroad*	Interpolated Episodes	Added Layers
A glimpse of the Celestial City				
33	181		***Martyn***, Solo Piano & Vla.	
The final leg				
34	184	[none]		***Beulah Land***, Tpt. III & Trb; also *Vc.; *In the Sweet Bye and Bye*, Picc., Fl., Cl., Orchestra Piano I, & High Bells; *"Massa's in de Cold Ground*, Cornet (mm. 186–89); *"Pig Town Fling*, Sax. (mm. 186–88)
Arrival at Beulah Land and vision of the Celestial City across the water				
36	190		***Martyn***, Solo Piano & Vla.	***Beulah Land***, Solo Vn. I
The ferry bound for Hell				
38	198	[none]		
Waking to reality: the Fourth of July in Concord				
39	205	[none]		*Throw Out the Life-Line*, Fl., Cl., & Vn. II; *Yankee Doodle*, Picc. (both to m. 209)

	m.		
	208	**Introductory figure** from Ives's *Country Band March*, Brass	
40	210	**Country Band March theme**, Tpts. (to m. 213)	*Marching Through Georgia*, Picc., Fl., & Cl.; *Throw Out the Life-Line*, Bells; *Turkey in the Straw*, Vn. I, Vla., Bsn., & Sax.; *'Long, Long Ago*, Cornet (from m. 211)
41	216	[none]	
42	219		*Marching Through Georgia*, Cornet & Tpt.I; *Throw Out the Life-Line*, Picc., Fl., & Cl. (to m. 220); *'Long, Long Ago* (to m. 220) and *St. Patrick's Day* (from m. 221), Vc. & Bsn.
44	225	"Street beat" variant, Solo Piano	**"Street beat,"** Percussion & Vc.; *Reveille*, Picc. & Fl.; *'Long, Long Ago*, Cornet; *'De Camptown Races*, Bsn.; *Throw Out the Life-Line*, High Bells; *'Nettleton*, Low Bells (to m. 237); *Garryowen* (to m. 228), *St. Patrick's Day* (mm. 229–30), and *Irish Washerwoman* (mm. 230–32), Vn. & Vla.
47	233	***Yankee Doodle***, tutti	
	235	[none]	*Marching Through Georgia*, Trb.; *'Long, Long Ago*, Cornet; *Irish Washerwoman*, Vn. I

mm. 109–13 in the violins; these "hidden" borrowings, which are unlikely to be heard or recognized, are designated in the table by asterisks.[69]

The episodes and multiple layers reflect, to some extent, the process of composition. As Ives turned the piano fantasy into an orchestral work, he added tunes at each stage, from sketches on the copy of *The Celestial Railroad* itself, to a sketch in short score, to a full score, to a copyist's score, with preliminary sketches and subsequent patches for many passages. The large episodes in mm. 38–61 and 89–95 and some shorter segments were inserted after the score-sketch; tunes marked with a prime sign appear in the autograph full score; and tunes marked with a double prime sign were added after the full score was complete.

The added tunes in this movement serve a variety of functions.

Some are clearly programmatic. The two main insertions (mm. 38–61 and 89–95) depict pilgrims making their slow journey to the Celestial City by foot, represented by the hymns *In the Sweet Bye and Bye* and *Nettleton*.[70] Recurrences of these tunes elsewhere may serve to recall the pilgrims; for example, when the railroad passengers take a rest stop at Vanity Fair (reh. 23), enjoying what they imagine is a foretaste of heavenly comforts, *In the Sweet Bye and Bye* hovers in the background as a symbol of the pilgrims and their goal, the Celestial City. Similarly, the many references to the hymn *Beulah Land* are presumably reminders of the train's destination, Beulah Land, and thus in some cases of the train itself. The hymn is heard for the last time and in its most complete form when the train arrives at Beulah Land (reh. 36). Its previous partial appearances and the use of *Martyn* as a countermelody lend this movement something of the shape of a cumulative setting, overlaid on top of the original episodic form that was created to suit the program of the piano fantasy. This quasi-cumulative form, counterpointing *Beulah Land* with *Martyn*, embodies the contrast between the railroad and its final stop in Beulah Land (the "exciting, easy, and wordly progress through life" of the program) and the foot-pilgrims and their goal, the Celestial City ("the trials of the Pilgrims in their journey through the swamp").

Other additions extend tunes already present in *The Celestial Railroad*. At the beginning, references to *Martyn* and *God Be With You* are expanded with insertions and added layers. *Throw Out the Life-Line*, cited briefly in the piano fantasy, appears throughout in many variants. "Marching Through Georgia," whose chorus is partly paraphrased in *The Celestial Railroad*, becomes prominent in this movement's closing section, in which the dreamer wakes to "reality—the Fourth of July in Concord." "De Camptown Races," "Columbia, the Gem of the Ocean," "Yankee Doodle," and the "street beat" drum pattern, developed in various sections of the piano piece, reappear elsewhere in the added layers of the orchestral work.

Some tunes are included apparently because they resemble tunes already present. A phrase from "Home! Sweet Home!" in m. 11 varies a few notes of *God Be With You*; the sketches for this passage show the transformation.[71] The first variant of *Throw Out the Life-Line* to appear (at m. 35)[72] features chromatic neighbor-note motion, and this idea recurs throughout, whether as part of an identifiable tune or as simple figuration. One tune that it seems to prompt is the introduction to Sousa's *Washington Post March* (mm. 56–59), and another is derived from "Hail! Columbia" (mm. 81–85). The pentatonic nature of *In the Sweet Bye and Bye* and *Nettleton* may have induced Ives to add other pentatonic tunes, such as *There Is a Happy Land* and *Westminster Chimes*; these may also be included for their heavenly associations. The opening phrase of *The Beautiful River* appears at mm. 112–15 in place of a portion of *Beulah Land* (mm. 5–6) that follows a similar contour.

The remaining tunes are included most likely because of their character or other associations. Three Irish jigs, "Saint Patrick's Day," "Garryowen," and "Irish Washerwoman," contribute to the festive bustle of the final section. So do the fiddle tune "Turkey in the Straw," the popular song "Long, Long Ago," and the bugle call "Reveille," each of which also appears at a noisy and busy moment earlier on. Another fiddle tune, "Pig Town Fling," joins in during the latter part of the trainride. Finally, the chorus of "Massa's in de Cold Ground" seems to play several roles: apparently suggested at m. 186 by its resemblance to m. 11 of *Beulah Land* in the horns; perhaps prompted at m. 79 by the preceding take-off on Foster's "Camptown Races"; possibly used throughout as a reminder of death; and perhaps intended as a symbol for the presence of Ives himself, as in *From Hanover Square North*.

The Celestial Railroad is an allegorical fantasy, a representation of a dream. In the orchestral version, all these added tunes reinforce the allegory and heighten the sense of dreamlike fantasy. Some flesh out the program with new episodes and references. Some intensify the contrasts of character between sections. Some mimic the moment-to-moment logic of dreams through melodic punning or other associations. And the great number of borrowings, along with the sheer thickness of texture in many sections, creates an impression of a vast and confusing dream, in which images fly by too rapidly to be understood fully, yet are capable of arousing strong and at times disturbing feelings. Although the Hawthorne tale provides a guide to the intended images and course of events, making this movement less abstract than the first, ultimately this movement also reflects an interior rather than an external experience, a dream about the inner struggle between spiritual laziness and discipleship.

QUODLIBET AND COLLAGE

Third Movement

Bellamann's program note calls the third movement "an expression of the reaction of life into formalism and ritualism." After the crowded, dissonant, and often raucous second movement, it sounds like a reaction: a tonal fugue, sober and restrained, with only a few added tunes. It is an orchestrated and expanded version of the first movement of the First String Quartet, a fugue on *Missionary Hymn* ("From Greenland's icy mountains"), with a phrase from *Coronation* as a countersubject and an episode borrowed from Bach's "Dorian" Toccata and Fugue in D minor BWV 538.[73] The most notable additions are a ten-measure insertion that includes a loud, dissonant caesura (mm. 95–104) and two hymn tunes in the coda: the chorus of *Welcome Voice* in the clarinet (reh. 14, mm. 111–17) and *Antioch* ("Joy to the World") in horn or trombone (mm. 116–20).[74] Two other added melodies may also be based on hymn tunes (possibly *Church Triumphant* in clarinet and *Brown* or *Lischer* in flute, both at mm. 89–92).[75] Ives also throws elements of the original contrapuntal fabric into relief by assigning them to horn or trombone: the fugue subject, the countersubject from *Coronation*, and a secondary line that resembles a phrase from the hymn *Christmas* (mm. 65–67), rendering as a conscious quotation what was apparently a coincidental similarity in the quartet movement.[76] The result is an extended meditation on *Missionary Hymn* surrounded by phrases from other tunes that fit with it contrapuntally or resemble it melodically. If the fugue represents the "formalism" of the program, perhaps the hymn fragments represent the "ritualism." The smooth fit of these other tunes onto the tonal structure of the fugue makes this movement less like the collages in the other movements than like parts of the Second Symphony in which several tunes can be heard together.

Fourth Movement

Ives described the finale as "an apotheosis of the preceding content, in terms that have something to do with the reality of existence and its religious experience."[77] It is both an apotheosis in programmatic terms, providing a solution to the problem posed in the first movement, and a synthesis in thematic terms, recalling and integrating material from the first two movements. Table 10.2 shows the thematic plan of the finale.

The focus of the movement is *Bethany* ("Nearer, my God, to Thee"), particularly its second half. In the first movement, this was played by the distant choir of harp and violins and by the celesta, all high, soft, and delicate, like a distant vision of the divine. Only at the end of that movement did the opening motive of *Bethany* briefly descend into the middle register in the main

TABLE 10.2: Borrowed Tunes in Ives's Fourth Symphony, fourth movement

Main themes: *Bethany, Missionary Chant,* Theme A
Theme A: Composite of *Bethany* 9–12, linking figure (perhaps from *Westminster Chimes*), and *Missionary Chant* 5–9

Section	Measure		Main key
1	1	Percussion "Battery Unit" begins, continues throughout ("street beat" in snare drum)	
		Bethany 9–12, Dbs.	
	5	First movement mm. 1–4, recapitulated and developed; Distant Choir (mm. 6–7) with *Bethany* 9–10	
2	11	*Dorrnance* 1–3, punning with *Missionary Chant* 1–5, Vns., Distant Choir, celesta, Ob.; *Bethany* 9–11, Fl., Vns. (mm. 12–14)	B major over first-movement motives (mm. 11–12), then G pedal
	15	*Dorrnance* 4–8, Vns.	
	17	Extension with *Bethany* 9–10 variants	
3	20	Theme A elements (*Bethany* 9–12 varied), Vns., Solo Piano, Tpt. IV	modulatory
	24	Theme A elements continued (linking figure, *Missionary Chant* 5–7), Tpt. I; *Martyn* 11–13, Cl. & Vn. II; *Bethany* 9–12, Fl. & Ob.	
	27	Theme A elements (*Bethany* 9–10, linking figure), Pianos, Tpt. I, Vns.; Unknown Tune H205, Distant Choir Vn., Fl.; *Westminster Chimes,* Vns. (m. 28)	
	29	*Martyn* 11–13, Tpt. I, Vns. (m. 29); *Martyn* 19–21, Vns. (mm. 30–31)	

Table 10.2, continued:

Section	Measure		Main key
4	32	Theme A variant (*Missionary Chant* 1–5 replaces same, mm. 5–9), Vn. II, Solo Piano, Fl., Ob., with proper conclusion (*Missionary Chant*, mm. 6–8) softly in Tpt, mm. 37–39; *Bethany* 9–10, Distant Choir, Celesta	Ab major over descending chromatic scales to m. 35, then Db pedal
5 >	40	**Missionary Chant complete**, Hns, Tpts, Vla., punning on *Dorrnance* in Tpt. II (mm. 40–43); *Bethany* 9–10 variants, Vns., Ob. II, Bells; Unknown H205, Picc. (mm. 42–45); *Westminster Chimes*, Bells, Celesta (mm. 45–49)	C major, descending C scales
	47	*Missionary Chant* cadence elided with first half of *Azmon*, Hns., Tpts., Vla.; *Bethany* 1–2, Vn. II, Fl., Cl.; *Missionary Chant* 1, Vn. II, Fl., Cl. (m. 49)	
6 >	50	**Theme A complete**, Vla., Tpt. I; *Missionary Chant* 1–5, Vns., punning with *Dorrnance*, Vns., Cl. I (to m. 53); *Martyn* 11–18, Ob., Cl. II; *Bethany* 1–8 variants, low bell, also Fl. & distant choir Vns.; *Westminster Chimes* variants, High Bells (to m. 55) & Picc. (56–58); *Antioch* variant, Bsn. II (to m. 53); *Nettleton* 1–4, Celesta (mm. 52–58)	A major, descending A scales
	59	Theme A first half (*Bethany* 9–12, linking figure), Solo Piano, High Bells I; *Bethany* 9–12, Harp; ostinato on *Bethany* 1–2, Vns., Winds, High Bells II, Celesta	mixed keys, chromatic chords
	64	*Westminster Chimes*, Solo Piano; *Bethany* 1, Low Bells	

7	>	65	**Bethany 1–5 elided with Missionary Chant 4–9**, Trb. I, Vn. II & III lower line; **Martyn 11–20 complete**, Tpt., Vn. III; Theme A first half (*Bethany 9–12*, linking figure), upper Vn. I; *Bethany 9–15*, lower Vn. I; *Bethany 9–12* (mm. 65–67), *Proprior Deo/Something for Thee* blend (mm. 67–71), Celesta; *Westminster Chimes*, High Bells I; *Westminster Chimes* and *Bethany 1–2* variants, Fl., Vn. II; *Bethany 1–2* elided with Westminster Chimes, Bsn. I/Ether Organ; *Bethany 1* ostinato, Low Bells; *There Is a Happy Land*, High Bell II, Cl., Ob.; *St. Hilda 1–6*, Hn.; *Dorrnance 1–3*, Picc.	D major, descending whole-tone scales on D
8	>	72	**Bethany 9–16 complete**, voices, Tpt., Vn. III; *Bethany 1–6*, Fls. (to m. 77); Bethany elements, variants, and derived ostinatos, Fls., Cls., Orchestra Piano, Trbs., Low Bells, Organ, Solo Piano, Vn. III, Vla., Vc.; Theme A first half (*Bethany 9–12*, linking figure), Vn. I (from m. 73); Bethany/Westminster Chimes elements, Celesta; Unknown Tune H205, Picc. (to m. 74); *Proprior Deo/Something for Thee* blend, Ob. (to m. 77)	D major, D pedal, descending whole-tone scales on D
		79	Coda, repeating figures from preceding	D major, D pedal, scales cease

orchestra, offering a hint of what was to come. This hymn is absent from the intervening movements; in programmatic terms, their false paths of spiritual laziness or faith in outward ritual do not lead us nearer to God. As the finale begins, *Bethany* reappears, but it is still distant: first in the string basses (mm. 1–4), growling in their lowest octave at the opposite extreme from the former high tessitura; then in the distant choir of violins and harp, as part of a reprise and extension of the invocation that opened the first movement (mm. 5–10). Other hymns begin to appear, but *Bethany* is a constant presence, gradually moving down from the high to the middle register in the main orchestra (by mm. 20–23). The first half of the movement uses only the third phrase of *Bethany* (mm. 9–12, "Still all my song shall be, Nearer, my God, to Thee"); then the motive that begins the first, second, and fourth phrases is introduced (m. 47, violin II) and both motives are combined with each other and with other hymns (from m. 50). At the culmination of the movement (m. 72), in a passage adapted from the conclusion of the Second String Quartet, a wordless chorus enters with the second half of *Bethany* in D major while the flute plays the first half, accompanied by ostinatos derived from the hymn over descending whole-tone scales on D. Over the course of this movement, the hymn that in the first movement was distant, within our sight but beyond our reach, draws close and ultimately suffuses the music. This symbolizes the fulfillment of the yearning, expressed from the beginning of the symphony, to *be* "Nearer, my God, to Thee." This apotheosis simultaneously proclaims the attainment of the goal envisioned in the first movement and reveals the fruitlessness of the paths suggested in the second and third movements, with their eyes on the external goals of getting into Heaven or conforming to religious custom. The progress of the symphony's music, combined with the hints in the program, suggests that for Ives the aim of the spiritual quest is nearness to the divine. This interpretation is supported by the many references to a journey and to reaching the Promised Land or coming close to God in the texts associated with the hymn tunes used in this symphony, particularly in the finale.[78]

Other hymns play significant thematic roles in the movement as well. One prominent theme, called Theme A in Table 10.2 and shown in Example 10.1, combines the third phrase of *Bethany* with the second half of *Missionary Chant*, punning on the latter's melodic similarity to the fourth phrase of *Bethany*. The two phrases are joined by a linking figure that may derive from *Westminster Chimes*. An early sketch for this movement shows this theme in combination with the first half of *Missionary Chant*, as the two appear at m. 50 of the finale.[79] Other early sketches try out contrapuntal combinations of *Missionary Chant* with the second half of *Martyn*, the two halves of *Bethany* with each other, and *Bethany, Martyn,* and *Missionary Chant* together, as at

EXAMPLE 10.1: Fourth Symphony, finale, Theme A and its sources

m. 65 and elsewhere.[80] In the final version, *Bethany, Missionary Chant*, and their composite in Theme A all serve as leading themes, and the second half of *Martyn* serves as an important countersubject, as shown in the table. Although their good contrapuntal fit and melodic similarities are enough to justify their presence, the words of *Missionary Chant* and this portion of *Martyn* are appropriate to the program:

> *Missionary Chant:*
> Ye Christian heralds, go, proclaim
> Salvation in Emmanuel's Name:
> To distant climes the tidings bear,
> And plant the Rose of Sharon there.

> *Martyn*, mm. 11-20:
> Hide me, O my Saviour, hide,
> Till the storm of life is past;
> Safe into the haven guide;
> O receive my soul at last.

QUODLIBET AND COLLAGE

The movement begins quietly, with a percussion ostinato that continues throughout. This is in layers, with the "street beat" in the snare drum in an independent meter while the other drums, cymbal, and gong each play a different figure, repeating in cycles of varying lengths.[81] After the anticipations of *Bethany* in the opening section, *Missionary Chant* appears in m. 11, in tandem with its close melodic relative, *Dorrnance*. The next section (m. 20) develops elements of Theme A and *Martyn*. A variant of Theme A, using the first instead of the second half of *Missionary Chant*, appears next (m. 32), with the trumpet softly providing the theme's proper conclusion. There follows a complete statement of *Missionary Chant* at m. 40, again punning on *Dorrnance* and eliding its cadence with the first half of *Azmon*. Theme A appears complete in m. 50, in counterpoint with *Missionary Chant/Dorrnance, Martyn*, and variants of the first half of *Bethany*. The peak of complexity is reached in the next section (m. 65), which combines a composite of the opening of *Bethany* and the conclusion of *Missionary Chant* with *Martyn*, Theme A, the second half of *Bethany, Dorrnance*, and several other tunes. This creates a kind of cumulative form for this movement, as the elements of this contrapuntal complex are introduced one by one, first in fragments and then whole, and are finally combined. The complete statement of the second half of *Bethany* at m. 72 functions as a chorus or refrain, asserting the primacy of this theme over the others. Each of the major thematic statements unfolds in a firmly established key above descending scales in the bass, closing on a rich D major with whole-tone inflections. Around this basic structure hover various other tunes and fragments, beyond the almost omnipresent elements and variants of *Bethany*. These include an unidentified tune (H205, at mm. 27, 40, and 72), *Westminster Chimes, Antioch, Nettleton, There Is a Happy Land, St. Hilda* (H51, also called *St. Edith*, arranged by Edward Husband from a tune by Justin H. Knecht), and the blend of the opening phrases of *Proprior Deo* and *Something for Thee* that Ives used in the first movement.[82] Once again, the addition of numerous tunes and tune fragments around a simpler thematic structure creates a dreamlike impression.

A number of musical factors lend a sense of unity and cohesion to this movement that supports the programmatic ideas of attainment and apotheosis. The constant presence of the percussion ostinato and the near omnipresence of *Bethany* provide a consistency the other movements lack. All of the tunes used in this movement are interrelated in an intricate web of melodic resemblance.[83] Besides providing a unified group of themes, this helps to integrate the many simultaneous layers of the music and create a single impression, unlike the contrasting simultaneous images in the first and second movements. The finale also unifies the whole symphony by recalling material from the first two movements, including the symphony's opening bars, *Bethany* itself, and the *Proprior Deo/Something for Thee* blend from the first movement; *Martyn, Nettleton,* and *There Is a Happy Land* from the second; and *Westminster Chimes* from both.[84] The vertical combination of *Bethany* and *Martyn* at several points links thematic material from the first two movements to create not only cyclic repetition but a genuine synthesis. The echo of the symphony's opening motive near the beginning of the finale, the many motivic similarities between tunes used in the outer movements, and the establishment at the end of the finale of a firm D major, recalling the key in which *Watchman* appeared in the first movement, are all traditional devices for achieving a sense of unity and arrival.[85] Together with the quasi-cumulative form culminating in *Bethany,* these aspects of the music embody a process of coming into fulfillment and completion, an apt musical metaphor for coming into the divine presence at the end of the spiritual journey described in the symphony as a whole.

The Fourth Symphony is a very unusual piece, even for Ives. It is programmatic, but its program is not as explicit as those of Strauss or of some other Ives pieces. For long stretches, neither the program nor the music makes clear what events are being depicted, and those that are clear are largely allegorical. Not every event in the music is motivated by the program, nor can every borrowing be explained in its terms. The music does not represent real happenings, as do *The General Slocum* and *Central Park in the Dark,* nor remembered events, as do *The Fourth of July* and *Washington's Birthday.* The Fourth Symphony is a musical representation of a mystical experience, a spiritual journey, that can only partially be captured in musical terms. We literally cannot understand this music completely. There is too much in it, too many things to grasp all at once. That is its point, for it represents events that cannot be fully comprehended or described, only experienced.

In order to create this impression of a spiritual journey through an inner, imagined landscape, Ives takes procedures that he had cultivated over his career to new extremes and achieves new syntheses. There is more contrast and diversity among the four movements of this symphony with respect to performing forces, texture, tonal language, level of complexity, and musical material than in any other multi-movement work. The second movement has a greater number of independent layers, incorporates more diverse styles and types of music, and borrows a greater number of different tunes than any other Ives work. The symphony uses a wider variety of borrowing procedures than any other work, including paraphrase, setting, cantus firmus, medley, quodlibet, modified cumulative setting, programmatic quotation, patchwork, and collage, as well as self-borrowing. The largely symbolic and allegorical use of borrowed music in the *Concord Sonata* and *The Celestial Railroad* here converge with the explorations of inner thoughts embodied in *Washington's*

Birthday and *The Fourth of July*. In many respects, the Fourth Symphony is like Beethoven's Ninth: a late work representing the high development of ideas that its composer had been exploring for two decades, but unlike anything else the composer wrote.

The Uniqueness of Collage

In all his collages, Ives exploits the ambiguity of melodic allusion that he had explored in his works based on modeling, paraphrase, and cumulative setting to make explicit melodic relationships which in earlier works might have remained implicit. A newly composed theme that sounds like a fiddle-tune or a march will remind listeners to some extent of other fiddle-tunes or marches they have heard; in *Washington's Birthday* and *Country Band March*, Ives makes that link for us through collage. In the process, a whole world is thrown open. It is as if Ives shows us the interrelationships among a number of tunes, arranging them in ways that make the relationships obvious, and invites us to continue the process ourselves. The way is open to hearing music that is not in fact alluded to, because so much is already there. Moreover, tunes appear in all degrees of paraphrase, from virtually unchanged and immediately recognized, like a clear memory; to distorted but still recognizable, like a misremembered melody; to a distant reworking that sounds familiar but goes unrecognized, like a half-forgotten face. In this music, as in life itself, some things come easily, others with more difficulty, and our efforts to comprehend draw us deeper into the complex musical fabric, confronting ambiguity and uncertainty to achieve a fuller understanding. Following Ives's dreamlike allusions, we are brought into our own memories and dreams, as we are reminded of the way we think about music and indeed about life, hearing resemblances, drawing relationships, confusing similar things and then sorting them out, noticing and half-noticing the swirl of experience as it goes by, and picking new elements out of the mix each time we rehear it, as we might gradually come to know more facets of our closest friends. Collage is the most amazing and perhaps most intuitive and unchartable of Ives's many techniques of using existing music. Although unusual in Ives's music, appearing in only ten works, collage is the borrowing technique we most closely associate with him.

Collage is also a procedure that Ives seems to have invented. His other uses of existing music have precedents. His use of models is like that of other composers. His paraphrased themes recall those in Beethoven's Razumovsky Quartets, Brahms's *Academic Festival Overture*, and Stravinsky's *Rite of Spring*. His cumulative form is anticipated by Smetana's *Tábor*, and he shares patchwork technique with George M. Cohan. But his collages are unlike any other music before younger composers began to imitate his techniques in the 1950s and 1960s, most famously Luciano Berio, in the third movement of his *Sinfonia* (1968). The nearest approximation in earlier music is the episode late in *Ein Heldenleben* (1897–98) in which Strauss interweaves the work's themes in a quodlibet or medley with more than a dozen themes from his own previous works. The effect is like some of Ives's collages in its serious nature and sense of reminiscence, but Strauss's smooth counterpoint and pointed citations of his own works are far from Ives's juxtaposition of mutually incompatible layers of well-known tunes at different levels of recognizability, in a musical metaphor for the stream of consciousness. It is no wonder that his collages have generated a great deal of attention and have led to a view of Ives as a composer who uses quotation chiefly for evocative allusion.

In most of Ives's music, however, that is not its main purpose. Most borrowed material is used to construct themes and countermelodies, whether in standard forms or in new forms such as cumulative setting. Other borrowed melodies are used to suggest a certain character or illustrate a text or a program. Even collage has been misunderstood as a loose jumble of tunes. For despite initial impressions of illogic and disorder, the various tunes are carefully organized, and each serves a distinct function. Some are major themes or countermelodies, varied and developed as part of the central musical structure. Others that share a similar character, common associations, or melodic resemblance are added around this core to create the impression of inner thoughts, whether memories or dreams. Placing Ives's collage movements in the context of his other work, we can see both how unusual they are—only ten of almost two hundred movements or independent works that use existing music in some way—and yet how dependent each collage is on his earlier, simpler uses of existing music, from modeling to cumulative setting. They are extraordinary works, and collage is an extraordinary procedure. But it is the culmination of a logical and gradual development, the fusion of all the techniques he had practiced.

CHAPTER 11

The Significance of Ives's
Uses of Existing Music

The prevailing view of Ives's borrowings has been to see them as part of a musical crazy-quilt, where borrowed and newly composed elements are mixed virtually without discrimination and stitched together by loose association, if at all. This process has been explained as an outgrowth of Ives's transcendentalism,[1] ascribed to programmatic intentions,[2] and even used to justify the suggestion that Ives did not really know what he was doing.[3] An alternative view has recognized that borrowed tunes indeed contribute to the musical basis for many of Ives's works, but sees them primarily as providing motives or scraps of music for Ives to develop.[4] Although showing that Ives's stitchery is better than had been thought, even this approach does not ultimately explain why Ives relied so heavily on existing music for his own.

The difficulties begin with the attempt to account for all of Ives's borrowings from one point of view. What is true of one Ives piece is not necessarily true of another. His practices are so diverse that no one approach will account for all of them, and even works of the same type show unique features. There is no one reason Ives borrowed; there are several, corresponding to the many different procedures he used. Thus the first step in explaining Ives's borrowings is to recognize the variety of approaches he used and distinguish between them. The second step is to survey all of Ives's works based on existing music, not merely a few works that are asserted to be representative, to discover the range of variation within and between these categories. Having done this in the preceding chapters, we are now in a position to reconsider why Ives used existing music in the ways and to the extent that he did.

Starting Points

The view of Ives's music as a crazy-quilt of motivically interrelated borrowed fragments does approximate what is happening in some pieces. We have seen that fourteen works can be described as patchworks, in which a melody is stitched together from fragments of many tunes, and ten others as collages, in which a flurry of borrowed tunes related by resemblance or association is overlaid on an already coherent musical structure. In some thirty pieces or movements, the borrowings can be explained as largely programmatic. But most of Ives's procedures for using existing music do not depend on patchwork, collage, or programmaticism, and so have rather simpler explanations than those commonly offered for Ives's borrowings.

In most instances, it is clear that Ives is not adding quotations at the end of his compositional process. Rather, the existing music is where he starts: using it as a model; transcribing or arranging it; treating a given tune in variations, a new setting, or a medley; creating a new melody from an existing one through paraphrase and using it as the basis for a work; or basing a cumulative setting on a borrowed or paraphrased tune. Even in patchwork and collage, the starting point is often a particular kind of music with strong emotional and social associations. For instance, in the barn dance episodes in the second movement of the Second Violin Sonata and in *Washington's Birthday*, Ives's original themes are modeled on dance tunes he knew. These tunes can be taken as the starting point for the music just as surely as the variation sets and symphonies that served him as models were the starting points for his *Variations on "America"* and First Symphony. When Ives brings in a number of fiddle tunes later in these movements, he makes audible the relationship between his music and his models that might otherwise remain implicit.

Indeed, he consistently makes his starting points clear, but often in retrospect: more overtly citing the source for a theme after a rather distant paraphrase in the opening period, as in the first themes of the second movement of the First String Quartet and the finale of the Second Symphony; arriving at the theme at the end of a cumulative setting; or quoting a work's chief model or melodic source most directly at the end, as in *Down East* and *West London*. Ives was heir to the Beethovenian tradition of beginning, not with a clear statement, but with a problem to be solved over the course of a movement. In his uses of existing music, as in many other aspects of his work, he requires of his listeners that they work at his music, interpreting what they hear. His more overt citations of his sources provide clues whose full significance can be understood only by the active, inquiring, and open mind he imagines as his ideal listener. Thus, like Beethoven, Ives invites his audience to participate in an experience of the piece as an unfolding process rather than a closed structure. This does not require us to explain these overt citations through appeals to transcendentalism, programmaticism, or indeed anything beyond being part of the core thematic structure of the music.

Just as Ives's starting point in composition is often existing music, so the starting point of his development is the procedures he learned from tradition: once again, the use of models, transcription or arrangement, variation, resetting, medley, quodlibet, stylistic allusion, and the use of paraphrased themes in extended works. From this beginning, his evolution is clear. Modeling is the central thread, influencing everything else through its example of the numberless ways in which one work can borrow and rework ideas from another work. Paraphrase technique, with roots in variation, setting, transcription, and fugue, gave a flexible method of reworking given melodies into all sorts of guises. The new form of cumulative settings grew from many sources, including paraphrase, variation, the traditional idea of composing a new setting for a familiar tune, and the thematic and developmental principles of sonata form. Imitation of a model or a style changed in focus during his apprenticeship from learning new styles and genres to evoking familiar ones in works of a different type, either as a commentary on music and how we use and experience it or as an expressive gesture. This in turn provided the basis for many of Ives's later works. His patchworks, which blend paraphrase with the old idea of medley, use familiar tunes to evoke associations certain types of music carry. More specific associations with individual tunes are exploited in several of his programmatic works. A small group of quodlibets shows Ives's occasional delight in quotation for its own sake. Finally, his collages bring together all the strands: the structural use of borrowing in the modeling, paraphrase, or cumulative setting that usually underlies the themes and their development; the evocation of tunes with strong emotional or cultural associations typical of his later use of models, his patchworks, and his programmatic works; and the texture of multiple quotation explored in his quodlibets.

Each technique has its individual characteristics and origins. But all are interrelated in the ways they spring from existing music and recreate borrowed material in a new context, and each technique influences the others. The later procedures and the later music in general exhibit a growing tendency to explore more fully the ramifications of borrowing and to exploit more openly the ambiguities built into the re-creation of existing music.

European Parallels

That Ives drew on existing music is less unusual than it first appears. Neely Bruce long ago called attention to the frequent use of borrowed material in nineteenth-century American music, a tradition that has still not been adequately explored.[5] But it has also been common practice among European composers of the nineteenth and twentieth centuries, as well as in earlier periods. Beethoven, for instance, used most of the procedures that Ives did:

1 he modeled works on pieces by other composers, such as his String Quartet in A Major, Op. 18, No. 5, based on a Mozart quartet;[6]
2 he wrote variations on existing tunes, including *God Save the King* (the same tune as *America*);
3 he used paraphrased themes, as in two themes in his Razumovsky Quartets that are based on Russian songs;
4 he wrote numerous settings of Irish, Welsh, Scottish, and other folk songs for voice and piano trio;
5 he composed at least one humorous quodlibet, adding quotations from *Don Giovanni* ("Notte e giorno faticar") and a waltz tune (titled *Keine Ruh bei Tag und Nacht*) to variation 22 of the *Diabelli Variations*, Op. 120, as a sly response after Diabelli pressured him to finish the work more quickly;[7]
6 he alluded to distinctive styles for expressive or descriptive ends, as in the evocations of peasant music in the "Pastorale" Symphony and of Renaissance motet style and operatic recitative in the third and fourth movements of the String Quartet in A Minor, Op. 132;
7 he arranged his own music for new media, for example, transcribing his Piano Sonata in E Major, Op. 14, No. 1, as a string quartet in F, and he recast material from many of his compositions in new guises;[8] and
8 he used programmatic quotation in *Wellington's Victory*.

Many European composers active during Ives's lifetime also used borrowed music, in a variety of ways. Bruckner's symphonies carry symbolic meanings through allusions to works by Haydn, Liszt, and Wagner and to his own religious music.[9] Brahms used similar allusions in a number of works, including his First Piano Concerto and *German Requiem*,[10] as well as writing numerous variations and transcriptions. Tchaikovsky wrote settings of Russian folk songs, recast works of Mozart in his Orchestral Suite No. 4 ("Mozartiana"), adapted Russian and Ukrainian folktunes as themes in his First and Second Symphonies, and used programmatic quotation in the *1812 Overture*. Mahler evoked the styles of marches and waltzes, paraphrased folk songs, alluded to works of Beethoven, Schubert, Donizetti, Wagner, and Brahms, and reworked his own songs in his symphonies.[11] Debussy borrowed from folk songs, popular songs, gamelan music, ragtime, national anthems, and classical composers such as Grieg, Wagner, and the Russian Five.[12] Satie quoted from a variety of sources in his humorous piano pieces and imitated the style of contemporary Gregorian chant settings in works on religious subjects.[13] Schoenberg arranged works by Bach, Brahms, Johann Strauss, and other composers, quoted "Ach, du lieber Augustin" in his Second String Quartet, mimicked the styles of a Chopin waltz and a Bach aria in *Pierrot Lunaire*, and recomposed a Handel concerto grosso as a concerto for string quartet and orchestra and a G. B. Monn keyboard concerto as a cello concerto. Bartók used works by Beethoven, Wagner, Strauss, Debussy, and other composers as models,[14] made numerous settings of peasant tunes (sometimes altered to suit Western taste),[15] adapted folk tunes as themes for his own music, wrote music in folk styles, and used gestures and procedures derived from peasant music in his concert works, using peasant tunes as models rather than as sources of melodic material. Stravinsky modeled some early works on pieces by his teacher Rimsky-Korsakov, the Symphony in C on Haydn and Beethoven, and *The Rake's Progress* on the operas of Mozart; used themes paraphrased from folk tunes in *The Rite of Spring* and other works; evoked styles as varied as the Baroque concerto, ragtime, and circus music; and recast eighteenth-century music in *Pulcinella* and Tchaikovsky in *The Fairy's Kiss* to create works that sound much more like Stravinsky than like their sources.[16] D'Indy, Elgar, Delius, Richard Strauss, Vaughan Williams, Rachmaninov, Holst, Ravel, de Falla, Palmgren, Bloch, Webern, Berg, and many other composers of Ives's generation might equally well be mentioned here.

As these composers' uses of existing music become better understood, it increasingly appears that borrowing is much more widespread and significant in the music of the nineteenth and twentieth centuries than we have thought. In such company, Ives's more thoroughgoing and diverse uses of existing music make him seem, not an exception, but a paramount case of a common condition.

Why So Much Borrowing?

What is unusual in Ives is not that he borrowed, but the extent to which he borrowed and the innovative ways he found to use existing music. The question we should ask is not why Ives borrows, but rather why he borrows so often, more frequently and more prominently than any of his European contemporaries. What is all this borrowing for? Why does it increase in his later music, so that over half the pieces and over two-thirds of the instrumental movements composed after 1902 use borrowed material?

The first reason is a practical one. Musical composition requires a starting point, and the growing importance of musical borrowing over Ives's career shows that he found reworking existing models and melodies to be one of the most fruitful sources of inspiration. Like the other ideas Ives used as a springboard for composition—a text, a technical problem requiring innovative solutions, or an extramusical idea—his dependence on reworking existing music seems to have replaced the starting points normally available to composers in the tradition of art music: received forms, shared conventions, and accepted procedures for the invention, development, and repetition of musical material. His approach to composition seems to have been in essence a process of elaboration. Whether working out a technical experiment, creating a musical analogue to a text or a program, or reworking borrowed material, he followed a similar pattern of elaborating a central, usually simple idea that served as the starting point.[17]

A second reason lies in the demands imposed on composers of his generation. In questioning shared conventions and seeking new bases for composition, Ives was at one with his European contemporaries from Debussy to Webern. Forced to compete for performance and recognition with a permanent repertoire of classics from the eighteenth and nineteenth centuries, these composers devised individual solutions to the common problem of how to write music that could find a place in that repertoire or create an alternative to it. They worked under opposing constraints: a new work must be enough like the recognized masterpieces to claim a place in the same tradition, yet distinctive enough to offer something new and recognizably their own. The typical strategy was to minimize or reject some elements from the past and extend others in new directions or to new extremes; thus, Webern, for instance, rejected tonality, focused emotion in the smallest gesture, extended the structural functions of tone color, register, and dynamics, saturated his music with unifying motives and harmonies, and resurrected Renaissance canonic procedures and textures in a new guise, arriving at a music that had strong connections to the music of the past yet sounded completely new and unlike anyone else's music.[18] Ives's increasing dependence on borrowed music provided a way to write music of exceptional individuality that nonetheless had strong ties to tradition, both in using familiar tunes and styles (and the tonal gestures they inevitably invoked) and in extending and transforming the traditional methods of reworking existing music. No earlier generation is more diverse or more characterized by individuality than composers born from the 1860s through the 1880s, and Ives's famous individualism puts him right in the mainstream.[19]

Surrounded by past masterpieces as these composers were, they endured a heightened sense of what Harold Bloom has termed "the anxiety of influence," the struggle of younger artists to achieve independence from the work of their predecessors and become original.[20] As David Hertz has pointed out, Ives's reworking of American tunes allowed him to escape being overwhelmed by the influence of European composers and to achieve originality within the tradition of art music.[21] At the same time, of course, his adoption of the genres and ethos of art music freed him from the limitations of the American utilitarian music he had known as a youth.[22]

Third, the increase in Ives's use of borrowed material over the course of his career is in part the result of his own innovation. As Emerson says in "Quotation and Originality," "only an inventor knows how to borrow." Emerson's point throughout the essay is that virtually everything we say or do borrows from what we have heard and seen, and the mark of true originality lies in how we suit it to our current situation and make it our own.[23] Ives's originality is never more clear than in the many ways he found to rework borrowed material into something fresh and to adapt it to the requirements of each individual composition. He would not have borrowed so much had he not had such a wide variety of techniques at hand, or had he not developed procedures that could create large forms, such as cumulative setting, patchwork, and extended paraphrase. Each procedure uses existing material in different ways and for different reasons, covering the whole range from almost wholly structural to almost purely programmatic and from essential to ornamental. Having so many methods at hand, each responsive to different compositional needs, made it possible for Ives to use borrowed music in a wider range of circumstances than any of his contemporaries.

Most important, however, is that Ives found that his artistic goals required using borrowed music. We can trace parallels in Ives's uses of existing music to the development of his artistic aims, including especially his interest in American music and subjects.[24]

In his youth (to 1894), Ives sought to assimilate the styles and genres around him in Danbury. His uses of existing music were those of common practice, from the imitation of models to variation and medley. The music he encountered and the music he composed was utilitarian, valued not for its own sake but for its contribution to worship, public celebrations, or entertainment. His youthful music was American without his thinking about it, not written in a deliberately nationalist style, but created for a specific need, using the forms and styles current in the region and traditions within which Ives was working.

During his apprenticeship (1894–1902), Ives learned the forms, procedures, and aesthetic ideals of European art music, chiefly from Horatio Parker. He soon abandoned the marches and anthems of his youth for the art song, sonata, symphony, and tone poem, giving himself over completely to the Romantic ideas of music as an art for its own sake and of composition as self-expression. His First Symphony shows his allegiance to this tradition, and the First String Quartet, with its themes paraphrased from American hymn tunes, was his first foray into overt musical nationalism. Both in evoking European models and in suffusing the quartet with the flavor of American hymnody, thematic paraphrase was indispensable.

The years of innovation and synthesis (1902–8), after Ives left his last post as a church organist in 1902, were marked by experimentation and a growing diversity of means, including the first cumulative setting (*Fugue in Four Keys on "The Shining Shore,"* ca. 1902), patchwork (*Largo cantabile (Hymn)*, begun ca. 1904), and collage (*Overture and March "1776,"* begun ca. 1903, or *Country Band March*, begun ca. 1905). The major work of this period was the Second Symphony, which extended to a new height the nationalism and use of thematic paraphrase explored in the First Quartet. Like other nationalists, Ives used native elements to create a distinctive sound and achieve the originality and individuality necessary for success. Yet reworking American tunes to fit the style and structure of European forms, like all forms of nineteenth-century exoticism, was a way to control the exotic elements, to discipline them and place them within rather than outside European culture.

In his mature period (1908–18), Ives inverted these values.[25] Having developed cumulative setting, Ives now applied it to the Third Symphony and a series of sonatas. In the context of concert music, using developmental procedures borrowed from sonata and variation forms to build up to a complete statement of the theme raised the simple American tunes that Ives used as themes to a level of seriousness associated with art music. This marks a new level of Americanism for Ives. Here he goes beyond claiming an American identity within the European tradition and uses the methods of European art music to assert the value of the American vernacular tradition in its own right.

This period also saw a deepening interest, nurtured by his wife Harmony, in depicting in music the people, places, scenes, holidays, events, and literature of America, particularly of Ives's own region, from New York City to Boston. This is Ives's principal subject. As John Kirkpatrick has noted, "Ives is the great American impressionist, in many ways parallel to Debussy, but Ives's subject matter is primarily people, their thoughts, feelings, and actions, whereas Debussy's people usually fade into the landscape or the medieval story or the blur of the carnival."[26] People make music, and Ives found in references to types of music or to actual pieces of music a way to evoke the people in a certain place and what they are doing and feeling. These experiences are diverse, and require different procedures. Many of them are experiences of music itself:

> waiting for the curtain to go up at a show, or hearing the song an uncle used to sing, evoked through stylistic allusion in *Memories;*
> watching a college football game and hearing the cheers and songs of the crowd, depicted through programmatic quotation in *Yale-Princeton Football Game;*
> hearing snatches of a hymn from across a river, captured through extended paraphrase in *The Housatonic at Stockbridge;*
> remembering the holiday celebrations of one's childhood in a flood of memories, evoked through collage in *The Fourth of July;*
> standing on an elevated train platform as a crowd slowly comes together to sing as one a tune that captures what is on their hearts, recreated through cumulative setting in *From Hanover Square North;*
> reminiscing about the songs of an older generation and the values they embodied, described through patchwork in *The Things Our Fathers Loved.*

None of these experiences could be captured in music without referring to existing music. What Kurt Stone calls Ives's "reluctance to operate with his own thematic ideas"[27] is no lack of originality but an almost inevitable result of his choice of subject matter. As Ives commented about *Yale-Princeton Football Game,* "in picturing the excitement, sounds and songs across the field and grandstand, you could not do it with a nice fugue in C."[28] His references to existing music in his mature period are part of Ives's attempt to write music that is about human experiences and is true to that experience.[29]

Even experiences that are not about music directly can be more clearly described by using music with strong associations, as such music inevitably calls forth images of people and their actions and feelings:

a woman, on the day her brother sails to war in Europe, recalling him as a
   child, her conflicting emotions of patriotism, pride, sadness, loss, and
   nostalgia perfectly limned in *Tom Sails Away* by the poignant
   juxtaposition of an old sentimental song with patriotic songs whose
   stirring inspiration is undermined by a slow tempo and soft dynamics;
the "Concord bards . . . pound[ing] away at the immensities with a
   Beethoven-like sublimity,"[30] evoked in the *Concord Sonata* through the
   development and ultimate exposition of a theme that blends the most
   famous Beethoven motive with familiar hymns;
an inner spiritual journey, mapped out in the Fourth Symphony in part
   through gradually stronger references to "Nearer, my God, to Thee."

In all of these, Ives is essentially a Romantic composer, trying to capture
an emotional experience in music. He recognized the pitfalls in trying to picture anything in music, asking in his *Essays Before a Sonata*, "Can a tune literally represent a stone wall with vines on it or even with nothing on it, though
it (the tune) be made by a genius whose power of objective contemplation is
in the highest state of development? Can it be done by anything short of an
act of mesmerism on the part of the composer or an act of kindness on the
part of the listener?"[31] But familiar tunes or types of music bring along
instant associations, which Ives then manipulates to suggest the feeling and
situation he wants to evoke: for instance, bands playing different tunes in different tempos to suggest the deck orchestras on *The General Slocum*, or fragments and paraphrases of dance tunes flitting by to suggest memories of a
barn dance, in *Washington's Birthday*.

In the period of his last works (1918–26), Ives at times achieves a great subtlety of allusion, particularly in his late songs. Here Ives's subject is often an
experience of the spirit, as in *The White Gulls*, and the hints of hymns and
other musical styles convey the right feeling with admirable efficiency. In this
time and in the period of revising (1927–54), as he reworked music composed
earlier, he occasionally added new tunes, thickening an existing collage with
new references (as in the second movement of the Fourth Symphony) or creating a collage or counterpoint where none had been before (as with the
"shadow" hymn tunes in *Thanksgiving*).

Borrowing, Americanism, and Authenticity

Particularly in his mature works on American subjects, Ives reaches a final
level of Americanism, one that transcends claiming a national identity within

the international tradition, as in the Second Symphony, and asserting the centrality of American music, as in the Third. In *The Housatonic at Stockbridge, The Fourth of July, From Hanover Square North, The Things Our Fathers Loved*, and many other works, Ives achieves a kind of musical autobiography, telling of his own experiences and those of people like him.[32] He is an American, indeed a white Anglo-Saxon old-family Protestant from the northeast, a member of a particular class and clan born and raised in a smallish city, and it is his particular experience that he tells us about.

This is a far cry from the other composers of his generation who sought to create a distinctively American music by incorporating native materials into European forms. Two of the most prominent were Henry F. Gilbert (1868–1928), who used black spirituals and ragtime as sources, and Arthur Farwell (1872–1952), who championed the use of the songs and dance music of American Indians. In *Essays Before a Sonata*, Ives addressed their approach, without mentioning them by name, and distinguished his own from theirs. What he says makes even more clear why he had to use musical borrowing and why he chose the hymns, patriotic songs, popular songs, and other types of vernacular music that were disdained by the musical establishment.

Ives allows that black spirituals or Indian tunes may be useful to a composer, but he rejects the idea of using such melodies simply to provide an exotic sound or to achieve a distinctive American identity. He insists that it is what he calls the *substance* of this music that is useful—its idealism, its spirit, not merely its sounds—and he says that the composer must have a deep identification with the idealism and spirit that underlay the creation and performance of the tunes and sounds he borrows. Ives argues that simply using a certain tune does not make a piece American. What makes it American is that it authentically reflects the experience of Americans, including the composer's own experiences.

For instance, Ives writes, in apparent reference to Gilbert,

> A composer born in America, but who has not been interested in the "cause of the Freedmen," may be so interested in "negro melodies" that he writes a symphony over them. He is conscious . . . that he wishes it to be "American music." . . . [But] if this composer isn't as deeply interested in the "cause" as Wendell Phillips was, when he fought his way through that anti-abolitionist crowd at Faneuil Hall, his music is liable to be less American than he wishes.[33]

Ives at one point planned a composition on this famous abolitionist speech by Phillips, part of a set on the abolitionist cause. Although this piece never materialized, he had memorialized the "cause of the Freedmen" in his own

"*St.-Gaudens*" *in Boston Common (Col. Shaw and his Colored Regiment)*, a tribute to the first black regiment in the Union Army. From Ives's point of view, a piece like Gilbert's *Comedy Overture on Negro Themes* (ca. 1906), based on the Uncle Remus stories, or his symphonic poem *The Dance in Place Congo* (ca. 1908, revised 1916) had nothing to offer musically or spiritually, for Gilbert's music did not manifest a deep identification with the idealism and spirit that underlay the black struggle for freedom and equality. Quite the contrary, it was part of a long tradition of using white versions of black culture for the entertainment of white audiences.

Ives goes on:

> Again, if a man finds that the cadences of an Apache war-dance come nearest to his soul—provided he has taken pains to know enough other cadences, for eclecticism is part of his duty . . .—let him assimilate whatever he finds highest of the Indian ideal so that he can use it with the cadences, fervently, transcendentally, inevitably, furiously, in his symphonies, in his operas, in his whistlings on the way to work, so that he can paint his house with them, make them a part of his prayer-book—this is all possible and necessary, if he is confident that they have a part in his spiritual consciousness. With this assurance, his music will have everything it should of sincerity, nobility, strength, and beauty, no matter how it sounds; and if, with this, he is true to none but the highest of American ideals (that is, the ideals only that coincide with his spiritual consciousness), his music will be true to itself and incidentally American, and it will be so even after it is proved that all our Indians came from Asia.[34]

Only if the composer identifies completely with both the music and the spirit behind the music does he earn the right to use Indian materials in his music, in Ives's view. Although the Indians may live in the same country, as far as white Americans like Farwell are concerned they represent a foreign culture. According to Ives, white composers have no right to wrap themselves in Indian garb unless they can convey the special genius of that culture, which requires an intimate knowledge a white urban composer is not likely to have.

Ives used the music of white Americans, rather than that of Indians or blacks, because it was the flavor of his own people and region that he sought to capture. He used popular music, rather than genuine folk music (except for some fiddle tunes), because that was the music of small-town and urban America. In order to portray these people in music, he used the music they were familiar with, from hymns and Stephen Foster ballads to the Tin Pan Alley hits of his own time, and he attempted to reveal the power this music had for them:

The man "born down to Babbitt's Corners" may find a deep appeal in the simple but acute Gospel hymns of the New England "camp meetin'" of a generation or so ago. He finds in them . . . a vigor, a depth of feeling, a natural-soil rhythm, a sincerity—emphatic but inartistic—which . . . carries him nearer the "Christ of the people" than does the *Te Deum* of the greatest cathedral. . . . If the Yankee can reflect the fervency with which "his gospels" were sung—the fervency of "Aunt Sarah," who scrubbed her life away for her brother's ten orphans, the fervency with which this woman, after a fourteen-hour work day on the farm, would hitch up and drive five miles through the mud and rain to "prayer meetin'," her one articulate outlet for the fullness of her unselfish soul—if he can reflect the fervency of such a spirit, he may find there a local color that will do all the world good. If his music can but catch that spirit by being a part with itself, it will come somewhere near his ideal—and it will be American, too —perhaps nearer so than that of the devotee of Indian or negro melody. In other words, if local color, national color, any color, is a true pigment of the universal color, it is a divine quality, it is a part of substance in art— not of manner.[35]

Ives sought to give his own culture articulate speech within the language of art music. By the time he wrote these words in early 1919, nationalism no longer interested him as an end in itself. Rather, his music was American because he sought to communicate the experience of Americans like himself, especially their experience of and emotional involvement with the music of their everyday life. He wrote art music because it was the only type of music that could serve as a framework for conveying such experiences, the only type of music that could coordinate such a breadth of styles and materials within a unified discourse, the only type of music one listened to with rapt attention, so that the composer could talk in the music itself about his experience with music. But the music he talked about was the music of his own people, the people of small-town and urban America in the northeast in the late nineteenth century. Through his music, Ives celebrates what American music means to Americans and thus, in a broader sense, what anyone's music means to them. This is the "true pigment of the universal color" that Ives saw in his use of the local materials he knew and loved intimately.[36]

In the end, it is Ives's desire to be himself that best explains his increasing use of borrowed material in his later music. He grew up surrounded by music, but upon entering the world of art music he found that the music he had known as a youth was excluded from that world. He stopped composing marches, anthems, and sentimental parlor songs, but he could not abandon what they had meant to him. By introducing the music he had known in his

THE SIGNIFICANCE OF USING EXISTING MUSIC

youth into his art songs, sonatas, and symphonies, he integrated the two sides of his musical personality and brought into the classical tradition the vitality of American vernacular music, with all of the emotions and associations it carried. In his mature music, he is speaking for himself, in a language that is his own, one that assimilates all the musical tongues he had learned. What he has to say could not be said in any other way.

Notes

CHAPTER 1: IVES'S USES OF EXISTING MUSIC

1. E.g., Gerald Abraham, *The Concise Oxford History of Music* (London: Oxford University Press, 1979), 824, dismisses Ives's music as a "bizarre unintegrated mixture of daring sophistication and homespun crudity."

2. John Kirkpatrick, *A Temporary Mimeographed Catalogue of the Music Manuscripts and Related Materials of Charles Edward Ives 1874–1954* (New Haven: Library of the Yale School of Music, 1960; reprint, 1973), hereafter cited as *Catalogue*; see also the "Index of Tunes Quoted," 264–66. Kirkpatrick's later findings, along with those of James B. Sinclair, are collated in Sinclair's "Microfilm Concordance to the JK Catalogue" (typescript and manuscript, 1976), which correlates Kirkpatrick's *Catalogue* to the microfilms of musical materials in the Ives Collection, John Herrick Jackson Music Library, Yale University.

3. Clayton W. Henderson, *The Charles Ives Tunebook* (Warren, Mich.: Harmonie Park Press, 1990), hereafter cited as *Tunebook*. This draws on Kirkpatrick's catalogue; on Henderson's dissertation, "Quotation as a Style Element in the Music of Charles Ives" (Washington University, 1969); and on Sinclair's concordance. The careful work of these three scholars in identifying and indexing hundreds of borrowings has made the present discussion possible. My debt to all three is deep.

4. E.g., Sydney Robinson Charles, "The Use of Borrowed Material in Ives' Second Symphony," *The Music Review* 28 (May 1967): 102–11; Dennis Marshall, "Charles Ives's Quotations: Manner or Substance?," *Perspectives of New Music* 6/2 (Spring–Summer 1968): 45–56; Gordon Cyr, "Intervallic Structural Elements in Ives's Fourth Symphony," *Perspectives of New Music* 9/2 and 10/1 (Spring/Summer–Fall/Winter 1971): 291–303; Laurence Wallach, "The New England Education of Charles Ives" (Ph.D. diss., Columbia University, 1973), 249–61; Mary Ellison, "Ives' Use of American 'Popular' Tunes as Thematic Material," in *South Florida's Historic Ives Festival 1974–1976*, ed. F. Warren O'Reilly (Coral Gables, Fla.: University of Miami at Coral Gables, 1976), 30–34; Nors S. Josephson, "Charles Ives: Intervallische Permutationen im Spätwerk," *Zeitschrift für Musiktheorie* 9/2 (Fall 1978): 27–33; and Lora L. Gingerich, "A Technique for Melodic Motivic Analysis in the Music of Charles Ives," *Music Theory Spectrum* 8 (1986): 75–93.

5. E.g., Colin Sterne, "The Quotations in Charles Ives's Second Symphony," *Music and Letters* 52 (January 1971): 39–45; Rosalie Sandra Perry, *Charles Ives and the American Mind* (Kent, Ohio: Kent State University Press, 1974), 51–53; Stuart Feder, "Decoration Day: A Boyhood Memory of Charles Ives," *The Musical Quarterly* 66 (April 1980): 234–61.

6. E.g., Henry Cowell and Sidney Cowell, *Charles Ives and His Music*, 2nd ed. (New York: Oxford University Press, 1969), 147–49 and 164; Charles Ward, "The Use of Hymn Tunes as an Expression of 'Substance' and 'Manner' in the Music of Charles E.

Ives, 1874–1954" (M.M. thesis, University of Texas at Austin, 1969); Clayton Henderson, "Structural Importance of Borrowed Music in the Works of Charles Ives: A Preliminary Assessment," in *Report of the Eleventh Congress of the International Musicological Society Held at Copenhagen, 1972*, ed. Henrik Glahn, Soren Sorensen, and Peter Ryom (Copenhagen: Wilhelm Hansen, 1974), 1:437–46; Charles Ward, "Charles Ives: The Relationship Between Aesthetic Theories and Compositional Processes" (Ph.D. diss., University of Texas at Austin, 1974), 155–73, particularly p. 157; and Christopher Ballantine, "Charles Ives and the Meaning of Quotation in Music," *The Musical Quarterly* 65 (April 1979): 167–84. The best recent overview of borrowing in Ives is in Wolfgang Rathert, *Charles Ives* (Darmstadt: Wissenschaftliche Buchgesellschaft, 1989), 95–110.

7. David Wooldridge, *From the Steeples and the Mountains: A Study of Charles Ives* (New York: Knopf, 1974), 17–18.

8. This list is an expansion of the categories proposed in two of my earlier works on musical borrowing in Ives: "Ives's Uses of Existing Music," part 2 of "The Evolution of Charles Ives's Music: Aesthetics, Quotation, Technique" (Ph.D. diss., University of Chicago, 1983), 212–460, especially 216–18; and "'Quotation' and Emulation: Charles Ives's Uses of His Models," *The Musical Quarterly* 71 (1985): 1–26, especially 2–3. A version of this list was published in my article "The Uses of Existing Music: Musical Borrowing as a Field," *Music Library Association Notes* 50 (March 1994): 854, using the traditional dates for Ives's works provided by John Kirkpatrick; the list given here uses the revised dates based on Gayle Sherwood's preliminary redating, as described below in note 15. Ives also borrowed frequently from himself, reworking finished or unfinished pieces into new compositions. This is not listed as a separate category, but it will be addressed in relation to individual works.

9. The second movement represents the "dissolute company" of soldiers before the battle, singing eight different folk songs in five different keys, entering at different times and clashing in casual dissonance, down to the closing six-note chord. The effect, to modern ears, is strikingly Ivesian.

10. Ives's career was outlined in my earlier study of his aesthetics, *Charles Ives: The Ideas Behind the Music* (New Haven: Yale University Press, 1985), 43–44, and chaps. 5–10.

11. Works too fragmentary to describe include the projected Third Orchestral Set in three movements (ca. 1919–26), Studies Nos. 16 and 19 (ca. 1914), a song fragment (item 6B45c in Kirkpatrick's *Catalogue*, renumbered 6B77a and dated ?1926 in Sinclair's "Microfilm Concordance," 192 and 212), and four unidentified fragments (7E1, 7E67c, 7E69b, and 7E92 in the *Catalogue*). See the listings for these works in Kirkpatrick, *Catalogue*, 24–25, 97–99, 192, 224, and 229–31, and Henderson, *Tunebook*, 197–98, 204, 212, and 213. The *Take-Off* on the Andante of Haydn's "Surprise" Symphony (ca. 1909, 7C22 in Kirkpatrick, *Catalogue*, 221) involves the addition of text, not music, and so is not discussed here.

12. Kirkpatrick, *Catalogue*, and "Ives, Charles E(dward)," in *The New Grove Dictionary of Music and Musicians*, ed. Stanley Sadie (London: Macmillan, 1980); the latter was slightly revised for *The New Grove Dictionary of American Music*, ed. H. Wiley Hitchcock and Stanley Sadie (London: Macmillan, 1986). See Kirkpatrick's comments on the dating problem, *Catalogue*, vii–viii.

13. Maynard Solomon, "Charles Ives: Some Questions of Veracity," *Journal of the American Musicological Society* 40 (Fall 1987): 443–70. For responses to Solomon, see J. Peter Burkholder, "Charles Ives and His Fathers: A Response to Maynard Solomon," *Institute for Studies in American Music Newsletter* 18/1 (November 1988): 8–11; J. Philip Lambert, "Communication," *Journal of the American Musicological Society* 42 (Spring 1989): 204–9, answered by Solomon in the same issue, 209–18; Stuart Feder, "On the Veracity of Ives's Dating of His Music," in *Charles Ives, "My Father's Song": A Psychoanalytic Biography* (New Haven: Yale University Press, 1992), 351–57; and David Nicholls, "Unanswerable Questions/Questionable Answers," *Music and Letters* 75 (May 1994): 246–52, which includes an overview of this and other recent issues in Ives scholarship.

14. For example, Wayne Shirley demonstrates that the fundamental harmonic and thematic structure of *The Fourth of July* is present from the first draft, although other borrowed tunes were added later, in "'The Second of July': A Charles Ives Draft Considered as an Independent Work," in *A Celebration of American Music: Words and Music in Honor of H. Wiley Hitchcock*, ed. Richard Crawford, R. Allen Lott, and Carol J. Oja (Ann Arbor: University of Michigan Press, 1990), 391–404. Carol K. Baron uses handwriting analysis to date *Putnam's Camp, Country Band March, Overture and March "1776,"* and the *Three-Page Sonata* to within half a decade of the dates Ives claimed for them, in "Dating Charles Ives's Music: Facts and Fictions," *Perspectives of New Music* 28/1 (Winter 1990): 20–56.

15. For Baron, see ibid. The music paper types and their dates are listed in chap. 2 of Gayle Sherwood, "The Choral Works of Charles Ives: Chronology, Style, and Reception" (Ph.D. diss., Yale University, in progress). Sherwood lists the datable manuscripts used to establish benchmarks for Ives's handwriting in 1892, 1898, 1902, 1907, ca. 1914, 1919, 1923, 1929, 1934, and 1942. A summary of her approach and of the handwriting data, including the list of benchmark manuscripts, appears in her article "Questions and Veracities: Reassessing the Chronology of Ives's Choral Works," *The Musical Quarterly* 78 (Fall 1994): 429–47. By combining paper-type dating with dating of handwriting, she is able to place each Ives manuscript with reasonable certainty near one of these dates or between two successive benchmark dates. Dates for the works with chorus are discussed in chap. 3 of her dissertation. She provided preliminary estimated dates for other manuscripts at my request, and hopes soon to establish a new chronology for Ives's music. I am very grateful for her help.

CHAPTER 2: EMULATING MODELS AND
LEARNING MUSICAL STYLES

1. The literature on the use of models is vast. Recent work relevant to music mentioned in this paragraph includes Howard Mayer Brown, "Emulation, Competition, and Homage: Imitation and Theories of Imitation in the Renaissance," *Journal of the American Musicological Society* 35 (Spring 1982): 1–48, on the imitation of models in fifteenth-century secular music; J. Peter Burkholder, "Johannes Martini and the Imitation Mass of the Late Fifteenth Century," *Journal of the American Musicological Society* 38 (Fall 1985): 470–523, and Leeman L. Perkins, "The L'homme armé Masses of

Busnoys and Okeghem: A Comparison," *The Journal of Musicology* 3 (Fall 1984): 363–96, on fifteenth-century masses; Patrick Macey, "Josquin as Classic: *Qui habitat, Memor esto*, and Two Imitations Unmasked," *Journal of the Royal Musical Association* 118 (1993): 1–43, and Michele Fromson, "A Conjunction of Rhetoric and Music: Structural Modelling in the Italian Counter-Reformation Motet," *Journal of the Royal Musical Association* 117 (1992): 208–46, on sixteenth-century motets; George J. Buelow, "Handel's Borrowing Techniques: Some Fundamental Questions Derived from a Study of 'Agrippina' (Venice, 1709)," *Göttinger Händel-Beiträge* 2 (1986): 105–28, on Handel's borrowings; A. Peter Brown, "*The Creation* and *The Seasons*: Some Allusions, Quotations, and Models from Handel to Mendelssohn," *Current Musicology*, no. 51 (1993): 26–58, on Haydn's models and influence; Charles Rosen, "Influence: Plagiarism and Inspiration," *19th-Century Music* 4 (Fall 1980): 87–100, and Kevin Korsyn, "Towards a New Poetics of Musical Influence," *Music Analysis* 10 (March–July 1991): 3–72, on borrowing as it relates to influence, with a particular focus on Brahms; J. Peter Burkholder, "Brahms and Twentieth-Century Classical Music," *19th-Century Music* 8 (Summer 1984): 75–83, and Raymond Knapp, "The Finale of Brahms's Fourth Symphony: The Tale of the Subject," *19th-Century Music* 13 (Summer 1989): 3–17, on the Brahms Fourth Symphony finale; Carolyn Abbate, "Tristan in the Composition of Pelléas," *19th-Century Music* 5 (Fall 1981): 117–41, on Debussy's debt to Wagner; and Joseph N. Straus, *Remaking the Past: Musical Modernism and the Influence of the Tonal Tradition* (Cambridge, Mass.: Harvard University Press, 1990), which considers a variety of ways in which modern composers reflect on music of the past and discusses the relationship between the Schoenberg Third Quartet and the Schubert A-Minor Quartet on pp. 161–68.

2. See Lawrence Morton, "Stravinsky and Tchaikovsky: *Le baiser de la fée*," *The Musical Quarterly* 48 (July 1962): 313–26.

3. Dates follow Kirkpatrick, *Catalogue* and the work-list in *New Grove*. Psalm 42 may also be this early; Kirkpatrick places it in 1888 or before, based on a note on one copy (*Catalogue*, 129), although he dates the extant sources to late 1890; Sherwood, "Choral Works," chap. 3, dates them ca. 1892. Few pieces during this early period can be securely dated to a single year. Individual dates are discussed below.

4. The date is confirmed by a notice in the *Danbury News* of a performance on 16 January 1888; see Kirkpatrick, *Catalogue*, 35. Given the awkwardness of Ives's other music from 1887 or earlier, he may have had help in composing this from his father George, who copied the extant sources; Kirkpatrick, ibid., suggests that George may have arranged or corrected this work.

5. James B. Sinclair, "Preface," in Charles E. Ives, *Holiday Quickstep*, ed. Sinclair (Bryn Mawr: Merion Music, 1975), 1, notes the relationship but calls it a quotation. Ives does not quote the Reeves but reworks it more subtly.

6. Charles E. Ives, *Essays Before a Sonata*, in *Essays Before a Sonata, The Majority, and Other Writings*, ed. Howard Boatwright (New York: W. W. Norton, 1970), 30 (see also Boatwright's note 15, p. 245); and Ives, *Memos*, ed. John Kirkpatrick (New York: W. W. Norton, 1972), 102. The impromptu performance in Ives's house is cited by John Kirkpatrick in Ives, *Memos*, 280.

7. Jonathan Elkus discusses its importance for Ives and for American band music in *Charles Ives and the American Band Tradition: A Centennial Tribute* (Exeter: American

Arts Documentation Centre, University of Exeter, 1974), 27, citing a typescript monograph on Reeves by Charles G. Richardson.

8. Neither Ives's hymn nor its model is included in Henderson's *Tunebook*.

9. Ives's hymn (item 5C1 in Kirkpatrick, *Catalogue*, 129) is transcribed in Wallach, "New England Education," 331, and discussed on pp. 123–25. Sherwood, "Choral Works," dates it before 1892 but cannot fix a more specific date by handwriting. It appears on manuscript page f5837/n2210c&n2209. Each Ives manuscript page is identified by one or by two numbers: the frame number (f) assigned to it in the master microfilms of Ives's music manuscripts in the Ives Collection, John Herrick Jackson Music Library, Yale University; and, where one exists, the number assigned to the negatives of Ives's manuscripts made between 1927 and 1960. Kirkpatrick, *Catalogue*, uses the latter to identify each manuscript page listed; the corresponding frame number is given in Sinclair's "Microfilm Concordance." The initial letter of each negative number indicates where and when it was made: q at Quality Photoprint Studio, New York, about 1927–50 (capital Q indicates a page on which Ives made additions after it was photographed, and qm indicates that the negative is missing); n at New York Public Library in 1955; and y at Yale since 1957. See Kirkpatrick, "Index of Negative Numbers in Numerical Order," in *Catalogue*, 247–63.

10. Ives dated the work 1887 or 1888; see Kirkpatrick, *Catalogue*, 157. Gayle Sherwood, personal communication, 26 May 1994 (hereafter Sherwood, 26 May 1994), confirms that it was composed before 1892 but cannot date the hand to a given year.

11. Ives may have learned the Handel march from *Fourteen Celebrated Marches*, a book of piano transcriptions (p. 23), stamped "Chas E Ives / Danbury, Conn." and now in the Ives Collection; see Wallach, "New England Education," 131. Feder, *Charles Ives*, 39 and 104, notes that the "Dead March" from *Saul* was "invariably" performed at military funerals during the Civil War and suggests that Ives associated it with his father's wartime service.

12. Wallach, "New England Education," 112–13. His interpretation is laudable in that it avoids interpreting an early piece, almost certainly sincere in its expression, in terms of Ives's later music, which can be satirical or ironic.

13. David Gooding, "A Study of the Quotation Process in the Songs for Voice and Piano of Charles Edward Ives" (M.A. thesis, Western Reserve University, 1963), 27, 31, and Example 10.

14. Ives offered no date for the work; Kirkpatrick, *Catalogue*, 62, guesses ?1887. Since the manuscript is in George Ives's hand, it is impossible to date the work exactly, and it may be as late as 1892. If it was written as early as 1887 or 1888, George might have corrected or helped to compose it. The excerpts from the Polonaise that appear in Examples 2.3, 2.5, and 2.6 are transcribed from George Ives's manuscript (f3019/y6068).

15. Stephen Foster, *The Social Orchestra* (New York: Firth, Pond, 1854; reprint, New York: Da Capo Press, 1973).

16. Henderson, *Tunebook*, 172, shows the opening accompanimental vamp (H179) as the material quoted from *Lucia* but does not mention the melodic resemblances. Wallach, "New England Education," 120, refers to the Polonaise as "an arrangement" of the Donizetti, which is clearly not the case.

17. *Hymnal of the Methodist Episcopal Church With Tunes* (New York: Nelson and Phillips, 1878), pp. 23 and 76. See the list in Charles Ward, "Use of Hymn Tunes," 129, of the hymnals used by Ives. The tune here is not *Toplady* ("Rock of Ages," H60), as claimed by Henderson, *Tunebook*, 208. Ives dated this song 1890 in his first surviving list of works, in *Memos*, 147. This is questioned by Kirkpatrick (ibid., n. 5, and *Catalogue*, 159), noting that the extant copy is in a hand of ca. 1892, as confirmed by Gayle Sherwood, personal communication, 19 May 1994 (hereafter Sherwood, 19 May 1994). Kirkpatrick, *New Grove*, dates the song ?1891.

18. No other surviving works from before 1892 have been shown to incorporate existing music. Henderson, "Quotation," 14, tentatively suggests that the first four notes of Ives's song *Abide with Me* (ca. 1890–92) may be an allusion to Mendelssohn's "Hark, the herald angels sing," but this can scarcely be credited; it is a musical commonplace, and four notes are not enough to prove a derivation in this case. Only a little longer and probably no more credible is the derivation of the opening notes of *At Parting* (ca. 1889) from "Flow Gently, Sweet Afton," suggested by Feder, *Charles Ives*, 367, n. 26. Two lost works that Ives said were composed before 1891 may also have used borrowed material: a *Slow March* for band on the cantus firmus *Adeste fideles* (1D2 in Kirkpatrick's *Catalogue*), which Ives said was composed in 1886 or 1887 and played soon afterwards by the Danbury Band and a band from Carmel, New York; and *The American Woods* (Kirkpatrick 1C2), overture for orchestra or band, composed and played in 1889 and later adapted as part of the Second Symphony finale (see Kirkpatrick, *Catalogue*, 54 and 35). Exactly how these lost pieces used borrowed material is unknown. *The American Woods* is discussed in chap. 4 with the Second Symphony.

19. The clear cases in the 1890s of melodic quotation from a model are treated in later chapters, the First Symphony (1898–1902) in chapter 4, the song *Waltz* (ca. 1895) and an Invention in D for piano (ca. 1897–98) in chapter 7.

20. On the rise of originality as a desired characteristic of music, see George J. Buelow, "Originality, Genius, Plagiarism in English Criticism of the Eighteenth Century," in *Florilegium musicologicum: Festschrift Hellmut Federhofer zum 75. Geburtstag*, ed. Cristoph-Hellmut Mahling (Tutzing: Hans Schneider, 1988), 57–66.

21. Ives dated the ink copy January–February 1892; composition may have begun in 1891, the date given in Ives's lists of his works in *Memos*, 154, and of a concert recorded on the ink copy. The work was submitted to a publisher in August 1892. See Kirkpatrick, *Catalogue*, 105–6.

22. On the variation sets in Ives's repertoire, see Wallach, "New England Education," 146–49. See also William Osborne, "Charles Ives the Organist," *The American Organist* 24/7 (July 1990): 58–64, especially p. 61.

23. Wallach, "New England Education," 156–58 and 161–62.

24. Osborne, "Ives the Organist," 58.

25. On Ives's polytonal experiments, see J. Peter Burkholder, "The Critique of Tonality in the Early Experimental Music of Charles Ives," *Music Theory Spectrum* 12 (Fall 1990): 203–23. On the bitonal interludes in the *Variations on "America,"* see Wallach, "New England Education," 159–63. The two interludes are added in pencil on empty staves of Ives's 1892 ink copy and do not appear in the ink copy by George Ives from later 1892, suggesting that they were composed after the rest of the work. According to Sherwood, 26 May 1994, they are in Ives's hand of ca. 1902.

26. See the list of hymn texts used by Ives in Kirkpatrick, "Index of Standard Song-texts and Hymn-texts," *Catalogue*, 241.

27. Ives listed an 1890 performance of his *Abide with Me*, and Kirkpatrick (*Catalogue*, 159 and *New Grove*) suggests a date of ?1890. Sherwood, 19 May 1994, dates the manuscript ca. 1892.

28. Ives noted an 1890 performance, and Kirkpatrick (*Catalogue*, 132 and *New Grove*) suggests ?1890. Sherwood, "Choral Works," dates it ca. 1894–95 on the basis of music paper, handwriting, and musical style.

29. "Editor's Note," in Charles E. Ives, *Turn Ye, Turn Ye*, ed. John Kirkpatrick (Bryn Mawr: Mercury Music, 1973), 2.

30. Other hymn tunes that repeat the middle phrase are for six-line stanzas, as in *Toplady* and *Pilot*. These share a pattern of ABCCAB, essentially a ternary structure with internal repetition in the middle phrase. Some tunes for eight-line stanzas, such as *Bethany* and *Nettleton*, have a similar internal repetition in the third phrase, but *Expostulation* seems to be the only tune for a hymn in four- or eight-line stanzas with phrase repetition that straddles the midpoint of the stanza.

31. Kirkpatrick, "Index of Standard Song-texts and Hymn-texts," *Catalogue*, 240, lists these texts and the composers of previous settings. In most cases, Ives probably knew the earlier works. Of the art song texts, most are in German, some in French, and a few only in English translation. Ives dated *Minnelied* to 1892 and a few others to the mid-1890s, but at least the German songs seem to date from Ives's last year at Yale through ca. 1902 (Sherwood, 26 May 1994). The French songs seem to postdate Yale.

32. Kirkpatrick (*Catalogue*, 167 and *New Grove*) guesses ?1895, but the sole surviving manuscript, an ink copy, dates from ca. 1898–1902 (Sherwood, 26 May 1994). Ives later adapted words from George Meredith's "Night of Frost in May" to this music and published it, transposed, in *114 Songs* (Redding, Conn.: By the Author, 1922), 193–94, following a group of German songs.

33. In *114 Songs*, Ives dated *Feldeinsamkeit* 1900 and *Ich grolle nicht* 1899, perhaps the dates of the final versions; Kirkpatrick, *New Grove*, suggests 1897 and 1898 respectively. Sherwood, 26 May 1994, places the *Feldeinsamkeit* sketch ca. Spring 1898 and the *Ich grolle nicht* material a little later, while noting that it may not be Ives's first draft.

34. Memo on f6570/q5002&2549, as edited by Kirkpatrick (his insertions) in Ives, *Memos*, 183–84. See also the differently edited version in Kirkpatrick, *Catalogue*, 175.

35. The example is taken from *114 Songs*, 190. All surviving manuscripts are in A♭ but otherwise differ little from the published version.

36. Of the two previous comparisons of these two settings, Philip Edward Newman, "The Songs of Charles Ives" (Ph.D. diss., University of Iowa, 1967), 151–54, emphasizes the differences, and Nachum Schoffman, "The Songs of Charles Ives" (Ph.D. diss., Hebrew University of Jerusalem, 1977), 13–20, stresses the similarities.

37. It is notable that the surviving draft (f6556–58/n2573–75) has only a two-bar introduction, the same length as in Brahms's song; mm. 3–6 are added at the top of the second page, as an afterthought. Here, too, in a structural detail, Ives seems determined to distinguish his song from its model.

38. Similarly, Ives's setting of *Die Lotusblume* is rhythmically varied whereas Schumann's is not, and Ives's *Wie Melodien zieht es mir* maintains a consistent accompanimental figuration throughout, unlike Brahms's more varied setting.

39. Schoffman's assertion, "Songs of Charles Ives," 17–18, that "the plan of tonalities" is similar is incorrect; the initial and final chords for each line of text are in every case different except for the opening and closing tonic in the first verse.

40. For other melodic and harmonic parallels, see ibid., 15–17.

41. Ives, *114 Songs*, 192. Perhaps it was this sort of criticism that spurred Ives to put new English words to many songs he first wrote to German texts.

42. Letter of 28 February 1778, as edited and translated by Emily Anderson, *The Letters of Mozart and His Family*, 3rd rev. ed., ed. Stanley Sadie and Fiona Smart (London: Macmillan, 1985), 497.

43. According to Sherwood, "Choral Works," Ives's second and third movements seem earliest, ca. 1898 or 1899, and the rest ca. 1898–1902. Kirkpatrick, *New Grove*, dates the whole work 1898–99; it was performed 1902.

44. Victor Fell Yellin, review of the first recording of *The Celestial Country*, *The Musical Quarterly* 60 (July 1974): 500–508. Yellin's comments on the texts appear on p. 504.

45. Yellin, 504–5, mentions the resemblance between these two movements. He further asserts that Ives's tenor aria (No. 6) "derives much of its material, as well as concept," from Parker's tenor aria (No. 7), a derivation I cannot see.

46. See Parker, *Hora novissima* (London: Novello, 1900; reprint, Earlier American Music, 2, New York: Da Capo Press, 1972), 46–47, reh. B–D; Ives, *The Celestial Country* (New York: Peer International, 1973), 27–32, mm. 38–75. John Kirkpatrick mentions Ives's "possible indebtedness to Parker" for this metric pattern in his edition of Ives's *Memos*, 63, n. 8, and Yellin points out the resemblance on p. 505 of his review. In *Memos*, 140, Ives attributed the idea of alternating $\frac{4}{4}$ and $\frac{3}{4}$ measures, not to Parker, but to his father, George Ives. This is typical of Ives's apparent attempts after about the mid-1920s to disguise his debt to the composers whose music had influenced him most, in part by ascribing their ideas to his father. See Solomon, "Some Questions of Veracity" (he mentions this case on p. 462, n. 13), and Burkholder, "Charles Ives and His Fathers."

47. David Eiseman, "Charles Ives and the European Symphonic Tradition: A Historical Reappraisal" (Ph.D. diss., University of Illinois at Urbana-Champaign, 1972), 267. While at Yale, Ives probably attended the performances of this group, founded and conducted by his teacher.

48. Yellin, 504–6.

49. Burkholder, *Charles Ives*, 78–82.

50. Ibid., 81 and 138–39, n. 84.

51. Links between Ives and these composers have been proposed for decades, although Ives denied any influence. Leo Schrade, "Charles E. Ives: 1874–1954," *Yale Review*, n.s., 44 (June 1955): 535–45, compares Ives to Debussy, and Wulf Konold, "Neue Musik in der Neuen Welt: Der Komponist Charles Ives," *Musica* 26 (May–June 1972): 240, compares him to Mahler. Gianfranco Vinay, "Charles Ives e i musicisti europei: Anticipazioni e dipendenze," *Nuova revista musicale italiana* 7 (July–December 1973): 417–29, shows parallels with Mahler and Debussy and suggests that Ives knew and was influenced by their music, but is unable to prove this. Donald Mitchell, *Gustav Mahler: The Wunderhorn Years* (London: Faber and Faber, 1975), 169–71, and Robert P. Morgan, "Ives and Mahler: Mutual Responses at the End of an Era," *19th-*

Century Music 2 (July 1978): 72–81, compare Ives and Mahler without suggesting mutual influence. Recently, John Jeffrey Gibbens, "Debussy's Impact on Ives: An Assessment" (D.M.A. diss., University of Illinois at Urbana-Champaign, 1985), has assembled persuasive though circumstantial evidence that Ives probably encountered Debussy's music sometime after 1902 and was influenced by it, mostly negatively. David Michael Hertz, *Angels of Reality: Emersonian Unfoldings in Wright, Stevens, and Ives* (Carbondale and Edwardsville: Southern Illinois University Press, 1993), 93–113, presents an excellent analysis of the influence on Ives of modern composers, especially Debussy, and Ives's ambivalence toward and attempts to disguise that influence.

CHAPTER 3: THE ART OF PARAPHRASE

1. Wallach, "New England Education," 146.

2. For the church engagements, see Kirkpatrick, "Chronological Index of Dates," in *Memos*, 325. Cowell and Cowell, *Charles Ives*, 26, say Ives began studying organ at eleven; this may be a year too early, as are their dates for his appointments at the Congregational and Baptist Churches, pp. 26-27. Osborne, "Charles Ives the Organist," gives a brief account of Ives's career as organist.

3. Wallach, "New England Education," 146–48.

4. In the earliest extant list of his works, written on the back of a December 1928 calendar and printed in *Memos*, 148, Ives names this among his pieces for brass band and dates it to before the Ives family moved from Stevens Street to Chapel Place on 9 May 1889. In the "Conductor's Note" to the Fourth Symphony, second movement, published in the January 1929 issue of *New Music* and reprinted in Charles E. Ives, *Symphony No. 4* (New York: Associated Music Publishers, 1965), 13, Ives mentions an outdoor band performance of "a kind of paraphrase of 'Jerusalem the Golden,' a rather elaborate tone poem for those days," without naming himself as the composer.

5. f5018–22/n1920–24. Like George Ives's copy of the Polonaise, this cannot be dated by handwriting more closely than ca. 1888–92.

6. "New England Education," 144.

7. At two spots, this figure appears on a third stave, implying just such an effect. Of course, this could be rendered on the organ by using another manual with different registration.

8. f4723/Y6571&Q2154 and f4724–28/Y6572–76. The title "March or Two Step No I in F & B♭" appears on f4767/Y6570&Q2153, with "Danbury Band / Standard Orchestra / 1890—D[anbury] Fair" added in the upper right hand corner. Kirkpatrick, *Catalogue*, 93, and Sherwood, 19 May 1994, date the hand at ca. 1892, though this may be a later copy. Whichever date is correct, Ives's numbering suggests that this was his first march after *Holiday Quickstep*.

9. Two pieces reworked into the Second Symphony may have been medley overtures; see chapter 4, note 50. Later "medleys" are more like humorous quodlibets, such as the middle movement of the Trio for violin, cello, and piano; these are treated in chapter 10.

10. Henderson, *Tunebook*, 136–37, prints the original 1880 version of "That Old Cabin Home Upon the Hill" by Frank Dumont. But in both this march and the Trio

(mm. 68-83, cello), Ives uses a different version. The latter is printed anonymously under the title "Far Away in the South" (the opening words) in *The New Yale Song-Book: A Collection of Songs in Use by the Glee Club and Students of Yale University*, ed. G. Frank Goodale (New York: G. Schirmer, 1918), 40. I have been unable to trace its origins, but this version must have been current by ca. 1890. Ives identifies the tune in the manuscript of the march (at m. 65) as "Give me a home in the dear old South," the first words of the chorus in both versions.

11. The C♯ in m. 15 appears in all three manuscript copies, but the sharp is missing in the published score, an error that is repeated in the orchestration by William Schuman, who even inserts a cautionary natural sign. In the copies prepared by Ives and his father in 1892, the chord in m. 16 is the expected D major; it was originally so in the third copy, prepared by a copyist much later, perhaps in the 1940s, but the F♯ was then altered to F natural, perhaps at Ives's suggestion. The original reading is preferable.

12. Kirkpatrick (*Catalogue*, 222–23 and *New Grove*) dates these between ca. 1889 and 1893. Sherwood, 19 May 1994, dates the handwriting ca. 1898 (the Schubert Impromptu perhaps a bit later). Ives registered for Parker's course in instrumentation in both his junior and senior years, and these transcriptions may have been made for one of those classes; see *Memos*, appendix 6, pp. 181–82. Cowell and Cowell, *Charles Ives*, 26, say that Ives arranged music for his father's ensembles, but none of this material survives.

13. f7459–64/n1947–52.

14. For the date, see chapter 4, note 52.

15. Rather than treat the reworking of his own music as a separate category of borrowing, individual instances will be noted as we encounter them throughout this study. Very different from this reworking of an entire piece is Ives's occasional self-quotation, as in his use of the *Country Band March* theme in several later works. In this study, such borrowings are identified and treated like borrowings from any other source.

16. Earlier studies of the use of hymn tunes in this quartet appear in Charles Ward, "Use of Hymn Tunes," 41–49, and Wallach, "New England Education," 251–61 and 268–72. Ives dated the work 1896 in his lists of works, *Memos*, 149 and 154; so does Kirkpatrick (*Catalogue*, 57–59 and *New Grove*), basing his date on Ives's manuscript note that the last two movements were played in 1896 at New Haven's Center Church either by organ or by two violins with organ (for this performance, see also *Memos*, 54). Gayle Sherwood, personal communication, 23 May 1994 (hereafter Sherwood, 23 May 1993), dates the first movement sketches at 1898 and the score between 1898 and 1902. The extant sketches for movements 2, 3, and 4 are mainly on music paper 16:BC4, not found in dated manuscripts before 1900. (For the music paper types Ives used, see the "Index of Music Paper" in Kirkpatrick, *Catalogue*, 242-46, and Sherwood, "Choral Works," chap. 2.) Ives's scores are on paper of indeterminate date, but the handwriting is all ca. 1902. The earliest surviving sketches of the first sections of movements 3 and 4 and of the middle sections of movements 4 and 2 (which are substantially similar) are mostly continuous and show few changes, making it possible that Ives was working ca. 1902 from earlier versions of this music. This is not true of the middle section of the third movement, which is sketched from its embryonic

stages on f2892/n1347 and f2893/n1349+n1370 (as discussed below), and is unlikely to be true of the first section of the second movement; both of these probably date from ca. 1902, along with the final forms of all three movements as string quartet movements in ABA form. Despite Ives's implication in *Memos*, 73, the pieces played in Center Church in 1896 were probably not conceived for string quartet; Ives's string quartet transcription of the Beethoven Adagio, discussed above, was likely his first essay in the medium and is securely dated at ca. 1898.

17. In his list of works, *Memos*, 154. The Copyist 9 score of the quartet in this three-movement form is undated, and the keyboard reduction by the same copyist is on music paper 12:GS2, available no sooner than 1907. For the church performances, see the previous note.

18. The echoes of this motive in cello (m. 1) and viola (mm. 2 and 4) were after-thoughts; they do not appear in the first extant draft of the opening (f2890/n1363b), which resembles the reprise at m. 79.

19. See Arnold Schoenberg, "Brahms the Progressive," in *Style and Idea: Selected Writings of Arnold Schoenberg*, rev. ed., ed. Leonard Stein, trans. Leo Black (London: Faber & Faber, 1975), 398–441, especially pp. 399–401 and 408 on avoiding repetition and pp. 409–29 on asymmetrical phrasing and "musical prose." Ives admired Brahms, whom he regarded with Bach and Beethoven as "the best music we know" and "among the strongest and greatest in all art" (*Memos*, 100 and 135). See also *Memos*, 95; *Essays*, 22 and 73; and the reminiscences of his nephew Brewster Ives in Vivian Perlis, *Charles Ives Remembered: An Oral History* (New Haven: Yale University Press, 1974), 79. Ives kept a picture of Brahms on the door of his studio in West Redding (see the photograph in ibid., 90). For Brahms's influence on Ives, see the discussion of *Feldeinsamkeit* in chap. 2 and of the First and Second Symphonies in chap. 4.

20. *Memos*, 54.

21. Henderson, *Tunebook*, 199, finds *Bringing in the Sheaves* in the cello, m. 18. This is a variant of mm. 2 and 3 of the theme, implying that *Bringing in the Sheaves* was a source for that motive, though Henderson does not say so directly.

22. See, for example, Henderson's comment that this theme "might well be a quotation [whose] source, if there is one, could not be traced" ("Quotation," 96). In his *Tunebook*, 182, Henderson lists this theme (H206) in the category of "Unknown Tunes," a group that includes several themes from the First Quartet that are paraphrased from hymn tunes.

23. It is primarily this that lies behind the metric irregularity of this movement, rather than an emulation of Emerson's rhetorical style, as Wallach attempts to argue in "New England Education," 95–109, especially p. 107.

24. Henderson, *Tunebook*, 184, lists mm. 1–2 as Unknown Tune H212 and does not relate it to *Coronation* or *Shining Shore*.

25. The sketch for the coda (f2916/n1374) is in $\frac{4}{4}$ only; the polymeter first appears in Ives's full score (f2926/n1384). The sketch shows that Ives first tried to use the middle-section theme unchanged, but this did not make good counterpoint, and he could not save it through the inner parts (as he does elsewhere). His second attempt resembles the final version in adding a bar to the middle-section theme after its fourth bar to improve the fit.

26. Henderson, *Tunebook*, 199, identifies this as *Azmon* (H5), which resembles *Shining Shore*. It is more likely the latter because of its many other appearances throughout the movement. See the discussion below of similarities between *Azmon* and *Shining Shore*.

27. Henderson, *Tunebook*, 183, includes the reference in mm. 59–60 at the end of H208; the rest of this "unknown tune" uses parts of the middle-section theme as counterpoint to the cello, which has the leading melody at his point.

28. Henderson, *Tunebook*, 183, lists this theme as Unknown Tune H207.

29. The measure numbers here and below follow Ives's own, maintained by Kirkpatrick in his *Catalogue*, with the first ending as m. 56 and the first measure of the second ending as m. 57.

30. Henderson, "Quotation," 98; Wallach, "New England Education," 254. The comparison with *Nettleton* in the next example is adapted from Henderson.

31. The classic demonstration of Ives's preference for using melodically related tunes is Dennis Marshall's pathbreaking "Charles Ives's Quotations: Manner or Substance?" Another is Gordon Cyr, "Intervallic Structural Elements." "Modulating" from one tune to another, and the ambiguity it depends on, are discussed in the final two sections of this chapter.

32. For the sake of clarity, Ives's D♯–C♯–B♯–B♮ in mm. 44–45 have been changed to their enharmonic equivalents.

33. Indeed, in the first sketch of these passages (f2892/n1347), discussed below and transcribed in Example 3.16, the opening two measures of the theme appear in their original form, with a rising fourth; only in later drafts is the first note of the second measure raised an octave.

34. f2892/n1347 (the earlier of the two) and f2893/n1349+1370. These are part of a double folio (ff. 2r and 1r, respectively), interleaved with sketches for the retransition and coda of the second movement (ff. 1v and 2v). Ives seems to have filled these pages in the order 1v, 2v, 2r, 1r. There are exceptions to the two-stave arrangement on f2892, where the melody on staff 3 continues into staff 4, staves 9–11 comprise a single system, and staff 16 stands alone.

35. In this and other transcriptions from sketches, the clefs and the key and time signatures that Ives apparently assumed have been supplied in brackets, along with some accidentals and rests. When the passage parallels one in the published version, the latter has been used as a guide. Other cases are less certain. The apparent B♯ after the *Beulah Land* fragment suggests that Ives may have been thinking in a key other than C major. If D major were held over from the beginning of the staff, these measures would resemble a statement of mm. 3–4 of *Beulah Land* in B minor. Whatever the key, the rhythm and contour of *Beulah Land* are unmistakable.

36. In the final version, this reference is less obvious, just four notes in parallel thirds repeated in sequence and extended in a longer descending line.

37. Henderson, *Tunebook*, 184, gives mm. 49–52 as Unknown Tune H211. In this passage in this sketch, many of the flags are askew and may have been added later to change even rhythms to dotted ones; many of the dots are missing and have been supplied in the transcription in Example 3.16. The beginning of staff 9 (before the key change) apparently offers a revision of the material beneath it on staff 10.

38. The material on this page of sketches is laid out in seven systems of two staves each and was apparently entered in this order: A, on systems 1–3; B, on systems 4–5; C, on the right half of system 5; D, at the end of system 6 and the beginning of system 7, leaving the remainder of system 6 temporarily vacant; E, at the end of system 7; and (not transcribed here) three measures of sketches for the first section of this movement (mm. 20–22), on the left half of system 6. Each draft is continuous; the gaps in Example 3.17 result from the alignment of parallel measures and show where later versions inserted new material.

39. The first eight measures of version A differ significantly from the final score only in m. 42, shortened to $\frac{2}{4}$ in the final version after Ives noted the change on a copyist's keyboard arrangement (f2908/q4677) made in or after 1907 (for the date, see note 17, above). The numbers under the last three measures of version A indicate an attempt to shorten the passage by one measure by dropping the beats that lack numbers written under them (beat 1 of m. 10 and beats 2 and 3 of m. 11).

40. See Ives's annotations, Kirkpatrick, *Catalogue*, 57–59, and note 16 above.

41. See Sinclair, "Microfilm Concordance," 57 and 59. If the fourth movement is adapted from a work of 1896, the thematic link to the fugue may have been fortuitous and perhaps was a factor in the decision to group the two existing movements together. The reference later in the fourth movement to the episode in the first movement—part of a section of the fourth movement that was apparently first sketched about 1902—goes beyond coincidence and was probably added to reinforce the cyclic connection to the first movement.

42. Wallach discusses fugue in "New England Education," 261–72, including a thorough analysis of the present movement. Especially relevant is his observation (p. 261) that "the ability to combine a germ motive with itself, work contrasting material against it, and abstract its rhythmic and motivic properties to create thematic transformations [is] acquired in the study of fugue." His comments on the relation between motivic coherence and "quotation" are on pp. 249–51.

43. Henderson, *Tunebook*, 199, finds *Christmas* (H12, arranged from Handel) in the viola, mm. 12–13. The contour here is like the first seven notes of *Christmas* in a somewhat different rhythm, but the resemblance seems to be an unintended result of the development of Ives's countersubject (in violin II, mm. 11–14). The figure recurs only once (mm. 62–63, viola), in a similar context, and nothing else in the movement seems to resemble *Christmas*. Nor did Ives use this tune in any other work, other than the revision of this movement as the third movement of the Fourth Symphony. It seems likely that he did not intend to use *Christmas* in the quartet movement but recognized the resemblance of this passage to the hymn tune when scoring the quartet movement for the symphony and assigned the second statement of this passage to horn or trombone (mm. 65–67), converting a coincidental similarity into a conscious reference.

44. Reinbert de Leeuw, "Charles Ives—Zijn Muziek: Inleidung, Ives' Gebruik van Muzikall Materiaal," in J. Bernlef and Reinbert de Leeuw, *Charles Ives* (Amsterdam: De Bezige Bij, 1969), 142; the partial translation by Bertus Polman, *Student Musicologists at Minnesota* 6 (1975–76): 136, omits the musical example. Henderson, *Tunebook*, 199, does not list this borrowing. On Ives's performances of this fugue, see Osborne, "Charles Ives the Organist," 58–59. Ives's borrowing of a Bach episode for an episode

in his own fugue is like his paraphrasing of symphonic transition sections in his Second Symphony, discussed in the next chapter, and the conflation here of Bach with Lowell Mason parallels that of Bach with Stephen Foster in the symphony's finale.

45. This is anticipated in violin II, mm. 48–49 and 52–53, as Wallach points out, "New England Education," 271. This movement was revised as the third movement of the Fourth Symphony, and in his review of the premiere and first recording of that work, Kurt Stone identified this third phrase of *Missionary Hymn* as part of Brahms's Alto Rhapsody, which it coincidentally resembles; see his "Ives's Fourth Symphony: A Review," *The Musical Quarterly* 52 (January 1966): 8, and Henderson, "Quotation," 13, which repeats the attribution. This is a "phantom quotation," heard by a competent listener though almost certainly unintended by Ives. See the discussion of this phenomenon in the final section of this chapter.

46. See Wallach, "New England Education," 269–70.

47. Kirkpatrick, *Catalogue*, 58. See also Wallach, "New England Education," 250.

48. Perhaps coincidentally, several images in *Missionary Hymn* are echoed in the hymns of the middle movements: a mountain or mount (*Beulah Land* and *Nettleton*), a strand or shore (*Shining Shore* and *Beulah Land*), a fountain or fount (*Nettleton*), a river or stream (*Beulah Land, Nettleton*, and perhaps *Shining Shore*, which refers to the Jordan), and a sea (*Beulah Land*).

49. See Kirkpatrick, *Catalogue*, 57–59.

50. See ibid., 206, on *The Side Show* and p. 112 for the lost earlier version. The text may date from as late as 1921. See also Kirkpatrick's note on this song in the liner notes to *Charles Ives: The 100th Anniversary*, sound recording (New York: Columbia M4 32504, 1974).

51. For the American performances, see H. Earle Johnson, *First Performances in America to 1900: Works with Orchestra* (Detroit: Information Coordinators, 1979), 357–58.

52. As does Henderson in his discussion of this piece, "Quotation," 21.

53. See his criticism of Tchaikovsky's repetitiveness in *Essays*, 99.

54. Henderson, "Quotation," 168.

55. There are many others; Henderson gives several examples in "Quotation," 169–74 and 30–32. Example 3.20 follows the published score, Charles E. Ives, *Fugue in Four Keys on "The Shining Shore,"* ed. John Kirkpatrick (Bryn Mawr, Pa.: Merion Music, 1975). Wallach, "New England Education," 371–73, prints a partial edition, breaking off before this point. Despite Wallach's objections (p. 370), Kirkpatrick's version is convincing. See chap. 5, note 27.

56. *114 Songs*, 36, where it is dated 1920, perhaps for the final revision. Kirkpatrick, *Catalogue*, 194, suggests ?1910 on the basis of a later memo and notes a lost earlier version for vocal quartet and organ (Kirkpatrick 5C40, ibid., p. 142). Gayle Sherwood, personal communication, 27 May 1994 (hereafter Sherwood, 27 May 1994), dates the handwriting of the surviving sketch to ca. 1914.

57. This part of Example 3.21 is adapted from Henderson, "Quotation," 173, but uses the version of *Bethany* in $\frac{6}{4}$ meter, more common in the hymnals Ives used than the $\frac{4}{4}$ meter version given by Henderson here and in his *Tunebook*, 17.

58. Henderson, "Quotation," 14. He does list the allusion in his *Tunebook*, 212. See also the analysis in Schoffman, "Songs of Charles Ives," 174–84, who notes the refer-

ences in mm. 3–4 and 7 described below. It is unlikely that Ives had in mind the "Lebe wohl" motive from Beethoven's Piano Sonata in E♭ Major, Op. 81a ("Les Adieux"), as suggested by Feder, *Charles Ives*, 313.

59. Neither sketches nor manuscript survive; see Kirkpatrick, *Catalogue*, 208. The date 1921 is from *114 Songs*, 6.

60. Ives dated the quartet 1911 in *Memos*, 73, and 1911–13 (1907 for the second movement) in his work-lists (ibid., 161). Gayle Sherwood, letter of 15 July 1994, confirms that the extant sketches for the first two movements are in a hand of between 1907 and 1914, close to the 1914 hand; the finale is in a hand of ca. 1914.

61. Wolfgang Rathert, *The Seen and Unseen: Studien zum Werk von Charles Ives* (Munich: Emil Katzbichler, 1991), 140–50, especially the examples on pp. 144 and 147; quoting from p. 145 ("das geheime Hauptthema des Satzes").

CHAPTER 4: MODELING AND PARAPHRASE IN THE FIRST AND SECOND SYMPHONIES

1. Thomas Willis, liner notes for *Charles Ives, Symphony No. 1*, sound recording by the Chicago Symphony Orchestra, conducted by Morton Gould (New York: RCA Victor LSC-2893, 1966). For an analysis of the First Symphony, see Roy V. Magers, "Aspects of Form in the Symphonies of Charles Ives" (Ph.D. diss., Indiana University, 1975), 28–79.

2. Ives states in *Memos*, 51 and 87, that he wrote the symphony in college, and in his lists of works dated it 1896–98 (ibid., 149 and 155). In memos on the scores (printed in Kirkpatrick, *Catalogue*, 1–3) he indicated that the work was begun in 1897 (an 1895 date of completion for the first movement is certainly too early), that the second and fourth movements were accepted as part of his thesis for Parker's course in June 1898, and that the full score was copied in 1903. Sherwood, 23 May 1994, dates the handwriting on the surviving manuscripts slightly later: the sketch and score-sketch for the first movement ca. 1898 and all other work on the symphony between 1898 and 1902. If Ives did submit movements of this symphony to Parker, perhaps earlier versions than those in the extant manuscripts, Parker would likely have kept them, as he did most student work; see Sherwood, "Choral Works," chap. 5.

3. Ives Collection, box 60, folder 10. See *Charles Ives Papers*, ed. Vivian Perlis (New Haven: Yale University Music Library, 1983), 188.

4. Henderson, *Tunebook*, 190, does not cite this or any other allusions in Ives's First Symphony to other symphonies; the only borrowing he lists is that of *Shining Shore* in the first movement (discussed below). Eiseman, "Charles Ives and the European Symphonic Tradition," 246–47, notes the similarity of these two themes in mood, scoring, and largely pentatonic character, and Paul Echols, "The Music for Orchestra," *Music Educators Journal* 61/2 (October 1974): 32–33, mentions the resemblance between the two passages.

5. In the earliest extant sketch (f6422/n2697, staves 10–12), m. 2 is first written as F–G–A–A–G, like m. 4 but an octave lower; this is then replaced by the final version. The first version also derives from the Dvořák theme, following the

Db–Eb–F–(Ab)–F–Eb contour in mm. 15–16 of the latter, but the revision makes Ives's theme more shapely and interesting.

6. The dotted rhythm in m. 6 was a late revision, showing that Ives originally planned to avoid citing Dvořák's rhythmic pattern entirely. In the first sketch (f6422/n2697, staves 10–12) and score-sketch (f0085/n0375), m. 6 has two eighths and a quarter on D–C–A, the D tied over from the previous measure. Dotted rhythm at this spot in the theme first appears later in the score-sketch (f0089/n0141), where the horn plays the melody; here (m. 86) the rhythm is as in the final version, but the notes are C–Bb–A (as in the trombone in the published score). The dotted figure on C–C–A is finalized in the next stage, the full score (m. 86 on f0098/n0138 and m. 109 on f0101/n0151; pp. 1 and 3, which would include the first statements of the theme, are missing).

7. See, for example, his comments on Tchaikovsky in *Essays*, 99; on Stravinsky and Ravel in ibid., 39, and *Memos*, 138; and on a violinist's comparison of an Ives sonata to one of Daniel Gregory Mason, ibid., 123. Feder, *Charles Ives*, 147–49, notes Ives's ambivalence towards Dvořák, as the older composer's "emulator and rival" (p. 149).

8. More common is the presence in the second theme of an element that has appeared in both first theme and transition. For example, in the first movement of Schubert's "Unfinished" Symphony, the rhythmic figure that begins the second theme (quarter, dotted quarter, eighth, m. 44) appears in the first theme (m. 18) and throughout the transition. Dvořák prepares his second-theme motive by developing a figure from the first theme; m. 28, clarinets and bassoons, is treated in sequence in mm. 63–72 in the violins, slightly altered in m. 73, and varied again to become the new motive in m. 74. This places Dvořák in the century-old tradition of linking the first and second themes, although such gradual variation is unusual. In the Ives, there is little or no apparent relation between the anticipated motive and anything in the first theme, although Eiseman suggests a subtle intervallic link in "Charles Ives and the European Symphonic Tradition," 174–75. Despite apparently following Dvořák's lead, Ives ends up doing something even more unusual.

9. Eiseman, "Charles Ives and the European Symphonic Tradition," 247–48, likens the Ives passage to Tchaikovsky's Fourth Symphony, fourth movement, mm. 245–47, but the resemblance to the *Pathétique* is much closer.

10. Lawrence Starr, "The Early Styles of Charles Ives," *19th-Century Music* 7 (Summer 1983): 76, compares the two movements in general terms.

11. See the list of New Haven Symphony concerts in Eiseman, "Charles Ives and the European Symphonic Tradition," 166–69.

12. The earliest extant sketch of this theme (f0001/n0104, top, where it is a fourth higher than in the final version) includes only the first two measures of *Shining Shore* (mm. 10–11 of the published score), followed immediately by the figure from reh. J, mm. 137–41 of the final version (shown in Example 4.7), in B minor. Thus, the latter was first conceived as part of the opening theme and may owe its shape as much to *Shining Shore* as to the motives from Schubert's "Unfinished" Symphony shown in Example 4.7.

13. Henderson, *Tunebook*, 190, lists the motive from *Shining Shore* but not these references to *Beulah Land*.

14. The English horn melody from the "New World" Symphony, paraphrased in Ives's second movement, acquired its text ("Goin' home") and its status as a pseudo-spiritual only later, in the adaptation by William Arms Fisher, *Goin' Home: From the Largo of the New World Symphony* (Philadelphia: Oliver Ditson, 1922).

15. Henderson, *Tunebook*, omits both songs. Kirkpatrick dates *On Judges' Walk* 1893–98? (*Catalogue*, 177, and *New Grove*) and suggests that Ives derived the symphonic theme from the song (see *Memos*, 37, n. 10). However, Ives and Henry Bellamann both stated that the song was adapted from the symphony; see Ives's memo on the ink copy of the song, in Kirkpatrick, *Catalogue*, 177, and Henry Bellamann, "Charles Ives: The Man and His Music," *Musical Quarterly* 19 (January 1933): 53. According to Sherwood, 27 May 1994, the only extant manuscript of the song, a fair ink copy, is on 12:OD2 paper, available from 1899, in a hand of ca. 1902. If Ives and Bellamann are correct, this is a likely date for the song. There is no manuscript for *Rough Wind*, which Ives dated 1902 in *114 Songs*, 155.

16. William K. Kearns, *Horatio Parker, 1863–1919: His Life, Music, and Ideas* (Metuchen, N.J., and London: Scarecrow Press, 1990), 241. The first to suggest that Ives's use of borrowed music might stem from Parker's was Perry, *Charles Ives*, xvii, 9–10, and 12.

17. See the comments quoted and cited in Gilbert Chase, *America's Music: From the Pilgrims to the Present*, 2nd ed. (New York: McGraw-Hill, 1966), 377, and 3rd ed. (Urbana: University of Illinois Press, 1987), 380, and Kearns, *Horatio Parker*, 117–18 and 129–30.

18. Kearns, *Horatio Parker*, 241; see also p. 117 for a defense of Parker's originality by a critic writing in 1899.

19. See datings on the manuscripts, cited in Kirkpatrick, *Catalogue*, 3–7. The 1909 copyist's copy is lost but for pp. 13–14 of the third movement (f7791–92), for which a new ending was substituted about 1910; see note 34, below. In his work-lists, Ives dated the symphony variously at 1899–1902 and 1897–1901 (*Memos*, 150 and 155).

20. Personal communication, 23 May 1994. The first movement sketches are on unidentified paper in handwriting from ca. 1902–7. The first sketches for the second movement are on 18:GS5 paper, not available before 1907, and the hand is ca. 1907 for all sketches. The first sketches for the third movement are on paper available by the early 1890s but in a hand of ca. 1902–7; later sketches and the score-sketch are on 16:gS4 paper, not available before 1907, and are in the 1907 hand. There are no sketches for the fourth movement prior to the score-sketch, which is in the 1907 hand. The sketches and score-sketch for the finale are in a hand from ca. 1907 or possibly later, and the score-sketch and some of the sketches are on paper not available before 1907. Ives's full score for the whole work is ca. 1907.

21. The fourth movement was at one time not a separate movement but a slow introduction at the start of the finale. In the score-sketch, the present fourth movement is marked "IV Intro" and the final Allegro "V or IV." The full score has continuous pagination through both movements (from p. 1), entitles the gathering "S #2 Intro IV," and has no indication of a new movement beginning at the Allegro. For these annotations, see Kirkpatrick, *Catalogue*, 6–7.

22. f0362, quoted in Kirkpatrick, *Catalogue*, 4.

23. Most notable are Leonard Bernstein, comments at a concert of the New York Philharmonic, printed as liner notes on his recording of the symphony (New York: Columbia ML 6289/MS 6889, 1966); Charles, "Use of Borrowed Materials"; Henderson, "Quotation," 207 and 102–9; Charles Ward, "Use of Hymn Tunes," 49–65 and 131–32; Sterne, "Quotations"; Eiseman, "Charles Ives and the European Symphonic Tradition," 239–49; and J. Peter Burkholder, "'Quotation' and Paraphrase in Ives's Second Symphony," *19th-Century Music* 11 (Summer 1987): 3–25, on which the rest of this chapter is based.

24. Sterne, "Quotations," 43; Charles, "Use of Borrowed Materials," 108, Example 9c. I adapt their examples in my own. William W. Austin, *"Susanna," "Jeanie," and "The Old Folks at Home": The Songs of Stephen C. Foster from His Time to Ours,* 2nd ed. (Urbana: University of Illinois Press, 1987), 317–30, explores the significance to Ives of this and other borrowings from Foster.

25. fo353/no303, fo354/no319, and fo356/no349a+o301. Henderson, *Tunebook,* 190, does not list *Nettleton* as a source for this movement.

26. The decision to borrow from Foster may have been prompted in part by Ives's desire to allude to Brahms's First Symphony at the opening of the fourth movement, which parallels the opening of the first movement. See the discussion below.

27. Noted by Sterne, "Quotations," 43, although he appears unaware that the violin motive in m. 23 is based on an existing fiddle tune.

28. In the earliest sketch for this passage (fo357/no296), this theme appears in its original note values, syncopated against the triple-time bar lines, like the phrases from "Massa's in de Cold Ground" and "Columbia, the Gem of the Ocean" in this movement. This was canceled before the other parts were filled in and replaced with the altered version in the published score.

29. See Sterne, "Quotations," 43.

30. It is possible that Ives had the hymn in mind here, rather than the college song. The hymn text would fit better with the other sources for this movement.

31. See Charles, "Use of Borrowed Materials," 106–107.

32. In the full score (fo438/qo236) and in later versions, Ives modifies the opening of *Hamburg* in cello I at mm. 329–32 to produce what seems to be a brief allusion to *America,* while *Hamburg* continues in the other low strings and trombones; see Charles, "Use of Borrowed Materials," 106. This is hardly audible with everything else going on, and it suits the harmony so perfectly that it may be an accident, or perhaps a private joke with the cellists.

33. f6569/q5001&n2324. Only the top line is given here. Other early drafts of this passage appear in fo444/q3118&n2323 and fo445/n2322. Both use ideas apparently first tried in f6569, suggesting they are later.

34. This coda was apparently added in 1909 or 1910. The original ending appears on pp. 12–13 of the 1907 full score (fo469–70/qo254–55), where it is crossed out; on a single leaf of a copyist's score (f7791–92, numbered pp. 13–14), probably part of the 1909 Tams copy, the rest of which is lost (see Kirkpatrick, *Catalogue,* 7); and in the parts (fo474–91), apparently copied at Tams from the 1909 score. The new coda appears in full score on a separate double leaf (fo471–73/qo256–58) and is added in Ives's hand to one of the copyist's parts for violin I (fo480). If the original ending was part of the 1909 score, it must have been detached and the new ending substituted before Ives

sent the score in 1910 to Walter Damrosch, who never returned it; see Frank R. Rossiter, *Charles Ives and His America* (New York: Liveright, 1975), 152. The note on the last page of the short-score sketch (f0453/n0345), "from 112 to end about or [added at?] 1909–10, but can't find," may refer to a sketch of this coda.

35. That Ives heard this similarity is shown by a sketch (f0448/n1299, staves 4–5) in which the first *Materna* motive is replaced by the figure from m. 10 of *Beulah Land*. Compare this to the parallel passage in mm. 5–13 of f0445/n2322.

36. The Wagner allusion was suggested by Bernstein and echoed by Sterne, "Quotations," 41, and Ballantine, "Charles Ives and the Meaning of Quotation," 179; the possible reference to Brahms was also first noted by Bernstein and repeated by Charles, "Use of Borrowed Materials," 105. Henderson, "Quotation," 11, and *Tunebook*, 190, repeats the latter suggestion and posits the reference to *There is a Happy Land*.

37. See Kenneth Robert Mays, "The Use of Hymn Tunes in the Works of Charles Ives" (M.M. thesis, Indiana University, 1961), 47, and Charles Ward, "Use of Hymn Tunes," 58 and 131. Other instruments echo the figure in mm. 40–42.

38. Henderson, "Quotation," 137. Bernstein and others have mistaken the reference to this tune at movement's end for the motto of Beethoven's Fifth Symphony.

39. In *Stephen Foster Song Book: Original Sheet Music of 40 Songs by Stephen Collins Foster*, ed. Richard Jackson (New York: Dover, 1974), 14–17.

40. f0508/n3119. The Roman-numeral chord indications of Example 4.21 are in the sketch in Ives's hand. Internal evidence strongly argues for this as the earliest extant sketch, for it shows Ives trying out ideas not repeated elsewhere and groping toward and fixing upon ideas that recur in the other sketches.

41. Henderson, "Quotation," 106, and *Tunebook*, 191, finds the first two measures of the fiddle tune "The Kerry Dance" (H165) in m. 11. Although the reference, if any, is distorted and fleeting, Ives may have first intended to suggest a fiddle tune in this theme.

42. They first appear in what seems to be the next surviving sketch (f2349/q0313 and f2350/q0309&0311), a continuity draft of the complete first theme area with "Columbia" in the bass in mm. 1–13. Ives identified this as a draft or reconstruction of *The American Woods Overture*, from which he said the finale was partly derived, and wrote his Yale address on both pages. But the address on f2350 was added after about 1927, when a photostat was made, and the music of at least the first theme must postdate the first sketch of the theme (f0508/n3119), which is on music paper not available before 1907. See Kirkpatrick, *Catalogue*, 35, and the discussion of this case of retrospective dating in Solomon, "Some Questions of Veracity," 454–55.

43. The fife tune first appears in the sketches on staff 9 of the same page as the draft of the theme shown in Example 4.21, apparently as a substitute for mm. 3–4 of the theme in counterpoint with mm. 3–4 of "Columbia." Henderson notes the drum figure in his *Tunebook*, 7 (he calls it a "roll-off"), but omits it from his indices because, strictly speaking, it is not a tune. For the distinction between the street beat and the roll-off, see chap. 6, note 75.

44. There are many variants of "Turkey in the Straw," also known as "Old Zip Coon"; Example 4.22 follows Henderson, *Tunebook*, 163. The retrograde form of the cell featured in mm. 37–40 is present from the cell's first appearance in the symphony; see Examples 4.11 and 4.12.

45. The first draft of these measures appears on f2349/q0313.

46. f0507/n0299. In this sketch, the first period of the countermelody is similar to the final version. The references to "Turkey in the Straw" and "Long, Long Ago" in the middle of the countermelody and to the former at mm. 37ff first appear in the final sketch in short score (f0514–15/n0362–63).

47. As noted by Garry Clarke, *Essays on American Music* (Westport, Conn.: Greenwood Press, 1977), 119.

48. When this theme reappears in the present context, it can be heard as a transformation of the B phrase of the second theme of the finale; see the discussion and musical example in Sterne, "Quotations," 45.

49. The earliest sketch of this passage is f0504/n0307, part of a two-stave continuity draft for the latter half of the movement. The next version is the short-score sketch, f0526/n0374, followed by the full score, f0557/q0292.

50. Kirkpatrick, *Catalogue*, 3–7. As noted above, all the surviving sources are from 1902 or later, but it is possible that some of the music was adapted from earlier works that are lost. Which movements derive from which overtures is not clear. On the short-score sketch of the present fourth movement, Ives wrote "from Overture 'Town, Gown & State' in These United States for Brass Band 1896 played Savin Rock NH Ct." On the title page of the second sketch of the first movement, he wrote "Down E[ast] Overture . . . 2nd part 1898." These attributions would be clear were not the first and fourth movements adaptations of the same music. A possible solution, though not the only one, is that "Town, Gown and State" referred to an earlier form of the fifth movement, for which the fourth is an introduction, while "Down East Overture" was the name for the "2nd part" of the symphony, meaning the second movement, to which the first movement serves as an introduction. This is not entirely satisfactory as an explanation of either the overtures' titles or the borrowed tunes. While "Columbia, the Gem of the Ocean" is a logical culmination for "Town, Gown and State," representing patriotism, and "De Camptown Races" might represent the town, the tune most closely associated with the academic gown is "Where, O Where are the Verdant Freshmen," which is an important theme in the second, not the fifth, movement (though it appears in passing in the latter).

51. Charles E. Ives, "Notes on the Symphony," in *Symphony No. 2* (New York: Peer International, 1951), 1. A similar note appears in *Memos*, 155.

52. Ives dated the Postlude to 1895, and Kirkpatrick guessed the same date for the Overture (*Catalogue*, 29, and *New Grove*). Gayle Sherwood, personal communication, 1 June 1994 (hereafter Sherwood, 1 June 1994), dates both ca. 1898 by handwriting.

53. f0354/n0319.

54. In the first sketch of the first movement (f0356/n0349a+0301), the transition at m. 93 was altogether different; the allusion to Bach first appears in the second sketch (f0360/n0317). What appears to be the earliest extant draft for the complete first theme area of the finale (f2349/q0313) gives violin I as in m. 25 of the published version and continues this idea in sequence, but lacks the lower parts, which confirm the reference to Bach. These first appear in the short-score sketch (f0513/n0361). The notes that fall on the beats in violin I alternate falling steps and rising minor thirds, as in the top line of mm. 28–29 of the Bach Sinfonia. The resemblance in the first full sketch may have suggested the borrowing here, which in

turn may have prompted the borrowings from the same Bach episode in the first and fourth movements.

55. Henderson, *Tunebook*, 179, lists this as Unknown Tune H192. It is identified in Sterne, "Quotations," 41, and Magers, "Aspects of Form," 86.

56. That the motive is the exposition's closing tag is easier to see in the sketch, score-sketch, and full score (f0386/no322, f0395/no330, and f0421–22/q0221–22 respectively), all of which call for a reprise of the exposition and present first and second endings, as does the Brahms. The reprise is suppressed in the published version of the Ives, making the end of the exposition less clear; it will be restored in Jonathan Elkus's forthcoming critical edition. The first ending (missing in the sketch) consists of a two-measure bridge following a slightly modified m. 127. Note that Ives borrows from Brahms not the closing tag itself, but a figure from another place, which he then treats exactly as Brahms treats the closing tag in the model.

57. Charles, "Use of Borrowed Materials," 106; see Henderson, *Tunebook*, 190 for the Brahms motive (H177). The resemblance consists of the 3–2–1 descent in dotted rhythm that opens Ives's melody and is paralleled by notes 3–5 of the Brahms. In mm. 149–51, Ives alters the second period of his theme, rhythmically augmented, so that it resembles the Brahms motive, despite the very different metric and harmonic context. The allusion is probably intentional, given all the direct references to Brahms in Ives's symphony.

58. Kirkpatrick, *Catalogue*, 4, suggests that the main motive for this passage derives from the opening four notes of "Blessed Assurance"; Sterne, "Quotations," 41, disputes this. The motive is much closer to Brahms, and the resemblance to the gospel song is probably fortuitous.

59. See Ives's comments about his father's teaching, in *Memos*, 237. Of the classical allusions noted above, Sterne, "Quotations," 41, lists the Brahms references in the first and second movements and the longer of the two *Tristan* references in the third movement; Charles, "Use of Borrowed Materials," 105–6, notes the Bach quotation in the finale and the passage from Brahms's Third Symphony in the second movement; Henderson, *Tunebook*, lists the *Tristan* borrowings in the third movement; and John Kirkpatrick noted the reference in the first and fourth movements to Bach's F Minor Sinfonia in his own copy of the Second Symphony score, which he kindly permitted me to consult. The references to Brahms's *Vier ernste Gesänge* and First Symphony at the end of the fourth movement (the latter repeated in the finale) have apparently not been identified before. It is perhaps not surprising that every commentator has arrived at a different list of borrowings in the Second Symphony. Sterne, 42, mentions the problem of securely identifying all the references to other music and notes "the desirability of seeking safety behind Kirkpatrick's convenient phrase: 'what else?,'" used in Kirkpatrick's *Catalogue* at the ends of lists of borrowings for several works.

60. On the first two, see note 36 above. Bernstein finds the opening motive of Beethoven's Fifth Symphony in the third movement but does not say where; the closest approximation is in the horn at m. 130, part of a last reference to *Missionary Chant*, the source for the similar figures in the middle section of the movement.

61. Bernstein includes the "New World" Symphony in his list of quotations, as does Ballantine, "Charles Ives and the Meaning of Quotation," 179. Both also say that Ives

quotes Bruckner, without making clear where or what they mean; see the comment in Charles, "Use of Borrowed Materials," 103.

62. See the comment on this resemblance by Hugh Arthur Scott, "Indebtedness in Music," *The Musical Quarterly* 13 (October 1927): 504.

63. Compare the last nine measures of the Dvořák with mm. 274–78 of the Ives: they share a 1–3–5–6 rising bass figure in quarter notes moving through two octaves (on the tonic, rising and falling, in the Dvořák; on the subdominant, rising only, in the Ives) and an identical rhythm of closing tonic chords (twice as fast in the Ives). Ives's 1907 full score ends with a sustained tonic chord on the downbeat of m. 278, tied over to the next measure, and this ending closely resembles Dvořák's. Measures 278–80 of the published score, including the dissonant last chord, an eleven-note crunch, were substituted for the original ending at a much later date, probably in the 1940s (see Kirkpatrick's note in *Memos*, 155). Henry Cowell, reviewing the symphony's premiere in "Current Chronicle," *The Musical Quarterly* 37 (July 1951): 402, notes that Ives told him that such a dissonance "was the formula for signifying the very end of the very last dance of all: the players played any old note, good and loud, for the last chord." The original ending is preferable; the final dissonance in the published version is a Bronx cheer out of the spirit of the rest of the work.

64. The first movement of Tchaikovsky's *Pathétique* Symphony includes a similar modulation around the circle of minor thirds from B minor through D, F, and G♯ minor and back to B minor (at reh. A, mm. 30–37). Both the Fourth and the Sixth Symphonies may have served as models for this type of key relationship and for Ives's choice of keys.

65. See the manuscript annotations cited in note 21 above and in Kirkpatrick, *Catalogue*, 6–7.

66. Perhaps it was his desire to allude to Brahms here that led Ives to change the opening theme of the first and fourth movements, which had originally been paraphrased from *Nettleton*, to the theme based on "Massa's in de Cold Ground." Brahms's opening motive is later transformed into his major-mode principal theme, and the resemblance between this theme and Ives's opening motive has been pointed out by Brunhilde Sonntag, *Untersuchungen zur Collagetechnik in der Musik des 20. Jahrhunderts* (Regensburg: Gustav Bosse, 1977), 121.

67. Thanks to Jonathan Elkus for insisting to me that the form of Ives's finale was not a modified sonata-rondo but a sonata without development, which led me to discover its close relationship to the Brahms First Symphony finale.

68. For an extended argument emphasizing European influences on Ives's First and Second Symphonies, see Eiseman, "Charles Ives and the European Symphonic Tradition."

69. Sterne, "Quotations," 43–44.

70. Ibid., 45.

71. Since some of the borrowings in the Second Symphony were added after Ives began composing his first collages, the influence may go both ways; just as reworking all the themes and countermelodies of the symphony from borrowed tunes prepared the way for collage, so the later additions to the symphony may have been inspired by his experience with collage.

72. Ives, *Essays*, 81.

1. Although both cumulative form and cumulative setting are forms, the latter is also a way of using existing music. Thus, the latter term will be used more often in this study, although the two are to some extent interchangeable in discussing Ives's music. Other composers have used cumulative form with original themes; some examples are discussed in chap. 6.

2. Cowell and Cowell, *Ives*, 142. See also p. 163 ("Ives habitually regards clarity as an ultimate, not a beginning") and p. 186, on *Paracelsus*.

3. The first to note this tendency was apparently Henry Bellamann, "Charles Ives," 49, who observed that in some works "the development leads into the theme which, not infrequently, is stated in its entirety only at the end." Others include Adeline Marie Logan's pioneering study of Ives's musical borrowings, "American National Music in the Compositions of Charles Ives" (M.M. thesis, University of Washington, 1943), 71–72; Mays, "Use of Hymn Tunes," 20; Gooding, "A Study of the Quotation Process," 3 and 6; Newman, "Songs of Charles Ives," I: 169–75; de Leeuw, "Charles Ives," 172 and 174 (pp. 160 and 161 in Polman's translation); Eugene Gratovich, "The Sonatas for Violin and Piano by Charles Ives: A Critical Commentary and Concordance of the Printed Editions and the Autographs and Manuscripts of the Yale Ives Collection" (D.M.A. diss., Boston University, 1968), 343; Henderson, "Quotation," 115, 183, and 193; Charles Ward, "Use of Hymn Tunes," 30–31; Robert P. Morgan, "Rewriting Music History: Second Thoughts on Ives and Varèse," *Musical Newsletter* 3/1 (January 1973): 9; Eugene Gratovich, "The Violin Sonatas," *Music Educators Journal* 61/2 (October 1974): 58 (reprinted as "The Violin Sonatas of Charles E. Ives," *The Strad* 85 [December 1974]: 471); H. Wiley Hitchcock, *Ives* (London,: Oxford University Press, 1977), 26; Stephen Blum, "Ives's Position in Social and Musical History," *The Musical Quarterly* 63 (October 1977): 468–69; William Masselos, "Preface," in Charles E. Ives, *Sonata No. 1 for Piano*, rev. ed., ed. Lou Harrison, William Masselos, and Paul Echols (New York: Peer International, 1979), iii; Lora Louise Gingerich, "Processes of Motivic Transformation in the Keyboard and Chamber Music of Charles E. Ives" (Ph.D. diss., Yale University, 1983), 272–77; Henderson, *Tunebook*, 8; and many of the studies mentioned in the following note. In a 1974 interview, Robert Shaw spoke of Ives's "reverse sort of sense of development in which fragmentation precedes assembly or statement," saying "there must be a musicological name for it"; Gordon H. Lamb, "Interview with Robert Shaw," *Choral Journal* 15/8 (April 1975): 6. The first to define a distinctive form based on this idea was Burkholder, "The Evolution of Charles Ives's Music," 385–407, which introduced the terms "cumulative setting" and "cumulative form."

4. For more extensive analyses of the movements treated in this chapter, see particularly the following: Charles Ward, "Use of Hymn Tunes," 66–103; on the Third Symphony, Magers, "Aspects of Form," 143–92, Ellison, "Ives' Use of American 'Popular' Tunes," 30–32, and James Vincent Badolato, "The Four Symphonies of Charles Ives: A Critical, Analytical Study of the Musical Style of Charles Ives" (Ph.D. diss., Catholic University of America, 1978), 113–51; on the violin sonatas, Laurence Perkins, "The Sonatas for Violin and Piano by Charles Ives" (M.M. thesis, Eastman School of Music, 1961), Lee Cyril Rosen, "The Violin Sonatas of Charles Ives and the Hymn" (B.M. the-

sis, University of Illinois at Urbana-Champaign, 1965), and Andrew Reed Rangell, "The Violin-Piano Sonatas of Charles Ives: An Analytical Discussion" (Ph.D. diss., The Juilliard School, 1976); on the Fourth Violin Sonata, William Edgar McCandless, "Cantus Firmus Techniques in Selected Instrumental Compositions, 1910–1960" (Ph.D. diss., Indiana University, 1974), 155–77; on the Fourth Violin Sonata and First Piano Sonata (first, third, and fifth movements), Gingerich, "Processes of Motivic Transformation," 56–125 and 156–271; on the First Piano Sonata, D. Robert Mumper, "The First Piano Sonata of Charles Ives" (D.M.A. document, Indiana University, 1971); on this sonata's second movement, Paul Franklyn Taylor, "Stylistic Heterogeneity: The Analytical Key to Movements IIa and IIb from the First Piano Sonata by Charles Ives" (D.M.A. diss., University of Wisconsin-Madison, 1986); on the third movement of the same sonata, Michael J. Alexander, *The Evolving Keyboard Style of Charles Ives* (Ph.D. diss., University of Keele, 1984; verbatim reprint, New York and London: Garland, 1989), 132–33 and 226–45; on *The Innate*, Schoffman, "Songs of Charles Ives," 53–63.

5. Ives dated the Third Symphony 1911 in his earlier work-lists, 1904 in his later ones (see *Memos*, 150 and 160), and noted on a copy that it was "finished summers Elk Lake 1910–1911" (Kirkpatrick, *Catalogue*, 7). According to Sherwood, 26 May 1994, the outer movements are sketched on 16:gS4 music paper, first available in 1907, in a hand dating from soon after ca. 1907, perhaps ca. 1908–9; the full score is in a slightly later hand on paper 16w:BC18, available ca. 1900–1912, so that ca. 1908–11 for movements 1 and 3 is a date range that conforms well to the extant sources and Ives's own rough date. Kirkpatrick, *Catalogue*, 111, tentatively identifies manuscript page f0633/n0441 as a possible sketch for the 1901 organ piece, but this cannot be the case; this sketch, like the rest of the symphony finale, is on paper not available before 1907. Since the countermelody is first developed on this page, as described in note 8 below, the organ work cannot have had the same shape as the finale. For John Kirkpatrick's analysis of how the source tunes are used in the Third Symphony, see the critical edition of Charles E. Ives, *Symphony No. 3: "The Camp Meeting,"* ed. Kenneth Singleton (New York: Associated Music Publishers, 1990), vi–ix. This edition restores the "shadow parts" that Ives wrote in the full score, then crossed out, and later thought to include as an option (see ibid., iv). These are dissonant lines that may be played softly or omitted at the conductor's discretion. They do not change the thematic structure, although they sometimes echo or parallel themes presented in other parts.

6. On the bell part, see Ives, *Symphony No. 3*, 39–41. Despite Ives's contradictory statements, which led Henry Cowell to conclude that the bells need not play "any particular rhythm or pitch," each notated version of the bell part features alternating B and G#/A♭ minor triads in close position, stated two, three, or four times. This echoes the hymn's final notes, F and D ("I come!"), at the tritone. Ives often used bitonality, especially at the tritone, to suggest distance between two events. By using minor triads, Ives imitates the overtone structure of church bells and suggests bitonality, which single tones could not do. Thus he creates the effect of distant church bells answering the hymn. Ives's intentions are clear: the bell part should be performed as notated.

7. Henderson, "Quotation," 207, and *Tunebook*, 192, finds *Erie* (H17) in the flute in mm. 45ff. Although *Erie* is featured in the symphony's first movement, the resemblance here in the finale is vague and very brief.

8. The earliest extant page of sketches (f0633/n0441+n3246) has two drafts of settings for *Woodworth*, both in $\frac{3}{4}$ time and with the hymn in the key and register of the final version (B♭ major, bass clef). The first draft combines the tune with a free descant not based on an existing tune. The second replaces this with the countermelody paraphrased from *Azmon* and harmonizes the theme much as in the final version, but without the figured accompaniment. The next set of sketches presents drafts of all main sections, close to the final version and now in $\frac{6}{8}$: on one page (f0630/n1693), the opening (mm. 1–11) and its partial reprise in the third section (mm. 37–42); on another (f0631/n0473), the partial statement of the countermelodies together near the end of the first section (mm. 11–15) and the final section with theme and main countermelody, now with the accompanimental figuration; on a third page (f0632/n0435b+n0443), three drafts of the second section with the countermelody alone, trying out different extensions, the last of which continues through the start of the third section with the paraphrase of the theme. The final section of the piece is the only one of these passages not to go through two or three drafts on these pages. It seems clear that Ives had settled on his main theme and countermelody in the earlier sketch and was here working out the other sections in which those ideas were developed. Moreover, since all sections appear here in the same key as in the final version, it appears that by the time he wrote out these pages, Ives had already determined the order of events; the development of fragments of the theme and countermelody would not appear in the tonic if he had not planned to begin with it, nor would the countermelody appear transposed if he had intended to use it as his opening theme, as he had used the countermelody to "Columbia, the Gem of the Ocean" in the Second Symphony finale.

9. The Third and Fourth Violin Sonatas offer several examples. Work on the first movement of the Fourth Violin Sonata began with Ives's combination of the hymn *Old, Old Story*, which serves as the theme, with one of his father's fugues, which serves as the countermelody. What is apparently the earliest sketch of the second movement (f3251) shows Ives developing the main ingredients of his form: the opening of the countermelody; the final combination of theme, countermelody, and harmonization; and the theme of the contrasting middle section. Near the bottom of a page of sketches for the third movement (f3259/n1300), after various rejected ideas, appears the opening of the movement's theme with the accompaniment that serves as its rudimentary countermelody. An early sketch for the first movement of the Third Sonata (f3476/n1134a+b+1221a+b) shows drafts of the refrain theme, which replaces the countermelody in this movement, and its combination with the main theme at movement's end. The earliest surviving sketch of the second movement (f3502/Q5021&n1217–f3503/n1256) is a continuity draft that breaks off at the entrance of the theme at m. 47 with the annotation "etc.," suggesting that the theme, countermelody, and accompaniment were already worked out in a sketch that is no longer extant; the draft then continues after the theme. The earliest sketches for the finale are on two sides of a leaf. At the top of one side (f3530/n2855), the theme, countermelody, and accompaniment appear in combination, close to their form at the end of the finished piece (though in a different key). The rest of the page contains sketches toward the movement's first section. The opening bars appear at the top of the other side (f3529/n3219), which continues with fragmentary sketches. Later pages draft longer passages, including most of the landmarks of the form.

10. See Keith D. Miller, "Martin Luther King, Jr., and the Black Folk Pulpit," *The Journal of American History* 78 (June 1991): 120–23, and Bruce A. Rosenberg, *Can These Bones Live?: The Art of the American Folk Preacher*, rev. ed. (Urbana: University of Illinois Press, 1988).

11. Magers, "Aspects of Form," 330–34, argues that the work can be considered programmatic, quoting Harold Farberman's program for the first two movements and adding his own for the finale and the symphony as a whole. To the extent that these interpretations go beyond mood or character to suggest a course of events, they have no support from Ives. See chap. 6 on extramusical aspects of cumulative settings.

12. For example, one student reported to me that *Woodworth* ("Just as I am") was frequently used for the weekly altar call in her small country Baptist church, and hearing the hymn as the culmination of this movement inevitably evokes a strong personal reaction for her.

13. Measures 1–4 of the song correspond to mm. 12–16 of the symphony finale; the first half of m. 5 is new; mm. 5–10 correspond to mm. 1–5 of the finale; mm. 10–16 to mm. 29–36; and mm. 17–34 to mm. 44–62. There is no manuscript of the song, so Ives's 1912 date cannot be independently confirmed, but it conforms well to the ca. 1911 date for the Third Symphony full score.

14. Singleton's edition includes a "shadow part" for solo violin, paralleling the flute in the key of A♭ major (the key of the countermelody at its earlier appearance) and repeating the opening of *Erie* in the last two measures of the piece. For the alternative text for *Erie* (also known as *Converse*), see Ives, *Memos*, 94. It appears with this text in a hymnal Ives may have known, since he used others by the same editor: *The New Laudes Domini*, ed. Charles S. Robinson (New York: Century, 1892), p. 127.

15. This was a later revision. The score-sketch (f0569/n0446) has the opening bars of the first-movement countermelody in a wind instrument, including the first measure of *Erie*. The full score (f0577/Q0380) omits this line.

16. Henderson, "Quotation," 111–17, sees the first movement in modified ternary form and the last in three non-repetitive sections. Charles Ward, "Use of Hymn Tunes," relates the first to ABA form (p. 66) and the last to "a free-flowing formal plan" (p. 72). Magers, "Aspects of Form," says the first combines aspects of ternary, rounded binary, and sonata forms (pp. 149–51 and 164) and the third is through-composed (pp. 182–83). Badolato, "Four Symphonies," calls the first movement "a modified sonata allegro" (pp. 115 and 120) and the last through-composed in four sections (pp. 140–51).

17. Ives dated the Third Violin Sonata 1907–14, 1902–14, and 1905–14 in various work-lists (printed in *Memos*, 150 and 163) and elsewhere wrote that it was finished in the fall of 1914 (*Memos*, 69, and manuscript annotations in Kirkpatrick, *Catalogue*, 79–80). Kirkpatrick, *New Grove*, suggests 1913–?14. According to Sherwood, 26 May 1994, the manuscripts confirm the 1914 date: the sketches for the first two movements and pencil sketch for the third are on 16:GS4 music paper, available 1913; earlier sketches for the finale are on 16:G4 paper, first available 1912; and the sketches and ink copies for all three movements are in a hand from ca. 1914. Sherwood, "Questions and Veracities," 440, lists the ink copy as one of the benchmark manuscripts for establishing Ives's handwriting.

18. Henderson, *Tunebook*, 202, identifies the rising figure in m. 8 (C–F–G–A) as the opening of *Happy Day* (H27), implying that the countermelody is partly based on that tune. Since no other portions of *Happy Day* are present in the movement, and since this motive is part of *Need*, the movement's theme, it is likely that the resemblance to *Happy Day* is of little or no significance.

19. This is true of works that are not cumulative settings as well. See Nors Josephson, "Zur formalen Struktur einiger später Orchesterwerke von Charles Ives (1874–1954)," *Die Musikforschung* 27 (January–March 1974): 57–64.

20. *Memos*, 69, §24, n. 1. The piece was played by David Talmadge and Stuart Ross "at a small invited concert in Carnegie Chamber Music Hall," probably on 22 April 1917 (*Memos*, 69, n. 1, and p. 118). Talmadge taught violin to Ives's nephew Moss White Ives.

21. See the letter from Coolidge of 15 March 1921 and Ives's sketch for a reply in *Memos*, 99–100, n. 7. Kirkpatrick surmised that this correspondence refers to the recently published *Concord Sonata*, although the work involved is not named in either letter.

22. The distinction matters. For example, the sophisticated analyses in Gingerich, "Processes of Motivic Transformation," are in general accurate and illuminating but treat most movements as if they were at base motivic rather than thematic. This makes it difficult to recognize formal similarities, just as a purely motivic approach to Beethoven would see less in common between his sonata-form movements than does an approach that recognizes most motives as deriving from themes. Without a sense of the themes, the number of apparently unconnected motives proliferates, leading to analyses that are more complex and hard to grasp than they need to be.

23. "Developing variation" is a term coined by Arnold Schoenberg for a process in which "variation of the features of a basic unit produces all the thematic formulations which provide for fluency, contrasts, variety, logic and unity on the one hand, and character, mood, expression, and every needed differentiation, on the other hand —thus elaborating the *idea* of the piece" (Schoenberg, "Bach," in *Style and Idea*, 397). See the discussion of the concept in Walter Frisch, *Brahms and the Principle of Developing Variation* (Berkeley and Los Angeles: University of California Press, 1984).

24. Thus Ives solves the problem of using "folkloristic" material as articulated by Arnold Schoenberg, "Folkloristic Symphonies," in *Style and Idea*, 161–66: "The discrepancy between the requirements of larger forms and the simple construction of folk tunes has never been solved and cannot be solved. . . . Structurally, there never remains in popular tunes an unsolved problem, the consequences of which will show up only later" (pp. 163–64). Evan Rothstein, "'What Its Signs of Promise Are': Ives, the Tradition of 'Developing Variation' and the Problem of 'Folkloristic' Music in Ives's First Violin Sonata, Third Movement" (unpublished typescript), offers an excellent treatment of this issue and of Ives's solution.

25. *Memos*, p. 69, §24, n. 1.

26. Kirkpatrick, *New Grove*, suggests a date of 1897; Sherwood, 23 May 1994, suggests ca. 1902 by handwriting.

27. This description follows the published score, Ives, *Fugue in Four Keys on "The Shining Shore,"* ed. John Kirkpatrick, which reconstructs this concluding passage (see

Kirkpatrick's "Editorial Notes," 4). Laurence Wallach, "New England Education," 371–73, offers another edition and dismisses Kirkpatrick's reconstruction of mm. 58–77: "Contrary to Kirk[patrick], there is no workable continuation in adjoining pages of the MS; our version is the end of the sketch, and is satisfactory in itself" (p. 370). If Wallach were correct, this work would not be a cumulative setting, for the culminating statement of the two tunes occurs in mm. 59–72 of Kirkpatrick's edition. However, Kirkpatrick's reconstruction is almost certainly correct in its general outlines, for mm. 58–77 are clearly sketched on the same page as the previous twenty-two measures; see the description of sources in Kirkpatrick's "Editorial Notes," 2, or see manuscript pages f3036/q1889 and f3037/q1890&1081.

28. Ives gave several dates for this movement. On the score, he wrote that it was finished in 1906 (Kirkpatrick, *Catalogue*, 75), but elsewhere he said he started the first theme in 1902 (*Memos*, 68) and that the sonata "was composed mostly in 1903 and completed in detail in 1908" (ibid., n. 1); his work-lists date the sonata at 1908 or 1903–8 (in ibid., 150 and 160). Kirkpatrick, *New Grove*, dates this movement 1902–?6. Sherwood, 26 May 1994, indicates that the paper on which the sketches appear is unidentified, but the hand suggests ca. 1907 or a bit later for the fragmentary early sketches, including the opening theme, and early in the years ca. 1907–14 for the pencil sketch. The ink copy is on 16:G4 paper, available 1912–14, in a hand of ca. 1914. The years 1906–8 are possible, but it cannot be true that the movement "was composed mostly in 1903." Emil Hanke's ink copy of the entire sonata is from ca. 1922 or later; it is on 12S:S9 paper, available 1919–23, and uses in the finale two pages from *114 Songs*, published in 1922.

29. Kirkpatrick, *Catalogue*, 74, and Henderson, *Tunebook*, 201, find *Bringing in the Sheaves* (H10) in the second half of the countermelody (mm. 65–69). There is a similarity of rhythm and pitch at m. 66, but thereafter Ives's melody follows the contour of *Shining Shore*, not *Bringing in the Sheaves*. Ives may have intended a reference to the latter, but it is more likely that he had in mind the tune on which the bulk of the movement is based.

30. Sinclair, "Microfilm Concordance," 74, suggests borrowings from *Autumn* (H4) and *Westminster Chimes* (H170). Motive W resembles the opening of the countermelody in the Second Violin Sonata, first movement, which was based on *Autumn*, but the hymn itself does not appear. A motive in the piano, mm. 4–5, that resembles part of *Westminster Chimes* is more likely derived from mm. 1–2 of *Shining Shore*.

31. Ives dated the version of this movement in his "Pre-First" Violin Sonata ca. 1903, revised 1907 or 1908, and the later version at 1908–10 (Kirkpatrick, *Catalogue*, 72 and 77); in his work-lists, he gave various dates for the whole Second Sonata ranging between 1902–9 and 1907–10 (*Memos*, 150 and 161). According to Sherwood, 26 May 1993, the earliest sketches for the first version are on 16:gS4 paper, available 1907–13, in a hand of ca. 1907–14, perhaps about 1910; the pencil sketch and ink copy are on 16:G4 paper, available 1912–14, in a ca. 1914 hand; patches for the later revision are on 16:SN4 paper, available 1917–20, in a hand of ca. 1919; and the ink copy is in a hand of ca. 1919–23 on paper that was available by 1911 at the latest. It is unlikely that work on this movement predated 1907.

32. Gratovich, "Sonatas for Violin and Piano," 94, gives a second countermelody that Ives added in pencil to the autograph. This is a dissonant "shadow part" like

those in the Third Symphony, unrelated to *Autumn*. It was omitted from the copyist's copy and the published score, following Ives's instruction to "leave out all the pencil parts in copying" (quoted in ibid., 76).

33. This introduction replaced an earlier one, shown on f3218/n1334 and f3227/n1171, which did not refer to the countermelody's headmotive but included later fragments of it. Laurence Perkins, "Sonatas for Violin and Piano," 37–41, was apparently the first to derive this headmotive from *Autumn*.

34. Henderson, *Tunebook*, 201, finds Stephen Foster's "Oh! Susanna" (H127) in the violin in m. 19. Ives probably did not intend such a reference: the resemblance is brief (ten notes); there are differences of rhythm and pitch; no other point in the movement resembles the Foster melody; the passage can be derived from the theme and countermelody (compare especially the end of the countermelody in its solo appearance, violin, mm. 40–42); the earliest sketch of this measure (f3220/n1336) indeed shows a transposition of mm. 40–42, of which the final version of m. 19 is a variant; there is no reason of program or character for introducing this minstrel song into a movement based on this hymn; and Ives did not use "Oh! Susanna" in any other work, making a fleeting reference in this one less likely.

35. No manuscript of the song survives, so Ives's date of 1913 (in *114 Songs*, 97) cannot be confirmed independently, but it is close to the date for the sonata movement.

36. *Memos*, p. 69, §24, n. 1. On ragtime as a stylistic influence on Ives, see Judith Tick, "Ragtime and the Music of Charles Ives," *Current Musicology*, no. 18 (1974): 105–13. Tick points out that treating hymn tunes in ragtime style was part of ragtime tradition, citing a ragtime arrangement of *Nettleton* from 1897 (p. 107).

37. Kirkpatrick, *Catalogue*, 79 finds *Happy Day* here as well, no doubt because of the addition of a pickup note that makes the 1–2–3 opening of *There'll Be No Dark Valley* into the 5–1–2–3 opening motive of *Happy Day*. However, no other signs of the latter hymn appear, and it is probably best to regard this as a case of an added note rather than a further borrowing.

38. In the program note on this piece, Ives referred to the hymn by its second verse, "There'll be no more sorrow"; see *Memos*, 69, §24, n. 1.

39. See Kirkpatrick, *Catalogue*, 74. Ives wrote in *Memos* that the Fourth Sonata was "composed quickly within two or three weeks in the fall of 1916," and in his work-lists he dated it 1916 and 1914–15 (see *Memos*, 72, 151, and 165). Kirkpatrick, *New Grove*, suggests 1914–?16 for the first and third movements. The only extant sketches are a few jottings on an ink copy of his father's fugue in B♭ (f7397/n1933) showing ways to combine *Old, Old Story* with the fugue.

40. For these fugues, see Kirkpatrick, *Catalogue*, 214 and 216. Complete transcriptions of this fugue (differing from each other in some details) appear in Laurence Perkins, "Sonatas for Violin and Piano," 166–67; Gratovich, "Sonatas for Violin and Piano," 337–38; and Gingerich, "Processes of Motivic Transformation," 75.

41. Kirkpatrick, *Catalogue*, 216. Either the date "1890–91" at the top of the page or "Dec 25, 1892" at the bottom may refer to the sketch combining the two themes, which Sherwood, 22 July 1994, dates ca. 1892 or shortly thereafter by handwriting.

42. Charles Ives, "Notes on Fourth Violin Sonata," in *Sonata No. 4 for Violin and Piano ("Children's Day at the Camp Meeting")* (New York: Arrow Music Press, 1942), 21.

43. Gingerich, "Processes of Motivic Transformation," 78–79.

44. In the lithographed printing of this movement (made by a copyist in or after 1917, according to Sherwood, 26 May 1994), the similarity of these motives is made even more obvious. The motive from mm. 5–6 of the hymn appears in the violin in mm. 47–48, just before it states the fugal answer in mm. 48–49. Gratovich, "Sonatas for Violin and Piano," 190, prints the variant of mm. 46–48. The published edition reflects Ives's later revisions.

45. Kirkpatrick, *New Grove*, dates this movement 1906–?16. Sherwood, 26 May 1994, notes that the preliminary sketches are on 16:GS4 paper, available 1913–16, and 16:G4 paper, available 1912–14 (or a similar paper available 1907); the pencil sketch is on unidentified paper; and all are in a hand of ca. 1914. Kirkpatrick's 1906 date is based on his observation that *In the Night*, which Ives dated 1906, was entered after sketches for the sonata movement, on the same page (f2608/n2857). However, Sherwood notes that the paper was not available before 1913 and that the hand for the *In the Night* sketch is ca. 1914. Thus the sonata movement can be dated fairly firmly to ca. 1914.

46. See McCandless, "Cantus Firmus Techniques," 168–69, for a discussion of this passage.

47. Example 5.20 is based on Lee Cyril Rosen, "Violin Sonatas," 35 (Example 24).

48. Ives, "Notes on Fourth Violin Sonata." See also the briefer note in *Memos*, 72.

49. Gratovich, "The Violin Sonatas," 58. Gratovich does not indicate which movements he means to include in this category, but it fits this movement well. Lee Cyril Rosen, "Violin Sonatas," 33–36, similarly describes this movement as a set of variations whose theme appears at the end.

50. Ives dated *Thanksgiving* 1897–1904 in his first list of works and 1904 in the later ones (in *Memos*, 149 and 160) and on the manuscripts (Kirkpatrick, *Catalogue*, 12–14). He noted its derivation from the earlier organ works on the manuscripts (ibid.) and in *Memos*, 39. The only extant page of the Postlude is f5094/q0904, which is on 16:KSOD paper, available from 1899, in a hand similar to that of 1898 (Sherwood, 23 and 26 May and 22 July 1994). Since the paper postdates Ives's employment at Center Church in New Haven, this is likely a revision of the Postlude that Ives played at the 1897 Thanksgiving service, his last in New Haven. Another sketch, fo878/no895, which Kirkpatrick, *Catalogue*, 109, suggests may be toward the Postlude, is on unidentified paper in a hand from between ca. 1907 and ca. 1914; this is probably among the first sketches toward *Thanksgiving*. Other sketches are on 16:GS4 paper, available 1913–16, in a hand of ca. 1913–14, and on unidentified paper in a comparable hand. The score-sketch and extra score-sketch pages are in a hand of ca. 1914–19, and the full score dates from 1932–33, as recalled by Ives's wife Harmony (*Memos*, 95, n. 5) and confirmed by the handwriting. Since the 1904 dates were entered retrospectively, one wonders whether Ives was mistaken or was referring to a version that, like the 1897 prototypes, was lost or discarded.

51. See fo892–93/q0913–14, which show that the work originally flowed directly from m. 152 to m. 180; mm. 154–62 are sketched in pencil on empty staves on the first of these pages, and the section is further worked out on empty staves on fo878/no895.

52. Gustave J. Stoeckel, ed., *The College Hymn Book: For Use in the Battell Chapel at Yale College* (New York: Wm. A. Pond, 1886), p. 58.

53. f5094/q0904; see Kirkpatrick, *Catalogue*, 109.

54. fo889/Qo906.

55. Henderson, *Tunebook*, 192, finds *Eventide* (H19, "Abide with me") in the bass parts at m. 229, but this is the start of the third phrase of *Duke Street*.

56. fo878/no895, sketch for mm. 244–57, from ca. 1907–14.

57. fo900/no903.

58. On the holidays, see Jonathan Elkus's "Preface" to his critical edition of Charles E. Ives, *Thanksgiving and Forefathers' Day* (New York: Peer International, 1991), iii.

59. Ives dated the first movement 1902–9 (see Kirkpatrick, *Catalogue*, 82–83), gave the same date for the entire sonata in his work-lists (in *Memos*, 150 and 156), and said in *Memos* that the sonata was finished in 1909 or 1910 (p. 74). Kirkpatrick, *New Grove*, suggests 1901–9 for this movement. According to Sherwood, 26 May 1994, the sketches are in a hand of ca. 1907–14, close to 1914; the first ink copy is on music paper types 16:GS4 (available 1913–16) and 16:G4 (available 1912–13) in a hand of ca. 1914; the second ink copy is on paper available from 1917 in a hand of ca. 1919 or a little later; and supplementary patches are much later, in a hand of between 1923 and 1929. If there were earlier forms of this movement, they may have been worked out by memory rather than on paper.

60. See Charles Ward, "Use of Hymn Tunes," 78, for a different interpretation of the textual link. Most studies identify Lowry's tune as Ives's source, and this is used in Example 5.21. But Gingerich, "Processes of Motivic Transformation," 186, prints the chorus of a tune by W. A. Williams whose opening two bars are quite like those of Lowry's verse and whose cadential figure is closer to that used by Ives than is Lowry's. However, Williams's tune lacks the dotted rhythm that characterizes Lowry's and that Ives uses throughout his paraphrase of *Lebanon*, which does not have it. Moreover, Williams's tune, a take-off on Lowry's, is not a hymn but a temperance song, published as "Down in the Licensed Saloon: An answer to 'Where is My Wandering Boy To-night?'" in *Silver Tones: A Temperance and Prohibition Song Book*, ed. C. H. Mead, G. E. Charles, and W. A Williams (Warnock, Ohio: W. A. Williams, 1892), 92 (no. 67). This would be a unique instance of a temperance song in Ives's music, if he intended to use it here.

61. Gingerich, "Processes of Motivic Transformation," 171, notes this anticipation.

62. Ives dated this movement 1902–9; see Kirkpatrick, *Catalogue*, 84–85. According to Sherwood, 26 May 1994, the sketches and first ink copy for the third movement appear on paper types 16:GS4 (available 1913–16) and 16:G4 (1912–14) in a hand from ca. 1914; the second ink copy is in a hand from ca. 1919.

63. In the pencil full score of the symphony, Ives modified this motive at every major appearance in the same way as in the sonata movement; the other versions of the symphony movement are not so consistent. These passages include mm. 75–77, oboe; mm. 77–78, flute, in the full score but not in the score-sketch or published versions; mm. 91–92, horn II; mm. 92–93, horn I, in the full score but not in the published versions; and mm. 119–20, flute, in the full score and first two published versions, but not in the score-sketch or the new critical edition. See the comparison of sources in Ives, *Symphony No. 3*, 34–38.

64. See H. Wiley Hitchcock, *Ives*, 51; Gingerich, "Processes of Motivic Transformation," 205–7; and Alexander, *Evolving Keyboard Style*, 132–33 and 226–45. Gingerich

points out (p. 207, n. 14) that such a substitution of a similar element from a melodically related tune also occurs in the first movement, where part of *Where Is My Wandering Boy?* is blended with *Lebanon*.

65. Sherwood, 26 May 1994, notes that the sketches appear on unidentified paper in a hand of ca. 1914.

66. Lee Cyril Rosen, "Violin Sonatas," 39–40, derives the opening of the countermelody from permutations of mm. 11–12 of the hymn. Gingerich, "Processes of Motivic Transformation," 67–69, and idem, "Technique for Melodic Motivic Analysis," 91–92, derives the countermelody from transformations of a motive of a falling whole step, minor third, and whole step found across phrases of the hymn tune (C–B♭–G–F in Ives's mm. 50–51, violin). Neither relationship is close enough to claim that the countermelody is paraphrased from the hymn, though it may be that Ives intended to create a motivic link between theme and countermelody.

67. Lee Cyril Rosen, "Violin Sonatas," 37–38, derives the accompanimental motives (piano, m. 1, left hand and m. 2, right hand) from mm. 9–10 of the hymn tune. Gingerich, "Motivic Transformation," 56–73, and "Technique for Melodic Motivic Analysis," 85–93, shows the motivic interrelations that underlie much of the motivic material in this movement.

68. No manuscript of the song survives, so Ives's date of 1916 (in *114 Songs*, 95) cannot be independently confirmed, but it is close to the date for the sonata movement.

69. Kevin O. Kelly, "The Songs of Charles Ives and the Cultural Contexts of Death" (Ph.D. diss., University of North Carolina at Chapel Hill, 1988), 362.

70. Ives dated the instrumental version 1908 in his work-lists (in *Memos*, 157) and on a manuscript (Kirkpatrick, *Catalogue*, 66); this is confirmed by Sherwood, 19 May 1994, who dates the handwriting at ca. 1907. No manuscript of the song survives to confirm Ives's 1916 date, from *114 Songs*, 87. Revisions in the song are minor, beyond the change of medium. The song is mostly unbarred; measure numbers here refer to the instrumental version. There are two versions of the text, the earlier in *114 Songs*, 87–88, and a revision in Charles E. Ives, *Nineteen Songs* (Bryn Mawr, Pa.: Merion Music, 1935), 16–17; see Schoffman, "Songs of Charles Ives," 53–54 and 60–63 for a comparison of the two published versions of the song. Henderson, *Tunebook*, 201, omits the instrumental version from his index.

71. Ives dated the unfinished overture 1904 on a manuscript (in Kirkpatrick, *Catalogue*, 90), in *Memos*, 65, and in his work lists (ibid., 163). He provided various dates for the movements of the *Concord Sonata* between 1909 and 1915; see Kirkpatrick, *Catalogue*, 88–91, and *Memos*, 79–82, 150, and 162–63. Sherwood, 15 July 1994, dates the earliest extant sketches for all four movements ca. 1914, with further sketching in the period 1914–19 and final ink copies ca. 1919 or shortly before, just prior to the work's 1920 publication; for "The Alcotts," only two early sketches survive from before ca. 1919. Kirkpatrick fixes the main work on the sonata at ca. 1911–12 (in *Memos*, 163), based on Ives's claim in a memo to have "played the whole sonata to Max Smith last year (1912)" (printed in ibid., 186). This date seems too early, given the preliminary nature of some of the extant sketches of ca. 1914, but a 1911–12 version, perhaps worked out by ear, may have existed.

72. This analysis is similar to that of Geoffrey Block, "Ives and the 'Sounds Beethoven Didn't Have,'" to be published in *Charles Ives and the Classical Tradition*,

ed. Geoffrey Block and J. Peter Burkholder (New Haven: Yale University Press, forthcoming). Henderson, *Tunebook*, 205, mentions only the Fifth Symphony and *Missionary Chant*. H. Wiley Hitchcock, *Ives*, 55–56, notes the role of *Missionary Chant* and *Martyn*. Fred Fisher, *Ives' Concord Sonata* (Denton, Texas: C/G Productions, 1981), 30–32, notes the "Hammerklavier" motive and suggests that the last part of Ives's melody is from the close of *Crusader's Hymn* ("Fairest Lord Jesus"), which has the same closing contour as *Martyn* with a rhythm closer to that of the Ives; however, given the prominent use of *Martyn* in the sonata's second movement ("Hawthorne") and the resemblance of its opening motive to that of the Fifth Symphony, it seems more likely that *Martyn* is the source. (To bolster his case, Fisher finds references to *Crusader's Hymn* elsewhere in the sonata; see pp. 33–35.) Fisher also suggests that the opening four notes of the melody, two rising whole steps and a descending perfect fifth, echo the similar motive in Brahms's Piano Sonata No. 2 in F♯ Minor, Op. 2; Fisher first offered this idea in "Ives's Concord Sonata," *Piano Quarterly* 92 (Winter 1975–76): 26. This seems less likely, for the Brahms and Ives motives are quite different in rhythm and in their relation to the surrounding melodic context, and they are developed in very different ways.

73. Both sketches are in C major, the first (f3252/n2856, bottom three staves) with jottings toward an accompanying ostinato, the second (f3993/n3176) with the ostinato fully fleshed out and the theme stated twice. In both, the first half of the theme is the same as in the final version except for a couple of rhythmic details; the Fifth Symphony motive is missing; the next unit is like the final version (and repeated in the second sketch); and the final segment is somewhat different but recognizable. Both sketches are in a hand of ca. 1914, the first on paper available 1913–16 and the second on older paper, available 1907–13. If Ives's date of 1904 for the lost *Orchard House Overture* is correct, perhaps the Fifth Symphony motto did not play a role in that work, but was introduced as Ives reworked the overture for his sonata movement.

74. Charles E. Ives, *Piano Sonata No. 2: "Concord, Mass., 1840–1860,"* 2nd ed. (New York: Arrow Music Press, 1947).

75. The pencil sketch (f3979/n1624) and the ink copy (f3986/n1625) show the complete theme here, which would negate the cumulative form. On the ink copy, this is canceled and replaced by a patch on the facing page (f3985/n3174a+b, now fragmentary), which shows the passage as in the final version: partly taken up an octave, which disrupts the melodic continuity, and with several notes omitted.

76. Henderson, *Tunebook*, 205, omits this attribution, first offered by Cowell and Cowell, *Charles Ives*, 198. The latter also suggest "Loch Lomond" as a source, but there is only a scant resemblance, a shared 4–3–2–1–6 descent (m. 7 of the tune and the first five notes of p. 55, bottom stave, m. 2).

77. H. Wiley Hitchcock, "Charles E. Ives," in *Music in the United States: A Historical Introduction*, 2nd ed. (Englewood Cliffs, N.J.: Prentice-Hall, 1974), 167.

78. *Essays*, 47. E.g., John Kirkpatrick, "Preface," in Charles E. Ives, *Symphony No. 4* (New York: Associated Music Publishers, 1965), viii, calls the Beethoven/*Missionary Chant* complex and the human-faith-melody "the two main themes" of the *Concord Sonata*, and Hitchcock, *Ives*, 54–55, notes that "This ['human-faith'] melody often precedes the appearance of another one, universally recognized: the opening motif of

Beethoven's Fifth Symphony." Hertz, *Angels of Reality*, 103–4, interprets the first four notes alone as "the 'human faith melody.'"

79. *Essays*, 47. Fred Fisher, *Ives' Concord Sonata*, 44, distinguishes between the Fifth Symphony motive and the human-faith-melody but notes that the former "can probably be considered an integral part of the melody, in view of Ives['s] professed concern with its metaphysical and symbolic implications." Betty E. Chmaj, "Charles Ives and the Concord Sonata," in *Poetry and the Fine Arts: Papers from the Poetry Sessions of the European Association for American Studies Biennial Conference, Rome 1984*, ed. Roland Hagenbüchle and Jaqueline S. Ollier (Regensburg: Friedrich Pustet, 1989), 42, was apparently the first to identify the whole "Alcotts" theme as the "human-faith-melody." Rathert, *The Seen and Unseen*, 169 and 183–85, refers to the theme at the end of "The Alcotts" as the "human-faith-melody," but seems to consider the entire flute melody at the end of "Thoreau" as its definitive statement. The latter is a developed reminiscence of the "Alcotts" theme with much internal repetition and without the last few notes. Since the theme of "The Alcotts" is the principal theme of the sonata as a whole, and Ives refers to the "human-faith-melody" only in his essay on "The Alcotts," it is most likely the "Alcotts" theme that he had in mind.

80. Hertz, *Angels of Reality*, 124–29, likewise emphasizes how Ives in the *Concord Sonata* reclaims Beethoven's motive as his own.

81. Ives dated this movement 1906, 1909–10 (Kirkpatrick, *Catalogue*, 78). But according to Sherwood, 26 May 1994, the early sketches (listed by Kirkpatrick, *Catalogue*, 73 as a rejected fourth movement for the Fourth Violin Sonata) are on 16:G4 paper (available 1912–14) in a hand of ca. 1914; subsequent sketches are on 16:GS4 paper (1913–16) in a hand of ca. 1914–19; a patch on 16:SN4 paper (1917–20) is in a hand of ca. 1919; and the ink copy is in a hand of ca. 1919–23.

82. Laurence Perkins, "Sonatas for Violin and Piano," 9 and 133, analyses this movement as a series of verses (based on mm. 1–4 of *Nettleton*) and refrains (based on mm. 8–10); this is repeated in Charles Ward, "Use of Hymn Tunes," 94, and Henderson, "Quotation," 86–88. This seems forced, an attempt to apply on a small scale a format that Ives used in much longer works: the Third Violin Sonata, third movement; the compound scherzo (movements IIa, IIb, IVa, and IVb) of the First Piano Sonata; and the *Ragtime Dances*. See the discussion of these works below.

83. A lithograph printing of the Fourth Violin Sonata (prepared by a copyist in or after 1917) includes this movement as a fourth movement. In this version, eight measures are added between the second and third sections (before the present m. 25) in which motives from *Nettleton* are further developed.

84. Kirkpatrick, *New Grove*, dates this movement 1906–?8, but Sherwood, 26 May 1994, dates the sketches ca. 1914. Ives's ink copy is on 16:G4 paper, available 1912–14, in the 1914 hand, with some later insertions.

85. Ives also mentioned a lost 1905 piece for horns and strings, apparently on this same melody. See Kirkpatrick, *Catalogue*, 20, 42, 75, and 186.

86. Ives dated *Watchman* at 1913 in *114 Songs*, 93, close to and possibly before the composition of the sonata movement in ca. 1914; no manuscript of the song version is extant. For the date of the first movement of the Fourth Symphony, see the discussion of the symphony in chap. 10.

87. The appearance of text in the sonata beneath the violin's statement of the theme in mm. 91–109 is unusual, and may be explained by Emil Hanke's use of the pages of *114 Songs* on which the song *Watchman* appeared for mm. 89–111 in his ink copy of the sonata. See Kirkpatrick, *Catalogue*, 76. The text and its relationship to John Bowring's hymn text are discussed in chap. 10.

88. *114 Songs*, 93. The First and Second Sonatas overlap, as both share motive W and include movements that originated in the "Pre-First" Violin Sonata (both middle movements and the first movement of the Second Sonata).

89. This was first noted by Marshall, "Ives's Quotations," 49 and 54.

90. According to Ives, the first three verse-refrain pairs were played as separate preludes in November 1901. See Kirkpatrick, *Catalogue*, 79 and 111.

91. See Charles E. Ives, *Ragtime Dances: Set of Four Ragtime Dances*, ed. James B. Sinclair (New York: Peer International, 1990). For the uncertain chronology of these pieces, see note 94, below.

92. Contrary to H. Wiley Hitchcock, *Ives*, 52, the chorus of "Massa's in de Cold Ground" is not a source for the chorus, despite its similarity to *Welcome Voice*. When Ives uses related tunes, he emphasizes not only what they have in common but also what differentiates them, as in his simultaneous use of *Missionary Chant* and *Dorrnance* in the Fourth Symphony finale, described in chap. 10. Nothing like that happens here, for Ives includes no element of "Massa," rhythmic or melodic, that is not also in *Welcome Voice*.

93. Marshall, "Ives's Quotations," 53.

94. On the various pieces mentioned here as related to the *Ragtime Dances*, see Kirkpatrick, *Catalogue*, 18–19, 39, 40–41, 45–46, 83–85, and 103. Ives dated the *Drum Corps or Scuffle* and *Skit for Danbury Fair* September 1902, the *Ragtime Dances* 1902–4, the movements of the First Piano Sonata 1902–9, *In the Inn* 1904–11, and *The Rockstrewn Hills* 1909 or 1912–15. Sherwood, 15 July 1994, confirms that *Drum Corps or Scuffle* and *Skit for Danbury Fair* date from ca. 1902. But surviving materials for the other works are later than the dates Ives provided. According to Sherwood, 19 and 26 May 1994, the single extant leaf of the orchestral score for the *Ragtime Dances* is on paper available 1903–10 in a hand that may be ca. 1907, although Ives's date on the manuscript is 1911; the sketches and pencil sketch (grouped by Kirkpatrick with the *Ragtime Dances* but apparently intended for the sonata), including the new movement IVa, are on papers available 1912–14 and 1913–16 in a hand of ca. 1913–14; the ink and pencil manuscript is later, in a hand of ca. 1919, and the ink copy of movements IIa and IIb is on paper available 1922–33 in a hand of ca. 1923. The orchestral version of *In the Inn* is in a hand of ca. 1914, with extra score-pages on paper available 1922–33 in a hand of about 1923. According to Sherwood, 31 May 1994, *The Rockstrewn Hills* developed in stages: sketches ca. 1914 and 1919, score-sketch ca. 1923, full score between 1923 and 1929, and patches for the score ca. 1929.

95. Marshall, "Ives's Quotations," 46.

96. Ibid., 50–51. Mumper, "First Piano Sonata," 40, finds *Welcome Voice* in C major hidden in the left half at mm. 36–40, missing its first note and with interpolations. Henderson, *Tunebook*, 204, finds *Bringing in the Sheaves* in the right hand at the same place. Neither is likely; many diatonic melodies can be extracted from these ostinatos

if one chooses freely from either top or bottom notes, omits notes, and ignores rhythm, as does Mumper.

97. Henderson, "Quotation," 149–50, compares the trumpet in mm. 77–82 to "The Girl I Left Behind Me." The latter portion may owe something to that tune, but mm. 77–78 are certainly closer to *Welcome Voice*, especially as Ives paraphrases it in this and other movements of the *Ragtime Dances*. Perry, *Charles Ives*, 77–78, points out that secular songs were sometimes sung at revivals, making these additions seem less incongruous than they may appear to be in a movement that reflects the spirit of an outdoor revival. Perhaps "Rock-a-bye Baby" is meant to suggest the presence of young children.

CHAPTER 6: THE DEVELOPMENT AND SIGNIFICANCE
OF CUMULATIVE SETTINGS

1. For a discussion of these and other experimental works as they relate to traditional tonality, see Burkholder, "Critique."

2. Described in ibid., 205–7; the setting in F over G♭ appears on p. 207. Kirkpatrick, *Catalogue*, 219, assigns the number 7C5 to all three settings and dates them 1891?. Sherwood, 27 May 1994, dates the first and second ones between 1892 and 1898, the third between 1898 and 1902.

3. Kirkpatrick, *Catalogue*, 107, groups these as 3D6 and suggests a date of 1892?. Sherwood, 26 May 1994, dates the *Nettleton* and *Bethany* interludes later, ca. 1898–1902, the other two possibly before 1898. Cowell and Cowell, *Charles Ives*, 35, print the interlude on *Bethany* (reprinted in Henderson, *Tunebook*, 10) but omit the *ppp* marking in the treble clef, which drastically changes the sonority.

4. On Ives's youthful experiences with bands, see Elkus, *Charles Ives and the American Band Tradition*. The best accounts of George Ives's band activities are in Wallach, "New England Education," 40–69, and Feder, *Charles Ives*, 31–61.

5. Titles follow Kirkpatrick, *Catalogue*, 36–37 and 93–95, and dates are based on Sherwood, 27 May and 15 July 1994.

6. The pieces mentioned here are recorded by The American Brass Quintet, assisted by John Stevens, on *American Brass Music of the 1850's* (Cambridge, Mass.: Titanic Records Ti/81, 1980), with helpful liner notes by H. Wiley Hitchcock. See also Pauline Norton, "March Music in Nineteenth-Century America" (Ph.D. diss., University of Michigan, 1983), 159–64, 307–11, and 320–24. I am grateful to my student John Q. Ericson and his unpublished paper "Ives and the Band March" (1988) for helping me to understand the early history of this form of march and for other insights into Ives's place in the American band music tradition.

7. See Paul E. Bierley, *John Philip Sousa: A Descriptive Catalog of His Works* (Urbana: University of Illinois Press, 1973).

8. David L. Stackhouse, "D. W. Reeves and His Music," *Journal of Band Research* 5/2 (1969): 15; see also pp. 19 and 22.

9. Ives uses a version of "That Old Cabin Home Upon the Hill" different from the one in Henderson, *Tunebook*, 136–37. See chapter 3, note 10.

10. f2370 and f2370A/q2195. Ives was ambivalent about presenting the counter-melody first. Sometime after writing out the full score, he added a note over the six-teen-measure initial statement of the countermelody: "(These 16 meas. may be omit-ted)" (see f2375/n2097 and f2376/n2084). Both marches on "Here's to Good Old Yale" use the same countermelody, but one introduces it before the borrowed tune and one does not. If Kirkpatrick is correct that the latter march is the second version (*Cata-logue*, 95), this is a case of Ives dropping the initial statement of the countermelody upon revision; if the reverse is true, this parallels the first and final versions of the march with "My Old Kentucky Home."

11. The manuscript of the march is too fragmentary to indicate whether it followed the same form as the song, but what survives suggests that it did. Ives appears to have reworked the march directly into the song, marking changes in pencil on his fair ink copy. At the start of the second strain (on f4730/n2172a), the bass line is labeled "Air (Son of a Gambolier)" and marked with accents. Ives later penciled in the tune and text in the treble clef and changed several bass notes to create a new bass line; these added notes appear to be in a hand of ca. 1919 (Sherwood, 15 July 1994), suggesting that the song was adapted from the march while Ives was preparing *114 Songs* in 1919–21. No other manuscript exists for the song, which Ives dated 1895 in *114 Songs*, 122; this may be the date of the march.

12. Ives may have first encountered this work in his volume of *Fourteen Celebrated Marches* in piano transcription, pp. 30–31; see chap. 2, note 11.

13. There is no manuscript for *The Collection*, but Kirkpatrick, *Catalogue*, 202, sug-gests its origin in church music from the early 1890s. Ives dated his setting of *Adeste fideles* 1897 in his work-lists (see *Memos*, 154) and recorded an 1898 performance (Kirkpatrick, *Catalogue*, 109). Sherwood, 26 May 1994, dates the handwriting for both sketch and pencil copy between 1898 and 1902 but notes that the copy is on music paper that was not available before 1899. Since the sketch does not include the first half of the piece, in which the countermelody appears alone, this may have been added at the time of the copy, ca. 1899.

14. Ives dated this movement 1906 (*Memos*, 58), but Sherwood, 31 May 1994, notes that the sketch is on paper available 1913 and in a hand of ca. 1914, and the score-sketch on paper available 1912 in a hand that is just after 1914.

15. See Ives's description of these pieces, including a 1902 performance of the ver-sion with male chorus, in *Memos*, 57–59. Kirkpatrick, *Catalogue*, 63, suggests 1899 for the Prelude; this is confirmed by Sherwood, 15 July 1994, who dates the handwriting between 1898 and 1902.

16. Ives dated the Trio 1904–11 in his work-lists (*Memos*, 158). According to Sher-wood, 15 July 1994, the surviving sketches for the first two movements are ca. 1914 or a little earlier; those for the finale are in a hand of 1907–14, closer to 1914, and many are on 16:gS4 paper, first available in 1907. These probably represent the version of ca. 1911. If an earlier version existed, its form is not known. Measures 13–40, 58–67, and 91–125 of the Trio finale are drawn from mm. 7–34, 92–106, and 46–82 of the song, constituting just over half of both works. See John Kirkpatrick, "Critical Commen-tary," in Charles E. Ives, *Trio for Violin, Violoncello, and Piano*, ed. John Kirkpatrick (New York: Peer International, [1984]), 14. *The All-Enduring* appears in Charles E.

Ives, *Forty Earlier Songs*, ed. John Kirkpatrick (New York: Associated Music Publishers, Peer International, and Theodore Presser, 1993), 35–43. The "unknown tune" that Henderson lists as H218 (*Tunebook*, 185) is from *The All-Enduring*, mm. 55–58, and is apparently not borrowed from elsewhere. Ives listed an 1896 performance of the song (Kirkpatrick, *Catalogue*, 171). Sherwood, 27 May 1994, notes that the surviving pencil draft of the song is on paper not found before 1900 in a hand between 1898 and 1902, but this may be a later copy.

17. Theme X appears in Henderson, *Tunebook*, 185, as Unknown Tune H217. Kirkpatrick, "Critical Commentary," 3, suggests that it is a paraphrase of *Toplady*, varied "so freely as to be cryptic." If this were so, this movement might be classed as a cumulative setting of a unique type. The opening 5–6–5–3 pitch motive of *Toplady* is present in theme X but could also be found in many pentatonic tunes, and the shape of theme X as a whole is quite far from *Toplady*. Kirkpatrick's suggestion that theme Y is anticipated at mm. 15 and 66 of the first movement and m. 43 of the second is also hard to credit; these seem to share only an opening chromatic neighbor-note figure.

18. Charles E. Ives, *Eleven Songs and Two Harmonizations*, ed. John Kirkpatrick (New York: Associated Music Publishers, 1968), 48–51.

19. See Eiseman, "Symphonic Tradition," 4, 7, and 35–36, and William K. Kearns, "Horatio Parker 1863–1919: A Study of His Life and Music" (Ph.D. diss., University of Illinois at Urbana-Champaign, 1965), 658.

20. An edition of this movement is in Wallach, "New England Education," 370 and 379–95; he discusses it on pp. 273–77. Ives dated it variously between ca. 1898 and 1907; see *Memos*, 67, 150, and 156. Sherwood, 26 May 1994, notes that some sketches are on undated paper in a hand ca. 1907 or just before, and pp. 5–7 of the sketches and the ink copy are on 16:gS4 paper, available 1907–13, in a hand of ca. 1907 (the ink copy perhaps a bit later). Either the first or the second movement of the "Pre-First" Sonata was Ives's first completed work for violin and piano, finished no earlier than ca. 1906–7.

21. Thanks to Jonathan Elkus for these examples from Sousa.

22. The first draft of this movement (f3111–12/q1700–1701) is of the final section only, with annotations in the left margin indicating the order of performance: "1st Time" the cello and piano right hand play; "2nd Time" the violin and piano left hand; and "3rd All." The first page of this is shown in Kirkpatrick, "Critical Commentary," 6. The appearance of this draft suggests that Ives sketched these measures before deciding on the additive form. For the date, see note 16 above.

23. Ives dated the work 1911 in his work-lists, but Kirkpatrick suggests 1 April 1906 or 1907 on the basis of a note on the manuscript; see *Memos*, 157, and Kirkpatrick, *Catalogue*, 65. Sherwood, 15 July 1994, notes that the sketch is on 16:gS4 paper, available 1907–13, in a hand from between 1907 and 1914, closer to 1914, supporting Ives's 1911 date; a later patch is from ca. 1914.

24. Ives played this work in two recitals in June 1890; see Wallach, "New England Education," 152.

25. I am grateful to George Brandon, personal communication, 7 May 1992, for helping me to clarify both the importance of the tradition of church organist improvisation and its limits as an influence on Ives.

26. See Ives's comments on Franck and d'Indy in *Essays*, 72 and 73. Ives kept a picture of Franck on the inside door of his West Redding studio; see the photograph in Perlis, *Ives*

Remembered, 90. H. Wiley Hitchcock, *Ives*, 58, compares the second and third movements of the Fourth Violin Sonata to *Istar*, and Alexander, *Evolving Keyboard Style*, 90, mentions this and the Franck *Variations symphoniques* as possible precedents for Ives's "notion of variations trying to 'find' their tune." The Franck received its first United States performance in 1898 in New York, the d'Indy in 1898 in Chicago and in 1899 in Boston and New York; see Johnson, *First Performances*, 140 and 199.

27. See Konrad Wolff, *Masters of the Keyboard*, enlarged ed. (Bloomington: Indiana University Press, 1990), 213–14.

28. John Daverio, "Schumann's 'Im Legendenton' and Friedrich Schlegel's *Arabeske*," *19th-Century Music* 11 (Fall 1987): 150–63. In an earlier version of the Fantasy, the passage with the Beethoven quotation was reprised at the end of the third movement; see Alan Walker, "Schumann, Liszt and the C major Fantasie, Op. 17: A Declining Relationship," *Music and Letters* 60 (April 1979): 156–165. My thanks to Geoffrey Block for suggesting the Fantasy and to Andreas Giger for drawing these articles to my attention.

29. Maynard Solomon, "The Ninth Symphony: A Search for Order," in *Beethoven Essays* (Cambridge, Mass.: Harvard University Press, 1988), 3–32; quotation from p. 14. Thanks to Geoffrey Block for suggesting the similarity of Solomon's findings to Ives's procedures.

30. See mm. 9–11, 22-27, 39–42, 51–53, 66–72, and 82–87 for the gradual growth of the theme. See Cecil Gray, *Sibelius*, 2nd ed. (London: Oxford University Press, 1934), 135–36 and 142–43, and Constant Lambert, *Music Ho!: A Study of Music in Decline* (London: Faber and Faber, 1934), 130–32, for early studies that stress Sibelius's formal innovations in these two symphonies. Recently, James Hepokoski has identified several Sibelius works, including the scherzo and finale of the Third Symphony (1907), *Luonnotar* (1913), and the whole Fifth Symphony (1915, rev. 1916 and 1919), that are characterized by a process of "teleological genesis," the gradual generation of a *telos* that is the final goal of the work; see Hepokoski, *Sibelius: Symphony No. 5* (Cambridge: Cambridge University Press, 1993), especially pp. 26–27 and 58–84, and "The Essence of Sibelius: Creation Myths and Rotational Cycles in *Luonnotar*," in *The Sibelius Companion*, ed. Glenda Dawn Goss (Westport, Conn.: Greenwood Press, forthcoming). Thanks to Professor Hepokoski for providing me with a typescript of the latter prior to publication. The two composers provide an interesting comparison. Although Sibelius's approach resembles Ives's, Sibelius seems more oriented to a process of gradual revelation, producing different formal results in each work, whereas Ives settled on a formal pattern that produced a series of movements in similar form, despite individual differences.

31. My thanks to John Barker for introducing me to this work.

32. Ives, comments on the finale of the Third Violin Sonata, in *Memos*, 69, §24, n. 1.

33. Kirkpatrick, *Catalogue*, 63 and 109–11, and *Memos*, 38–39, 55, 69–70, and 72.

34. f0878/n0895, handwriting dated ca. 1907–14 by Sherwood, 26 May 1994. See the discussion of *Thanksgiving* and its origins in chap. 5.

35. See the discussion of this sketch in chap. 5, notes 5 and 8.

36. Printed in Kirkpatrick, *Catalogue*, 80 and 110.

37. Ives dated this movement 1901; see Kirkpatrick, *Catalogue*, 71. Sherwood, 26 May 1994, dates the sketches ca. 1906–7 and the ink copy ca. 1907 by handwriting; the ink

copy is on 12SLCF10 paper, first available in 1906. This movement was later rescored by Ives or a copyist and published as *Largo for Violin, Clarinet and Piano* (New York: Southern Music, 1953). It is also published in its original scoring as *Largo for Violin and Piano*, ed. Paul Zukofsky (New York: Southern Music, 1967).

38. Ives dated this movement "1903—finished Feb 1908" and said it was copied in 1909; see Kirkpatrick, *Catalogue*, 75. Sherwood, 26 May 1994, confirms the 1908–9 date, as the pencil sketch (described on Kirkpatrick, *Catalogue*, 71) is in a hand between 1907 and 1914, closest to 1907, and the ink copy (p. 75) is on 16:gS4 paper, available 1907, in a hand early in the 1907–14 period.

39. Ives dated the rejected scherzo 1902 and said it was revised in 1907 or 1908; see Kirkpatrick, *Catalogue*, 71 and 77. According to Sherwood, 26 May 1994, the sketch is on paper not available before 1907, in a hand of ca. 1907; the first ink copy of the Second Violin Sonata version is on 16:G4 paper, available 1912–14, in a hand from between 1914 and 1919; and the second ink copy is in a hand from between 1919 and 1923. For the date of the finale, see chap. 5, note 31.

40. Early sketches for the finale suggest that it was first conceived in G major (see especially f3214/n1692, f3216/n1331, and f3225/n1341), but the surviving fragmentary sources for the completed finale show that it ended in A (see f3227–31/n1171–75 and f3232–34).

41. Sherwood, 26 May 1994, dates the first sketches for this movement ca. 1907 by handwriting, the score-sketch soon after, and the full score at the same time as that for the outer two movements, ca. 1911. Ives wrote that it was based on an organ postlude played May 1901; see Kirkpatrick, *Catalogue*, 8.

42. Perhaps coincidentally, all three of these hymn tunes were arranged by Lowell Mason from existing melodies.

43. Kirkpatrick, *Catalogue*, 8, and Henderson, *Tunebook*, 192, find *Blessed Assurance* (H9) in the figure treated in fugato in mm. 70–75, but this is unconvincing; the rhythmic resemblance does not outweigh the differences in melodic contour. Gianfranco Vinay, *L'America musicale di Charles Ives* (Torino: Giulio Einaudi, 1974), 91, suggests that the march tune at m. 100 is based on the Welsh hymn *Ar Hyd Y Nos* ("All Through the Night"), but the resemblance is brief, consisting of only four notes.

44. Magers, "Aspects of Form," 182–83, makes a similar point and calls *Woodworth* "the major unifying element of the symphony." There is a fragmentary sketch for a fourth movement in F based on *The Beautiful River* (see Kirkpatrick, *Catalogue*, 9), but this would have been superfluous, standing outside the thematic and harmonic scheme of the work.

45. For the date of the Trio, see note 16, above. The pencil sketch of the *Three-Page Sonata*, which Ives dated August 1905 (Kirkpatrick, *Catalogue*, 96), is in a hand of between 1907 and 1914, according to Sherwood, 22 July 1994; the patches are in a much later hand, ca. 1923.

46. Hitchcock, *Ives*, 44. See the analyses in ibid., 44–48; David Nicholls, *American Experimental Music, 1890–1940* (Cambridge: Cambridge University Press, 1990), 34–40; Mary Ann Joyce, "The *Three-Page Sonata* of Charles Ives: An Analysis and a Corrected Version" (Ph.D. diss. [part II], Washington University, 1970); Gingerich, "Processes of Motivic Transformation," 126–55; and Carol K. Baron, "Ives on His Own

Terms: An Explication, a Theory of Pitch Organization, and a New Critical Edition for the *3-Page Sonata*" (Ph.D. diss., City University of New York, 1987).

47. See Gingerich, "Processes of Motivic Transformation," 126–55, and J. Philip Lambert, "Compositional Procedures in the Experimental Works of Charles E. Ives" (Ph.D. diss., Eastman School of Music, 1987), 205–12 and 239–41. After completing his *Catalogue*, John Kirkpatrick searched through Ives's works for direct, transposed, and varied statements of BACH and found dozens. Many are listed in Sinclair's "Microfilm Concordance." In the other works, the motive is not as prominent as it is here, nor is it developed, nor does it have any apparent significance, nor are there signs that Ives intended to allude to Bach; rather, in most or all other cases it appears to be an artifact of chromatic counterpoint and so is not noted here. See also Henderson, *Tunebook*, 8.

48. H. Wiley Hitchcock, *Ives*, 45, relates the Andante to *Westminster Chimes*. John Kirkpatrick, "Editor's Notes," in Charles Ives, *Three-Page Sonata for Piano*, ed. John Kirkpatrick (Bryn Mawr, Pa.: Mercury Music, 1975), 17–18, suggests three possible borrowings: the hymn tunes *Proprior Deo* at mm. 31–32 (endorsed by Henderson, *Tunebook*, 204) and *Need* at mm. 36ff, and at m. 41 a cornet fantasy by Carl Foeppl, Ives's father's teacher, on "Ever of Thee" by Foley Hall. All of these are brief and remain speculative; Hitchcock's hint that Ives is ringing changes on the bell tune seems more likely.

49. This follows Kirkpatrick's edition, cited above. See the similar analyses in Gingerich, "Processes of Motivic Transformation," 144–45, and Baron, "Ives on His Own Terms," 42.

50. This group of four excludes the projected fifth sonata reconstructed by John Kirkpatrick and recorded by him with violinist Daniel Stepner on *Charles Ives: Five Violin Sonatas* (Tinton Falls, N. J.: Musical Heritage Society MHS 824501, 1982). On this sonata, which features alternate versions of movements from the *Holidays Symphony*, see Kirkpatrick's note on this recording. Only *Decoration Day* was ever sketched; see Kirkpatrick, *Catalogue*, 81.

51. The final passage (mm. 81–85), with its reference to the theme of the following movement of the First Violin Sonata, was added only when the present movement was transferred there from the "Pre-First" Sonata; see f3210/y6635 for the first version and f3374–75/n1118 for the revision.

52. See Kirkpatrick, *Catalogue*, 74.

53. *Memos*, 70–71.

54. *Memos*, 69, §24, n. 1.

55. Ives wrote that this movement was finished in 1908 (see Kirkpatrick, *Catalogue*, 85–87), but the surviving sketches are in a hand that Sherwood, 26 May 1994, identifies as ca. 1919. The best analysis is in Gingerich, "Processes of Motivic Transformation," 225–71. Mumper, "First Piano Sonata," 79, reports that the right-hand figure on the first beat of mm. 146 and 147 was thought by John Kirkpatrick to be a reference to "Home! Sweet Home!" (H108), on the basis of Ives's marginal memo on one manuscript that "I used to play more of 'there's no place like Home' here." Sinclair, "Microfilm Concordance," 85, lists this as a quotation. The resemblance is too vague and fleeting to be significant, if it is intended at all. Henderson, *Tunebook*, 204–5, finds

Happy Day in *Scene Episode*, the fourth of the *Set of Five Take-Offs* for piano, but not in the parallel passage in the First Piano Sonata finale, mm. 126–39; the passing similarity to the hymn tune is too slight to credit. Kirkpatrick, *Catalogue*, 96, and *New Grove*, dates the *Take-Offs* late 1906 to January 1907 on the basis of a manuscript memo. This is corroborated by Sherwood, 15 July 1994, who dates the handwriting ca. 1907 or a little earlier. The incorporation of part of this 1906 piece into the First Piano Sonata finale suggests that other portions of the movement and perhaps an early version of it may also have been composed by 1908, which would explain Ives's date.

56. See H. Wiley Hitchcock, *Ives*, 51; Masselos, "Preface," in Ives, *Sonata No. 1 for Piano*, iii; Mumper, "First Piano Sonata," 10 and throughout; and, most clearly and convincingly, Gingerich, "Processes of Motivic Transformation," 225–71.

57. Neely Bruce, "Ives and Nineteenth-Century American Music," in *An Ives Celebration: Papers and Panels of the Charles Ives Centennial Festival–Conference*, ed. H. Wiley Hitchcock and Vivian Perlis (Urbana: University of Illinois Press, 1977), 39–40, links Ives's interest in nonrepetitive musical structures to the nineteenth-century American tradition of narrative pieces, in which "the unity of the piece is achieved purely by the narrative; there are no large-scale repetitions of musical ideas, or even key areas, to create the kind of unity one normally expects in music" (p. 40). But cumulative settings do feature motivic development and the return of themes (such as the countermelody) and of keys (in many cases), suggesting that the European tradition of thematic forms that avoid exact repetition may be a stronger influence.

58. Kirkpatrick's note, *Memos*, 75.

59. Kirkpatrick prints this at the point of a lacuna in *Memos*, 75. The punctuation is Ives's (including the ellipsis), the bracketed matter Kirkpatrick's. "Dan S." remains unidentified.

60. According to Kirkpatrick's note, *Memos*, 75, this probably refers to the sketch on p. 15 of the same copy, a "rambunctious variant of the arpeggi in the 2nd and 3rd lines of page 3 of the Peer edition." In his *Catalogue*, 83, Kirkpatrick suggests that this was a rejected patch for p. 3 or p. 4 of the Peer edition, a passage which could scarcely be farther in mood from shouting and rambunctiousness.

61. See Charles E. Ives, *Sonata No. 1 for Piano*, rev. ed., ed. Lou Harrison, William Masselos, and Paul Echols (New York: Peer International, 1979), 10.

62. For Ives's programmatic comments on the First and Third Violin Sonatas, see *Memos*, 68, n. 1, and 69, §24, n. 1; for the Fourth Sonata, see *Memos*, 72, and Ives's "Notes on Fourth Violin Sonata," 21; on "The Alcotts," see *Essays*, 48.

63. *Memos*, 68, n. 1.

64. Mark Sumner Harvey, "Charles Ives: Prophet of American Civil Religion" (Ph.D. diss., Boston University, 1983), 219–26.

65. Thus I take issue with the argument in Charles Ward, "Use of Hymn Tunes," that the words are of central importance. His attempt to identify "manner" with the way in which tunes are treated in the music and "substance" with the extramusical meanings imparted by their texts gravely misconstrues and oversimplifies the famous distinction that Ives draws in *Essays*, 74–77. In these cumulative settings, the substance lies equally in the emotional significance carried by the hymn tunes and in the way they are developed in the music.

66. *Memos*, 132.

67. *Memos*, 132–33. See also the discussion of revivalism and Ives's use of hymn tunes in Perry, *Charles Ives*, 73–78 and 80–81.

68. Harvey, "Charles Ives," 210–19.

69. For such criticism, see, for instance, Elliott Carter, "Shop Talk by an American Composer," *The Musical Quarterly* 46 (April 1960): 199–200 (reprinted in *Problems of Modern Music*, ed. Paul Henry Lang [New York: W. W. Norton, 1962], 61–62). Carter's notion that "too often [Ives] had to let hymn tunes and patriotic songs stand for his experience without comment" shows no grasp of how Ives conveys his experiences of music through the ways he reworks it and the forms he uses.

70. In a recent article, James Hepokoski proposes that Ives's cumulative settings are memory pieces hearkening back to a time of lost childhood innocence that can never be regained; see Hepokoski, *"Temps Perdu," The Musical Times* 135 (December 1994): 746–51. My thanks to Professor Hepokoski for sharing his article before publication and for fruitful conversations about what I call "cumulative form" and what he calls "teleological genesis." He may read too much into the fade-outs that often follow the final statement of the theme, which he hears as denoting "loss, unsustainability, and the irretrievability of a cherished past." First, a quiet close is far from unusual at the end of a movement in the late Romantic tradition; for example, eleven of Brahms's sixteen symphony movements end softly. Thus, Ives's quiet endings are part of the tradition, a signal that the thematic process is complete, and not an anomaly that necessarily requires explanation. Second, there is no correlation in Ives's music between fade-outs and remembrance of his childhood. *Putnam's Camp*, a piece about childhood memories, ends with a bang, yet several pieces about Ives's experiences as an adult, including *The Housatonic at Stockbridge* and *From Hanover Square North*, end with fade-outs. So do pieces about imagined spiritual experiences as an adult, such as the Second String Quartet and the Fourth Symphony, second movement and finale. Although a fade-out may suggest the fading of an image or the ending of a moment of contemplation, what is being contemplated in one of Ives's cumulative settings is the experience of the hymn and the values it embodies, not Ives's lost childhood. Hepokoski also argues that the lack of melodic and harmonic closure in the finales of the Second and Fourth Violin Sonatas symbolizes an inability to achieve the desired goal. This is possible, but these are special cases; the great majority of cumulative settings end on the local tonic after a complete statement of the paraphrased theme or borrowed tune or phrase used as a theme. For the most part, Ives's cumulative settings seem to proclaim the value of a usable past, not the loss of an irretrievable one.

71. Nicholas Vachel Lindsay, *General William Booth Enters into Heaven and Other Poems* (New York: Mitchell Kennerley, 1913), 1. Ives uses a slightly different version of the poem, as indicated below.

72. *Vachel Lindsay Reading The Congo, Chinese Nightingale, and Other Poems* (New York: Caedmon LP TC-1041, n.d.). The recording was made in New York in 1931.

73. "A Poet of Promise" (review of *General William Booth Enters into Heaven and Other Poems*, by Nicholas Vachel Lindsay), *The Independent*, 12 January 1914, 72. See Kirkpatrick, *Catalogue*, 198.

74. For this and other aspects of the song, see the brief but perceptive analysis in H. Wiley Hitchcock, *Ives*, 24–27. Henderson, "Quotation," 65–71, shows the transfor-

mations of the hymn tune in the song. Robert P. Morgan analyses the song in six parts, each ending with a statement of the refrain paraphrased from *Fountain*. See his *Anthology of Twentieth-Century Music* (New York: W. W. Norton, 1993), 77–79.

75. This analysis is based on the voice and piano version in Ives, *Nineteen Songs*, 2–7. Ives dated the ink copy September 1914 (Kirkpatrick, *Catalogue*, 198); Sherwood, 27 May 1994, confirms the date. The sketches suggest unison voices and orchestra, and John J. Becker later made such an arrangement under Ives's supervision. On imitating drumming in the piano with dissonant chords, see *Memos*, 42–43, and J. Philip Lambert, "Ives's 'Piano-Drum' Chords," *Intégral* 3 (1989): 1–36. The figure used here is the simpler form of the "street beat." The more complex form, used in the Second Symphony finale (mm. 27–29), *Country Band March* (mm. 45–48), and elsewhere, is typically used for moving musicians in step; the simpler form, played by the bass drum under the more complex form in the higher drums, may also be used alone for moving troops, using the rhythm of the leader's call, "Left, left, left-right-left." Both forms can be played in either $\frac{2}{4}$ or $\frac{6}{8}$ meter, and the simpler form may also appear with the fourth measure replaced by a single stroke on the downbeat. Thanks to Wilber England for this information. That Ives knew the simple form as the "street beat" is confirmed by his use of that term for this figure in a memo to John J. Becker on *General Booth* (f5689/n2948). Henderson, *Tunebook*, 7, prints the more complex form and calls it a "roll-off," but this is incorrect. A roll-off is a figure that signals the other players to raise their instruments and play; see Elkus, *Charles Ives and the American Band Tradition*, 22. The snare drum pattern for the standard roll-off is one Ives apparently never used (in $\frac{2}{4}$ meter, two eighth notes and a quarter rest for two measures, a measure-long drumroll accented on both beats, and a return to the opening pattern for the fourth measure). However, the bass drum part is essentially the same as that of the street beat, so that the first two measures of *General Booth* can be heard as a roll-off.

76. See Larry Starr's analysis in *A Union of Diversities: Style in the Music of Charles Ives* (New York: Schirmer Books, 1992), 93–103, especially pp. 94–98.

77. Lindsay's original has "lasses"; "lassies" is one of several variants introduced in the printing of the poem in *The Independent*.

78. Lindsay closed the quotation after the refrain, leaving "Hallelujah!" to the narrator; Ives omits the close quotation mark, leaving it ambiguous, but implies by repeating "Hallelujah" to a figure akin to that on the preceding phrase that it is sung by the same singers. Gooding, "A Study of the Quotation Process," 35, finds a reference to the Hallelujah chorus from Handel's *Messiah* in this outburst, as does Starr, *Union of Diversities*, 98.

79. The similarity of text and music makes it likely that Ives intended the reference. However, the melody is like that at "Saints smiled gravely" (mm. 13–14) and "Lurching bravoes" (m. 23); since these passages are derived from the opening notes of the song's vocal line and have no textual links to *Onward, Upward*, the later reference may be coincidental. Probably Ives recognized the similarity of his motive to the gospel song and intended the reference here as a musical and textual pun.

80. This follows the text as it appeared in *The Independent*. Lindsay's original has "out" between "from" and "the" in the first line.

81. The third stanza of the poem, which Ives did not have, notes that "Booth died blind," explaining why he "saw not."

82. See my discussion of this in "Evolution," 679–83, and my consideration of the larger problem in J. Peter Burkholder, "Rule-Breaking as a Rhetorical Sign," in *Festa musicologica: Essays in Honor of George J. Buelow*, ed. Benito Rivera and Thomas J. Mathiesen, 369–89 (New York: Pendragon Press, 1995).

83. Ives and Kirkpatrick dated this movement to 1915, the year of the incident that inspired it; see *Memos*, 93; Kirkpatrick, *Catalogue*, 19; and idem, *New Grove*. Sherwood, 31 May 1994, dates the hand in the sketches between 1914 and 1919, closer to 1919; in the score-sketch ca. 1919; and in the full score ca. 1929, perhaps a bit earlier, on paper types available after 1925 and 1922. A brief formal analysis and chart appear in Josephson, "Zur formalen Struktur," 61–62.

84. *Memos*, 92.

85. *Memos*, 92–93. The italic parentheses are used by Kirkpatrick to indicate Ives's later additions to the text, and brackets enclose Kirkpatrick's own editorial additions. Kirkpatrick's footnotes have been omitted.

86. For a complete list, see Henderson, *Tunebook*, 118–19.

87. For a compelling discussion of autobiography in music as expressed through the reinterpretation of musical material from a composer's own earlier music, see David Carl Birchler, "Nature and Autobiography in the Music of Gustav Mahler" (Ph.D. diss., University of Wisconsin-Madison, 1991).

CHAPTER 7: MODELING AND STYLISTIC ALLUSION
TO EVOKE A STYLE OR GENRE

1. See chap. 2 above and Burkholder, *Charles Ives*, 83–88.

2. Ives dated *Waltz* 1895 in *114 Songs*, 252, and "about 1893, 1894" on the sketch (Kirkpatrick, *Catalogue*, 165). Kirkpatrick, *New Grove*, guesses ?1894, and Sherwood, 27 May 1994, confirms that the hand is between 1892 and 1898.

3. Text from *Little Annie Rooney*, arr. J. C. Mayseder (Boston: Oliver Ditson, 1889). Several editions exist with slightly different words and punctuation.

4. *Invention* is Kirkpatrick's title, *Allegretto* the tempo marking. Thanks to Geoffrey Block for providing me with a copy of his edition prior to publication. Kirkpatrick (*Catalogue*, 96, and *New Grove*) suggests a date of ?1896. Sherwood, 27 May 1994, identifies the hand as ca. 1898, close to that of the fugue that Ives wrote for Parker's class in Strict Composition that spring.

5. According to Sherwood, "Choral Works," chap. 5, the first-semester assignment for Strict Composition was an invention in three voices in D.

6. Ives dated *Memories* 1897 in *114 Songs*, 236; no manuscript survives.

7. Ives dated the song 1894 in *114 Songs*, 128, but no manuscript of that version is extant. According to Sherwood, 27 May 1994, the march from which the song was arranged was sketched on 16:KSOD paper, first available in 1899, in a hand that is likely ca. 1899.

8. These bars (mm. 41–44) were added at a later time to the first page of the original sketch of the march (f4749/n2165, staves 13–14), in a hand of ca. 1902 or a little earlier (Gayle Sherwood, personal communication, 6 August 1994).

9. Ives dated this song 1900 in *114 Songs*, 219. Sherwood, 27 May 1994, dates the hand on the extant manuscript ca. 1907, though this may be a later copy.

10. *114 Songs*, 219, citing Hunt's essay "Rhyme and Reason."

11. See Newman, "Songs of Charles Ives," 2:166, for Hunt's text and a discussion of Ives's changes. The best analysis of the song is in Schoffman, "Songs of Charles Ives," 21–27. Cassandra I. Carr stresses the parodistic nature of this and several other songs in "Charles Ives's Humor as Reflected in His Songs," *American Music* 7 (Summer 1989): 123–39. Another song Carr discusses that spoofs a musical style is *In the Alley* (1896), whose title and tale of seeing "Sally" in an "alley" window suggests it may have been modeled on the popular song "Sally in Our Alley," a copy of which Ives had in his collection of music (listed in Perlis, *Charles Ives Papers*, 189).

12. *114 Songs*, 220.

13. Ives's annotation in one of his copies of *114 Songs*, printed in *Memos*, 174.

14. Ives dated the song 1902 in *114 Songs*, 149. Kirkpatrick (*Catalogue*, 187, and *New Grove*) guesses 1900–?2. Sherwood, 27 May 1994, dates the sketches ca. 1907 or a little earlier by handwriting. See the analysis of this song in Starr, *Union of Diversities*, 35–43.

15. Ives dated this work 1901 in his work-lists (in *Memos*, 158). Kirkpatrick, *New Grove*, guesses 1901–?2. Sherwood, 31 May 1994, dates the main sketches between ca. 1902 and ca. 1907 by handwriting; the last page is later. For analyses, see J. Philip Lambert, "Compositional Procedures," 182–87 and 288–90, and Nicholls, *American Experimental Music*, 21–25.

16. Noted by J. Philip Lambert, "Compositional Procedures," 184–86.

17. Henderson, *Tunebook*, 200, derives these descending scales from Henry Lahee's hymn tune *Wild Bells* (H65, "Ring out, wild bells"), which begins with an octave leap up and a descent through the major scale, immediately repeated. But this tune imitates pealing bells in the manner of change ringing, so that both it and the Ives are modeled on the same source; the Ives is not apparently modeled on the hymn tune directly.

18. See Burkholder, "Critique."

19. The dates in this paragraph are based on Sherwood, "Choral Works," chap. 3.

20. For an analysis of the first section of *Psalm 67*, including deeper parallels with Anglican chant, see Burkholder, "Critique," 209–15.

21. For a list of parallel passages and locations of the (twice borrowed) borrowings, see John Kirkpatrick's "Editor's Notes," in Charles E. Ives, *Study No. 21: Some South-Paw Pitching!*, ed. John Kirkpatrick (Bryn Mawr, Pa.: Mercury Music, 1975), 7. Ives dated the work 1908 (see *Memos*, 155). Kirkpatrick, *New Grove*, guesses ?1909. Sherwood, 27 May, 1994, dates the hand ca. 1914 or a little later. H. Wiley Hitchcock, *Ives*, 48, notes that "the title uses the American baseball slang for a pitcher who is left-handed" and suggests that the juxtaposition of "Massa's in de Cold Ground" and "Joy to the World" may symbolize "one team murdered, the other jubilant." Keith C. Ward offers an analysis in "Musical Idealism: A Study of the Aesthetics of Arnold Schoenberg and Charles Ives" (D.M.A. diss., Northwestern University, 1985), 135–46.

22. Ives dated the second movement 1923–24 in his work-lists (in *Memos*, 165), and said the third was arranged from a lost quarter-tone chorale for strings, dated 1913–14 in his early lists and 1903–14 in his later ones (ibid., 150 and 163). These two move-

ments were premiered in February 1925 (ibid., 110). Sherwood, 27 May 1994, confirms that the hand is ca. 1923 in all sketches for both movements.

23. Measures 7–11 adapt mm. 1–2 of *The New River*, and mm. 12–26 develop this material. Measures 27–39 adapt the piano part of *The Indians*, mm. 1–10, and mm. 39–41 repeat and vary the last two chords of this passage. Measures 46–48 quote mm. 9–10 of "The Battle Cry of Freedom," augmenting the first three notes, and mm. 48–50 develop its motives. Measures 57–60 borrow and vary mm. 4–5 of *The Seer*, beginning the long ragtime episode, and mm. 61–64 develop a figure from m. 6 of the same song. Measures 65–72 elaborate motives from mm. 96–98 of the First Piano Sonata, movement IIb (or mm. 71–72 of *Ragtime Dance No. 1*), presenting the borrowed passage most directly in mm. 69–70. (Ives borrows his own music here, not *Happy Day* as indicated in Henderson, *Tunebook*, 205, although Ives's theme uses a rising 5–1–2–3 motive from either *Happy Day* or *Bringing in the Sheaves*.) Measures 73–80 seem to paraphrase mm. 84–87 of movement IIb (or mm. 57–60 of *Ragtime Dance No. 1*); the pitches differ, but the rhythm and melodic contour are very similar. Measures 83–86 borrow mm. 97–98 of movement IVb of this sonata (or mm. 54–55 of *Ragtime Dance No. 4*) and repeat the second measure twice in quarter-tone transpositions. Measures 90–97 return to *The Seer*, drawing from mm. 4–6 of the latter (at mm. 90–92 and 96–97) and from its transposed, varied reprise at mm. 25–29 (mm. 27–28 are borrowed literally in mm. 93–94, and m. 95 echoes m. 94; the entire passage is a variant of mm. 25–29 of *The Seer*). The last portion of the movement is derived from other parts of *The Seer*: mm. 119–23 paraphrase mm. 12–16; mm. 124–28 extend these ideas; mm. 129–37 are based on mm. 20–24 of *The Seer*, with the most direct borrowing at mm. 130–34; and mm. 139–41 repeat and vary mm. 4–5 one last time.

24. Gibbens, "Debussy's Impact on Ives," 53. He also notes the parallel between the citation of this phrase from "La Marseillaise" and the similar quotation in Debussy's prelude *Feux d'artifice*; see pp. 53–54 and Example 11 (pp. 90–91).

25. *Memos*, 111. The italic parentheses, supplied by Kirkpatrick, indicate a later insertion.

26. In the "Notes" to his edition of *Study No. 20 for Piano* (Bryn Mawr, Pa.: Merion Music, 1981), 17, note to m. 82, John Kirkpatrick points out the relationship, commenting that the chorus of "Alexander" "has quite a different shape, though it is unmistakably the tune Ives is quoting." Kirkpatrick, ibid., 12, guesses a date of 1908? for the pencil sketch and after 1914 for the ink copy; Sherwood, 27 May 1994, confirms that the sketch is in a hand between 1907 and 1914, closer to the 1914 form, and the ink copy in a hand of ca. 1914 or later.

27. See James Sinclair, "Preface," in Charles Ives, *Study No. 23 for Piano*, ed. John Kirkpatrick (Bryn Mawr, Pa.: Merion Music, 1990), 3. Sherwood, 27 May 1994, dates the paper for *Study No. 23* at 1912–14 and the hand ca. 1914 or a little later. Henderson, *Tunebook*, omits this work. Ives dated *Rube trying to walk* 1906 on a photostat and *Over the Pavements*, which incorporates the earlier work, 1906–13 in his work-lists (*Memos*, 158). Sherwood, 15 July and 31 May 1994, corroborates these dates, dating the handwriting for both *Rube trying to walk* and the sketch of *Over the Pavements* ca. 1907 and the handwriting for the sketch of the latter's cadenza somewhat later, closer to 1914.

28. Kirkpatrick, "Critical Commentary," in Ives, *Study No. 23*, 13, notes to mm. 53–56.

29. *114 Songs*, 38.

30. Gibbens, "Debussy's Impact on Ives," 43–51. See also Schoffman, "Songs of Charles Ives," 144–58, who views the song as a criticism of modern ideas of nature, using Debussy as a symbol of modern attitudes.

31. Gibbens, "Debussy's Impact on Ives," 82. See also Ives's discussion of Debussy in *Essays*, 24–25 and 81–82. David Michael Hertz describes Ives's attitude toward Debussy along very similar lines in *Angels of Reality*, 93–113; he considers *Grantchester* on pp. 106–7.

32. Dates from Kirkpatrick, *New Grove*. Sherwood, 22 July 1994, confirms that the first song was composed before 1892 in a hand like that of the "First Hymn," which Ives dated 1887; the second version consists primarily of the addition of words and cannot be precisely dated, and the final version is in a hand of ca. 1898–1902.

33. *114 Songs*, 206.

34. f6920/n2663; *114 Songs*, 68. There are many musical Smiths, but this one seems most likely, as a composer of the same generation and similar aesthetic, style, and quality as Nevin and Hawley. Other candidates include composer and singer H. Wakefield Smith (1865–1956) and lyricist Harry B. Smith (1860–1936); the latter is probably excluded by Ives's text, which seems to refer to the music alone.

35. Kirkpatrick, *New Grove*, dates this song 1923, and Sherwood, "Choral Works" and "Questions and Veracities," 440, accepts this date, using this manuscript as one of her benchmarks for Ives's hand.

36. Kirkpatrick, unpaginated notes to the 1974 recording *Charles Ives: The 100th Anniversary*. See also Kirkpatrick's similar comment in his edition of Ives, *Eleven Songs and Two Harmonizations*, iii, that "it is just possible that the chorus is a take-off of the style of Oley Speaks's *On the Road to Mandalay*."

37. Quoted by Gooding, "A Study of the Quotation Process," 19. Kirkpatrick quotes the same annotation in his *Catalogue*, 210, and in his edition of Ives, *Eleven Songs and Two Harmonizations*, 29, but omits the names of the composers both times. Much of LaForge's name is now missing from the manuscript (f7006/Q2668). LaForge (1879–1953) and Speaks (1874–1948), both American contemporaries of Ives with successful performing careers, composed songs to rather earnest texts in a conservative style little different from popular songs.

38. Joseph W. Reed, *Three American Originals: John Ford, William Faulkner, and Charles Ives* (Middletown, Conn.: Wesleyan University Press, 1984), 129. See Reed's discussion of genre in American art, pp. 129–49.

39. Ives calls it "a unison chant" in *114 Songs*, 89. There is no manuscript for the song, which Ives dated at 1919 (ibid.). Kirkpatrick, *Catalogue*, 122, guesses 1909 for the fragment of a sketch with orchestra, and Sherwood, 22 July 1994, confirms that the paper was available 1907–13 and the hand is ca. 1907–14, closer to 1914. For a stimulating analysis that takes a very different approach from the one taken here, see Starr, *Union of Diversities*, 143–48.

40. The version given in Example 7.6 is from Robinson, *The New Laudes Domini*, p. 152, which begins with this stanza. The $\frac{6}{8}$ version also appears (with a different text) on p. 310 of the *Hymnal of the Methodist Episcopal Church With Tunes*, used at the

church Ives attended in Danbury until 1889. Henderson, *Tunebook*, 50, prints the $\frac{3}{4}$ version as H53. That Ives knew this text is confirmed by his quotation from its next stanza at the end of "The Majority," in *Essays*, 199. Since this text seems to appear with no other tune than *Serenity*, it is likely that Ives identified this tune with this text.

41. An analogous substitution occurs in *General William Booth Enters into Heaven* (see chap. 6). In both cases, the two tunes share similarities of text, mood, and meaning as well as melodic contour.

42. The quotation of the harmony in the piano confirms that the source is *Serenity* rather than George C. Stebbins's *There is a Green Hill Far Away*, as suggested by Gooding, "A Study of the Quotation Process," 26–27 and Examples 4 and 5; Newman, "Songs of Charles Ives," 2:320; Henderson, "Quotation," 45–46 and 217; and Kelly, "Songs of Charles Ives," 347.

43. For another view of the alternating chords in the piano, see Douglass M. Green, "*Exempli Gratia*: A Chord Motive in Ives's 'Serenity,'" *In Theory Only* 4/5 (October 1979): 20–21.

44. Henderson, *Tunebook*, 212, suggests that the vocal line at the words "Dad won't kill a lark 'r thrush" (mm. 22–23) borrows the English horn melody in the pastoral section of Rossini's *William Tell* overture, m. 176 (H186). The gesture is similar, but the rhythm and harmony are different. If the allusion was intended, perhaps Ives meant to evoke the imagery of woods and singing birds that this section of the overture seems to convey. However, he may also have used a horn-call figure here to evoke nature, using the same traditional associations but not intending to allude to the Rossini in particular.

45. Although Ives prints the opening words of the chorus, the music corresponds more closely to the beginning of the verse.

46. Ives inscribed the sketch for orchestra to his wife "on her first birthday in Redding, June 4 1914" (Kirkpatrick, *Catalogue*, 49). Sherwood, 31 May 1994, confirms the handwriting is ca. 1914; the patches are in a slightly later hand.

47. *Memos*, 46.

48. Ives dated *Luck and Work* 1920 in *114 Songs*, 49, but dated the chamber orchestra version on his forty-second birthday, 20 October 1916 (Kirkpatrick, *Catalogue*, 51). Kirkpatrick, *New Grove*, guesses ?1913 for the song. According to Sherwood, 27 May and 22 July 1994, both versions are on paper available 1917–20 in a hand of ca. 1919. See the analysis by J. Philip Lambert, "Compositional Procedures," 138–44.

49. Neither Kirkpatrick, *Catalogue*, 51 and 192, nor Henderson, *Tunebook*, identifies this as a borrowing, though Sinclair, "Microfilm Concordance," 192, suggests it as a possibility.

50. f6765/n2906.

51. Dates from Ives, *114 Songs*. Manuscripts survive only for *Afterglow*, confirmed at ca. 1919 by Sherwood, 27 May 1994, and *Two Little Flowers*. Henderson, *Tunebook*, 212, identifies *St. Peter in Immortality* and *Two Little Flowers* but does not include *Afterglow* or *Disclosure*. Gooding, "A Study of the Quotation Process," 28, 33, and Example 19, notes the resemblance to *Olivet* in *Disclosure*; he also suggests two much less likely sources, the second theme of Tchaikovsky's Sixth Symphony, first movement, and "My Heart at Thy Sweet Voice" from Saint-Saëns's *Samson and Delilah*. Gooding also suggests (p. 31) that *Immortality* borrows from *Lux Benigna* ("Lead, kindly Light") by

John B. Dykes, presumably in the first melody notes in the piano, a rising 5–1–2–3 figure. Ives uses this figure in the Third Violin Sonata and the First Piano Sonata, but derives it from other hymns; in this case, it is probably not from any hymn, but its contour and harmonization may suggest the general style of hymns.

52. Feder, *Charles Ives*, 315–16, suggests that, in both *Immortality* and *Two Little Flowers*, "in the allusion to Saint Peter as keeper of the gates of heaven Ives is signaling his trust in an idyllic afterlife." This may overinterpret the reference, as listeners who recognize the hymn are more likely to think of a text they have sung to it than of its title.

53. f2956/q1392. Mischa Elman (1891–1967), born in Russia, was already a world-class virtuoso when he settled in the United States in 1911. He was renowned for his rich tone and expressive Romantic playing style, the obvious targets of Ives's satire. For the date of the quartet, see chap. 3, note 60.

54. Ives dated the song 1921 in *114 Songs*, 13, but 1913 on the pencil sketch (Kirkpatrick, *Catalogue*, 196), perhaps dating the final and first versions, respectively. Sherwood, 27 May and 22 July 1994, dates the handwriting in the same sketch between 1914 and 1919, closer to 1919, and the orchestral version ca. 1914 or a little later. The versions for chamber orchestra and for chorus and chamber orchestra include programmatic quotations of popular songs as well, as discussed in chap. 9.

55. In his work-lists, Ives dated the earlier versions of *The Indians* and *Majority* 1912 and 1915 respectively (*Memos*, 159, 151, and 164). Sherwood, 31 May 1994, confirms that the handwriting for the former dates from ca. 1914 or a little earlier and notes that the earliest source for the latter is a pencil full score in a hand from between 1914 and 1919, closer to 1919.

56. See the analyses of *On the Antipodes* in John McLain Rinehart, "Ives' Compositional Idioms: An Investigation of Selected Short Compositions as Microcosms of His Musical Language" (Ph.D. diss., The Ohio State University, 1970), 71–86; Dominick Argento, "A Digest Analysis of Ives' 'On the Antipodes,'" *Student Musicologists at Minnesota* 6 (1975–76): 192–200; Schoffman, "Songs of Charles Ives," 209–34; Burkholder, "Evolution," 553–63; J. Philip Lambert, "Compositional Procedures," 375–91, summarized in idem, "Interval Cycles as Compositional Resources in the Music of Charles Ives," *Music Theory Spectrum* 12 (Spring 1990): 75–81; and Starr, *Union of Diversities*, 86–93. Ives dated the work 1915–23 in his work-lists (in *Memos*, 162). Sherwood, 27 May 1994, dates the hand in the earlier sketches ca. 1919–23, but the first sketch of mm. 14–19 is in a somewhat later hand of ca. 1923. Sherwood further notes that mm. 14–15 may be a self-quotation, as they closely match mm. 84–85 of *The Celestial Country*, third movement, in both melody and harmony; this could be unintentional, or could be a kind of self-mockery akin to Ives's sendup of *A Song—for Anything* in *On the Counter*.

57. Harmony Ives suggested a date of 1911–13 for *Duty*; see Kirkpatrick, *Catalogue*, 124. Sherwood, 31 May 1994, dates the sketch 1912 or later by paper type and ca. 1914 by handwriting, and the score-sketch between 1914 and 1919 by handwriting. Kirkpatrick, *New Grove*, guesses ?1923 for *Varied Air and Variations*. Sherwood, 27 May 1994, dates the hand between 1914 and 1919 in the early sketches and between 1923 and 1929 in the later ones.

58. Starr first proved the importance of stylistic heterogeneity and contrast as a determinant of form in Ives's music in "Charles Ives: The Next Hundred Years—Towards a Method of Analyzing the Music," *The Music Review* 38 (May 1977): 101–11, and "Style and Substance: 'Ann Street' by Charles Ives," *Perspectives of New Music* 15/2 (Spring–Summer 1977): 23–33. He examines this aspect of Ives's music in detail in *Union of Diversities*. See also the discussion of this issue in Burkholder, "Evolution," 551–66.

59. See Leonard Ratner, *Classic Music: Expression, Form, Style* (New York: Schirmer Books, 1980), 3–30.

CHAPTER 8: PATCHWORK AND EXTENDED PARAPHRASE

1. "Patchwork" has been used in the Ives literature in different senses. In Rinehart, "Ives' Compositional Idioms," 180–81, it refers to Ives's custom of piecing together works from fragments he had composed somewhat independently. In Keith C. Ward, "Musical Idealism," 66–67, it refers to the succession of different ideas without apparent relation; Perry, *Charles Ives*, 63, seems to use it with a similar meaning. Gingerich, "Processes of Motivic Transformation," 1, compares Ives's compositions to "patchwork quilts comprising fragments of his heritage and experience," but argues that his works "are not haphazard patchwork: they contain patterns of melodic figuration repeated in an organized, coherent manner."

2. Ives dated the orchestral sketch "June 4 1911" (Kirkpatrick, *Catalogue*, 49). Sherwood, 31 May 1994, dates the handwriting ca. 1914 or a little earlier. Ives dated the song arrangement 1921 in *114 Songs*, 8; no manuscript survives.

3. See also the analysis by Kelly, "Songs of Charles Ives," 401–9, who interprets the song as deriving solely from *Cherith* and *Manoah*.

4. See the discussion of quodlibet in chap. 10.

5. Ives dated the instrumental version 1904 on a manuscript and in his work-lists; see Kirkpatrick, *Catalogue*, 66, and *Memos*, 157. Sherwood, 15 July 1994, dates the first two pages of the sketch ca. 1907 or perhaps earlier and the remainder between 1907 and 1914.

6. Henderson, *Tunebook*, 186, lists this as Unknown Tune H219. For the identity of this tune, see the discussion of *The Pond* in chap. 9.

7. Ives dated *Adagio sostenuto* "before 1914" in his work-lists and referred on a manuscript to a 1912 performance of an earlier version; see *Memos*, 158, and Kirkpatrick, *Catalogue*, 51. Yet the instrumental version that survives is an arrangement in a hand from ca. 1919 or a little later, according to Sherwood, 15 July 1994. Henderson, *Tunebook*, includes neither *Adagio sostenuto* nor *At Sea*. Gooding, "A Study of the Quotation Process," 28, and Sinclair, "Microfilm Concordance," 204, list *Bethany* as being quoted in *At Sea*. Schoffman, "Songs of Charles Ives," 73–83, offers a good analysis, without mentioning possible borrowings.

8. Ives dated the song 1917 in *114 Songs*, 91, and the orchestral prototype by 1907 by a memo on the ink copy (Kirkpatrick, *Catalogue*, 43 and 201). Sherwood, 27 May 1994,

dates the handwriting in the song sketch between 1914 and 1919, closer to 1919, which confirms Ives's date; but the earliest sketch for the orchestral prototype is on 16:GS4 paper, not available before 1913, in a hand of ca. 1914 (Sherwood, 6 August 1994). See the analyses of this work in Stuart Feder, "The Nostalgia of Charles Ives: An Essay in Affects and Music," *The Annual of Psychoanalysis* 10 (1982): 301–32, reprinted in *Psychoanalytic Explorations in Music*, ed. Stuart Feder, Richard L. Karmel, and George H. Pollock (Madison, Conn.: International Universities Press, 1990), 233–66; in Robert P. Morgan, "Charles Ives und die europäische Tradition," in *Bericht über das Internationale Symposion "Charles Ives und die amerikanische Musiktradition bis zur Gegenwart," Köln 1988*, ed. Klaus Wolfgang Niemöller, Manuel Gervink, and Paul Terse, Kölner Beiträge zur Musikforschung Vol. 164 (Regensburg: Gustav Bosse, 1990), 17–36 (a briefer discussion appears in Morgan, *Twentieth-Century Music: A History of Musical Style in Modern Europe and America* [New York: W. W. Norton, 1991], 141–43); and in Lloyd Whitesell, "Reckless Form, Uncertain Audiences: Responding to Ives," *American Music* 12 (Fall 1994): 304–19. Starr, *Union of Diversities*, 57–67, analyses the song without reference to its borrowings.

9. Early sketches for this work appear on f2489/n3271+3213 and f2490/n2743+1533a. Kirkpatrick, *Catalogue*, 201, Henderson, *Tunebook*, 211, and Morgan, "Charles Ives und die europäische Tradition" identify the opening gesture as "Dixie." Ives uses "Dixie" in the Trio, second movement (m. 145, violin), *The Fourth of July* (m. 109, piccolo), the Second String Quartet, first movement (m. 60, viola), and *He Is There!* (m. 21, obbligato); all are in a rapid tempo, and only the last omits the arpeggiated upbeat.

10. Feder, "Nostalgia," analyzes the song as nostalgic, and in *Charles Ives*, 253–56, Feder treats it as one of many works marked with nostalgia, which he calls "the affect perhaps most characteristically associated with the music of Ives" (p. 253). But Reed, *Three American Originals*, 54–55, offers a more convincing view, arguing that Ives's works are not "just exercises in nostalgia" marked by yearning for the past, but attempts to "rediscover old-fashioned virtue" and to explore what we in the present can gain from encountering the past directly.

11. Ives dated the song 1920 in *114 Songs*, 115. Sherwood, 27 May and 6 August 1994, dates the main sketch (f6800/y6264) ca. 1914–19 by handwriting and the ink copy ca. 1919–21. A note on the score led Kirkpatrick, *Catalogue*, 197, and *New Grove*, to suggest that 1920 was the date of a revision and that the song was composed ca. 1913–14. The note appears to refer to *The Fourth of July*, which uses the same melody as mm. 9–18 of the song in a passage (mm. 44–63) first sketched ca. 1913–14 (f0783/n0805; date according to Sherwood, 31 May 1994). If the orchestral work borrowed from the song, as seems to be the case from internal evidence, this supports Kirkpatrick's guess that there was an earlier draft of the song from ca. 1913–14, now lost. But it is also possible that the song dates from after 1914 and borrows from the orchestral work.

12. Schoffman, "Songs of Charles Ives," 89, identifies the vocal line in m. 18 as a variant of the closing motive of "The Battle Cry of Freedom," but this is probably either not borrowed or based on "The Battle Hymn of the Republic"; it first appears in mm. 12–13 as the cadential motive for the apparently original first phrase of the verse, is varied in m. 15 as part of the paraphrase of "The Battle Hymn," and returns in mm. 17–18 to conclude the verse. Kirkpatrick, *Catalogue*, 197, and Newman, "Songs

of Charles Ives," 2:273, also find "The Battle Cry" in this song but may have interchanged it with the melodically similar "Battle Hymn," which they do not list.

13. Henderson, *Tunebook*, lists this as Unknown Tune H221 (p. 186) and the "tune from Todd's opera house" as Unknown Tune H199 (p. 181, citing its appearance in *The Fourth of July*).

14. The obbligato appears to be a late addition. The only extant sketch (f6800/y6264) does not include it, and the ink copy (f6802–4/n2652–54) was completed without it. A separate page on the same paper and in the same hand (f6805/n2285) gives an alternate version of the chorus with the obbligato and the words for the second verse. The end of the obbligato was then revised and completed on the last page of the ink copy. The similarity of paper and handwriting suggests the obbligato was added soon after the ink copy was completed.

15. See the analysis by Schoffman, "Songs of Charles Ives," 84–93, particularly the eloquent conclusion on pp. 92–93.

16. Ives dated the choral version 1912 in his work-lists (*Memos*, 150 and 164) and the song 1921 in *114 Songs*, 23. According to Sherwood, 27 May 1994, the extant sketches for the song version are on paper available in 1919 in a hand of 1919–21. The sketches for the choral version do not survive, and the full score is on paper available only in 1922, suggesting that the choral version may have developed from the song rather than the other way around (Sherwood, 6 August 1994).

17. Measure numbers are for the choral-orchestral version, as the solo song version is unbarred. However, the vocal line is easier to follow in the song, which lacks the complex divisis of the choral version. Many of these borrowings are doubled in the orchestral accompaniment.

18. "Columbia, the Gem of the Ocean" appears at mm. 12–13 (flute), 22 (violin I), and 28 (clarinet); "The Star-Spangled Banner" at 14–16 (flute); some bugle-call figures at 20–22 (trumpet); and "Hail! Columbia" at 28–30 (winds). Some of these are doubled in other instruments. Not all of these appear in the piano version, which is generally sparser. Henderson, *Tunebook*, 207, finds "The Battle Cry of Freedom" at mm. 35–37 in the flute, but this is mm. 13–15 of "The Battle Hymn of the Republic," a similar tune. Nor does "The Battle Cry" appear anywhere in the voice, as Henderson asserts on p. 209. Kirkpatrick, *Catalogue*, 123, and Newman, "Songs of Charles Ives," 2: 270, also find "The Battle Cry" in this song but again may be confusing it with "The Battle Hymn." Wendell C. Kumlien, "The Music for Chorus," *Music Educators Journal* 61/2 (October 1974): 52, finds "When Johnny Comes Marching Home" in this work, perhaps meaning the bass line in mm. 4–7, which resembles mm. 1–3 of that tune; but this also derives from "The Battle Hymn," mm. 3–4 (in the version commonly sung in Ives's day and our own, which differs slightly from the 1862 version in Henderson, *Tunebook*, 68–69).

19. f5755/Q2981&n0150–f5756/Q2982. The sketch is laid out for solo voice and piano, but at the end Ives adds indications for chorus and instruments. The date "Columbus Day 1914" appears on the first page. Sherwood, 31 May 1994, dates the hand slightly later than the works known to be from 1914.

20. Henderson, *Tunebook*, 207, also finds "The Battle Cry of Freedom" in the ostinato at m. 22, but this is "Marching Through Georgia."

21. Rossiter, *Charles Ives and His America*, 153–54. The song was revised in 1919, the date Ives gives in *114 Songs*, 104. At the end of a complete sketch (of which only the last two staves survive), Ives wrote that some material in the song was "from a march for Dewey Day, NY Oct 2 1899 / from March—'National' (Inter County Festival / later used in Flanders Fields" (quoted in Kirkpatrick, *Catalogue*, 200). It is unclear which parts of the song were based on this lost work, which may have included some of the borrowed material.

22. What may be an early sketch for the piano introduction (f6858/n2562, second system, on the reverse of a draft of mm. 8–33) shows a segment of "Hail! Columbia," not used in the final version, that overlaps the beginning phrase of "Columbia, the Gem of the Ocean." This suggests that Ives had a patchwork of patriotic tunes in mind from the beginning.

23. Ives dated *He Is There!* 30 May 1917 (i.e., Decoration Day) in *114 Songs*, 107. Sherwood, 27 May 1994, dates the paper for the pencil sketch 1913–18 and the hand 1914–19, closer to 1919, which confirms Ives's date; an ink patch with the instrumental obbligato to the chorus is somewhat later, in a hand of ca. 1919–21. *They Are There!* appears in Charles E. Ives, *Nine Songs* (New York: Peer International, 1956), 19–24, and the choral version in Charles E. Ives, *"They Are There!": A War Song March*, ed. Lou Harrison (New York: Peer International, 1961).

24. Ives, *114 Songs*, 111.

25. Henderson, *Tunebook*, 210, identifies the fanfare figures in mm. 28–29 as "Reveille" and "Over There," but they are too distant from those tunes to be certain. As Henderson notes, the sketches all featured a fragment of George F. Root's "Just Before the Battle, Mother" (H111) at this point in the obbligato. One sketch (f6881/y6102) includes "Over There" in the obbligato in mm. 24–25. An ink copy by a copyist identifies most of the quotations in the obbligato (f6885–88).

26. f57778–79/Q2960–61 and f5786–88/Q2987–89. For the coda, see also Newman, "Songs of Ives," 1: 79.

27. The end of the second verse (on f5773–74) originally read "Hip Hip Hooray! for old Carl Schurz, / his soul is ever marching on."

28. f5775.

29. To the following might be added the brief patchwork melodies in two quodlibets discussed in chapter 10, the Scherzo for string quartet and *Study No. 20*. These are treated there rather than here because, like most quodlibets, they are humorous and thus differ in tone and function from the pieces discussed here, despite similarities in technique.

30. The first sketch (f3212–13/n3158–59) differs in several respects: it begins right away with the theme, including an opening eight-measure period that was later replaced by the introduction; the second reference to "Sailor's Hornpipe" is less overt; there is no ragtime episode; and all of "The White Cockade" appears, not just its second half. The sketch breaks off after this tune. A later sketch (f3440/n1186b+1185+) includes "Turkey in the Straw" in G in the piano, complete though a little distorted; this was replaced with the partial and altered references in mm. 70–80. Thus, Ives first planned to use both fiddle tunes complete and only later fragmented them. In the ragtime episode, Ives borrows his own music, not *Happy Day* as indicated in Sinclair, "Microfilm Concordance," 77; Henderson, *Tunebook*, 201–2, omits this borrowing.

31. Ives dated this movement 1909 on the manuscript, 1912–15 in his work-lists, and 1913 or earlier in *Memos*; see Kirkpatrick, *Catalogue*, 18, and *Memos*, 164 and 91–92. Sherwood, 31 May 1994, dates the sketches ca. 1914 and the score-sketch soon after that by handwriting, and the full score between 1923 and 1929 by paper type and handwriting. See the brief discussion of this work in Austin, "*Susanna*," 326–28.

32. Henderson, *Tunebook*, 196, finds *Nettleton* in the zither in this passage, but this is part of "Massa's in de Cold Ground."

33. Ives dated this movement 1911–12 on the manuscripts (Kirkpatrick, *Catalogue*, 14–15). Sherwood, 31 May 1994, notes that the sketches and score-sketch are on 16:SH4 paper, available 1915–18, in a hand from between 1914 and 1919, with later revisions to the score-sketch; subsequent patches and the full score are in a hand of between 1919 and 1923. It was rescored and revised ca. 1929 in preparation for its 1931 premiere. For another analysis, see Henderson, "Quotation," 60–64, summarized in his "Structural Importance," 441, and "Ives' Use of Quotation," *Music Educators Journal* 61/2 (October 1974): 24–28. See also Ellison, "Ives' Use of American 'Popular' Tunes," 32–34; Alan Stein, "The Musical Language of Charles Ives' Three Places in New England" (D.M.A. diss., University of Illinois at Urbana-Champaign, 1975); Austin, "*Susanna*," 328–29; and Feder, *Charles Ives*, 232–37.

34. See Peter Burchard, *One Gallant Rush: Robert Gould Shaw and His Brave Black Regiment* (New York: St. Martin's Press, 1965). For a study of the regiment and of Saint-Gaudens's statue as subjects in literature and other arts, see Chadwick Hansen, "One Place in New England: The Fifty-Fourth Massachusetts Volunteer Infantry as a Subject for American Artists," *Student Musicologists at Minnesota* 6 (1975–76): 250–71, reprinted as "The 54th Massachusetts Volunteer Black Infantry as a Subject for American Artists," *Massachusetts Review* 16 (Autumn 1975): 37–44.

35. In Example 8.3, mm. 2 and 10 of "Marching Through Georgia" differ in small details from the original 1865 print used by Henderson, *Tunebook*, 76. The variants given here are used consistently by Ives, suggesting that he knew a later version of the tune. For m. 2, see the Trio, second movement, mm. 43–46; the Second String Quartet, first movement, mm. 62–63; and *Decoration Day*, mm. 39–40. For m. 10, see *Putnam's Camp*, mm. 31–34; *Decoration Day*, mm. 37–39; and *The Fourth of July*, mm. 34–36. The references to "Marching Through Georgia" in mm. 6–9 were not present in the first sketch of this melody (f1011/n0963), which was based more directly on "Old Black Joe." The references in mm. 8–9, which embellish and obscure the "I'm coming" motive from "Old Black Joe," were added to the score-sketch (f1014/n0967) and the full score (f1024). The reference to the verse of "Marching Through Georgia" in mm. 6–7 is a late revision, first appearing in a patch (f1020/n0966) in a hand of ca. 1919–23.

36. For a brief formal analysis and chart, see Josephson, "Zur formalen Struktur," 57–58.

37. H. Wiley Hitchcock, *Ives*, 86–87, derives this ostinato from the two Civil War tunes.

38. So identified by Henderson, *Tunebook*, 194, but it may only be a motive in the style of spirituals. Logan, "American National Music," 39–40, suggests "Swing Low, Sweet Chariot." Ellison, "Ives' Use of American 'Popular' Tunes," 33–34, finds "Swing

Low, Sweet Chariot" elsewhere as well, including in the flute at m. 5, violin I at reh. C, and the ostinato at reh. D.

39. This is a late addition, added in pencil on the full score (f1034) and filled out in a patch (f1020/n0966) from ca. 1919–23.

40. Stone, "Ives's Fourth Symphony," 14–15.

41. E.g., by Cyr, "Intervallic Structural Elements"; William Brooks, "Unity and Diversity in Charles Ives's Fourth Symphony," *Yearbook for Inter-American Musical Research* 10 (1974): 5–49; and more recently by Rathert, *The Seen and Unseen*, 209–46.

42. Stone, "Ives's Fourth Symphony," 15.

43. William W. Austin, *Music in the 20th Century from Debussy through Stravinsky* (New York: W. W. Norton, 1966), 59, asserts that "To guess what Ives is getting at in his sonatas and symphonies, it is essential to recognize the tunes he quoted" and "desirable to know the texts." The issue was a point of sharp disagreement between Americans and Europeans at the 1974 Ives Festival-Conference in New Haven, where some American scholars and composers argued for variants of Austin's view and Europeans insisted that knowing the tunes was unnecessary for appreciating the music. See Laurence Wallach, "The Ives Conference: A Word from the Floor," *Current Musicology*, no. 19 (1975): 35–36, and the transcript in H. Wiley Hitchcock and Vivian Perlis, eds., *An Ives Celebration: Papers and Panels of the Charles Ives Centennial Festival-Conference* (Urbana: University of Illinois Press, 1977), 55–57. From a listener's point of view, I side with the Europeans; from an analyst's point of view, with the Americans. See Starr, *Union of Diversities*, 78–79, for a strong assertion that it is not necessary to recognize the borrowed material.

44. Mentioned in Charles Hamm, *Music in the New World* (New York: W. W. Norton, 1983), 346.

45. An exception is Harris's "Fly Away Birdie to Heaven" (1905), which closes with *Bethany* ("Nearer, my God, to Thee") as a piano postlude.

46. This survey was based on the extensive collection of American sheet music from this period in the Starr Collection at the Lilly Library, Indiana University, Bloomington, Indiana.

47. See Charles Hamm, *Yesterdays: Popular Song in America* (New York: W. W. Norton, 1979), 284–325. Sherwood, "Choral Works," chap. 2, points out that Ives lived near Tin Pan Alley (W. 28th St.) in the summer of 1898, bought music paper through the popular song publishers Tams and Witmark, and used copyists that worked for Tams. All the evidence suggests that Ives was well aware of trends in popular song.

48. See the comments on *The Things Our Fathers Loved* in Morgan, "Charles Ives und die europäische Tradition," 25–31.

49. Kirkpatrick, *Catalogue*, viii.

50. Robert Underwood Johnson, *Poems*, 2nd ed. (New York: Century, 1908), 105–7. For the inspiration of the work, see *Memos*, 87–88, where Ives dates its origin in 1908 and its completion in 1914, and his comments on f1125/n0998b and f1126/Q1016, partly transcribed in Kirkpatrick, *Catalogue*, 17. For the gestation of the orchestral version, see James B. Sinclair, "Preface," in Charles Ives, *A New England Symphony: Three Places in New England*, ed. James B. Sinclair (Bryn Mawr, Pa.: Mercury Music, 1976), iii–iv. Sherwood, 31 May 1994, dates the first sketch ca. 1908, some score-sketches ca. 1913–14 and others between 1914 and 1919 (partially confirming Ives's dates), and the

full score soon after 1919, with later patches and score pages between 1923 and 1929. Starr, *Union of Diversities*, 115–26, provides an excellent analysis focused on the layering of two divergent styles in the work.

51. This tune appears in many variants and with many different texts in hymnals of Ives's time. The barring also varies, as some versions begin the opening two quarter notes on the downbeat, for a rhythmic pattern like that of *Shining Shore* or *Azmon*, and others begin with those same notes acting as a pickup, for a rhythm like that of *Nettleton*. Ives uses the version in the hymnal used at Yale (Stoeckel, *The College Hymn Book*, 189, printed with halved note-values in Henderson, "Quotation," 253), rather than the one in Henderson, *Tunebook*, 23–24, which differs in its last three notes. In Example 8.6, the F naturals in mm. 1–2 of the Ives have been respelled as E sharps and several flags have been changed to beams to make the example easier to follow.

52. This movement must be one of Ives's songs that were composed first for instruments, with the text fully in mind, and later arranged as a song, for the scansion of Johnson's poem is perfect, and Ives inserted the words of the song and some other lines drawn from the poem as a preface to the score.

53. Ives pairs these two hymns in the Fourth Symphony finale, where he states both completely and distinctly, exploiting their shared opening. That does not happen here; the extra note is the only feature of *Missionary Chant* that appears, and it is prompted by the text. Thus, the resulting melody is a paraphrase of *Dorrnance* and not a fusion of the two, as claimed by Henderson, "Quotation," 64 and 172–73. Ives does not seem to have had the opening motive of Beethoven's Fifth Symphony in mind here, as has occasionally been suggested, for that takes quite a different form.

54. Ives dated the song 1919 in *114 Songs*, 126. Sherwood, 27 May 1994, confirms the handwriting at ca. 1919. Kirkpatrick, *Catalogue*, 38 and 202, and *New Grove*, suggests that this song may derive from the lost *Down East Overture* of 1896. This is almost certainly only a coincidence of names, as Ives attributed parts of the Second Symphony to that overture, and there is no connection whatsoever between this song and any section of that symphony.

55. Cf. Gooding, "A Study of the Quotation Process," 29, and H. Wiley Hitchcock, *Ives*, 11. Gooding, p. 56 (Example 9), also notes the chromatic variant of *Bethany* in mm. 1–2. Henderson, *Tunebook*, 186, lists the main melody of *Down East* (mm. 8ff.) as Unknown Tune H222, overlooking its derivation from *Bethany*.

56. As described by, e.g., Henderson, "Quotation," 47 and 64.

57. Henderson, *Tunebook*, 5 and 23.

58. Ballantine, "Charles Ives and the Meaning of Quotation," 173–74. Only the first page and part of the coda remain of the overture, which began with sixteen measures of different music and then followed the course of the song. Ives dated the overture 9–15 December 1912 on the incomplete extant manuscript (Kirkpatrick, *Catalogue*, 8), but Sherwood, 15 July 1994, dates the handwriting between 1914 and 1919, closer to 1919. The remainder of this chapter is adapted from the final section of my article "'Quotation' and Emulation," 20–26.

59. Jacques van Nieuwstadt, "Charles Ives: realisme en pragmatisme (I): Muzikale citaten," *Mens & Melodie* 46 (November/December 1991): 603, adopts a similar view of Ives's intent, regarding the setting of the last line as parodistic and Ives's purpose as

an attack on Victorian hypocrisy, but comments that the meaning of the quotation is not clear.

60. For a similar interpretation, see Schoffman, "Songs of Charles Ives," 171–73.

61. *Memos*, 77.

62. That hand-organs played hymns on the streets of New York is clear from Ives's story about the origins of *From Hanover Square North* (discussed in chap. 6; see *Memos*, 92–93). Although Ives did not visit London before 1924, he probably knew or assumed that street organists played hymns there as well.

63. This collection is listed and its inscription noted in a hand-written inventory of the books at the Ives house outside West Redding, Connecticut, which Vivian Perlis kindly provided to me.

64. On Twichell and Bushnell, see Burkholder, *Charles Ives*, 102–4.

65. Kelly, "Songs of Charles Ives," 244–50, also interprets the song as sincere social criticism.

66. Ballantine, "Charles Ives and the Meaning of Quotation," 180–84.

CHAPTER 9: PROGRAMMATIC QUOTATION

1. See the very clear discussion of this issue by Roger Scruton, "Programme Music," in *The New Grove Dictionary of Music and Musicians,* ed. Stanley Sadie (London: Macmillan, 1980).

2. The term "quotation" is used here because, as noted in the next paragraph, these references typically stand out as quotations. However, here as in his other uses of existing music, Ives rarely quotes exactly, tending rather to vary or paraphrase his sources.

3. *The Battle of Trenton* (1797), in James Hewitt, *Selected Compositions,* ed. John W. Wagner (Madison: A-R Editions, 1980), 88–106, includes imitations of drum patterns, trumpet fanfares, and the fife and drum corps playing "Yankee Doodle." *The Battle of Manassas* is printed in *Piano Music in Nineteenth Century America,* vol. 1, ed. Maurice Hinson (Chapel Hill, N.C.: Hinshaw Music, 1975), 5–13. It suggests the armies leaving home through the music that accompanies them: an imitation of the drums' "street beat" in the bass and "The Girl I Left Behind Me" and "Dixie" (used, surprisingly, for the Northern army) in a high register, imitating the fife. The approaching battle is heralded by trumpet calls from both sides, and during the battle bass clusters depict cannon fire while "Yankee Doodle," "La Marseillaise," "The Star Spangled Banner," and "Dixie" are heard above.

4. For the program, see the liner notes by James Sinclair to his recording with Orchestra New England of *The Orchestral Music of Charles Ives* (Westbury, N.Y.: Koch International 3-7025-2, 1990). Ives discusses the piece in *Memos,* 40 and 61, where he dates a lost ink score to 1899; Kirkpatrick, New Grove, suggests ?1898 for the music. The first part of the work survives in three sketch pages on paper available by 1892 in a hand of ca. 1898–1902, confirming Ives's date, but the remainder exists only in two pages of orchestral score on paper available by 1900 in a hand of ca. 1914–1919 (dates from Sherwood, 1 June 1994). In a memo of about 1934–36, Ives wrote out the cheers and songs used in the work (f2208–9/n2871–72). Sinclair's recording is of his own

realization; another reconstruction by Gunther Schuller appears on a recording made during the Charles Ives Festival at New England Conservatory, *Charles Ives Festival* (Boston: New England Conservatory NEC-122, 1983).

5. Published as "Dear Old Yale" in *Yale Songs: A Collection of Songs in Use by the Glee Club and Students of Yale College,* ed. Frank B. Kellogg and Thomas G. Shepard (New Haven: Shepard & Kellogg, 1882), 95, where the words are credited to H. S. Durand, Yale 1881. Henderson, *Tunebook,* 145–46, titles this song "Bright College Years" and gives Durand's first verse on p. 146.

6. See the liner note by James Sinclair to *The Orchestral Music of Charles Ives.* Ives's statements about the date of this work are vague as to whether it was written at Yale or in the spirit of his Yale days; see *Memos,* 40, 60, and 61. Kirkpatrick, *Catalogue,* 48, suggests ca. 1907, based on an address on the manuscript, but in *New Grove* dates this work at summer 1911. Sherwood, 1 June 1994, notes that the extant sketch is on paper not available before 1912 and that the sketch and score-sketch are in a hand of after 1914 and close to 1919.

7. See the analysis in J. Philip Lambert, "Compositional Procedures," 160–64, and the discussion in Feder, *Charles Ives,* 161–64.

8. For the program, see *Memos,* 62. In his work-lists, Ives writes "date uncertain, some time before 1912" (ibid., 158), and Kirkpatrick (*Catalogue,* 47, and *New Grove*) suggests ?1911. Sherwood, 1 June 1994, dates the music paper 1907 or later and the hand ca. 1914 or a little later.

9. Henderson, *Tunebook,* 194, omits "Few Days." Rinehart, "Ives' Compositional Idioms," 193–203, offers a good analysis but misidentifies "Few Days" as a composite of parts of "Columbia, the Gem of the Ocean" and "Jingle Bells." He also finds a possible fragment of "The Battle Cry of Freedom" in clarinet and trumpet II at m. 26.

10. *Memos,* 105. Ives dated the sketch July 1904 (Kirkpatrick, *Catalogue,* 30), but Sherwood, 1 June 1994, dates the hand between 1907 and 1914, closer to 1914.

11. Nicolas Slonimsky, *Music Since 1900,* 4th ed. (New York: Charles Scribner's Sons, 1971), 1491. The effect is also described by Robert P. Morgan, "Spatial Form in Ives," in *An Ives Celebration: Papers and Panels of the Charles Ives Centennial Festival-Conference,* ed. H. Wiley Hitchcock and Vivian Perlis (Urbana: University of Illinois Press, 1977), 151–52, and by Keith C. Ward, "Musical Idealism," 71, among others.

12. Ives's "Note," in *Central Park in the Dark,* ed. Jacques-Louis Monod with notes by John Kirkpatrick (Hillsdale, N.Y.: Boelke-Bomart, 1973), 31. My brackets. Quotations throughout this paragraph are from Ives's "Note" unless otherwise indicated. For programmatic annotations on the sketches, referred to below, see Kirkpatrick's "Comparison of Sources," ibid., 32. For an analysis of this piece, see Burkholder, "Evolution," 494–520. Ives dated the sketch 1906 (Kirkpatrick, *Catalogue,* 44), perhaps for the first concept or the events depicted; Sherwood, 1 June 1994, dates the hand in both sketches ca. 1914.

13. The waltz paraphrases the last phrase of "Ben Bolt." In the first sketch (f2527/Q2826), only one phrase appears, with a melody like that at m. 59 of the published score; in the final version, Ives varies this to create the two earlier phrases for a tune in AA′A″ form based on "Ben Bolt" but unlike it in form or contour. Henderson, *Tunebook,* 180, lists the flute and oboe melody as Unknown Tune H196, quoting a later variant rather than its first appearance. Healy's was a restaurant remembered by

Ives's insurance partner Julian Myrick as being on Columbus Avenue and 66th Street, near Columbus Circle and the "Poverty Flat" apartment at Central Park West and 66th Street where Ives lived with several roommates in 1901–7; see *Memos*, 264.

14. Ives dated the work 1913 in his early work-lists, 1912 in his later ones (see *Memos*, 150 and 160). James B. Sinclair, "Preface," in Charles E. Ives, *Decoration Day: Second Movement of "A Symphony: New England Holidays,"* ed. James B. Sinclair (New York: Peer International, 1989), III–IV, suggests that the work was begun in 1912 for violin and piano, recomposed for full orchestra in 1912–13, copied 1919 for a reading the next year, and revised 1931. But Sherwood, 1 June 1994, supports Ives's 1913 date and his claim on a manuscript (quoted in Kirkpatrick, *Catalogue*, 10) that the violin sonata version was arranged from the orchestral version rather than the reverse: the first sketch is in a hand of ca. 1914, perhaps 1913; several patches are on paper available 1915, in a hand after 1914 and close to 1919; the draft for violin and piano is in a hand of ca. 1919 or a little later; and the full score and subsequent patches are in a hand of ca. 1919–23, presumably before the 1920 reading. Although Henderson, *Tunebook*, 202, lists only two tunes borrowed in the version for violin and piano, the borrowings in this version (f0712–19/n0857–64) are substantially the same as in the orchestral version except that "Taps" is not present under the trio from Reeves's *Second Regiment March*.

15. The program is printed as "Postface" in the edition cited in note 14 (p. 33). See Feder, "Decoration Day," and *Charles Ives*, 237–41, on the relation of this piece to Ives's memories of his father. Starr, *Union of Diversities*, 103–9, offers an illuminating non-programmatic analysis, but Nicholls, "Unanswerable Questions," 252, questions his attempt to deal with the piece in abstract terms.

16. Henderson, *Tunebook*, 186, lists the motive as Unknown Tune H220. It is listed with the violin and piano version on p. 202 but accidentally omitted from the listing on p. 195 of tunes in the orchestral version. Sinclair, "Preface," in Ives, *Decoration Day*, v, suggests that it "may well be a quotation from a now-forgotten song (perhaps relating to the gathering of flowers, the 'early morning flower-song,' in Ives's scenario)." Vinay, *L'America musicale*, 81, suggests that it is a variant of the *Dies irae* chant; indeed, its pitch contour resembles the chant's first five notes with the first two intervals changed to whole steps, or its first seven notes with the first and third notes omitted.

17. Henderson, *Tunebook*, 195, finds "The Battle Cry of Freedom" in mm. 37–39, but this is the chorus (mm. 9–10) of "Marching Through Georgia." He also finds m. 3 of Stephen Foster's "Nelly Bly" (H124) in flute and clarinet in m. 41. Although the resemblance is almost exact, there is no reason for this tune to appear in this context; since mm. 41–42 are a close variant of mm. 3–4 of "Marching Through Georgia," the latter seems to be the intended reference, although Ives may be making a musical pun. The first four notes of a minor-mode "Yankee Doodle" found in m. 46 in violin I by Sinclair, "Preface," in Ives, *Decoration Day*, v, constitute too brief a reference to be certain; this is more likely a reference to m. 5 of "Marching Through Georgia." In an earlier section, the three-note triadic figure played by muted trumpet in mm. 22–23 is part of a longer melody in the strings and is unlikely to be "Over There," as suggested by Henderson and by Logan, "American National Music," 37; the rhythm is different, and neither the text nor the World War I tune would have any place in a piece memorializing celebrations of Decoration Day in the latter nineteenth century. Ives wrote

on one manuscript that the hymn tune *Lambeth* (H32, "People of the living God") was present at or near m. 24 (see Sinclair, "Preface," in Ives, *Decoration Day*, v, and the editorial note on p. 35); Sinclair finds no related material, but Henderson identifies the melody at m. 20 in violin I as a variant of *Lambeth*, although it is unrecognizable as a version of the hymn tune.

18. Henderson, *Tunebook*, 195.

19. The composite melody produced by the linear combination of these two songs in mm. 61–68 parallels that in the "Pre-First" Violin Sonata, first movement, mm. 126–31. Ives used the same fragments in the same order at the end of *He Is There!* (1917), first and second endings (mm. 35–39, broken off, and 41–46). The appearance of this composite melody in three otherwise unrelated works suggests that Ives thought of this as an independent melody created from fragments of the two Civil War tunes.

20. On the idea of fictional music, see Peter J. Rabinowitz, "Fictional Music: Toward a Theory of Listening," in *Theories of Reading, Looking, and Listening*, ed. Harry R. Garvin (*Bucknell Review* 26/1; Lewisburg: Bucknell University Press, 1981), 193–208, and Burkholder, *Charles Ives*, 84–86.

21. For Ives's programmatic interpretations of this work, see *Memos*, 57–59, and Charles Ward, "Use of Hymn Tunes," 25–27.

22. Kirkpatrick (*Catalogue*, 47, and *New Grove*) dates the work summer 1907 based on a memo on the manuscript, but this dates the event, not the work. Sherwood, 1 June 1994, dates the hand between 1907 and 1914, closer to 1907.

23. Quotations from the sole surviving manuscript, f2660/q2835.

24. Ives dated the overture 1911 in his work-lists (*Memos*, 156) and 1912 in *Memos*, 76. Gayle Sherwood, personal communication, 15 August 1994, dates the handwriting ca. 1914, perhaps as early as 1912 for the early sketches and ca. 1915 for the second half of the piece; the passage in mm. 370–76 first appears in the full score, in a hand of ca. 1914–15. Josephson, "Zur formalen Struktur," 60, identifies *Adeste fideles*. To my knowledge, the presence of *Christmas* has not been noted previously. Renate Hüsken, "Charles Ives' 'Robert Browning Overture,'" *Neuland* 1 (1980): 20–21, suggests parallels between two motives in the Ives and two leitmotives from Wagner's *Ring* cycle, but in both cases the similarity is mainly one of contour and is too brief and unspecific to be certain that a reference is intended.

25. See Burkholder, *Charles Ives*, 88. For the date of composition, see chap. 3, note 60.

26. *Memos*, 74. On Ives's use of gendered terms to discuss music, see Hertz, *Angels of Reality*, 178–83, and Judith Tick, "Charles Ives and Gender Ideology," in *Musicology and Difference: Gender and Sexuality in Music Scholarship*, ed. Ruth A. Solie (Berkeley: University of California Press, 1993), 83–106.

27. See Kirkpatrick, *Catalogue*, 60; missing punctuation supplied. In the *Memos*, 74, Ives does not provide a program but gives the following titles for the movements: "I. Four Men have Discussions, Conversations, II. Arguments and Fight, III. Contemplation."

28. For analyses of the quartet, see H. Wiley Hitchcock, *Ives*, 61–67, and Rathert, *The Seen and Unseen*, 139–64. In the first movement, Rathert finds allusions to *Bethany* that are probably illusory (discussed above in chap. 3). Henderson, *Tunebook*, 176, identifies the viola's first four notes as the opening of Wagner's prelude to *Tristan und Isolde;*

Rathert, p. 143, makes a similar comment. Although the intervals are identical, the different rhythm and harmony render the resemblance almost unrecognizable, suggesting that it is unintended. Henderson, p. 202, finds the opening motive of "Taps" in violin I, first movement, mm. 81–84. But similar dotted figures appear throughout the work, beginning in mm. 4–6 (viola, then violin II), often with different intervals, and a more complete rendition of "Taps" never appears. Thus this figure seems to be part of the quartet's idiom rather than a borrowing; Rathert, 146 and 308, n. 6, supports this view. Henderson also finds mm. 13–14 of "Columbia, the Gem of the Ocean" in violin II, first movement, mm. 8–10, but this may simply be a descending diatonic scale fragment.

29. Perry, *Charles Ives*, 49, suggests the argument may be about the Civil War.

30. Rathert, *The Seen and Unseen*, 155 and 157, presents a convenient table and musical example but misidentifies "Hail! Columbia" as "The Red, White and Blue" (the alternative title for "Columbia, the Gem of the Ocean").

31. Measure numbers follow the corrected Peer edition. The tune that Henderson, *Tunebook*, 164 provides for *Westminster Chimes* is not that used in most clock towers. These require a cycle of five four-note units, of which the first (3–2–1–5) sounds at the quarter-hour; the second (1–3–2–5) and third (1–2–3–1) at the half-hour; the fourth (3–1–2–5), fifth (5–2–3–1), and first at the three-quarters-hour; and the second through fifth at the hour. Of these, Ives uses only the fourth and fifth units (mm. 1–4 of Henderson's version).

32. See Ballantine, "Charles Ives and the Meaning of Quotation," 171–72, for a moving description of this passage and its meaning.

33. *Essays*, xxv. For the date, see chapter 5 above, note 71. Interpretations of the *Concord Sonata* abound. Particularly notable are Sondra Rae Clark, "The Transcendental Philosophy of Charles E. Ives as Expressed in *The Second Sonata for Pianoforte*, 'Concord, Mass., 1840–1860'" (M.A. thesis, San Jose State College, 1966); Betty E. Chmaj, "Sonata for American Studies: Perspectives on Charles Ives," *Prospects: An Annual of American Cultural Studies* 4 (Winter 1978): 1–58, and Chmaj, "Charles Ives and the Concord Sonata"; Fred Fisher, *Ives' Concord Sonata*; Lawrence Kramer, *Music and Poetry: The Nineteenth Century and After* (Berkeley: University of California Press, 1984), 171–91; Felix Meyer, *"The Art of Speaking Extravagantly": Eine vergleichende Studie der "Concord Sonata" und der "Essays before a Sonata" von Charles Ives* (Berne and Stuttgart: Paul Haupt, 1991); and Rathert, *The Seen and Unseen*, 165–208. The present analysis focuses only on the function of the borrowed material. On sources, sketches, and variants for the sonata, see Sondra Rae Clark, "The Evolving *Concord Sonata*: A Study of Choices and Variants in the Music of Charles Ives" (Ph.D. diss., Stanford University, 1972).

34. *Essays*, 47.

35. Fred Fisher, *Ives' Concord Sonata*, finds other motivic links between movements, but these are obscure and may be fortuitous: a chromatic idea related to B–A–C–H used in several movements (discussed in ibid., pp. 10–15); an opening wedge (two lines in contrary motion opening out from a common starting tone) in "The Alcotts" like that which opens "Emerson" (pp. 10–11, 13–14, and 44–45); hints of "Massa's in de Cold Ground" in "Emerson" as well as "Thoreau" (pp. 18–19); and a descending line in "Thoreau" that resembles the middle-section theme of "Emerson" (pp. 35–37).

36. *Essays*, xxv. See also Ives's comments in a letter to John Kirkpatrick printed in *Memos*, 199, and in a note on a copy of the sonata's first edition (in *Memos*, 199, n. 2).

37. *Memos,* 77. See also Kirkpatrick, *Catalogue,* 31. In one work-list, Ives dated the Emerson concerto 1907; see *Memos,* 163. Sherwood, 1 June 1994, dates the paper for the sketches 1907–13 and the hand ca. 1907–14, closer to 1914 in most cases; the cadenzas and patches are much revised and appear to date mostly from 1919 and later.

38. Since the work is largely unbarred, reference is made to the page and system numbers of the most widely available published edition, Ives, *Piano Sonata No. 2,* 2nd ed. Following the passages shown in Example 9.1, motive a appears alone as follows and perhaps elsewhere: three times on p. 2, system 3 (in octaves); p. 6, system 1; p. 13, system 3, three times in treble; p. 15, last quarter note (D♯), through p. 16, top, in the highest register; and p. 17, system 5, several times in top line and inner voices. Motive b appears alone on p. 2, system 3; p. 3, system 4, middle line and bass (bass in augmentation); p. 4, systems 1 and 3, bass (in augmentation), and systems 4–5, treble; p. 6, system 5, to p. 7, system 1, bass; p. 7, systems 3–4 (threefold high C♯ in left hand), to p. 8, first measure (A); p. 10, system 4, top line; p. 12, system 2, top and alto lines, and system 4, top line; p. 16, system 2, alto; several times on p. 18, leading up to the closing statements of the second half of the theme; p. 19, system 1, second measure, and system 3, last measure; and in the last three notes in the bass, p. 19, system 4.

39. Rathert, *The Seen and Unseen,* 168 and 186–87, notes how the movement combines four movements in one.

40. For Ives's note on the middle section theme, see *Piano Sonata No. 2,* 2nd ed., 73. For the "Tolerance" theme, see Kirkpatrick's note in *Memos,* 199, n. 3, which refers to the first, fragmentary entrance of the theme on p. 2, systems 4–5. Hertz, *Angels of Reality,* 106–9, suggests that part of the middle section is modeled on Debussy's prelude *La cathédrale engloutie.*

41. Fred Fisher, *Ives' Concord Sonata,* 33–34.

42. Of these three melodic similarities, Rathert, *The Seen and Unseen,* 188, notes the first and second, Fred Fisher, *Ives' Concord Sonata,* 22, notes the second, and Chmaj, "Charles Ives and the Concord Sonata," 42, notes the second and third.

43. Schoenberg's original formulation of the idea of developing variation suggested that later themes would be derived from the idea presented at the outset; see Schoenberg, "Bach," in *Style and Idea,* 397.

44. Kirkpatrick, "Preface," in Ives, *Symphony No. 4,* VIII. Thomas M. Brodhead offers a speculative program for the movement based on Kirkpatrick's suggestion and other available evidence in "Ives's *Celestial Railroad* and His Fourth Symphony," *American Music* 12 (Winter 1994): 419–22. I am grateful to Mr. Brodhead for sharing with me drafts of this article prior to publication.

45. Motive a appears as follows: p. 21, systems 3–4, alto; p. 22, systems 2–3 and 3–4, bass; p. 23, system 1, and p. 24, system 1, top-sounding line (divided between the hands); p. 25, end of system 2, soprano; p. 26, system 1, bass; p. 33, systems 2 and 4, and p. 34, systems 4–5, tenor; p. 47, system 4, bass (with its continuation); p. 49, *passim;* and p. 50, systems 4 and 5, and p. 51, systems 1 and 3–4, top line. Motive b appears only once (p. 46, system 4, bass) outside its statements as part of the "Alcotts" theme.

46. *Essays,* 42. Compare the similar program in an earlier memo printed in *Memos,* 187–88, which indicates that the movement begins with the image of "the 'Magical Frost Waves' on the Berkshire dawn window." The other images are difficult to connect with the music, except for the hymn and the march discussed below. For possible

identification of some episodes, including some annotations in published copies of the sonata, see Kirkpatrick's comments in *Memos*, 81, n. 7, and Brodhead, "Ives's *Celestial Railroad*," 420.

47. A similar passage later appeared in Ives's song "*1, 2, 3*" (1921), as noted by Rathert, *The Seen and Unseen*, 200. Sinclair, "Microfilm Concordance," 89, lists "Pig Town Fling" as another borrowing, but nothing in the movement clearly resembles it.

48. *Essays*, 48.

49. See the discussion of this movement in chap. 5.

50. *Essays*, 47.

51. *Essays*, 67–69; most of this is reprinted in Ives, *Piano Sonata No. 2*, 2nd ed., 58. Hertz, *Angels of Reality*, discusses the relation of the music to the program (pp. 197–203) and identifies passages in two Debussy preludes as possible models for passages in *Thoreau* (pp. 106–11).

52. *Essays*, 68; Boatwright supplies the passage from *Walden* on p. 249, n. 38. Ives identifies this as a reference to "Down in de cornfield" in his notes (*Piano Sonata No. 2*, 2nd ed., 74). For a different interpretation of this passage, linking it not only to Foster but to the hymn *Come, Ye Disconsolate*, see Fred Fisher, *Ives' Concord Sonata*, 18–21. Rathert, *The Seen and Unseen*, 205 and p. 311, n. 35, suggests that this tune is meant to evoke "the simplicity of the authentic," with Foster serving as a musical counterpart to Thoreau.

53. Ives dated the song 1915 in *114 Songs*, 103; no manuscript survives.

54. In the *Essays*, see chiefly the prologue, pp. 3–8, and epilogue, pp. 70–102.

55. See Ives's letter to John Kirkpatrick, in *Memos*, 200. A sketch toward the first Emerson transcription was made ca. 1919, and sketches toward all four were made in a copy of the published sonata; the ink copy is on 16:F7 paper, available 1925–27, in a hand of 1925–29 (Kirkpatrick, *Catalogue*, 101–2, and Sherwood, 6 August 1994). Thomas M. Brodhead discusses this work and its relation to the *Emerson Concerto* and the two editions of the *Concord Sonata* in "Ives's *Celestial Railroad*," 411–16.

56. Brodhead, "Ives's *Celestial Railroad*," 394–410 and 415–19, especially 418. See also Ives's comments in *Memos*, 64–66, 81–82, 164–65, and 204, and Kirkpatrick's note on the gestation of the *Concord Sonata* in *Memos*, 163; Brodhead explains the apparent discrepancies between these and his own account on pp. 418–19. Sherwood, 31 May and 1 June 1994, dates work on *The Celestial Railroad* between 1919 for the first sketches and ca. 1923 for the ink copy. Using different means, Brodhead also dates the ink copy between 1921 and 1923 (p. 398). Essentially, Brodhead argues that the ink copy of the piano work must be the main source for the score-sketch of the Fourth Symphony, second movement, the earliest extant source for that movement, for two main reasons. First, there are several layers of revision in ink on the ink copy. The final version in ink was the basis for George Price's copy of the fantasy, showing that it represented Ives's conception of the fantasy. It also matches the music in the score-sketch, suggesting that the latter was written out only after the final version of the fantasy had been created. Second, lines added in pencil to the fantasy, which were not part of *The Celestial Railroad* as copied by Price, appear in the score-sketch assigned to instruments other than the piano; thus Ives must have used the ink copy to make sketches toward the instrumental expansion that he later copied out as the score-sketch. Brodhead's scenario is complicated, however, by the existence of a few

sketches toward the symphony movement that predate 1919 and by the presence of several layers of writing on the score-sketch, the earliest between 1919 and 1923, which appears to predate the ink copy of the fantasy (information from Sherwood, 6 August 1994). It may be that Ives used the early layers on the score-sketch in writing the piano fantasy, then used the revisions and additions on the fantasy to revise the score-sketch, so that each work is a source for the other; this conforms fairly closely to Brodhead's conclusions. In any case, the symphonic movement as it stands in its final version is an orchestration and expansion of the fantasy.

57. See *Essays*, 42, and *Memos*, 81–82, 187, and 204.

58. Brodhead, "Ives's *Celestial Railroad*," 389–90. See also the "Editor's Preface" to Charles E. Ives, *The Celestial Railroad*, ed. Thomas M. Brodhead (New York: Associated Music Publishers, forthcoming). I am grateful to Mr. Brodhead for giving me a copy of his edition prior to publication. For other discussions of the relation of Hawthorne's tale to the symphony movement, see Magers, "Aspects of Form," 338–49, summarized in "Charles Ives's Optimism: or, The Program's Progress," in *Music in American Society 1776-1976: From Puritan Hymn to Synthesizer*, ed. George McCue (New Brunswick, N.J.: Transaction Books, 1977), 76–80, and Feder, *Charles Ives*, 277–78. Rathert, *The Seen and Unseen*, 94–106, considers the relation of Hawthorne's story and philosophy to both the symphonic movement and the "Hawthorne" movement of the *Concord Sonata*.

59. The list of borrowings given here differs from those in Henderson, *Tunebook*, 205–6; in Brodhead, "Ives's *Celestial Railroad*," 390–93; and in the "Editor's Preface" to Brodhead's edition. What Henderson identifies as "Massa's in de Cold Ground" is part of "Old Black Joe," and what he identifies as "Hello! Ma Baby" is a ragtime version of *Throw Out the Life-Line*. He also finds *Beulah Land* at mm. 159ff.; although this tune is on the manuscript, it is not part of the ink score of *The Celestial Railroad* but is part of the pencil sketches towards the Fourth Symphony, second movement. Brodhead finds *Bethany* in mm. 19–21, but this is more likely part of *God Be With You*. He also suggests that mm. 43–47 paraphrase *Throw Out the Life-Line* (mm. 3–4 or 7–8 of the verse) over "Peter Peter Pumpkin Eater" (the melody called Unknown Tune H201 by Henderson, p. 181). This is possible, though the latter tune is hard to explain programmatically. This melody also appears in "Hawthorne" (p. 23, last beat of system 2 through system 3), and an annotation in one of Ives's printed copies of the sonata links this to the image in Hawthorne's "Feathertop" of demons (the right hand) dancing around the rim of a pipe (the left hand); see *Memos*, 81, n. 7, and *Essays*, 42. Finally, Brodhead hears *The Beautiful River* in mm. 87–88, which is unlikely. As always, there may be other references not yet identified.

60. Brodhead's edition marks these points, based on annotations in Ives's manuscripts. Compare the different interpretation in Magers, "Aspects of Form," 338–49.

61. Charles E. Ives, *The Pond* (Hillsdale, N.Y.: Boelke-Bomart, 1973), 2. Ives dated *The Pond* 1906 in his work-lists (see *Memos*, 157) and *Remembrance* 1921 in *114 Songs*, 27. Sherwood, 1 June 1994, dates the first sketch for *The Pond* between 1907 and 1914, closer to 1907, and the remaining sketches and score ca. 1914 by handwriting; the score is on paper not available before 1912. No manuscript for the song is extant.

62. The early sketches have a longer segment from "Taps" and place it in the cornet, which also plays the main melody. In the first sketch (f2660/Q2835), the figure from

"Taps" is marked "in the distance"; in the first complete draft (f2516/Q2681&2916b and f2517/Q2682&2915a), "Taps" appears in m. 10 with all other instruments tacet and is echoed in the upper register by violin. These variants are printed in the notes to mm. 9a and 10 in John Kirkpatrick, "Comparison of Sources," in Ives, *The Pond*, 8. Both variants are more naturalistic than the final version.

63. Stuart Feder, "Charles and George Ives: The Veneration of Boyhood," *The Annual of Psychoanalysis* 9 (1981): 306–9; and Feder, *Charles Ives*, 2–3 and 227. Henderson, *Tunebook*, 192, endorses this identification of the tune.

64. *Hymnal of the Methodist Episcopal Church With Tunes*, p. 52. Gooding, "A Study of the Quotation Process," 28, 29, and 53, suggests that Ives's melody is based on the hymn tune *Camden* (one of at least two tunes by that name), although he admits it is "obscure" and has located only one publication of it, in *The Mozart Collection of Sacred Music*, ed. Eli Ives, Jr. (New York: Cady and Burgess, 1848), p. 141. Since it begins exactly like *David*, mm. 1–3, and has a different continuation, the obscurity of *Camden* suggests that *David* is the more likely source.

65. Stoeckel, *The College Hymn Book*, p. 164 (see also *St. John*, an adaptation of this melody for a six-line stanza, on p. 97); and Louis F. Benson et al., eds., *The Hymnal, Published by Authority of the General Assembly of the Presbyterian Church in the United States of America* (Philadelphia: The Presbyterian Board of Publication and Sabbath-School Work, 1895), no. 538.

66. Stoeckel, *The College Hymn Book*, p. 234. See also *Prince* in Roswell D. Hitchcock et al., eds., *Hymns and Songs of Praise for Public and Social Worship* (New York and Chicago: A. S. Barnes, 1874), p. 33, and in Robinson, *The New Laudes Domini*, p. 221; the latter also includes a different adaptation, *Raynolds*, on p. 330. John Stainer's *Rest*, which appears in Benson et al., *The Hymnal*, as nos. 422, 596, and 616, is another possible candidate, opening with a similar pitch contour but rather different rhythm. It is also possible that Ives's tune is a more distant paraphrase of a better-known hymn. For example, the third phrase of *Eventide* ("Abide with me") has the same pitch contour as mm. 3–6 of *The Pond* but a different rhythm.

67. Kirkpatrick (*Catalogue*, 146, and *New Grove*) suggests a date of 1897–?98 and notes that *The Bells of Yale* was published in *Yale Melodies* in 1903. Sherwood, "Choral Works," chap. 3, dates the sketches and first two copies ca. 1898, the third and fourth copies on paper available 1899–1902 in a hand from between 1898 and 1902.

68. For the note, see Ives, *Nineteen Songs*, 52. Ives dated the song Nov. 1911 on a copy (see Kirkpatrick, *Catalogue*, 195) and in *Nineteen Songs*, 9. Sherwood, 27 May 1994, dates the handwriting ca. 1914.

69. Kirkpatrick, *Catalogue*, 201, suggests "Deep River" (H14) as the source for this figure, but the match of rhythm and text with "The Old Oaken Bucket" confirms the latter as the most likely source. Ives dated *Tom Sails Away* "Sep 1917" on a copy (ibid.) and 1917 in *114 Songs*, 112. Sherwood, 27 May 1994, confirms that the hand is between 1914 and 1919.

70. That the speaker is a woman is implied by the character of her feelings and by the fact that, if a man, he would likely be heading to war himself. But see Starr's opposing view in *Union of Diversity*, 71.

71. These words appear in the original version, in *114 Songs*, 114. In *Nineteen Songs*, 22, this line reads "But today! Today Tom sailed away," an unfortunate change that deemphasizes the ambivalence in the speaker, who feels pride as well as regret.

72. Thus, while agreeing with most of Starr's analysis of the song in *Union of Diversity*, 71–78, I believe that he underestimates the significance of the borrowed material; as is clear in his discussion of the quotation from "Over There" (p. 78), recognizing the borrowed text and tune enriches our understanding of this passage, for, without being familiar with the "boisterous, affirming quality" of Cohan's song, we would not catch the irony, ambiguity, and poignancy that Starr points out in Ives's reinterpretation.

73. Ives dated the song 1921 in *114 Songs*, 50. Sherwood, 31 May 1994, dates the full score 1922 or later by paper type and ca. 1923–29 by handwriting.

74. *Nov. 2, 1920* begins with the first part of this same passage from *Lincoln*. Ives could count on his audience's recognizing the reference, for in *114 Songs* he placed *Nov. 2, 1920* (no. 22, pp. 50–55) a few songs after *Lincoln* (no. 11, pp. 23–26).

75. H. Wiley Hitchcock, "Ivesiana: The Gottschalk Connection," *Institute for Studies in American Music Newsletter* 15/1 (November 1985): 5. The earliest extant sketch for the sixth verse (on f6020/n2607) has completely different music, suggesting that the lost earlier version did not borrow this tune. Ives dated *Psalm 90* 1923–24 in his first list of works (see *Memos*, 148) but elsewhere referred to a lost earlier version (see ibid., 47, and Kirkpatrick, *Catalogue*, 140–41). Sherwood, "Choral Works," chap. 3, confirms the hand at ca. 1923.

76. Robert Offergeld, "More on the Gottschalk Connection," *Institute for Studies in American Music Newsletter* 15/2 (May 1986): 1–2 and 13.

77. *Hymnal of the Methodist Episcopal Church With Tunes*, p. 42. The tune also appears in the Yale college hymnal (Stoeckel, *The College Hymn Book*, p. 139, as *Last Hope*) and in the last hymnal that Ives used as an organist (Benson et al., *The Hymnal*, nos. 281 and 516, as *Mercy*), printed with texts that have no apparent relation to the imagery of this portion of Psalm 90.

78. Kirkpatrick, in *Memos*, 147, n. 1, and *New Grove*, dates the work 1925; Sherwood, 31 May 1994, dates the hand ca. 1929.

79. John Kirkpatrick, "Commentary," in Charles E. Ives, *Johnny Poe*, realized and ed. John Kirkpatrick (New York: Peer International, 1978), 18–22, suggests that the bassoon and clarinet line in mm. 13–14 may be a disguised quotation of the Siegfried leitmotive from Wagner's *Ring* cycle, finds B–A–C–H transposed in mm. 22–23, and sees the second phrase of "Taps" in the viola in mm. 61–62. Of these, the first is unlikely, the second is possible (but may be coincidental), and the last is simply not present in the score.

80. Bruce, "Ives and Nineteenth-Century American Music," 34–35 and 38–39. Bruce's claim that Stephen Foster's "Song of All Songs" uses borrowed music is unsupported; the later verses string together titles and phrases of text from several dozen different songs, making it a textual patchwork, but the music to each verse is the same and apparently original.

81. See Roger Lax and Frederick Smith, *The Great Song Thesaurus*, 2nd ed. (New York: Oxford University Press, 1989), 24 (on "Hoochy-Koochy") and 378 (on "Streets of Cairo").

82. Laurence Bergreen, *As Thousands Cheer: The Life of Irving Berlin* (New York: Viking, 1990), mentions the borrowings in "Alexander's Ragtime Band" (p. 40) and "That Mesmerizing Mendelssohn Tune" (pp. 45–46). Berlin's use of the Mendelssohn in at least three different songs again parallels Ives's tendency to use some tunes repeatedly in work after work.

1. For comparisons to Joyce, see Lou Harrison, "On Quotation," *Modern Music* 23 (Summer 1946): 166–69; Cowell and Cowell, *Charles Ives*, 147 (who also mention Eliot); Henderson, "Quotation," 31; Morgan, "Rewriting Music History," 11; Peter Dickinson, "A New Perspective for Ives," *The Musical Times* 115 (October 1974): 837–38; and H. Wiley Hitchcock, *Ives*, 10. Both "collage" and "stream of consciousness" are terms that appear frequently in the Ives literature, with varying meanings. See for instance Newman, "Songs of Charles Ives," 1:171 (on the song *Religion*, a patchwork); Monika Tibbe, "Musik in Musik: Collagetechnik und Zitierverfahren," *Musica* 25 (November–December 1971): 562–63; Konold, "Neue Musik," 240 and 242; Morgan, "Rewriting Music History," 11; Vinay, *L'America musicale*, 79–80; David Wooldridge, "Charles Ives and the American National Character: 'Musical Spirit of '76,'" in *South Florida's Historic Ives Festival 1974-1976*, ed. F. Warren O'Reilly (Coral Gables, Fla.: University of Miami at Coral Gables, 1976), 29; Morgan, "Spatial Form," 154; and H. Wiley Hitchcock, *Ives*, 10 (which refers to *The Things Our Fathers Loved* and *He Is There!*, both patchworks, as "collage-like assemblages") and 62 (which uses "collage" for certain passages of the Second String Quartet). The most thorough treatment of "stream of consciousness" in Ives's music is in Perry, *Charles Ives*, XVIII and 40–55, but she applies the concept to virtually all of Ives's mature music and includes a variety of techniques. Howard Isham, "The Musical Thinking of Charles Ives," *Journal of Aesthetics and Art Criticism* 31 (Spring 1973): 402, suggests "montage" as "the basic constructive principle in Ives's music." Perry also uses the term (pp. 53–54). Europeans writing on collage often mention Ives as a progenitor or early practitioner without always distinguishing between his various procedures for multiple quotation; see for example Zofia Lissa, "Historical Awareness of Music and Its Role in Present-Day Musical Culture," *International Review of the Aesthetics and Sociology of Music* 4 (June 1973): 26–32, and Sonntag, *Untersuchungen zur Collagetechnik*, who defines "collage" very broadly (p. 16) and treats the Concord Sonata, the Second Symphony, and all three movements of *Three Places in New England* as examples of collage.

2. See Maria Rika Maniates (with Peter Branscombe), "Quodlibet," in *The New Grove Dictionary of Music and Musicians*, ed. Stanley Sadie (London: Macmillan, 1980). Successive combination is clearly related to patchwork in technique, but Ives's patchworks generally adopt a serious tone, in strong contrast to the characteristic humor of quodlibets.

3. Kirkpatrick, *Catalogue*, 216. See the discussion of this movement and the date of this sketch in chap. 5.

4. Charles Ives, *The Circus Band*, arr. George F. Roberts (New York: Peer International, 1969), 15. Cully Kernochan was a fraternity brother of Ives's; see the program for the DKE play "Hells Bells" (f5106/y6099), for which Kernochan acted the part of Noey Wont and Ives provided the music.

5. Ives, *Circus Band*, 16.

6. *Memos*, 39; italic parentheses used by Kirkpatrick to indicate a later insertion by Ives.

7. For the date, see chap. 6, note 16; for the title, see Kirkpatrick, *Catalogue*, 67.

8. See *Memos*, 166, and Kirkpatrick, "Critical Commentary" to the Trio, 2. The list of borrowings given below is based in part on Kirkpatrick's list on pp. 2–3.

9. Kirkpatrick describes this last as "the tune [Ives's copyist] George Roberts remembered as a take-off of a man limping" (ibid., 3). See the discussion of this tune in chap. 9. Henderson, *Tunebook*, 200, fails to recognize "Few Days" and relates this melody to "Columbia, the Gem of the Ocean" and "Jingle Bells"; for a musical example, see his "Quotation," 29–30.

10. As in *March No. 1*, Ives uses a different version of the latter tune than that in Henderson, *Tunebook*, 136–37. See chap. 3, note 10.

11. Quoted in Kirkpatrick, "Critical Commentary," 2.

12. Henderson, *Tunebook*, 184–85, lists the first unknown tune as H214 but does not list the others. On p. 200, he identifies part of the second, at its varied recurrence in m. 108, as "Turkey in the Straw," but the similarity is slight and probably coincidental. Ulrich Maske, *Charles Ives in seiner Kammermusik für drei bis sechs Instrumente* (Regensburg: Gustav Bosse, 1971), 26–27, identifies the cello tune at m. 107 as a paraphrase of "Marching Through Georgia"; if so, it is a masterly transformation of a mid-nineteenth-century tune into a melody characteristic of 1890s popular song.

13. Kirkpatrick, "Critical Commentary," 3.

14. Ibid. Maske, *Charles Ives in seiner Kammermusik*, 25–26, 33–34, and 118, suggests that the two references to *In the Sweet Bye and Bye*, together with the extended quotations that precede them, are pillars of the movement's form.

15. See the annotations in Kirkpatrick, *Catalogue*, 66, and Ives's brief discussion of the piece in *Memos*, 34. Ives dated the work 1903 or 1904, revised by 1914 (see the above and his work-lists, ibid., 157). Sherwood, 15 July 1994, dates the sketch between 1907 and 1914 with revisions ca. 1934.

16. For this tune, see the discussion of "Streets of Cairo" in chap. 9.

17. On motivic links between the quoted tunes, see Rinehart, "Ives' Compositional Idioms," 189–93.

18. See Kirkpatrick's notes in Ives, *Study No. 20*, 17. The composite melody here and the cello melody of the Scherzo for string quartet both resemble the patchworks discussed in chap. 8 in technical terms, but the intended effect in both works is clearly humorous, placing them in the genre of quodlibet.

19. Kirkpatrick, *Catalogue*, 100, dates this work 1911 by an address on the manuscript. Sherwood, 1 June 1994, confirms that the piece is on paper available by 1907 in a hand of ca. 1907–14.

20. The episodes are cited in the coda in their original order except for the fourth, which is abridged in the last four bars of the work. For the precise relationship of the coda to the rest of the work, see the note for m. 150 in Charles E. Ives, *Waltz-Rondo for Piano*, ed. John Kirkpatrick and Jerrold Cox (New York: Associated Music Publishers, 1978), IV.

21. Ives dated *The Fourth of July* between 1911 and 1913 (see *Memos*, 83 and 104; his work-lists in ibid., 150 and 160; and his manuscript notes in Kirkpatrick, *Catalogue*, 11–12). But Sherwood, 31 May 1994, dates the extant sketches ca. 1914, no earlier than 1913 by handwriting (one page is on 16:GS4 paper, not available before 1913); the score-sketch ca. 1914–19, closer to 1919; the full pencil score and extra pages in pencil ca. 1919–23; and extra score pages in ink and extra patches 1922 or later by paper and ca. 1923–29 by handwriting.

22. *Memos,* 104. For analyses of the work, see Arthur Maisel, *"The Fourth of July* by Charles Ives: Mixed Harmonic Criteria in a Twentieth-Century Classic," *Theory and Practice* 6/1 (August 1981): 3–32; Mark D. Nelson, "Beyond Mimesis: Transcendentalism and Processes of Analogy in Charles Ives' The Fourth of July," *Perspectives of New Music* 22/1–2 (Fall/Winter 1983-Spring/Summer 1984): 353–84; and Shirley, "'The Second of July.'"

23. Ives mentions this tune, also called "The Red, White and Blue," in his program, printed in *Memos,* 104, n. 1, and in Charles E. Ives, *The Fourth of July,* ed. Wayne D. Shirley (New York: Associated Music Publishers, 1992), VII. Marshall, "Charles Ives's Quotations," 54–56, discusses the use of this tune in *The Fourth of July* as a source for motives and harmonies, noting that it "serves as a structural framework for the entire movement in much the same way that a Lutheran chorale melody would serve as the formal model and motivic source for a cantata movement or an organ chorale of J. S. Bach."

24. *Memos,* 104, n. 1.

25. Maisel, *"The Fourth of July,"* presents a Schenker-based harmonic analysis that supports the thematic analysis given here. Maisel sees the piece in B♭ major, the key of the final statement of the theme and countermelodies, and analyzes the first two main sections (up to m. 80) as embellished dominant preparation. As he points out (p. 15), the long dominant prolongation coordinates with the form, which begins with development and leads to the theme.

26. See J. Philip Lambert, "Interval Cycles," 67–70.

27. Maisel, *"The Fourth of July,"* 19, finds "large-scale references" to "The Battle Hymn" in his middleground analysis of mm. 12–44 and 52–62 (Example 2b, pp. 8–9) but admits these are "speculative." Since they involve plucking out notes from several instruments amid changing figuration, they are very likely artifacts of Maisel's analysis and not part of Ives's structure.

28. Henderson, *Tunebook,* 181, lists this as "unknown tune" H199. It is identified by Maisel, *"The Fourth of July,"* 16 and 18, and Shirley, "'The Second of July,'" 395–97, and in the preface to Shirley's edition of *The Fourth of July,* IV. As pointed out in chap. 8, note 11, it is not entirely clear whether the song was written first, but that seems to be the case, to judge from the way in which the shared musical material is used in each work.

29. Measures 66a-73a in the piccolo and percussion are measures that are delayed in respect to mm. 66–73 in the rest of the orchestra by an added ⅔ measure, counted here as m. 65a. The piccolo part involves yet another borrowing from *Old Home Day,* for here "The Girl I Left Behind Me" follows the variant used in the song's obbligato, mm. 22–23.

30. In Shirley's critical edition, these lines are given to the xylophone alone.

31. As before, in Shirley's edition this is given to the xylophone alone.

32. *Essays,* 22.

33. The terms "foreground" and "background" are here used in a spatial sense, the former indicating the elements or events that seem nearest or most prominent from the perceiver's point of view, the latter the more distant or less prominent elements or events. No reference is meant to the quite different meaning these terms have in Schenkerian analysis. See Ives's "Conductor's Note," in *Symphony No. 4,* 13, for a comparison of this layered effect in music to receding hills in a landscape: "As the distant

hills, in a landscape, row upon row, grow gradually into the horizon, so there may be something corresponding to this in the presentation of music. Music seems too often all foreground even if played by a master of dynamics." On layering as a reflection of the multidimensionality of life, see also Morgan, "Spatial Form," 152–53; Perry, *Charles Ives*, 60; Keith C. Ward, "Musical Idealism," 65; and Starr, *Union of Diversities*, 115–26.

34. See the similar descriptions of the effect of *Putnam's Camp* in Robert M. Crunden, "Charles Ives' Innovative Nostalgia," *Choral Journal* 15/4 (December 1974): 10–11, reworked in Crunden, *Ministers of Reform: The Progressives' Achievement in American Civilization 1889-1920* (New York: Basic Books, 1982), 128–30, and of the *Holidays Symphony* in H. Wiley Hitchcock, *Ives*, 84. On free association as a representation of the flow of consciousness in the Fourth Symphony, see Perry, *Charles Ives*, 44. Ives's manner later in life of reminiscing out loud while improvising at the piano, reported in Feder, *Charles Ives*, 350, has strong parallels to the way in which memory is suggested in his collages: the tunes used in his improvisation would stimulate spoken memories, which in turn would suggest other tunes.

35. The *Quodlibet* appears on Peter Schickele, *P. D. Q. Bach (1807–1742)?*, sound recording (New York: Vanguard VRS-9195/VSD-79195, 1965), and the *"Unbegun" Symphony* on *An Hysteric Return: P. D. Q. Bach at Carnegie Hall*, sound recording (New York: Vanguard VRS-9223/VSD-79223, 1966).

36. See Burkholder, "Rule-Breaking as a Rhetorical Sign."

37. Shirley, "'The Second of July,'" 393–97, and the score-sketch, fo789–96/no811–18+n3240A-B. As usual in cumulative settings, the theme and its countermelody were apparently worked out first (fo785/no891+2781a+3154). At this early stage, the countermelody drew more heavily on the chorus of "Marching Through Georgia." As Shirley points out in the preface to his edition of *The Fourth of July*, iv, the combination of "Columbia, the Gem of the Ocean" with "The Battle Hymn of the Republic" was tried out earlier in the trio of *Overture and March "1776"* (ca. 1903–7), mm. 42–56, which is similar in concept but different in detail.

38. Shirley, "'The Second of July,'" 392 and 400. The unidentified horn tune at mm. 94–98 is part of the original ink score-sketch. The first appearance of "Marching Through Georgia," though a later addition, can be considered a part of the central thematic complex; the portion that is borrowed here is the same as that incorporated into the principal countermelody, and it appears in conjunction with the paraphrase of the main theme.

39. Nelson, "Beyond Mimesis," shows some of these on pp. 375–76 and 383 and in Figures 15 and 18.

40. Shirley, "'The Second of July,'" 397.

41. *Thanksgiving* and *The Rockstrewn Hills*, discussed in chap. 5, also have collage-like sections. In addition, at least the middle movement of the Third Orchestral Set, sketched between 1919 and 1926 and left unfinished, may have been intended as a collage. Henderson, *Tunebook*, 197–98, lists five borrowed tunes in the first movement and twenty for the second but omits the third movement, for which Kirkpatrick, *Catalogue*, 25, lists four borrowed tunes.

42. Quotations from Ives's postface, in *Memos*, 96–97, n. 1. Ives dated the work 1913 in *Memos*, 97, and his first work-list (ibid., 150), but changed this to "1909, rescored in 1913" in later lists (ibid., 160). A note on the score-sketch says it was begun in October

1909 (Kirkpatrick, *Catalogue*, 9), and Kirkpatrick accepts 1909 as the date in *New Grove*. But Sherwood, 31 May 1994, dates the partial extant sketch ca. 1913–14, the score-sketch between 1914 and 1919, and the full score between 1923 and 1929 by handwriting. See the discussion of this work in Hertz, *Angels of Reality*, 130–37.

43. Henderson, *Tunebook*, 181, prints this as Unknown Tune H198, without its first four measures.

44. Henderson, *Tunebook*, 180, prints this as Unknown Tune H197.

45. *Memos*, 97.

46. Henderson, *Tunebook*, 180, prints the second unidentified tune and the Von Tilzer as Unknown Tunes H194 and H195. Von Tilzer's song, about a rube come to the city, was published in 1916; its late date and Von Tilzer's propensity to quote existing tunes make it possible that he and Ives are quoting from a common source. Indeed, Von Tilzer used the same phrase again in "Oh You Can't Fool an Old Hoss Fly" (1924). Henderson, p. 193, identifies the clarinet tune in mm. 101–4 as "The Girl I Left Behind Me," but this is doubtful; this traditional fife tune would be an unlikely choice for a movement titled "In the Inn," and although the contour is vaguely similar, the clarinet tune has a different meter and character and sounds more like a Tin Pan Alley tune. The suggestion in Cowell and Cowell, *Charles Ives*, 150, that near the end "the tune of the fast barn dance continues merrily against snatches from *We Won't Go Home until Morning* and *Good-night, Ladies*," seems to refer to the end of *Washington's Birthday*, in which at least the latter appears; neither tune is in *In the Inn*, despite the attempt of Rinehart, "Ives' Compositional Idioms," 247–48, to find them in the piano and violin in mm. 89–94.

47. See Nicholls, *American Experimental Music*, 45–46 and Example 2.30.

48. Ibid., 44–51, building on the approach suggested by Brooks, "Unity and Diversity in Charles Ives's Fourth Symphony."

49. Hitchcock, *Ives*, 73. Ives dated one manuscript page 1905, wrote on another an address valid 1909–14, and two or more decades later wrote the year 1903 on a photostat (Kirkpatrick, *Catalogue*, 39); Kirkpatrick, *New Grove*, adopts 1903 as the date. Sherwood, 1 June 1994, dates pp. 1–4 of the sketch ca. 1907 or earlier by handwriting and the rest between 1907 and 1914; some of these are on paper not available before 1907.

50. Jonathan Elkus has suggested models for both themes (letter of 28 December 1990). The trio of William Nassann's *Connecticut March* (New York: Carl Fischer, 1913, but probably available earlier) and the upper countermelody in the trio of R. B. Hall's *New Colonial March* (Philadelphia: John Church, 1901) begin with a chromatic lower-neighbor-note motion on the third scale degree, as does Ives's first tune, and the second strain of O. R. Farrar's *March "Indiana State Band"* (New York: Carl Fischer, 1939, but first copyrighted 1896) begins with a figure similar to Ives's second tune. In each case, the continuation is different from that in the Ives, and these melodic figures are common in the music of the time, making it possible but far from certain that any of these served Ives as models. Elkus has also identified several further works that parallel the Ives (letter of 6 September 1993). This suggests that Ives's tunes derive from a family of similar tunes rather than from any one model. I am grateful to Jonathan Elkus for sharing his research with me.

51. The borrowings given below are identified in Henderson, *Tunebook*, 191, and in James B. Sinclair, "Index of Tunes Quoted," in Charles Ives, *"Country Band" March*,

ed. James B. Sinclair (Bryn Mawr, Pa.: Merion Music, 1976), III. Sinclair also lists a number of tunes or fragments that may be borrowed.

52. In his preface to his edition of Ives, *Ragtime Dances*, III, James Sinclair identifies mm. 170–73 of *Country Band March* as a quotation from *Ragtime Dance No. 1*. The figuration in mm. 172–73 is much like that in mm. 64–66 of the *Ragtime Dance*, but this may simply be part of Ives's stock of typical ragtime figures; the resemblance is less close for mm. 170–71.

53. *Memos*, 83. For the play, see ibid., 281–317. For an analysis of this work, see Nicholls, *American Experimental Music*, 25–30. Ives dated the work 1903–4 on the manuscripts (see Kirkpatrick, *Catalogue*, 42). According to Sherwood, 1 June 1994, the first two pages of the score-sketch date from between 1902 and 1907, closer to 1902, which confirms Ives's date, but the rest seems to be ca. 1907 or a little later.

54. Ives mentions this in his program for *Putnam's Camp*, and Kirkpatrick supplies one version of the words in *Memos*, 84–85.

55. Memo on f2485/q2409. Henderson, *Tunebook*, 191, finds "Saint Patrick's Day" in the violin at m. 44, but this is a completely unrelated figure.

56. Ives dated *Putnam's Camp* 1912 on one manuscript (see Kirkpatrick, *Catalogue*, 16) and revised it ca. 1929 for small orchestra. Sherwood, 31 May 1994, dates the sketches 1914–19, closer to 1919; the score-sketch 1919–23, closer to 1919; the first full score 1919–23; subsequent patches ca. 1923 or later; the second full score ca. 1929 or a bit earlier (using paper not available before 1925); and extra score pages ca. 1929.

57. For the correspondences, see Sinclair, "Table of Correlative Measures," in his edition of *"Country Band" March*, and Sinclair, "Table of Correlative Measures," in Charles E. Ives, *Overture and March "1776,"* ed. James B. Sinclair (Bryn Mawr, Pa.: Merion Music, 1976), 34. The overture's trio found a home in *The Fourth of July*.

58. "The British Grenadiers" replaces "London Bridge" and "The Girl I Left Behind Me" in the flute and other instruments at mm. 14–16 (mm. 24–29 of *Country Band March*), substitutes for "London Bridge" as a countermelody in the winds at the reprise of the principal theme in mm. 126–30 (mm. 131ff. of *Country Band March*), and reappears in the trumpet at mm. 133–37 and in violin I in mm. 144–45 (mm. 160–63 of *Country Band March*) and 148–55 (adapted from the tune as it appears in mm. 63–66 of *Overture and March "1776"*). Other changes include the addition of Sousa's *"Liberty Bell" March* and *Semper Fideles* at mm. 27ff. and the latter's omission at mm. 31ff. (mm. 44ff. and 53ff. of *Country Band March*), the omission of "Violets," the addition of some fanfare figures, and the appearance of "Marching Through Georgia" in the flute at m. 147 (barely hinted at in m. 166 of *Country Band March*). Henderson, *Tunebook*, 194, finds the hymn tune *Happy Day* in the bassoon at mm. 8–9, but this four-note figure is probably part of the march rather than a reference to the hymn.

59. For the program and its connection to the music, see Charles Ives, *A New England Symphony: Three Places in New England*, ed. James B. Sinclair (Bryn Mawr, Pa.: Mercury Music, 1976), 20, with helpful annotations by Sinclair.

60. The descriptions that follow are based on the 1965 edition, Charles E. Ives, *Symphony No. 4* (New York: Associated Music Publishers, 1965) for movements 1, 3, and 4 and on the original publication of the second movement in Charles E. Ives, "The Fourth Symphony for Large Orchestra," *New Music* 2/2 (January 1929). It is not possible to offer an analysis of such a work in the space available here; the following

attempts to describe only the use of collage as an aspect of its meaning. Cyr, "Intervallic Structural Elements," has shown motivic interrelationships in the work. James Wm. McClenden, Jr. explores its message in theological terms, focusing on the use of hymn tunes and their associated texts, in "Expanding the Theory: Charles Edward Ives— Theologian in Music," in *Biography as Theology: How Life Stories Can Remake Today's Theology* (Nashville and New York: Abingdon Press, 1974), 150–69. Magers, "Aspects of Form," 193–266, surveys the symphony and offers a programmatic interpretation based in part on the texts of the hymns, summarized in "Charles Ives's Optimism." Feder, *Charles Ives,* 273–81, explores the psychological meaning of the work for Ives. Perhaps the best analysis is that of Rathert in *The Seen and Unseen,* 209–46, building on his earlier "Charles Ives, Symphonie Nr. 4, 1911–1916," *Neuland* 3 (1982–83): 226–41.

61. For the history of the work and its many sources, see Kirkpatrick, "Preface," in Ives, *Symphony No. 4,* VII–X. On preparations for the 1927 partial premiere, see William Brooks, "A Drummer-Boy Looks Back: Percussion in Ives's *Fourth Symphony,*" *Percussive Notes* 22/6 (September 1984): 10–11. Kirkpatrick, *New Grove,* dates the four movements 1910–11, 1911–16, 1909–11, and 1911–16, respectively. Sherwood, 31 May 1994, dates the first movement sketches and score-sketch between 1914 and 1919, closer to 1919; the second movement sketches and score-sketch close to 1919 or later; patches for the third movement ca. 1919; the fourth movement sketches and first and second score-sketches ca. 1919, patches 1919–23, and first full score ca. 1923, with subsequent extra pages; and the full score of the entire symphony (and second full score of the finale) on paper available 1922 in a hand of 1923 or later, before the 1927 premiere of the present first two movements.

62. Henry Bellamann, program notes to Ives's Fourth Symphony, *Pro Musica Program,* 29 January 1927. This is most readily available as excerpted by Kirkpatrick, "Preface," in Ives, *Symphony No. 4,* VIII, from which this and the following quotations are drawn. Bellamann was a close confidant of Ives in this period, and the program he offered presumably reflected Ives's own ideas. In 1927, the middle movements were in reversed order, the fugal movement second, and the comedy movement based on *The Celestial Railroad* third.

63. Brooks, "Unity and Diversity," 22.

64. See f1386/n0481, f1389/Q1685&n0479, and f1391–92/n0484–85 for the evolution of this melody. Henderson, "Quotation," 31–32, shows an example of this patchwork melody, but labels the last unit as mm. 9–10 of *Bethany*. Brooks, "Drummer-Boy," 20–21, notes the "street beat" in this passage.

65. Kirkpatrick, "Preface," in Ives, *Symphony No. 4,* VIII–IX. See also the interpretation of Ballantine, "Charles Ives and the Meaning of Quotation," 174–76.

66. For an outstanding analysis of this movement, including a searching investigation of the network of musical borrowings, see Brooks, "Unity and Diversity."

67. For a comparison of the two works, see Brodhead, "Ives's *Celestial Railroad,*" 392–93, or his "Table of General Correspondence" in his edition of *The Celestial Railroad* (New York: Associated Music Publishers, forthcoming). All but the first six measures of the piano work are incorporated in the orchestral version. On the complex interrelated gestation of these two works, see chap. 9. Rathert, *The Seen and Unseen,* 228–29, shows a formal chart of the symphony movement that compares it to the "Hawthorne" movement of the *Concord Sonata*.

68. The table uses the measure numbers of the 1929 version published in *New Music* and of Kirkpatrick's *Catalogue*, not those of the 1965 performing edition (used in Henderson's list). It draws on other analyses, notably Henderson, *Tunebook*, 196–97, and an unpublished "Color-Coded Quotation Analysis" by Thomas Brodhead, but differs from them, as they do with each other. I am grateful to Mr. Brodhead for sharing his analysis with me. Every analyst may see and hear new allusions in this music or be blind and deaf to what others are convinced they have found, in part because Ives included many conventional melodic ideas that suggest more than one tune without resembling any closely enough to identify it.

69. Most of these were detected by Thomas Brodhead.

70. Brodhead, "Ives's *Celestial Railroad*," 422, n. 3, suggests that the first of these passages shifts to the point of view of the pilgrims journeying on foot while the train roars by.

71. See f1439/n0507.

72. In his "Critical Commentary," in Ives, *Study No. 23*, 13, Kirkpatrick identifies this tune as "at once a variant of *Throw Out the Lifeline* and *Hello! Ma Baby*." Rhythmically and melodically it seems much closer to the former, making the connection to the latter more tenuous.

73. See the analysis in chap. 3. For the phantom quotation of Brahms's *Alto Rhapsody*, see chap. 3, note 45. Jonathan Elkus has suggested that Ives may have meant the "icy mountains" of the hymn subject to evoke "something cold, academic, about rules and ritual . . . i.e., inhuman/non-divine" (letter of 26 December 1993).

74. Magers, "Aspects of Form," 264, suggests a programmatic justification for the added quotations based on the hymn texts: the first symbolizes the journey toward God ("I am coming Lord"), the second a reciprocation from God ("the Lord is come").

75. These are in the Presbyterian hymnal that Ives used in his last position as an organist; see Benson, et al., *The Hymnal*, nos. 99, 591, and 38, respectively. However, the match between these and Ives's melodies is not very extensive, and the latter may be based on different hymn tunes or none at all. Both melodies imitate the opening of the phrase from *Missionary Hymn* being developed at this point in the fugue.

76. See the discussion in chap. 3, note 43.

77. Quoted in Kirkpatrick, "Preface," in Ives, *Symphony No. 4*, VIII. William Anson Call, "A Study of the Transcendental Aesthetic Theories of John S. Dwight and Charles E. Ives and the Relationship of These Theories to Their Respective Work as Music Critic and Composer" (D.M.A. diss., University of Illinois at Urbana-Champaign, 1971), 82–144, offers a Schenker-based harmonic and formal analysis of this movement.

78. See Magers, "Aspects of Form," 334–54, and "Charles Ives's Optimism."

79. f1689/n0735.

80. f1690/n0716 and f1691/n0777. In these early sketches for the passage at m. 65, all of *Missionary Chant* appears, its opening measures later replaced by the opening of *Bethany*.

81. See Brooks, "Drummer-Boy," 19–32, on percussion in the symphony, including this ostinato and the role of marching band drum cadences. The "street beat" in the snare drum is hidden by the notation; five eighth notes as written would equal one $\frac{2}{4}$ measure of the normally notated pattern.

82. Kirkpatrick, "Preface," in Ives, *Symphony No. 4*, ix, identifies the melody at mm. 65ff in oboe, clarinet, and high bells II as "As Freshmen first we came to Yale" (published as "Eli Yale" in Kellogg and Shepard, eds., *Yale Songs*, 7), but this is the hymn *There Is a Happy Land*. The Yale song would certainly be incongruous in this context.

83. See for instance the discussion in Cyr, "Intervallic Structural Elements."

84. The third and fourth movements use different phrases from *Antioch*. Although the same hymn is borrowed in both movements, no motivic repetition is involved.

85. Rathert, *The Seen and Unseen*, notes the tonal plan (p. 210) and the similarity between the tunes used in the outer movements (pp. 213–14). He further suggests (pp. 216–18) that the opening motive of the symphony, recalled in mm. 5–12 of the finale, also appears at the beginning of the second movement, mm. 1–5, bassoons, but this melody, a variant of *God Be With You*, is quite different in shape.

CHAPTER 11: THE SIGNIFICANCE OF IVES'S USES OF EXISTING MUSIC

1. E.g. by Kirkpatrick, *Catalogue*, viii, and *New Grove*, 415; H. Wiley Hitchcock, *Ives*, 51–52; Henderson, "Structural Importance," 437; Perry, *Charles Ives*, 18–22 and 35–37; Clarke, *Essays on American Music*, 116–17; and Meyer, "*Art of Speaking Extravagantly*," 30. The most sophisticated and nuanced linking of Ives's borrowing practices to the Emersonian tradition is in Hertz, *Angels of Reality*, 114–59.

2. E.g. by Henderson, "Structural Importance," 437; Sterne, "Quotations"; Austin, *Music in the 20th Century*, 59; and Peter S. Hansen, *An Introduction to Twentieth Century Music*, 4th ed. (Boston: Allyn and Bacon, 1978), 93 and 95.

3. E.g., Stone, "Ives's Fourth Symphony," 14–15; Elliott Carter, "Forecast and Review: The Case of Mr. Ives," *Modern Music* 16 (March–April 1939): 175; and idem, "Shop Talk by an American Composer."

4. E.g., Marshall, "Charles Ives's Quotations"; Charles, "Use of Borrowed Material"; Cyr, "Intervallic Structural Elements"; and Wallach, "New England Education," 250–52.

5. Bruce, "Ives and Nineteenth-Century American Music," 34–35 and 38–39.

6. See J. A. Watson, "Beethoven's Debt to Mozart," *Music and Letters* 28 (July 1937): 248–58, and Jeremy Yudkin, "Beethoven's 'Mozart' Quartet," *Journal of the American Musicological Society* 45 (Spring 1992): 30–74. The citations here and in the following several notes only begin to sample the vast literature on the subject of musical borrowing.

7. See William Zoor, "Correspondence," *Gramophone* 61 (October 1983): 416.

8. See Myron Schwager, "Some Observations on Beethoven as an Arranger," *The Musical Quarterly* 60 (January 1974): 80–93, and Lilani Kathryn Lutes, "Beethoven's Reuses of His Own Compositions, 1782–1826" (Ph.D. diss., University of Southern California, 1975).

9. Constantin Floros, "Zur Deutung der Symphonik Bruckners: Das Adagio der Neunten Symphonie," in *Bruckner-Jahrbuch 1981*, ed. Franz Grasberger (Linz: Druck- und Verlagsanstalt Gutenberg, 1982), 89–96, and idem., "Die Zitate in Bruckners Symphonik," in *Bruckner-Jahrbuch 1982/83*, ed. Othmar Wessely (Linz: Akademische Druck- und Verlagsanstalt, 1984), 7–18.

10. Christopher Reynolds, "A Choral Symphony by Brahms?," *19th-Century Music* 9 (Summer 1985): 3–26.

11. Hans Ferdinand Redlich, "The Creative Achievement of Gustav Mahler," *The Musical Times* 101 (July 1960): 418–21; Fritz Egon Pamer, "Die Lieder Gustav Mahlers," *Studien zur Musikwissenschaft* 16 (1929): 116–38 and 17 (1930): 105–27; Miriam K. Whaples, "Mahler and Schubert's A Minor Sonata D. 784," *Music and Letters* 65 (July 1984): 255–63; Alexander L. Ringer, "'Lieder eines fahrenden Gesellen': Allusion und Zitat in der musikalischen Erzählung Gustav Mahlers," in *Das musikalische Kunstwerk: Geschichte, Ästhetik, Theorie: Festschrift Carl Dahlhaus zum 60. Guburtstag*, ed. Hermann Danuser et al. (Laaber: Laaber-Verlag, 1988), 589–602; Rosamund McGuinness, "Mahler und Brahms: Gedanken zu 'Reminiszenzen' in Mahlers Sinfonien," *Melos/Neue Zeitschrift für Musik* 3 (May–June 1977): 215–24.

12. See Gibbens, "Debussy's Impact on Ives," 74–77, and Charles-Henry Combe, "Les citations d'hymnes nationaux chez Debussy," *Revue musicale de Suisse romande* 39 (March 1986): 19–27.

13. Alan M. Gillmor, "Musico-poetic Form in Satie's 'Humoristic' Piano Suites (1913–14)," *Canadian University Music Review* 8 (1987): 1–44; András Wilheim, "Erik Satie's Gregorian Paraphrases," *Studia musicologica* 25 (1983): 229–37.

14. Ferenc Bónis, "Quotations in Bartók's Music: A Contribution to Bartók's Psychology of Composition," *Studia musicologica* 5 (1963): 355–82; John A. Meyer, "Beethoven and Bartok—A Structural Parallel," *The Music Review* 31 (November 1970): 315–21; Mark A. Radice, "Bartók's Parodies of Beethoven: The Relationships between Opp. 131, 132 and 133 and Bartók's Sixth String Quartet and Third Piano Concerto," *The Music Review* 42 (1981): 252–60; A. Batta, "A Nietzsche Symbol in the Music of Richard Strauss and Bela Bartok," *The New Hungarian Quarterly* 23 (Spring 1982): 202–7.

15. Ingrid Arauco, "Bartók's *Romanian Christmas Carols*: Changes from the Folk Sources and Their Significance," *The Journal of Musicology* 5 (Spring 1987): 191–225.

16. Edward T. Cone, "The Uses of Convention: Stravinsky and His Models," *The Musical Quarterly* 48 (July 1962): 287–99; Lawrence Morton, "Footnotes to Stravinsky Studies: *Le Sacre du Printemps*," *Tempo*, no. 128 (March 1979): 9–16; Richard Taruskin, "Russian Folk Melodies in *The Rite of Spring*," *Journal of the American Musicological Society* 33 (Fall 1980): 501–43; Uwe Kraemer, "Das Zitat bei Igor Strawinsky," *Neue Zeitschrift für Musik* 131 (1970): 135–41; Joseph N. Straus, "Recompositions by Schoenberg, Stravinsky, and Webern," *The Musical Quarterly* 72 (1986): 301–28; Morton, "Stravinsky and Tchaikovsky."

17. For a thoroughgoing demonstration of this in respect to his experimental music, see J. Philip Lambert, "Compositional Procedures."

18. This view of twentieth-century music is laid out in J. Peter Burkholder, "Museum Pieces: The Historical Mainstream in Music of the Last Hundred Years," *The Journal of Musicology* 2 (Spring 1983): 115–34, and "The Twentieth Century and the Orchestra as Museum," in *The Orchestra: Origins and Transformations*, ed. Joan Peyser (New York: Charles Scribner's Sons, 1986), 408–33.

19. This is the burden of my dissertation, "The Evolution of Charles Ives's Music," especially pp. 1–8, 462–68, and 684–94.

20. Harold Bloom, *The Anxiety of Influence: A Theory of Poetry* (New York: Oxford University Press, 1973). Straus, *Remaking the Past*, applies Bloom's approach to composers of this generation, particularly Schoenberg, Bartók, Stravinsky, Webern, and Berg.

21. Hertz, *Angels of Reality,* 114–17, 124–37, and 156–59.

22. Burkholder, *Charles Ives,* 64–66.

23. Ralph Waldo Emerson, "Quotation and Originality," in *The Complete Works of Ralph Waldo Emerson,* Concord Edition, vol. 8, *Letters and Social Aims* (Boston and New York: Houghton, Mifflin, 1904), 175–204, quoting from p. 204. It is not certain that Ives knew this essay, for he does not appear to quote or refer to it, but its view of artistic creation as essentially re-creation is certainly in line with Ives's approach.

24. For Ives's aesthetic development, see Burkholder, *Charles Ives.* For a different interpretation of his aims, see MacDonald Smith Moore, *Yankee Blues: Musical Culture and American Identity* (Bloomington: Indiana University Press, 1985). Although Moore's illuminating work shows how Ives's aesthetic aims parallel those of other Yankee composers of his generation, the focus here is on explaining traits that distinguish his work from that of others: why Ives borrowed so often and why he used the particular sources that he did.

25. For a similar comment, see Hertz, *Angels of Reality,* 116.

26. Kirkpatrick, "Preface," in Ives, *Symphony No. 4,* VIII.

27. Stone, "Ives's Fourth Symphony," 14.

28. *Memos,* 40. Rabinowitz, "Fictional Music," 204–5, suggests that listeners and critics who approach Ives without taking into account the "fictionality" of his music (i.e., his attempt to convey in music an experience of hearing music) will misunderstand and devalue it. See also the conclusion of Ballantine, "Meaning of Quotation," 183–84.

29. See Wilfred Mellers, "Realism and Transcendentalism: Charles Ives as American Hero," in *Music in a New Found Land: Themes and Developments in the History of American Music,* rev. ed. (New York: Oxford University Press, 1987), 38–64, especially 39–45. Mellers links Ives to the artistic and philosophical traditions of realism, an idea that is further developed by Perry, *Charles Ives,* 56–71, and Jacques van Nieuwstadt, "Charles Ives: realisme en pragmatisme (I): Muzikale citaten" and "Charles Ives: realisme en pragmatisme (II): Vernieuwende nostalgie," *Mens & Melodie* 46 (November–December 1991): 601–5 and 47 (January 1992): 13–17.

30. *Essays,* 47.

31. Ibid., 3.

32. Vinay, *L'America musicale,* 75–93, argues that Ives uses quotation to speak of his own experiences, especially memories from childhood; I would limit this to only some of Ives's mature works and note that not all of the experiences he describes are his own, nor are they all from the distant past. Hertz, *Angels of Reality,* 261–86, places Ives's desire to represent everyday experience in a broader Emersonian tradition. As Emerson says in "Quotation and Originality," 201, originality "is being, being one's self, and reporting accurately what we see and are."

33. *Essays,* 79.

34. Ibid., 79–80.

35. Ibid., 80–81.

36. Hertz, *Angels of Reality,* 34, shows that Ives drew on Emerson for this interest in achieving universality through contemplating his own culture. Isham, "Musical Thinking," 402, points out that Ives's "search for universality is, as it was for Emerson, . . . the romantic search for self."

Bibliography

Abbate, Carolyn. "Tristan in the Composition of Pelleas." *19th-Century Music* 5 (Fall 1981): 117–41.

Abraham, Gerald. *The Concise Oxford History of Music.* London: Oxford University Press, 1979.

Alexander, Michael J. *The Evolving Keyboard Style of Charles Ives.* Ph.D. diss., University of Keele, 1984. Verbatim reprint. New York and London: Garland, 1989.

Arauco, Ingrid. "Bartók's *Romanian Christmas Carols:* Changes from the Folk Sources and Their Significance." *The Journal of Musicology* 5 (Spring 1987): 191–225.

Argento, Dominick. "A Digest Analysis of Ives' 'On the Antipodes.'" *Student Musicologists at Minnesota* 6 (1975–76): 192–200.

Austin, William W. *Music in the 20th Century from Debussy through Stravinsky.* New York: W. W. Norton, 1966.

———. *"Susanna," "Jeanie," and "The Old Folks at Home": The Songs of Stephen C. Foster from His Time to Ours.* 2nd ed. Urbana: University of Illinois Press, 1987.

Badolato, James Vincent. "The Four Symphonies of Charles Ives: A Critical, Analytical Study of the Musical Style of Charles Ives." Ph.D. diss., Catholic University of America, 1978.

Ballantine, Christopher. "Charles Ives and the Meaning of Quotation in Music." *The Musical Quarterly* 65 (April 1979): 167–84.

Baron, Carol K. "Dating Charles Ives's Music: Facts and Fictions." *Perspectives of New Music* 28/1 (Winter 1990): 20–56.

———. "Ives on His Own Terms: An Explication, a Theory of Pitch Organization, and a New Critical Edition for the *3-Page Sonata.*" Ph.D. diss., City University of New York, 1987.

Batta, A. "A Nietzsche Symbol in the Music of Richard Strauss and Bela Bartók." *The New Hungarian Quarterly* 23 (Spring 1982): 202–7.

Bellamann, Henry. "Charles Ives: The Man and His Music." *The Musical Quarterly* 19 (January 1933): 45–58.

———. Program notes to Ives's Fourth Symphony. *Pro Musica Program,* 29 January 1927.

Benson, Louis F., et al., eds. *The Hymnal, Published by Authority of the General Assembly of the Presbyterian Church in the United States of America.* Philadelphia: The Presbyterian Board of Publication and Sabbath-School Work, 1895.

Bergreen, Laurence. *As Thousands Cheer: The Life of Irving Berlin.* New York: Viking, 1990.

Bernlef, J., and Reinbert de Leeuw. *Charles Ives.* Amsterdam: De Bezige Bij, 1969.

Bernstein, Leonard. Liner notes for *Charles Ives: Second Symphony,* by the New York Philharmonic, conducted by Leonard Bernstein. Sound recording. New York: Columbia ML 6289/MS 6889, 1966.

Bierley, Paul E. *John Philip Sousa: A Descriptive Catalog of His Works.* Urbana: University of Illinois Press, 1973.

Birchler, David Carl. "Nature and Autobiography in the Music of Gustav Mahler." Ph.D. diss., University of Wisconsin-Madison, 1991.

Block, Geoffrey. *Charles Ives: A Bio-Bibliography.* Bio-Bibliographies in Music, 14. New York: Greenwood Press, 1988.

———. "Ives and the 'Sounds That Beethoven Didn't Have.'" In *Charles Ives and the Classical Tradition,* ed. Geoffrey Block and J. Peter Burkholder. New Haven: Yale University Press, forthcoming.

Bloom, Harold. *The Anxiety of Influence: A Theory of Poetry.* New York: Oxford University Press, 1973.

Blum, Stephen. "Ives's Position in Social and Musical History." *The Musical Quarterly* 63 (October 1977): 459–482.

Bónis, Ferenc. "Quotations in Bartók's Music: A Contribution to Bartók's Psychology of Composition." *Studia musicologica* 5 (1963): 355–82.

Brodhead, Thomas M. "Editor's Preface" and "Table of General Correspondence." In Charles E. Ives, *The Celestial Railroad,* ed. Thomas M. Brodhead. New York: Associated Music Publishers, forthcoming.

———. "Ives 4th Symphony 2nd Movement: Color-Coded Quotation Analysis." Unpublished manuscript.

———. "Ives's *Celestial Railroad* and His Fourth Symphony." *American Music* 12 (Winter 1994): 389–424.

Brooks, William. "A Drummer-Boy Looks Back: Percussion in Ives's *Fourth Symphony.*" *Percussive Notes* 22/6 (September 1984): 4–45.

———. "Unity and Diversity in Charles Ives's Fourth Symphony." *Yearbook for Inter-American Musical Research* 10 (1974): 5–49.

Brown, A. Peter. "*The Creation* and *The Seasons:* Some Allusions, Quotations, and Models from Handel to Mendelssohn." *Current Musicology,* no. 51 (1993): 26–58.

Brown, Howard Mayer. "Emulation, Competition, and Homage: Imitation and Theories of Imitation in the Renaissance." *Journal of the American Musicological Society* 35 (Spring 1982): 1–48.

Bruce, Neely. "Ives and Nineteenth-Century American Music." In *An Ives Celebration: Papers and Panels of the Charles Ives Centennial Festival-Conference,* ed. H. Wiley Hitchcock and Vivian Perlis, 29–43. Urbana: University of Illinois Press, 1977.

Buelow, George J. "Handel's Borrowing Techniques: Some Fundamental Questions Derived from a Study of 'Agrippina' (Venice, 1709)." *Göttinger Händel-Beiträge* 2 (1986): 105–28.

———. "Originality, Genius, Plagiarism in English Criticism of the Eighteenth Century." In *Florilegium musicologicum: Festschrift Hellmut Federhofer zum 75. Geburtstag,* ed. Cristoph-Hellmut Mahling, 57–66. Tutzing: Hans Schneider, 1988.

Burchard, Peter. *One Gallant Rush: Robert Gould Shaw and His Brave Black Regiment.* New York: St. Martin's Press, 1965.

Burkholder, J. Peter. "Brahms and Twentieth-Century Classical Music." *19th-Century Music* 8 (Summer 1984): 75–83.

———. "Charles Ives and His Fathers: A Response to Maynard Solomon." *Institute for Studies in American Music Newsletter* 18/1 (November 1988): 8–11.

————. *Charles Ives: The Ideas Behind the Music.* New Haven: Yale University Press, 1985.

————. "The Critique of Tonality in the Early Experimental Music of Charles Ives." *Music Theory Spectrum* 12 (Fall 1990): 203–23.

————. "The Evolution of Charles Ives's Music: Aesthetics, Quotation, Technique." Ph.D. diss., University of Chicago, 1983.

————. "Johannes Martini and the Imitation Mass of the Late Fifteenth Century." *Journal of the American Musicological Society* 38 (Fall 1985): 470–523.

————. "Museum Pieces: The Historical Mainstream in Music of the Last Hundred Years." *The Journal of Musicology* 2 (Spring 1983): 115–34.

————. "'Quotation' and Emulation: Charles Ives's Uses of His Models." *The Musical Quarterly* 71 (1985): 1–26.

————. "'Quotation' and Paraphrase in Ives's Second Symphony." *19th-Century Music* 11 (Summer 1987): 3–25.

————. "Rule-Breaking as a Rhetorical Sign." In *Festa musicologica: Essays in Honor of George J. Buelow,* ed. Benito Rivera and Thomas J. Mathiesen, 369–89. New York: Pendragon Press, 1995.

————. "The Twentieth Century and the Orchestra as Museum." In *The Orchestra: Origins and Transformations,* ed. Joan Peyser, 408–33. New York: Charles Scribner's Sons, 1986.

————. "The Uses of Existing Music: Musical Borrowing as a Field." *Music Library Association Notes* 50 (March 1994): 851–70.

Call, William Anson. "A Study of the Transcendental Aesthetic Theories of John S. Dwight and Charles E. Ives and the Relationship of These Theories to Their Respective Work as Music Critic and Composer." D.M.A. diss., University of Illinois at Urbana-Champaign, 1971.

Carr, Cassandra I. "Charles Ives's Humor as Reflected in His Songs." *American Music* 7 (Summer 1989): 123–39.

Carter, Elliott. "Forecast and Review: The Case of Mr. Ives." *Modern Music* 16 (March–April 1939): 172–76.

————. "Shop Talk by an American Composer." *The Musical Quarterly* 46 (April 1960): 189–201. Reprinted in *Problems of Modern Music,* ed. Paul Henry Lang, 51–63. New York: W. W. Norton, 1962.

Charles, Sydney Robinson. "The Use of Borrowed Materials in Ives' Second Symphony." *The Music Review* 28 (May 1967): 102–11.

Charles Ives Festival. Sound recording. Boston: New England Conservatory NEC-122, 1983.

Chase, Gilbert. *America's Music: From the Pilgrims to the Present.* 2nd ed. New York: McGraw-Hill, 1966. 3rd ed., Urbana: University of Illinois Press, 1987.

Chmaj, Betty E. "Charles Ives and the Concord Sonata." In *Poetry and the Fine Arts: Papers from the Poetry Sessions of the European Association for American Studies Biennial Conference, Rome 1984,* ed. Roland Hagenbüchle and Jaqueline S. Ollier, 37–60. Eichstätter Beiträge, 24. Regensburg: Friedrich Pustet, 1989.

————. "Sonata for American Studies: Perspectives on Charles Ives." *Prospects: An Annual of American Cultural Studies* 4 (Winter 1978): 1–58.

Clark, Sondra Rae. "The Evolving *Concord Sonata:* A Study of Choices and Variants in the Music of Charles Ives." Ph.D. diss., Stanford University, 1972.

———. "The Transcendental Philosophy of Charles E. Ives as Expressed in *The Second Sonata for Pianoforte,* 'Concord, Mass., 1840–1860.'" M.A. thesis, San Jose State College, 1966.

Clarke, Garry. *Essays on American Music.* Contributions in American History, No. 62. Westport, Conn.: Greenwood Press, 1977.

Combe, Charles-Henry. "Les citations d'hymnes nationaux chez Debussy." *Revue musicale de Suisse romande* 39 (March 1986): 19–27.

Cone, Edward T. "The Uses of Convention: Stravinsky and His Models." *The Musical Quarterly* 48 (July 1962): 287–99.

Cowell, Henry. "Current Chronicle." [Review of Second Symphony, first performance.] *The Musical Quarterly* 37 (July 1951): 399–402.

Cowell, Henry, and Sidney Cowell. *Charles Ives and His Music.* 2nd ed. New York: Oxford University Press, 1969.

Crunden, Robert M. "Charles Ives' Innovative Nostalgia." *Choral Journal* 15/4 (December 1974): 5–12.

———. *Ministers of Reform: The Progressives' Achievement in American Civilization 1889–1920.* New York: Basic Books, 1982.

Cyr, Gordon. "Intervallic Structural Elements in Ives's Fourth Symphony." *Perspectives of New Music* 9/2 and 10/1 (Spring/Summer–Fall/Winter 1971): 291–303.

Daverio, John. "Schumann's 'Im Legendenton' and Friedrich Schlegel's *Arabeske.*" *19th-Century Music* 11 (Fall 1987): 150–63.

de Leeuw, Reinbert. "Charles Ives—Zijn Muziek: Inleidung, Ives' Gebruik van Muzikall Materiaal." In *Charles Ives,* by J. Bernlef and Reinbert de Leeuw, 131–209. Amsterdam: De Bezige Bij, 1969. Trans. Bertus Polman, in *Student Musicologists at Minnesota* 6 (1975–76): 128–91.

Dickinson, Peter. "A New Perspective for Ives." *The Musical Times* 115 (October 1974): 836–38.

Echols, Paul. "The Music for Orchestra." *Music Educators Journal* 61/2 (October 1974): 29–41.

Eiseman, David. "Charles Ives and the European Symphonic Tradition: A Historical Reappraisal." Ph.D. diss., University of Illinois at Urbana-Champaign, 1972.

Elkus, Jonathan. *Charles Ives and the American Band Tradition: A Centennial Tribute.* Exeter: American Arts Documentation Centre, University of Exeter, 1974.

———. "Preface." In Charles E. Ives, *Thanksgiving and Forefathers' Day,* ed. Jonathan Elkus, iii–iv. New York: Peer International, 1991.

Ellison, Mary. "Ives' Use of American 'Popular' Tunes as Thematic Material." In *South Florida's Historic Ives Festival 1974–1976,* ed. F. Warren O'Reilly, 30–34. Coral Gables, Fla.: University of Miami at Coral Gables, 1976.

Emerson, Ralph Waldo. "Quotation and Originality." In *The Complete Works of Ralph Waldo Emerson,* Concord Edition, vol. 8, *Letters and Social Aims,* 175–204. Boston and New York: Houghton, Mifflin, 1904.

Ericson, John Q. "Ives and the Band March." Unpublished typescript, 1988.

Farrar, O. R. March *"Indiana State Band."* New York: Carl Fischer, 1939.

Feder, Stuart. "Charles and George Ives: The Veneration of Boyhood." *The Annual of Psychoanalysis* 9 (1981): 265–316. Reprinted in *Psychoanalytic Explorations in Music*, ed. Stuart Feder, Richard L. Karmel, and George H. Pollock, 115–76. Madison, Conn.: International Universities Press, 1990.

———. *Charles Ives, "My Father's Song": A Psychoanalytic Biography*. New Haven: Yale University Press, 1992.

———. "Decoration Day: A Boyhood Memory of Charles Ives." *The Musical Quarterly* 66 (April 1980): 234–61.

———. "The Nostalgia of Charles Ives: An Essay in Affects and Music." *The Annual of Psychoanalysis* 10 (1982): 301–32. Reprinted in *Psychoanalytic Explorations in Music*, ed. Stuart Feder, Richard L. Karmel, and George H. Pollock, 233–66. Madison, Conn.: International Universities Press, 1990.

Fisher, Fred. *Ives' Concord Sonata*. Denton, Texas: C/G Productions, 1981.

———. "Ives's Concord Sonata." *Piano Quarterly* 92 (Winter 1975–76): 23–27.

Fisher, William Arms. *Goin' Home: From the Largo of the New World Symphony*. Bryn Mawr, Pa.: Oliver Ditson, 1922.

Floros, Constantin. "Die Zitate in Bruckners Symphonik." In *Bruckner-Jahrbuch 1982/83*, ed. Othmar Wessely, 7–18. Linz: Akademische Druck- und Verlagsanstalt, 1984.

———. "Zur Deutung der Symphonik Bruckners: Das Adagio der Neunten Symphonie." In *Bruckner-Jahrbuch 1981*, ed. Franz Grasberger, 89–96. Linz: Druck- und Verlagsanstalt Gutenberg, 1982.

Foster, Stephen. *The Social Orchestra*. New York: Firth, Pond, 1854. Reprint, Earlier American Music, 13. New York: Da Capo Press, 1973.

Frisch, Walter. *Brahms and the Principle of Developing Variation*. Berkeley and Los Angeles: University of California Press, 1984.

Fromson, Michele. "A Conjunction of Rhetoric and Music: Structural Modelling in the Italian Counter-Reformation Motet." *Journal of the Royal Musical Association* 117 (1992): 208–46.

Gibbens, John Jeffrey. "Debussy's Impact on Ives: An Assessment." D.M.A. diss., University of Illinois at Urbana-Champaign, 1985.

Gillmor, Alan M. "Musico-poetic Form in Satie's 'Humoristic' Piano Suites (1913–14)." *Canadian University Music Review* 8 (1987): 1–44.

Gingerich, Lora Louise. "Processes of Motivic Transformation in the Keyboard and Chamber Music of Charles E. Ives." Ph.D. diss., Yale University, 1983.

———. "A Technique for Melodic Motivic Analysis in the Music of Charles Ives." *Music Theory Spectrum* 8 (1986): 75–93.

Goodale, G. Frank, ed. *The New Yale Song-Book: A Collection of Songs in Use by the Glee Club and Students of Yale University*. New York: G. Schirmer, 1918.

Gooding, David. "A Study of the Quotation Process in the Songs for Voice and Piano of Charles Edward Ives." M.A. thesis, Western Reserve University, 1963.

Gratovich, Eugene. "The Sonatas for Violin and Piano by Charles Ives: A Critical Commentary and Concordance of the Printed Editions and the Autographs and Manuscripts of the Yale Ives Collection." D.M.A. diss., Boston University, 1968.

———. "The Violin Sonatas." *Music Educators Journal* 61/2 (October 1974): 58–63. Reprinted as "The Violin Sonatas of Charles E. Ives." *The Strad* 85 (December 1974): 471–77.

Gray, Cecil. *Sibelius.* 2nd ed. London: Oxford University Press, 1934.

Green, Douglass M. *"Exempli Gratia:* A Chord Motive in Ives's 'Serenity'." *In Theory Only* 4/5 (1979): 20–21.

Hall, R. B. *The New Colonial March.* Philadelphia: John Crouch, 1901.

Hamm, Charles. *Music in the New World.* New York: W. W. Norton, 1983.

———. *Yesterdays: Popular Song in America.* New York: W. W. Norton, 1979.

Hansen, Chadwick. "One Place in New England: The Fifty-Fourth Massachusetts Volunteer Infantry as a Subject for American Artists." *Student Musicologists at Minnesota* 6 (1975–76): 250–71. Reprinted as "The 54th Massachusetts Volunteer Black Infantry as a Subject for American Artists." *Massachusetts Review* 16 (Autumn 1975): 37–44.

Hansen, Peter S. *An Introduction to Twentieth Century Music.* 4th ed. Boston: Allyn and Bacon, 1978.

Harrison, Lou. "On Quotation." *Modern Music* 23 (Summer 1946): 166–69.

Harvey, Mark Sumner. "Charles Ives: Prophet of American Civil Religion." Ph.D. diss., Boston University, 1983.

Henderson, Clayton W. *The Charles Ives Tunebook.* Bibliographies in American Music, 14. Warren, Mich.: Harmonie Park Press, 1990.

———. "Ives' Use of Quotation." *Music Educators Journal* 61/2 (October 1974): 24–28.

———. "Quotation as a Style Element in the Music of Charles Ives." Ph.D. diss., Washington University, 1969.

———. "Structural Importance of Borrowed Music in the Works of Charles Ives: A Preliminary Assessment." In *Report of the Eleventh Congress of the International Musicological Society Held at Copenhagen, 1972,* ed. Henrik Glahn, Soren Sorensen, and Peter Ryom, 1: 437–46. Copenhagen: Wilhelm Hansen, 1974.

Hepokoski, James. "The Essence of Sibelius: Creation Myths and Rotational Cycles in *Luonnotar.*" In *The Sibelius Companion,* ed. Glenda Dawn Goss. Westport, Conn.: Greenwood Press, forthcoming.

———. *Sibelius: Symphony No. 5.* Cambridge Music Handbooks. Cambridge: Cambridge University Press, 1993.

———. *"Temps Perdu."* *The Musical Times* 135 (December 1994): 746–51.

Hertz, David Michael. *Angels of Reality: Emersonian Unfoldings in Wright, Stevens, and Ives.* Carbondale and Edwardsville: Southern Illinois University Press, 1993.

Hewitt, James. *Selected Compositions.* Ed. John W. Wagner. Madison: A-R Editions, 1980.

Hinson, Maurice, ed. *Piano Music in Nineteenth Century America.* Vol. 1. Chapel Hill, N.C.: Hinshaw Music, 1975.

Hitchcock, H. Wiley. "Charles E. Ives." In *Music in the United States: A Historical Introduction,* 2nd ed., 149–72. Englewood Cliffs, N.J.: Prentice-Hall, 1974.

———. *Ives.* Oxford Studies of Composers, 14. London: Oxford University Press, 1977. Reprinted with corrections, Brooklyn: Institute for Studies in American Music, 1985.

———. "Ivesiana. The Gottschalk Connection." *Institute for Studies in American Music Newsletter* 15/1 (November 1985): 5.

———. Liner notes to *American Brass Music of the 1850's,* by The American Brass Quintet, assisted by John Stevens. Sound recording. Cambridge, Mass.: Titanic Records Ti/81, 1980.

Hitchcock, H. Wiley, and Vivian Perlis, eds. *An Ives Celebration: Papers and Panels of the Charles Ives Centennial Festival-Conference*. Urbana: University of Illinois Press, 1977.

Hitchcock, Roswell D., et al., eds. *Hymns and Songs of Praise for Public and Social Worship*. New York and Chicago: A. S. Barnes, 1874.

Hüsken, Renate. "Charles Ives' 'Robert Browning Overture.'" *Neuland* 1 (1980): 16–24.

Hymnal of the Methodist Episcopal Church With Tunes. New York: Nelson and Phillips, 1878.

Isham, Howard. "The Musical Thinking of Charles Ives." *Journal of Aesthetics and Art Criticism* 31 (Spring 1973): 395–404.

Ives, Charles E. *The Celestial Country*. New York: Peer International, 1973.

——. *The Circus Band*. Arr. George F. Roberts. New York: Peer International, 1969.

——. "Conductor's Note." In *Symphony No. 4*, 12–14. New York: Associated Music Publishers, 1965.

——. *Eleven Songs and Two Harmonizations*. Ed. John Kirkpatrick. New York: Associated Music Publishers, 1968.

——. *Essays Before a Sonata*. New York: Knickerbocker Press, 1920.

——. *Essays Before a Sonata, The Majority, and Other Writings*. Ed. Howard Boatwright. New York: W.W. Norton, 1970.

——. *Forty Earlier Songs*. Ed. John Kirkpatrick. New York: Associated Music Publishers, Peer International, and Theodore Presser, 1993.

——. *The Fourth of July*. Ed. Wayne Shirley. New York: Associated Music Publishers, 1992.

——. "The Fourth Symphony for Large Orchestra." [Second movement of Symphony No. 4.] *New Music* 2/2 (January 1929).

——. *Fugue in Four Keys on "The Shining Shore."* Ed. John Kirkpatrick. Bryn Mawr, Pa.: Merion Music, 1975.

——. *Largo for Violin and Piano*. Ed. Paul Zukofsky. New York: Southern Music, 1967.

——. *Largo for Violin, Clarinet and Piano*. New York: Southern Music, 1953.

——. *Memos*. Ed. John Kirkpatrick. New York: W. W. Norton, 1972.

——. *A New England Symphony: Three Places in New England*. Ed. James B. Sinclair. Bryn Mawr, Pa.: Mercury Music, 1976.

——. *Nine Songs*. New York: Peer International, 1956.

——. *Nineteen Songs*. Bryn Mawr, Pa.: Merion Music, 1935.

——. "Note." In *Central Park in the Dark*. Ed. Jacques-Louis Monod with notes by John Kirkpatrick, 31. Hillsdale, N.Y.: Boelke-Bomart, 1973.

——. "Notes on Fourth Violin Sonata." In *Sonata No. 4 for Violin and Piano ("Children's Day at the Camp Meeting")*, 21. New York: Arrow Music Press, 1942. Reprint, New York: Associated Music Publishers, n.d.

——. "Notes on the Symphony." In *Symphony No. 2*, 1. New York: Peer International, 1951.

——. *114 Songs*. Redding, Conn.: By the Author, 1922. Reprint, New York: Peer International, Associated Music Publishers, and Theodore Presser, 1975.

——. *Piano Sonata No. 2: "Concord, Mass., 1840–1860."* 2nd ed. New York: Arrow Music Press, 1947. Reprint, New York: Associated Music Publishers, n.d.

————. *The Pond.* Hillsdale, N.Y.: Boelke-Bomart, 1973.

————. "Postface." In *Decoration Day: Second Movement of "A Symphony: New England Holidays,"* ed. James B. Sinclair, 33. New York: Peer International, 1989.

————. *Ragtime Dances: Set of Four Ragtime Dances.* Ed. James B. Sinclair. New York: Peer International, 1990.

————. *Sonata No. 1 for Piano.* Rev. ed. Ed. Lou Harrison, William Masselos, and Paul Echols. New York: Peer International, 1979.

————. *Symphony No. 3: "The Camp Meeting."* Ed. Kenneth Singleton. New York: Associated Music Publishers, 1990.

————. *Symphony No. 4.* New York: Associated Music Publishers, 1965.

————. *"They Are There!": A War Song March.* Ed. Lou Harrison. New York: Peer International, 1956.

————. *Waltz-Rondo for Piano.* Ed. John Kirkpatrick and Jerrold Cox. New York: Associated Music Publishers, 1978.

Ives, Eli, Jr., ed. *The Mozart Collection of Sacred Music.* New York: Cady and Burgess, 1848.

Jackson, Richard, ed. *Stephen Foster Song Book: Original Sheet Music of 40 Songs by Stephen Collins Foster.* New York: Dover, 1974.

Johnson, H. Earle. *First Performances in America to 1900: Works with Orchestra.* Bibliographies in American Music, 4. Detroit: Published for The College Music Society by Information Coordinators, 1979.

Johnson, Robert Underwood. *Poems.* 2nd ed. New York: Century, 1908.

Josephson, Nors S. "Charles Ives: Intervallische Permutationen im Spätwerk." *Zeitschrift für Musiktheorie* 9/2 (Fall 1978): 27–33.

————. "Zur formalen Struktur einiger später Orchesterwerke von Charles Ives (1874–1954)." *Die Musikforschung* 27 (January–March 1974): 57–64.

Joyce, Mary Ann. "The *Three-Page Sonata* of Charles Ives: An Analysis and a Corrected Version." Ph.D. diss. (Part II), Washington University, 1970.

Kearns, William K. "Horatio Parker 1863–1919: A Study of His Life and Music." Ph.D. diss., University of Illinois at Urbana-Champaign, 1965.

————. *Horatio Parker, 1863–1919: His Life, Music, and Ideas.* Composers of North America, 6. Metuchen, N.J., and London: Scarecrow Press, 1990.

Kellogg, Frank B., and Thomas G. Shepard, eds. *Yale Songs: A Collection of Songs in Use by the Glee Club and Students of Yale College.* New Haven: Shepard & Kellogg, 1882.

Kelly, Kevin O. "The Songs of Charles Ives and the Cultural Contexts of Death." Ph.D. diss., University of North Carolina at Chapel Hill, 1988.

Kirkpatrick, John. "Commentary." In Charles E. Ives, *Johnny Poe,* realized and edited by John Kirkpatrick, 18–22. New York: Peer International, 1978.

————. "Comparison of Sources." In Charles E. Ives, *Central Park in the Dark,* ed. Jacques-Louis Monod with notes by John Kirkpatrick, 32. Hillsdale, N.Y.: Boelke-Bomart, 1973.

————. "Comparison of Sources." In Charles E. Ives, *The Pond,* 8. Hillsdale, N.Y.: Boelke-Bomart, 1973.

————. "Critical Commentary." In Charles Ives, *Study No. 23 for Piano,* ed. John Kirkpatrick, 11–13. Bryn Mawr, Pa.: Merion Music, 1990.

————. "Critical Commentary." In Charles E. Ives, *Trio for Violin, Violoncello, and Piano,* ed. John Kirkpatrick. New York: Peer International, [1984].

————. "Editor's Note." In Charles E. Ives, *Turn Ye, Turn Ye,* ed. John Kirkpatrick, 2–4. Bryn Mawr: Mercury Music, 1973.

————. "Editor's Notes." In Charles E. Ives, *Study No. 21: Some South-Paw Pitching!,* ed. John Kirkpatrick, 7–12. Bryn Mawr, Pa.: Mercury Music, 1975.

————. "Editor's Notes." In Charles E. Ives, *Three-Page Sonata for Piano,* ed. John Kirkpatrick, 14–22. Bryn Mawr, Pa.: Mercury Music, 1975.

————. "Ives, Charles E(dward)," in *The New Grove Dictionary of Music and Musicians,* ed. Stanley Sadie. 20 vols. London: Macmillan, 1980. Revised as "Ives, Charles (Edward)," with additions to the work-list by Paul C. Echols, in *The New Grove Dictionary of American Music,* ed. H. Wiley Hitchcock and Stanley Sadie. 4 vols. London: Macmillan, 1986.

————. Liner notes to *Charles Ives: Five Violin Sonatas,* by Daniel Stepner, violin, and John Kirkpatrick, piano. Sound recording. Tinton Falls, N.J.: Musical Heritage Society MHS 824501, 1982.

————. Liner notes to the songs, in *Charles Ives: The 100th Anniversary.* Sound recording. New York: Columbia M4 32504, 1974.

————. "Notes." In Charles E. Ives, *Study No. 20 for Piano,* ed. John Kirkpatrick, 12–18. Bryn Mawr, Pa.: Merion Music, 1981.

————. "Preface." In Charles E. Ives, *Symphony No. 4,* vii-x. New York: Associated Music Publishers, 1965.

————. *A Temporary Mimeographed Catalogue of the Music Manuscripts and Related Materials of Charles Edward Ives 1874– 1954.* New Haven: Library of the Yale School of Music, 1960; reprint, 1973.

Knapp, Raymond. "The Finale of Brahms's Fourth Symphony: The Tale of the Subject." *19th-Century Music* 13 (Summer 1989): 3–17.

Konold, Wulf. "Neue Musik in der Neuen Welt: Der Komponist Charles Ives." *Musica* 26 (May–June 1972): 239–44.

Korsyn, Kevin. "Towards a New Poetics of Musical Influence." *Music Analysis* 10 (March–July 1991): 3–72.

Kraemer, Uwe. "Das Zitat bei Igor Strawinsky." *Neue Zeitschrift für Musik* 131 (1970): 135–41.

Kramer, Lawrence. *Music and Poetry: The Nineteenth Century and After.* Berkeley: University of California Press, 1984.

Kumlien, Wendell C. "The Music for Chorus." *Music Educators Journal* 61/2 (October 1974): 48–52.

Lamb, Gordon H. "Interview with Robert Shaw." *Choral Journal* 15/8 (April 1975): 5–7.

Lambert, Constant. *Music Ho!: A Study of Music in Decline.* London: Faber and Faber, 1934.

Lambert, J. Philip. "Communication." *Journal of the American Musicological Society* 42 (Spring 1989): 204–9.

————. "Compositional Procedures in the Experimental Works of Charles E. Ives." Ph.D. diss., Eastman School of Music, 1987.

————. "Interval Cycles as Compositional Resources in the Music of Charles Ives." *Music Theory Spectrum* 12 (Spring 1990): 43–82.

———. "Ives's 'Piano-Drum' Chords." *Intégral* 3 (1989): 1–36.

Lax, Roger, and Frederick Smith. *The Great Song Thesaurus.* 2nd ed. New York: Oxford University Press, 1989.

Lindsay, Nicholas Vachel. *General William Booth Enters into Heaven and Other Poems.* New York: Mitchell Kennerley, 1913.

———. *Vachel Lindsay Reading The Congo, Chinese Nightingale, and Other Poems.* Sound recording. New York: Caedmon, LP TC-1041, n.d.

Lissa, Zofia. "Historical Awareness of Music and Its Role in Present-Day Musical Culture." *International Review of the Aesthetics and Sociology of Music* 4 (June 1973): 17–32.

Logan, Adeline Marie. "American National Music in the Compositions of Charles Ives." M.M. thesis, University of Washington, 1943.

Lutes, Lilani Kathryn. "Beethoven's Re-uses of His Own Compositions, 1782–1826." Ph.D. diss., University of Southern California, 1975.

Macey, Patrick. "Josquin as Classic: *Qui habitat, Memor esto,* and Two Imitations Unmasked." *Journal of the Royal Musical Association* 118 (1993): 1–43.

Magers, Roy V. "Aspects of Form in the Symphonies of Charles Ives." Ph.D. diss., Indiana University, 1975.

———. "Charles Ives's Optimism: or, The Program's Progress." In *Music in American Society 1776–1976: From Puritan Hymn to Synthesizer,* ed. George McCue, 73–86. New Brunswick, N. J.: Transaction Books, 1977.

Maisel, Arthur. "*The Fourth of July* by Charles Ives: Mixed Harmonic Criteria in a Twentieth-Century Classic." *Theory and Practice* 6/1 (August 1981): 3–32.

Maniates, Maria Rika, with Peter Branscombe. "Quodlibet." In *The New Grove Dictionary of Music and Musicians,* ed. Stanley Sadie. 20 vols. London: Macmillan, 1980.

Marshall, Dennis. "Charles Ives's Quotations: Manner or Substance?" *Perspectives of New Music* 6/2 (Spring–Summer 1968): 45–56. Reprinted in *Perspectives on American Composers,* ed. Benjamin Boretz and Edward T. Cone, 13–24. New York: W.W. Norton, 1971.

Maske, Ulrich. *Charles Ives in seiner Kammermusik für drei bis sechs Instrumente.* Kölner Beiträge zur Musikforschung, 64. Regensburg: Gustav Bosse, 1971.

Masselos, William. "Preface." In Charles E. Ives, *Sonata No. 1 for Piano,* rev. ed. Ed. Lou Harrison, William Masselos, and Paul Echols. New York: Peer International, 1979.

Mays, Kenneth Robert. "The Use of Hymn Tunes in the Works of Charles Ives." M.M. thesis, Indiana University, 1961.

McCandless, William Edgar. "Cantus Firmus Techniques in Selected Instrumental Compositions, 1910–1960." Ph.D. diss., Indiana University, 1974.

McClendon, James Wm., Jr. "Expanding the Theory: Charles Edward Ives—Theologian in Music." In *Biography as Theology: How Life Stories Can Remake Today's Theology,* 150–69. Nashville and New York: Abingdon Press, 1974.

McGuinness, Rosamund. "Mahler und Brahms: Gedanken zu 'Reminiszenzen' in Mahlers Sinfonien." *Melos/Neue Zeitschrift für Musik* 3 (May–June 1977): 215–24.

Mead, C. H., G. E. Charles, and W. A Williams, ed. *Silver Tones: A Temperance and Prohibition Song Book.* Warnock, Ohio: W. A. Williams, 1892.

Mellers, Wilfred. "Realism and Transcendentalism: Charles Ives as American Hero." In *Music in a New Found Land: Themes and Developments in the History of American Music*, rev. ed., 38–64. New York: Oxford University Press, 1987.

Meyer, Felix. *"The Art of Speaking Extravagantly": Eine vergleichende Studie der "Concord Sonata" und der "Essays before a Sonata" von Charles Ives*. Berne and Stuttgart: Paul Haupt, 1991.

Meyer, John A. "Beethoven and Bartok—A Structural Parallel." *The Music Review* 31 (November 1970): 315–21.

Miller, Keith D. "Martin Luther King, Jr., and the Black Folk Pulpit." *The Journal of American History* 78 (June 1991): 120–23.

Mitchell, Donald. *Gustav Mahler: The Wunderhorn Years*. London: Faber and Faber, 1975.

Moore, MacDonald Smith. *Yankee Blues: Musical Culture and American Identity*. Bloomington: Indiana University Press, 1985.

Morgan, Robert P. "Charles Ives und die europäische Tradition." In *Bericht über das Internationale Symposion "Charles Ives und die amerikanische Musiktradition bis zur Gegenwart," Köln 1988*, ed. Klaus Wolfgang Niemöller, Manuel Gervink, and Paul Terse, 17–36. Kölner Beiträge zur Musikforschung, 164. Regensburg: Gustav Bosse, 1990.

———. "Ives and Mahler: Mutual Responses at the End of an Era." *19th-Century Music* 2 (July 1978): 72–81.

———. "Rewriting Music History: Second Thoughts on Ives and Varèse." *Musical Newsletter* 3/1 (January 1973): 3–12 and 3/2 (April 1973): 15–23 and 28.

———. "Spatial Form in Ives." In *An Ives Celebration: Papers and Panels of the Charles Ives Centennial Festival-Conference*, ed. H. Wiley Hitchcock and Vivian Perlis, 145–58. Urbana: University of Illinois Press, 1977.

———. *Twentieth-Century Music: A History of Musical Style in Modern Europe and America*. New York: W. W. Norton, 1991.

———, ed. *Anthology of Twentieth-Century Music*. New York: W. W. Norton, 1993.

Morton, Lawrence. "Footnotes to Stravinsky Studies: *Le Sacre du Printemps*." *Tempo*, no. 128 (March 1979): 9–16.

———. "Stravinsky and Tchaikovsky: *Le baiser de la fée*." *The Musical Quarterly* 48 (July 1962): 313–26.

Mozart, Wolfgang Amadeus. *The Letters of Mozart and His Family*. Ed. and trans. Emily Anderson. 3rd rev. ed. Ed. Stanley Sadie and Fiona Smart. London: Macmillan, 1985.

Mumper, D. Robert. "The First Piano Sonata of Charles Ives." D.M.A. document, Indiana University, 1971.

Nassann, William. *The Connecticut March*. New York: Carl Fischer, 1913.

Nelson, Mark D. "Beyond Mimesis: Transcendentalism and Processes of Analogy in Charles Ives' The Fourth of July." *Perspectives of New Music* 22/1–2 (Fall/Winter 1983–Spring/Summer 1984): 353–84.

Newman, Philip Edward. "The Songs of Charles Ives." Ph.D. diss., University of Iowa, 1967.

Nicholls, David. *American Experimental Music, 1890–1940*. Cambridge: Cambridge University Press, 1990.

————. "Unanswerable Questions/Questionable Answers." *Music and Letters* 75 (May 1994): 246–52.

Nieuwstadt, Jacques van. "Charles Ives: realisme en pragmatisme (I): Muzikale citaten" and "Charles Ives: realisme en pragmatisme (II): Vernieuwende nostalgie." *Mens & Melodie* 46 (November–December 1991): 601–5 and 47 (January 1992): 13–17.

[Nolan, Michael.] *Little Annie Rooney.* Arranged by J. C. Mayseder. Boston: Oliver Ditson, 1889.

Norton, Pauline. "March Music in Nineteenth-Century America." Ph.D. diss., University of Michigan, 1983.

Offergeld, Robert. "More on the Gottschalk Connection." *Institute for Studies in American Music Newsletter* 15/2 (May 1986): 1–2 and 13.

Osborne, William. "Charles Ives the Organist." *The American Organist* 24/7 (July 1990): 58–64.

Pamer, Fritz Egon. "Die Lieder Gustav Mahlers." *Studien zur Musikwissenschaft* 16 (1929): 116–38 and 17 (1930): 105–27.

Parker, Horatio. *Hora novissima.* London: Novello, 1900. Reprint, Earlier American Music, 2. New York: Da Capo Press, 1972.

Perkins, Laurence. "The Sonatas for Violin and Piano by Charles Ives." M.M. thesis, Eastman School of Music, 1961.

Perkins, Leeman L. "The L'homme armé Masses of Busnoys and Okeghem: A Comparison." *The Journal of Musicology* 3 (Fall 1984): 363–96.

Perlis, Vivian. *Charles Ives Remembered: An Oral History.* New Haven: Yale University Press, 1974. Reprint, New York: W. W. Norton, 1976.

————, ed. *Charles Ives Papers.* Yale University Music Library Archival Collection Mss. 14. New Haven: Yale University Music Library, 1983.

Perry, Rosalie Sandra. *Charles Ives and the American Mind.* Kent, Ohio: Kent State University Press, 1974.

"A Poet of Promise." [Review of *General William Booth Enters into Heaven, and Other Poems,* by Nicholas Vachel Lindsay.] *The Independent,* 12 January 1914, 72.

Rabinowitz, Peter J. "Fictional Music: Toward a Theory of Listening." In *Theories of Reading, Looking, and Listening (Bucknell Review* 26/1), ed. Harry R. Garvin, 193–208. Lewisburg: Bucknell University Press, 1981.

Radice, Mark A. "Bartók's Parodies of Beethoven: The Relationships between Opp. 131, 132 and 133 and Bartók's Sixth String Quartet and Third Piano Concerto." *The Music Review* 42 (August–November 1981): 252–60.

Rangell, Andrew Reed. "The Violin-Piano Sonatas of Charles Ives: An Analytical Discussion." Ph.D. diss., The Juilliard School, 1976.

Rathert, Wolfgang. *Charles Ives.* Erträge der Forschung, 267. Darmstadt: Wissenschaftliche Buchgesellschaft, 1989.

————. "Charles Ives, Symphonie Nr. 4, 1911–1916." *Neuland* 3 (1982–83): 226–41.

————. *The Seen and Unseen: Studien zum Werk von Charles Ives.* Berliner musikwissenschaftliche Arbeiten, 38. Munich: Emil Katzbichler, 1991.

Ratner, Leonard. *Classic Music: Expression, Form, Style.* New York: Schirmer Books, 1980.

Redlich, Hans Ferdinand. "The Creative Achievement of Gustav Mahler." *The Musical Times* 101 (July 1960): 418–21.

Reed, Joseph W. *Three American Originals: John Ford, William Faulkner, and Charles Ives.* Middletown, Conn.: Wesleyan University Press, 1984.

Reynolds, Christopher. "A Choral Symphony by Brahms?" *19th-Century Music* 9 (Summer 1985): 3–26.

Rinehart, John McLain. "Ives' Compositional Idioms: An Investigation of Selected Short Compositions as Microcosms of His Musical Language." Ph.D. diss., The Ohio State University, 1970.

Ringer, Alexander L. "'Lieder eines fahrenden Gesellen': Allusion und Zitat in der musikalischen Erzählung Gustav Mahlers." In *Das musikalische Kunstwerk: Geschichte, Ästhetik, Theorie: Festschrift Carl Dahlhaus zum 60. Guburtstag,* ed. Hermann Danuser et al., 589–602. Laaber: Laaber-Verlag, 1988.

Robinson, Charles S., ed. *The New Laudes Domini.* New York: Century, 1892.

Rosen, Charles. "Influence: Plagiarism and Inspiration." *19th-Century Music* 4 (Fall 1980): 87–100.

Rosen, Lee Cyril. "The Violin Sonatas of Charles Ives and the Hymn." B.M. thesis, University of Illinois at Urbana-Champaign, 1965.

Rosenberg, Bruce A. *Can These Bones Live?: The Art of the American Folk Preacher.* Rev. ed. Urbana: University of Illinois Press, 1988.

Rossiter, Frank R. *Charles Ives and His America.* New York: Liveright, 1975.

Rothstein, Evan. "'What Its Signs of Promise Are': Ives, the Tradition of 'Developing Variation' and the Problem of 'Folkloristic' Music in Ives's First Violin Sonata, Third Movement." Unpublished typescript, 1988.

Schickele, Peter. *An Hysteric Return: P. D. Q. Bach at Carnegie Hall.* Sound recording. New York: Vanguard VRS-9223/VSD-79223, 1966.

———. *P. D. Q. Bach (1807–1742)?* Sound recording. New York: Vanguard VRS-9195/VSD-79195, 1965.

Schoenberg, Arnold. *Style and Idea: Selected Writings of Arnold Schoenberg.* Rev. ed. Ed. Leonard Stein, with translations by Leo Black. London: Faber & Faber, 1975.

Schoffman, Nachum. "The Songs of Charles Ives." Ph.D. diss., Hebrew University of Jerusalem, 1977.

Schrade, Leo. "Charles E. Ives: 1874–1954." *Yale Review,* n.s., 44 (June 1955): 535–45.

Schwager, Myron. "Some Observations on Beethoven as an Arranger." *The Musical Quarterly* 60 (January 1974): 80–93.

Scott, Hugh Arthur. "Indebtedness in Music." *The Musical Quarterly* 13 (October 1927): 497–509.

Scruton, Roger. "Programme Music." In *The New Grove Dictionary of Music and Musicians,* ed. Stanley Sadie. 20 vols. London: Macmillan, 1980.

Sherwood, Gayle. "The Choral Works of Charles Ives: Chronology, Style, and Reception." Ph.D. dissertation, Yale University, forthcoming.

———. "Questions and Veracities: Reassessing the Chronology of Ives's Choral Works." *The Musical Quarterly* 78 (Fall 1994): 429–47.

Shirley, Wayne. "'The Second of July': A Charles Ives Draft Considered as an Independent Work." In *A Celebration of American Music: Words and Music in Honor of H. Wiley Hitchcock,* ed. Richard Crawford, R. Allen Lott, and Carol J. Oja, 391–404. Ann Arbor: University of Michigan Press, 1990.

Sinclair, James B. "Index of Tunes Quoted" and "Table of Correlative Measures." In *Charles Ives, "Country Band" March,* ed. James B. Sinclair, iii–iv. Bryn Mawr, Pa.: Merion Music, 1976.

———. Liner notes to *The Orchestral Music of Charles Ives,* by Orchestra New England, conducted by James Sinclair. Sound recording. Westbury, N.Y.: Koch International 3-7025-2, 1990.

———. "Microfilm Concordance to the JK Catalogue." [Annotations to John Kirkpatrick's *Catalogue.*] Typescript and manuscript, Ives Collection, John Herrick Jackson Music Library, Yale University, New Haven. Prepared 1975–76.

———. "Preface." In Charles E. Ives, *Decoration Day: Second Movement of "A Symphony: New England Holidays,"* ed. James B. Sinclair, iii–v. New York: Peer International, 1989.

———. "Preface." In Charles E. Ives, *Holiday Quickstep,* ed. James B. Sinclair, 1. Bryn Mawr: Merion Music, 1975.

———. "Preface." In Charles E. Ives, *A New England Symphony: Three Places in New England,* ed. James B. Sinclair, iii–vi. Bryn Mawr, Pa.: Mercury Music, 1976.

———. "Preface." In Charles E. Ives, *Study No. 23 for Piano,* ed. John Kirkpatrick, 3. Bryn Mawr, Pa.: Merion Music, 1990.

———. "Table of Correlative Measures." In Charles E. Ives, *Overture and March "1776,"* ed. James B. Sinclair, 34. Bryn Mawr, Pa.: Merion Music, 1976.

Slonimsky, Nicolas. *Music Since 1900.* 4th ed. New York: Charles Scribner's Sons, 1971.

Solomon, Maynard. "Charles Ives: Some Questions of Veracity." *Journal of the American Musicological Society* 40 (Fall 1987): 443–70.

———. "Communication." *Journal of the American Musicological Society* 42 (Spring 1989): 209–18.

———. "The Ninth Symphony: A Search for Order." In *Beethoven Essays,* 3–32. Cambridge, Mass.: Harvard University Press, 1988.

Sonntag, Brunhilde. *Untersuchungen zur Collagetechnik in der Musik des 20. Jahrhunderts.* Regensburg: Gustav Bosse, 1977.

Stackhouse, David L. "D. W. Reeves and His Music." *Journal of Band Research* 5/2 (Spring 1969): 15–28 and 6/1 (Fall 1969): 29–41.

Starr, Lawrence. "Charles Ives: The Next Hundred Years—Towards a Method of Analyzing the Music." *The Music Review* 38 (May 1977): 101–11.

———. "The Early Styles of Charles Ives." *19th-Century Music* 7 (Summer 1983): 71–80.

———. "Style and Substance: 'Ann Street' by Charles Ives." *Perspectives of New Music* 15/2 (Spring–Summer 1977): 23–33.

———. *A Union of Diversities: Style in the Music of Charles Ives.* New York: Schirmer Books, 1992.

Stein, Alan. "The Musical Language of Charles Ives' Three Places in New England." D.M.A. diss., University of Illinois at Urbana-Champaign, 1975.

Sterne, Colin. "The Quotations in Charles Ives's Second Symphony." *Music and Letters* 52 (January 1971): 39–45.

Stoeckel, Gustave J., ed. *The College Hymn Book: For Use in the Battell Chapel at Yale College.* New York: Wm. A. Pond, 1886.

Stone, Kurt. "Ives's Fourth Symphony: A Review." *The Musical Quarterly* 52 (January 1966): 1–16.

Straus, Joseph N. "Recompositions by Schoenberg, Stravinsky, and Webern." *The Musical Quarterly* 72 (1986): 301–28.

———. *Remaking the Past: Musical Modernism and the Influence of the Tonal Tradition.* Cambridge, Mass.: Harvard University Press, 1990.

Taruskin, Richard. "Russian Folk Melodies in *The Rite of Spring*." *Journal of the American Musicological Society* 33 (Fall 1980): 501–43.

Taylor, Paul Franklyn. "Stylistic Heterogeneity: The Analytical Key to Movements IIa and IIb from the First Piano Sonata by Charles Ives." D.M.A. diss., University of Wisconsin–Madison, 1986.

Tibbe, Monika. "Musik in Musik: Collagetechnik und Zitierverfahren." *Musica* 25 (November–December 1971): 562–63.

Tick, Judith. "Charles Ives and Gender Ideology." In *Musicology and Difference: Gender and Sexuality in Music Scholarship*, ed. Ruth A. Solie, 83–106. Berkeley: University of California Press, 1993.

———. "Ragtime and the Music of Charles Ives," *Current Musicology*, no. 18 (1974): 105–13.

Vinay, Gianfranco. *L'America musicale di Charles Ives.* Torino: Giulio Einaudi, 1974.

———. "Charles Ives e i musicisti europei: Anticipazioni e dipendenze." *Nuova revista musicale italiana* 7 (July–December 1973): 417–29.

Walker, Alan. "Schumann, Liszt and the C major Fantasie, Op. 17: A Declining Relationship." *Music and Letters* 60 (April 1979): 156–165.

Wallach, Laurence. "The Ives Conference: A Word from the Floor." *Current Musicology*, no. 19 (1975): 32–36.

———. "The New England Education of Charles Ives." Ph.D. diss., Columbia University, 1973.

Ward, Charles. "Charles Ives: The Relationship Between Aesthetic Theories and Compositional Processes." Ph.D. diss., University of Texas at Austin, 1974.

———. "The Use of Hymn Tunes as an Expression of 'Substance' and 'Manner' in the Music of Charles E. Ives, 1874–1954." M.M. thesis, University of Texas at Austin, 1969.

Ward, Keith C. "Musical Idealism: A Study of the Aesthetics of Arnold Schoenberg and Charles Ives." D.M.A. diss., Northwestern University, 1985.

Watson, J. A. "Beethoven's Debt to Mozart." *Music and Letters* 28 (July 1937): 248–58.

Whaples, Miriam K. "Mahler and Schubert's A Minor Sonata D. 784." *Music and Letters* 65 (July 1984): 255–63.

Whitesell, Lloyd. "Reckless Form, Uncertain Audiences: Responding to Ives." *American Music* 12 (Fall 1994): 304–19.

Wilheim, András. "Erik Satie's Gregorian Paraphrases." *Studia musicologica* 25 (1983): 229–37.

Willis, Thomas. Liner notes for *Charles Ives: Symphony No. 1*, by the Chicago Symphony Orchestra, conducted by Morton Gould. Sound recording. New York: RCA Victor LSC-2893, 1966.

Wolff, Konrad. *Masters of the Keyboard.* Enlarged ed. Bloomington: Indiana University Press, 1990.

Wooldridge, David. "Charles Ives and the American National Character: 'Musical Spirit of '76.'" In *South Florida's Historic Ives Festival 1974–1976*, ed. F. Warren

O'Reilly, 27–29. Coral Gables, Fla.: University of Miami at Coral Gables, 1976.

————. *From the Steeples and the Mountains: A Study of Charles Ives.* New York: Knopf, 1974. Republished as *Charles Ives: A Portrait.* London: Faber and Faber, 1975.

Yellin, Victor Fell. Review of the first recording of *The Celestial Country. The Musical Quarterly* 60 (July 1974): 500–508.

Yudkin, Jeremy. "Beethoven's 'Mozart' Quartet." *Journal of the American Musicological Society* 45 (Spring 1992): 30–74.

Zoor, William. "Correspondence." *Gramophone* 61 (October 1983): 416

Index of Ives's Compositions

The principal discussions or listings of the uses of existing music within the listed work are indicated by **boldface** page numbers. Page numbers in ***boldface italics*** indicate the principal discussions or listings of completed, extant works of his own that Ives borrows from, uses as a model, or reworks in a new piece (other than a transcription to another medium). Works not followed by boldface page numbers are lost or fragmentary or are not known to use borrowed material.

457n55, 497n41; compared to other Ives works, 80, 187, 198, 206; sketches, 185, 186, 234, 456n51

Housatonic at Stockbridge, The. See *Three Places in New England*

Hymn. See *Largo cantabile*

Hymn-Anthem (lost), 225, 463n15

Hymn interludes, **218,** 462n3

Hymns, 14

—"First Hymn, Op. 2, No. 1," **16,** 431n9, 474n32

Ich grolle nicht, **27–31,** 32–33, 33, 433nn33,35

Immortality, **289, 291,** 475–76n51, 476n52

Improvisations, 49

Indians, The, **294,** 476n55; Ives borrows from, *276, 473–23*

In Flanders Fields, **313,** 326, 370, 371–72, 480n21; Ives borrows from, *276;* sketches for, 480n22

Innate, The. See *Adagio cantabile*

Instrumental music, 11

In Summerfields. See *Feldeinsamkeit*

In the Alley, **472n11**

In the Inn. See *Set for Theater or Chamber Orchestra*

In the Mornin', **226**

In the Night. See *Set for Theater or Chamber Orchestra*

In These United States (lost), 125–26, 446n50

Invention in D, **270,** 471n4

Johnny Poe, **365,** 367, 493nn78,79

Largo, violin and piano, 11, 465–66n37

Largo, violin, clarinet, and piano, 11, 134, 465–66n37

Largo cantabile (Hymn), 4, **305–6,** 326, **361, 362,** 477n5

Last Reader, The, 7, **301–5,** 325, 326, 370, 477nn2,3

Lincoln, the Great Commoner, 135, **312,** 326, 370, 479nn16,17,**18;** Ives borrows from, *364, 493n73*

"London Bridge" settings, **218,** 274, 462n2

Lotusblume, Die, **433n38**

Luck and Work, **288, 290,** 291, 475n48; sketches, 288

Majority, **294–95,** 476n55

Marches, 6, 10, 13, 22, 36, 47; lost, 14; incorporate popular tune, 38, 41, **218–24,** 228, 232

March for Dewey Day (lost), 480n21

March in F and C (theater orchestra, 1C5), 222

March in F and C (theater orchestra, 1C7), 222

March in F and C, with "Omega Lambda Chi" (band), **221**

March in F and C, with "Omega Lambda Chi" (piano), **221**

March in G and C, with "Here's to Good Old Yale" (first version of 3B13?), **221, 222, 223,** 463n10

March in G and C, with "See the Conquering Hero," **221, 224**

March in G and D (third version of 3B13?), 222

March "Intercollegiate," 219, **220, 222**

March No. 1 in F and B♭, with "The Year of Jubilee," 3, **41–43,** 75, **220, 222, 223–24,** 435n8, 462n9

March No. 2 in C and F, with "The Son of a Gambolier" (piano), **220,** 224, 463n11

March No. 2 in F and B♭, with "The Son of a Gambolier" (theater orchestra), **220**

March No. 3 in F and C, with "My Old Kentucky Home," **220, 222, 223–24;** sketches, 224, 463n10

March No. 5 in C and A♭, with "Annie Lisle" (band), 219, **220, 222**

March No. 5 in D and B♭, with "Annie Lisle" (piano), **220, 222**

March No. 6 in G and D, with "Here's to Good Old Yale" (second version of 3B13?), **221, 222,** 463n10

March: "The Circus Band," 222, 471n7; reworked as song *The Circus Band,* **271,** 471n8

Index of Compositions by Others

Works are listed by title, except for works known only by such generic titles as "Sonata" or "Symphony," which are listed by composer. All compositions mentioned in the text that are not by Ives are listed here. Principal discussions or mentions of Ives's use of compositions by others as sources or models are indicated by **boldface** page numbers.

INDEX OF COMPOSITIONS BY OTHERS

INDEX OF COMPOSITIONS BY OTHERS

General Index

Adams, John, 349
Alcott, Beth, 356, 357
Alford, Henry, 34–35
Allusion, stylistic. *See* Stylistic allusion
American Indian music, 294, 422, 423, 424
Americanism: in subject matter, 6, 135, 136, 418, 420; in sound, 126, 134, 253, 317, 419; in focus on American tunes, 135, 245, 246–47, 418, 419; and identity, 421–25
American music: and borrowing, 21–22, 38, 219, 300, 322–25, 365–67, 372, 415; evocation of, 36, 286; character of, retained in paraphrase, 55, 104, 108, 125, 134; used in European forms, 89, 99, 102–3, 104, 107, 124–25, 129, 133, 135, 419; integrated with European art music, 103, 124–33, 134, 135, 136; used in genres of European art music, 217, 246, 253, 316, 419; and music about experiencing music, 366, 367; and nonrepetitive form, 468n57. *See also* Vernacular music
Anglican chant, 274–75
Arne, Thomas, 186
Arnold, Matthew, 333, 337
Art music: and borrowing, 2, 3, 5, 9, 12–13, 37–38, 49, 75, 224–25, 229, 230, 231, 232, 342, 365, 367, 415, 416; aesthetics of, 2, 75, 136, 150, 284, 417; used by other composers, 5, 102, 331, 342, 366, 415, 416, 465n28, 493n82; Ives trained in, 6, 13, 27, 88, 89, 246, 267, 419; used as model, 16, 17–20, 21–22, 27–36, 89–99, 101, 102, 160, 228, 270, 276–77, 285, 433n38, 434–35n51, 441–42n5, 442nn6, 8,12, 444n26, 448nn64,67, 489n40, 490n51; transcriptions of, 46–47, 48, 54; vernacular music used in, 49–52, 75, 88–89, 99, 104, 124–25, 161, 217,

246–47, 252; Ives borrows from, 71, 76–79, 103, 126–33, 133–34, 195, 196–97, 198–200, 221, 224, 240, 276, 279, 341, 349, 351, 352, 354, 356, 402, 431n11, 446–47n54, 459n73, 463n12, 470n78; value of, 79; Ives writing, 101, 102, 107, 133, 325, 424; integrated with vernacular music, 103, 126, 129–30, 131, 134, 135, 136, 424–25; methods of, 126, 246, 252, 417, 419; vernacular tune raised to level of, 161, 246–47, 250, 419; elite status of, 247, 419; evoking vernacular music in, 268, 271, 282, 284–85, 286, 367
Art songs: by Ives, 6, 13, 22, 24–34, 36, 88, 325, 433n31; about vernacular music, 150, 268, 271, 282, 284–85; and borrowing, 322, 365, 367

Bach, Johann Christian, 12, 34
Bach, Johann Sebastian: as borrower, 5, 12, 49, 371, 496n23; as model or source for other composers, 13, 102, 416; as model for Ives, 22, 32, 72, 74, 124–25, 133, 252, 437n19; Ives borrows from, 71, 104, 126, 126–27, 128, 129, 131, 134, 270, 276, 439–40n44, 446–47n54, 447n59; and idealism, 136; as precedent for Ives's procedures, 224–25, 229, 232
Bacon, Leonard, 185
Baker, J. C., 366
Ballantine, Christopher, 333–38
Baron, Carol K., 10
Bartók, Béla, 298, 416
Bayly, Thomas Haynes, 120
Becker, John J., 470n75
Beckett, Thomas à, 108
Beethoven, Ludwig van: Ives transcription from, 4, 46–47, 54, 436–37n16; as borrower, 13, 38, 49, 75, 415; as model or source for other composers, 13, 95, 231, 416, 465n28; as model for Ives, 47,

Beethoven, Ludwig van (continued)
95, 97–98, 102, 109, 160, 161, 244, 252,
414, 437n19; compared to Ives, 75, 139,
145, 150–51, 154, 177, 187, 246, 410,
453n22; Ives borrows from, 80, 195,
196–97, 198–200, 349, 351, 359,
459–60n78, 460n80; as precedent for
Ives's procedures, 108, 225, 226, 227, 229,
230, 231, 232, 240, 298, 410; doubtful
borrowing from, 130, 440–41n58,
445n38, 447n60, 483n53; and coinciden-
tal similarity, 131; and idealism, 136, 350,
421; and program music, 248, 340, 415
Bellamann, Henry, 390, 392, 401, 500n62
Berg, Alban, 270–71, 298, 416
Berio, Luciano, 411
Berlin, Irving: as borrower, 324–25, 325,
331, 366, 493n83; Ives borrows from, 325
Berlioz, Hector, 226, 230, 248, 270
Bernard de Morlaix, Saint, 35
Bethune, Thomas (Blind Tom), 342
Biber, Heinrich, 5, 371
Bishop, Henry R., 383
Blake, James W., 343
Bland, James A., 255
Bliss, Philip P., 342
Bloch, Ernest, 416
Bloom, Harold, 418
Booth, William, 253
Borrowing: definition of problem, 2–3;
reasons for, 2, 3, 4, 5, 36, 75, 101, 114,
129, 133–34, 338, 376, 412–14, 417–25;
and aesthetics, 2, 3, 102; and originality, 2, 6, 75, 103, 136, 266, 368, 410, 418,
419; precedents for, 3, 5, 7, 8, 415–17;
and meaning, 11, 36, 49, 73–75, 84, 101,
135, 148–51, 193–94, 266, 299, 322, 338,
341, 363, 419–25; significance of, 11,
73–75, 101, 104, 133–36, 338, 412–25; and
listener response, 84–87, 114–15, 126,
130, 148–49, 248, 250, 299, 312, 367, 414,
440n45; Ives criticized for, 252, 321–22,
379, 412, 469n69
—and ambiguity: in identifying borrowed material, 38, 75, 80–81, 83,
85–86, 104, 293, 415; and linear combi-

nation of tunes, 75, 80, 85, 320;
between similar tunes, 213, 391, 410, 415
—amount and extent of: in Ives's music,
1–2, 7, 11, 86, 134, 337, 416–17; in individual works, 1–2, 75, 86, 87, 103, 104,
128, 133, 237, 239, 409; in other composers, 12–13, 324, 367, 416
—and compositional intent: shown in
sketches, 8, 87, 107, 118–19, 314, 330, 382,
439n41, 480n22, 480n27; shown in
manner of use, 27–28, 33–34, 43, 47,
86–87, 89, 95, 101, 131, 314, 439n43;
uncertain, 84, 214, 375–76, 445n41,
476n56; doubted, 85–86, 440n45,
454n29, 467–68n55, 487n24; not supported by sketches, 114–15, 455n34
—recognition of: not necessary in
understanding musical form, 49, 51, 87,
125, 199, 371, 482n43; necessary in text
illustration, 362
—recognizability of: varying levels of, 1,
46, 103, 104, 125, 128, 135, 143, 146, 317,
327, 367, 381, 410, 411; obscured, 54, 60,
64–65, 86, 110, 116, 134, 288–89, 312, 376;
level of, changed in process of composition, 63–70, 105, 111, 113, 115, 125, 306,
438n36, 448n63, 452n15, 480n30,
491–92n62
Borrowing procedures: described, 3–5;
development of, 3, 5–7, 7–8, 10–11, 13,
20, 38, 135–36, 327, 411, 414–15, 418–21;
variety of, 3–5, 326–27, 338–39, 360,
409, 413, 416–17, 418, 419. See also Cantus firmus; Collage; Cumulative setting; Medley; Modeling; Paraphrase;
Patchwork; Programmatic quotation;
Quodlibet; Self-borrowing; Setting;
Stylistic allusion; Transcription; Variations
Bowring, John, 390
Bradbury, William, 143, 181, 316
Brahms, Johannes: as borrower, 13, 49, 75,
125, 416; as model for Ives, 24–25,
27–28, 31–34, 51, 104, 109, 125, 132–33,
136, 160, 161, 244–45, 252, 433nn37,38,
437n19, 447nn56,57, 448nn66,67; com-

pared to Ives, 75, 213, 379; Ives borrows from, 104, 126, 127, 128, 130, 131, 132–33, 134, 349, 444n26, 447nn56,57,59; as precedent for Ives's procedures, 108, 353, 410, 469n70; doubtful borrowing from, 114–15, 130, 440n45, 458–59n72; meaning of references to, 133–34; as source or model for other composers, 416

Brewster, Lyman, 387

Brodhead, Thomas M., 358, 359, 490–91n56

Brooke, Rupert, 277–78

Browning, Robert, 347

Bruce, Neely, 365–66, 415

Bruckner, Anton, 416, 447–48n60

Buck, Dudley, 21–22, 38

Bugle calls and fanfares: as source, 1; and modeling, 15, 274; used by others, 15, 252, 298, 324, 325, 366, 484n3; in works with paraphrased themes, 89, 124; as text illustration, 257, 258, 341, 363, 364, 493n79; in patchworks, 312, 313, 314, 316, 320, 479n18, 480n25; in program music, 345–46, 347, 361–62, 486n14, 487–88n28, 491–92n62; in collages, 377, 378, 379, 381, 382, 387, 388, 401

Bunyan, John, 358

Bushnell, Horace, 337

Buxtehude, Dietrich, 13

Camp meetings, 148, 149–50, 161, 180, 250, 251, 252, 262, 424. *See also* Revivals

Cantos (Pound), 369

Cantus firmus: defined, 3, 4; precedents for, 5, 8; Ives uses, 41, 110–11, 238–39, 240, 392, 409; as musical device, 266

Carter, Elliott, 469n69

Center Church, New Haven, 185, 456n50

Central Presbyterian Church, New York, 36, 234, 361, 493n77, 501n75

Chadwick, George Whitefield, 27–28, 34

Change ringing, 273–74, 472n17

Charles, Sydney Robinson, 105, 127

Chopin, Frédéric, 230, 273, 416

Christy, Edwin P., 384

Civil War: and George Ives, 218, 431n11; and marches, 219; as subject, 250, 317, 321, 324, 345, 488n29; in American history, 314–15, 350, 356

—songs of: paraphrased as themes, 108, 226–27, 236, 237, 241, 242, 250, 487n19; and modeling, 276; in patchworks, 306–11, 312–22, 325, 478–79n12, 479nn18,20, 481n35, 487n19; borrowed by other composers, 322, 324, 325, 366; in extended paraphrase, 327; and program music, 343, 345–46, 347, 348–49, 359, 485n9, 486–87n17, 487n19; in quodlibets, 372, 373–74, 375; in collages, 377–79, 382, 386–87, 388, 400, 497nn37,38, 499n58

Classical tradition. *See* Art music

Cohan, George M.: Ives borrows from, 314, 325, 364; as precedent for Ives, 322, 410; as borrower, 322–24, 325, 325–26, 331, 367

Collage: defined, 4, 369–71; and modeling, 4, 7, 8, 287, 299, 368, 369, 370, 376, 383, 384, 410, 411, 414–15; and paraphrase, 4, 7, 86, 368, 369, 370, 376, 383, 410, 414–15; and cumulative setting, 4, 7, 139, 186, 214, 369, 370, 376, 383, 410, 411, 414–15; and program music, 4, 135, 360, 383, 389; as unprecedented and exceptional, 5, 348, 368, 410–11; place in Ives's development, 7, 8, 10–11, 411, 419, 421, 448n71; and extramusical meaning, 135, 299, 338, 342, 346, 367–68, 379–81; and resemblance between source tunes, 135, 370, 382, 385, 386, 387, 388, 391, 401, 402, 408, 410, 411; and music about experiencing music, 273, 275, 299, 346, 386, 410, 420; represents dreaming, 338, 368, 401, 408, 410, 411; and stream of consciousness, 338, 369–70, 382, 387, 391, 392, 410, 411; and medley, 368; and evocation of memory, 368, 369–70, 380–81, 382, 385, 411, 497n34; and programmatic quotation, 368, 369, 370, 376, 414–15; and quodlibet, 368, 369, 370, 376, 414–15; function

Collage (continued)
of borrowed tunes in, 370, 371, 376,
379–81, 382; and patchwork, 370, 384,
414–15; Ives uses, 376–411, 413, 497n41;
and layering, 379–81, 383, 390, 392, 400,
408; and fugue, 383, 402; conveys
events from participant's point of
view, 389; conveys mystical experience,
389, 391–92, 409; used by other composers, 411
College songs: paraphrased as themes,
110, 444n30, 446n50; in marches, 221,
222, 223; in programmatic works,
342–43, 344, 502n82; in texted works,
363, 365; in quodlibets, 372, 373–74
Collins, Anne Timoney, 286
Compositional process. *See* Ives, Charles:
compositional process; Sketches
Conkey, Ithamar, 20
Contrapuntal combination of tunes or
themes: in ternary forms, 57, 93, 217,
226–27, 236, 237, 238, 371; in cumulative
settings, 57, 139, 180–81, 213, 228, 316,
371, 451n9; in sonata forms, 94, 95, 104,
110–11, 116, 123–24, 124, 131, 217, 226,
236, 237, 238, 371; in collages, 135, 372,
402, 406–7; in quodlibets, 180–81, 370,
371–72; in marches, 222–24, 228; as
rudimentary cumulative forms,
227–28; in other works, 316, 351, 371–72,
388
Converse, Charles, 151
Coolidge, Elizabeth Sprague, 160
Corelli, Arcangelo, 12, 13
Cornelius, Peter, 24–25, 25–27
Cornell, Joseph, 370
Couperin, François, 12, 13
Cowell, Henry, 138
Cowell, Sidney, 138
Crockett, Effie I., 214
Crouch, Frederick, 361
Cumulative form: and cumulative set-
ting, 137–38, 449n1; based on contra-
puntal combination, 227–28; used by
Sibelius, 231. *See also* Cumulative
setting

Cumulative setting: defined and
described, 4, 135, 137–38, 161–62, 449n1;
paraphrased themes in, 4, 5, 137–38,
139, 146, 161, 187, 201, 213, 215; countermelody precedes theme, 4, 217, 223–26,
229–30; as innovative, 5, 6, 7, 135, 138,
160–61, 216, 232–33, 262, 418; place in
Ives's development, 6–7, 7, 8, 10–11, 135,
414, 419; thematic development in,
6–7, 137, 145–46, 147, 149, 150, 154, 159,
160, 161, 162, 187, 201, 207, 212, 215, 217,
228, 229, 232–33, 238, 244, 246, 247, 252,
262, 266, 414; frequency in Ives's
music, 6–7, 138, 159–60, 232, 236, 262,
275; development of, in Ives's music, 8,
57, 139, 147–48, 216–28, 232–33, 233–47;
as thematic form, 8, 137, 139, 146–47,
156, 160, 214–15, 244, 411, 414, 453n22;
precedents for, 8, 138, 139, 147–48,
216–17, 224–25, 226, 227–28, 228–33,
410; and contrapuntal combination of
themes, 57, 139, 213, 217, 226–28, 316,
371, 451n9; Ives uses, 71, 137–215,
253–66, 402–9, 413; and melodic transformation, 86, 135, 211, 217, 232, 410;
non-repetitive, 137, 146–47, 217, 231, 233,
238, 244–45; and developing variation,
137, 161, 217; paraphrased countermelodies in, 138, 139, 143, 146, 161–62,
163, 172, 174–75, 187, 377, 451n8, 458n66;
as process of discovery or clarification,
138, 146, 147, 148–49, 150–51, 159, 160,
181, 192, 212, 217, 230, 252, 262, 266, 284,
335, 337, 409, 414; flexibility of, 139, 161,
162, 177, 215, 262; in works with text,
139, 149–50, 194, 217, 245, 247, 253–62,
266; harmonic plan of, 143, 146, 162,
187, 200; and compositional process,
147, 451nn8,9, 459n75, 497n37; and text
of source, 149–50, 151, 174, 187, 191,
193–94, 217, 251–52, 263; raises stature
of borrowed tune, 150, 161, 246–47, 250,
419; and use of American vernacular
themes, 161, 217, 245, 246–47, 250, 419,
453n24; goal-oriented, 161, 228, 244,
246, 247, 250; and multi-movement

cycles, 162, 216, 233, 235–44, 245; and resemblance between source tunes, 163, 181, 185, 187, 191, 195, 205, 213, 254–55, 470n79, 475n41; role in Ives's music, 216, 233, 236, 244–45; used by Smetana, 232; extending over three movements, 240; Ives works with similar features compared to, 316, 320, 335, 350, 351, 386, 388, 400, 464n17
—and other forms of borrowing: and collage, 4, 7, 139, 369, 370, 376, 376–77, 380, 381–82, 383, 400, 408, 411, 414–15; and paraphrase, 6–7, 71, 139, 143, 146, 149, 155, 157, 161–62, 163, 172, 184, 187, 205–6, 217, 264, 327, 414; and variations, 6–7, 147, 213, 215, 217, 246, 414, 419, 456n49; and settings, 6–7, 138, 174, 194, 217, 217–26, 234, 239, 414
—meaning of: in program music, 5, 8, 139, 161, 184, 186, 216, 217, 245, 247–50, 253, 262–66, 341, 379, 400, 408, 409; in character pieces, 8, 148, 247–53; as purely musical form, 148, 151, 160, 199, 215, 217, 244–45, 250, 252–53, 262, 266, 338; and meaning, 148–51, 216, 245–66, 420, 468n65, 469n70
—and other musical forms: compared to other forms, 137–39, 146–47, 156, 160, 161, 200, 215, 231, 452n16, 468n57; compared to ternary form, 137, 138, 147, 154, 160, 215, 217, 227, 238, 245, 452n16; compared to sonata form, 137, 138, 139, 146–47, 154, 156, 160, 194, 200, 215, 217, 227, 232–33, 238, 245, 246, 419, 452n16, 453n22; compared to ritornello form, 139, 156, 215; and end-weighted forms, 161, 217, 226–28, 232, 233, 238, 244; combined with ternary form, 183–84, 185, 187, 194, 198, 201, 206, 215, 242; combined with variation form, 183–84, 187, 193, 215; replaced sonata and ternary forms, 232, 236, 238, 245
—sub-types of, 139, 162, 215, 235; with paraphrased countermelody, 138, 139–61, 161–62, 162–87, 194, 225, 235; with partial or rudimentary counter-

melody, 162, 187–94, 225, 235; without countermelody, 162, 194–200, 235; double, 162, 200–206; combined with verse-refrain form, 162, 201, 206–14, 215, 235, 460n82
Cutler, Henry S., 313
Cyclic unification, 70, 75, 95, 103, 131, 243, 350, 402, 408–9, 439n41; and borrowings shared between movements, 70, 70–71, 108, 123–24, 240, 242, 243, 244, 245, 408–9, 439n41; and resemblance between source tunes, 239, 239–40, 242

Damrosch, Walter, 444–45n34
Dance melodies. *See* Fiddle tunes and dance melodies
Debussy, Claude: as borrower, 13, 416, 473n24; ambivalence toward, 36, 278; compared to Ives, 136, 296, 298, 417, 420; Ives borrows from, 277–78, 474n30; as model for Bartók, 416; possible model for Ives, 434–35n51, 489n40, 490n51
de Leeuw, Reinbert, 71
Delius, Frederick, 416
Delta Kappa Epsilon, 76, 343, 372, 373, 494n4
Developing variation, 108, 161, 217, 330, 353, 453n23, 489n43
Diabelli, Anton, 415
D'Indy, Vincent, 49, 230, 416, 464–65n26
Doane, William H., 178, 305, 371
Dodworth, Allen T., 219
Donizetti, Gaetano, 17–20, 22, 285, 416
Donlin, Mike, 347
Dresser, Paul, 286, 306, 324, 325
Dumont, Frank, 435n10
Dvořák, Antonín: as model for Ives, 24–25, 70, 89–95, 101, 102, 125, 131, 133, 135, 228, 273, 441–42n5, 442nn6,8, 448n63; as borrower, 49, 75; as model for Parker, 102; Ives borrows from, 130–31; as precedent for Ives, 230; Ives as competitor to, 273, 442n7
Dykes, John B., 475–76n51

Harrison, Lou, 313
Harvey, Mark, 251
Hastings, Thomas, 226
Hatton, John, 185
Hawley, Charles Beach, 279, 474n34
Hawthorne, Nathaniel, 355, 358–60, 392, 401
Haydn, Franz Joseph: as borrower, 13, 49; compared to Ives, 244, 296; Ives borrows from, 301, 428n11; as model or source for other composers, 416
Heine, Heinrich, 28
Henderson, Clayton, 2, 14, 61, 80, 83, 115
Hepokoski, James, 465n30, 469n70
Herbert, Victor, 273
Hertz, David, 418
Hewitt, James, 342, 484n3
Hitchcock, H. Wiley, 199, 240, 364–65, 386
Hoffman, Elisha A., 253
Hoffman, E. T. A., 248
Holden, Oliver, 57
Holst, Gustav, 416
Hopkins, Josiah, 23–24
Howard, Joseph E., 277
Humor: and quodlibets, 4, 7, 322, 371, 372–76, 435n9, 480n29, 494n2, 495n18; and parody, 472n11
Hunt, Leigh, 271
Hymnals: used in Danbury, 20, 361, 365, 474–75n40; used at Yale, 185, 361, 483n51, 493n77; as popular music, 246; used at Central Presbyterian Church, 361, 493n77, 501n75; other, 440n57, 452n14, 483n51
Hymn texts: set by Ives, 20, 23, 34–35, 149–50, 174, 185, 193–94, 205, 247, 281, 390. *See also* Text of source
Hymn tunes: as source, 1, 2; by Ives, 14, 16; used as models, 14, 16, 20, 23–24, 83–84, 276, 277, 281–86, 287–94, 360–62, 421, 433n30, 440n57, 474–75n40, 476n52; used in variations, 21–22, 38–41, 43–46, 49, 230; in art music, 49–52, 161, 217, 246–47, 252, 284–85; paraphrased as themes, 49–75, 85, 87,

99–101, 103, 105–7, 109–15, 123, 125, 226–27, 236, 237–38, 238–40, 246, 276, 371, 419, 437n21, 438n35, 442n12, 444n32, 445n35, 447n60, 448n66; and linear combination of tunes, 80; in extended paraphrase, 81, 327–39, 483nn51,53; in patchworks, 82–83, 301–11, 313, 325; American character of, 126, 134, 246–47, 253; extramusical associations with, 126, 149, 151, 217, 245–53, 258–59, 262, 266, 284–86, 288, 293–94, 296, 338, 422, 423, 424, 452n12, 468n65; in cumulative settings, 135, 139–214, 229, 230, 233–35, 237, 239–40, 241–44, 245–53, 253–66, 450n6, 451nn8, 9, 452nn14,15, 455n39, 457n60, 458n66, 466n44, 468n65; in program music, 135, 340–41, 344, 345–46, 347, 349–50, 353, 355, 356, 357, 358–60, 360, 364–65, 389–409, 421, 491n59, 492nn64,66; improvised preludes on, 148, 229–30, 234; music about, 148–51, 245–53, 266, 285–86, 327–33, 420, 422; art songs about, 149–50, 268, 281–86, 325, 326; raised to level of art music, 161, 246–47, 250, 419; in settings, 174, 193–94, 205, 217, 218, 225–26, 233–35, 240, 274; treated in ragtime style, 213, 455n36; used by other composers, 219, 224–25, 229, 230, 232, 366, 482n45; style of, 288, 291, 294, 295, 296; in quodlibets, 371–72, 373–74, 495n14; in collages, 389–409, 439n43, 501n75
Hyperion Theater Orchestra, 373

Improvisation, 147–48, 229–30, 234, 372, 497n34
Independent, The, 254, 257
Ives, Charles: career, 5–7, 7, 9, 35–36, 267, 419–21; as organist, 6, 21, 36, 38, 71, 147–48, 180, 185, 234, 276, 361, 419, 435n2, 439n44, 456n50, 493n77; dating of works, 9–11, 233, 235, 428n8, 429nn14,15, 430n3, 445n42; aesthetic aims, 418–25, 504n24
—compositional process: revealed in

Ives, Charles (continued)
sketches, 8; borrowing central to, 11, 413, 417; in cumulative settings, 147, 451n8, 497n37; in collage, 381–82, 400, 429n14; and contrapuntal combination, 437n25, 463nn10,13, 464n22. *See also* Sketches

—reworking own music. *See* Self-borrowing

—writings: *Essays Before a Sonata,* 15, 199, 278, 337, 350, 357, 421, 422; *Memos,* 15, 287, 337, 351, 373

Ives, Edith, 226

Ives, George: as teacher and influence, 6, 15, 20, 128, 218–19, 430n4, 434n46; as copyist, 17, 38–39, 430n4, 431n14, 435n5; Ives borrows from, 167, 178–81, 371, 372, 451n9, 455n39; as musician, 218–19, 287, 365, 431n11, 467n48; memorials to, 361, 486n15; and transcriptions, 436n12

Ives, Harmony Twichell, 6, 327, 337, 420, 456n50

Ives, Moss White, 453n20

Johnson, Robert Underwood, 327
Johnson, Samuel, 304
Josquin des Prez, 102
Joyce, James, 369, 389

Kearns, William K., 102
Kelly, Kevin O., 194
Kernochan, Cully, 372, 494n4
Kiallmark, George, 170, 236
King, Martin Luther, Jr., 148
Kingsley, George, 186, 225
Kipling, Rudyard, 279
Kirkpatrick, John: *Catalogue,* 2, 9, 39, 219; and borrowings, 2, 23, 277, 279, 326, 374, 447n59, 467n47, 467–68n55; and dating Ives's works, 9–10, 428n8; and extramusical meanings, 248, 249, 353, 391, 420
Kittredge, Walter, 226, 366
Knapp, Mrs. Joseph F., 115
Kneass, Nelson, 344
Kneisel Quartet, 348

LaForge, Frank, 279, 474n37
Lahee, Henry, 472n17
Langlotz, Carl, 342
Lawlor, Charles B., 343
Layering, 379–81, 383, 389, 390, 392, 400, 408, 409, 450n6, 482–83n50, 496–97n33
Leslie, Edgar, 366
Lincoln, Abraham, 136, 312
Lindsay, Vachel, 253–59
Linear combination of tunes: and paraphrase, 61, 75, 76–80, 86; and resemblance between source tunes, 75, 76–80, 85, 86, 110, 235, 300, 320, 483n53; in quodlibet, 370, 371, 372–76, 494n2
Liszt, Franz: as borrower, 37, 342; as precedent for Ives, 108, 230, 244, 351; borrowed from by Bruckner, 416
Longfellow, Henry Wadsworth, 366
Low, Benjamin, 365
Lowry, Robert, 154, 174, 187, 193, 457n60
Lully, Jean-Baptiste, 12, 13
Lusitania, 262
Lyte, Henry F., 23

Mahler, Gustav: as borrower, 13, 49, 416; ambivalence toward, 36; compared to Ives, 213, 434–35n51; as precedent for Ives, 231, 296, 298
Main, Hubert Platt, 365
Maker, Frederick C., 282–83
Marches: Ives borrows from, 1, 180, 343, 344, 346, 347, 374, 387, 401, 431n11, 486n14, 499n58; by other composers, using borrowed tunes, 5, 219; by Ives, 6, 10, 14, 14–16, 47, 93, 218–24, 246, 285, 419, 424; used as model, 13, 14–16, 16, 22, 36, 221, 222, 498n50; use of popular tune in, 20, 38, 41–43, 46, 75, 218, 219–24, 228, 232; style of, 240, 277, 296, 311, 410; referred to, 249; music about, 271, 343, 345, 346, 355, 357, 359, 360, 380, 386
Markham, Edwin, 312
Marsh, Simeon, 195
Marshall, Dennis, 213
Mason, Huntington, 363

Mason, Lowell: Ives paraphrases, 71, 123, 201, 439–40n44; Ives borrows from, 80, 81, 110, 185, 205, 254, 289, 466n42; as arranger, 80, 110, 123, 254, 466n42; doubtful borrowing from, 114–15

Massenet, Jules, 24–25

McCrae, John, 313

Medley: defined, 3, 4; used by others, 5, 8, 219, 411; and patchwork, 7, 301, 414; place in Ives's development, 8, 414, 419; Ives uses, 41, 219, 373, 409, 413, 435n9; and collage, 368

Mendelssohn, Felix: as borrower, 13; as model or precedent for Ives, 24–25, 229; as model or source for other composers, 102, 331, 366, 493n83; as source for hymn tune Ives uses, 306, 361–62; doubtful borrowing from, 432n18

Meredith, George, 433n32

Milton, John, 84

Minor, George A., 52, 109

Modeling: defined, 3, 4; structural, 3, 6, 13, 20, 23, 24, 90, 93–95, 97, 98, 109, 120, 132–33; with quotation, 3, 6, 13, 14–20, 37, 268–70, 276–78, 294; and collage, 4, 7, 8, 287, 299, 368, 369, 370, 376, 383, 384, 410, 411, 414–15; underlies later procedures, 5, 6, 13, 20; in other composers, 5, 12–13, 37, 102, 133, 410, 415, 416, 429–30n1, 498n46; role in Ives's development, 6–7, 7, 10–11, 13, 20, 37–38, 414, 419; and learning by imitation, 6, 8, 12–36, 37, 88–89, 267, 270, 280, 285, 298–99; without quotation, 6, 13, 20–36, 37, 38, 268, 277, 278–80; to evoke a style or genre, 6, 13, 14, 36, 267–99; and music about music, 8, 13, 22, 36, 266, 268–70, 275–86, 298–99; for expression, 8, 266, 268, 286–94, 298–99; and meaning, 14, 36, 266, 281–82, 284–86, 294, 298–99, 341, 362; relation of work to model, 20, 21, 23, 25–27, 27–34, 36, 89, 102, 127, 133, 285–86, 413; and negative influence, 21, 23, 25–27, 28, 31–33, 34; and resetting a song text, 23–34; and competition,

33–34, 35, 36, 94, 95, 101, 267; and emulation, 34, 35–36, 89, 90, 101; and genre, 36, 268, 280–86; in symphonies, 88–99, 101–2, 125, 127, 130, 131–33, 228, 246; and patchwork, 301, 304, 305, 315, 317; and gradual clarification, 335

Monk, William H., 23, 225

Monn, G. B., 416

Monteverdi, Claudio, 270

Moody, Dwight, 251

Morris, George, 343

Mosses from an Old Manse, 358

Mozart, Wolfgang Amadeus: as borrower and emulator, 5, 12, 13, 34, 38; as model or source for other composers, 13, 37, 415, 416; and coincidental similarity, 131; as precedent for Ives's procedures, 226, 296, 298; compared to Ives, 385, 386

Music about music, 6, 13, 367, 420–25; modeling and, 8, 13, 22, 36, 266, 268–70, 275–86, 298–99; stylistic allusion and, 266, 268, 270–75, 414, 420; collage and, 273, 275, 299, 346, 386, 387, 410, 420; programmatic quotation and, 273, 275, 341, 342–46, 357, 360–63, 366, 420; patchwork and, 299, 305, 306–12, 316, 325–26, 367, 420; extended paraphrase and, 331, 333, 420; American music as influence on, 366, 367. *See also* Hymn tunes, music about; Marches, music about

Mussorgsky, Modest, 342, 365

Myrick, Julian, 313, 485–86n13

Nassann, William, 498n50

National Conservatory of Music, 89–90

Nationalism, 88, 126, 133, 135, 136, 246–47, 419, 424

Nettleton, Asahel, 50

Nevin, Ethelbert, 279, 341, 474n34

New Haven Symphony Orchestra, 35, 98

Nicholls, David, 386

Nijinsky, Vaslav, 278

Nolan, Michael, 268–70, 343

Offergeld, Robert, 365

Oliver, Henry K., 185

Originality: expected in art music, 2, 13, 21, 418; in using borrowed material, 6, 75, 103, 136, 266, 368, 410, 418, 419; defined by Emerson, 418, 504n32

Paine, John Knowles, 21–22
Palestrina, Giovanni Pierluigi da, 102
Palmgren, Selim, 416
Paradise Lost, 84
Paraphrase: defined, 3, 4, 41; in themes, 3, 6, 8, 10, 49–75, 86–87, 88–89, 90–93, 97–102, 104–26, 130–34, 136, 215, 226, 236, 238, 238–39, 241, 246, 327, 413, 419; in themes of cumulative settings, 4, 5, 137–38, 139, 146, 161, 187, 201, 213, 215; and collage, 4, 7, 86, 368, 369, 370, 376, 383, 410, 414–15; and patchwork, 4, 7, 86, 299, 300, 317, 320, 327, 414; underlies later procedures, 5, 6–7, 134–36, 299, 300, 327; used by other composers, 5, 75, 228–29, 410, 415, 416; and fugue, 6, 70–72, 133, 163, 414, 439n42; place in Ives's development, 6–7, 7, 8, 10–11, 36, 38, 327, 414; and cumulative setting, 6–7, 71, 139, 143, 146, 149, 155, 157, 161–62, 163, 172, 184, 187, 205–6, 217, 264, 327, 414; instead of exact quotation, 37–38, 80–81, 85, 104, 134, 484n2; and variation, 38–41, 43–46, 75, 327; and ambiguity, 38, 75, 80, 85–86, 410; omissions and elisions in, 39, 41, 46, 54, 86, 116, 330; interpolations in, 39, 41, 43, 54, 116, 330; key change or transposition in middle of, 39, 43–45, 46, 115, 116, 120, 157, 288, 301, 330, 374; and reordering material, 39, 41, 43, 46, 93; and reducing repetition, 41, 50, 55, 60, 92, 93, 104, 108, 114, 116, 124, 151, 161, 244–45; quoted fragment as clue for longer paraphrase, 41, 46, 58–59, 60, 120, 125, 331, 337; and adding repetition, 43, 46, 108, 330; and change of function or style, 43, 47, 49, 54–55, 126; and levels of resemblance to source, 45–46, 125, 410; and recognizability of borrowed material, 46, 49, 51, 54, 55,

58–59, 60, 64–65, 104, 105, 115, 116, 125, 134; and meaning, 49, 73–75, 136, 266, 338, 341; and rhythm, 50, 52, 60, 330; and harmony, 50–52, 108, 161; follows structure of source, 59, 109, 115, 120, 330, 331, 333, 335; and resemblance between source tunes in works with paraphrased themes, 61, 70, 74, 104, 107–8, 114, 120, 124, 126, 127, 128, 130; and linear combination of tunes, 61, 75, 76–80, 86; and text of source, 74, 79; of transitions and episodes, 126–30, 439–40n44; in countermelodies of cumulative settings, 138, 139, 143, 146, 161–62, 163, 172, 174–75, 187, 377, 451n8, 458n66; in other instrumental works, 225, 277, 387, 409; in songs, 283, 288, 364; in programmatic works, 359, 379, 485–86n13; in quodlibets, 374, 374–75, 376
—extended: defined, 4, 300, 327; place in Ives's development, 7, 8, 300, 418; Ives uses, 81, 299, 327–38, 483n53; follows structure of source tune, 330, 331, 333, 335; and music about experiencing music, 331, 333, 420; and gradual clarification, 335
Parker, Edwin Pond, 365
Parker, Horatio: as Ives's teacher, 6, 35, 71, 89, 436n12; and Ives's German songs, 27–28, 31, 33, 34; as model for Ives, 34–36, 102, 226, 285, 434n46; as conductor, 35, 98; class assignments, 46, 70, 441n2, 471n5; and art music, 88, 136, 419; and Dvořák, 90; as borrower, 102
Parody, 2, 472n11, 483–84n59
Patchwork: defined, 4, 300, 477n1; and paraphrase, 4, 7, 86, 299, 300, 317, 320, 327, 414; place in Ives's development, 7, 8, 10–11, 300, 418, 419; and medley, 7, 301, 414; and resemblance between source tunes, 83, 316, 317, 319, 320–22; Ives uses, 242, 301–22, 325, 409, 413, 480n22; and music about music, 299, 305, 306–12, 316, 325–26, 367, 420; and meaning, 299, 306, 315–16, 414; in Tin

Pan Alley songs, 300, 322–26, 410; and
quodlibet, 301, 304, 480n29, 494n2,
495n18; and modeling, 301, 305, 306–12,
315, 317; and stylistic allusion, 301, 305,
311; and form of source tune, 306; and
collage, 370, 384, 414–15

Patriotic songs: as source, 1, 422, 424;
used by others, 38, 219, 231, 322–25, 365,
366–67, 473n24, 484n3; and linear
combination of tunes, 80; in works
with paraphrased themes, 108, 116,
118–19, 120, 123–24, 125, 128, 147, 226–27,
236, 241, 242, 250, 444n28, 445nn42,43,
446n50, 451n8, 487n19; and American
character, 126; and modeling, 276,
473n24; in patchworks, 304–5, 306–11,
312–22, 325, 478–79n12, 479nn18,20,
480n22, 481n35, 487n19; in extended
paraphrase, 327; in program music,
343, 345–46, 347, 348–49, 355, 357, 358,
359, 485n9, 486–87n17, 487n19; to illustrate a text, 364, 421, 493n72; in quodlibets, 372, 373–74, 375–76; in collages,
376–79, 380–81, 381–82, 386–89,
400–401, 496n23, 497nn37,38, 499n58

Perkins, Theodore E., 391

Phile, Philip, 312

Phillips, Wendell, 422

Pilgrim's Progress, 358

Poe, Johnny, 365

Popular music. *See* Hymn tunes; Patriotic songs; Popular songs; Vernacular
music

Popular songs: as source, 1, 75, 192, 214,
249, 422, 423–25; used by other composers, 5, 37, 38, 49, 75, 219, 322–25,
325–26, 331, 366–67, 416; in marches,
20, 38, 41–43, 220–24, 225, 435–36n10,
463n10; and linear combination of
tunes, 76–80; paraphrased as themes,
89, 103, 104, 104–7, 115–24, 125, 126, 127,
128, 130–31, 133–34, 199, 236, 239, 241,
242, 250, 301, 444n26, 446nn46,50,
448n66, 451n8; American character of,
134, 253; in cumulative settings, 161,
246–47; settings of, 217, 218, 274; as text

illustration, 255, 257, 279, 361, 363,
363–64, 364, 367; and programmatic
quotation, 265, 341, 343–45, 346, 347,
349, 356, 357, 359–60, 462n97,
485–86n13, 491n59; and modeling,
268–70, 276, 277, 278–80, 281, 286–87,
472nn11,21, 475n45; and stylistic allusion, 271, 295–96; as influence on Ives,
300, 322–26, 365–67, 482n47, 493n82;
and patchwork, 301, 306–12, 316–22,
481n35; and meaning, 326; and quodlibet, 372, 373–74, 375, 435–36n10; and
collage, 378, 379, 380–81, 382, 383–84,
385, 386, 387, 388, 400–401, 498n46,
499n58

Pound, Ezra, 369

Price, George, 490–91n56

Princeton University, 365

Programmatic quotation: defined, 4,
340–41; and collage, 4, 8, 135, 338, 360,
367–68, 369, 370, 376, 383, 389, 390, 400,
401, 402, 409, 414–15; and cumulative
setting, 5, 8, 139, 161, 184, 216, 217, 245,
247–50, 253–66; used by other composers, 5, 341–42, 365–67, 415, 416; place
in Ives's development, 7, 8, 10–11, 266,
414; not involved, 74, 133–34, 150,
247–50, 293–94, 315–16, 341, 452n11; and
symbolic meanings, 265, 341, 342, 344,
346–60, 366–67, 421; used by Ives, 266,
299, 317, 319–22, 327, 330, 338, 340–41,
371, 376, 379–80, 411, 412, 413, 418,
491n59; and music about experiencing
music, 273, 275, 341, 342–46, 357,
360–63, 366, 420; and text-painting,
277–78, 279, 312, 341, 360–67, 476n52;
and text of source, 341, 359, 363–65, 367,
407

Prokofiev, Sergei, 13

Protestantism, 251, 252–53, 274

Putnam, Israel, 389

Quodlibet: defined, 3–4, 370–71; and
humor, 4, 7, 322, 371, 372–76, 435n9,
480n29, 494n2, 495n18; precedents for,
5, 8, 372, 411, 415; place in Ives's devel-

Quodlibet (continued)
opment, 7, 8, 414; and collage, 9, 368, 369, 370, 376, 414–15; Ives uses, 180–81, 240, 277, 371–76, 409; and contrapuntal combination, 180–81, 370, 371–72; and patchwork, 301, 304, 480n29, 494n2, 495n18; and linear combination of tunes, 370, 371, 372–76, 494n2

Quotation. *See* Borrowing; Programmatic quotation

Rachmaninov, Sergei, 416
Ragtime: style of, used by Ives, 174, 212, 242, 253, 273, 315, 316, 319–20, 386; figuration in Ives's music, 240, 276, 387, 499n52; borrowed by Ives, 277, 344, 375; used by others, 322, 326, 422, 455n36
Rathert, Wolfgang, 84
Ravel, Maurice, 416
Reed, Joseph W., 281
Reeves, David Wallis: Ives borrows from, 1, 180, 221, 343, 346, 347, 374, 486n14; as model for Ives, 14–16, 22, 222, 430n5
Reinagle, Alexander R., 289
Repetition: reducing, in paraphrasing themes, 41, 50, 55, 60, 92, 93, 104, 108, 114, 116, 124, 151, 161, 244–45; adding, in paraphrasing, 43, 46, 108, 330; avoidance of, in cumulative setting, 137, 146–47, 217, 231, 233, 238, 244–45; avoidance of, in nineteenth-century works, 217, 231, 244–45, 468n57; omission of, in marches, 222
Resemblance between source tunes: Ives exploits, 2, 85, 86, 134–35, 283, 321; in works with paraphrased themes, 61, 70, 74, 104, 107–8, 114, 120, 124, 126, 127, 128, 130; and cyclic unification, 70, 239, 239–40, 242; and linear combination of tunes, 75, 76–80, 85, 86, 110, 300, 320, 483n53; in patchwork, 83, 316, 317, 319, 320–22; in collage, 135, 370, 382, 385, 386, 387, 388, 391, 401, 402, 408, 410, 411; in cumulative settings, 163, 181, 185, 187, 191, 195, 205, 213, 254–55, 470n79, 475n41; in program music, 343, 349

Resemblance to existing work: coincidental or unintentional, 16–17, 75, 83, 86, 104, 131, 214, 291, 402, 439n43, 440n45, 445n34, 455n38, 470n79, 476n56; levels of, in paraphrase, 45–46
Reverse variation form, 184, 230, 456n49
Revivals, 214. *See also* Camp meetings
Rimsky-Korsakov, Nicolai, 416
Rinck, Johann Christian Heinrich, 21–22
Roberts, George F., 372, 495n9
Robinson, Robert, 174
Romantic tradition, 88, 103, 111, 136, 244, 419, 421, 469n70
Rondo form, 137, 215, 375
Rooney, Pat, 76–79
Root, George F., 57, 61, 226, 236, 239, 306, 480n25
Ross, Stuart, 453n20
Rossini, Gioachino, 475n44
Rovinsky, Anton, 358
Ruby, Harry, 366
Ruggles, Carl, 15
Ruggles, Charlotte, 15

Saint-Gaudens, Augustus, 317
Saint-Saëns, Camille, 342, 475–76n51
Sankey, Ira D., 174, 251, 257
Satie, Eric, 416
Sayers, Henry J., 347
Schickele, Peter, 381
Schiller, Friedrich von, 151
Schoenberg, Arnold: as borrower, 13, 416; compared to Ives, 50–51, 102, 136; and developing variation, 453nn23,24, 489n43
Schubert, Franz: as borrower, 13; songs, 24, 287, 340; as model for Ives, 24–25, 98, 99, 102, 442n12; Ives transcription from, 46; as source for other composers, 416; compared to Ives, 442n8
Schuller, Gunther, 484–85n4
Schuman, William, 436n11
Schumann, Robert: as model for Ives, 24–25, 27–31, 32–33, 33–34, 433n38; Ives transcription from, 46; as precedent

for Ives, 230, 231; as borrower, 231, 365, 465n28; and program music, 248

Schurz, Carl, 314–15, 480n27

Schwitters, Kurt, 370

Self-borrowing: and reworking entire works or movements, 47, 49, 212, 213–14, 219, 220–22, 225, 236–37, 241, 242, 281, 315, 350–51, 357–58, 374, 385, 386, 388–89, 389, 390, 392–401, 402, 409, 439n43, 440n45, 473n27, 499n58; and reworking instrumental works as songs, 47, 101, 149, 174, 193–94, 194, 205, 224, 305, 306, 357, 471nn7,8; from lost works, 125, 143, 151, 154, 174, 178, 185, 195, 205, 206, 225, 233–35, 306, 333, 432n18, 456n50, 472–73n22; of brief passages, 205, 276, 313, 325, 355, 387, 467–68n55, 476n56, 487n19, 490n47, 499n52; by other composers, 213, 322, 324, 325, 342, 411, 415, 416; of extended passages, 225, 276, 315, 355, 359, 360, 364, 377–78, 382, 388, 389, 406, 409, 463–64n16, 473n23, 496nn28,29, 497n37, 499n57; in modeling, 278–79, 280; in general, 428n8, 436n15

Setting: defined, 3, 4; used by others, 5, 38, 41, 219, 222, 229, 415, 416; place in Ives's development, 6, 8, 10, 37–38, 414; and cumulative setting, 6–7, 138, 174, 194, 217, 217–26, 234, 239, 414; in marches, 38, 41, 218, 218–24; Ives uses, 174, 194, 217–26, 234, 409, 413; experimental, 218; primacy of musical over extramusical concerns, 266, 338. *See also* Cumulative setting

Shadow parts, 185, 185–86, 450n5, 454–55n32

Shaw, David, 108

Shaw, Robert Gould, 317

Sherwood, Gayle, 10, 103, 428n8, 429n15

Shirley, Wayne, 382

Sibelius, Jean, 231, 465n30

Sinclair, James, 212, 214, 484–85n4

Sketches: and contrapuntal combination, 4, 180–81, 371, 406–7, 437n25, 445n43;

help identify borrowings, 8, 63–66, 87, 105–7, 306, 442n12, 455n34; and dating, 9, 10, 233; show process of adding borrowings, 63, 67, 68–69, 113, 114, 118–19, 120–22, 123–24, 126, 127, 128, 288, 381–82, 391, 392–99, 400, 401, 429n14, 437n18, 444n32, 444–45n34, 445n35, 446n46, 446–47n54, 459n73, 467n51, 471n8, 479n14, 480n30, 481n35, 482n39, 493n75, 497n38; show change in recognizability of borrowing, 63–70, 111, 113, 115, 125, 306, 438n36, 448n63, 452n15, 480n30, 491–92n62; not extant, 84, 162, 235; show change of borrowed tune, 105–7, 186, 501n80; reveal Ives's intentions, 8, 87, 107, 114–15, 118–19, 314, 330, 382, 439n41, 455n34, 480nn22,27; in cumulative settings, begin with theme and countermelody, 147, 180–81, 186, 234, 451nn8,9, 455n39, 497n37; show addition of passages, 185, 224, 432n25, 433n37, 444–45n34, 456n51, 463nn10,13, 464n22, 467n51, 471n8, 485–86n13; and key, 242, 466n40; and program, 327; and published editions, 436n11, 447n56; variant readings in, 438n33, 439n39, 441–42n5, 442n6, 444n28, 454–55n32, 455n33, 457n63, 468n60; about, 438nn34,35,37, 439n38, 444n33, 445nn40,42, 446n49, 463n11; and form, 443n21, 453–54n27, 459n75; show process of deleting borrowings, 480nn22,25. See also in Index of Ives's Compositions *Adeste Fideles in an Organ Prelude; Central Park in the Dark; Circus Band, The; Concord Sonata; Feldeinsamkeit; Fugue in Four Keys on "The Shining Shore"; He Is There!; Holidays Symphony; In Flanders Fields; Luck and Work; March No. 3 in F and C, with "My Old Kentucky Home"; Old Home Day; Pond, The; Psalm 90;* Quartets, strings: First; Sonatas, piano: First; Sonatas, violin: "Pre-First," First, Second, Third, *and* Fourth; *Son of a Gambolier, A;* Sym-

GENERAL INDEX